LITERARY RESEARCH GUIDE

Second Edition
Second Revised Printing

An evaluative, annotated bibliography of important reference books and periodicals on English, Irish, Scottish, Welsh, Commonwealth, American, Afro-American, American Indian, Continental, Classical, and World literatures, and sixty literature-related subject areas including

Bibliography	Little Magazines
Biography	Prosody
Book Collecting	Reviews
Film	Teaching Resources
Folklore	Textual Criticism
Linguistics	Women's Studies

Margaret C. Patterson

The Modern Language Association of America

New York   1984

Library of Congress Cataloging in Publication Data

Patterson, Margaret C.
  Literary research guide.

  Subtitle: An evaluative, annotated bibliography of important reference
books and periodicals on English, Irish, Scottish, Welsh, Commonwealth,
American, Afro-American, American Indian, continental, classical, and
world literatures, and sixty literature-related subjects including
bibliography, biography, book collecting, film, folklore, linguistics, little
magazines, prosody, reviews, teaching resources, textual criticism, women's
studies.
  Includes index.
  1. Literature—Bibliography. 2. Reference books—Literature.
I. Modern Language Association of America. II. Title.
Z6511.P37 1983 [PN43]   016.8   82-20386
ISBN 0-87352-128-5
ISBN 0-87352-129-3 (pbk.)

Second edition
First printing, 1983, 2,600 copies
Second printing, revised, 1984, 1,800 copies
Third printing, 1985, 2,000 copies
Fourth printing, 1987, 2,000 copies

Published by The Modern Language Association of America
10 Astor Place, New York, New York 10003

Learning how to learn is one of the best investments that can be made for an effective life.

Carnegie Foundation
for the Advancement of Learning

When we choose to become scholars, we join the guild of professional in-quirers, the guild of those who profess the rational habits [of honesty, courage, persistence, consideration, and humility].

Wayne C. Booth

Anyone engaged in research soon discovers that everything is related to everything else. . . . As Emerson's friend at Walden Pond suggested, though, it takes two to speak the truth: one to speak, and another to hear.

Joel Conarroe

Introduction to Scholarship in
Modern Languages and Literatures, 1981

I believe in . . . an aristocracy of the sensitive, the considerate, and the plucky. Its members are to be found in all nations and classes, and all through the ages, and there is a secret understanding between them when they meet. They represent the true human tradition, the one permanent victory of our queer race over cruelty and chaos.

E. M. Forster, *What I Believe*

Contents

Abbreviations

Abbreviations for selected books, periodicals, and organizations are listed here alphabetically, letter by letter. A comprehensive list of abbreviations for literary periodical titles may be found in the annual volumes of the *MLA International Bibliography* (D31). Other abbreviations and acronyms may be found in entries W1025–26. The abbreviations listed below are both the conventional form used by the *MLAIB* and a shortened version that can be recognized immediately by the reader. The entry number is provided for those who want more information.

ABELL; *Ann. Bibl. Eng. Lang. Lit.*	*Annual Bibliography of English Language and Literature* (D32) (sometimes erroneously referred to as MHRA)
Abst. Eng. Stud.; *AES*	*Abstracts of English Studies* (E38)
Abst. Folk. Stud.	*Abstracts of Folklore Studies* (W1274)
Abst. Pop. Cult.	*Abstracts of Popular Culture* (W1498)
ACRL	Association of College and Research Libraries (W1047)
ALA	American Library Association (W1047)
ALT	*African Literature Today* (R980)
America	*America: History and Life* (E43)
Am. Hum. Ind.	*American Humanities Index* (P738)
Am. Lit.; *AL*	*American Literature* (P744)
Am. Lit. Abst.	*American Literature Abstracts* (E42)
Am. Lit. Schol.	*American Literary Scholarship* (P734)
AQ	*American Quarterly* (P745)
Arts and Hum. Cit. Ind.; *AHCI*; *Arts and Humanities CI*	*Arts and Humanities Citation Index* (F47)
A-SD	*Anglo-Saxon Dictionary* (J233)
BC	*Book Collector* (W1168)
Bibl. Ind.	*Bibliographic Index* (C28)
Biog. Ind.	*Biography Index* (W1085)
BIP	*Books in Print* (W1170)
Bk. Rev. Dig.	*Book Review Digest* (W1558)
Bk. Rev. Ind.	*Book Review Index* (W1559)
BM	British Museum (B13)
Brit. Hum. Ind.; *BHI*	*British Humanities Index* (F49)
Brit. Mus. Cat.; *BM Cat.*	British Museum. *General Catalogue* (B13)
Brit. U.-C. of Per.	*British Union-Catalogue of Periodicals* (W1480)
CALL	*Current Awareness—Library Literature* (F53)
Can. Ess. Lit. Ind.	*Canadian Essay and Literature Ind.* (N673)

Abbreviations

CanL	*Canadian Literature* (N676)
Can. Per. Ind.	*Canadian Periodical Index* (N674)
CBEL	*Cambridge Bibliography of English Literature* (J175)
CBI; Cum. Bk. Ind.	*Cumulative Book Index* (D35, P717.16)
CC	*Current Contents* (F47)
CE	*College English* (W1599)
CEA	College English Association (W1047)
CEAA	Center for Editions of American Authors (W1177)
CFM	*Canadian Fiction Magazine* (N689)
CIJE; Current Ind. Jour. Ed.	*Current Index to Journals in Education* (W1224)
COM	Computer-output-microform (see COM in Glossary)
CSE	Center for Scholarly Editions (W1179)
Current Bk. Rev. Cit.	*Current Book Review Citations* (W1564)
DA	*Dissertation Abstracts* (W1214-15)
DA	*Dictionary of Americanisms* (W1210)
DAB	*Dictionary of American Biography* (W1087)
DAE	*Dictionary of American English* (W1206)
DAI	*Dissertation Abstracts International* (W1214–15)
DNB	*Dictionary of National Biography* (W1086)
ECW	*Essays on Canadian Writing*, ECW Press (N669, N679)
Ed. Ind.	*Education Index* (W1225)
EETS	Early English Text Society (W1046)
EIC	*Essays in Criticism* (H146)
ELH	*ELH: Journal of English Literary History* (H144)
ELN	*English Language Notes* (J186)
ERIC	Educational Resources Information Center (see ERIC in the Glossary)
Ess. Gen. Lit. Ind.; EGLI	*Essay and General Literature Index* (F46)
Expl.	*Explicator* (G56)
Hist. Abst.	*Historical Abstracts* (E43)
Hum. Ind.	*Humanities Index* (F45)
IMB	*International Medieval Bibliography* (J263)
Index of Am. Per. Ver.	*Index of American Periodical Verse* (P818)
Index to Bk. Rev. Hum.	*Index to Book Reviews in the Humanities* (W1560)
Index to Lit. Mag.	*Index to Little Magazines* (W1429)
JHI	*Journal of the History of Ideas* (W1305)
Jour. Can. Fict.; JCF	*Journal of Canadian Fiction* (N688)
K-SJ	*Keats-Shelley Journal* (J444)
KTO	Kraus-Thomson Organization
Lang. and Lang. Beh. Abst; LLBA	*Language and Language Behavior Abstracts* (W1332)
L.C.; LC	Library of Congress (B10, B12)
L.C. Catalog	*Library of Congress Catalog* (B10, B12)
Leary	*Articles on American Literature* (P727)
LHUS; Spiller	*Literary History of the United States* (P701)
Lib. Info. Sci. Abst.	*Library and Information Science Abstracts* (E43)
Lib. Lit.	*Library Literature* (F53)
Lib. Sci. Abst.	*Library Science Abstracts* (E43)
LRN	*Literary Research Newsletter* (W1421)
MARC	Machine Readable Cataloging (see MARC in the Glossary)
MD	*Modern Drama* (J563)
MED	*Middle English Dictionary* (J264)
MFS	*Modern Fiction Studies* (J544)
MHRA	Modern Humanities Research Association (D32, W1047, W1328)

MLA	Modern Language Association (see Index)
MLA Abst.	*MLA Abstracts* (E41)
MLAIB; MLA Int'l Bibl.	*MLA International Bibliography* (D31)
MLN	*Modern Language Notes* (Q890)
MLQ	*Modern Language Quarterly* (H149)
MP	*Modern Philology* (H150)
Music Ind.	*Music Index* (W1456)
NCTE	National Council of Teachers of English (W1047)
NED	*New English Dictionary* (W1205)
NEH	National Endowment for the Humanities (see Index)
NEQ	*New England Quarterly* (P756)
New CBEL	*New Cambridge Bibliography of English Literature* (J175)
New Yk. Tim. Ind.	*New York Times Index* (F50)
NST	*New Serial Titles* (W1478)
NUC	*National Union Catalog* (B10-11)
OCLC	Online Computer Library Center (see OCLC in the Glossary)
OED	*Oxford English Dictionary* (W1205)
OHEL	*Oxford History of English Literature* (J174)
PADS	*Publication of the American Dialect Society* (W1337)
PBSA	*Papers of the Bibliographical Society of America* (W1075)
Phil. Ind.	*Philosopher's Index* (W1489)
PMLA	*PMLA: Publications of the Modern Language Association* (D31, H152)
PQ	*Philological Quarterly* (H154)
PRO	Public Records Office (see Glossary)
Psych. Abst.	*Psychological Abstracts* (E39)
PTLA	*Publishers' Trade List Annual* (W1172)
RAL	*Research in African Literatures* (R981)
RG; Read. Gd.	*Readers' Guide* (F48)
RLG	Research Libraries Group (see RLG in the Glossary)
RQ	Journal of the Reference Services Division of ALA
RSR	*Reference Services Review* (W1569.1)
SEL	*Studies in English Literature* (J320)
SFS	*Science-Fiction Studies* (G100)
Soc. Abst.	*Sociological Abstracts* (E40)
Soc. Sci. Hum. Ind.; SSHI	*Social Sciences and Humanities Index* (F51)
Soc. Sci. Ind.	*Social Sciences Index* (W1579)
SP	*Studies in Philology* (J321)
SQ	*Shakespeare Quarterly* (J316)
SSF	*Studies in Short Fiction* (G80)
SSI	*Short Story Index* (G76)
STC; Pollard and Redgrave	*Short-Title Catalogue, 1475-1640* (J306)
STC; Wing	*Short-Title Catalogue, 1641-1700* (J370)
TLS	*Times Literary Supplement* (W1563)
ULS	*Union List of Serials* (W1479)
VP	*Victorian Poetry* (J490)
VS; Vict. Stud.	*Victorian Studies* (J470)
WLWE	*World Literature Written in English* (R960)
YCGL	*Yearbook of Comparative and General Literature* (T1014)
Year's Wk. Eng. Stud.; YWES	*Year's Work in English Studies* (D33)
Year's Wk. Mod. Lang. Stud.; YWMLS	*Year's Work in Modern Language Studies* (W1328)

Preface to the Second Edition

Many years ago Charles Evans wrote in the Preface to his *American Bibliography* "the true Bibliographer is tolerant of the foibles and weaknesses of the gentle art" (vol.1, p. vii; see entry number P717 in this guide). Evans probably wrote the preface after he had completed the remainder of his project, a common practice, because only then can an author determine how extensively the content has affected the shape of the original idea. We can assume that he was more than a little weary and chastened by the mental and physical demands required in the preparation of descriptions for some 26,000 books. The project was his life's work, the first heroic effort toward a comprehensive "American bibliography." Experience—exacting, frustrating, tedious experience, in which every word and all possible interpretations, every numeral and every comma, every spelling and space had to be checked again, and again, and yet again—experience had taught him that to err is human and to forgive, divine.

The same spirit prevails in the selection and evaluation of the books included in this guide for the literary scholar. There is nothing here of the theory that in order to be profound—or even perceptive—one must be obscure. There is only gratification that the need for literary research tools has been recognized and pride that so much has been accomplished. A veritable avalanche of bibliographies, indexes, and surveys has appeared in the past decade. Most of them are not definitive, nor do they claim to be, but many are remarkably accurate for first efforts. A word of caution: Those works should be accepted as just that—first efforts—with the expectation that they will be improved by a later edition or another generation of scholars who will profit from the errors and omissions of those who came before them. Future authors of literary tools will learn to adopt the minimum reference format that scholarly readers need and expect: an introductory statement of the book's scope and purpose; guidelines for locating information within the volume; a variety of ways to approach the contents, including detailed indexes and numerous cross-references; and, perhaps the most valuable by-product, suggestions for further research possibilities in their field.

Not a single reference book in this guide is flawless. Not a single one will satisfy the needs of all readers. Some will be too elementary for the seasoned warrior, some too specialized for the floundering beginner. But taken together, they can literally be a "guide," a *learning* guide that proposes new ideas and associations, that opens virgin territory to the curious, the determined, and the talented. Here new literature majors can come to comfortable terms with a variety of biographical dictionaries and discover that they can handle material far beyond the scope of *Readers' Guide* (F48) and the *MLA International Bibliography* (D31). They can revel in dozens of new bibliographies that focus on a single subject: the novel in any given country, the works of any one poet, the authors of any one nation, or the drama of the world. And they can explore for themselves the complexities of textual criticism, prosody, analytical bibliography, book collecting, comparative literature, linguistics, ethnic studies, and a hundred other literary puzzles. The only limits on intellectual growth are those of time and imagination. The worthy university student has the imagination and will find the time.

This second edition of the *Literary Research Guide* adds entries for about three hundred new titles published during the past five years. It greatly expands the sections on Commonwealth, Continental, Classical, and World literatures, Dictionaries, Film, Folklore, Book Collecting, Linguistics, Literary Handbooks and Encyclopedias, Little Magazines, Publishing, Women's Studies, and periodicals in all areas. Comparisons between old and new editions and between new and old reference books in the same area emphasize the contributions of recent scholarship. In a very few cases where the new work was not yet available or where the criticism seemed particularly appropriate, the annotations include brief comments from *Choice* (W1557) or the publishers' announcements. When publishers consistently produce splendid work, that fact is noted; when others fail to demand quality of their authors, that, too, is noted so that students will learn to look at the imprint on the title page and anticipate intelligently the quality of the scholarship. Most superseded works have been deleted, including many venerable masters who first brought order to the concept of literary research. A few cessations have been retained because their contribution is unique: *Abstracts of Folklore Studies* (W1274), *Abstracts of Popular Culture* (W1498), *American Literature Abstracts* (E42), *Canadian Essay and Literature Index* (N673), *MLA Abstracts* (E41), *Proof* (P760), *Studies in Black Literature* (P854), and *Journal of Spanish Studies* (Q947).

No attempt has been made to compile a totally comprehensive, totally international literary research guide. This selective list includes only those books that are

available in most large American university libraries,

capable of answering most of the factual and interpretive problems encountered by literature and humanities students in their reading and writing, and

suitable for students who want to make the best possible use of their library, their time, and their intellect.

If students need a label for this guide, they will see that it is a learning guide designed for the critical pluralist who believes in the value of widely differing approaches to an author's work and welcomes the opportunity to question the established, the accepted, and the traditional.

The preparation of an unannotated, nonevaluative list of a hundred (or a thousand) literature-related titles poses no challenge and no purpose; too many of those already exist. But a project that demands selection, comparison, evaluation, rejection, illustration, description, and explanation is fascinating because it requires decisions and satisfying because it results in focus and order. Since the guide's territory is limited to the evaluation of books useful in literary research, it does not encroach on Sheehy's hallowed ground. Veteran Sheehy (see entry A5) is the appropriate source for complete publication information and factual (not evaluative) accounts of books in dozens of disciplines, but students will find little comfort there when they need ideas for a literary thesis.

Each book in this guide has its own unique value to a literature student. Some are immensely interesting, with a thousand ideas and items that press urgently for comment. Each one, therefore, is given an annotation commensurate with its possibilities as an item of interest to students. No apologies will be made for the acknowledged differences in the annotations, whether they be in length or depth, because those strictures seem to have more to do with appearance and form than with quality of the text. The primary concern of this learning guide is the content of the best reference books in literature and the way in which that content can help literature students produce scholarly research. To choose only the best and most helpful; to describe potentialities and illustrate possibilities; to distinguish between the classic and the ephemeral, the elementary and the advanced, the general and the specialized; and, above all, to make these books come through to the reader as remarkably useful, remarkably well-done treasure houses of remarkably interesting information—it has been the best of times.

M.C.P.
Autumn 1982

Second Printing of the Second Edition

Thirty-seven new titles published between 1982 and 1984 have been added in this printing, and three titles have been dropped. Information has been inserted for about eighty new editions and supplements. Altogether, changes have been made on 272 pages. The second printing is contentedly up to date, yet still in consonance with the first printing.

M.C.P.
Spring 1984

Introduction

Vehicle and Tenor

Literary Research Guide is directed toward those students—whether undergraduate, graduate, or faculty—who want to be self-educating individuals. They are the ideal product of the American educational system, the independent intellectuals who recognize that our ever-widening circles of knowledge contain within them the added possibility and responsibility of an ever-increasing number of doors leading to the unknown. And students trained in logical research procedure will be able to open them. They will organize what they know about the subject with what they know about their information sources and use both so efficiently that the final product will be creative as well as factual scholarship. This process will in turn develop what may be the most valuable asset scholars can have—a well-deserved confidence in their own ability to handle any research problem.

The immediate purpose of this guide, then, is to be a reliable reference book. Readers will quickly grasp the facts about each book discussed here, but the long-term, more elusive goal is to encourage the habit of inquiry and the wisdom of perspective. The conviction that independent research is both a means to and an end of creative scholarship and the belief that accuracy, detail, and proof are essentials to be pursued with enthusiasm—these are the qualities that propel self-educating students toward their goals. And these are the qualities that this guide wants to awaken and encourage.

The subject and form of this guide make it suitable for the reference section of libraries. Its factual data on basic material used in bibliography and literary research make it a practical text for both English and library science graduate courses. It can help teachers involved in independent projects and can serve as a convenient desk source for quick reference when recommending books to students. It can assist English or education undergraduates who want to improve their personal research methods so they will be better prepared for future questions from future professors and students. Finally, it outlines procedures and titles that will be useful for theses, dissertations, and written or oral examinations.

The books selected for this guide have proved their value by use. They are books for the student, not the librarian, for the writer and teacher, not the library assistant. Most of them have been used by the author either in personal research projects or in methods of research and bibliography courses with graduate students. About two percent of the titles have not yet been published. They are included because they will contain important scholarship that should be utilized as soon as it is available.

Every book has been scrutinized for strong points and weak points, unique contributions, clarity, and authority. In general, long evaluative annotations accompany those books that, because of their complexity or importance, seem to warrant the space; short annotations point out the major features of the others. Most annotations refer to names, theories, or facts in literature to illustrate how the student can best use the time, knowledge, and wisdom that other scholars have contributed to their special fields. They are meant to spark the imagination, to show readers how they can use the reference material to make themselves better writers and scholars. To fulfill these purposes, this guide includes:

> **an evaluative, annotated bibliography** of the most important reference books and periodicals in English and American literature;
>
> **the most useful sources** for research in Irish, Scottish, Welsh, Commonwealth, Continental, world, classical, and comparative literature;
>
> **more than six hundred reference books in sixty subject areas** relating to literature, such as book collecting, education, film, folklore, history, music, paleography, and religion. These books cover specific problem areas ranging from biography, literary criticism, handbooks, terms, quotations, reviews, and textual criticism to works in progress. As a personal crusade against tunnel vision, the author includes a few basic sources that every educated person ought to use such as the *Encyclopedia of World Art* (W1038) and *World of Learning* (W1221);
>
> **an extensive glossary** of two hundred terms encountered in textual criticism, bibliography, and literary research. No other single reference book contains definitions for this particular group of terms;
>
> **a primer to the library's classification system** (which is all most scholars will ever need) with tables and illustrations to show how even a slight familiarity with its logic will lead to shortcuts and long results;
>
> **an analytical table of contents** that was inspired by Bateson's *Cambridge Bibliography of English Literature* (J175)—every important title in every important field is visible at one glance;
>
> **an analytical index** with many subject headings and subheadings so that both the first-term student who is interested in "the novel" and the professional who is ferreting out an elusive first edition can locate what they need;
>
> **lists of time-tested books for background reading** at the conclusion of most geographical, chronological, and genre sections; and
>
> **a list of abbreviations** for books and periodicals mentioned frequently in the text.

Positive Capability

When confronted with a research problem in literature, the first thing you, the student, should do is **analyze the question**. Does the nationality, genre, or date of your subject affect the choice of reference books? Do you need current or retrospective information? What *type* of information do you want—critical works, factual data, primary sources, summaries, definitions, background reading? Is it a bibliography you need? an index? a review of research? or a book review?

IF YOU have a *short*, easy question,
IF YOU need only a *little* information, and/or
IF YOU have a *limited* amount of time,

THEN YOU probably have a one-step research problem. That is, you will probably be able to go directly to a specific, specialized reference book and find in it the information you need, as, for instance:

- a **specialized encyclopedia** such as any one of the twelve Oxford Companions (see the Index) or the *Reader's Encyclopedia of World Drama* (R966), which treats drama as literature and thus provides information quite different from the Oxford Companion, which treats it as theater.
- a **handbook** such as Holman's *Handbook to Literature* (W1406) for a literary explanation of symbolism with illustrations from well-known titles.
- a **directory** such as *Directory of American Scholars* (W1146) for information about contemporary intellectuals or the *MLA Directory of Periodicals* (W1474) for a description of the contents and manuscript requirements of literary periodicals published all over the world.
- a **digest of data** such as *Famous First Facts* (W1199) or Steinberg's *Historical Tables* (W1203) for events of the 1850s that led up to that spectacular year for publishing—1859.
- a **geographical guidebook** such as the *Oxford Literary Guide to the British Isles* (W1049) to see where Jane Austen lived.
- one of the many **Who's Who biographical dictionaries** such as *International Authors and Writers Who's Who* (W1100) or *Who's Who in the Theatre* (W1098) for personal statistics.
- an **essay-style biographical** dictionary such as *Current Biography* (W1115) for a discussion of people in the news or *Notable American Women* (W1088) for enlightenment on women's contributions to American history.
- an **annual** like the *Yearbook of Comparative and General Literature* (T1014) for news of translations, conferences, and comparative literature scholarship completed during the past year.
- a **concordance** (W1194) such as those to Emily Dickinson's or Gerard Manley Hopkins' poems.
- a **dictionary** such as the *Oxford English Dictionary* (W1205) for a definition of "wit" as it was used in the eighteenth century, which is quite different from its meaning today.

IF YOU have a more difficult question,
IF YOU need several types of information, and/or
IF YOU have adequate time for extended research,

THEN YOU probably have a two-step research problem. That is, you will first consult a reference book that locates information in other sources, and then you will go to those sources for the information itself. For instance, you might use

- an **index** such as *Biography Index* (W1085) to locate several titles of periodical articles or books about Solzhenitsyn, *Essay and General Literature Index* (F46) for specific chapters about him in books, or *Humanities Index* (F45) for cross-disciplinary studies on his roles as author and national leader.
- an **abstracting service** such as *Abstracts of English Studies* (E38) or *Psychological Abstracts* (E39) for brief summaries of articles and books about *The Exorcist* and exorcism, for example.
- a **subject, genre, or author bibliography** such as *Afro-American Fiction, 1853-1976* (P856), *Research Guide to Science Fiction Studies* (G88), or the D. H. Lawrence bibliography, all of which cumulate many titles that relate to a single, specific area.
- a **review of research** such as *American Literary Scholarship* (P734) or those for Renaissance drama edited by Logan and Smith (J343-46).

In all research problems, analyze the question for depth and type, consider your own time limits, and then select the one or two reference books that answer your needs.

Research Project A: Flannery O'Connor

1.   Let us first consider the problems you face if you decide to investigate the life and works of Flannery O'Connor. Your first step, as you already know, is to assemble the basic facts about your subject. Individually and collectively these facts determine both the general type and the specific titles of the reference books you will need. If you are not comfortably familiar with O'Connor's life and works or if you want to verify your facts or expand your knowledge before you begin your research project, you have no less than five reliable sources that collect and summarize information about important people for quick reference purposes:

a.   *The Modern Period* is vol. 4 of *Notable American Women, 1607-1950* (W1088). In this volume you will find a judicious appraisal of O'Connor's contribution to the literary history of the United States. The three-page entry provides a biographical sketch, a brief explanation of O'Connor's works and themes, information on the best critical books and biographies, and the location of her private papers. This unquestionably is the most prestigious source for brief assessments of famous twentieth-century women until they are officially recognized by the *Dictionary of American Biography* (W1087). The latest supplement to the *DAB* covers through the year 1965 and is currently on its way from the publisher to library shelves. O'Connor will surely grace its pages.

    b.   *American Novelists since World War II* (vol. 2 of *Dictionary of Literary Biography*, W1121) provides a short sketch of O'Connor's life and then spends the greater part of six pages analyzing her works. It also includes a photograph, lists several critical works, many of them written in the 1970s, and briefly describes the collection of her manuscripts in the Georgia College Library.

    c.   For a factual account of O'Connor's life, including how she felt about her own works, go to *American Writers* (P721). The twenty-three-page entry (originally a University of Minnesota pamphlet) also suggests some of the subtleties of her language and themes and ends with a bibliography drawn mostly from the 1960s.

    d.   The long entry in *American Women Writers: A . . . Guide* (W1630) is both biographical and analytical. It includes a list of her works and selected criticism.

    e.   *Contemporary Literary Criticism* (J516) contains a seven-page entry on O'Connor in vol. 13 and cites additional entries in vols. 1, 2, 3, 6, and 10. Unlike the first four titles, which provide biographical and interpretive information, this volume reproduces excerpts from books and articles written by noted critics. Because the excerpts are unusually long—two or three pages—they generally convey an authentic impression of the critics' opinions. For a quick overview of O'Connor's reception and stature, they may be just what you need.

    2.   You already have an advantage over students who are not aware that the preceding five reference sources exist. Given the same assignment and the same need for basic information, they will probably reach for a general literary handbook such as the *Reader's Encyclopedia* (W1402), a general biographical dictionary such as *Webster's* (W1080), or, if they know O'Connor was American, a more specific handbook such as the *Oxford Companion to American Literature* (P736). All these are excellent for brief identification purposes, but they do not attempt to analyze the works or make suggestions for further study. You, on the other hand, have now had the opportunity to read several reliable assessments of O'Connor's literary contributions, and you know the following basic facts about her life:

Flannery O'Connor lived in the twentieth century.
She is an author.
      an American.
      a Southerner.
      a woman.
      a Catholic.
      deceased.
      admired especially for her short stories.
      interested mainly in the small Southern town and its
          cultural, social, ethnic, religious, and psychological
          conflicts.

    3.   Keeping in mind the fact that each of the above items suggests further

research in additional reference books, you next must consider two variables in your own situation:

How much background reading must you do to prepare for your assignment? Do you need only enough information to contribute intelligently to a one-hour class discussion of O'Connor's works? Do you need perhaps one book and a few articles so you can write a short paper analyzing the major themes in one of her stories? Or have you already completed all this preliminary research and come to the conclusion that you want to use O'Connor's Southern viewpoint as a dissertation topic? In other words, what is the *extent* of your needs?

Finally, how much *time* do you have for the required research? Must you prepare something for tomorrow's class? Or do you have a month to write a paper, a year to complete a dissertation?

4.   Only after you have established a timetable for yourself and a limit to the depth of your research do you proceed to the next logical step: determining how much material is readily available in your library. You have to assume two burdensome but inevitable tenets: First, your library is not going to own everything you want to use. Second, what it does own is not always going to be obvious or immediately available to you. Once you have learned to accept these two absolutely maddening facts with equanimity, you can counter the first limitation, if you have time, with interlibrary loan (W1312) and, if you have the services, with online information retrieval (see the Glossary). You can also overcome the second limitation, but only with training, experience, and imagination. You must learn to use sources that are unknown to other students who have not had the benefit of instruction in research methods.

5.   As a typical example, the card catalog at Wellesley College shows that the library owns nine books on O'Connor criticism. This sounds encouraging, but the circulation desk reports that six are checked out and the other three are on reserve (par for the course). As an optimistic research student, you naturally put in a request to be notified upon the return of the six (Eggenschwiler, Feeley, Hendin, Martin, May, and Stephen), and then you take notes on the three in the reserve room (Friedman, Hyman's University of Minnesota pamphlet, and Walters' volume in the United States Authors Series published by Twayne). Because the Twayne and Minnesota books are designed strictly for the student who is doing preliminary research or who has a limited amount of time or interest, you will use them with caution and only as a starting point, as they were intended. They are, however, generally acceptable sources for the basic facts about an author's life and works. And if you have waited until Sunday night to prepare yourself for an hour's discussion on Monday morning, they will be all you can handle.

6.   While you are at the card catalog, you will do one more thing: You will see whether there is an author newsletter or other serial publication devoted solely to Flannery O'Connor. If there is, you will locate it and read every word of every issue. If you do not find a card in the catalog, however, you must not assume that no such publication exists. You will instead double-check by consulting a reference book entitled *Author Newsletters and Journals* (W1476). There

you will find that a *Flannery O'Connor Bulletin* began publication in 1972. You will then have three options: (1) You can ask your librarian to subscribe (it will be months, however, before an issue arrives on your library shelves), (2) you can find a library that already has a subscription (Wellesley does not; Widener does), or (3) you can subscribe to the newsletter yourself (you will receive it the following week if you enclose a check). These author newsletters and journals ferret out and hoard information that is often unavailable elsewhere: news of private collections of manuscripts and papers; reports of seminars; reprints of inaccessible letters or other personal papers; photographs; specialized bibliographies of first editions, recent scholarship, or library holdings; lists of works in progress; activities of other scholars; reviews of new books; and articles of all kinds—biographical, interpretive, historical, textual, comparative, explicative—as well as source studies.

7.   If you are disappointed to find that no newsletter exists for your author, you have one recourse: You can create one. Scores of newsletters have been organized in the past few years, and the survival rate is remarkably high. The *Johnsonian News Letter, Mark Twain Journal, Conradiana, Shaw Review, Blake: An Illustrated Quarterly, John Updike Newsletter, Robinson Jeffers Newsletter*, and hundreds more were formed by scholars who were dissatisfied with the research materials available to them. These scholars will tell you that creating and nurturing a private literary publication is a memorable experience. The word "memorable" was deliberately selected rather than other more accurate but less elegant descriptors such as "frustrating," "exasperating," "mind-boggling," and "back-breaking." You will learn a lot about copyright laws, printing costs, paper shortages, layout, postal rates, binding problems, postponed deadlines, irate authors, and contemptuous reviewers, and you will understand why Strunk and White (W1188) ought to be taught annually beginning in the third grade. You will also become an authority on your subject.

8.   You are now at the point where most students stop. They have located a few books on their subject in the card catalog, and they believe they have exhausted their research possibilities. A little exposure to the library's reference collection, some counseling in the imaginative use of bibliographies and indexes, a healthy respect for cross-references, annotations, footnotes, catalog cards, cumulations, and updated supplements—these additional resources and capabilities will lead you, as an experienced researcher in a reasonably large university library, to at least forty more reference sources that contain information on O'Connor, and these forty will lead to dozens more.

9.   Keeping in mind the nine facts about O'Connor's life that you verified at the beginning of this project, you will probably decide to begin your research by consulting the latest annual volume of *American Literary Scholarship* (P734), an excellent survey of research in American literature that usually contains a three- or four-page essay review of the previous year's investigation of O'Connor's life and works. Its evaluations of the most significant books and articles by the most noted critics are so concisely and accurately prepared that you will probably want to browse through all the earlier annual volumes so you can have an overview of the trends in criticism. Like all "reviews of research" (W1556), this will acquaint you with the names of the best critics and guide you away from those

research areas that have already been well covered. Using it as a frame of reference, you now turn to more specific research aids.

10. Since O'Connor's most significant contribution was to the short story, you might choose as your next source Walker's fine bibliography and supplement of 1980, *Twentieth-Century Short Story Explication* (G78). Success, gratification, and joy, for there you find an astonishing ten full pages listing titles of articles, books, and essays containing explications of her stories. It lists, for example, forty-four titles that will help with "A Good Man Is Hard to Find" and twenty-four for "The Displaced Person." An equally valuable source is Weixlmann's new (1982) checklist of *American Short-Fiction Criticism* (G77.1), which complements Walker's concentration on "explication" by listing only historical, biographical, and other interpretive studies. If this is the area in which you wish to work, you will probably want to make xerox copies of all this material so you can have it at your side at every stage of your research.

11. Your next logical source—because it is remarkably comprehensive and relatively current—is the second supplement to Leary's *Articles on American Literature* (P727). This cumulates the criticism on American fiction published in periodicals between 1968 and 1975 (the main volume and the first supplement cover 1900–67). It will of course overlap to some extent with Walker and Weixlmann, but it is one of the most popular reference books in American literature, and, in spite of its occasional lapses in accuracy, it should be consulted early in the hierarchy of any research project.

12. Because Leary, Walker, and Weixlmann are of course limited by their own copyright dates and because no one reference work is ever completely comprehensive or completely accurate, you will want to check their coverage with the latest volume of one or all of the following four bibliographies:

a. The *MLA International Bibliography* (D31, *MLAIB*) can always be depended on for several new entries on O'Connor because it indexes almost three thousand periodicals, including most of those listed in the American literature section of this guide (Section P). And because it is now computer based, it appears regularly in the Autumn with information on the previous year's research and is available for online research back to 1969.

b. The *Annual Bibliography of English Language and Literature* (D32, *ABELL*) is equally important. It is usually three or four years behind in publication, but it does not overlap to a discouraging extent with *MLAIB* and will often contain twenty to forty titles on O'Connor.

c. *The Year's Work in English Studies* (D33) may also contain a few brief evaluations, but it, too, is slow to appear.

d. *American Literature* (P744) has in every quarterly issue a current bibliography of significant articles that may include one or two on O'Connor. In May 1979 it announced that it would cease publishing a list of works in progress, a regrettable decision, for this had long been an essential first checkpoint for anyone planning a dissertation in American literature. See Works in Progress (W1650) for possible help in that area.

Two predictions: Search in these four bibliographies will be so lucrative that (1) you will make copies of the O'Connor entries for your own use, and (2) you will decide to search through the volumes for previous years as well. No matter how much you find elsewhere on your subject, these bibliographies will always combine—to as great an extent as is realistically possible—the essential qualities of comprehensiveness, accuracy, and currency.

13. If you are doing extensive research you will still at this early stage in your labors be looking mainly for bibliographies, both primary (by the author) and secondary (about the author). You will, therefore, glance quickly through the most recent issues of *Bibliographic Index* (C28), an important basic source that you might even prefer to consult before you go to *Twentieth-Century Short Story Explication* or *American Short-Fiction Criticism*. Here you can hope to find entries that will lead you to book-length bibliographies as well as to any shorter lists that appear within books or periodicals. If your interest is in primary material, you will be delighted to find an entry for David Farmer's *Flannery O'Connor: A Descriptive Bibliography* (New York: Garland, 1981; 132pp.). This is a chronological record of all first appearances of her complete works including books, essays, articles, reviews, translations, film and television adaptations, even art work for college publications. If it is criticism you need, you may at first be disappointed when you find only one book listed in *Bibliographic Index*—in the 1978 volume—but it alone will make your search worthwhile, for it is a 342-page list of works by and about O'Connor and Caroline Gordon (Boston: Hall, 1977), and it will probably serve as your basic author bibliography for the duration of your research. If your library does not own this volume (Wellesley, for example, does not, but the University of Florida does), you may want to buy it yourself, depending on the extent of your intended research, because it is seldom possible to borrow bibliographies through interlibrary loan. *Bibliographic Index* also lists, in its April 1983 issue, one brief bibliography in Frederick Asals, *Flannery O'Connor: The Imagination of Extremity* (Athens: Univ. of Georgia Press, 1982), pp. 257–63.

14. Since what you need at this point is recently completed research, you will now go to the *Bulletin of Bibliography* (C29), a favorite quarterly specializing in up-to-date bibliographies on a remarkable variety of timely subjects and modern authors. Proper strategy is to start with the most recent issue (which cannot possibly have yet been indexed by any of the indexing services) and work backward to about two years *before* the publication date of the latest comprehensive bibliography, which in O'Connor's case is the Hall book you just located in *Bibliographic Index*. This time overlap is essential because the work required for the final editing, printing, and binding of a book consumes many months during which there is no opportunity to update the manuscript, so its contents are invariably, and regrettably, out of date long before it arrives in your library. That is why any *book* bibliography has to be updated with annual, quarterly, or monthly publications. Nothing on O'Connor is to be found in the most recent issues of the *Bulletin of Bibliography*. *BB*'s index for 1897–1975, however, shows that there is an O'Connor bibliography in the October-December 1975 issue, a five-page list of critical works that may or may not be in the Hall book. You would have to compare them to be sure. *BB* does not appear to be of much help in the O'Connor project, but it is often the best and only source for bibliographies, whether for major or minor authors, contemporary or historical issues. You should always consult it when you work on

any literary research project.

15. Returning now to your original quest for scholarship on the short stories, you may next want to browse through the current unbound issues of *Studies in Short Fiction* (G80, *SSF*) because they have not yet been in print long enough to have been indexed by *MLAIB* or other annual or quarterly bibliographies. The indexing procedure, like the printing process, takes time, so you always, in any literature search, plan to examine the current year's periodicals individually (and you have to catch them quickly before the library whisks them off to the binder, where they may stay for months). *SSF* will usually reward the O'Connor scholar. The Summer 1981 issue, for instance, contains a factual account of the journey in "A Good Man Is Hard to Find."

16. By this time you may have decided that it would be wise to read all the O'Connor short stories. Naturally, other students have come to the same conclusion, perhaps long before you did, so the library shelves are bare. Undaunted, you go directly to *Short Story Index* (G76, *SSI*), which provides information on where to find short stories in anthologies. The 1976 volume of *SSI*, for instance, shows that "Good Country People" is included in a collection entitled *Initiation* (New York: Harcourt, 1976). The 1977 *SSI* volume shows that "The Life You Save May Be Your Own" is in a McGraw-Hill publication, *The Realm of Fiction*. Older volumes of *SSI* will undoubtedly help you locate most of O'Connor's short stories in one or more anthologies, and your library will almost certainly own some of them.

17. If you cannot find all the O'Connor works that you need and if you want to refresh your mind on some of the details of her plots and characters, you may have to resort to the summaries in the latest editions of Magill's *Masterplots* (J518, R955, W1591). The cumulative indexes will indicate that O'Connor has entries in several of the volumes. Warnings about these sources: The quality of the interpretation varies greatly, the facts are not always accurate, your friends will snicker if you mention their existence, and, should you foolishly copy more than one word, you will be suspended instantly for plagiarism because your professors know Magill by heart. (You may read into this last sentence anything you wish.) The truth is that Magill, Salem (see Index), Monarch Notes, and other summarizing services are as familiar to most students as fraternity files. Acknowledging their existence is the best possible way to guard against their indiscriminate use.

18. Turning next to O'Connor's novels, you will find that the information in *American Novel* (P786) has been largely superseded because its copyright date is 1970. *Contemporary Novel* (J542) is more helpful, with three pages of general studies on her style and themes (about sixty entries), two and a half pages on *The Violent Bear It Away*, and one and a half pages on *Wise Blood*. Other sources for information on the novel do exist, such as Nevius (P784) and *Studies in the Novel* (G66), but they do not happen to be productive for O'Connor at this time. *Novel: A Forum on Fiction* (G64) does have an occasional helpful article.

19. You might find additional information on O'Connor's fiction in Rosa and Eschholz, *Contemporary Fiction in America and England, 1950-1970* (J536). Nine pages are devoted to her works, but most of the entries were written in

the 1960s and probably are included in the sources you have already consulted. *Contemporary Novelists* (W1130) and Woodress' *American Fiction* (P782) contain no information on O'Connor; *Studies in American Fiction* (P788) and *Modern Fiction Studies* (J544), very little; but the Gothic elements in her works might be considered in Louis Rubin's books (P711) or in the titles in Gothic Fiction (G81–82).

20.   Up to this point, the assumption has been that there are few if any limits on your time and interest. If you are limited, however, and if what you need is merely a brief critical overview of how O'Connor has been received by critics through the years, you need spend only ten minutes with *Modern American Literature* (P732), which is very much like *Contemporary Literary Criticism* (J516), mentioned in paragraph 1e. There you will find extracts from critics' reviews arranged chronologically so that you can trace the increased appreciation of O'Connor's talent and determine which critics first discerned her particular genius. Should an extract pique your interest, you can find and read the entire article because the citation appears at the end of each entry.

21.   If this limited search makes you want to read the reviews her books received when they were first published, two commonly available sources will help you locate them immediately. The *Author/Title Index, 1905–1974,* of *Book Review Digest* (W1558) leads to six different annual volumes containing excerpts from O'Connor's reviews. And once you have found the correct copyright date for her books in the *National Union Catalog* (B11) or *Books in Print* (W1170), you can look in the appropriate volume of *Index to Book Reviews in the Humanities* (W1560) for several more reviews. The 1961 volume, for instance, contains citations for six reviews of *The Violent Bear It Away*, published in 1960.

22.   An O'Connor project with a cross-disciplinary interest requires an entirely different approach. If you are pursuing her interest in religion, psychology, sociology, or history, for example, you will probably elect as your first reference source that excellent quarterly publication *Humanities Index* (F45) because it includes one or two entries on O'Connor in almost every issue. If the editors would expand their subject index to include proper names, *Psychological Abstracts* (E39), too, would be an excellent source for cross-disciplinary research. As it is, you will have to look in the table of contents for "Literature and Art" and turn to that section to browse through the entries. Once located, however, this section unearths fascinating studies on Kafka, Salinger, Swift, Brecht, black literature, Dickens, the Gothic novel, Proust, and dozens of other subjects. In addition, the *Catholic Periodical and Literature Index* (W1543) occasionally contains entries on O'Connor, and *Essay and General Literature Index* (F46) has something about her in almost every issue.

23.   Strangely, the women characters in O'Connor's works have received relatively little attention. Myers' *Women in Literature* (W1634) does list thirteen books and articles, but none of the other reference sources devoted to women is of any great help in this area (see Women's Studies, W1629–49). To the enterprising student this situation should suggest an immediate course of action.

24.   Interest in Flannery O'Connor's life, however, has remained constant

throughout the years. Almost every issue of *Biography Index* (W1085) contains two or three entries, a recent one listing articles in *Time, Newsweek, Commonweal,* and the *New York Times Book Review. Contemporary Authors* (W1127) provides no additional information, but it does make cross-references to *Contemporary Literary Criticism* (see paragraph 1e). And finally, the *New York Times Obituaries Index* (W1148) indicates that articles were published on O'Connor on 4 and 5 August 1964.

25.   At this stage in your research, you may feel obligated to check some of the time–honored older literary sources to see if they have any leads you ought to follow. In many cases, their age will nullify their usefulness; in others, the information is less complete and accurate than that provided by publications already discussed:

> Rubin (P711) has been superseded in most areas, but the subject approach may still be useful. *Southern Writers: A Biographical Dictionary* (P711) serves as both supplement and complement to Rubin.
>
> Jones (P707) makes only two brief references to O'Connor.
>
> *LHUS* (P701) neglects O'Connor shamefully. She is the subject of exactly six sentences, and the accompanying bibliography was out of date when *LHUS* was published.
>
> Callow and Reilly (P704) have a two-page discussion of O'Connor's works and a one-page bibliography. This is suitable for quick survey-type problems.
>
> *Reader's Adviser* (A4) gives only one page to O'Connor, but it supplies brief facts on her life, a list of her major works, and selected important criticism.
>
> *Encyclopedia of World Literature in the 20th Century* (J523) is an adequate source for the important facts of O'Connor's life and the salient themes of her works.
>
> Havlice (P702) offers no new material.
>
> Nilon (C27) has no new material.
>
> *Southern Literature, 1968-1975* (P755) overlaps with other sources (*MLAIB*, D31, for instance), but you will find this conflation from the *Mississippi Quarterly* useful for chronological studies, and it can be brought up to date with the periodical's annual bibliographies.

26.   Dissertations are easily handled. Go to McNamee (W1212), look in the subject index, and find—surprise—no titles listed in the main volume (c1968), twelve in the first supplement (c1969), and thirty in the second (c1974). Very few additional dissertations appear in the other basic sources (W1211-15), but more recent titles are of course reported in *DAI* (W1214).

27.   If you are interested in examining O'Connor's manuscripts and papers, the section in this guide on Library Collections (W1313-24) will help you select the appropriate sources. If you are interested in collecting first editions of her works, Book Collecting (W1153-69) contains the information you need. And of course you will read every word in the section on Women's Studies

(W1629–49). There are, as you can see, no limits to research possibilities except those of your imagination.

Research Project B: Lord Byron

1.   Scholarship on Byron is, in general, well organized and easily accessible. You may want to begin by considering the descriptions in this guide of the general reference books for Nineteenth-Century English Literature (J415–33):

   a.   The *New Cambridge Bibliography of English Literature* (*New CBEL*), vol. 3, 1800–1900 (J415), provides information on all important primary and secondary material on Byron up to its own preparation date.

   b.   The annual bibliographies *MLAIB* (D31), *Year's Work in English Studies* (D33), and *ABELL* (D32) will help you accumulate more recent or more extensive material than that found in the *New CBEL*.

   c.   *Poole's* (J416) and the *Wellesley Index* (J466) locate periodical articles written in the nineteenth century on Byron, and Madden and Dixon (J420) list nine titles that might be helpful.

2.   You might prefer, on the other hand, to focus on the titles listed in Romantic Literature (J434–52):

   a.   In the Oxford History of English Literature, the surveys on the Romantic period by Renwick (J434) and Jack (J435) provide reliable background information and bibliographies.

   b.   Jackson's volume for the Routledge History of English Poetry (J436) makes a valuable reassessment of Byron's contributions to poetry as a genre. The bibliographies on the Romantic poets by Reiman (J440), Jordan (J437), and Fogle (J439) also have special sections devoted to Byron scholarship. Reiman may be the only source you will need to use for some projects because his guide is up-to-date, accurate, and comprehensive.

   c.   The antagonism between Byron and his critics is legend. *Romantics Reviewed* (J441) and *Literary Reviews in British Periodicals* (J442) offer endless possibilities for investigation.

   d.   The *Romantic Movement Bibliography* (J443), both retrospective and current, will help you locate scholarship on Byron and on Romanticism in the broadest sense of the term.

   e.   If you want a periodical that supplies recent scholarship on both the poet and his times, see the *Keats-Shelley Journal* (J444) and the two cumulations of its annual bibliography, or *Studies in English Literature* (J320), Autumn issue.

   f.   Several books are useful for background reading (J449–52). Their distinguished authors have spent many years studying the primary and secondary material in their field. If the volumes you choose contain bibliographies, you would certainly be wise to consult the titles that they recommend.

3.   As a cautious researcher, you may prefer to begin with the *Reader's Adviser* (A4, vol. 1) for evaluations of the various editions or works pertaining to Byron so you will know what *type* of book you are looking for and which

scholars are most dependable.

4. You can also consult Section B, Basic Guides, and see that Bateson and Meserole (B17) indicate the preferred critical works and editions of Byron. A more extensive evaluation of Byron research in the Oxford University Press guide by Dyson (J216) is now ten years old, so, unless you are doing a retrospective project, it may not be of much help.

5. If your most urgent need is for a recently published author bibliography of works by and about Byron, you will of course look first in your library's card catalog. You will next consult Section C of this guide, Bibliographies of Bibliographies, to familiarize yourself with the *Bulletin of Bibliography* (C29) and *Bibliographic Index* (C28). They list information on the latest bibliographies of all kinds, and your librarian will probably be more than willing to buy a copy if you find one described in those sources. Finally, turn to the entry on Author Bibliographies (W1053–54) in the reference section of this guide, where you will find that Scarecrow publishers have issued a bibliography of works by and about Lord Byron (W1054). If you want advice on the most recent scholarship of *all* kinds, you should consult Reviews to find how to use *Choice* (W1557), *American Reference Books Annual* (W1568), and other review sources.

6. To save time, you may prefer to read summaries of critical articles about Byron. In Section E, Abstracting Services, you will see that *Abstracts of English Studies* (E38) is an appropriate source.

7. For an extensive project you may want to read pertinent chapters in books, or critical essays in collections. You will then use Section F, Indexing Services, and see that *Essay and General Literature Index* (F46) specializes in locating such material.

8. For the explication of specific passages from Byron's poetry, you will want to consult Section G, Genres, where the *Explicator* (G56–57) is cited as of possible use. Poetry—General (G125–37.1) recommends a variety of other authorities such as Preminger, Brooks, and Ciardi; but most important, that section describes two reference books that are favorites with students when they first begin doing research on poetry: *Poetry Explication* (G125) and *Index to Criticisms of British and American Poetry* (G126). See also the recent publication by Alexander (G137.1). More advanced researchers who are interested in the adventures of Don Juan and Childe Harold will need to use vol. 1 of *Epic and Romance Criticism* (G127).

9. If you are concerned with Byron's influence on the Continent, you will want to examine the titles listed in Section T, Comparative Literature (T1007–24).

10. You can find the latest biographical studies of Byron in *Biography Index* (W1085), while a quick source of reliable information on his life and contribution to English literature is the *Dictionary of National Biography* (W1086).

11. If you want to purchase copies of Byron's works, *Books in Print* (W1170) will give you information on currently available editions. If your research requires you to use originals, you should consult Library Collections (W1313–24) to learn where to locate his manuscripts and papers. And Interlibrary Loan (W1312) will show you how to go about borrowing materials.

12. When working on Byron's language and imagery in *Don Juan*, you may want guidance in the use of Concordances (W1194). You may also need to consult the *Oxford English Dictionary* (W1205).

13. For a quick overview of Byron's historical background, see Langer's *Encyclopedia of World History* (W1292) in this guide's section on History and the *Handbook of British Chronology* (W1201) in the section on Dates.

14. If you are doing a historical study of Byron and need to verify nineteenth-century reactions to his works, turn to the section on Literary Criticism and look for titles that specialize in reprinting excerpts from works by literary critics. The Critical Heritage Series (W1361) and *The Critical Temper* (W1358) will probably give you what you need.

15. For explanations of Byron's historical or literary allusions, you might look in Literary Encyclopedias such as the *Reader's Encyclopedia* (W1402) or the *Oxford Companion to English Literature* (J178).

16. When you need clarification of prosodic terms such as Byron's ottava rima, you should look for a definition in a Literary Handbook such as Holman's *Handbook to Literature* (W1406), in the titles concerned with Prosody (W1504–08.1), or in Preminger (G128).

17. For brief plot summaries of Byron's longest works, go to the appropriate titles listed in the section on Summaries (W1589–92).

The crucial point, as you can see from these examples, is that you must first **analyze the question**—and **then** start looking. The folly of expecting to find information about Byron in *Contemporary Authors* (W1127) is immediately obvious to everyone, but it is just as useless to waste time and energy confining your efforts to the *MLAIB* (D31)—excellent source though it is—if what you really need is a Review of Research (W1556), which for Byron's works is Jordan (J437, soon to be updated).

Research, in other words, must be orderly. The penalties for a haphazard approach are frayed nerves, foiled research, and, even worse, a regrettable determination never to enter the library again. The preventive, or antidote, is to **analyze the question**. Use this guide to pinpoint the books that you think are most likely to contain the answer, and then examine them. If you do not find what you want, consider your question again, think about the *type* of book you've selected, and criticize, too, the *way* in which you are using the book. Are you looking for a title in an author index? Would the table of contents quickly give you a clue to the solution? If an abbreviation baffles you, have you looked for an explanatory table in the front of the book (like the one that precedes this Introduction)? Would the author's introduction about scope and purpose tell you why you haven't found your answer in the book? Are you reading and rereading this guide to broaden your own knowledge of your chosen field?

Finally, try to convert every research problem into a positive learning experience. Before you get frustrated and decide to chuck the whole thing in favor of selling real estate, go to the humanities librarian and say, "Look, I can't find what I want. Why?" (Not, you will notice, "Find it for me.") Good librarians are also good teachers. They are trained to teach you how to select and use appropriate research tools. Listen to their analysis of your tactical errors, and profit from your peregrinations. Make mental and written notes of the books you consulted by mistake so that you can return to them when next you need their information. Jot down comments in the margin of this guide (unless it is a library copy!). There is strategy to research just as there is to a game of chess, a small slam, a good round of golf—and, surprisingly, a similar kind of triumph and satisfaction.

Acknowledgments

The first edition of the *Literary Research Guide* required the better part of six years to forge its way from scribbled notes to reference library shelf. The revision has taken another four years, easier years in some ways because the structure was there, but more difficult in others because hundreds of new books had to be scrutinized, dozens of titles removed from the manuscript, dozens more added, new sections inserted to answer the needs of the times, and all comparisons reevaluated. Of necessity this had to be the work of one memory through which everything could be recalled and associated, but fortunately a hardy crew of advisory editors was at hand, an articulate, demanding, knowledgeable, encouraging crew who helped to store the ballast, set the sails, and batten the hatches, so to speak, even though the solitary hand at the tiller was responsible for fetching the mark.

Those who were especially generous with their time and conscientious with their criticism were Kelsie B. Harder, professor of English at the State University College at Potsdam, New York; Mary George, reference librarian at Princeton University; Joan Stockard, reference librarian at Wellesley College; Thomas Clayton, professor of English at the University of Minnesota; James L. Harner, professor of English at Bowling Green State University; Dedria Bryfonski, editor at Gale Research, Detroit; and Walter S. Achtert, director of Book Publications and Research Programs, MLA. Some of these scholars concentrated on those specific parts of the manuscript that related to their own professional areas. Others read the entire manuscript for overall accuracy and consistency. Both points of view are essential. For their shared knowledge, cheerful cooperation, and enthusiastic encouragement, I wish to express my sincerest respect and gratitude. Others who helped to resolve specific research problems were Madge Tams, Annette Liles, Virginia Francis, Fleming Montgomery, Tim Lozier, Dolores Jenkins, and Marie Nelson of the University of Florida; Edith Alpers, Claire Loranz, Sally Linden, and Michael Hyde of Wellesley College; and Vincent Tollers of the State University of New York at Brockport. True scholarship drew these professors, librarians, and editors together as did the conviction that it is essential to present information accurately, to express arguments objectively, and to state ideas clearly. All the errors they reported have been corrected, and as many suggestions have been accepted as seemed appropriate to the needs of the student who will use this book. An insignificant number of librarians were uncooperative with their books, working room, or time. Let us consider them just that—insignificant.

More than a little assistance came from an unusual source—one or two indignant academics who were apparently offended by the reviewers' approval of the first edition. With the concerted effort of friends and students they found and reported a most helpful accumulation of errors and omissions which I have most gratefully accepted. The second edition will be much improved by their efforts; I extend my thanks. They also, unfortunately, reported as errors an unduly large number of items that were correct.

Finally, thanks must go to the *Harvard Concordance to Shakespeare*, which is exactly the right size to bring incredibly uncomfortable oak chairs into something resembling conformity with incredibly high oak tables at the institution of the same name. And to Jim Beam, who lightened my days and nights and who is responsible for every error in this book. Without him it would of course have been flawless.

M.C.P.
Autumn 1982

Guidelines for the Reader

Collecting a Personal Library

"Serious students of literature own a small personal library of basic reference books that can be consulted quickly as the need arises." So began the first edition of this book. Seven years have passed, yet there is no better opening statement for a working guide to efficient methods and essential tools of literary research. Scholars are not born; they are made. Library literacy does not come automatically, any more than does fine writing style with one semester of freshman English. It is a cumulative experience that prospers only in an encouraging atmosphere. It begins when children receive a copy of *The Wind in the Willows*, when they find pleasure in collecting the Sherlock Holmes stories, when they acquire a *Webster's Collegiate Dictionary* for their own room, when they discover Bartlett's *Familiar Quotations* on the family bookshelves, and when finally they go to scour the public library for their current reading passion. They have learned to enjoy reading, and they have learned to enjoy having books around them. And so it is that when they become "serious students of literature" they find that one of the most pleasant by-products of the literary profession is the privilege of hoarding books. Everyone approves—the family, their colleagues, even the IRS. The only question is, What books will they need most?

As undergraduates in literature they begin with three desk companions that will serve them for the rest of their professional careers:

Holman's *Handbook to Literature* (W1406)
Benét's *Reader's Encyclopedia* (W1402)
MLA Handbook for Writers (W1584)

In addition, no matter what field of literature they select for their own specialty, they will want the two classic literary histories:

Baugh's *Literary History of England* (J170)
Spiller's *Literary History of the United States* (P701)

As their reading assignments lengthen and their themes thicken, so does the need for reference sources that give quick solutions to identification and definition problems:

Webster's Biographical Dictionary (W1080)
Princeton Encyclopedia of Poetry and Poetics (G128)
Oxford Companions to thirteen subjects including English, American, French, Spanish, German, Canadian, and classical literature; art, music, film, and theater (see Index)

Trained now to appreciate the delicate balance of fine literary style, they concurrently become painfully aware of the deficiencies in their own writing. Many of their problems can be alleviated by these two books:

Watkins, *Practical English Handbook* (W1188)
Webster's New Dictionary of Synonyms (W1593)

For literature courses in a specialized area, students will probably find that one of the basic research guides in these series will be sufficient for a while:

Goldentree Bibliographies (W1291)
Gale Information Guide Library (A8)

More advanced courses may indicate the need for one of the volumes in specialized surveys such as

Oxford History of English Literature (J174)
Revels History of Drama in English (G114)
Perkins, *A History of Modern Poetry* (J568)

And a major advance is made toward professional status when students recognize the benefit of owning excellent reviews of research such as

Logan and Smith's four surveys in English Renaissance drama (J343–46)
Oxford University Press Select Bibliographical Guides (J204, novel; J212, drama; J216, poetry)
Bryer, *Sixteen Modern American Authors* (P728)

Knowledgeable professors will point out to their students the perils of inaccurate editions, the influence of proud relatives and profiteering publishers on the final form of the manuscript, the existence of expurgations, the folly of abridgments. For guidance in selecting best editions, not only in original works but in criticism, not only in literature but in all fields, students can go to a source that is revised frequently:

Reader's Adviser (A4)

This will continue to be a basic reference point as they gradually acquire a fine reference library centered solely on their own needs and preferences. Such expenditures can result only in profits.

Using This Guide

A good selection policy and full utilization of available materials are essential if the literature student wishes to become proficient in research methods. This guide encourages the development of both:

1. The **guide number** at the top margin of each page will help locate specific titles and general subject areas. Students may approach the information in this guide from either the Table of Contents or the Index. Professors may want to refer to the entry numbers when making assignments.

2. **Complete bibliographical information** is supplied for every title:

a. *Author's or editor's name.* The full name, including middle initial, is included whenever possible so that students can do name searches on their computer terminals. If they are uncertain of the exact wording of the title, for instance, they may decide that a computer search by author should be their first step. In entries for periodicals and other serials that characteristically have frequent administrative changes, the editor's name is not included.

b. *Edition number.* Students should always notice this important item, especially when their assignment requires the most recent information or an edition published in a specific year.

c. *Publisher, city, and date.* This information is absolutely necessary for accurate identification. When more than one publisher or city is cited on the title page of the book in question, only the first is noted here. When both publication date and reprint date are provided, they are written "1960; rpt. 1976." When both a recent publication date and an earlier copyright date for a previous edition are provided, they are written "1979, c1954." In citations of periodicals, only the current publisher and current publishing facts are provided.

d. *Bibliographies.* Most scholarly books contain bibliographies that have been compiled with great care by their scholarly authors. Students usually overlook them, but they can save hours of needless, repetitive searching. Their existence in a book is almost always noted on the catalog card, and they are noted in this guide.

e. *Number of pages.* Clever students realize that this item is a clue to comprehensiveness.

f. *Series title.* This is useful for identification purposes, but each book must be judged on its own merit, not on the general reputation of the publisher or of the entire series. Series titles are not italicized; they are set in roman type to distinguish them from the titles of individual volumes.

g. *Availability in paperback.* To own is better than to borrow.

h. *Library of Congress and Dewey numbers.* These are included because they may indicate a specific location or general area where the book may be shelved in the library. They are of course only indications, because at present every library has its own method of cataloging and shelving, but they may help the student develop the habit of intelligent browsing. Certain schools of thought hold that our increasing dependence on computer cataloging and searching will encourage standardization of book identification, for economic reasons as well as for search efficiency. For the sake of consistency, almost all L.C. and Dewey numbers in this guide come from one source (a computer terminal tied in with the Online Computer Library Center; see OCLC in the Glossary) and one staff (the Library of Congress in Washington, D.C.). The official Library of Congress number is cited first, followed by an alternative L.C. subject area number in brackets that some libraries may prefer, and then a suggested Dewey number that libraries on the Dewey system can adapt to their own needs (the prime, or apostrophe, in the number indicates a possible cutoff point):

Z5917.S36.T95   [PN3448.S45]   016.823'087

The Library of Congress does not usually append author numbers to the suggested Dewey numbers because each library's system contains too many variables that would affect that designation. In a few cases the L.C. or Dewey number is not provided because it has not yet been assigned.

3.   A **dash** after the date in the imprint statement means the work is a continuing publication. The fact that *Modern Fiction Studies* published its first issue in 1955 and has since then published continuously is indicated in this way: *Modern Fiction Studies*, 1955–   .

4.   The **title** appears first in the entry when readers customarily refer to the book by its title. The author's name is printed first when it is favored as a designation for the book. Changes in titles are not cited unless the previous title had a special significance. When a supplement, cumulation, or new edition has a different title, however, that information is included in the main entry, as in W1033 or W1088. In a very few cases, when a companion piece, superseded title, or less important book is closely related in scope to the main entry, it is mentioned and described in the same annotation rather than in a separate entry.

5.   **Abbreviations** for periodical titles are placed in parentheses after the title. They include both the conventional *MLAIB* (D31) abbreviation and a shortened version that will enable readers to recognize the title immediately when it is mentioned in the text, as, for example, *Abst. Eng. Stud.* (E38).

6.   **Arrangement of titles** in the chronological and genre areas generally begins with the most commonly used books and proceeds to the more specialized. The "See also" and "Background reading" lists at the end of most sections and subsections are arranged alphabetically for ease in consultation. In the periodical sections the outstanding periodical is often placed first, and the rest are listed alphabetically.

7.   **Titles** are listed only once and have only one main entry number. If the book covers material from several national, ethnic, religious, or cultural interests, it is placed in one of those sections with cross-references to and from all others. Cross-references to all related subject areas are an essential feature of this guide and of all research.

8.   An **entry number** without parentheses is the main entry. A number in parentheses is a cross-reference that refers the reader to the main entry for a full description and annotation.

9.   **Asterisks** indicate essential reference books that literary scholars use most

frequently. Students should put these titles and authors high on their investigation list because they will find that these books are mentioned again and again in their classes and in their reading. Those books marked with one asterisk (about four hundred) are familiar old friends of all experienced literature students; those with two (about forty) are generally for more advanced research. The asterisk can serve as a guide for readers who are looking for the most respected and most helpful titles in every area of literature. Usually at least one entry in each section and subsection has an asterisk, sometimes because of the work's unique contribution to that area (Bosworth and Toller, J233, for example) and sometimes because of its general acceptance (for instance, the Oxford History of English Literature, J174, a series whose main entry bears an asterisk because all students should be aware of its scope and purpose even though several of its volumes are not outstanding and do not merit an asterisk). These asterisks will unquestionably be the single most controversial feature of this guide, but controversy, too, can be useful. They are certain to prompt heated discussions, scornful derision, and classroom disagreements. They will, as as result, encourage debate on the merits of the entry, which is one of the reasons they are included.

10.   **Spelling** of titles is exactly as it appears on the title page. Readers will find, therefore, *Newsletters* and *News Letters*, *Eighteenth-Century Studies* and *20,000 Years of Fashion*, *Medieval Studies* and *Mediaeval Stage*, *1700-39* and *1740-1749*. **Capitalization** is normalized in accordance with the recommendations of the *MLA Handbook for Writers* (W1584) rather than as it appears on the title page, as the purist might prefer, especially for foreign periodicals or early reference books.

11.   Many **annotations** contain references to specific chapters or subject headings in the book under discussion so that the reader can better understand how that particular reference source can help in research. These chapter and subject titles are capitalized to distinguish them from other general areas covered in the same book.

12.   The **main sections** of this guide are designated by the letters *A* through *Z*. To avoid confusion with numbers, the letters *I*, *O*, *U*, and *V* have been omitted.

13.   At the **end of most sections** one or two entry numbers are omitted so that the owner of the guide can enter recent publications and favorite titles. Insertion of pertinent information in the Index and Table of Contents will keep this a current guide to literary research. Another strictly utilitarian reason for omitting an occasional number in each section is that while in transit from the author's desk to the binder and bookstore—a journey that now requires two or three years—the manuscript can accommodate the addition of recently published titles and new editions and thus be up to date when it finally reaches the student.

14.   Because the **glossary of bibliographical terms** (Section Y) contains so many phrases and abbreviations, it is arranged letter by letter. That is, "incipit" comes before "in preparation." This order will also give the student some practice in using that form of alphabetical arrangement.

15.   The **index** (Section Z) is in word-by-word alphabetical order, as are most card catalogs and reference books. When using this method, alphabetize

to the end of each word and then start over (New York comes before Newark).

    a.   When the first word is duplicated in several items, the order is always *a*uthor, *s*ubject, *t*itle (*a*, *s*, *t*, alphabetically):

French, William P.	P868
FRENCH LITERATURE	Q902–15, R957
French Literature: A Student's Guide	Q905

    b.   Subject headings are set in full capitals and placed to the left of the other items, as in the above example.

    c.   Abbreviations are placed at the beginning of the alphabet (MLA, therefore, is listed at the beginning of the *M*'s).

    d.   When looking for names beginning with *Mc* or *Mac*, ignore the real spelling and pretend they all are spelled *Mac*.

    e.   When looking for names beginning with *O'*, ignore the apostrophe.

    f.   Titles that include dates are arranged chronologically.

    g.   To distinguish a series from the individual volumes within that series, the series title is in roman and the individual titles are in italic.

Finally, when you are examining the reference books described in this guide, take notes on those features that are going to be useful to you in your field. Add those notes to the annotations in your own copy of the guide, and take it with you when you work on your research project. The handful of reference resources you could handle comfortably as a freshman will gradually and surely become the distinguished four hundred that receive asterisks in this guide. And by then you will know that "Learning how to learn is one of the best investments that can be made for an effective life" (Carnegie Foundation for the Advancement of Learning).

Short-Title Table of Contents

1

Literary Research Guide

A

General Guides to Reference Books and Research Procedures

General Research

For general research problems in any discipline, the student might first consult these basic reference sources:

A1.   Gates, Jean Key. *Guide to the Use of Books and Libraries*. 5th ed. New York: McGraw-Hill, 1983. 360pp. Paperback. Z710.G27   028.7
    The best possible source for clarifying any uncertainties about the use of the library. This begins with a brief history of the development of books and libraries from Nineveh to computers, then defines and discusses card and book catalogs, stresses the importance of learning to use Library of Congress subject headings, and explains the Dewey and L.C. systems for arranging books on the shelf. All literature students, for instance, should know how to locate a copy of Wordsworth's poems without resorting to the card catalog, which is generally upstairs or downstairs from wherever they are at the moment. Gates also illustrates the logic and availability of general and specific information sources that are so often ignored, defines the *types* of reference sources, and annotates the most popular titles in the humanities, social sciences, and sciences. Especially useful for the undergraduate who is taking courses in several disciplines and has not yet chosen a major.

A2.   Bell, Marion V., and Eleanor A. Swidan. *Reference Books: A Brief Guide for Students and Other Users of the Library*. 8th ed. Baltimore: Enoch Pratt Free Library, 1978. 179 pp. Paperback. Z1035.1.E35   028.7
    The best pocket-size (inexpensive) guide to reference books in all branches of the humanities, sciences, and social sciences, with exemplary descriptive and evaluative annotations. This will be of special interest to students with cross-disciplinary interests. If they can cultivate the habit of consulting this source for titles that might possibly answer their questions *before* they start groping

3

around the library, they will save time and ultimately become confident, knowledgeable researchers.

A3.   Cheney, Frances Neel, and Wiley J. Williams. *Fundamental Reference Sources.* 2nd ed. Chicago: American Library Assn., 1980. 351pp. Z1035.1.C5   011.02

The most lucid and readable of the scholarly general guides. This focuses only on bibliographies, biographical dictionaries, encyclopedias, and statistics and is not intended for the more complex problems in literary research. The arrangement reflects the library-trained mind of the author, for it is by type of question and then by type of possible source such as index, biography, handbook, or directory.

The annotations point out the strengths and weaknesses of each book and include good advice on how to use the information: *International Who's Who* (W1096) is "A good source for persons from countries without a national *Who's Who*, but not to be preferred to a national *Who's Who*." These suggestions are both wise and welcome, for the author has spent years in the research business. She gives over fifty pages to "Words," for example, explaining how and why dictionaries have been compiled over the centuries, comparing their merits, and designating which titles are best for language usage, synonyms, pronunciation, slang, dialect, and rhyme.

A3.1.   Baker, Nancy L. *A Research Guide for Undergraduate Students: English and American Literature.* New York: MLA, 1982. 40pp. PR56.B34   820'.72

A primer for students who need instruction in the use of a few basic reference books that will help them write better research papers. Here they learn why *Bibliographic Index* (C28) is an essential first step in research procedure, how the card catalog and subject headings can suggest research topics, and why the *Essay and General Literature Index* (F46) makes a unique and valuable contribution to any research project. The illustrations and annotated list of most frequently used reference books are important learning aids. Methodical, uncomplicated.

*A4.   *Reader's Adviser: A Layman's Guide to Literature.* 12th ed. 3 vols. New York: Bowker, 1974–77. Z1035.G73   016.028

The title indicates the purpose of this popular interdisciplinary book: to provide for the layman the most accurate and most respected titles by and about the greatest authors, with explanations and quoted criticism for many authors and titles, and subject summaries at the beginning of each chapter. The unexpectedly interesting comments are spiced with little-known facts of biographical or critical interest. Readable and witty, concise and convenient, this should be consulted when other guides seem cumbersome or perfunctory. Many scholars purchase it for their home libraries. Malcolm Muggeridge, no less, agrees that it is useful.

Vol. 1: *The Best in American and British Fiction, Poetry, Essays, Literary Biography, Bibliography, and Reference* (808pp.), ed. Sarah L. Prakken. Suggests the best titles for subjects ranging from bibliographies of early books to censorship (with a summary of past and current problems which admits that obscenity is still undefined). The thirty pages devoted to Modern British Poetry, for instance, progress from a brief summary of the state of affairs to critical comments on specific works devoted to individual authors such as Wilfred Owen, Robert Graves, and Lawrence Durrell.

Vol. 2: *The Best in American and British Drama and World Literature in English Translation* (774pp.), ed. F. J. Sypher. World literature here includes classical Greek as well as European, African, Middle Eastern, and Asian.

Vol. 3: *The Best in the Reference Literature of the World* (1034pp.), ed. Jack A. Clarke. Selects and describes the most helpful titles in religion, philosophy, science, social science, history, opera, dance, film, the media, folklore, humor, and travel.

Points to remember: The *Reader's Adviser* usually includes only those books currently available from publishers (see also the latest *Books in Print*, W1170). Its coverage of foreign literature is excellent, especially since it identifies the major works of non-English authors that have been translated into English, and it is gratifyingly comprehensive in all other fields. Its publishers schedule new editions regularly, but they make no attempt to supply complete bibliographical information, since that is easily available in other sources such as the *NUC* (B10–11). As an adviser to the reader, it is most successful in reporting on the best editions, the best biographies, the best criticism, and all recent publications of importance.

Advanced Research

—for advanced research by scholars and librarians:

**A5. Sheehy, Eugene P. *Guide to Reference Books.* 9th ed. Chicago: American Library Assn., 1976. 1015pp. Supplement 1 (1979), 305pp. Supplement 2 (1982), 243pp. Z1035.1.S43   011'.02

The librarians' bible. Advanced literature students who cannot find what they need in literary reference guides may also benefit from its suggestions, for it annotates and provides complete bibliographical information for over twelve thousand selected authoritative books essential to research in all fields.

The literature section describes important titles under such subject headings as Bibliography, Dictionaries, Atlases, History, Biography, Drama, Parodies, and Handbooks (an inadequate selection, however; see Literary Encyclopedias, W1402-05, and Literary Handbooks, W1406-14, in this guide). New entries for Women, Data Bases, and Science Fiction, but no citations for reviews, and almost no works concerned with individual authors. Library of Congress call numbers are included in each annotation, a great timesaver that sometimes enables students to bypass the card catalog and go directly to the library shelf. Every edition of this guide has had an excellent analytical index of titles, authors, and subjects. Two caveats: A few errors still persist, and the annotations are descriptive, not evaluative (except for the labeling of an occasional title as "important," "well selected," or "comprehensive"), so apprentice researchers are not given as much guidance as they might need. Introductions and prefaces are occasionally quoted, however, and the supplements may indicate a change in editorial policy because they include a handful of quotations from reviews.

Librarians still refer loyally to Mudge and Winchell, the editors of earlier editions of the *Guide to Reference Books*. Because there is usually an interval of several years between editions, students should anticipate occasional supplements. Supplements 1 and 2 of the ninth edition, for instance, bring coverage up to Fall 1980 and greatly enlarge, to the gratification of all, the sections on Ethnic Groups, Black Studies, Women, and Film. There are four more ways to keep up to date with new reference works: the annual list published in *Choice* (W1557) of outstanding reference books of the year, the timely *American Reference Books Annual* (W1568), reviews and notes in the highly specialized *Literary Research Newsletter* (W1421), and Sheehy's own column of reviews in the January and July issues of *College and Research Libraries* (W1324). See also Reviews of Reference Books (W1568–69.1).

A6.   Walford, Albert J. *Guide to Reference Material*. 3rd ed. 3 vols. London: Library Assn., 1973–77. Fourth edition in progress with new title, *Walford's Guide to Reference Material*: vol. 1, 1981; vol. 2, 1982; vol. 3 projected for 1984. Z1035.1.W33   011.02

Walford's Concise Guide to Reference Material. Phoenix, Ariz.: Oryx Press, 1981. 364pp.

A quality guide used by librarians for a comprehensive overview of materials in all fields for all centuries and all nations. Because this work emphasizes British contributions and gives ample space to European and Russian imprints, titles might be found here that are not mentioned in the American Sheehy (A5) or the French Malclès (A7). For instance, in addition to the expected titles in literary bibliography, periodicals, and genres, vol. 3 lists Tannenbaum's Elizabethan bibliographies plus the supplements written in the 1960s, and numerous titles for Irish, Australian, and many non-European literatures. Of particular value are the lengthy, carefully descriptive annotations for both general sources and individual authors. Occasional quotations from reviewing journals help to evaluate the unique contributions of new publications. Author, editor, compiler, title, and analytical subject indexes. Vol. 3 contains an excellent cumulated subject index for all three volumes. The *Concise Guide* contains selected, updated entries from the three volumes and adds some new material.

Most librarians find that Sheehy and Walford complement each other. Some feel that Sheehy is more accurate and easier to use because of its detailed index. Others prefer Walford because it emphasizes current scholarship, explains which titles are superseded and supplemented, defines the scope and limitations of all sources, and thus guides the student into methods of efficient research. Careful scholars use both.

A7.   Malclès, Louise-Noëlle. *Les Sources du travail bibliographique*. 4 vols. in 3. Genève: Droz, 1950–58; rpt. 1965. Abridged, updated edition, 1969. Z1002.M4   016.01
Malclès has attempted to be international and interdisciplinary in her three-

volume bibliography of reference materials, but of course she emphasizes Continental scholarship. The literary scholar should become acquainted not only with vol. 2, the Humanities, but also with vol. 1 and its excellent introduction to the problems of literary search with definitions, types of bibliography, history, official publications, professional journals, and learned societies. One of the most useful features is the chronological arrangement of the national bibliographies, which shows how easy it is to trace the fate of any one author or title, or how necessary it is to select the appropriate bibliography for research in a particular decade. Again, when logic is used, research is simple. In French. See French Literature (Q902–15) for additional titles.

Series—General

A8.   Gale Information Guide Library. American Literature, English Literature, and World Literatures in English: An Information Guide Series. Detroit: Gale, 1974– . In progress.

Research becomes both an art and a science in this ambitious project to produce a "guide to information sources" (the common subtitle) for every major area of current literary interest. Over three hundred volumes are under way, many of which are—note this—the first guides ever published in their subject areas. The quality varies, of course, but some are excellent and most are at least a good beginning. In general, they have been kindly received by reviewers. Their purpose: to be convenient sources for information on the handbooks, dictionaries, periodicals, surveys, various editions, and critical studies related to an author's life and works. In addition, each information guide has one or more of the following research aids: chronologies; annotations; indexes to titles, authors, and subjects; lists of periodicals; cross-references; definitions; prices, comments on availability, and indications of best editions; divisions according to geography, century, nationality, titles, author, and/or genre. The publication of each new title in this series will probably encourage a spate of enthusiastic projects and papers. Alert students will time their research accordingly. Unnumbered titles are in preparation or recently announced but not yet received.

Afro-American Fiction, 1853–1976. Ed. Edward Margolies and David Bakish (P856)
Afro-American Poetry and Drama, 1760–1975. Ed. William P. French et al. (P868)
American Drama to 1900. Ed. Walter J. Meserve (P796)
American Drama, 1900–1970. Ed. Paul J. Hurley
American Fiction to 1900. Ed. David K. Kirby (P781)
American Fiction, 1900–1950. Ed. James L. Woodress (P782)
American Poetry to 1900. Ed. Bernice Slote
American Poetry, 1900–1950. Ed. William White and Artem Lozynsky
American Prose and Criticism to 1820. Ed. Donald Yannella and John H. Roch (P793)
American Prose and Criticism, 1820–1900. Ed. Elinore H. Partridge (P793)

American Prose and Criticism, 1900-1950. Ed. Peter A. Brier and Anthony Arthur (P792)

Asian Literature in English. Ed. George L. Anderson (R983.1)

Australian Literature to 1900. Ed. Barry G. Andrews and William H. Wilde (N655)

Author Newsletters and Journals. Ed. Margaret C. Patterson (W1476)

Black African Literature in English. Ed. Bernth Lindfors (R972)

Contemporary Fiction in America and England, 1950-1970. Ed. Alfred F. Rosa and Paul A. Eschholz (J536)

Contemporary Irish Literature, 1940-1970. Ed. Patrick J. Keane

Contemporary Poetry in America and England, 1950-1975. Ed. Martin E. Gingerich. 1983

English-Canadian Literature to 1900. Ed. Robert G. Moyles (N664)

English Drama to 1660 (excluding Shakespeare). Ed. F. Elaine Penninger (J335)

English Drama, 1660-1800. Ed. Frederick M. Link (J399)

English Drama and Theatre, 1800-1900. Ed. Leonard W. Conolly and J. Peter Wearing (J426)

English Drama, 1900-1950. Ed. Edward H. Mikhail (J552)

English Fiction, 1660-1800. Ed. Jerry C. Beasley (J386)

English Fiction, 1800-1850. Ed. Duane DeVries

English Fiction, 1850-1900. Ed. Duane DeVries

English Fiction, 1900-1950 (2 vols.). Ed. Thomas J. Rice (J535)

English Literary Journal to 1900. Ed. Robert B. White, Jr. (J190)

English Literary Journal, 1900-1950. Ed. Michael N. Stanton (J533)

English Poetry, 1660-1800. Ed. Donald C. Mell (J409.1)

English Poetry, 1900-1950. Ed. Emily Ann Anderson (J570)

English Prose and Criticism, 1660-1800. Ed. John T. Shawcross

English Prose and Criticism in the Nineteenth Century. Ed. Harris W. Wilson and Diana Long Hoeveler (J423)

English Prose and Criticism, 1900-1950. Ed. Christopher C. Brown and William B. Thesing. 1983

English Prose, Prose Fiction, and Criticism to 1660. Ed. S. K. Heninger, Jr. (J324)

English Romantic Poetry, 1800-1835. Ed. Donald H. Reiman (J440)

Index to American Literature, English Literature, and World Literatures in English. Ed. Theodore Grieder

Indian Literature in English, 1827-1979. Ed. Amritjit Singh, Rajiva Verma, and Irene M. Joshi. 1981

Irish Literature, 1800-1875. Ed. Brian McKenna (K582)

Irish Literature, 1876-1950. Ed. Brian McKenna (K583)

Literary Journal in America to 1900. Ed. Edward E. Chielens (P741)

Little Magazines in America, 1950-1975. Ed. Robert Bertholf

Modern Australian Poetry, 1920-1970. Ed. Herbert C. Jaffa (N656)

Modern Australian Prose, 1901-1975. Ed. Arthur Grove Day (N657)

Modern Drama in America and England, 1950-1970. Ed. Richard H. Harris (P797)

Modern English-Canadian Poetry. Ed. Peter Stevens (N691)

Modern English-Canadian Prose. Ed. Helen Hoy (N693)
New Zealand Literature to 1977. Ed. John E. P. Thomson (N694)
Old and Middle English Poetry to 1500. Ed. Walter H. Beale (J241)
Renaissance Poetry to 1660. Ed. Walter H. Beale
Scottish Literature in English and Scots. Ed. William R. Aitken (L630)
Victorian Poetry, 1835–1900. Ed. Ronald E. Freeman
West Indian Literature in English. Ed. Priscilla Tyler

A8.1.   American Studies: An Information Guide Series, also published by
Gale, offers a few titles useful in literature projects:

Afro-American Literature and Culture since World War II. Ed. Charles D.
Peavy (P837)
American Folklore. Ed. Richard M. Dorson
American Humor and Humorists. Ed. M. Thomas Inge
American Literature and Language. Ed. Donald N. Koster. 1982
Jewish Writers of North America. Ed. Ira B. Nadel. 1981
Relationship of Literature and Painting. Ed. Eugene L. Huddleston and
Douglas A. Noverr (W1037)

B

National Literatures
Basic Guides and Bibliographies

Catalogs of National Libraries

Indispensable for verifying almost any bibliographical problem of any book from any country and century. The enormous holdings of national libraries and the accuracy of their catalogs render them the unchallenged arbiters in all matters of verification—dates, edition, publisher, spelling, accurate title, variants, pseudonyms, and, most important, availability for use, photoduplication, and interlibrary loan. No bibliography will ever be without its errors, of course, but these are the most comprehensive and most accurate *commonly available* sources for enlarging the information or unraveling the discrepancies found elsewhere. Pollard and Redgrave (J306), Wing (J370), and all the Evans clan (P717) are other favorite magistrates for verifying facts about early books.

American

**B10. *National Union Catalog, Pre-1956 Imprints*. 685 vols. London: Mansell, 1968–80. Supplements, vols. 686–754. Z881.A1.U518   021.6'4

The biggest library news of the twentieth century is that the *NUC, Pre-1956* project is finally completed. Fourteen years of work, twenty thousand carefully edited catalog cards delivered to the London flight every Friday (six hundred deadlines), $35 million, 754 massive volumes weighing eight pounds each, 528,000 pages—this is a permanent, distributable record of material from Gutenberg to 1956, a cumulative author list of the holdings of the Library of Congress in Washington, D.C., and one thousand other research-oriented libraries in the United States and Canada. The supplementary volumes add material accumulated since the original work was started in 1967 and record additional locations for items already listed. Scholars now have one source that tells them where in North America they can find more than five centuries' worth of the world's printed material.

The catalog's great strength lies in its comprehensiveness and the high degree of accuracy of the entries. The Library of Congress (L.C.), which provides the base information, is the largest in the country and acts as our national library. It has holdings of about 75 million titles including volumes, manuscripts, maps, prints, photographic items, broadsides, and other printed matter. Its collection is swelled annually by the law that requires deposit with the Library of any work for which copyright is registered (see Copyright in the Glossary).

Entries give full bibliographic descriptions of all editions reported by the cooperating libraries and then identify, by code, those libraries that own the books so that scholars can use them personally or, when possible, borrow them through interlibrary loan (see W1312). The main point for students to remember is that this is a *National* (including most large libraries), *Union* (with information accumulated from and available to everyone), *Catalog* (a record of the holdings of all participating libraries).

As a set, it cumulates and adds information to a series of Library of Congress catalogs published over the years. Some libraries unable to afford the massive Mansell publication may have the earlier sets or portions of them in reprint editions:

A Catalog of Books Represented by Library of Congress Printed Cards Issued to July 31, 1942 (L.C. Catalog). 167 vols. Ann Arbor, Mich.: Edwards Brothers, 1942–46. *Supplement: Cards Issued August 1, 1942–December 31, 1947.* 42 volumes. 1948. Z663.7.L512

Library of Congress Author Catalog: A Cumulative List of Works Represented by Library of Congress Printed Cards, 1948-52. 24 vols. Ann Arbor, Mich.: J. W. Edwards, 1953. Z663.7.L512

The National Union Catalog . . . 1953-57. 28 vols. Ann Arbor, Mich.: J. W. Edwards, 1958. Z663.7.L512

or

Library of Congress and National Union Catalog Author Lists, 1942-1962: A Master Cumulation. 152 vols. Detroit: Gale, 1969–71. Z881.A1.L63 018'.1'0973

A convenient cumulation of several cumbersome, multi-volume editions, including the basic set of the *L.C. Catalog* of 1942 and its four supplements. Many libraries will be content with this title because the *NUC* is so expensive.

**B11. *National Union Catalog: A Cumulative Author List Representing Library of Congress Printed Cards and Titles Reported by Other American Libraries (NUC).* Washington, D.C.: Library of Congress, 1958– . Monthly (9/yr.), with quarterly, annual, and five-year cumulations; since 1983, available on microfiche only (see COM in the Glossary), with quarterly author, subject, and title indexes. Z881.A1.U372

The *NUC* continues the bibliographic record of the previous entry (B10) for printed materials published after 1956. Additional libraries holding titles already recorded in the set can be located through the supplementary volumes in the *National Union Catalog: Register of Additional Locations,* 1963– .

Students who for one reason or another know only the *titles* of their research material have long had a valid complaint against the author-entry *NUC*. This problem has been alleviated by the publication of the *Cumulative Title Index to the Classified Collections of the Library of Congress* (Arlington, Va.: Carrollton, 1980; 132 vols.), which provides access to most of the entries in the *NUC*. Title access has of course always been possible through the *CBI* (D35). Coverage by online information retrieval—with access by title, author, and L.C. book number— is increasing daily (see Glossary). Beginning in 1983, the *NUC* paper editions will be replaced by computer output microform (COM); and the new microfiche publications, *NUC: Books* and *NUC: U.S. Books*, which will contain information from 1,500 institutions and the Library of Congress, will have cumulative indexes by name, title, series, and, most important, *subject*.

By pulling together information from most of the major libraries of America, the printed *NUC* has made an invaluable and historically important contribution to research methods. More and more frequently, however, scholars will be using libraries that have access to a computer data base of shared catalog information assembled from the holdings of all cooperating libraries. These data bases already exceed any available printed tools (including *NUC*) in comprehensiveness for post-1965 publications. The future world of literary research via computers is a brand-new ball game, happily charged with the pleasures of anticipation and satisfaction that are inherent in any battle of wits.

B12.   Library of Congress Catalogs. *Subject Catalog*. Washington: Library of Congress, 1976– . Quarterly, with annual and five-year cumulations; beginning in 1983, available on microfiche only (see COM in the Glossary). Z881.A1.U375

Since this series, and its predecessors under slightly varying titles, offers access by subject to books cataloged for the Library of Congress since 1950, it provides a very handy, if somewhat less comprehensive, bibliographic complement to *NUC* (B10–11). Entries provide the same full detail since they, too, are reproduced from catalog cards. See also L.C.'s newly published title index, referred to in B11.

English

**B13.   British Museum. *General Catalogue of Printed Books* (*Brit. Mus. Cat.*; *BM Catalogue*; *BM Cat.*). 263 vols. London: Trustees of the BM, 1965. Supplement, 1956–1965 (50 vols.); supplement, 1966–1970 (26 vols.); supplement, 1971–1975 (13 vols.). Z921.B87

The main set of 263 volumes contains photocopies of the catalog cards for all books owned by the British Library, London, up through 1955. (The British Library was formerly referred to as the British Museum because the library was housed in the national museum, but in 1973 an official reorganization was announced.) It is necessary to consult all three supplements at present for subsequent acquisitions, but a cumulated edition is under way (see B14). A series of subject indexes covers the years 1881 to 1960.

American researchers and librarians use the catalog mainly for verification of factual information. It is formidable in size and inimitable in fragrance but, in general, easy to use, having a simple, alphabetical-by-author arrangement with a few exceptions such as a listing of all periodicals by city of publication under "Periodicals," and certain subject groupings such as "England" and "Ireland." Both of the latter idiosyncrasies were abandoned in the third supplement, and henceforth the *BM Catalogue* will be computer-based and machine-readable. An era has ended.

**B14.   British Library. *General Catalogue of Printed Books to 1975*. 360 vols. New York: Saur, 1979–84.

Incorporates into one set the unwieldy *British Museum Catalogue* (B13) of 263 vols. and the first, second, and third supplements of 89 vols., together with recent additions and corrections amounting to another 900,000 entries, for a grand total of seven million books published before 1975. For the first time, the holdings of the British Library (formerly the British Museum) are available in a single alphabetical listing. Prepayment price: $23,040. This catalog is not as comprehensive as the *National Union Catalog, Pre-1956 Imprints* (B10), but the two sets will supplement each other. The computer has allowed prompt publication of 1976–82 British and overseas acquisitions (1983; 50 vols.).

Basic Guides Covering Two or More National Literatures

Literary guides devoted to one national literature are discussed in their own geographical sections. See, for example, these specialized guides:

English literature (J175)
American literature (P704–12.1)
Irish literature (K581–85)
Canadian literature (N663–69.1)
French literature (Q904–09)
African literature (R972–75)
Comparative literature (T1009–12)

*B15.   Altick, Richard D., and Andrew Wright. *Selective Bibliography for the Study of English and American Literature*. 6th ed. New York: Macmillan, 1979. 180pp. Paperback. Z2011.A4   016.82

A time-honored guide to literary research materials—handbooks, encyclopedias, histories, periodicals, indexes, and bibliographies—as well as a source of technical information helpful to graduate students. It includes a brief chapter explaining research procedure and basic reference tools, a glossary of terms encountered in literary research, and a list of books every student should read (most recent copyright date, 1961), but students will probably wish there were annotations to describe the contents and show them how this large selection of books might answer their specific questions. No L.C. or Dewey call numbers, no cross-references, and a subject index that could list many more specific subject headings, especially for American literature and drama. The book is, however, a convenient companion for those who already have some familiarity with the reference collection.

*B16.   Schweik, Robert C., and Dieter Riesner. *Reference Sources in English and American Literature: An Annotated Bibliography*. New York: Norton, 1977. 258pp. Paperback. Z2011.S415   [PR83]   016.82

This convenient bibliography of 1,217 major reference books in the field has several strong points: an introduction on the technique of using reference sources, perceptive analyses, high-quality selections, a reasonable price, and sections on materials related to literary studies such as film and textual bibliography. It has no title index, no L.C. or Dewey numbers, insufficient bibliographical information in the citations for both books and periodicals, very few cross-references, and a subject index that is occasionally broad or inexact. For example, if students are looking for criticism on English or American novels, they will find no cross-references in either the text or the index from "English Fiction" and "American Fiction" (both of which list secondary works) to another section entitled "Fiction—Secondary Materials," which also includes criticism on the English and American novel. A similar problem exists in the coverage of drama.

*B17.   Bateson, Frederick W., and Harrison T. Meserole, eds. *Guide to English and American Literature*. 3rd ed. London: Longman, 1976. 334pp. Z2011.B32   [PR83]   016.82

Excellent in its principal aim: to select for the beginning student the best books by and about the principal authors of English and American literature. It points out, for example, that the best edition of E. M. Forster's complete works is the Abinger edition now in progress and that the most useful critical studies are by Trilling, Crews, and Stone. Especially important are the brief essays that analyze the main currents of the literature for each era, the chronological approach by century and then by birth date of the author (unwieldy for some students), a new Shakespeare section, and uninhibited evaluations by experienced editors. All libraries will own this, but a new edition is needed. See *Reader's Adviser* (A4) for a similar concept but greater scope.

B18.   Bell, Inglis F., and Jennifer Gallup. *A Reference Guide to English, American, and Canadian Literature*. Vancouver: Univ. of British Columbia Press, 1971. 139pp. Paperback. Z2011.B42   016.82

A guide to literary research that is designed specifically for the undergraduate and is still valuable for its solid retrospective basis even though its copyright date is 1971. Section A is logically arranged by type of reference book, subject, and chronological period; Section B is an alphabetical listing of individual authors and selected critical works (for more recent information, see B17 or the *Reader's Adviser*, A4). As a source for information on Canadian literature, this is convenient but highly selective. See Canadian Literature (N662–93) for more complete coverage.

The editorial work is particularly fine; even the page numbers of critical works are frequently cited so that new researchers can go directly to the appropriate section. The volume includes occasional brief annotations and a glossary of literary terms as well as indexes of both primary and secondary authors.

B19.   Kennedy, Arthur, and Donald Sands. *Concise Bibliography for Students of English*. Rev. William E. Colburn. 5th ed. Stanford, Calif.: Stanford Univ. Press, 1972. 300pp. Paperback. Z2011.K35   016.82

An immense bibliography with fine chronological, genre, and subject approaches to literary research, but no annotations, no title index to its thousands of books, and an aging copyright date. Researchers must approach this guide through its subject index because there are no cross-references in the text to tie together the many titles with overlapping interests. The subject index, alas, is not as analytical as it needs to be to compensate for this omission of cross-references. The heading "Novel," for instance, has no national subdivisions, so much flipping back and forth is necessary to locate all American entries. And "Welsh Literature" contains a reference to "Periodicals 9, 10" that leads to exactly 127 periodicals, ninety-eight percent of which have nothing to do with Welsh literature, listing such publications as *Mississippi Quarterly*, *American Scholar*, and *Western American Literature*. The book is important because it is comprehensive, however, and students appreciate its L.C. and Dewey numbers.

*B20.   Somer, John L., and Barbara Eck Cooper. *American and British Literature, 1945-1975: An Annotated Bibliography of Contemporary Scholarship*. Lawrence, Kans.: Regents Press, 1980. 326pp. Z1227.S65 [PS221]   016.820'9'00914

A responsible guide to the trends and issues of contemporary literature is difficult to find. Here is one that combines good coverage with good organization. It provides access to fifteen hundred books arranged by genre and type (guide, handbook, biographical dictionary, etc.) so that students can study the theories, relationships, and developments of the past thirty years. For example, it briefly describes Elizabeth Hardwick's two collections of essays and Ihab Hassan's three books of criticism on American literature. Important research aids are an excellent index with specific subject headings, a list of critical works published *after* 1975, and a list (unannotated) of other reference works that might be helpful for research on contemporary literature. Students will find that very few guides are devoted to post-war material. This is a rare and indispensable trophy. See also Harris for contemporary drama (P797), Gingerich for contemporary poetry (A8), and others listed in A8.

C

Bibliographies of Bibliographies

—for locating subject, title, genre, and author bibliographies, both standard editions and recent supplements. Warning: Note the copyright dates. Because of the time required to collect, prepare, and print the information, these titles include only those works published at least one or two years before their own publication. For more up-to-date titles, see *Bibliographic Index* (C28), *Bulletin of Bibliography* (C29), and Section D—Annual, Monthly, and Weekly Bibliographies.

Basic Sources

C25. Besterman, Theodore. *A World Bibliography of Bibliographies, and of Bibliographical Catalogues, Calendars, Abstracts, Digests, Indexes, and the Like.* 4th ed. 4 vols. and index. Lausanne: Soc. Bibliographica, 1965. Supplement, 1964–1974, ed. Alice F. Toomey (Totowa, N.J.: Rowman, 1977; 2 vols). Z1002.B5685   016.01

The authoritative source for bibliographies of almost all countries and centuries with, says the author, less than one percent error or omission pre-1914 and perhaps as much as three percent post-1914. He has examined over ninety-nine percent of the almost 85,000 separately published bibliographies in fifty languages of books, letters, manuscripts, and patents. Excluded are booksellers' and sales catalogs, art lists, and general library catalogs. The descriptive entries include the number of pages as well as the number of items in each bibliography to aid in estimating its value. Under each heading, the entries are chronological, and first and last (but not intervening) editions are listed whenever possible. A monumental and invaluable work.

The supplement is merely a photographic reproduction of eighteen thousand catalog cards, with no index—a great disappointment to Besterman admirers. Currently under way, however, is a series of augmented reprints from the fourth edition. *A World Bibliography of African Bibliographies*, edited by James D. Pearson (1975), for instance, more than doubles the number of

16

entries in Besterman's original volume. And Pearson's *Bibliography of Oriental Bibliography* (1975) adds 4,500 entries to the original 6,500. The Eastern European sections are in need of a similar enlargement. See additional titles in this and the next section for ways to find other recent bibliographies.

C26.   Howard-Hill, Trevor H. *Index to British Literary Bibliography*. 7 vols. Oxford: Clarendon, 1969–   . In progress. Z2011.A1.H68 [PR83] 016.82

A guide to works on British literary and bibliographical history:

Vol. 1: *Bibliography of British Literary Bibliographies*. 1969. 570pp. Z2011.H6 016.01682

Vol. 2: *Shakespearian Bibliography and Textual Criticism: A Bibliography*. 1971. See J337.

Vol. 3: *British Bibliography to 1890: A Bibliography*. In preparation.

Vols. 4 and 5: *British Bibliography and Textual Criticism: A Bibliography*. 1979. See W1611.

Vol. 6: *British Literary Bibliography and Textual Criticism, 1890–1969: An Index*. 1980. See W1611.

Vol. 7: *British Literary Bibliography, 1970–1979: A Bibliography*. In preparation.

The coverage is extensive and reliable. Vol. 1 lists all bibliographies published since about 1890 of works written by British authors in English from 1475 to the 1960s (a new edition is in preparation). Arrangement is by author, chronological period, region, form and genre (such as Common prayer, Letter-writers, Forgeries), and subject (such as Alchemy, Witchcraft). Authors and subjects are listed alphabetically, and bibliographies chronologically. Descriptive notes and citations of book reviews are provided for many titles. A single alphabetical index of authors, compilers, editors, publishers, and subjects is extremely helpful, with such entries as Chaucer (six bibliographies on his life and works), Fielding (eight titles), Conrad (sixteen), courtesy books (four), and newspapers (over one hundred).

The title of vol. 2 indicates that it contains lists of Shakespearian bibliographies and textual studies, but fully half the volume is an extensive supplement to vol. 1 that brings the coverage up to 1969 (adding three more titles for Chaucer, for instance). Vols. 4 and 5 list nineteenth- and twentieth-century bibliographical studies of topics and authors. Vol. 6 is an index to the four volumes already published, arranged by author, editor, compiler, title, and subject (280 pages for the subject index alone). It also lists studies of how books were produced and disseminated.

Additional information on bibliographies for twentieth-century writers may be found in Mellown (J513–14). And of course all volumes can be brought up to date with the annual, monthly, and weekly bibliographies listed in Section D.

C27.   Nilon, Charles H. *Bibliography of Bibliographies in American Literature*. New York: Bowker, 1970. 483pp. Z1225.A1.N5 016.01681

A basic and comprehensive reference book that serves the same purpose for American literature as does Howard-Hill's *Bibliography of British Literary Bibliographies* (C26) for English literature. It includes book bibliographies of works by and about authors and culls articles from about one hundred journals. The major restriction on its value is its copyright date. Students will have to go to *Bibliographic Index* (C28), *Bulletin of Bibliography* (C29), and the Annual, Monthly, and Weekly Bibliographies (D31–36) to locate more recent publications.

General bibliographies are listed first, then individual author bibliographies in their appropriate chronological periods (with fifty-one for Melville and fourteen for Stevens). The last section lists bibliographies of miscellaneous genres, literary themes, and subjects such as Literary Criticism, Folklore, Book Collections, and Religion.

The work offers no cross-indexing and no annotations, but a sixty-seven-page subject, author, editor, and title index facilitates search. The format could be improved; choice of type and arrangement of entries do not permit easy location of information.

Serials
—for locating recent bibliographies.

*C28. *Bibliographic Index: A Cumulative Bibliography of Bibliographies* (*Bibl. Ind.*). New York: Wilson, 1937– . 3/yr. Z1002.B595   016.016

An international subject list of bibliographies that contain fifty or more entries and that are published either separately or as parts of books, pamphlets, and about 2,600 periodicals—an extremely important source that scholars should consult regularly. Since it comes out in April and August and cumulates in December, it is the obvious source for the latest comprehensive information. Individual authors are listed as subjects; bibliographies are of works both by and about the author. No annotations.

The subject heading "Literature" has numerous subdivisions for easy location of eras and themes such as Symbolism, Melodrama, Biography. The subject heading "Fiction," for example, leads to bibliographies in periodicals like the *Journal of Modern Literature* (J530), *Novel: A Forum on Fiction* (G64), *Nineteenth-Century Fiction* (J422), and *Modern Fiction Studies* (J544).

*C29. *Bulletin of Bibliography* (*BB*). Westwood, Mass.: Faxon, 1897– Quarterly. Z1007.B94   016.05

A small periodical that specializes in printing highly selective bibliographies. This is often the best place to go for the most recent and most exhaustive scholarship on a single author or subject, especially if it has become an issue of popular interest. See, for example, "Vietnam War Literature, 1958–1979," *BB* (Jan.-Mar. 1981), pp. 26–31, 51. The contents of the periodical are thoroughly indexed by an impressive number of indexing publications (see below), but alert researchers glance at the cover of each issue as *BB* arrives in the library to see if their fields of interest are being updated. Recent topics have included John Fowles, Louise Bogan, Little Magazines, Kay Boyle, Anne Tyler, Mari Sandoz,

Flannery O'Connor, the Gothic Novel, Drugs, and periodicals devoted to the works of one author. The last item has been enlarged into a book entitled *Author Newsletters and Journals* (W1476).

The special section on newly established and recently defunct magazines ceased in December 1978. Similar information may be verified in *Serials Updating Service* (W1483) with remarkable accuracy and currency or, after a delay of a year or two, in Ulrich's quarterly supplement (W1477), *Serials Review* (W1482), and *New Serial Titles* (W1478). Annual index. Cumulated index, 1897–1975 (1977), 137pp.; 1976–1980 (1981), 10pp.

Indexed in *ABELL* (D32), *Abst. Eng. Stud.* (E38), *America* (E43), *Am. Lit.* (P744), *Bibl. Ind.* (C28), *Biog. Ind.* (W1085), *CALL* (F53), *Hist. Abst.* (E43), *Library and Info. Sci. Abst.* (E43), *Lib. Lit.* (F53), *MLAIB* (D31), *Religion Index One: Periodicals* (F53), *Romantic Movement: A . . . Bibliography* (J443), *Vict. Stud.* (J470), *Year's Wk. Eng. Stud.* (D33).

C30.   *A Guide to Serial Bibliographies for Modern Literatures.* Ed. William A. Wortman. New York: MLA, 1982. 124pp. Paperback. Z6519.W67 [PN695]   016.805

Now that this has been published, it is difficult to imagine how any librarian or scholar was able to do efficient research without it. It assembles, for the first time, the titles of all sources that feature on-going bibliographies of interest to students of literature. The range is enormous, from the *Gypsy Scholar*, with its annual list of American dissertations, to the *Index to Australian Book Reviews*, *Revue des Langues Romanes*, and the *Heine-Jahrbuch*. Descriptions and evaluations of each of the seven hundred titles help readers select the one most suited to their needs, thus keeping research time to a minimum.

A briefer list that would be sufficient for the beginning student is *English Literature: A Guide to Serial Bibliographies* (Montreal: McLennan Library, McGill Univ., 1981; 10pp.). See ERIC, in the Glossary, for information on the reproduction, distribution, and purchase of the McGill bibliographies, and see the Index for additional titles.

See also

Annual, Monthly, and Weekly Bibliographies (D31–36)

D

Annual, Monthly,
and Weekly Bibliographies

Annual Bibliographies

—for supplementing older bibliographies and making comprehensive literature searches.

*D31.   *MLA International Bibliography of Books and Articles on the Modern Languages and Literatures (MLAIB, MLA Int'l Bibl.)*. New York: MLA, 1921–   . Annual. Z7006.M64   016.4

An annual bibliography noted for its excellent coverage of literary and linguistic scholarship in hundreds of countries all over the world. Until 1969 this appeared annually as a feature of the journal *PMLA* (H152), which itself is important for the scholarly articles and news notes published and distributed six times a year to MLA's 27,000 members in all fifty states, Canada, Latin America, Europe, Asia, and Africa. In 1970 the bibliography gained independent status and was computerized in an effort to keep up with the increased volume of scholarly works. The 1980 edition contains fifty-nine thousand entries, more than double the pre-computer figure, and the bibliography now aims at annual publication in the fall, making it the most timely of annual bibliographies.

Before 1956, the *MLAIB* was restricted to critical works by American authors only, but now coverage extends to more than three thousand international periodicals. In 1969 the publication was divided into four volumes: 1: *General, English, American, Medieval and Neo-Latin, Celtic Literatures, and Folklore*; 2: *General Romance, French, Italian, Spanish, Portuguese and Brazilian, Romanian, Netherlandic, Scandinavian, Modern Greek, Oriental, African, and East European Literatures*; 3: *Linguistics* (see W1329); 4: *ACTFL Annual Bibliography . . . on Pedagogy in Foreign Languages*. After 1972 vol. 4 was dropped because of limitations of time, space, and money. Since 1981 with the introduction of a computerized classification system for a more detailed arrangement and more efficient location of items, the bibliography has been published in five parts: 1: British, American, Canadian, Australian, New Zealand, and English Caribbean literatures; 2: European, Soviet, Asian, African, Spanish-American, and Portuguese-American; 3: Linguistics; 4: General Literature; and 5: Folklore.

The new system of subject descriptors introduced in 1981 enables researchers to look for books and articles not only by country, century, genre, and author as they did in all earlier volumes but also by themes, movements, influences, theories, methodological approaches, motifs, and other techniques. Users will therefore be able to locate quickly all documents relating to, for instance, Faulkner's *Light in August* or semantic theory in the German language. Each of the parts has a thesaurus of the indexing terms, a scholars' index, and a subject index with cross-references to the classified arrangement. Each national literature is arranged first chronologically and then alphabetically by the subject of the article. There are a few glosses but no annotations, no lists of research in progress, and no claim to be exhaustive in coverage. Students will still have to consult specialized bibliographies such as *Shakespeare Quarterly* (J316) and *Victorian Studies* (J470) for extensive literature searches.

For many reasons, literature students have always found the *MLAIB* to be their single most valuable aid to research. (1) When online information retrieval is finally in operation for all volumes, the *MLAIB* will unquestionably be the indispensable source for information on international scholarship (see Glossary, computerized literature search). The 530,000 citations listed in the 1969–81 volumes are now available for retrieval via computer. Further retrospective coverage back to 1921 will be complete by 1986–87. (2) Because of its international coverage, *MLAIB* is generally preferred over the *Annual Bibliography of English Language and Literature* (D32), which, however, indexes more book reviews, more minor figures, and more of the smaller author newsletters. (3) The *MLAIB* is also usually preferred over the less specialized *Essay and General Literature Index* (F46) for locating individual literary essays and articles published in larger works. (4) It contains an extensive list of abbreviations for periodical titles used most frequently in literary research (see also W1025–26). (5) Completed and accepted American doctoral dissertations abstracted in *DA/DAI* (W1214) are easy to locate, although the student may have to consult additional sources (see J465, P737, P810, W1211–13). For additional publications by MLA, see the Index of this guide.

*D32.   *Annual Bibliography of English Language and Literature (ABELL)*. Cambridge, Eng.: Modern Humanities Research Assn., 1920–   . Annual. Z2011.M69   016.82

An enumerative, international bibliography of books, reviews, dissertations, and articles from thirteen hundred periodicals written originally in English (with few exceptions) in the United States, Great Britain, and thirty other countries. A study that regrettably is several years old (a hint to some diligent scholar) shows only a twenty-one percent duplication of those titles covered by *MLAIB* (D31), so this, as well as the other annual bibliography for English literature, *Year's Work in English Studies* (D33), should be consulted for all serious research. It is a particularly good source—in fact, superior to *MLAIB*—for book reviews and author newsletters (W1476). It occasionally includes comparative, Continental, and Commonwealth studies, and it has a reputation for excellent coverage of "Bibliography" as a subject (see W1053 for *ABELL's* treatment of author bibliographies).

Arrangement is by subject (Biography, Learned Societies, Language, Syntax, etc.), then by century (Old English, Middle English, Fifteenth Century, etc.), with individual authors listed alphabetically under each heading. Entries are numbered and cross-referenced, but not annotated. Coverage is so comprehensive, both geographically and numerically (4,975 titles for the twentieth century in the 1978 volume), that publication is slow, but editors are trying to decrease the three- to four-year lag. The excellent layout earns commendations from researchers who spend their lives reading fine print. *ABELL* has large print, good arrangement of divisions and subdivisions, good use of white space, and high quality paper. It is a pleasure to use.

Each volume contains one index of authors and subjects and another of contributing scholars. Because there is no cumulative index, students will have to check all the annual volumes, which of course can be tedious and discouraging. The same situation exists in *MLAIB* (D31) and *YWES* (D33). Online information retrieval will eventually eliminate that little problem (see *MLAIB*, D31, and the Glossary, computerized literature search).

*D33.   *The Year's Work in English Studies* (*Year's Wk. Eng. Stud.*, *YWES*).
London: Murray, for the English Assn., 1921-   . Annual. PE58.E6

An annual review that features scholarly essays summarizing and evaluating notable and controversial work completed the previous year in English, American, Commonwealth, and some Continental literatures. Critical objectivity is the obvious review policy, a commendable stand that rejects the academic satire or old school loyalty of so many periodical reviews. Arrangement is chronological. An American literature chapter that was added in 1958 has been expanded to two chapters (pre-1900 and post-1900). Each period is covered by an authority in the field who directs the criticism toward bibliographies, surveys, genre studies, individual authors, and individual titles. Separate sections are devoted to Chaucer, Shakespeare, Milton, English Drama: 1550–1660, English Language, and Literary History.

The unique value of this bibliography is that it provides a critical overview of trends in criticism and scholarship from year to year. Coverage is admittedly erratic, but most of the important bibliographies, editions, biographies, critical books, and articles from over four hundred periodicals are given frank, though brief, evaluations. All faculty and graduate students, as well as librarians who select and purchase these titles, should at least browse through each annual volume, especially when they are unable to locate book reviews in any other source.

Index I is by critic's name; Index II, by author and subject. Since 1966 (vol. 47) the analytical subject index has been much more detailed and has included all references to individual titles, so busy students can now save time by glancing through the index columns to see whether the editors have reviewed anything in their field. It is necessary to examine the author and subject indexes of each annual volume because there is no cumulative index. No attempt is made to provide complete bibliographical information because it is so easily available in *CBI* (D35), *NUC* (B10–11), and other specialized sources. Since the contributing scholars must read all the recommended books and articles and then write their evaluations, there is an unavoidable time lag of three or more years. This is the publication's only weakness.

Indexed in *Brit. Hum. Ind.* (F49), *Hum. Ind.* (F45), *MLAIB* (D31).

Additional annual bibliographies

American Literary Scholarship (P734), sections for American, black, foreign, and bibliographical scholarship

Köttelwesch (Q927), for Continental criticism

Year's Work in Modern Language Studies (W1328), international coverage of both literature and linguistics studies

Monthly Bibliographies

—for locating information on the most recently published scholarship.

*D35. *Cumulative Book Index* (*Cum. Bk. Ind.*, *CBI*). New York: Wilson, 1928– . Monthly except August, with quarterly and annual cumulations. Z1219.M78   015.73

The only author-subject-title international bibliography of books published in the English language—especially those in print in the United States—with information on the publisher, date, price, pagination, and paperback edition. Factual information is obtained from publishers in dozens of countries, but no attempt is made to include pamphlets, small editions, or any local or ephemeral material.

The work is valuable to literature students for several reasons. (1) It permits a title search if the author's name in unknown or difficult to spell—a unique capability until the publication of the *Cumulative Title Index* of the L.C. collections (B11). (2) It provides the publication date of first and important subsequent editions so students can go to the proper volume of the book-reviewing services (see Reviews, W1557–70, in this guide for further information; see *NUC*, B10–11, for additional verification sources). (3) It serves as a standard current or retrospective bibliography on any given subject or author, such as the eighteenth century or the Enlightenment. (4) It gives the latest easily available information on new publications (for even more timely factual data, see P717.17–.19). (5) And it suggests related ideas, as with the fifty "See also" subject headings under "Literature."

Weekly Bibliographies

D36. *British National Bibliography*. London: British Library, Bibliographic
Services Division, 1950– . Weekly with monthly, quarterly, and
five-year cumulations. Z2001.B75 015.42

An author, title, and series list of newly published books in the British Isles
that is comparable to our *CBI* (D35). Because it is prepared weekly as the titles
are submitted to the Copyright Receipt Office of the library for registration, the
information is gratifyingly accurate and remarkably recent. Arrangement is by
the Dewey Decimal system (Section X). Most large countries have similar accounts
of new books, such as the *Australian National Bibliography*, *Livres du Mois*,
and *Canadiana*.

E

Abstracting Services

Basic Sources

—for locating summaries of published articles and books.

*E38.   *Abstracts of English Studies* (*Abst. Eng. Stud.*, *AES*). Calgary, Alta.,
Canada: Univ. of Calgary, 1958- . 10/yr. PE25.A16   820.5

Before 1970 there were two ways to use this monthly publication: by consulting an author index that was cumulated annually or by finding the title of the periodical in alphabetical order. Since 1970, arrangement has been only by subject, era, and genre (not by periodical title), with primary authors listed separately under each section. The publication does not include books but does include general and specific studies in periodicals and monographs concerned with English, American, Commonwealth, and related literatures. About three thousand articles are abstracted each year from several hundred sources, but selection is on a random, not an orderly, basis, so the work has predictable errors of omission. It is an important source, however, because it covers some periodicals such as individual author newsletters and interdisciplinary studies that are not indexed by other services.

The student should remember that these abstracts merely summarize the contents of the articles without making recommendations or evaluations (see *Choice*, W1557, for that service). The issues are slow to appear—sometimes several years after the article's initial publication—but they do have an important timesaving feature: They indicate to students immediately whether the article is pertinent to their subject and whether it is worth an interlibrary loan request if their institution does not have the periodical on its shelves. This is the source to use if, when working on sea imagery in Yeats, imagism in Twain, or modern interpretations of Chaucer, for instance, the student decides to scan all the more important articles in order to select a few for concentrated study.

The monthly index is by author and subject. The cumulative annual index is by secondary author, subject (primary author listed as subject), proper names within the abstracts, and titles—all in one alphabetical arrangement.

E39.   *Psychological Abstracts: Nonevaluative Summaries of the World's
       Literature in Psychology and Related Disciplines (Psych. Abst.).*
       Washington, D.C.: American Psychological Assn., 1927– . Monthly
       with semiannual, annual, and larger cumulations. BF1.P65   150'.5

A random sampling of the subject index under "Literature" leads to entries for the psychological novel, the quest for a father-god in Wolfe, the role
of sensory deprivation and monotony in Conrad's *The Secret Sharer*, Ruskin as
psychotic, and problems in Shakespeare, Dostoevsky, Arthur Miller, Kafka,
Orwell, Dickinson, Salinger, and the Gothic novel. International in scope—
and important. It is too often ignored by students who are genuinely interested
in the subject but unaware that such a source exists. A cumulative index of
authors, subjects, and abstractors appears every six months.

E40.   *Sociological Abstracts (Soc. Abst.).* New York: Sociological Abstracts,
       1952– . 8/yr. HM1.S67   301

The best approach to this publication is through the analytical subject index, where under "Literature" are entries on realism in the novel, black literature,
the teaching of literature, and the writing of criticism with reference to Arnold
and Newman.

E41.   *MLA Abstracts of Articles in Scholarly Journals.* New York: MLA,
       1970–75. Annual. P1.M64   408

A worthy project this was, but limitations of time and money, and the
difficulty of obtaining abstracts from busy authors, resulted in an early demise.

E42.   *American Literature Abstracts: A Review of Current Scholarship in the
       Field of American Literature (ALA, Am. Lit. Abst.).* San Jose: Califor-
       nia State Coll., 1967–72. Semiannual. PS1.A63   016.81

Similar in purpose to the older and respected *Abst. Eng. Stud.* (E38), but
ALA limited itself to American literature and covered only about one hundred
journals. No cumulated index, which is regrettable. Like *MLA Abstracts* (E41),
it succumbed to the lack of time, money, and cooperation by the contributing
critics and editors.

Abstracting Services—Specialized

E43.   *Abstracts of Folklore Studies* (W1274)
       Abstracts of Popular Culture (W1498)
       America: History and Life. Santa Barbara, Calif.: Clio Press, 1964– .
           Abstracts about nineteen hundred periodicals in the United States
           and Canada
       College Composition and Communication (W1598)
       Computer Abstracts (W1190)
       Current Index to Journals in Education (W1224)
       Historical Abstracts. Santa Barbara, Calif.: American Bibliographical
           Center, 1955– . Computer searchable file, 1973– . World history
           retroactive to 1775

Journalism Abstracts. Minneapolis: Univ. of Minnesota, 1963–   .
Language and Language Behavior Abstracts (W1332)
Language Teaching and Linguistics: Abstracts (W1333)
Library and Information Science Abstracts. London: Library Assn.,
   1969–   . Former title: *Library Science Abstracts*
Resources in Education (W1223)
—and many other titles in many other fields (see Sheehy, A5)

F

Indexing Services

Basic Sources

—for locating articles published in periodicals, newspapers, or collections. Students might note that abstracts and indexes have a value far beyond the obvious one of locating single titles on a single subject. It is possible, for instance, to trace the entry for any author or any subject down through the years, noting type of research, facets, trends, growth and fading of popularity, and branching of knowledge. This can be summarized and analyzed to produce important conclusions on trends in literary style, criticism, and influence of external pressures on authors—social, cultural, religious, and political. John Cleland, for example, was avoided for decades until mid-twentieth century sophisticates could accept *Fanny Hill*, and nineteenth-century Victorian criticism of Byron was predominantly biographical and, therefore, quite naturally derogatory.

*F45. *Humanities Index (Hum. Ind.)*. New York: Wilson, 1974–   . Quarterly, with annual cumulations. AI3.H85   016.0013

Especially suitable for research in interdisciplinary studies because it indexes the contents of almost three hundred English-language and a few European periodicals in folklore, classical studies, language and literature, literary criticism, philosophy, religion, and the performing arts, including music, drama, and film. Since it is a quarterly publication with information on relatively current research, it is an appropriate source for updating the annual *MLAIB* (D31) and for covering 125 periodicals which the *MLAIB* does not index. It is also a good source for "Moving Picture Reviews" (under M), "Book Reviews" (in a separate section at the back of each issue, arranged by author of the book reviewed), and reviews of opera, ballet, drama, and television. Material published before 1974 on the humanities was indexed by *Soc. Sci. Hum. Ind.* (F51).

*F46.   *Essay and General Literature Index* (*Ess. Gen. Lit. Ind., EGLI*). New York: Wilson, 1900– . Semiannual, with annual and five-year cumulations. AI3.752   080.1'6

Miscellaneous essays and chapters in *books* would be difficult or impossible to locate if it were not for this invaluable index, which literature students should note emphasizes literary, drama, and film criticism. If, for instance, T. S. Eliot's essay on *The Jew of Malta* cannot be found in his collected works, this index will locate the essay in an anthology. Contents are listed by subject and author, with author's works listed first, then titles about the author, and then titles about the individual works.

Only books and annuals are indexed, not periodicals. These books are listed in the back with full bibliographical information, and, in some libraries, the call numbers will be noted in the margin next to the titles so that the student can go to the shelf immediately without consulting the card catalog. The cumulative index for works indexed between 1900 and 1969 is useful for retrospective research (New York: Wilson, 1972; 437pp.).

The contributions made to research by this title are unique. It cumulates bibliographies of hard-to-locate essays by a given author, locates essays when only the title is known, collects analytical material on any given subject, organizes biographical or critical material about titles and persons, and cites numerous collections where a given essay may be found. Sample subject headings: Chinese Fiction, Mark Twain (under Clemens), Jonathan Edwards, Ireland in Literature, Northrop Frye, Robin Hood, the Short Story, Romanticism, and Moving Picture Criticism.

Other publications that index books as opposed to *periodicals* are *Biography Index* (W1085), *Canadian Essay and Literature Index* (N673), *Film Criticism* (W1258), and *Authors* (W1119).

*F47.   *Arts and Humanities Citation Index* (*Arts and Hum. Cit. Ind.; AHCI*). Philadelphia: Inst. for Scientific Information, 1977– . 3/yr., including annual cumulation. Z5937.A795

The great value of this publication is that there are three ways to approach its contents. (1) Through the Permuterm Subject Index it permits "permuted title searching" similar to the major dissertation indexes (W1211, W1214-15), which means that the searcher can look up any key word in the title and be directed to the related entry. These key words thus have the potential for creating an elaborate subject access system whose efficiency of course depends entirely on the foresight of the authors in selecting accurate, meaningful words for their titles. Unfortunately, they do not always do so, and, since the indexers do not read or examine the contents, the material is often not entered under the subject heading where scholars would logically look for it.

(2) The Source Index locates authors of the articles, reviews, letters, notes, creative works, bibliographies, or illustrations in over eleven hundred international periodicals and many books and series.

(3) The Citation Index locates all works mentioned in the book under consideration—whether in the text, footnotes, or bibliography—and thus identifies other authors who are working on related subjects. It is especially useful.

therefore, for cross-disciplinary studies. It also indexes a great many author newsletters that are not covered elsewhere (see also *Author Newsletters and Journals*, W1476). Very small print, however.

See the *Proceedings* volume for information on literature produced by conferences, seminars, symposia, and workshops. The subject indexes in the weekly issues of *Current Contents: Arts and Humanities* (same publisher) keep this up to date. *CC*'s unique function is to reproduce tables of contents from over one thousand journals in the arts and humanities. In 1983, Bibliographic Retrieval Services made *AHCI* available online (see computerized literature search in the Glossary).

*F48.   *Readers' Guide to Periodical Literature: An Author and Subject Index (RG; Read. Gd.).* New York: Wilson, 1900– . 2/month. AI3.R4   051

A satisfactory first source for the undergraduate student because it indexes material in 150 to 200 popular periodicals such as the *New Yorker, Ebony, Reader's Digest,* and *Newsweek.* Plays and fiction are listed under the author's name and some subject headings. An excellent feature is the cumulation of current reviews of musical comedies and moving pictures (for additional sources see Salem, P806, and Film, W1229–68). Book reviews are in a separate section in the back of the book. *RG* is also useful for retrospective searches because it indicates, by sheer number of articles, the actual popularity of the subjects. See also *Nineteenth Century Readers' Guide* (J468) and *Poole's Index* (J416).

F49.   *British Humanities Index (Brit. Hum. Ind., BHI).* London: Library Assn., 1962– . Quarterly. AI3.B7   011'.34

This quarterly index supersedes the *Subject Index to Periodicals* (1915–61). It lists, by subject, material in about three hundred British publications such as *British Book News, Essays in Criticism, Hermathena, Kipling Journal, Medium Aevum, Notes and Queries, Spectator, Times Literary Supplement, Welsh Historical Review,* and *Year's Work in English Studies.* Under "Linguistics" and "Literature," for instance, may be found entries on Noam Chomsky, Charles Dickens, René Wellek, Iris Murdoch, and Frank Leavis.

*F50.   *New York Times Index (New Yk. Tim. Ind.).* New York: New York Times, 1913– . 2/mo. AI21.N452   071'.47'1

Every student should be familiar with this subject index to the late city edition and the Sunday supplement sections of the leading American newspaper. It comes out every other week, cumulates quarterly and annually, and provides brief synopses of the articles, which frequently have all the information that the inquirer needs. Articles are placed chronologically under small subject headings with many cross-references. Dating of the news facilitates search in other newspapers that are not able to afford the luxury of indexing. After locating subjects in this index, which has cumulated annually since 1851, students will be able to go to the correct date in other sources.

Students should also be aware of two additional shortcuts: (1) Over three million names mentioned in America's most important newspaper can now be located with ease in the twenty-two-volume *Personal Name Index to the* New York Times Index, *1851-1974* (Succasunna, N.J.: Roxbury Data Interface,

1980-83; ed. Byron A. Falk and Valerie R. Falk). Five-year supplements will keep it up to date. (2) The New York Times Information Bank (Infobank) now provides the instant retrieval of abstracts of articles in the *Times* and a few other newspapers. When the request is typed on a computer terminal, the answer is either displayed on a screen or printed out. Convenient but expensive, so many libraries prefer to subscribe to the *National Newspaper Index* (Los Altos, Calif.: Information Access, 1979–   ), which indexes the *Christian Science Monitor, Wall Street Journal*, and *New York Times*.

Literature students should note that reviews are listed under "Book," "Theater," "Opera," and "Music," not under "reviews." For a cumulation of all book reviews from 1896 to 1970, see *New York Times Book Review Index* (W1561). See also Reviews (W1557–70) for additional review sources. For information on obituaries published in the *New York Times*, see W1148.

F51.   *Social Sciences and Humanities Index (Soc. Sci. Hum. Ind., SSHI).* New York: Wilson, 1965-74. Quarterly. Former title, 1907–65: *International Index.* AI3.R282   016.3

This has now been superseded by the greatly enlarged *Humanities Index* (F45) and *Social Sciences Index* (W1579), but it is still a valuable retrospective index for interdisciplinary approaches to literature that may relate to anthropology, archaeology, economics, geography, history, philosophy, political science, religion, and sociology.

Experience has shown that this quarterly publication provided the quickest, most accurate access to many periodicals that had no cumulative indexes of their own and that were not carefully indexed by other services. *MLAIB* (D31) duplicated some, but not all, titles found here. Articles were indexed from over two hundred periodicals, including *Speculum* (J265), *SQ* (J316), *PQ* (H154), *Times Literary Supplement* (W1563), and the *Spectator.* About eighty percent of the sources were published in the United States.

This is mainly a subject index (that is, articles are about Nabokov rather than by him), but it contains a few author and anonymous title entries—all in one alphabetical list. Articles may be located here, for instance, on science fiction, the editions of Goethe, original short stories, the manuscripts of Boethius, and every aspect of Shakespeare from authorship and characters to influence studies and individual plays.

F52.   *New Periodicals Index.* Boulder, Colo.: Mediaworks, 1977–   . 2/yr. Z1219.N45

Important because it indexes many periodicals not covered by popular indexes such as *Readers' Guide* (F48) and because it is interested in contemporary issues such as energy, diet, feminism, life-styles, and grass-roots politics.

Indexing Services—Specialized

F53.   *American Humanities Index* (P738)
   Annual Bibliography of the History of the Printed Book and Libraries (W1072)

Art Index (W1042)
Author Biographies Master Index (W1117)
Bibliographic Index (C28)
Biography Index (W1085)
Book Review Index (W1559)
CALL: Current Awareness—Library Literature. Framingham, Mass.:
   Goldstein Assoc., 1972–   .
Canadian Essay and Literature Index (N673)
Canadian Periodical Index (N674)
Children's Book Review Index (W1183)
Comprehensive Index to English-Language Little Magazines (W1427)
Cumulative Book Index (D35)
Cumulative Book Review Index (W1565)
Current Book Review Citations (W1564)
Drama Scholars' Index (G108)
Education Index (W1225)
Film Literature Index (W1252)
French Periodical Index (Q913)
Guide to the Performing Arts (W1469)
Index of American Periodical Verse (P818)
Index to Australian Book Reviews (N658)
Index to Black American Literary Anthologies (P848)
Index to Black Poetry (P870)
Index to Book Reviews in the Humanities (W1560)
Index to Commonwealth Little Magazines (N647)
Index to Literature on the American Indian (P877)
Index to Little Magazines (W1429)
Index to Periodical Articles by and about Blacks (P847)
Index to Periodical Fiction in English (G77)
Index to Science Fiction Anthologies (G96)
International Index to Film Periodicals (W1253)
Library Literature. New York: Wilson, 1921–   .
Music Index (W1456)
New York Times Book Review Index (W1561)
Nineteenth Century Readers' Guide (J468)
Ottemiller's Index to Plays (G107)
Palmer's Index to the Times (J419)
Philosopher's Index (W1489)
Play Index (G109)
Plot Summary Index (W1589)
Poole's Index (J416)
Religion Index One: Periodicals. Chicago: American Theological Library
   Assn., 1949–   . Former title: *Index to Religious Periodical Literature*
Science Fiction Book Review Index (G97–98)
Short Story Index (G76)

Social Sciences Index (W1579)
Speech Index (W1580)
Wellesley Index to Victorian Periodicals (J466)
—and many others.

G

Genres

General

Only those comprehensive titles that span several centuries, countries, or genres are listed here. Those that concentrate on one century, country, or genre are cited in their specific chronological, national, or genre section. *British Novel: Conrad to the Present* (J537), for instance, is located in the section on Twentieth-Century English Literature—Fiction.

Series

*G55.   Critical Idiom Series. New York: Methuen, 1969– . 70–120pp. In progress.

The quality of this remarkable series varies, of course, but the approach is so orderly and the content so useful that it is well worth the attention of anyone interested in genre studies or in need of an extensive explanation with numerous examples. Volumes have been published so far on the following subjects:

Absurd	Metre, Rhyme, and Free Verse
Allegory	Modern Verse Drama
Ballad	Modernism
Biography	Myth
Burlesque	Naturalism
Classicism	Ode
Comedy	Pastoral
Comedy of Manners	Picaresque
Dada and Surrealism	Plot
Drama and the Dramatic	Realism
Dramatic Monologue	Rhetoric
Epic	Romance
Expressionism	Romanticism
Fancy and Imagination	Satire
Farce	Short Story
Genre	Sonnet
Grotesque	Stanza
Irony and the Ironic (2nd ed.)	Symbolism
Melodrama	Tragedy
Metaphor	Tragicomedy

Criticism—Poetry and fiction

*G56.   *Explicator (Expl)*. Washington, D.C.: Heldref, 1942–   . Quarterly.
PR1.E9   820.5

Short explications de texte (interpretations of the language) that are useful
for students who are making close studies of specific phrases or images in poems
or prose works and who are unsatisfied with the critical titles listed in such sources
as Cline and Baker's *Index to Criticisms of British and American Poetry* (G126),
Poetry Explication (G125), or Alexander (G137.1). A cumulative index to vols.
1–20 (1942–62; 1,237 items) and subsequent annual cumulative indexes provide easy access to the contents. A cumulative index for vols. 21–40 (1962–82)
would certainly be a convenience on the shelves next to the periodical. Mean-
while, students can locate most entries in the *Explicator* by consulting the third
edition of *Poetry Explication*.

The *Explicator* also provides an annual list of explication on American and
English literature and film culled from other sources. The list for 1979, for instance, gives information for eight explications on Hardy and one on Polanski
published that year in other literary periodicals. It is arranged alphabetically by
poet, novelist, or filmist, and it limits itself to explications of "unquestioned
merit."

Indexed in *ABELL* (D32), *Abst. Eng. Stud.* (E38), *Arts and Hum. Cit. Ind.*
(F47), *Hum. Ind.* (F45), *MLAIB* (D31), *Romantic Movement: A . . .
Bibliography* (J443).

G57.   *The Explicator Cyclopedia*. 3 vols. Chicago: Quadrangle, 1968.
PR401.E9

Selected important explications that appeared originally in vols.1–20
(1942–62) of *Explicator* (G56), grouped here for the convenience of the literature
student:

Vol. 1: *Modern Poetry*. 366pp.
Vol. 2: *Traditional Poetry: Medieval to Late Victorian*. 387pp.
Vol. 3: *Prose*. 181pp.

Arrangement is alphabetical by author. An unexpectedly interesting introduction traces the development of explication as a method of interpretation,
saying it is a by-product of New Criticism that begins with syntax and encompasses punctuation, shades of meaning, literary allusions, puns, tone, point of
view, and a great deal of "mother wit and patience" (p. xvi).

Periodicals

G58.   *Genre: A Quarterly Devoted to Generic Criticism*. Norman: Univ. of
Oklahoma, 1967–   . Quarterly. AP2.G493   805

Genre—its concept, historical development, and relation to the interpretation of specific literary works. This journal covers a host of subjects including
the novels of Frances Brooke, the long poem in the twentieth century, fragments
of Keats's letters, autobiography, and cannibalism in fiction.

Indexed in *Am. Hum. Ind.* (P738), *Arts and Hum. Cit. Ind.* (F47), *Index
to Bk. Rev. Hum.* (W1560), *MLAIB* (D31).

Fiction—General

Basic guides

G60.   Cotton, Gerald B., and Hilda M. McGill. *Fiction Guides, General: British and American*. Hamden, Conn.: Shoe String, 1967. 126pp. Z5916.C77   016.823009

Completely out of date, of course, but retained here to illustrate the phenomenal explosion in bibliographical publications during the past few years. In 1967, when Cotton and McGill published their book, it was one of the few "guides" in existence. Their one thin volume has now been superseded by a dozen or more hefty bibliographies, each one devoting several hundred pages to a subject that in Cotton and McGill may have required only two or three pages. See, for example, Kirby, *American Fiction to 1900* (P781); Woodress, *American Fiction, 1900-1950* (P782); Rosa and Eschholz, *Contemporary Fiction in America and England, 1950-1970* (J536); Beasley, *English Fiction, 1660-1800* (J386); and Rice, *English Fiction, 1900-1950* (J535). Or see historical fiction (G83-84), the Gothic novel (G81-82, J387), and other subject areas. Our next prudent step should be to temper this enthusiastic, sometimes hasty, assumption of scholarship with strident demands for accuracy and organization. The end product of a good reference book is an informed scholar.

Bibliographies of primary works

G61.   *Author Bibliography of English Language Fiction in the Library of Congress through 1950*. Comp. R. Glenn Wright. 8 vols. Boston: Hall, 1973. Z5918.W74   016.823'008

Over 120,000 novels and short stories published in English from the eighteenth century through 1950 are here arranged by country and then by author, with place of birth, birth and death dates (a noteworthy feature for students working on an obscure author), and indexes to translators and pseudonyms. Companion volumes provide alternatives for approaching this material: *Chronological Bibliography of English Language Fiction in the Library of Congress through 1950* (8 vols., 1974) and *Title Bibliography of English Language Fiction in the Library of Congress through 1950* (9 vols., 1976).

G62.   *Fiction Catalog*. 10th ed. New York: Wilson, 1980. 797pp. Annual supplements. Z5916.W74   016.823

An author, subject, and title index of selected works of fiction in the English language with information on publisher, date, price, size, translations, extracts from reviews, and table of contents or brief plot summary. It is kept up to date with annual supplements so students can look up subject headings such as Sea Stories, Russia, Family Life, and Large Print Books, observe what has been published through the years on these subjects, and read short summaries or evaluations of the most popular recent fiction. It is important to remember that this is a list of titles recommended by librarians for purchase by libraries, so comprehensiveness must not be expected. Index of publishers and distributors.

Novel—General

Periodicals

G64. *Novel: A Forum on Fiction*. Providence, R.I.: Brown Univ., 1967– .
3/yr. PN3311.N65
A fine periodical that covers the whole field of fiction, from *Giles Goat-Boy* and *Catch-22* to the picaresque and Fielding. The long book reviews and the cumulative annual index of authors, articles, book reviews, and subjects are valuable features. The format is particularly imaginative and attractive, with wide inner margins and large pages for comfortable reading. Cumulative indexes for vols. 1–5 by subject, author, article, and book review.
Indexed in *ABELL* (D32), *Abst. Eng. Stud.* (E38), *Arts and Hum. Cit. Ind.* (F47), *Hum. Ind.* (F45), *Index to Bk. Rev. Hum.* (W1560), *MLAIB* (D31), *Romantic Movement: A . . . Bibliography* (J443).

G65. *Journal of Narrative Technique (JNT)*. Ypsilanti: Eastern Michigan Univ., 1971– . 3/yr. PE1425.J68   820.9
Articles and notes concerned with the narrative elements of literature, including characterization, style, biographical background, and historical influences.
Indexed in *ABELL* (D32), *Arts and Hum. Cit. Ind.* (F47), *MLAIB* (D31), *Romantic Movement: A . . . Bibliography* (J443).

*G66. *Studies in the Novel (SNNTS)*. Denton: North Texas State Univ., 1969– . Quarterly. PN3311.S82   809.3'3'05
Every aspect of the novel including early American fiction, picaresque novels, textual criticism, and essays about Austen, Styron, Faulkner, Hardy, Defoe, Dostoevsky, Tolstoy, Heller, and Pynchon. Each issue contains several scholarly book reviews and long review essays on such subjects as "Women and Fiction." Annual index to authors, subjects, and books reviewed.
Indexed in *ABELL* (D32), *Abst. Eng. Stud.* (E38), *Arts and Hum. Cit. Ind.* (F47), *Current Bk. Rev. Cit.* (W1564), *Hum. Ind.* (F45), *Index to Bk. Rev. Hum.* (W1560), *MLAIB* (D31).

Background reading for the novel

G67. Booth, Wayne C. *The Rhetoric of Fiction*. 2nd ed. Chicago: Univ. of Chicago Press, 1983. 552pp. Paperback. PN3451.B6   808.3
A treatise on subtlety—how point of view controls the reader's responses, and other niceties of the language. The second edition adds an analysis of recent criticism and a supplemental bibliography.

*G68. Forster, E[dward] M. *Aspects of the Novel*. New York: Harcourt, 1927. 250pp. Paperback. PN3353.F73   809
Forster referred to this series of lectures as "informal, indeed talkative" in tone. They are. They are also so inspiring that, in spite of what he says (p. 23),

true scholarship does indeed seem to be communicable. This book should be required reading, preferably at five-year intervals.

G69.   Lubbock, Percy. *The Craft of Fiction.* New York: Scribners, 1921. 277pp. Paperback. PN3355.L8   808.3
A classic that emphasizes the role of the creative reader and the creative critic.

G70.   Lukács, Georg. *Studies in European Realism.* New York: Grosset, 1964. 267pp. PN601.L8
A classic text. Lukács' interest is in "the encounter of a superior individual with a society unequal to his sense of possibility" (p. vi). Quality reading, much superior to most of the more recent efforts to grasp the intellectual significance of the modern novel.

G71.   Muir, Edwin. *The Structure of the Novel.* London: Hogarth, 1946, c1928. 151pp. Paperback. PN3353.M8
A valuable discussion of how writing style and structure are used by various novelists to frame the development of character and action.

G72.   Scholes, Robert, and Robert Kellogg. *The Nature of Narrative.* New York: Oxford Univ. Press, 1966. 326pp. Paperback. PN3451.S3 809.3923
The best introduction to narrative for undergraduates.

G73.   Stevick, Philip, ed. *Theory of the Novel.* New York: Free Press, 1967. 440pp. Paperback. PN3331.S9   808.3
A collection of about fifty essays on the art of the novel. The interesting aspect of this collection is that the essays are written by the novelists themselves, from Fielding to Joyce, and by contemporary literary critics, such as Frye and Schorer. Future novelists, especially, should note what is said here.

Additional reference sources for the novel

Abstracting and Indexing Services (E38–43, F45–53)
Afro-American Fiction (P856–59)
American Fiction (P778–91)
Annual, Monthly, and Weekly Bibliographies (D31–36)
Art of the Novel (W1369)
Commonwealth Literature (N687–90)
Contemporary Novelists (W1130)
Continental Novel (Q895)
English Fiction
    General (J196–205)
    Renaissance (J323–25)
    Eighteenth century (J386–95)
    Nineteenth century (J422, J477–84)
    Twentieth century (J535–48)
International Fiction Review (R963)

Irish Fiction (K601#03)
MLAIB (D31), vol. 1, General IV, Prose Fiction, and subsections in most
of the major divisions
Twentieth-Century Spanish-American Novel (R991)
Women's Studies (W1647, W1649.1)

Short Story—General

Surveys

G74.   Allen, Walter. *The Short Story in English.* New York: Oxford Univ.
Press, 1981. 376pp. PR829.A47   823'.01'09
The development of the short story in the United States and England, with
discussions of Stevenson, Dickens, Conrad, Flaubert, Poe, Hawthorne, James,
Mansfield, Cheever, Updike, Morley Callaghan, Gordimer, and others.

G75.   Harris, Wendell V. *British Short Fiction in the Nineteenth Century:
A Literary and Bibliographic Guide.* Detroit: Wayne State Univ. Press,
1979. 209pp. PR861.H35   823'.01
A fine survey of the development of the short story from loosely woven
sketches and tales to the carefully structured literary form of today, with discussions of Le Fanu, Collins, Carleton, Fiona Macleod, H. G. Wells, and others.
Harris offers an exceptionally long bibliography of general studies and primary
and secondary works of individual authors (pp. 164–203). A good starting point.

Bibliographies of primary works

*G76.   *Short Story Index: An Index to Stories in Collections and Periodicals*
(*SSI*). New York: Wilson, 1953–   . Five-year cumulations (the latest
for 1979–83); annual supplements. Z5917.S5.C62   016.80883'1
An index to about 135,000 short stories published since 1900 in hundreds
of anthologies and also, since 1974, in the periodicals indexed by *RG* (F48) and
Hum. Ind. (F45). When students cannot find the required short story on the
library shelves among the author's works, they should look in this index to see
if it has been included in a collection elsewhere. The 1977 volume, for instance,
shows that Isaac Bashevis Singer, the Nobel Prize winner, had stories in four
issues of the *New Yorker* that year. Other indexes do exist such as the *Chicorel
Index to Short Stories* (New York: Chicorel, 1974–   ), but *Short Story Index*
is considered the most accurate and convenient. The cumulated index to collections, 1900–78 (1980) lets the student know which anthologies and periodicals
have been searched for short stories. A few of the anthologies actually were
published before 1900.
    The author, title, and subject index also facilitates research, for it provides
a ready-made author bibliography, assists students who cannot remember the
author's name (who wrote "Gimpel the Fool"?), and serves as a guide to teachers
who want to build a lesson plan around a theme such as Prejudice, Single
Women, Musicians, Symbolism, or The West. In the back of each volume is
a list of the indexed collections, where some libraries insert the library call
numbers so the student can go directly to the shelf for the anthology.

G77.   *Index to Periodical Fiction in English, 1965-69.* Ed. Douglas Messerli
and Howard N. Fox. Metuchen, N.J.: Scarecrow, 1977. 764pp.
Z2014.F5.M475   [PR821]   016.813

Different from the *Short Story Index* (G76) in the following ways: Before
1974, *SSI* indexed only collections and anthologies, not periodicals; this indexes
many more journals (405) than *SSI* (45); and it indexes more scholarly journals
such as the *Virginia Quarterly Review* and the *Kenyon Review*. The next volume
in this index will cover 1970 to 1974. Since no other source has this coverage,
it may eventually become an extremely important research tool, especially for
minor authors whose works generally are not anthologized. It emphasizes
American material but includes some British, Canadian, and foreign literature.
The indexes to little magazines (W1427-30) of course have still a different scope.

Criticism

*G77.1. Weixlmann, Joe, ed. *American Short-Fiction Criticism and Scholarship,
1959-1977: A Checklist.* Chicago: Swallow, 1982. 638pp.
Z1231.F4.W3   [PS374.S5]   016.813'01'09

This may well be the only reference book that students of the American
short story will need to use. Explication of short stories has for many years been
well covered by Walker's splendid volumes (see G78), but the only comprehensive index of psychological, biographical, source, influence, and historical studies
has been Thurston's outdated checklist of 1960 (G79). This has now been brought
up to date in part by Weixlmann, who locates scholarship in 5,000 books and
325 periodicals on over 500 American short fictionists. His checklist includes
entries for interviews and bibliographies as well as for criticism, and it makes
a special effort to give good coverage to minority authors.

*G78.   Walker, Warren S., ed. *Twentieth-Century Short Story Explication: In-
terpretations 1900-1975 of Short Fiction since 1800.* 3rd ed. Hamden,
Conn.: Shoe String, 1977. 880pp. Supplement 1 (1980), 257pp. Supplement 2 (1984), 360pp. Z5917.S5.W33   [PN3373]   016.8083'1

Contemporary interest in the short story makes this a particularly valuable
bibliography of critical articles, books, and monographs, most of which have
been published since 1920 and so reflect the New Criticism's emphasis on "explication" (the analysis of structure, symbolism, and theme) rather than on
biographical, source, or background studies (see Weixlmann, G77.1, for that
aspect). The main volume covers about 850 authors from forty-five countries
including Camus, Chopin, Heinlein, Hughes, Kipling, Melville, Poe, Salinger,
Tolstoy, Kafka (15pp.), and Conrad (20pp., with 175 entries on "Heart of
Darkness," which some critics refer to as a short novel). Authors are listed
alphabetically, and then individual titles alphabetically with their critical works,
so it is possible to trace changing attitudes and preferences.

The supplements add explication published through 1981 on 432 authors.
They also include an index of short story writers and a list of the journals and
books consulted by the editor. The annual bibliographies in *Studies in Short
Fiction* (G80) are of course one of the basic sources. Every literature student should
be thoroughly familiar with this book and with its complement by Weixlmann.

G79.   Thurston, Jarvis, ed. *Short Fiction Criticism: A Checklist of Interpretation since 1925 of Stories and Novelettes (American, British, Continental), 1800-1958.* Denver: Swallow, 1960. 265pp. Z5917.S5.T4

The checklists by Weixlmann (G77.1) and Walker (G78, restricted to explication) are much more comprehensive and up to date, of course, but Thurston may be the source to use if students need early criticism for comparison or historical purposes. Arrangement is alphabetical by author, with titles and critical works listed alphabetically under each name. By Thurston's definition, a short story is less than 150 pages long.

Periodicals
—for updating the preceding scholarship.

*G80.   *Studies in Short Fiction (SSF).* Newberry, S.C.: Newberry Coll., 1963– . Quarterly. PN3311.S8

A periodical devoted to English, American, and Continental short story and novella writers of the nineteenth and twentieth centuries. It contains articles, news, a lengthy book review section, and a cumulative index in the back of each annual volume. An important feature for students is the selective bibliography of short fiction criticism that appears in the Summer issue. This is the source to use in bringing up to date Weixlmann's *American Short-Fiction Criticism* (G77.1), Walker's *Twentieth-Century Short Story Explication* (G78), and Thurston's *Short Fiction Criticism* (G79). Its all-inclusive scope covers Flannery O'Connor, Flaubert, James, Disraeli, Wilde, Welty, Ruskin, Eliot, Crane, Bellow, Azorín, Kafka, Jackson, Conrad, Thackeray, and dozens of others.

The Winter 1970 and 1971 issues are special cross-referenced indexes of short fiction anthologies. Their author-title indexes are valuable for teachers who want to select the right anthology and for students who are trying to locate a specific title. Since 1976 this has been a regular annual supplement.

Indexed in *ABELL* (D32), *Abst. Eng. Stud.* (E38), *Arts and Hum. Cit. Ind.* (F47), *Current Bk. Rev. Cit.* (W1564), *Hum. Ind.* (F45), *Index to Bk. Rev. Hum.* (W1560), *MLAIB* (D31), *Romantic Movement: A . . . Bibliography* (J443).

Quotations
For titles and procedure useful in locating quotations in prose, drama, and poetry, see Quotations (W1527-37).

Additional reference sources for short fiction
Abstracting and Indexing Services (E38-43, F45-53)
American Indian in Short Fiction (P878)
American Literature—Fiction (P778-91), occasional entries on the short story
Annual, Monthly, and Weekly Bibliographies (D31-36)
Explicator (G56-57)
Fiction (G60-62)
Journal of Narrative Technique (G65)
MLAIB (D31), vol. 1, General IV, Prose Fiction, and subsections in the national literatures

41

Gothic Fiction

Basic sources

G81.   *Gothic Novels of the Twentieth Century: An Annotated Bibliography.*
Ed. Elsa J. Radcliffe. Metuchen, N.J.: Scarecrow, 1979. 272pp.
Z1231.F4.R32   016.823'0872

A bibliography of about nineteen hundred Gothic novels by over five hundred authors—Anya Seton, Barbara Mertz, Anne Maybury, Eleanor Hibbert, August Derleth, and other, mainly contemporary, authors of mysteries, ghost stories, and romances. Not scholarly and not comprehensive, but better than nothing at all. Brief biographical facts for some of the authors, candid comments on some of the novels. The author thoroughly enjoyed preparing this bibliography, that is obvious, but she also seems, in the critics' opinion, to have indulged her preference for recent best-sellers, with the result that the term "Gothic" becomes somewhat amorphous, and the project judges itself to have been something less than serious. A pity.

Additional reference sources for Gothic fiction

G82.   *Crime Fiction, 1749–1980* (G85)
Eighteenth-Century Gothic Novel: An Annotated Bibliography (J387)
Frank, Frederick S. "The Gothic Novel: A Checklist of Modern Criticism." *BB*, 30 (1973), 45–54.
———. "The Gothic Novel: A Second Bibliography of Criticism." *BB*, 35 (1978), 1–14, 52.
Spector, *The English Gothic* (J387.1)
Twentieth-Century Romance and Gothic Writers (W1130)

Historical Fiction

G83.   *World Historical Fiction Guide: An Annotated Chronological, Geographical and Topical List of Selected Historical Novels.* Ed. Daniel D. McGarry and Sarah Harriman White. 2nd ed. Metuchen, N.J.: Scarecrow, 1973. 629pp. Z5917.H6.M3   016.80883'81

Disappointing. Graduate students in search of a project might consider compiling a twentieth-century scholarly bibliography on this subject because this second edition is noticeably "weak on recent editions, strong on out-of-print books, and middling on the one-sentence annotation," as one critic said. It lists about 6,400 titles, however.

G84.   *Dickinson's American Historical Fiction.* Ed. Virginia B. Gerhardstein. 4th ed. Metuchen, N.J.: Scarecrow, 1981. 328pp. Z1231.F4.D47 016.813'081

American Literature (P744) states that this work has "immense value." It provides an annotated, chronological list of over 2,700 novels that use American history as background and setting. An excellent subject index permits entry by geographical location, ethnic group, and individual.

Mystery Fiction

G85.   *Crime Fiction, 1749-1980: A Comprehensive Bibliography*. Ed. Allen
J. Hubin. New York: Garland, 1984. 712pp. Z2014.F4.H82
[PR830.D4]   016.823'0872

All crime novels, plays, and short story collections published during the
past two centuries are listed here by author with title, settings, and series indexes. This corrects the errors and omissions in Ordean A. Hagen's *Who Done
It?* (New York: Bowker, 1969) and will probably be the standard primary
bibliography for quite some time, although Hagen may still be useful for certain statistics. Hubin includes Gothic literature (see also G81-82, J387-87.1),
pseudonyms, birth and death dates, information on English translations, a series
character chronology, and five-year supplements. MLA members who look up
Carolyn Heilbrun will find a referral to the entry for Amanda Cross with several
titles listed and information on the series' main character. The entry for Emma
Lathen contains information on the real names of the co-authors, their other
pseudonyms, their works, and data on the main character John Putnam Thatcher.
Well done, with a moment's vision of quiet rainy evenings and a room full of
books yet unread.

G85.1.   *What about Murder? A Guide to Books about Mystery and Detective
Fiction*. Ed. Jon L. Breen. Metuchen, N.J.: Scarecrow, 1981. 175pp.
Z5917.D5.B73   [PN3448.D4]

Now that the mystery story has been accepted as a topic worthy of discussion by MLA, this annotated guide to criticism through 1980 is certain to become
popular with students who have to do research on the subject. It includes information on histories, criticism, and a host of authors such as Haycraft, Symons,
and Nevins.

G86.   *Encyclopedia of Mystery and Detection*. Ed. Chris Steinbrunner and
Otto Penzler. New York: McGraw-Hill, 1976. 436pp. PN3448.D4.E5
808.8'016

This subject seemed to warrant something more sympathetic than a mere
list of recommended books. The editors, therefore, have prepared an encyclopedia
that can be read and enjoyed from cover to cover for facts about the authors,
summaries of the plots, comments on movie versions, photographs from films,
and reproductions of dust wrappers. Pleasant reading.

Picaresque Literature

G87.   *Bibliography of Picaresque Literature from Its Origins to the Present*.
Ed. Joseph L. Laurenti. Metuchen, N.J.: Scarecrow, 1973. 262pp. Supplement, 1973-78. New York: AMS, 1980. Z5917.P5.L35   808.83'3

This one source, designated as "definitive" by *Choice* (W1557), will probably supply information on everything needed by the student of picaresque
literature. It draws not only on Spanish literature but also on the literatures of
Germany, France, England, Italy, and Latin America. The first volume cites 2,400

entries. The second, with 850, adds some annotations, some library locations where obscure items may be found, and Spanish translations for the introduction and table of contents. Other leads to picaresque literature may be found in *Novel: A Forum on Fiction* (G64) and *Studies in the Novel* (G66).

Science Fiction

Basic sources

*G88.   *Research Guide to Science Fiction Studies: An Annotated Checklist of Primary and Secondary Sources for Fantasy and Science Fiction.* Ed. Marshall B. Tymn, Roger C. Schlobin, and Lloyd W. Currey, with a bibliography of dissertations by Douglas R. Justus. New York: Garland, 1977. 165pp. Z5917.S36.T93   [PN3448.S45]   016.823'0876

A practical guide with well-annotated entries for the four hundred most useful reference books in science fiction, including histories, periodicals, dissertations, general studies, and works on individual authors like Bradbury, Howard, and Lovecraft. This supplements Clareson's *Checklist* (G90). Author and title index. Students may want to buy this one—a handsome, handy volume.

G89.   *Science Fiction and Fantasy Literature: A Checklist, 1700–1974, with Contemporary Science Fiction Authors II.* Ed. Robert Reginald. 2 vols. Detroit: Gale, 1979. Supplement, 1975–82 (1984), 600pp. Z1231.F4.R42   [PS374.S35]   016.823'0876

Two parts: (1) a remarkably complete list of fifteen thousand science fiction first editions (prose, not drama or poetry; books, not articles, anthologies, or foreign translations), with criticism on the genre as a whole, and (2) fourteen hundred biographical sketches of authors, both living and dead. Lists of awards, annotations of critical works, and a title index help to make this a well-edited reference book for serious science fiction students. It overlaps somewhat with Everett F. Bleiler's *Checklist of Science-Fiction and Supernatural Fiction* (Glen Rock, N.J.: Firebell, 1978; 266pp.), but Bleiler describes his five thousand first editions and is, therefore, more valuable to the book collector.

Criticism

*G90.   *Science Fiction Criticism: An Annotated Checklist.* Ed. Thomas D. Clareson. Serif Series 23 (P722). Kent, Ohio: Kent State Univ. Press, 1972. 225pp. Z5917.S36.C55   016.80938'76

Science-wise summaries of critical articles and books in the field of science fiction, including criticism of a general nature; analyses of science fiction as it appears in works by Nabokov, Greene, Twain, Miller, Vonnegut, Orwell, Burroughs, Lovecraft, Donne, Bradbury, and others; book reviews; lists of books in need of further research or available for browsing right now. Supplement this with Tuck (G93), Tymn (G88), and *Extrapolation* (G99) and its cumulations.

G91.   *Science Fiction Writers: Critical Studies of the Major Authors from the Early Nineteenth Century to the Present Day.* Ed. Everett F. Bleiler.

New York: Scribners, 1982. 623pp. PS374.S35.S36   823'.0876'09

A survey of the contributions of Mary Shelley, Verne, Wells, Orwell, Lewis, Le Guin, Disch, Lem, Tiptree, and about seventy other authors. This includes biographical information, historical background, and selected bibliographies, so is a good one-volume source for anyone interested in science fiction.

Identification problems

G92.   *Who's Who in Science Fiction*. Ed. Brian Ash. New York: Taplinger, 1976. 220pp. PN3448.S45.A83   809'.3'876

Not only the expected brief biographical sketches but also a glossary of terms (android?, cyborg?), a list of science fiction magazines, and a bibliography. The approach is chronological.

Encyclopedias

G93.   Tuck, Donald H. *The Encyclopedia of Science Fiction and Fantasy through 1968*. 3 vols. Chicago: Advent, 1974–82. Supplements at five-year intervals. Z5917.S36.T83   016.80883'876

A comprehensive, important work that supersedes all earlier titles covering the same material. Author-editor-artist biographies; checklists of the works, including series and paperbacks; information on periodicals, international publications, pseudonyms, films, listings in anthologies. Vol. 2 includes a title index for vols. 1 and 2. Vol. 3 includes information on weird fiction, lists of periodicals and series, pseudonyms, films, authors by country, and other helpful material. Good editorial management, well received by the critics.

Summaries

G94.   *Survey of Science Fiction Literature: Five Hundred 2,000-Word Essay Reviews*. Ed. Frank N. Magill. 4 vols. Englewood Cliffs, N.J.: Salem, 1979. PN3448.S45.S88   809.3'876

Focuses on the major science fiction of the last two centuries from Mary Shelley to Ray Bradbury—470 novels and plays and thirty short story collections. Each entry provides factual data, a one-sentence synopsis, a list of characters, a four- to five-page summary and critique, a brief list of sources for further study, and citations for contemporary reviews. Like the other Magill productions, this does not attempt to be scholarly and will not produce scholarly papers. It is, however, convenient for quick reference when your library does not own the book you need, when your memory needs refreshing on names of characters, or when you are trying to decide which books to use for class. It is not a substitute for the books themselves, of course, but it will often be the only quick source available for the information you need.

Series

G95.   Masters of Science Fiction and Fantasy. Ed. Lloyd W. Currey and Marshall B. Tymn. Boston: Hall, 1979–   . In progress.

A series of primary and annotated secondary bibliographies on major science fiction writers such as André Norton, Clifford D. Simak, Theodore Sturgeon,

Jules Verne, Brunner, Clarke, Delany, Silverberg, Zelazny, Jack Williamson, Alexander, Ensley, and Morris. Both fiction and nonfiction are included, and all important criticism. Indexes for titles and critics.

Indexes

G96.   *Index to Science Fiction Anthologies and Collections.* Ed. William Contento. Boston: Hall, 1978. 608pp.   Z1231.F4.C65   [PS374.S35] 016.813'0876

The author began this work when he accumulated eight hundred anthologies in his own library and then, like Sadleir (J480), found he had difficulty locating individual stories. It will undoubtedly be a popular book in science fiction courses because it locates about twelve thousand stories that are presently collected in two thousand English-language one-author anthologies. About 2,500 different authors are represented, including Disch, Russ, Silverberg, Aldiss, Asimov, and Zelazny. Superseding Siemon, Cole, Collins, and all other earlier indexes, it is accepted as the standard source in this field and is complemented by Fletcher (G96.1). Author and title indexes. Very small print, however.

G96.1.   *Science Fiction Story Index, 1950-1979.* Ed. Marilyn P. Fletcher. 2nd ed. Chicago: American Library Assn., 1981. 610pp.   Z5917.S36.65 [PN3433.5]   016.823'0876

A title and author index to a thousand science fiction anthologies published between 1950 and 1979. Since this includes reprints and "best" works, Plato, Kipling, Voltaire, and Verne are here as well as Goulart, Knight, and Padgett. Good editorial features: updating supplements and identification of pseudonyms.

G97.   *SFBRI: Science Fiction Book Review Index.* Bryan, Texas: H. W. Hall, 1970-   . Annual.   Z5917.S36.S19

An excellent index that annually locates hundreds of reviews of science fiction books. Like the *Bk. Rev. Ind.* (W1559), it gathers only factual information on the reviews so that students can find and read the entire review in the journal. Author arrangement with cross-references from the title. Indispensable and well done. For a fifty-year cumulation and supplements of science fiction book reviews, see the following entry.

G98.   *Science Fiction Book Review Index, 1923-1973.* Ed. Halbert W. Hall. Detroit: Gale, 1975. 438pp. Index, 1974-1979 (1981), 391pp. Z5917.S36.H35   016.80883'876

The easiest way to locate reviews of science fiction. The first volume lists over fourteen thousand reviews that appeared in 250 different periodicals, reporting on 6,900 books. The second volume adds 15,600 citations to over six thousand books reviewed in the same number of periodicals. Two or three assignments in this index could easily and wisely be worked into every class schedule, either concurrently as the science fiction is being read or as a special research project for papers and theses. College students need to consider the fact that experienced critics differ in their evaluations of literature.

Periodicals

*G99.   *Extrapolation*. Kent, Ohio: Kent State Univ. Press, 1959–   . Quarterly. PN3448.S45.E9   808.83'876'05

This began as a newsletter of the MLA seminar on science fiction and soon
developed into a respected journal that contains analytical articles, bibliographic
studies, and an annual bibliography of international research that brings up to
date the parent volume, *Science Fiction Criticism* (G90). These bibliographies
are now being updated, revised, and consolidated into one alphabetical listing
for publication every four to five years:

> *Year's Scholarship in Science Fiction and Fantasy, 1972-75*. Ed. Marshall
> B. Tymn and Roger C. Schlobin. Serif Series 36 (P722). Kent, Ohio: Kent
> State Univ. Press, 1979. 222pp. Z5917.S36.T95 [PN3448.S45]
> 016.823'087

> Indexed in *ABELL* (D32), *Abst. Eng. Stud.* (E38), *Arts and Hum. Cit. Ind.*
> (F47), *Hum. Ind.* (F45), *Index to Bk. Rev. Hum.* (W1560), *MLAIB* (D31).

*G100.   *Science-Fiction Studies* (*SFS*). Montreal: McGill Univ., 1973–   . 3/yr.
PN3448.S45.S34   809.3'876

The leading scholarly periodical in science fiction, with interpretations,
theories, news notes, and reviews on the science fiction of all countries and all
centuries. Outstanding foreign articles are translated into English. *SFS* and *Extrapolation* (G99) should be read regularly for the latest news and opinions on
current scholarship concerning individual authors, their works, and themes such
as science fiction by and about women or science fiction and teaching.

Indexed in *ABELL* (D32), *Abst. Eng. Stud.*   (E38), *Abst. Pop. Cult.*
(W1498), *Am. Hum. Ind.* (P738), *Arts and Hum. Cit. Ind.* (F47), *Hum. Ind.*
(F45), *MLAIB* (D31).

Background reading for science fiction

G101.   Bretnor, Reginald, ed. *Science Fiction, Today and Tomorrow*. New
York: Harper, 1974. 342pp. Paperback. PN3448.S45.B7   809.3876

A collection of essays by science fiction authors on the nature of their craft.
A good introduction to the field.

See also

> *Dictionary of Literary Biography* (W1121), vol. 8
> *MLAIB* (D31), vol. 1, General IV, Prose Fiction, and twentieth-century
> sections of English and American literature
> *Studies in Short Fiction* (G80), Fifth Supplement to a Cross-Referenced
> Index of Short Fiction Anthologies and Author-Title Listings (Spring
> 1979), and ensuing Spring issues, which will include listings of science
> fiction

Sea Fiction

G103.   *Sea Fiction Guide.* Ed. Myron J. Smith, Jr., and Robert C. Weller. Metuchen, N.J.: Scarecrow, 1976. 286pp. Z5917.S4.S64   [PR830.S4]   016.823'008'032

This guide should prompt a spate of courses in sea fiction, for it includes about 2,500 author-arranged entries on books published from the eighteenth century to the present, from Smollett to Marryat, Cooper, Melville, Stevenson, Conrad, Henty, Roberts, and Wouk. Even recreational reading can be organized to advantage. Excellent index by subject, title, pseudonym, and joint authors, but regrettably brief and sometimes inexact annotations.

Additional areas

Additional areas in fiction in need of investigation: business in literature, ethnic literatures, sports in literature, war and (or in) literature, the western.

Prose—General

Periodicals

G105.   *Prose Studies (PS; PSt).* Leicester, Eng.: Univ. of Leicester, 1977–   . 3/yr. Former title: *Prose Studies, 1800-1900.* PN4500.P76   PR1.P96

Scholarly articles and a bibliography of English and American scholarship on nonfiction prose of all periods, including essays, political treatises, philosophical works, theological writings, letters, diaries, biographies, autobiographies, and history. Occasional special issues treat such subjects as Walter Pater or travel literature.

Indexed in *MLAIB* (D31).

See also

MLAIB (D31), vol.1, General IV

Drama—General

Bibliographies of primary works

*G107.   *Ottemiller's Index to Plays in Collections: An Author and Title Index to Plays Appearing in Collections Published between 1900 and Early 1975.* Ed. John M. Connor and Billie M. Connor. 6th ed. Metuchen, N.J.: Scarecrow, 1976. 523pp. 7th ed. in preparation. Z5781.08 [PN1655]   016.80882

Useful for locating duplicate copies in anthologies for class assignments and production groups, and for verifying authors, names, dates, titles, and publishing information. Arrangement is alphabetical by author and then by title. Each entry gives the title, date, variant titles, and an abbreviation that leads to the alphabetically arranged collections index in the back of the book, where full bibliographical information is given for all anthologies.

Ottemiller is selective in scope, but it indexes 3,700 plays by more than 1,900 authors (some foreign) in 1,240 collections. If, for instance, students are unable to find a twentieth-century edition of Jonson's *Volpone* (1606) on the library shelf, they can usually locate a copy in an anthology by using either this source or the *Drama Scholars' Index* (G108). Other indexes do exist, such as the *Chicorel Theater Index to Plays* (New York: Chicorel, 1970–   ), *Index to Plays in Periodicals* (rev. ed., Metuchen, N.J.: Scarecrow, 1979), and *Plays in Periodicals* (Boston: Hall, 1970), but Ottemiller and Samples are usually more up to date and accurate.

*G108. Samples, Gordon. *Drama Scholars' Index to Plays and Filmscripts: A Guide to Plays and Filmscripts in Selected Anthologies, Series, and Periodicals.* Metuchen, N.J.: Scarecrow, 1974. 448 pp. Vol. 2 (1980), 705pp. Z5781.S17   016.80882

When a dramatist's collected works have disappeared from the library shelf, this is probably the first source students will consult to locate a copy of a play in an anthology or periodical because (1) its coverage goes back to collections published in the eighteenth century, in contrast to Ottemiller's coverage of anthologies from 1900 (G107), (2) it continues its coverage through 1977, (3) it indexes many important foreign periodicals and some English and American periodicals not found in other drama indexes, and (4) its scope ranges over ancient Greek, early American, black, and recent Latin American playwrights; radio, television, and film scripts; dramatic works of Byron, Keats, and Shelley; Chinese, Japanese, and other Asian works; and translations of Poe and Albee. Vol. 2 adds new titles, including many in their original language or in translation, makes corrections to the material found in vol. 1, and provides a cumulative title index to both volumes. Together they unearth works heretofore unknown because of lack of indexes. Easy to consult, like all other Scarecrow publications. Arranged alphabetically by author and title.

G109. *Play Index.* New York: Wilson, 1953–   . Irregular supplements, the most recent for 1978–82 (1983; 480pp.). Z5781.P53   016.80882

Author, subject, and title entries with facts about twenty thousand plays from Sophocles to Stoppard, with complete publishing information, a one-sentence summary, number of acts, number of men and women characters, scene location, set and music requirements. Additional plays, with citations for anthologies where they may be located and read, are listed in Samples (G108), Ottemiller (G107), and Firkin and Logasa (see Sheehy, A5).

G110. Salem, James M. *Drury's Guide to Best Plays.* 3rd ed. Metuchen, N.J.: Scarecrow, 1978. 421pp. Z5781.D8   [PN1655]   016.80882

Obviously designed for the amateur group that wants to put on a play, with all necessary information on nonmusical popular plays from the beginning to Tom Stoppard and Alan Ayckbourn. It includes the publisher's name, fee, number of men and women characters, requirements for scenery, and brief synopses. Interesting indexes arrange the plays by number in the cast (one actor in *Krapp's Last Tape*), sex (all men in *Clouds*), subject (war—*Antigone*), most popular (*You're a Good Man, Charlie Brown*), long-running, prize-winning, and recommended. If drama groups need to purchase copies of the play for production purposes or if they want information on royalties, they should get in touch with one of the publishers listed in the back of the book. The *National Playwrights Directory* (W1140) also includes production information.

See also

Microtext (G112–13)

Criticism

*G111. Coleman, Arthur, and Gary R. Tyler. Vol. 1: *Drama Criticism: A Checklist of Interpretation since 1940 of English and American Plays.* Denver: Swallow, 1966. 457pp. Vol. 2: *Drama Criticism: A Checklist of Interpretation since 1940 of Classical and Continental Plays.* Chicago: Swallow, 1971. 446pp. Z5781.C65   016.8

Excellent up to its own copyright date. No other single source accumulates so much critical work on so many plays from so many countries. In some areas, of course, it is now either supplemented or superseded by more recent publications in the Gale Information Guide Library (A8), American drama (P804), English drama (J212–13, J334–37, J343–48, J403, J551–58), classical drama (S996–98), world drama (R965), Continental drama (Q897), and others. Because the editors intended to be "broad, nearly definitive," they researched 1,050 periodicals and 1,500 books, all of which are listed in appendixes with indication of those titles that contained most critical material. Coverage is confined to explication de texte, which excludes historical, biographical, plot, and source studies. An interesting conclusion by the editors is that the formalist approach (aesthetic, textual, or New Criticism) was more popular in the 1960s than the moral, psychological, sociological, or archetypal.

Vol. 1 first cites anonymous plays (arranged by title, as *Arden of Faversham*), then playwrights with titles of individual plays (as Congreve, Eliot, Marlowe, Milton, Osborne, Shelley, Yeats), and then 155 pages on the plays of Shakespeare.

Vol. 2 extends from Greek plays (by Aeschylus and Aristophanes) to Continental plays of all periods and countries (by Calderón de la Barca, Samuel Beckett, Goethe, Ionesco, Lope de Vega, Molière, Pirandello, Strindberg, Racine). As an indication of this bibliography's comprehensive nature, note that it lists fifty-seven critical works for Sartre's *The Flies*.

Microtext

G112. Wells, H. William. *Three Centuries of English and American Plays, 1500–1830.* New York: Readex Microprint, 1952– . Irregular.

Reproductions of about 5,350 British and 250 American plays, an almost complete collection that few libraries can ever hope to have in the original. This collection must be used in conjunction with Bergquist's *Index* (G113), which lists all available first and later significant editions, plus translations and adaptations from foreign works. The plays are arranged alphabetically by author (if known), editor, title, and all variants. Both Greg and Woodward and McManaway numbers are included for scholars who wish to do further research. In verifying the bibliographical facts for this index, the editors identified several anonymous titles and pseudonyms (see also W1033–35). These, too, are clearly cross-referenced for easy use. For information on microprints of nineteenth-century drama, see J429.

G113.   Bergquist, G. William. *Three Centuries of English and American Plays: A Checklist, England: 1500–1800, United States: 1714–1830*. New York: Readex, 1963. 281pp. Z2014.D7.B45
See G112.

Theater (Stage)—General

Surveys

*G114. *Revels History of Drama in English*. London: Methuen, 1975–83.
    Some may prefer this new survey to Nicoll's *History of English Drama* (J208) because it has longer and more evaluative criticism of specific works. For annotations of vols. 2–8, see the appropriate entry numbers.

Vol. 1, *Medieval Drama*. Ed. L. Potter. 1983. 300pp.
Vol. 2, 1500–1576 (J328)
Vol. 3, 1576–1613 (J328)
Vol. 4, 1613–1660 (J328)
Vol. 5, 1660–1750 (J397)
Vol. 6, 1750–1880 (J425)
Vol. 7, 1880 to the Present Day (J549)
Vol. 8, American Drama (P794)

Basic guides

G115.   Hunter, Frederick J. *Drama Bibliography: A Short-Title Guide to Extended Reading in Dramatic Art for the English-Speaking Audience and Students in Theatre*. Boston: Hall, 1971. 239pp. Z5781.H84 016.7921
    Limited by its own copyright date, of course, but still a reliable source for scholars who need a quick guide to reference books on theater history, biography, techniques, and criticism of theater art in general. It includes lists of theatrical periodicals and encyclopedias, sections arranged according to nation and century, and bibliographies of dramatists, directors, and actors such as David Garrick, Sarah Bernhardt, Goethe, Shaw, Yeats, and Tennessee Williams. For broader coverage of the theater world, see Performing Arts (W1468–72).

G116.   *Modern World Theatre: A Guide to Productions in Europe and the United States since 1945*. Ed. Siegfried Kienzle. New York: Ungar,

1970. 509pp. PN112.5.K513   808.82
Performance and publishing information on plays produced since World War II. The synopses are useful, especially for the less well-known works.

Identification problems

*G117. *Oxford Companion to the Theatre*. Ed. Phyllis Hartnoll. 4th ed. London: Oxford Univ. Press, 1983. 934pp. PN2035.H3   792'.03'21

Emphasizes staged, not literary, drama, so most of the entries are on actors (such as David Garrick), producers (Florenz Ziegfeld), theaters (Old Vic), history of the stage in different countries, and terms (theater-in-the-round). There are 200 illustrations and an extensive bibliography arranged by both subject and nation. Many of the long entries were written by noted scholars and are signed. A concise, less expensive paperback edition was published in 1972.

The *Oxford Companion* is scholarly and comprehensive, but the *Penguin Dictionary of the Theatre* (New York: Penguin, 1966; 295pp.) defines theater terminology more thoroughly, and the *Encyclopedia of World Theater* (R970) may provide additional information on contemporary or less well-known individuals. For more extensive study of the theater, see Performing Arts (W1468–72) and other titles listed in the Index under "Theater (Stage)."

Periodicals

*G118. *Theatre Journal*. Baltimore: Johns Hopkins Univ. Press for the American Theatre Assn., 1979– . Quarterly. Former title, 1949–78: *Educational Theatre Journal (ETJ)*. PN3171.E38   371.332505

Rosmersholm, James Shirley, renovation of the Yale repertory theater, the nineteenth-century actress Julia Glover, regional drama, *Faust*, Brecht, *The Homecoming*, and Mexican theater are some of the subjects covered in these spirited articles and reviews of performances and books. An unusually fine periodical, with evidence of experienced, imaginative editing. Since 1952 it has featured an annual international "Doctoral Projects in Progress in Theatre Arts." Annual index and ten-year index for 1949–58.

Indexed in *ABELL* (D32), *Abst. Eng. Stud.* (E38), *Arts and Hum. Cit. Ind.* (F47), *Current Ind. Jour. Ed.* (W1224), *Ed. Ind.* (W1225), *Hum. Ind.* (F45), *MLA Abstracts* (E41), *MLAIB* (D31).

G119.   *Theatre Research International (ThR)*. Oxford: Oxford Univ. Press, 1975– . 3/yr. Former title, 1958–75: *Theatre Research*. PN2001.T436   790.2'05

Articles and reviews on the history and criticism of theater, with reference to art, architecture, design, music, and dramatic literature. International editorial board members and contributors. In English with summaries in French.

Indexed in *ABELL* (D32), *Arts and Hum. Cit. Ind.* (F47), *Current Bk. Rev. Cit.* (W1564), *Hum. Ind.* (F45), *Index to Bk. Rev. Hum.* (W1560), *MLAIB* (D31).

Background reading for drama

*G120. *Aristotle: Rhetoric*, trans. W. Rhys Roberts; *Poetics*, trans. Ingram Bywater. Ed. Friedrich Solmsen. New York: Modern Library, 1954. 289pp. PN173.A7.R6   881

The best of the many translations, with an admirable blend of accuracy and readability that is envied by other translators who all too often have sacrificed one for the other. The summaries at the beginning of each chapter and the introduction that surveys the historical background make this an ideal text for the classroom. Aristotle's famous concepts of tragedy, plot, character, epic, style, and the unities are required reading, of course.

G121.   Stratford-upon-Avon Studies. New York: St. Martin's, 1960– . Irregular (vol.19, 1980). 250pp.

A series concerned with literary and theatrical subjects of major interest. Each volume treats a different area, such as Jacobean Theatre, Elizabethan Theatre, Contemporary Theatre, American Theatre, Early Shakespeare, Decadence and the 1890s, and the Contemporary English Novel.

*G122. Brockett, Oscar G. *History of the Theatre*. 4th ed. Boston: Allyn and Bacon, 1982. 768pp. PN2101.B68   792'.09

The most readable, entertaining history of world drama available. Its scope extends to theater of the Byzantine Empire, the Orient, and all other major countries, with stress on the political, social, and intellectual forces that have influenced theater since 1960. Numerous illustrations and a timesaving seventeen-page bibliography.

Quotations

For titles and search procedure appropriate for the location of quotations, see Quotations (W1527–37).

Additional reference sources for drama as genre

ABELL (D32), Literary History and Criticism
American drama (P795–800, P810)
Classical drama (S995, S997, S1005)
Continental drama (Q897)
English drama
  General (J208, J212–13)
  Medieval (J278–80)
  Renaissance (J328–37, J343–48)
  Eighteenth century (J397–99, J401)
  Nineteenth century (J425–26)
  Twentieth century (J549–52)
Gerstenberger and Hendrick (W1475), drama periodicals
MLAIB (D31), vol. 1, General IV, and subsections in the national literatures
Performing Arts (W1468–72)
World Literature—Drama (R965)

Poetry—General
Criticism

*G125. *Poetry Explication: A Checklist of Interpretation since 1925 of British and American Poems Past and Present.* 3rd ed. Ed. Joseph M. Kuntz and Nancy C. Martinez. Boston: Hall, 1980. 570pp. Z2014.P7.K8 [PR502]   016.821'009

For thirty years Kuntz's *Poetry Explication* has been the single most popular source for students who need help in understanding poetry. This third edition, therefore, is greeted with enthusiasm and relief. Gratitude must also be extended to the publishers for their decision to give poetry the dignity and respect it deserves by presenting their bibliography with a fine binding, quality paper and print, and attractive layout. It incorporates all the information from the 1950 and 1962 editions and presents new information on criticism published up to 1978 in the most convenient way possible—alphabetically by poet and then by title of the specific poem (such as Eliot, "The Hollow Men") followed by a list of relevant critical articles and books. It claims to include interpretation by "phenomenologists, new literary historians, Marxist or dialectical critics, psychological critics, linguists, stylistic experts, rhetoricians, and prosodists, as well as by formalists and avowed 'new critics.' " Titles of the books and periodicals used by the editors are listed in the back of the book, sometimes with the library call numbers inserted so the students can go directly to the shelf and read the explication.

This work claims to be selective, but it contains three times the number of entries as the second edition. It does, however, confine itself strictly to explications (close readings of the text), omitting all poems over five hundred lines and all works by contemporary authors who have not yet been widely recognized. It also omits studies of only part of a poem (see *Explicator*, G56) and all books devoted solely to one author because that material is easy to locate. Additional information may possibly be found in Cline and Baker (G126) and the new publications by Alexander and Donow (G137.1). To bring it up to date, see the annual cumulative indexes and recent monthly issues of the *Explicator* (G56).

*G126. *Index to Criticisms of British and American Poetry.* Comp. Gloria S. Cline and Jeffrey A. Baker. Metuchen, N.J.: Scarecrow, 1973. 307pp. PR89.C5   821'.009

This indexes criticism on 285 poets that was published mainly from 1960 through 1970 in thirty specialized journals, giving particular attention to living authors. It covers the entire range of poetry from the anonymous medieval "Battle of Maldon" to the contemporary works of Eberhart and Ginsberg. The editors list forty-seven of Wallace Stevens' poems, for instance, and cite from one to four critical works for each title. Very little duplication with the previous entry by Kuntz and Martinez, who limit themselves strictly to explication whereas Cline and Baker locate historical, source, and interpretive studies.

Teachers who want to encourage good habits of research will require students to use this source so that they can consider the opinions of numerous experienced critics before arriving at a final conclusion of their own. Scholars who are interested in efficient methods of research will urge the editors to expand their coverage. Their use of only thirty periodicals was undoubtedly the result of restrictions of book size and price (and perhaps energy), but their idea is excellent. It warrants more confidence on the part of the publisher. See also G137.1.

*G127. *Epic and Romance Criticism.* Vol. 1: *A Checklist of Interpretations, 1940–1972, of English and American Epics and Metrical Romances.* Vol. 2: *A Checklist of Interpretations, 1940–1973, of Classical and Continental Epics and Metrical Romances.* Ed. Arthur Coleman. Searingtown, N.Y.: Watermill, 1973–74. Z7156.E6.C64   016.8091

A long-awaited source that fills a glaring research gap. Works are listed alphabetically with their related criticism—expected epics like *Beowulf, Sir Gawain, Paradise Lost* (Book 1, Book 2, etc.), *Faerie Queene* (Book 1, Book 2, etc.) as well as unexpected works like Whitman's *Leaves of Grass,* Hopkins' "Wreck of the Deutschland," Chaucer's *Canterbury Tales,* Williams' *Paterson,* and Ginsberg's *Howl.* Dryden, Pope, Keats, Blake, Coleridge, Browning, Eliot, and dozens of other authors of all centuries are cited in vol. 1. Vol. 2 brings the total number of citations up to twenty thousand and covers material from *Gilgamesh* and the *Iliad* to the *Mahabharata, Cid, Edda,* and *Divine Comedy.*

Encyclopedias

*G128. *Princeton Encyclopedia of Poetry and Poetics.* Ed. Alex Preminger. Rev. ed. London: Macmillan, 1975. 992pp. Paperback. Title of first edition: *Encyclopedia of Poetry and Poetics.* PN1021.E5   808.1'02

The best source available. This absolutely indispensable encyclopedia includes one thousand signed entries written by two hundred scholars about the history, technique, and criticism of poetry and poetics from earliest times. No entries on individual authors, poems, or allusions. For those research problems students must consult *Poetry Explication* (G125), Cline and Baker's *Index* (G126), Alexander (G137.1), Donow (G137.1), or the sections on Biography or Literary Encyclopedias in this guide (W1080–1152 or W1402–05).

Subject headings include classicism (5pp.), baroque poetics, Austrian poetry, imagery (8pp.), metaphor (5pp.), sound in poetry (6pp.), religion and poetry. The scholarly explanations are illustrated and clarified with numerous quotations and titles. A short definition is usually given first followed by more detailed explanations with distinctions, historical development, and applied critical theory. It has many cross-references, and bibliographies of both books and articles for further study follow most entries. It is essential to remember that *contemporary* topics are found in the appendix at the back of this edition—such subjects as computer poetry, hermeneutics, the Geneva school (3pp.), metacriticism (5pp.), rock lyrics (2pp.), and semiotics (2pp.). All students of literature should own this book.

Series

G129.   Poet and His Critics. Chicago: American Library Assn., 1975–   . Irregular.

A useful series that surveys and evaluates existing criticism on major English and American authors. Completed volumes deal with William Carlos Williams, Dylan Thomas, Langston Hughes, Robert Frost, and Wallace Stevens. In preparation are volumes on W. B. Yeats, Ezra Pound, Robert Lowell, E. E. Cummings, and T. S. Eliot.

Periodicals

G130.   *Concerning Poetry (CP)*. Bellingham: Western Washington Univ. Press, 1968–   . 2/yr. PS301.C64   810

Everything focuses on the poem, its criticism, and theories of criticism, from *The Dream of the Rood* to the sestina, from Taylor and Donne to Dickey, Duncan, Rich, and Plath. Book reviews and some original poetry.

Indexed in *ABELL* (D32), *Abst. Eng. Stud.* (E38), *Arts and Hum. Cit. Ind.* (F47), *Index to Bk. Rev. Hum.* (W1560), *MLAIB* (D31).

Background reading for poetry

*G131.   Brooks, Cleanth. *The Well Wrought Urn: Studies in the Structure of Poetry*. New York: Harcourt, 1947. 300pp. Paperback.   PR502.B7 821.09

The classic study of poetry as a "miracle of communication," with an exhortation that readers attempt to determine the original meaning of the poet's language and to suppress their own convictions so they can enjoy the total experience.

G132.   Ciardi, John, and Miller Williams. *How Does a Poem Mean?* 2nd ed. Boston: Houghton, 1975. 408pp. PS586.C53   821'.008

Explanations and questions written with a discerning ear and a responsive heart.

G133.   Eliot, T[homas] S[tearns]. *On Poetry and Poets*. London: Faber, 1957. 262pp. Paperback. PN511.E435   808.1

Students should become familiar with the theories of Eliot even though they may not necessarily agree with him: "Explanation . . . can distract us altogether from the poem as poetry instead of leading us in the direction of understanding."

G134.   Nims, John. *Western Wind: An Introduction to Poetry*. 2nd ed. New York: Random, 1983. 624pp. Paperback. PN1111.N5   809'.1

A logical analysis, but written with the touch of a poet. The author begins where we begin—with our senses. From imagery he goes to emotions, to the language that we use to express these emotions, to the sound and rhythm of this language, to the mind as an organizer, and to poems as sense and, naturally but inexplicably, as more than sense. He ends by considering the process of writing poetry: How much is inspiration and how much is design?

G135.   Ransom, John Crowe. *The World's Body*. Baton Rouge: Louisiana State Univ. Press, 1968. 390pp. Paperback. PN1136.R3   809.1

"True poetry . . . only wants to realize the world, to see it better" (p. x). This noted critic interprets the vision of Milton, Donne, I. A. Richards,

Shakespeare, Rebecca West, Santayana, and many others. See also Ransom's ideas on *The New Criticism* (W1389).

G136.   Wimsatt, William K., Jr. *The Verbal Icon: Studies in the Meaning of Poetry*. Lexington: Univ. Press of Kentucky, 1954. 299pp. Paperback. PN1031.W517   808.1
   A collection of sixteen essays on the history, theory, and practice of literary criticism.

G137.   Yu, Anthony C., ed. *Parnassus Revisited: Modern Critical Essays on the Epic Tradition*. Chicago: American Library Assn., 1973. 360pp. PN1305.Y8   809.1'3
   This anthology of essays by C. S. Lewis, E. M. W. Tillyard, Northrop Frye, and eighteen other twentieth-century scholars contains a four-page bibliography of books and articles on the epic.

Quotations
For titles and procedure useful in locating quotations in either prose or poetry, see Quotations (W1527–37).

Additional reference sources for poetry
G137.1 *ABELL* (D32)
   Abrams (J449)
   Alexander, Harriet, comp. *American and British Poetry: A Guide to the Criticism, 1925-1978*. Gen. eds. George Hendrick and Donna Gerstenberger. Athens: Ohio Univ. Press (Swallow), 1984. 550pp.
   A guide to research on specific poems; 20,000 entries.
   Contemporary Poets (W1129)
   International Who's Who in Poetry (W1101)
   Location of individual poems: *Granger's Index to Poetry* (W1536)
   MLAIB (D31), vol. 1, General IV, and subsections in the national literatures
   Poetry—General (G55–58)
      English, General (J215–19)
         Old English (J240–44)
         Medieval (J283, Q899)
         Seventeenth century (J355–56)
         Eighteenth century (J408–09)
         Romantic (J434–52)
         Victorian (J488–92)
         Twentieth century (J568–77)
      American (P814–24, P866–70)
   Prosody (W1504–08.1)
   The Sonnet in England and America: A Bibliography of Criticism. Comp. Herbert S. Donow. Westport, Conn.: Greenwood, 1982. 447pp.

Comedy and Tragedy

G138.   Mikhail, Edward H. *Comedy and Tragedy: A Bibliography of Critical Studies*. Troy, N.Y.: Whitston, 1972.   54pp.   Z5784.C6.M55 016.8092'52

Psychological and historical studies on comedy and tragedy as genre. As the editor says, this is only a beginning toward a comprehensive list, but it already comprises an interesting range from Aristotle to Bentley, from Nietzsche to Chesterton, from Eberhart to Meredith.

See also

ABELL (D32), English Literature, General; chronological sections, General
MLAIB (D31), General Literature, and English Literature, Themes and Types

H

Periodicals—General

Periodicals devoted to a specific country, century, or genre are discussed in their own specific sections. The entry for *Modern Fiction Studies* (J544), for instance, is located in the section on twentieth-century fiction. Reference books devoted to the analysis of periodicals are discussed in the reference section at the back of this guide under Periodicals (W1474–84). There the student will find that the most recent and most comprehensive annotated list of current literary periodicals is the *MLA Directory of Periodicals* (W1474). The representative titles discussed below have been selected because they make special contributions to specific areas of literary research.

H140. *American Notes and Queries (AN&Q)*. Owingsville, Ky.: Erasmus, 1962– . 10/yr. Z1034.A4 031'.02

Brief, problem-solving notes on sources, allusions, interpretations, and names from all national literatures and eras; queries and replies; brief book reviews. Supplement of the backlog of accepted material (Troy, N.Y.: Whitston, 1980).

Indexed in *ABELL* (D32), *Abst. Eng. Stud.* (E38), *Abst. Folklore Stud.* (W1274), *Am. Hum. Ind.* (P738), *Arts and Hum. Cit. Ind.* (F47), *Bk. Rev. Ind.* (W1559), *Hum. Ind.* (F45), *MLAIB* (D31), *Vict. Stud.* (J470), *Year's Wk. Eng. Stud.* (D33).

*H141. *Bulletin of Research in the Humanities (BRH)*. New York: Readex Books, 1978– . Quarterly. Former title, 1897–1977: *Bulletin of the New York Public Library*. Z881.N6.B8 001.3'05

Very Important. A glittering array of articles for the perfectionist—on the revelation that Virginia Woolf actually wrote "Man too can be emancipated," not, as the phrase is usually printed, "manipulated"; on accidentals in nineteenth-century texts as proposed by the CEAA (with stern references to Bowers, Greg, and McKerrow); on Blake's illustrations, Yeats's curious altera-

tions, and other delights for those who are blessed with inquiring minds.
Indexed in *ABELL* (D32), *Abst. Eng. Stud.* (E38), *Am. Hum. Ind.* (P738), *Arts and Hum. Cit. Ind.* (F47), *Bibl. Ind.* (C28), *Biog. Ind.* (W1085), *Hum. Ind.* (F45), *Lib. Lit.* (F53), *MLAIB* (D31).

H142. *College Language Association Journal (CLAJ; CLA Journal)*. Baltimore: CLA, Morgan State Univ., 1957– . Quarterly. P1.A1.C22   400
Scholarly articles, book reviews, and until 1976 an annual bibliography of Afro-American, African, and Caribbean literary studies, both creative and critical, in English. The volume for 1975 contained over fifty pages of scholarship. Articles are in various languages.
Indexed in *ABELL* (D32), *Abst. Eng. Stud.* (E38), *Arts and Hum. Cit. Ind.* (F47), *Current Bk. Rev. Cit.* (W1564), *Hum. Ind.* (F45), *Index to Bk. Rev. Hum.* (W1560), *MLAIB* (D31).

H143. *Criticism: A Quarterly for Literature and the Arts*. Detroit: Wayne State Univ. Press, 1959– . Quarterly. AS30.W3.A2   809
Analyzes and evaluates writers of all periods and nations—Chaucer, Arnold, Sartre, Thoreau, Edmund Wilson, Barthes, Hardy, Richardson, Virginia Woolf, Jonson, Hesse, even poststructuralists. Numerous book reviews.
Indexed in *ABELL* (D32), *Abst. Eng. Stud.* (E38), *Arts and Hum. Cit. Ind.* (F47), *Current Bk. Rev. Cit.* (W1564), *Hum. Ind.* (F45), *Index to Bk. Rev. Hum.* (W1560), *MLAIB* (D31).

H144. *ELH: Journal of English Literary History*. Baltimore: Johns Hopkins Univ. Press, 1934– . Quarterly. PR1.E5   820.9
Articles only—no reviews, no news, no bibliographies, no indexes of any kind. This covers the whole range of English literature from The Clerk's Tale to Holden Caulfield, from Gulliver to Beckett, from Ophelia to Leopold Bloom, from Pope to Pater, with occasional items on American works. See also J443.
Indexed in *ABELL* (D32), *Abst. Eng. Stud.* (E38), *Arts and Hum. Cit. Ind.* (F47), *Hum. Ind.* (F45), *MLAIB* (D31).

H145. *English Studies: A Journal of English Language and Literature (ES)*. Lisse, Netherlands: Swets and Zeitlinger, 1919– . 6/yr.   PE1.E55   420.5
Articles and reviews on English language and literature (including Commonwealth and some American) of all centuries, ranging from the Cotton Library manuscripts to specific verses in *Beowulf*, a line in *King Lear*, discussions of Trollope and Virginia Woolf, and an explanation of the difference between *dare* and *need* in Australian English. Research students want to look for its two annual bibliographical surveys of "Current Literature," one on original prose, poetry, and drama and the other on criticism and biography. Strictly for specialists and their special problems.
Indexed in *ABELL* (D32), *Arts and Hum. Cit. Ind.* (F47), *Current Bk. Rev. Cit.* (W1564), *Hum. Ind.* (F45), *Index to Bk. Rev. Hum.* (W1560), *Language and Lang. Beh. Abst.* (W1332), *MLAIB* (D31).

H146.   *Essays in Criticism: A Quarterly Journal of Literary Criticism (EIC)*. Lisse,
Netherlands: Swets and Zeitlinger, 1951– . Quarterly. PR1.E75
804.E78
Articles and reviews on all aspects of literature in English: *The Cloud of
Unknowing*, Shakespeare, Marvell, Wordsworth, James, Lawrence, Marianne
Moore. Cumulative index to vols. 1–15 (1951–66).
   Indexed in *ABELL* (D32), *Arts and Hum. Cit. Ind.* (F47), *Brit. Hum. Ind.*
(F49), *Current Bk. Rev. Cit.* (W1564), *Hum. Ind.* (F45), *Index to Bk. Rev. Hum.*
(W1560), *MLAIB* (D31).

H147.   *Essays in Literature (ELWIU)*. Macomb: Western Illinois Univ.,
   1973– . 2/yr. PN2.E84   805
Articles on English, American, and modern European language and
literature of all periods: Falstaff, Greene, Fielding, Vonnegut, Vargas Llosa,
Butler, Odets, Nabokov, Goethe, the Arthur ballads, Rousseau. No reviews.
Index to vols. 1–5 in vol. 5, no. 2 (Fall 1978).
   Indexed in *ABELL* (D32), *Abst. Eng. Stud. (E38)*, *Am. Hum. Ind.* (P738),
Arts and Hum. Cit. Ind. (F47), *MLAIB* (D31).

H148.   *Georgia Review (GaR)*. Athens: Univ. of Georgia, 1947– . Quarter-
   ly. AP2.G375   051
For interdisciplinary interests, with no limits on subject or century. Articles
on Bellow, Thoreau, theories on artists and critics, Dostoevsky's *The Possessed*
(by Oates), language in diaries, book reviews, original fiction and poetry.
   Indexed in *ABELL* (D32), *Abst. Eng. Stud.* (E38), *Arts and Hum. Cit. Ind.*
(F45), *Film Literature Index* (W1252), *Hum. Ind.* (F45), *Index to Bk. Rev. Hum.*
(W1560), *MLAIB* (D31), *Romantic Movement: A . . . Bibliography* (J443).

H149.   *Modern Language Quarterly (MLQ)*. Seattle: Univ. of Washington,
   1940– . Quarterly. PB1.M642   405
Especially important because of its contributions from international sources.
This journal is for those interested in English, American, French, Italian, and
other literatures, with articles and long, scholarly reviews on D. H. Lawrence,
Howells, Céline, Malraux, Blake, and Trollope. Its Arthurian literature
bibliography was an annual feature from 1936 through 1962, when it relin-
quished coverage of the field to the *Bulletin Bibliographique de la Société In-
ternationale Arthurienne* (see J267). No annotations, but a subject, author, and
title index.
   Indexed in *ABELL* (D32), *Arts and Hum. Cit. Ind.* (F47), *Hum. Ind.* (F45),
Index to Bk. Rev. Hum. (W1560), *MLAIB* (D31), *Romantic Movement:
A . . . Bibliography* (J443).

*H150.   *Modern Philology: A Journal Devoted to Research in Medieval and
   Modern Literature (MP)*. Chicago: Univ. of Chicago Press, 1903– .
   Quarterly. PB1.M7   405
Emphasis is on source, textual, and historical criticism, with subjects rang-
ing from Middle English alliterative verse to dating problems in manuscripts,
from literary and linguistic investigations of Chaucer to studies of Jonson,

Collins, Rimbaud, Dostoevsky, Johnson, and Faulkner. English is the main concern, but some articles deal with American, Romance, and Germanic literatures. News, numerous notes, and long book reviews contribute timely information.
Indexed in *ABELL* (D32), *Abst. Eng. Stud.* (E38), *Arts and Hum. Cit. Ind.* (F47), *Bk. Rev. Dig.* (W1558), *Bk. Rev. Ind.* (W1559), *Current Bk. Rev. Cit.* (W1564), *Hum. Ind.* (F45), *Index to Bk. Rev. Hum.* (W1560), *MLAIB* (D31), *Soc. Sci. Ind.* (W1579).

H151.   *Names: Journal of the American Name Society.* Potsdam, N.Y.: State Univ. Coll., 1953– . Quarterly. P769.N3   929
Scholarly, investigative articles on the origin and meaning of all names (personal, commercial, geographic, and scientific) from the Hittites and Romans to Spanish shrines, Proust, and South Carolina counties. Annual international bibliography.
Indexed in *ABELL* (D32), *America* (E43), *Hist. Abst.* (E43), *Index to Bk. Rev. Hum.* (W1560), *MLAIB* (D31), *Romantic Movement: A . . . Bibliography* (J443).

*H152.   *PMLA (Publications of the Modern Language Association of America).* New York: MLA, 1884– . 6/yr. PB6.M68   406
Editorial policy is to publish "the best of its kind, whatever the kind," but it favors essays that address a significant problem, that examine the implications of the thesis, and that, through a "concise, readable presentation," engage the attention of its audience (Jan. 1981, p. 7). This is the most prestigious literary journal in America. If your article appears here, you have arrived. See also D31 and W1029. Index to vols. 1–50, 1884–1935 (1964, c1936) and to vols. 51–79, 1936–64 (1966).
Indexed in *ABELL* (D32), *Abst. Eng. Stud.* (E38), *Arts and Hum. Cit. Ind.* (F47), *Hum. Ind.* (F45), *Language and Lang. Beh. Abst.* (W1332), *MLAIB* (D31), *Year's Wk. Eng. Stud.* (D33).

H153.   *Papers on Language and Literature: A Journal for Scholars and Critics of Language and Literature (PLL).* Edwardsville: Southern Illinois Univ., 1965– . Quarterly. PR1.P3   820'.5
Long scholarly studies on subjects ranging from the Corpus Christi cycles to Marvell, Aphra Behn, T. S. Eliot, Hemingway, and Yannis Ritsos. Review articles, news notes, and an annual index.
Indexed in *ABELL* (D32), *Abst. Eng. Stud.* (E38), *Arts and Hum. Cit. Ind.* (F47), *Hum. Ind.* (F45), *Language and Lang. Beh. Abst.* (W1332), *MLAIB* (D31).

*H154.   *Philological Quarterly: A Journal Devoted to Scholarly Investigation of the Classical and Modern Languages and Literatures (PQ).* Iowa City: Univ. of Iowa, 1922– . Quarterly. P1.P55   410'.5
Scholarly articles on English, Continental, and some American literature of all eras; book reviews; news and notes; and lists of new books received. Annual table of contents.
From 1926 to 1975 a special July issue entitled "Eighteenth Century: A

Current Bibliography" was probably the most valuable research aid in the field. See J375 for a description of the issues and the compilation of 1926–70 scholarship in six volumes. Since 1975, the bibliography has appeared as a separate publication (see J374), but *PQ* continues to feature essay reviews of the previous year's scholarship in English drama (1660–1800), Restoration literature, eighteenth-century fiction, Augustan literature, literary criticism, and the Age of Johnson. See also J443.

Indexed in *ABELL* (D32), *Abst. Eng. Stud.* (E38), *Arts and Hum. Cit. Ind.* (F47), *Bk. Rev. Ind.* (W1559), *Hum. Ind.* (F45), *Index to Bk. Rev. Hum.* (W1560), *Language and Lang. Beh. Abst.* (W1332), *MLAIB* (D31).

H155.   *Tennessee Studies in Literature (TSL)*. Knoxville: Univ. of Tennessee Press, 1956–   . Annual. PS1.T43   809

Scholarly essays on literary criticism, literary critics, and English and American literature; reviews. Beginning in 1982 each annual volume will be limited to a single subject such as Sexuality in the Victorian Age (1982) and Popular Literature of Medieval England, 1150–1450 (1983).

Indexed in *ABELL* (D32), *Am. Hum. Ind.* (P738), *Arts and Hum. Cit. Ind.* (F47), *MLAIB* (D31).

H156.   *Texas Studies in Literature and Language: A Journal of the Humanities (TSLL)*. Austin: Univ. of Texas Press, 1959–   . Quarterly. Former title, 1911–58: *Texas Studies in English*. AS30.T4   820.5

Articles only—long studies on literature, linguistics, philosophy, social studies, nontechnical science, Erasmus, Patrick White, Milton, Cowley, Magic, Mario Vargas Llosa, the Modern Comic Novel, and editing problems in Yeats.

Indexed in *ABELL* (D32), *Abst. Eng. Stud.* (E38), *Arts and Hum. Cit. Ind.* (F47), *Hum. Ind.* (F45), *MLAIB* (D31).

H157.   *Western European Specialists Section Newsletter*. Evanston, Ill.: Northwestern Univ. Library, 1977–   . 2/yr. Assn. of College and Research Libraries and American Library Assn.

News and notes concerning the journal's sponsor, the Western European Specialists Section of ACRL, which is a forum for the communication and exchange of ideas for librarians working with library materials in the English, Germanic, and Romance languages. The journal is interested in policies regarding the development and evaluation of library collections, in graduate level bibliographic instruction, and in other related subjects.

J

English Literature

General

Surveys

*J170.   Baugh, Albert C., et al. *A Literary History of England*. 2nd ed. New York: Prentice-Hall, 1967. 1605pp. PR83.B3   820.9

Critics agree that this is the standard against which most other criticism is measured. Some chapters, including that by George Sherburn on the eighteenth century, are still regarded as definitive in their field. The book is heavily weighted with facts and footnotes. Reading time: one year, in small doses.

J171.   Daiches, David. *A Critical History of English Literature*. 2nd ed. 2 vols. New York: Ronald, 1970. 1211pp. PR83.D29   820.9

Not everyone will agree with Daiches in all of his arguments, but this survey—through a combination of experience, perspective, and conversational writing style—is both authoritative and readable.

*J172.   Day, Martin S. *History of English Literature*. 3 vols. Garden City, N.Y.: Doubleday, 1963. Paperback. PR83.D35   820.903

Graduate students should still buy and read this in preparation for their M.A. and Ph.D. exams. It is the ultimate in convenience—uncluttered factual content and methodical physical arrangement. A best buy for very little money.

J173.   Ford, Boris, ed. *A Guide to English Literature*. 7 vols. London: Cassell, 1963. Penguin. Paperback. PR83.F6   820.9

This comprehensive survey of the whole field of English literature places authors and their works in their social context, surveys trends in literary forms, studies style and themes, and includes a list of books for further reading. In the preface the editor states that he tried to answer the questions of why, where, what, and which.

Vol. 1: *Age of Chaucer*; vol. 2: *Age of Shakespeare*; vol. 3: *From Donne*

64

to Marvell; vol. 4: *From Dryden to Johnson*; vol. 5: *From Blake to Byron*; vol. 6: *From Dickens to Hardy*; vol. 7: *The Present Age*. Critics seem to agree that the whole series is well planned, well written, and well documented. The section on Gerard Manley Hopkins, for instance, summarizes his philosophy and work accurately and mentions the best critical works.

*J174.   Oxford History of English Literature (OHEL). Oxford: Oxford Univ. Press, 1945– . In progress. For full annotations, see appropriate guide number.

> Vol. 1, pt. 1: *English Literature before the Norman Conquest*. In preparation (J246); pt. 2: *Middle English Literature*. In preparation (J252).
> Vol. 2, pt. 1: Henry S. Bennett. *Chaucer and the Fifteenth Century*. 1947 (J250); pt. 2: Sir Edmund K. Chambers. *English Literature at the Close of the Middle Ages*. 1945 (J251).
> Vol. 3: C[live] S[taples] Lewis. *English Literature in the Sixteenth Century excluding Drama*. 1954 (J301).
> Vol. 4, pt. 1: Frank P. Wilson. *The English Drama, 1485–1585*. 1968 (J330); pt. 2: *The English Drama, 1585–1642*. In preparation (J333).
> Vol. 5: Douglas Bush. *English Literature in the Earlier Seventeenth Century, 1600–1660*. 2nd ed. 1962 (J300).
> Vol. 6: James R. Sutherland. *English Literature of the Late Seventeenth Century*. 1969 (J362).
> Vol. 7: Bonamy Dobrée. *English Literature in the Early Eighteenth Century, 1700–1740*. 1959 (J361).
> Vol. 8: John E. Butt and Geoffrey Carnall. *The Mid-Eighteenth Century*. 1979 (J360).
> Vol. 9: William L. Renwick. *English Literature, 1789–1815*. 1963 (J434).
> Vol. 10: Ian R. Jack. *English Literature, 1815–1832*. 1963 (J435).
> Vol. 11: *The Mid-Nineteenth Century*. In preparation (J456).
> Vol. 12: John I. M. Stewart. *Eight Modern Writers*. 1963 (J510).

Basic guides

*J175.   *New Cambridge Bibliography of English Literature (New CBEL)*. Ed. George Watson. 4 vols. and index. Cambridge, Eng.: Cambridge Univ. Press, 1969–76. Z2011.N45 [PR83] 016.82

An extensive revision of the original four-volume *CBEL* of 1941 (ed. Frederick W. Bateson) and its supplement of 1957. This is the most comprehensive bibliography available to students of English literature, but the editor of the first revised volume, vol. 3 (J415), states frankly that the work treats only literature, that it does not include social, historical, political, scientific, and psychological titles, and that scholars must consult the earlier edition for those interests. Students must remember that even the scope in literature is limited. Not included are dissertations, reviews of secondary works, brief notes, antiquated articles that have been superseded, and the literature of certain Commonwealth states that have their own national bibliographies such as Canada, South Africa, Australia, and New Zealand (see Commonwealth Literature, N645–95). Coverage is occasionally uneven and dated, and there are few critical comments to distinguish the significant from the trivial items. Primary authors must be native to or resident in the British Isles (Auden and James are included, for instance, but no Canadians). There are, however, no national restrictions on authors of the secondary material.

Arrangement is generally in six main categories: general works, poetry, the novel (including children's books), drama, prose, and Anglo-Irish literature. The categories have chronological, major, and minor author subdivisions, with bibliographies for important individual titles. Under each major author (such as T. S. Eliot) a brief paragraph indicates the location of manuscripts in libraries (Houghton). This is followed by lists of bibliographies, collections of works, translations, editions, letters, incorrectly ascribed works, and international coverage of criticism—all in chronological order. Numbering is by column, not by pages.

Each volume has its own index of primary authors and some major subjects. The cumulative index for the entire work (vol. 5) increases the scope of the indexes in the four individual volumes to include minor authors, major anonymous works, certain subject headings, editors, foreign writers, pseudonyms, and titles of periodicals as well as of books. A full description of the scope of each volume appears in the appropriate entry:

Vol. 1, 600–1660 (J227), ed. George Watson. 1974.
Vol. 2, 1660–1800 (J363), ed. George Watson. 1971.
Vol. 3, 1800–1900 (J415), ed. George Watson. 1969.
Vol. 4, 1900–1950 (J511), ed. Ian R. Willison. 1972.
Vol. 5, Index, ed. J. D. Pickles. 1977. 542 cols.

The Shorter New CBEL (1981; 850pp.) is a one-volume abridgment that some professors may want to use as a classroom text.

The editor worked twenty years on this project. Fifty scholars contributed their time and experience. And one heroine spent seven years typing the entire four-volume bibliography. All literature students know that the *New CBEL* is the most important reference work in their field. The *MLAIB* (D31) is a close second.

A few reviewers have enjoyed expressing their dissatisfaction with this revision. Most frequently criticized are the editors' selection of critical material, their "bias" and uneven coverage, the chronological arrangement, the separation of major and minor authors, and the elimination of some of the categories found in the original *CBEL*. Nevertheless, the *New CBEL* remains what it has always been—the best. The publication of vol. 5 (the Index) invalidates many of the critics' complaints (it had been planned from the beginning; they need only have waited). The remainder of the objections have been eclipsed by the approval of scholars who find that repeated use and the resultant familiarity with arrangement and contents produce satisfactory research results.

See also

Altick and Wright, *Selective Bibliography for the Study of English and American Literature* (B15)

Bateson and Meserole, *Guide to English and American Literature* (B17)

Bell and Gallup, *Reference Guide to English, American, and Canadian Literature* (B18)

Kennedy and Sands, *Concise Bibliography for Students of English* (B19)

Schweik and Riesner, *Reference Sources in English and American Literature* (B16)

Somer and Cooper, *American and British Literature, 1945-1975* (B20)

Bibliographies of primary works

J176.   *Annals of English Literature, 1475-1950: The Principal Publications of Each Year Together with an Alphabetical Index of Authors with Their Works*. 2nd ed. Ed. Robert W. Chapman and W. K. Davin. Oxford: Clarendon, 1961; rpt. with corrections, 1969. 380pp. Z2011.A5 016.82

This simplified table of dates and titles shows immediately the major works that people were reading at any one time. It is interesting to ponder the influence of and competition between contemporaries, to note that Caxton printed his *Canterbury Tales* the same year that Thomas More was born, and to find that the year 1929 produced books by Hemingway, Woolf, Yeats, Wharton, Lawrence, Faulkner, Greene, Eliot, Powys, Thomas Wolfe, and a dozen more of our best authors. This bibliography will of course have to be brought up to date by the Rogal *Outline* (J177) and other more recent chronologies such as those in the *Revels History of Drama in English* (G114).

J177.   Rogal, Samuel J. *A Chronological Outline of British Literature*. Westport, Conn.: Greenwood, 1980. 341pp. PR87.R57   820'.9

Students will probably want to use both this and the *Annals* (J176) because, while Rogal covers a longer time span (A.D. 516 to 1979) and is much more up to date, he omits the United States. *Annals* has a better index, with authors' dates and titles.

Identification problems

*J178.   *Oxford Companion to English Literature*. Ed. Sir Paul Harvey. 4th ed., rev. Dorothy Eagle. Oxford: Clarendon, 1967; rpt. with corrections, 1983. 961pp. PR19.113   820'.3

English authors such as Sons of Ben, literary works such as *Ancrene Wisse*, literary societies, allusions, terms, mythical and fictional characters such as Fagin, a few American authors and their works, important persons, literary movements—in fact, any item found in English literature that might need clarification. Students should note the important appendixes on Censorship and the Law of the Press, the History of English Copyright, the Julian and Gregorian Calendars (including table), movable feast days, and saints' days frequently used in dating documents.

Series

J180.   British Book News. Bibliographical Series of Supplements. London: Longman, for the British Council and the National Book League, 1950– . In progress (over 270 had been published by 1982). Paperback.
Brief studies (30–60pp.) of individual English authors, philosophers, historians, genres, and movements. Each study includes a biographical or historical sketch, an analysis of style, comments on a few major works, and a selective bibliography. The quality of the evaluation varies, of course, but the contributing critics include T. S. Eliot writing on George Herbert, Ian Jack on Pope, and Jeffares on George Moore, so students, especially undergraduates who need only minimum information or have limited time, will find that these little booklets at least give them a good foundation. The unnumbered titles are in preparation.
The card catalog files these items under British Book News, Writers and Their Work, or the name of the author-subject. Between 1964 and 1967, most of the early booklets were bound in eleven volumes with updated bibliographies and published under the series title British Writers and Their Work (ed. Bonamy Dobrée and Thomas O. Beachcroft). Fifteen years later, they are once again being revised and updated for publication under the title *British Writers* (New York: Scribners, 1979–84; 7 vols. and index). British Book News also publishes every month the reviews of about 230 new books, a list of forthcoming books, and general articles on books and publishing (cumulative annual index).
Indexed in *Brit. Hum. Ind.* (F49), *MLAIB* (D31).

***J181.   Twayne's English Authors Series (TEAS). Boston: Twayne, 1964– .
Paperback.**

During the first eighteen years of this project, the editors published about 330 surveys on English and Irish authors. For a complete annotation on the Twayne Authors Series, see P720. Unnumbered titles are in preparation.

J182.   British and Irish Authors Series. Cambridge, Eng.: Cambridge Univ. Press,
        1969–   . In progress. Paperback. Former title: British Authors Series.
        Scholarly studies have been published so far on

Jane Austen   George Eliot
William Blake   E. M. Forster
Joseph Conrad   Thomas Hardy

John Keats
D. H. Lawrence
Alexander Pope

Sir Walter Scott
William Wordsworth

*J183.   Essential Articles Series. Ed. Bernard N. Schilling. Hamden, Conn.:
Archon, 1961– .
Collections of those articles that over the years have proved essential. Sub-
jects so far include

Francis Bacon
John Donne
John Dryden
English Augustan Backgrounds
George Herbert
Saint Thomas More

Old English Poetry (J243)
Alexander Pope
Edmund Spenser
Jonathan Swift (in preparation)
Henry Vaughan (in preparation)

See also

Author Bibliographies (W1053–55)

Periodicals

Periodicals that focus on English literature and have no restrictions by subject
or century are discussed in this section. Those devoted to English literature within
a limited subject area or time span (such as *Modern Fiction Studies*, J544) are
discussed in the appropriate chronological or subject subdivision. Those that
cover two or more national literatures are discussed in Periodicals—General
(H140–57), Continental Literature (Q890–92), and World Literature (R959–63).

J185.   *English*. London: Oxford Univ. Press, for the English Assn., 1935– .
3/yr. PR5.E5   820.5
A few critical articles and original poems, a great many scholarly reviews,
but it is the editorial column that makes this periodical memorable, for here
the scholar's voice affirms that research is pleasure, and discovery, delight. Subjects range from Owen to Thackeray, Eliot, Marvell, Keats, and Shakespeare.
Indexed in *ABELL* (D32), *Abst. Eng. Stud.* (E38), *Arts and Hum. Cit. Ind.*
(F47), *Brit. Hum. Ind.* (F49), *Index to Bk. Rev. Hum.* (W1560), *Language and
Lang. Beh. Abst.* (W1332), *MLAIB* (D31), *Romantic Movement: A . . . Bibliography* (J443).

*J186.   *English Language Notes (ELN)*. Boulder: Univ. of Colorado, 1963– .
Quarterly. PE1.E53   420'.5
English literature, linguistics, and textual criticism are *ELN*'s main interests.
It offers articles, reviews, and one outstanding feature: the regular September
supplement, "The Romantic Movement: A Selective and Critical Bibliography,"
which contains critical annotations and review citations for books concerned with
Continental and English Romanticism (see J443).
Indexed in *ABELL* (D32), *Abst. Eng. Stud.* (E38), *Arts and Hum. Cit. Ind.*
(F47), *Current Bk. Rev. Cit.* (W1564), *Hum. Ind.* (F45), *Index to Bk. Rev. Hum.*
(W1560), *MLAIB* (D31).

*J187.   *Notes and Queries: For Readers and Writers, Collectors and Librarians* (*N§Q*). Pembroke Coll., Oxford: Oxford Univ. Press, 1849– . 6/yr. AG305.N7   032

Devoted principally to English (not American) language and literature, lexicography, history, and scholarly antiquarianism, with emphasis on the factual rather than the speculative. Questions and answers, chastisements and apologies, notes and reviews.

Indexed in *ABELL* (D32), *Abst. Eng. Stud.* (E38), *Arts and Hum. Cit. Ind.* (F47), *Brit. Hum. Ind.* (F49), *Current Bk. Rev. Cit.* (W1564), *Hum. Ind.* (F45), *Index to Bk. Rev. Hum.* (W1560), *MLAIB* (D31).

J188.   *Review of English Studies: A Quarterly Journal of English Literature and the English Language* (*RES*). Oxford: Clarendon, 1925– . Quarterly. PR1.R4   820'.9

Scrupulously frank book reviews on a variety of English (not American) literary subjects: Anglo-Saxon poetry, Old English vocabulary, editions of Gawain, Scottish language and literature, Sidney, Lady Montagu, Smollett, E. M. Forster, James Stephens. Only one or two critical essays but an unusual, very convenient list of the contents of about thirty-five other contemporary literary periodicals. This feature is the type of research tool that students should consult regularly to make their own research less time-consuming and more productive.

Indexed in *ABELL* (D32), *Abst. Eng. Stud.* (E38), *Arts and Hum. Cit. Ind.* (F47), *Bk. Rev. Ind.* (W1559), *Brit. Hum. Ind.* (F49), *Current Bk. Rev. Cit.* (W1564), *Hum. Ind.* (F45), *Index to Bk. Rev. Hum.* (W1560), *MLAIB* (D31).

See also
    Articles on American and British Literature (P733.1)

Periodicals—Reference works

J190.   *English Literary Journal to 1900: A Guide to Information Sources.* Ed. Robert B. White, Jr. Vol. 8 of Gale Information Guide Library (A8). Detroit: Gale, 1977. 311pp. Z6956.G6.W47   [PN5114]   016.81'05

A valuable, carefully indexed bibliography of two thousand books, articles, and dissertations including nonfiction and genre studies written since 1890 on early British journals. All research should begin here. For bibliographies on American periodicals during this era, see Kribbs (P742) and Chielens (P740–41). A similar study of twentieth-century English periodicals has just been published: *English Literary Journal, 1900–1950* (J533).

Author newsletters, journals, and other serial publications devoted to individual English authors

J195.   Additional author newsletters are listed in this guide for American (P777), Canadian (N685), Continental (Q893), Irish (K600), Scottish (L627), and Welsh (M640) authors. For full bibliographical information and descriptive annotations on these and other periodicals concerned with one person, see *Author Newsletters and Journals* (W1476).

Aldington, Richard
  New Canterbury Literary Society Newsletter, 1973– .
Arnold, Matthew
  Arnold Newsletter, 1973–75.
  Arnoldian, 1975– .
Austen, Jane
  Jane Austen Newsletter, 1980– .
  Jane Austen Society. *Report*, 1940(?)– .
Bacon, Francis
  American Baconiana, 1923–31.
  Baconiana, 1892– .
Bennett, Arnold
  Arnold Bennett Newsletter, 1975–79.
  Era of Arnold Bennett, 1979– .
Bentham, Jeremy
  Bentham Newsletter, 1978- .
Blackmore, Richard
  Blackmore Studies, 1969–(?).
Blake, William
  Blake: An Illustrated Quarterly, 1977– .
  Blake Newsletter, 1967–77.
  Blake Studies, 1968– .
The Brontës
  Brontë Society. *Transactions*, 1895– .
Browning, Robert and Elizabeth
  Baylor Browning Interests, 1927– .
  Browning Institute Studies, 1973– .
  Browning Newsletter, 1968–72.
  Browning Society. London. *Papers*, 1881–91.
  Browning Society Notes, 1970– .
  Bulletin of the New York Browning Society, 1907–65.
  Studies in Browning and His Circle, 1973– .
  Through Casa Guidi Windows, 1975– .
Bulwer-Lytton, Edward
  Bulwer-Lytton Chronicle, 1973– .
Butler, Samuel
  Samuel Butler Newsletter, 1978– .
Byron, Lord
  Byron Foundation Lecture, 1912– .
  Byron Journal, 1973– .
  Byron Society. *Newsletter*, 1973– .
Carroll, Lewis. See Dodgson, Charles Lutwidge.
Chaucer, Geoffrey
  Chaucer Newsletter, 1978– .
  Chaucer Research Report. See J268.
  Chaucer Review, 1966– .
  Studies in the Age of Chaucer, 1979– .
Chesterton, G. K.
  Chesterton Review, 1974– .

Conrad, Joseph
  Conradiana, 1968– .
  L'Époque Conradienne, 1975– .
  Italian Joseph Conrad Society Newsletter, 1975– .
  Joseph Conrad Society Journal, 1975– .
  Joseph Conrad Society Newsletter, 1973–75.
  Joseph Conrad Today, 1975– .
  Pamphlet Series (England), 1975– .
Dickens, Charles
  Dickens Studies, 1965–69.
  Dickens Studies Annual, 1970–80.
  Dickens Studies Annual: Essays on Victorian Fiction, 1980– .
  Dickens Studies Newsletter, 1970– .
  Dickensian, 1905– .
Disraeli, Benjamin
  Disraeli Newsletter, 1976– .
Dodgson, Charles Lutwidge (Lewis Carroll)
  Bandersnatch, 1973– .
  Carroll Studies, 1975– .
  Jabberwocky, 1969– .
  Knight Letter, 1974– .
Doyle, Sir Arthur Conan
  Adventuresses of Sherlock Holmes Newsletter, 1975– .
  Arnsworth Castle Business Index, 1960–64.
  Baker Street Cab Lantern, 1963– .
  Baker Street Christmas Stocking, 1953–56; 1958–60; 1962– .
  Baker Street Journal, 1946–49; 1950– .
  Baker Street Miscellanea, 1975– .
  Baker Street Pages, 1965–70.
  Canadian Holmes, 1973– .
  Commonplace Book, 1964–69.
  Devon County Chronicle, 1964– .
  Feathers from the Nest, 1971– .
  Gamebag, 1965–69.
  Garroter, 1972– .
  General Communication, 1972– .
  Holmesian Observer, 1971–74; annual, 1975– .
  Holmeswork, 1974– .
  Irregular Report (Copenhagen), 1960–65.
  Kansas City Journal, 1976– .
  Lens, 1975– .
  Northumberland Dispatch, 1974– .
  Pontine Dossier, 1967– .
  Report Card, 1971– .
  Sherlock Holmes Journal, 1952– .
  Sherlockiana, 1956– .
  Sidelights on Holmes, 1966–69.
  Vermissa Herald, 1962–63; 1967– .
  Victorian Journal, 1970–71.

Dudevant, Mme. (George Sand)
George Sand Newsletter, 1977/78– .
Durrell, Lawrence
Deus Loci, 1977– .
Eliot, George. See Evans, Mary Ann.
Evans, Mary Ann (George Eliot)
George Eliot Fellowship Review,
1970– .
Forster, John
John Forster Newsletter, 1978– .
Freeman, R. Austin
Thorndyke File, 1976– .
Gissing, George
Gissing Newsletter, 1965– .
Graves, Robert
Focus on Robert Graves, 1972– .
Greenaway, Kate
Under the Window, 1971–(?).
Hardy, Thomas
Monographs on . . . Hardy, 1968– .
Thomas Hardy Society Review, 1975– .
Thomas Hardy Year Book, 1970– .
Herbert, George
George Herbert Journal, 1977– .
Hopkins, Gerard Manley
Annual Hopkins Lecture, 1970–76.
Annual Hopkins Sermon, 1969–75.
Hopkins Quarterly, 1974– .
Hopkins Research Bulletin, 1970–76.
Housman, A. E.
Housman Society Journal, 1974– .
Johnson, Samuel
Johnsonian News Letter, 1940– .
Johnson Society. Lichfield. *Transactions*,
1911– .
New Rambler, 1941– .
Keats, John
Keats-Shelley Journal, 1952– .
Keats-Shelley Memorial Bulletin, 1910,
1913, 1950– .
Kipling, Rudyard
Kipling Journal, 1927– .
Lamb, Charles
Charles Lamb Bulletin, 1973– .
C.L.S. Bulletin, 1941–72.
Lawrence, D. H.
D. H. Lawrence News and Notes,
1959–62.
D. H. Lawrence Newsletter, 1977– .
D. H. Lawrence Review, 1968– .
D. H. Lawrence Studies (Japan),
1973– .
Journal of the D. H. Lawrence Society,
1976– .
Nethermere News, 1973– .
Lawrence, T. E.
T. E. Lawrence Studies, 1976– .

Leacock, Stephen
Newspacket, 1970– .
Lessing, Doris
Doris Lessing Newsletter, 1976– .
Lewis, C. S.
*Bulletin of the New York C. S. Lewis
Society*, 1969– .
Canadian C. S. Lewis Journal, 1979– .
*Chronicle of the Portland C. S. Lewis
Society*, 1972– .
Lamppost, 1976– .
Lewis, Wyndham
Enemy News, 1978 (no.9)– .
Lewisletter, 1974–77(?).
Locke, John
Locke Newsletter, 1970– .
Lydgate, John
Lydgate Newsletter, 1972–(?).
Mill, John Stuart
Mill News Letter, 1965– .
Milton, John
Milton and the Romantics, 1975–78;
1980.
Milton Newsletter, 1967–69.
Milton Quarterly, 1970– .
Milton Society of America: Proceedings,
1948– .
Milton Studies, 1969– .
More, Saint Thomas
Moreana, 1963– .
Morris, William
Journal of the William Morris Society,
1961– .
News from Anywhere, 1958– .
William Morris Society. *Report*, 1955– .
Newman, Cardinal John Henry
Newman Studien, 1948– .
Pater, Walter
Pater Newsletter, 1980– .
Peake, Mervyn
Mervyn Peake Review, 1975– .
Mervyn Peake Society Newsletter,
1975–76.
Pope, Alexander
Scriblerian: A Newsjournal, 1968–71.
Scriblerian and the Kit-Cats, 1972– .
Powys, Llewelyn, John, and Theodore
Powys Newsletter, 1970– .
Powys Review, 1977– .
Read, Sir Herbert
Herbert Read Series, 1961– .
Rohmer, Sax. See Ward, Arthur S.
Russell, Bertrand
Bertrand Russell Society Newsletter,
1974– .
*Russell: The Journal of the Bertrand
Russell Archives*, 1971– .

Sand, George. See Dudevant, Mme.
Sayers, Dorothy
Sayers Review, 1980– .
Shakespeare, William
Bard, 1975– .
*Bulletin of the Shakespeare Association
of Japan*, 1930–33(?).
Deutsche Shakespeare-Gesellschaft.
Jahrbuch. Heidelberg, 1965– .
Deutsche Shakespeare-Gesellschaft.
Schriftenreihe. Heidelberg, 1904– .
Folger Library Newsletter, 1969– .
Folger Shakespeare Library. *Report*,
1948–68.
*Journal of the Cincinnati Shakespeare
Club*, 1860–72.
New Shakespeareana, 1901–11.
On-Stage Studies, 1976– .
Publications (London), 1874–92.
Report of the International Shakespeare
Conference, 194(?)– .
Schriften (Weimar), 1904–12.
Schriftenreihe (Bochum), 1931– .
Shakespearakan, 1966– .
Shakespeare Association Bulletin,
1924–49.
Shakespeare Association of Japan.
Bulletin, 1930–36.
Shakespeare Fellowship News-Letter,
1939–43.
Shakespeare Fellowship Quarterly.
1944–48.
Shakespeare-Jahrbuch (Heidelberg),
1965– .
Shakespeare-Jahrbuch (Weimar),
1864– .
Shakespeare News (Japan), 1961– .
Shakespeare Newsletter, 1951– .
Shakespeare on Film Newsletter,
1976– .
Shakespeare Pictorial, 1928–39.
Shakespeare Problems, 1920–41;
1952–(?).
Shakespeare Quarterly, 1950– .
Shakespeare Quarterly (Austria),
1948–(?).
Shakespeare-Schriften. Vienna, 1954–(?).
Shakespeare Stage, 1953–54.
Shakespeare Studies (Tokyo), 1962– .
*Shakespeare Studies: An Annual Gather-
ing of Research*, 1965– .
Shakespeare Studies Monograph Series,
1969–(?).
Shakespeare Survey, 1948– .
Shakespeare Survey (London), 1923–28.
Shakespeare-Tage Weimar, 1971– .
Shakespeare Translation, 1974– .

Shakespearean Authorship Review,
1959–75.
Shakespearean Quarterly (Australia),
1922–24.
*Shakespearean Research and Oppor-
tunities*, 1968– .
Shakespearean Research Opportunities,
1965–67.
Shakespeare's Proclamation, 1968– .
Shakespeariana, 1883–93.
Stratford Papers on Shakespeare,
1960–69.
Shelley, Percy Bysshe. See Keats, John.
Spenser, Edmund
Spenser Newsletter, 1968– .
Spenser Studies, 1980– .
Sterne, Laurence
Shandean, 1979– .
Tennyson, Alfred
Tennyson Research Bulletin, 1967– .
Tennyson Society. *Annual Report*,
1961– .
Tennyson Society. *Monographs*, 1969– .
Tennyson Society. *Occasional Papers*,
1974– .
Tennyson Society. *Publications*, 1963– .
Tennyson Society. *Tennyson Memorial
Sermon*, 1968– .
Thackeray, William Makepeace
Thackeray Newsletter, 1975– .
Thompson, Francis
Francis Thompson Society. *Journal*,
1964/65–74/75.
Tolkien, John R. R.
Amon Hen.
Anduril, 1972– .
Green Dragon, 1965–(?).
Mallorn, 1970– .
Mythlore, 1969– .
Mythprint, 1967– .
New Tolkien Newsletter, 1980– .
Niekas, 1962–78.
Orcrist, 1966– .
Tolkien Journal, 1965–72.
Trollope, Anthony
Trollopian, 1945–49.
Wallace, Edgar
Edgar Wallace Newsletter, 1969– .
Ward, Arthur S. (Sax Rohmer)
Rohmer Review, 1968– .
Waugh, Evelyn
Evelyn Waugh Newsletter, 1967– .
Wells, H. G.
Bulletin. H. G. Wells Society, 1963;
1964–71.
Journal of the H. G. Wells Society,
1972–73.

Wells, H. G. (continued)
  Newsletter, 1975– .
  Occasional Papers, 1973– .
  Wellsian, 1960–68.
  Wellsian: The Journal of the H. G.
    Wells Society, 1976– .
  Wellsian: World of H. G. Wells,
    1904(?)– .

Wollstonecraft, Mary
  Mary Wollstonecraft Newsletter,
    1972–74.
Woolf, Virginia
  Virginia Woolf Miscellany, 1973– .
  Virginia Woolf Newsletter, 1971– .
  Virginia Woolf Quarterly, 1972– .
Wordsworth, William
  Wordsworth Circle, 1970– .

FICTION

Surveys

*J196.   Allen, Walter. *The English Novel: A Short Critical History*. New York: Dutton, 1954. 454pp. Paperback. PR821.A4 823.09

Interesting viewpoints and pleasant reading—probably the best comprehensive survey from the beginnings of prose fiction in the Renaissance to Woolf, Joyce, and Lawrence.

J197.   Baker, Ernest A. *The History of the English Novel*. 10 vols. London: Witherby, 1924–39. PR821.B33 823.09

This helpful survey ranges from Anglo-Saxon fiction to full discussions of Conrad and Lawrence, with summaries, footnotes, indexes, and bibliographies for further study. Stevenson (J198) extends the survey to post-World War II authors.

J198.   Stevenson, Lionel. *The History of the English Novel*. Vol. 11: *Yesterday and After*. New York: Barnes and Noble, 1967. 431pp. PR881.S7 823'.9'109

The latest volume in the series initiated by Baker in 1924 (see previous entry). Stevenson covers Wells, Forster, and Joyce thoroughly before going into Beckett, Orwell, Golding, Iris Murdoch, and dozens of other modern novelists. A readable book—crowded with facts and provocative observations on trends and influences, analyses of many specific titles, and interpretations of style and themes. Footnotes, index, and bibliography.

J199.   Wagenknecht, Edward C. *Cavalcade of the English Novel*. Rev. ed. New York: Holt, 1954, c1943. 686pp. Supplementary bibliography. PR821.W25 823.09

A dependable survey of the novel from Shakespeare's time through the beginnings of realism, the novels of humors and sensibility, the romances, and the spate of nineteenth-century novelists to Woolf. An appendix of brief biographies for minor authors not mentioned in the text.

Basic guides

J200.   Booth, Wayne C., and Gwin J. Kolb. *The British Novel through Jane Austen*. Goldentree Bibliographies (W1291). In preparation.

See also

> Watt, *British Novel: Scott through Hardy* (J479)
> Wiley, *British Novel: Conrad to the Present* (J537)

Bibliographies of primary works

J201.   Bonheim, Helmut, ed. *The English Novel before Richardson: A Checklist of Texts and Criticism to 1970.* Metuchen, N.J.: Scarecrow, 1971. 145pp. Z2014.F4.B65   016.823'03

Students who think that the English novel began with *Pamela* and *Tom Jones* should consult this work for it includes prose fiction by Dekker, Greene, Lodge, and Congreve as well as the expected Lyly, Sidney, and Defoe.

Criticism

*J202.   *English Novel Explication: Criticisms to 1972.* Ed. Helen H. Palmer and Anne J. Dyson. Hamden, Conn.: Shoe String, 1973. 329pp. Supplement 1, ed. Peter L. Abernethy, Christian J. W. Kloesel, Jeffrey R. Smitten (1976), 305pp. Supplement 2 through 1979, ed. Kloesel and Smitten (1981), 228pp. Z2014.F5.P26   016.823'009

Students enrolled in courses on the English novel should use this regularly—the exposure to work of experienced critics will help them formulate solid ideas of their own. Both the basic volume and the supplements have a broad interpretation of the words "novel" and "explication." *Le Morte d'Arthur* is included as well as *The Lord of the Rings*, and all criticism is listed except source, influence, biographical, and bibliographical studies. The supplements, however, exclude book reviews, dissertations, all short novels such as *Animal Farm* that are already indexed in Walker's *Twentieth-Century Short Story Explication* (G78), and authors who did not live in Great Britain most of their creative years, such as Henry James and Brian Moore. Exceptionally well edited, with excellent format. Complements Bell and Baird (J203).

*J203.   Bell, Inglis F., and Donald Baird. *The English Novel, 1578–1956: A Checklist of Twentieth-Century Criticisms.* Rev. ed. Hamden, Conn.: Shoe String, 1974. 168pp. Z2014.F5.B44   016.823'03

Indexes about one hundred periodicals as well as books and monographs for twentieth-century criticism of English novels from Lyly's *Euphues* to contemporaries like Graham Greene. This was inspired by the success of Kuntz's *Poetry Explication* (G125) and, like it, is selective with no annotations. A short introduction gives background information on the development of critical theory (pre- and post-James), and the entries are arranged alphabetically, with individual titles listed alphabetically under each author.

Invaluable for locating critical works published before the original copyright date of 1958. The above "revised edition" appears to be only a reprint. For more recent scholarship, consult the sources described in the preceding and following entries.

*J204.   Dyson, Anthony E., ed. *The English Novel: Select Bibliographical Guides*. London: Oxford Univ. Press, 1974. 372pp.   Z2014.F5.D94 016.823'03

A group of experienced researchers recommend the best biographies, best critics, best editions, and best bibliographies for twenty novelists from Bunyan to Joyce. Dyson's other collection of reviews of research on *English Poetry* (J216) has proved its value. This guide is most welcome.

*J205.   Schlueter, Paul, and June Schlueter. *English Novel: Twentieth Century Criticism*. Vol. 2, *Twentieth Century Novelists*. Athens: Ohio Univ. Press (Swallow), 1982. 416pp.

The most nearly complete list of criticism on the twentieth-century British novel, covering eighty-three major and minor British novelists and 7,500 titles of critical works. It even includes entries for special issues of periodicals that are devoted to individual authors, and for outstanding criticism that is devoted to specific novels. It does not overlap with Palmer and Dyson (J202), which is restricted solely to "explication," and of course is more up to date than any other guide or bibliography for the English novel. Students who are doing extensive work in this field should definitely begin their research with this book. Vol. 1, *Defoe through Hardy*, ed. Richard J. Dunn (Chicago: Swallow, 1976), lists forty-five novelists, their major novels, related criticism, and general studies.

DRAMA

Surveys

*J208.   Nicoll, Allardyce. *A History of English Drama, 1660-1900*. 6 vols. Cambridge, Eng.: Cambridge Univ. Press, 1952-59.   PR625.N52   822'.009

Very few errors in this excellent work by a respected scholar. Vols. 3-5 are second editions, vol. 2 a third edition, and vol. 1 a fourth edition. In vol. 5, *A History of Late Nineteenth-Century Drama, 1850-1900*, Nicoll gives the Victorian background, discusses the plays by decade, lists the theaters in operation during that time, and provides a five-hundred-page author bibliography with titles of plays and location and date of first performance. Students who need a more manageable treatment of the subject may prefer to use Nicoll's one-volume survey, which has been recently revised by John C. Trewin: *British Drama: An Historical Survey from the Beginnings to the Present Time*, 6th ed. (New York: Barnes and Noble, 1978; 311pp.).

Nicoll has also written many other studies on various aspects and eras of the drama (see Index). Students will probably want to supplement this particular history with the more recent *Revels History of Drama in English*, vols. 5, 6, 7 (J397, J425, J549).

Bibliographies of primary works

**J209.   Stratman, Carl J., C.S.V. *Bibliography of English Printed Tragedy, 1565-1900*. Carbondale: Southern Illinois Univ. Press, 1966. 843pp.   Z2014.D7.S83   016.822051

This scholarly, copiously detailed bibliography of 1,483 tragedies listed alphabetically by author includes 175 titles not found elsewhere but excludes all Shakespeare. Each entry cites title, subtitle, imprint, pagination, staging information, identifying numbers in the *STC* (J306, J370), Greg numbers, entries for all editions, symbols indicating location in libraries, and editor's comments on textual and historical problems.

A chronological table reveals that in the nineteenth century, for instance, about seven hundred tragedies were written by such authors as Arnold, Byron, Coleridge, Disraeli, Hardy, Keats, Lamb, Tennyson, and Wordsworth. To facilitate further research, the editor includes a table locating extant manuscripts and a list of the anthologies he consulted for his own research. Some inaccuracies have been noted, but when used in conjunction with Nicoll's and Revels' histories (J208, G114) this bibliography provides complete background information for English tragedy up to 1900.

J210.   Arnott, James F., and John W. Robinson. *English Theatrical Literature, 1559-1900: A Bibliography Incorporating Robert W. Lowe's A Bibliographical Account of English Theatrical Literature (1888)*. London: Soc. for Theatre Research, 1970. 486pp. Z2014.D7.A74 016.792'0942

A subject arrangement (as Government Regulation of the Theatre, Morality, London, Periodicals, History) of all theatrical literature published in the British Isles up to 1900. Students will find this a promising source for studies either by subject (436 titles are concerned with morality in the theater between 1577 and 1898) or by public response (almost three hundred theatrical periodicals are listed for London alone). Each edition is described briefly and is located in an English or American library. This scholarly work is remarkably interesting and readable. The title index, for instance, leads to an entry on the performance of Shelley's *Cenci* in 1886, and the author index cites two lectures written by Byron for delivery at the Drury Lane Theatre in 1812 and 1816. Information on periodicals is supplemented by the following title (J211).

J211.   Stratman, Carl J., C.S.V. *Britain's Theatrical Periodicals, 1720-1967: A Bibliography*. 2nd ed. New York: New York Public Library, 1972. 160pp. Title of first edition, 1962: *A Bibliography of British Dramatic Periodicals, 1720-1960*. Z6935.S76   016.792'0942

A chronological list of drama periodicals published in England, Scotland, and Ireland betwen 1720 and 1967. It supplements Arnott's bibliography (J210), which also locates the periodicals in English and American libraries.

Criticism

*J212.   Wells, Stanley, ed. *English Drama (excluding Shakespeare): Select Bibliographical Guides*. London: Oxford Univ. Press, 1975. 320pp. Paperback. Z2014.D7.E44   [PR625]   822'.009

A survey of research that is similar in approach and usefulness to those edited by Dyson on English poetry (J216) and the English novel (J204). These essays evaluate contemporary scholarship and major trends in the criticism of individual dramatists and types of drama. Footnotes, bibliography, and index—a well-edited, reliable handbook by experienced researchers that students should purchase for their private collections. For extended research in Renaissance, Jacobean, and Caroline drama that requires information on textual studies, editions, and other problem areas, students will have to go to the more comprehensive (and more expensive) volumes edited by Logan and Smith (J343–46). For more information on the review of research as a genre, see W1556.

J213.   *English Tragedy, 1370–1600: Fifty Years of Criticism.* Comp. Harry B. Caldwell and David L. Middleton. Checklists in the Humanities and Education. San Antonio: Trinity Univ. Press, 1971. 89pp. Z2014.D7.C3 016.822'051

A selective bibliography of criticism on nondramatic verse (for example, Chaucer's *Troilus and Criseyde*), dramatic tragedy exclusive of Marlowe and Shakespeare (Kyd's *Spanish Tragedy*), and special topics like revenge, the tyrant, and Senecan influence. Of special value to the graduate student is an appendix listing works that need further research such as Skelton's *Kynge Edwarde the Forth* and Drayton's contributions to *I, II Sir John Oldcastle*. Primary and secondary author index.

See also

American and British Theatrical Biography (W1138)
Salem, *Foreign Drama* (R969)

POETRY

Surveys

*J215.   Routledge History of English Poetry. Ed. Reginald A. Foakes. 6 vols. Boston: Routledge, 1977–   . PR502.R58   821'.009

The first critical history of English poetry written in the last three-quarters of a century. Each volume will reassess the historical and social milieu that produced the poetry, with a new evaluation of the poets as judged by current taste in criticism. See the specific entry numbers for additional information.

Vol. 1: Pearsall, Derek. *Old English and Middle English Poetry.* 1977 (J240).
Vol. 2: *English Renaissance Poetry: Spenser to Milton.* In preparation.
Vol. 3: *From Dryden to Cowper.* In preparation.
Vol. 4: Jackson, James R. de J. *Poetry of the Romantic Period.* 1980 (J436).
Vol. 5: *Critical History of Victorian Poetry.* In preparation.
Vol. 6: *The Twentieth Century in English Poetry.* In preparation.

Criticism

*J216.   Dyson, Anthony E., ed. *English Poetry: Select Bibliographical Guides.* London: Oxford Univ. Press, 1971. 378 pp. Z2014.P7.E53   016.821

This review of research on twenty authors from Chaucer to Joyce contains essays by such reliable critics as Erdman (Blake), Jack (Browning), and Storey (Hopkins). Every essay makes recommendations on the best critics, editions, biographies, bibliographies, background reading, and special studies available at the time the collection was published, but unfortunately it now needs updating badly. The researcher's first step should always be to determine whether specific guides like these are available and the next, to assess their usefulness. See, for instance, the other "select guides" on the English novel (J204) and English drama (J212). See also Review of Research (W1556) and Author Bibliographies (W1053-55).

Background reading for poetry

J217.   Fairchild, Hoxie Neale. *Religious Trends in English Poetry*. 6 vols. New York: Columbia Univ. Press, 1939-68. PR508.R4.F3   821.09
A survey of the extent to which poets from the eighteenth to the twentieth century responded to religious influences of the times. Special chapters on the major authors and on such subjects as Protestantism, Evangelicalism, the Catholic Revival, and Aestheticism.

J218.   Leavis, Frank R. *Revaluation: Tradition and Development in English Poetry*. Westport, Conn.: Greenwood, 1975, c1936. 275pp. PR503.L4 821.09
Leavis exhorts students to deal with the "concrete" in poetry: the wit in Carew, the many tones of Pope's satire, the consciousness of Wordsworth's creativity, the feeling (not thinking) of Shelley's poetry. Even if students don't agree with this book, they should read it. It is a landmark.

J219.   Miles, Josephine. *Eras and Modes in English Poetry*. 2nd ed. Westport, Conn.: Greenwood, 1976. 292pp. Paperback. PR502.M48   821'.009
The author believes there is a pattern of artistic progression, an interrelationship in time and manner, and a potential metaphor in every word. She explores the complexities of these beliefs in the work of Donne, Dryden, Hopkins, Yeats, and dozens of other poets. The tables illustrating a count of the verbs, nouns, and adjectives in selected works of two hundred poets have provoked a flurry of heated discussions.

Old English Literature

Surveys

*J225.   Greenfield, Stanley B. *Critical History of Old English Literature*. New York: New York Univ. Press, 1965. 237pp. Paperback. PR173.G7 829.09
The reviewer in *Choice* (W1557) gives this work highest praise—"succinct," "lucid," "discriminating." Greenfield's study of Anglo-Saxon religious poetry is particularly discerning and convincing. Students of Joyce, Pound, Stein, and Auden will be interested in his arguments.

J226.   Ker, William P. *The Dark Ages.* London: Nelson, 1904; rpt. Westport,
Conn.: Greenwood, 1979. 361pp. PN671.K4   809'.02

There are more recent studies of this period, but none more authoritative
or lucid.

Basic guides

*J227.   *New Cambridge Bibliography of English Literature (New CBEL).* Ed.
George Watson. Vol. 1, 600–1660. Cambridge, Eng.: Cambridge Univ.
Press, 1974. 2491 cols. Z2011.N45   [PR83]   016.82

This volume covers three literary periods: the Anglo-Saxon to 1100 (Old
English, writings in Latin, Anglo-Saxon and Irish authors), the Middle English,
1100–1500 (romances, Chaucer and the Chaucerians, prose, ballads, medieval
drama), and Renaissance to Restoration, 1500–1660 (literary relations with the
Continent, book production, the sonnet, Milton, drama, religion, the pamphleteers, Scottish literature). The index is to main subject headings and major
authors only. See vol. 5, the main index to all four volumes of the *New CBEL*
(J175), for detailed subjects and minor authors.

J228.   Matthews, William, ed. *Old and Middle English Literature.* Goldentree Bibliographies (W1291). New York: Appleton (Meredith), 1968.
112pp. Paperback. Z2012.M32   016.8209'001

A selective guide to scholarship on literature and culture up to 1525. This
includes translations, histories, religion, art, language, both major and minor
authors, and many specific titles (*Beowulf, Dream of the Rood,* Caedmon,
Wulfstan, Malory, Chaucer, Gower, Rolle). The two parts (Old and Middle
English) are subdivided into sections concerning general background, manuscripts
and printing, genres, prosody, themes, and authors. Arranged chronologically,
then by subject, then alphabetically by critical author. This book is particularly
good for a panoramic study of the trends and attitudes in scholarship since World
War II. Two indexes: modern authors, and medieval authors and anonymous
titles.

Bibliographies of primary works

**J229.   Ker, Neil R. *Catalogue of Manuscripts Containing Anglo-Saxon.* Ox-
ford: Clarendon, 1957. 567pp. Supplement in *Anglo-Saxon England,*
5 (1976) (J237). Z6605.A56.K4   016.829

A scrupulously detailed, word-by-word, letter-by-letter description and
analysis of the language, handwriting, and format of the less than two hundred
extant literary manuscripts written entirely or mainly in Old English before 1200.
After expressing gratitude to the eighteenth-century paleographer, Wanley, for
cataloging and describing so many manuscripts that have since been lost or
destroyed, the author explains the scribe's procedure in preparing the parchment, the change from Anglo-Saxon minuscule to caroline minuscule in the
tenth and eleventh centuries, punctuation, drawings, problems of provenance,
bindings, neglect of the manuscripts between 1200 and 1500 because of swift
changes in the language, and the revival of interest after Henry VIII's dissolu-
tion of the monasteries in the mid–sixteenth century.

Criticism

*J231. Greenfield, Stanley B., and Fred C. Robinson. *Bibliography of Publications on Old English Literature from the Beginnings through 1972.* Toronto: Univ. of Toronto Press, 1980. 437pp. Paperback. Supplement, 1973–82, ed. Carl T. Berkhout, in preparation. Z2012.G83 [PR173] 016.829

The first exhaustive bibliography on Old English literature since 1885. This volume lists every relevant book, monograph, article, note, and review published between the fifteenth century and 1972. Fifty years in the making, it contains items never before listed in a bibliography. Arranged chronologically by genre with some annotations, numerous cross-references, and an index of reviewers, authors, and subjects. Extremely important.

*J232. *Anglo-Saxon Scholarship: The First Three Centuries.* Ed. Milton McC. Gatch and Carl T. Berkhout. Boston: Hall, 1982. 150pp. PE103.A5 429

A collection of essays on the history of Anglo-Saxon scholarship ranging from a discussion of sixteenth-century studies to evaluations of the contributions of noted antiquarians, the rediscovery of Old English poetry by the Romantics, and consideration of various grammars and glossaries. The first such collection in sixty-five years, well received by experts, this assembles ideas that may stimulate renewed interest in the birthing of our literary history.

Annual bibliographies that will update the preceding works

ABELL (D32) has a special section for Old English literature.
MLAIB (D31) has a section on Old English literature in vol. 1 and, beginning in 1969, a section on Old English in vol. 3, *Linguistics* (W1329). *Year's Wk. Eng. Stud.* (D33) devotes one chapter to reviewing the previous year's research on Old English literature.

Researchers should also consult the appropriate abstracting services (E38–43) and indexing services (F45–53) for recent publications.

Dictionaries

**J233. Bosworth, Joseph, and T. Northcote Toller, eds. *Anglo-Saxon Dictionary* (A-SD). Oxford: Clarendon, 1882–98. 1302pp. Supplement, 1921. Addenda and Corrigenda enlarge and revise the supplement, ed. Alistair Campbell (1973). 76pp. PE279.B5 429.3

A dictionary of the English language as it existed before 1100. Preliminary computer work is now under way for a new edition that will be called the *Dictionary of Old English* (J248).

*J234. *English–Old English, Old English–English Dictionary.* Ed. Gregory K. Jember et al. Boulder, Colo.: Westview, 1975. 178pp. PE279.J4 429'.3'21

Seasoned professors may forget that beginning students need a source like this, the first double-entry dictionary of Old English—simple, accurate, specific, nontechnical, essential.

Concordances

**J235. *Concordance to the Anglo-Saxon Poetic Records*. Ed. Jess B. Bessinger, Jr. Ithaca, N.Y.: Cornell Univ. Press, 1978. 1503pp.   PR1506.B47 829'.1

A computer-generated alphabetical list of 175,000 words in all their appearances in the six volumes of the most complete and reliable edition of the poetry by Krapp-Dobbie (1931–53), not the manuscripts. This is an essential tool that will open up a whole new world of scholarly investigation. Most reviewers agree that it is well done but that there is room for more work before it can be termed a definitive concordance.

Periodicals

*J236.   *Old English Newsletter* (*OENews*). Binghamton: State Univ. of New York, 1967– . 2/yr. Center for Medieval and Early Renaissance Studies. Sponsored by MLA. 429.05

Concentrates on Old English language and literature, with brief articles, notes, abstracts, and two features of interest to researchers: The first issue of each year contains an enumerative international bibliography of books, articles, and dissertations arranged by subject (the "Old English Bibliography") and the second contains a long essay evaluating the major scholarship in that list ("Year's Work in Old English Studies").

Indexed in *ABELL* (D32), *MLAIB* (D31).

J237.   *Anglo-Saxon England* (*ASE*). London: Cambridge Univ. Press, 1972– . Annual. DA152.2.A75   914.2'03'105

Collections of interdisciplinary studies on the Anglo-Saxon world, with emphasis on Anglo-Saxon literature, sagas, and manuscripts, language (Latin and vernacular), documents (lost and found), artifacts, the influence of the Roman occupation, and the artistic revival of the tenth century. Each volume contains a bibliography of the previous year's international scholarship on language, literature, numismatics, paleography, ecclesiastical texts, archaeology, history, specific towns, cemeteries, ships, pottery—in short, all of Anglo-Saxon life. Index to vols. 1–5 in vol. 5.

Indexed in *ABELL* (D32), *Arts and Hum. Cit. Ind.* (F47), *MLAIB* (D31).

POETRY

Surveys

*J240.   Pearsall, Derek. *Old English and Middle English Poetry*. Vol. 1 of Routledge History of English Poetry (J215). Boston: Routledge, 1977. 352pp. PR201   821'.1'09

Heralded by *TLS* as a "remarkable achievement," this survey is scholarly, well argued, and supported by many footnotes, quotations, a glossary, chronological table, and index. It also is written with a sensitive understanding of the poetry and is, therefore, everything a fine literary history should be.

Basic guides

J241.   *Old and Middle English Poetry to 1500: A Guide to Information Sources.* Ed. Walter H. Beale. Vol. 7 of the Gale Information Guide Library (A8). Detroit: Gale, 1976. 454pp. Z2014.P7.B34 [PR161] 016.829'1

A guide to general reference collections, significant background studies, primary texts, commentaries, and specific genres, with accurate, frank annotations. Students should note, however, that as a reference book it would be improved if the numerous repeated entries were replaced with a simple system of cross-references.

*J242.   Fry, Donald K. *Beowulf and* The Fight at Finnsburh: *A Bibliography.* Charlottesville: Univ. Press of Virginia, 1969. 222pp. Z2012.F83 016.829'3

This gem of scholarship started as a dissertation, was abandoned, and finally resulted in the best bibliography available on these two poems. Research on *Beowulf* has been updated to 1978 by Douglas D. Short in *Beowulf Scholarship: An Annotated Bibliography* (New York: Garland, 1980; 353pp.). Fry lists a total of 2,280 international books and articles covering all significant criticism on the two poems up to July 1967, even a few early works by famous authors such as Sir Walter Scott in 1824. For every title, the editor indicates the nature of the contents, its scope (including imagery, themes, language, kennings), references to specific lines, other articles on the same subject, and critical reviews of the secondary scholarship.

Two excellent indexes—one by subject (over forty different classifications) and the other by every line of the poems that has received critical attention. If students have trouble understanding line 224 of *Beowulf*, therefore, they need only look in this index to locate articles that will clarify it. Because arrangement is alphabetical by the name of the critic, it is easy to ascertain who are the most prolific and best authorities in the field. Dedication is to Fredson Bowers, "Winedryten" (friendly lord)—see W1066, W1419, W1619.

Criticism

*J243.   *Essential Articles for the Study of Old English Poetry.* Ed. Jess B. Bessinger and Stanley J. Kahrl. Hamden, Conn.: Archon, 1968. 570pp. PR176.B4   829'.1'09

A collection of articles that over the years have proved to be of lasting value. It includes studies by Chambers, Bloomfield, Sisam, Sievers, Greenfield, Schlauch, and other respected scholars who have made important critical statements and discerning assessments that need to be remembered. Even the footnotes are valuable. This is essential reading.

J244.   Greenfield, Stanley B. *The Interpretation of Old English Poems.* Boston: Routledge, 1972. 188pp. PR201.G7   829'.1

Controversial but/and important. Substantially different interpretations of the poetry will be found in other sources, but these interpretations are well founded, well argued, and must be considered. Students with a good background in the Old English language will use this as their all-purpose handbook. They should pay attention to the notes and use the bibliography.

Works in progress

J246.   *English Literature before the Norman Conquest.* Vol. 1, pt. 1 of OHEL (J174). In preparation.

*J247.   *Dictionary of the Middle Ages.* Ed. Joseph R. Strayer. 12 vols. New York: Scribners, 1982–   . In progress (vols. 5–6, 1984).

Sponsored by the National Endowment for the Humanities, which awarded a grant to the American Council of Learned Societies for the purpose of producing a twelve-volume dictionary on the accomplishments of Western and Eastern Europe from the year 500 to 1500. It includes long biographical entries on such personages as Chaucer, Dante, and Augustine; surveys of major topics such as Old English literature and the Spanish language; brief definitions, illustrations, up-to-date bibliographies at the end of most entries; and an index volume. No other reference book covers this era so thoroughly.

**J248.   *Dictionary of Old English.* Ed. John Leyerle. Toronto: Univ. of Toronto Press. Centre for Medieval Studies. In progress.

An ambitious project that has been under way for over a decade. As a first step, Roberta Frank and Angus Cameron published *A Plan for the Dictionary of Old English* (1973; 384pp.; PE273.P5   429'.3). Just recently, announcement was made that *A Microfiche Concordance to Old English*, compiled by Richard L. Venezky and Antonette di Paolo Healey, can be purchased from the *Dictionary of Old English*, Robarts Research Library, University of Toronto. As evidence that the computer is being used to full advantage, take note that in 1978 it produced 850,000 slips for this dictionary. How many years would it have taken to do this by hand? See also Bosworth and Toller (J233).

Medieval Literature

Surveys

J250.   Bennett, Henry S. *Chaucer and the Fifteenth Century.* Vol. 2, pt. 1 of OHEL (J174). Oxford: Clarendon, 1947; rpt. with corrections, 1970. 326pp. PR255.B43   821.17

A survey of Chaucer's contributions to literary history and of the background that produced him. Chronological tables and bibliography (pp. 219–318).

J251.   Chambers, Sir Edmund K. *English Literature at the Close of the Middle Ages.* Vol. 2, pt. 2 of OHEL (J174). Oxford: Clarendon, 1945; rpt. 1964. 247pp. PR291.C5   820.902

A study of drama, the lyric, the ballad, the narrative, and major authors as they contributed to English literary history at the end of the fifteenth century. Bibliography (pp. 206–31).

J252. *Middle English Literature.* Vol. 1, pt. 2 of OHEL (J174). In preparation.

Basic guides

*J253. *Medieval Studies: An Introduction.* Ed. James M. Powell. Syracuse, N.Y.: Syracuse Univ. Press, 1976. 389pp. D116.M4 940.1'07'2

A collection of surveys written specifically for graduates or undergraduates who, as they embark on their medieval studies, realize that they need to familiarize themselves with the cultural background in order to understand the literature. This is a worthy complement to Fisher's review of research on medieval literature (J255) and to Paetow's revered but aged classic on medieval history (J254). Scholarly essays by noted authorities evaluate the state of research and show how to interpret evidence and solve problems in Latin paleography, numismatics, genealogical materials, the computer and social and economic documents, art, music, and other areas. Paul Theiner, for instance, tells students why they need to use Wells's *Manual* (in its latest edition by Severs and Hartung, see J260) and how they should begin doing research on Chaucer. Very important bibliographies and biographies are cited at the end of every chapter. Title, subject, and author index. A well-edited, scholarly book.

*J254. Paetow, Louis J. *A Guide to the Study of Medieval History.* Rev. and corrected, with errata and addendum. New York: Appleton, 1959, c1931; rpt. Millwood, N.Y.: Kraus, 1980. 643pp. Z6203.P25 016.9401

Literature of Medieval History, 1930-1975: A Supplement to Louis John Paetow's A Guide to the Study of Medieval History. Ed. Gray C. Boyce. 5 vols. Millwood, N.Y.: Kraus, 1981. Sponsored by the Medieval Academy of America.

Paetow's guide is the basic text for the study of medieval history in eleven different countries and seven different subjects. It describes the value of general reference books and specific titles on paleography, numismatics, philology, history of the church, the Renaissance, Christendom and the papacy, and then it makes a detailed chronological approach to materials useful for research on every country of Western Europe. Each section begins with a brief outline, makes special recommendations for reading of interest to the less advanced student, and ends with an extensive bibliography of the best scholarship available at that time.

Paetow has been brought up to date by Boyce's supplement, which is an exhaustive list of 55,000 works on medieval culture published between 1930 and 1975.

*J255. Fisher, John H., ed. *The Medieval Literature of Western Europe: A Review of Research, Mainly 1930-60.* New York: New York Univ. Press, for MLA, 1966. 432pp. PN671.F5 809.02

All students should read this basic guide before attempting to do research in medieval literature, whether it be Latin, English, French, German, Norse, Italian, Spanish, Catalan, Portuguese, or Celtic, for, as the editor points out, the study of medieval literature is by necessity a comparative study. The medievalist must know not only primary works but also the scholarship of all the medieval nations that were influenced by the Latin Christian culture.

Each chapter is written by an authority in the field: Old English, pp. 37-71, by George K. Anderson; and Middle English, pp. 75-123, by Robert W. Ackerman. After evaluating the general reference books and studies, the authors turn to genres and discuss both major and minor individual titles—for example, Mysticism (*Ancrene Riwle*), Heroic Poetry (*Beowulf*), and Elegies ("The Seafarer"). *Piers Plowman* and the works of Chaucer receive especially careful consideration. For all titles, critical works are compared, themes linked, and trends of scholarship defined. Philology, however, is neglected; see Linguistics (W1325-53). Clever researchers will make good use of the index of proper names, for in addition to locating people mentioned in the text, it offers clues to the activity of both primary and secondary authors.

J256.   Robb, Allan P. "The Middle Ages: An Annotated Bibliographical Supplement." *Literary Research Newsletter*, 4 (1979), 73-94.   PN73.L57 809

Good judgment is evident here, both in the selection of titles and in the exceptionally fine annotations. This is concerned not with indexes and bibliographies but with histories, handbooks, criticism of drama and poetry, saints' lives, and linguistics—"the needs and wants of students." The author summarizes, evaluates, and recommends. See *LRN* (W1421).

*J257.   Baugh, Albert C. *Chaucer*. 2nd ed. Goldentree Bibliographies (W1291). Arlington Heights, Ill.: AHM, 1977. 160pp. Paperback. Z8164.B33 [PR1905]   016.821'1

An exceptionally fine guide to Chaucer bibliographies, surveys, societies, journals, reference works, biography, political and social environment, collective editions, criticism, language and versification, lost and apocryphal works, sources and influences such as Boccaccio, Boethius, and Macrobius. Because it lists each title (for example, *The Parlement of Foules*, with seventy-seven critical works) and all the Canterbury pilgrims (ninety-four entries for the Wife of Bath's tale), this could easily be the only source the undergraduate student of Chaucer would have to consult. No asterisks, however, to help the student select the most distinguished scholarship.

See also

Matthews, *Old and Middle English Literature* (J228)
New CBEL (J227), vol. 1, 600-1660

Bibliographies of primary works

**J260.   *A Manual of the Writings in Middle English, 1050-1500*. 10 vols. Hamden, Conn.: Shoe String, 1967–   . MLA. In progress. PR255.M3 [PR255.S4]   016.820'9'001

The revision of John Edwin Wells's original *Manual*, which covered only to 1400 and which, with its nine supplements, had become unmanageable. The first two volumes of this new edition (1967, 1970) were edited by J. Burke Severs;

the third (1972), fourth (1973), fifth (1975), and sixth (1979) by Albert E. Hartung (pages are numbered consecutively).

> Vol. 1: Romances—Arthurian Legends, Charlemagne Legends, Legends of Troy and Alexander the Great, Breton Lays.
> Vol. 2: *Pearl* poet, Wyclyf and his followers, the Bible, Saints' Legends, Instructions for Religious (as *Ancrene Riwle*).
> Vol. 3: Dialogues (on the Supernatural, Death), Debates (on Love and Women), and Catechisms (on Science and Biblical Lore); Thomas Hoccleve; Malory and Caxton.
> Vol. 4: Middle Scots Writers; Chaucerian Apocrypha.
> Vol. 5: Dramatic Pieces, Mysteries, Moralities, Folk Drama, and Poems Dealing with Contemporary Conditions.
> Vol. 6: Carols, Ballads, Lydgate.
> Vol. 7: In preparation.

Part 1 of each volume is composed of essays by authorities that discuss the problems pertinent to each title, with a historical account of the manuscript, dates, sources, form, an analysis of the subject and style, and a summary of the trends in interpretation. Part 2 is a comprehensive, international bibliography of critical articles for each title. Important authors are given separate treatment. Title, author, printer, and subject index, and many cross-references. A volume on private letters is forthcoming.

**J261. Goff, Frederick R., ed. *Incunabula in American Libraries: A Third Census of Fifteenth-Century Books Recorded in North American Collections.* Millwood, N.Y.: Kraus, 1973, c1964. 798pp.   Z240.G58 016.093

An invaluable location list of 51,000 incunabula (fifteenth-century printed books in all languages) that are now held in American public and private libraries. An interesting introduction traces the history of incunabula in America and provides statistics showing that twenty-five libraries hold seventy percent of the titles, the first few being the Library of Congress, Huntington, Harvard, Yale, Pierpont Morgan, and Newberry.

This edition is a reprint of Goff's personal copy of the Third Census (1964) with all the marginalia he added over a period of eight years—his corrections, recent prices, names of dealers, changes in ownership, and numerous new titles (four thousand more than the 1964 edition). Many libraries and researchers prefer, for obvious reasons, to use this personally annotated reprint rather than the Third Census of 1964 and its supplement (New York: Bibliographical Soc. of America, 1972).

Arrangement is alphabetical by author or title, then chronological by publication date of the various editions. The entries include the place of publication, publisher, date, size, location of owners in the United States, and references in bibliographical works. For instance, thirteen different American libraries own copies of the first folio edition of Gower's *Confessio Amantis*, which was published by Caxton in 1483.

**J262. de Ricci, Seymour. *Census of Medieval and Renaissance Manuscripts in the United States and Canada*. 2 vols. and Index. New York: Wilson, 1935–40. Supplement (2 vols.), 1962. American Council of Learned Societies. Z6620.U5.R5

In this alphabetical list of libraries in the United States and Canada with their holdings of medieval and Renaissance manuscripts (pre-1600), each entry includes the manuscript number, author, title, date, physical description of contents and binding, name of scribe, provenance, and references to the manuscript in scholarly literature. The supplement brings up to date the changes in ownership.

After stating that the present location of many manuscripts is unknown, the editor expresses his hope that his volume will call attention to this fact and that scholars will assist in the continuing search. Students might be interested in knowing that some of the best collections of these early MSS are at Widener, Yale, Huntington, Newberry, the New York Public Library, and the Walters Gallery in Baltimore.

See also

Editing the Middle English Manuscript (W1615)

Annual bibliographies that will update the preceding reference works

*J263. *International Medieval Bibliography* (*IMB*). Leeds: Univ. of Leeds, 1968–   . 2/yr. Z6203.I63   016.914′031

Indispensable for locating current scholarship. This bibliography lists articles and notes (but not reviews) published in 950 periodicals, one hundred festschriften, and many papers and anthologies devoted to the medieval period (500–1500). It covers all of Europe and Russia, including the Byzantine Empire and other countries when they have a bearing on medieval Europe. Subject headings for folklore, language, manuscripts, and literature lead to Caedmon, *The Cloud of Unknowing*, Rolle, Gerald of Wales, Wulfstan, Tennyson, and Malory. In his list of consulted periodicals, the editor marks with asterisks those that do not contain relevant medieval material, and he provides the issue number for those that do. Scholars and librarians appreciate such care for detail. Critic and subject indexes in each issue.

See also

ABELL (D32) has special sections on Middle English and fifteenth-century scholarship.

MLAIB (D31) has a section on Middle English literature and, beginning in 1969, a section on Middle English as a language in vol. 3, *Linguistics* (W1329).

Year's Wk. Eng. Stud. (D33) features one chapter reviewing the year's research on Middle English literature and another on Chaucer.

See also appropriate abstracting services (E38–43) and indexing services (F45–53).

Dictionaries

**J264. *Middle English Dictionary (MED)*. Ed. Hans Kurath, Sherman M. Kuhn, and John Reidy. Ann Arbor: Univ. of Michigan Press, 1952— . In progress. PE679.M54 427.02

A monumental work that will, when finished, supersede the *OED* (W1205) for the language as it was used between approximately 1100 and 1475. It seeks to establish meaning and shades of meaning by citing hundreds of thousands of passages from Middle English literature in a logical sequence of ideas, as opposed to the chronological approach of the *OED*. It may, for instance, be able to explain why, in the first few pages of *Sir Gawain and the Green Knight*, twelve different words are used for the concept of "man."

Each entry indicates part of speech, derivation, definition, compounds, historical notes, and cross-references. The total work will comprise about ten volumes when finished, but at present (1982) the most recent fascicle has progressed only through the word "Phitoun." This represents fifty years of work, support by the NEH, a current staff of eighteen, and, recently, a million dollars from the Mellon Foundation. The projected completion date is 1983.

See also

Dictionary of the Middle Ages (J247)

Periodicals

*J265. *Speculum: A Journal of Mediaeval Studies*. Cambridge, Mass.: Medieval Academy of America, 1926– . Quarterly. PN661.S6 805

Specializes in all phases of medieval culture in all nations, with several significant articles in each issue that tend toward the historical. A good source for information on *Beowulf* and Chaucer as well as on religion, politics, and all Continental literatures of the era. About half of the periodical is given to long, scholarly book reviews, and there is always a list of "Books Received" to keep the student up to date on recent international publications. Until 1972 it included a short, unannotated "Bibliography of American Periodical Literature" on medieval studies. Since 1973 it has featured a bibliography of editions and translations in progress of medieval texts. Because there are, regrettably, no cumulative indexes for these bibliographies or for the periodical itself, the best way to approach the content is through the indexes listed below.

Indexed in *ABELL* (D32), *Abst. Eng. Stud.* (E38), *Arts and Hum. Cit. Ind.* (F47), *Art Ind.* (W1042), *Bk. Rev. Ind.* (W1559), *Current Bk. Rev. Cit.* (W1564), *Hum. Ind.* (F45), *Index to Bk. Rev. Hum.* (W1560), *MLAIB* (D31).

J266.   *Annuale Mediaevale (AnM)*. Atlantic Highlands, N.J.: Humanities, 1960– . Annual. D111.A55 940.105

Interested in the medieval literature and history of England and France.

Indexed in *ABELL* (D32), *Abst. Eng. Stud.* (E38), *Arts and Hum. Cit. Ind.* (F47), *MLAIB* (D31).

J267.   *Bibliographical Bulletin (BBSIA)*. St. Louis, Mo.: Bulletin Bibliographique de la Soc. Internationale Arthurienne, Washington Univ., 1949– . Annual. International Arthurian Society. Z8045.I5

Critical articles, news of translations and other research projects, lists of the nine hundred society members devoted to Arthurian studies, and (the outstanding feature) a definitive bibliography arranged by country, then form. It includes new editions, translations, criticism, reviews, and theses in English, French, or German, with occasional descriptive annotations. Author and subject indexes. Text in English, French, and German. Additional Arthurian studies may be located in *ABELL* (D32, under Arthurian Romance and Legend), *MLAIB* (D31, vol. 1, General IV, under Themes and Types), and *Modern Language Quarterly* (H149, for the years 1936–62).

Indexed in *MLAIB* (D31).

*J268.   *The Chaucer Review: A Journal of Medieval Studies and Literary Criticism (ChauR)*. University Park, Pa.: Pennsylvania State Univ. Press, 1966– . Quarterly. MLA. PR1901.C48

An important source for Chaucer scholars not only for its six or eight articles each quarter but also for its annual report of "Chaucer Research" (ed. Thomas A. Kirby), which includes titles from *MLAIB* (D31) as well as many more critical works, with particular emphasis on American scholarship. It also gives a detailed account of research in progress, projects approved and completed, and projects being encouraged. This is not an annotated bibliography, but it is comprehensive and should be the first source consulted by all Chaucer scholars. It qualifies its recommendation of Robinson as the best text, for instance, by warning against the typographical errors in the second edition. And it is the best (only) source that reports regularly on the progress of the *Variorum Chaucer*: (1) the general editor is Paul G. Ruggiers, (2) about thirty-five other editors have been selected, one for each of Chaucer's works, (3) it will be published by the University of Oklahoma Press, (4) a facsimile has already been published of the Hengwrt text and Ellesmere variants, which will be used as the basic text for the variorum edition. This will unquestionably be as helpful to research scholars as the Shakespeare variorum (J340). Students should watch its progress eagerly.

Students must also remember that the *Chaucer Review* is subtitled a *Journal of Medieval Studies*. It usually includes, therefore, material that is important for anyone working with early English literature—for instance, "The Alliterative *Morte Arthure*: An Annotated Bibliography, 1950–1975," ed. Michael Foley, in vol. 14, no. 2 (1979), 166–86. Index to vols. 1–10 (1966–76) in vol. 11, no. 1.

Indexed in *ABELL* (D32), *Abst. Eng. Stud.* (E38), *Arts and Hum. Cit. Ind.* (F47), *Hum. Ind.* (F45), *MLAIB* (D31), *Year's Wk. Eng. Stud.* (D33).

J269.   *14th Century English Mystics Newsletter (FCEMN)*. Iowa City: Univ. of Iowa, 1975– . Quarterly. B728.F687

Extends into the fields of philosophy, theology, history, psychology, the history of ideas, art history, and the mass media. Students should watch for the

reports of work in progress that are sent in by the international editorial board. A valuable by-product emerged from the mass of material assembled for the periodical: *The 14th-Century English Mystics: A Comprehensive Annotated Bibliography* (New York: Garland, 1981; 300pp.), edited by Ritamary Bradley and Valerie M. Lagorio.
Indexed in *MLAIB* (D31).

J270.   *Journal of Medieval and Renaissance Studies (JMRS)*. Durham, N.C.:
        Duke Univ. Press, 1971– . Quarterly. CB351.J78   940.1'05
Interdisciplinary and comparative studies. Scholarship focuses primarily on the processes of change observable in late medieval and Renaissance culture, art, history, literature, music, philosophy, and theology.
Indexed in *ABELL* (D32), *Arts and Hum. Cit. Ind.* (F47), *MLAIB* (D31).

J271.   *Medieval Studies (MS)*. Toronto: Pontifical Inst. of Medieval Studies,
        1939– . Annual. D111   901.42
An excellent periodical with scholarly articles, report of works in progress, lists of the institute's publications, standard editions, and sources in translation, but no book reviews. Two general indexes: vols. 1–25 and 26–30.
Indexed in *ABELL* (D32), *Abst. Eng. Stud.* (E38), *MLAIB* (D31).

J272.   *Medievalia et Humanistica: Studies in Medieval and Renaissance Culture*
        (M&H). Totowa, N.J.: Rowman, 1943– . Annual. D111.M5   940.105
Critical articles and book reviews on Malory, Chaucer, dissent in medieval literature, Towneley plays, Beowulf, More, Boccaccio, Norman studies, saints, Thomas Hoccleve, and many more. But no index.
Indexed in *ABELL* (D32), *Index to Bk. Rev. Hum.* (W1560), *MLAIB* (D31).

*J273.   *Medium Aevum (MÆ)*. Oxford: Blackwell, for the Soc. for the Study
        of Medieval Languages and Literature, 1932— . 3/yr. PB1.M4   405
A scholarly periodical that features English and foreign language articles on religion, politics, history, and literature. Half of every issue is devoted to long, critical book reviews, so all medieval literature students should consult it regularly. There is a cumulative index to vols. 1–25 (1932–57), but entry into the volumes since 1957 is easiest through the indexing services listed below.
Indexed in *ABELL* (D32), *Abst. Eng. Stud.* (E38), *Arts and Hum. Cit. Ind.* (F47), *Brit. Hum. Ind.* (F49), *Hum. Ind.* (F45), *Index to Bk. Rev. Hum.* (W1560), *MLAIB* (D31), *Year's Wk. Eng. Stud.* (D33).

*J274.   *Neuphilologische Mitteilungen (NM)*. Helsinki: Modern Language Soc.,
        1899– . Quarterly. PB10.N415   405
Articles, reviews, and three important annual bibliographies: Old English research in progress, Middle English research in progress, and Chaucer research in progress. The Chaucer list is adapted from that in the *Chaucer Review* (J268), which is concerned mainly with the work of American Chaucerians.
Indexed in *ABELL* (D32), *Abst. Eng. Stud.* (E38), *Arts and Hum. Cit. Ind.* (F47), *Index to Bk. Rev. Hum.* (W1560), *Language and Lang. Beh. Abst.* (W1332), *MLAIB* (D31).

J275.   *Nottingham Mediæval Studies (NMS)*. Nottingham: Univ. Press, 1957– . Annual. PN661.N6   809.02
Articles on the literature, language, history, painting, economics, and music of the Middle Ages. No index.
Indexed in *Brit. Hum. Ind.* (F49), *MLAIB* (D31).

J276.   *Traditio: Studies in Ancient and Medieval History, Thought, and Religion*. New York: Fordham Univ. Press, 1943– . Annual. D111.T7 940.1058
Articles in several languages, occasional specific subject bibliographies, and a long annual bibliography of current scholarship.
Indexed in *ABELL* (D32), *Abst. Eng. Stud.* (E38), *Arts and Hum. Cit. Ind.* (F47), *MLAIB* (D31).

PROSE

Works in progress

J277.   *Index to Middle English Prose, 1476–1976*. Ed. Norman F. Blake, Anthony S. G. Edwards, and Robert E. Lewis. New York: Garland. In preparation.
The complex issues of identification and organization confronting the editors of this project are explained in *Middle English Prose: Essays on Bibliographical Problems* (New York: Garland, 1981; 150pp.), edited by Edwards and Derek Pearsall. No publication date has been projected for the *Index*, but scholars should anticipate its appearance because it will make Middle English prose more accessible, unquestionably unearth new information, and inspire a flood of research papers.

DRAMA

Surveys

J278.   Chambers, Sir Edmund K. *The Mediaeval Stage*. 2 vols. Oxford: Oxford Univ. Press, 1903. PN2152.C4   792.09401
This venerable landmark was one of the first studies to emphasize the development of "the theater" as a permanent institution in English literature and life. More recent surveys by Wickham (J279, J329) evaluate the same era from a later twentieth-century viewpoint. To get an overview of the origin of today's drama, use all of these in conjunction with Stratman's bibliography (J281).

*J279.   Wickham, Glynne W. *The Medieval Theatre*. New York: St. Martin's, 1974. 245pp. PN2152.W5   809.2
The development of dramatic art in Europe between the tenth and the sixteenth century, especially as it was affected by changing ideas in religion, recreation, and commerce. Manageable in size and style for both classroom and leisure reading. See also Wickham's more elaborate examination of *Early English Stages* (J329).

J280.   Young, Karl. *The Drama of the Medieval Church.* 2 vols. Oxford: Clarendon, 1933. PN1751.Y6   792.1
Students should use this basic source for background reading because of the valuable comments on the extant texts.

Bibliographies of primary works

**J281.   Stratman, Carl J., C.S.V. *Bibliography of Medieval Drama.* 2 vols. 2nd ed., rev. enl. New York: Ungar, 1972. Z5782.A2.S8   .016.80882
"Medieval drama" here means all liturgical, mystery, miracle, morality plays, and interludes written in England, France, Germany, Italy, and Spain up to the seventeenth century.

Until Stratman compiled this bibliography, there was no single comprehensive source of accurate information. The editor says it is not exhaustive, but he locates almost every title in a library in the United States, England, Ireland, or Canada, lists collections of plays and festschriften, cites general studies in book and periodical form as well as critical works on all individual titles. He also marks important items with asterisks, supplies book review information for controversial titles, includes dissertations and master's theses, indicates where the manuscripts are located, and even provides a serial-location list. In his first edition, for instance, he located 138 entries on *The Towneley Plays* (manuscript in Huntington Library) and 121 on *Everyman.* The second edition adds five thousand entries and is chronological rather than alphabetical. Author-subject index, so easy to use. No annotations.

J282.   *Records of Early English Drama (REED).* Toronto: Univ. of Toronto, 1978– . Irregular. Centre for Medieval Studies. PR1262.R31 [PR621]   822'.009
This research project locates, transcribes, and publishes the surviving unedited or badly edited performance records of dramatic, minstrel, ceremonial, and related entertainment activities in Britain before 1642. The first three volumes published were the records of York, Chester, and Coventry. A newsletter reports regularly on progress and problems.
Indexed in *MLAIB* (D31).

See also

English Tragedy, 1370–1600: Fifty Years of Criticism (J213)
Medieval Drama (G114)
Research Opportunities in Renaissance Drama (J349), medieval supplement

POETRY

**J283.   *Index of Middle English Verse.* Ed. Carleton F. Brown and Rossell H. Robbins. New York: Columbia Univ. Press, for the Index Soc. of MLA, 1943. 785pp. Supplement, ed. Robbins and John L. Cutler (Lexington: Univ. of Kentucky Press, 1966), 551pp. Z2012.B86   016.821'1
Entries for six thousand poems written in English before 1500 are arranged alphabetically by first line, with bibliographical description and indication of the manuscript's present location or ownership. Subject and title index. The editors note, for instance, that the *Pricke of Conscience* was apparently a best-

seller in medieval England (117 extant manuscripts)—or perhaps it was well preserved because it was purchased but not read? Other favorite titles were *The Canterbury Tales*, *Piers Plowman*, and *Confessio Amantis*. They point out that only about two hundred of the poems date from or before the thirteenth century, which suggests that tremendous strides were made in skillful use of the language, public interest in the poetic form, and perhaps, too, in the desire and ability to preserve manuscripts from all kinds of destructive forces. A few additions and emendations to the *Index* are listed in *Anglia*, 99 (1981), 394–98.

See also
   Medieval Lyric (Q899)

Background reading for the medieval era

*J287.   Ackerman, Robert W. *Backgrounds to Medieval English Literature*. New York: Random, 1966. 171pp. Paperback. P255.A3   820.9'001
   Still highly recommended for students who realize they will come to a more personally satisfying appreciation of Chaucer and Langland if they know something about the facts and feeling of the environment that produced early English literature.

J288.   Jackson, William T. H. *The Literature of the Middle Ages*. New York: Columbia Univ. Press, 1960. 432pp. PN671.J3
   Reliable background reading for beginning students.

J289.   Ker, William P. *English Literature: Medieval*. London: Oxford Univ. Press, 1962, c1912. 192pp. PR255.K4   820.9'001
   A survey of Anglo-Saxon and medieval literature that is still both valid and readable.

J290.   ———. *Epic and Romance: Essays on Medieval Literature*. 2nd ed. New York: Dover, 1957, c1908. 398pp. PN671.K39   809.02
   Still the classic model for interpretation of medieval literature.

*J291.   Lewis, C[live] S[taples]. *The Allegory of Love: A Study in Medieval Tradition*. Oxford: Clarendon, 1936. 378pp. Paperback.   PN600.L4   809
   An interesting, valid genre history of allegory, written by an interesting, popular critic. Lewis works with love poetry of the Middle Ages such as the *Romance of the Rose*, and with exponents of courtly love in the Renaissance such as *The Faerie Queene*. This is a memorable book, a thoughtful, helpful book.

J292.   ———. *The Discarded Image: An Introduction to Medieval and Renaissance Literature*. Cambridge, Eng.: Cambridge Univ. Press, 1964. 232pp. Paperback. PN671.L4   809'.02
   The best background reading for facts and feeling of the times.

J293.   Robertson, Douglas W., Jr. *A Preface to Chaucer: Studies in Medieval Perspectives.* Princeton: Princeton Univ. Press, 1962. 519pp. PR1924.R58   821.1
All students should read this important survey of background influences.

Additional reference sources for medieval literature

J294.   Early English Text Society (W1046)
Lives before the Tudors (W1144)
Oxford History of English Literature, Bennett (J250), Chambers (J251)
Present State of Scholarship in Fourteenth-Century Literature. Ed. Thomas D. Cooke. Columbia: Univ. of Missouri Press, 1982. 319pp.
Whiting, *Proverbs, Sentences, and Proverbial Phrases* (W1532)
Who's Who in the Middle Ages (W1107)

Renaissance Literature

Surveys

*J300.   Bush, Douglas. *English Literature in the Earlier Seventeenth Century, 1600-1660.* 2nd ed. Vol. 5 of OHEL (J174). Oxford: Clarendon, 1962. 621pp. Paperback. PR431.B8   820.903
English reviewers referred to this as "a new model of literary history" when it first appeared. As a survey, it encompasses all aspects of seventeenth-century life. As a critical work, it treats all significant writing with learning, wit, and acumen. As valuable background reading for the period, it has not been surpassed. Bibliographies of general subjects and specific authors (pp. 440–610), and a chronological table (pp. 406–39).

J301.   Lewis, C[live] S[taples]. *English Literature in the Sixteenth Century excluding Drama.* Vol. 3 of OHEL (J174). Oxford: Clarendon, 1954. 696pp. Paperback. PR411.L4   820.903
An overwhelming accumulation of facts about English literature as it developed during the turbulent years of the sixteenth century. Lewis always brings to his works an essential familiarity with Continental cultural influences. Students should try to read as many of his works as possible, keeping in mind that more than one critic objects to his "notorious bias" (pride in all things English?). Warning: The valuable bibliographies (pp. 594–685) and chronological table (pp. 560–93) are not included in the paperback edition.

Basic guides

J302.   Barker, Arthur E. *Seventeenth Century: Bacon through Marvell.* Goldentree Bibliographies (W1291). Arlington Heights, Ill.: AHM, 1979. 132pp. Paperback. Z2012   [PR431.A1.B3]   016.82'08004
Another of the Goldentree paperbacks of works by and about selected authors and subjects, convenient in size, selectivity, and price. This focuses on thirty-nine poets and prose writers of the seventeenth century, including Jonson, Taylor, Donne, Herbert, Marvell, Andrewes, Kynaston, and many minor authors not researched elsewhere. Careful readers will note those critics who have

done the most intensive work in this area and the numerous possibilities for future research in unexplored poems and poets. Two regrettable facts—the cutoff date is 1975, and many entries are duplicated several times, needlessly.

J303.   Lievsay, John L. *The Sixteenth Century: Skelton through Hooker.* Goldentree Bibliographies (W1291). New York: Appleton (Meredith), 1968. 132pp. Paperback. Z2012.L5   016.8209'002
A convenient, selective bibliography of background studies, festschriften, anonymous works, translations, and works by and about Skelton, More, Marlowe, Lyly, Kyd, Raleigh, Elizabeth I, Wyatt, Spenser, Sidney, and about one hundred other major and minor writers of the century. No Shakespeare except in relation to other writers. Arranged by subject (Literary Histories, Bibles, Special Topics), and then alphabetically by primary author. Index of both primary and secondary authors.

J304.   Levine, Mortimer. *Tudor England, 1485-1603.* Cambridge, Eng.: Cambridge Univ. Press, 1968. Conference on British Studies. 115pp. Z2017.5 016.9
This guide is helpful for cross-disciplinary or background studies because it provides a subject approach to the period, with entries for the historical, social, economic, scientific, religious, military, and cultural elements.

J305.   Jones, William M., ed. *The Present State of Scholarship in Sixteenth-Century Literature.* Columbia: Univ. of Missouri Press, 1978. 257pp. PN731.P7 809'.031
A collection of bibliographical essays on Italian, French, Spanish, English, German, and Neo-Latin Renaissance literature, especially valuable because it permits a comparison of the national literatures within a single century. It illustrates, yet again, that scholars tend to research the major authors and ignore the minor, thus perpetuating our limited vision of the period.

See also
New *CBEL* (J227), vol. 1, 600–1660

Bibliographies of primary works

**J306. Pollard, Alfred W., and Gilbert R. Redgrave. *A Short-Title Catalogue of Books Printed in England, Scotland, and Ireland and of English Books Printed Abroad 1475-1640 (STC).* London: Bibliographical Soc., 1926; rpt. 1969. 609pp. 2nd ed. (Oxford Univ. Press), begun by William A. Jackson and Frederic S. Ferguson, and completed by Katharine F. Pantzer: vol. 1 (A–H), scheduled for publication in 1985; vol. 2 (I–Z), 1976 (494pp.); vol. 3, Additions and Printers' Index, scheduled for publication in 1986. Z2002.P77   010.6
The original edition lists, briefly describes, and locates in American and British libraries all editions of all books (26,143) printed between 1475 and 1640 that are now extant in institutions queried by the editors (not, as many scholars think, all books that are reputed to have been published). The revised edition

adds several hundred new titles, makes many corrections, and lists Continental locations.

Entries are arranged alphabetically by author with original spelling preserved. Each entry gives the *STC* number (which is now quoted in all important bibliographies and sales catalogs), the size, date, date of entry in the *Stationers' Register* (J308), printer, and abbreviated notes on current ownership (those before the semicolon are British or Continental; after, American). The title index is described in entry J307. All these titles are or soon will be available from University Microfilms. Many librarians enter the reel number in the margin next to the title as soon as the film arrives in the library so students can go directly to the film files and film viewer (see W1438).

Donald Wing has prepared a similar bibliography for the years 1641 to 1700 (J370), and an eighteenth-century *STC* is under way (J373).

**J307. *Titles of English Books (and of Foreign Books Printed in England): An Alphabetical Finding List by Title of Books Published under the Author's Name, Pseudonym, or Initials*. Ed. Antony F. Allison and Valentine F. Goldsmith. Hamden, Conn.: Archon, 1976–77. Vol. 1, 1475–1640; vol. 2, 1641–1700. Z2001.A44 015.42

This is, quite simply, a title index, vol. 1 being keyed to both the old edition of Pollard and Redgrave and the new edition that is in progress (J306), and vol. 2, to the first edition of Wing (J370). Since both Pollard and Wing are author catalogs, the student who knows only the title would come to this book first and then be directed to the proper entry in Pollard or Wing for the remaining available information. During their research, the editors located in the *BM Catalogue* (B13) and several other sources a number of titles not included in Wing's bibliography. They added these to the title index and marked them with asterisks for the reader's information.

**J308. London. Stationers' Company. *A Transcript of the Registers of the Company of Stationers of London, 1554–1640*. Ed. Edward Arber. 5 vols. 1875–94; rpt. New York: Smith, 1950. Z2002.L64 655.442

The introduction discusses the problems of printing in Elizabethan times and the history and purpose of the Company of Stationers. Vols. 1–4 are chronological transcripts of the registers; vol. 5 contains a list of London publishers and a bibliographical summary through 1603. Included are detailed cash accounts (salaries, fines for errors and objectionable language), notices on seditious literature, information on apprenticeships and licensing of printers. This is the place to go when looking for facts concerning the publishing history of books and the records of booksellers of this era.

To locate an entry in the *Stationers' Register*, the student can go first to the *Short-Title Catalogue* (J306) or its title index (J307) to obtain the exact date when the author or publisher "registered" the title. Since a title had to be registered before it could be printed, and since occasionally the title either never did succeed in getting printed or else copies have never been found, the *Stationers' Register* is sometimes the only place in which certain works are mentioned. The entry itself will include the names of the clerk, publisher, and other concerned individuals, the fee for registering (vij^s—seven shillings, for example), and, sometimes, a list of the contents.

Its successor, *Stationers' Register: 1640-1708* (London, 1913-14), has been provided with a computer-generated index by William P. Williams (Laurence McGilvery Publishers, P.O. Box 852, La Jolla, Calif.). This provides access to all authors, titles, editors, pseudonyms, translators, compilers, and anyone connected with the mechanical production of the books. It is useful, therefore, for locating all references to a particular work or person, stationers' activities, and licensing and censorship policies. Forthcoming is the *Stationers' Register: 1710-1746*, ed. David F. Foxon (Oxford Univ. Press).

Annual bibliographies that will update the preceding reference works

ABELL (D32) has annual bibliographies of scholarly work on both the sixteenth and seventeenth centuries.

MLAIB (D31) has a section on Renaissance and Elizabethan literature.

Year's Wk. Eng. Stud. (D33) has special chapters reviewing the previous year's research on the early Renaissance, Shakespeare, English drama: 1550-1660, the later Tudor period, and the earlier seventeenth century.

The appropriate abstracting services (E38–43) and indexing services (F45–53) should also be checked regularly for recent publications.

Identification problems

*J309. *Crowell's Handbook of Elizabethan and Stuart Literature*. Ed. James E. Ruoff. New York: Crowell, 1975. 468pp. PR19.R8   820'.9'003

Designed for the "general reader" who is interested in English literature from 1558 to 1660. It is especially appreciated because no other single volume attempts to cover this same material in such breadth and depth. The editor provides long entries on an unexpected variety of subjects such as Bible translations, Cavalier poets, literary criticism, and the pastoral tradition as well as the expected summaries of lives and works, critical comments, and recommendations for best editions. A few inconsistencies and omissions, but the lively style and provocative ideas make this handbook a comforting desk companion.

Periodicals

*J311. *English Literary Renaissance* (*ELR*). Amherst: Univ. of Massachusetts, 1971- . 3/yr. PR1.E43   820.9'002

Textual studies, critical articles, and bibliographies on the literary achievements of Tudor and early Stuart England, 1485-1660. Of special interest to researchers are the bibliographical articles that combine a "reasonably complete" bibliography with an essay review of the most important research listed by *MLAIB* (D31), *ABELL* (D32), and *Year's Wk. Eng. Stud.* (D33). Subjects range from special topics such as Early Tudor Drama to Renaissance figures such as Sidney and John Rastell. About twenty of these bibliographies are now available as individual reprints.

Indexed in *ABELL* (D32), *Abst. Eng. Stud.* (E38), *Am. Hum. Ind.* (P738),

Arts and Hum. Cit. Ind. (F47), *Milton Quarterly, MLAIB* (D31), *Review of Eng. Stud.* (J188), *Seventeenth-Century News* (J314), *Shakespeare Newsletter* (J315), *Spenser Newsletter, Year's Wk. Eng. Stud.* (D33).

J312.   *Renaissance and Modern Studies (RMS).* Nottingham: Sisson and Parker,
        for the Univ. of Nottingham, 1957– . Annual. AS121.R4.042   042
Long scholarly articles that focus on the humanities. No cumulative index.
Indexed in *Brit. Hum. Ind.* (F49), *MLAIB* (D31).

J313.   *Renaissance Quarterly (RenQ).* New York: Renaissance Soc. of America,
        1948– . Quarterly. CB361.R45   940.2'1'005
Scholarly articles on Savonarola, Erasmus, politics in Milan, women in Tudor England, and other Renaissance interests; numerous book reviews; news of awards, member activities, and conferences; and two lists—of recent bibliographical tools and of books received—that do not begin to equal the usefulness of the former excellent bibliography of new Renaissance books.
    The *Renaissance Quarterly* absorbed *Studies in the Renaissance* in 1975. No annual index, but an author and subject index of both the articles and book reviews cumulates every two or three years.
    Indexed in *ABELL* (D32), *Abst. Eng. Stud.* (E38), *Arts and Hum. Cit. Ind.* (F47), *Current Bk. Rev. Cit.* (W1564), *Hum. Ind.* (F45), *Index to Bk. Rev. Hum.* (W1560), *MLAIB* (D31).

J314.   *Seventeenth-Century News (SCN).* University Park: Pennsylvania State
        Univ., 1942– . Quarterly. PR1.S47
The official organ of the Milton Society of America and the Milton section of MLA. It is interested in all aspects of English, American, and European seventeenth-century culture, with emphasis on literature and history. Scope is broad—Herbert, Dryden, Milton, Spenser, Kepler, Galileo, Edward Taylor, Michael Wigglesworth, the metaphysical poets, and all dramatists except Shakespeare. Articles, abstracts of recent books and articles, book reviews, news notes, and *Neo-Latin News*, which covers all scholarship on literature and ideas in Latin from 1500 to the present.
    Indexed in *ABELL* (D32), *Am. Hum. Ind.* (P738), *Arts. and Hum. Cit. Ind.* (F47), *Index to Bk. Rev. Hum.* (W1560), *MLAIB* (D31).

*J315.   *Shakespeare Newsletter (ShN).* Chicago: Univ. of Illinois at Chicago
        Circle, 1951– . 6/yr. PR2885.S48   822.33
Short articles on new publications, performances, awards, conferences, and festivals; occasional bibliographies on special subjects such as Shakespeare's fools; book and periodical reviews; and an annual cumulated index. For extensive, consistent, accurate, lively coverage of international news and views, this author newsletter has no equal except perhaps the *Johnsonian News Letter* (J382). Even more remarkable is the fact that it has been shepherded throughout its entire life span of over thirty years—168 issues—by just one editor, Louis Marder.
    Indexed in *ABELL* (D32), *Abst. Eng. Stud.* (E38), *MLAIB* (D31), *Year's Wk. Eng. Stud.* (D33).

*J316.   *Shakespeare Quarterly (SQ)*. Washington D.C.: Folger Shakespeare
    Library, 1950–   . Quarterly, with bibliographical supplement. Former
    title, 1924–49: *Shakespeare Association Bulletin*. PR2885.S63   822.33
    High standards in scholarship and editorial policy make this one of the
outstanding literary periodicals. The quarterly issues contain critical articles,
queries, long scholarly book reviews, notes and comments, and occasional illustrations. The bibliographical supplement is an annotated world bibliography
for the preceding year of critical books, articles, festschriften, new editions and
translations, book, film, and stage reviews from about thirty countries including
Russia, India, and Japan. The subject arrangement of the bibliography, which
is 100 to 250 pages long, is outlined in the table of contents. There is a valuable
analytical index of critics, actors, dramatists, and descriptive terms that leads
to the numbered entries. Cumulative index for vols. 1–15 (1950–64). Students
should note that a computerized, cumulative *World Shakespeare Bibliography*
sponsored by NEH is currently being planned. The editors hope it will ultimately
make accessible all scholarship back to 1900 (University Park: Pennsylvania State
Univ.).
    Indexed in *ABELL* (D32), *Abst. Eng. Stud.* (E38), *Am. Lit.* (P744), *Arts
and Hum. Cit. Ind.* (F47), *Current Bk. Rev. Cit.* (W1564), *Film Literature Ind.*
(W1252), *Hum. Ind.* (F45), *Index to Bk. Rev. Hum.* (W1560), Leary (P727),
MLAIB (D31), *Year's Wk. Eng. Stud.* (D33).

J317.   *Shakespearean Research and Opportunities (SRO)*. New York: City
    Univ. of New York, 1965–   . Annual. PR2885.S655   822.33
    Every issue contains a bibliography, numerous book reviews, and the an-
nual report of the MLA conference, including work in progress. The first six
bibliographies have been compiled by William R. Elton and Giselle Neuschloss
into a convenient volume entitled *Shakespeare's World: Renaissance Intellectual Contexts, a Selective, Annotated Guide, 1966–1971* (New York: Garland,
1977). Z8813.E38   [PR2910]   016.94105'5
    Indexed in *ABELL* (D32), *Abst. Eng. Stud.* (E38), *MLAIB* (D31).

J318.   *Shakespeare Studies: An Annual Gathering of Research, Criticism, and
    Reviews (ShakS)*. Nashville, Tenn.: Vanderbilt Univ., 1965–   . Center
    for Shakespeare Studies. PR2885.S64   822.33
    A fine source for a quick survey of annual accomplishments. Each volume
contains about twenty scholarly articles, an occasional evaluation of recent significant scholarship, numerous lengthy book reviews which occupy about a third
of the four hundred pages, and sometimes a directory.
    Indexed in *ABELL* (D32), *Abst. Eng. Stud.* (E38), *Ess. Gen. Lit. Ind.* (F46),
Hum. Ind. (F45), *MLAIB* (D31).

*J319.   *Shakespeare Survey: An Annual Survey of Shakespearian Study and Pro-
    duction (ShS)*. Cambridge, Eng.: Cambridge Univ. Press, 1948–   . An-
    nual. PR2888.C3   822.33
    Numerous scholarly essays and a valuable review of scholarship entitled ''The
Year's Contribution to Shakespearian Study,'' which evaluates recent textual
studies, productions, and selected critical works on Shakespeare's life and times.

Some issues are devoted to a single subject such as *Macbeth* in vol. 19, *Othello* in vol. 21, and *Shakespeare's Language* in vol. 23. Most issues also include articles on related subjects such as the influence of Lyly, and new ideas on Inigo Jones's designs (vol. 30, 1977). Author and title index. Cumulative index for vols. 1–10 in vol. 11, and for vols. 11–20 in vol. 21. This is a convenient and efficient source that all Shakespeare scholars should consult annually.

Indexed in *ABELL* (D32), *Abst. Eng. Stud.* (E38), *Arts and Hum. Cit. Ind.* (F47), *Ess. Gen. Lit. Ind.* (F46), *Hum. Ind.* (F45), *MLAIB* (D31), *Romantic Movement: A . . . Bibliography* (J443), *Year's Wk. Eng. Stud.* (D33).

See also: For additional Shakespeare criticism

Author Newsletters and Journals (W1476)
Chambers, *Elizabethan Stage* (J331)
Coleman and Tyler, *Drama Criticism* (G111, vol. 1, pt. 2)
Howard-Hill, *Shakespearian Bibliography* (J337)
Shakespeare (Goldentree Bibliographies, W1291)
Shakespeare Criticism. Detroit: Gale, 1983–   . In progress.

*J320.   *Studies in English Literature, 1500–1900 (SEL)*. Houston, Tex.: Rice Univ., 1961–   . Quarterly. PR1.S82   820'.9
An outstanding periodical that devotes each issue to a different period: Winter, Renaissance; Spring, Elizabethan and Jacobean drama; Summer, Restoration and eighteenth century; and Autumn, nineteenth century. Each quarterly publication contains ten to twelve scholarly articles, an evaluative, authoritative review of the previous year's research that is ten to thirty-five pages long, and a list of books received. Annual index but no cumulative index, which is regrettable.

Indexed in *ABELL* (D32), *Arts and Hum. Cit. Ind.* (F47), *Hum. Ind.* (F45), *MLAIB* (D31), *Romantic Movement: A . . . Bibliography* (J443).

*J321.   *Studies in Philology (SP)*. Chapel Hill: Univ. of North Carolina Press, 1906–   . Quarterly. P25.S8   405
From 1918 to May 1969, this scholarly periodical featured an annual spring bibliography of the previous year's studies in the English and European Renaissance to 1660. The editors terminated it because of duplication in other bibliographies. It was an excellent reference tool, however, with national divisions, international contributors, and 300 to 500 pages covering linguistics, literary criticism, histories, and interpretations found in books, articles, dissertations, and book reviews. The index of proper names provided easy access to critics, historical persons, and all important authors of the British Isles and Continent such as Lope de Vega, Sidney, Cervantes, Donne, Milton, Spenser, Boccaccio, du Bellay, Leonardo da Vinci, and Montaigne. The periodical itself publishes only long, scholarly articles on literature and language, no reviews or news notes. Vol. 25 includes an index for vols. 1–25 (1906–28).

Indexed in *ABELL* (D32), *Abst. Eng. Stud.* (E38), *Arts and Hum. Cit. Ind.* (F47), *Hum. Ind.* (F45), *MLAIB* (D31).

PROSE AND PROSE FICTION

Basic guides

*J323. *English Renaissance Prose Fiction, 1500-1660: An Annotated Bibliography of Criticism.* Ed. James L. Harner. Boston: Hall, 1978. 556pp. Z2014.F4.H37 [PR833] 016.823'2'09

Impressive in appearance, well researched, thoroughly annotated, with everything necessary for extensive research on Greene, Dekker, Middleton, Sidney, and many others. This is the first comprehensive bibliography on the subject, and it is excellent. The 3,200 entries include every edition of the works and all studies published since 1800 throughout the world. A supplement for 1976–83 is projected for 1985.

J324. *English Prose, Prose Fiction, and Criticism to 1660: A Guide to Information Sources.* Ed. Simeon K. Heninger, Jr. Vol. 2 of Gale Information Guide Library (A8). Detroit: Gale, 1975. 255pp. Z2014.P795.H45 [PR707] 016.08

This list of primary and secondary works for English prose from Aelfric through 1660 has an unusually and needlessly complex arrangement that may discourage all but the most desperate reader. For information on English prose authors and their works, this complements Sterg O'Dell's *Chronological List of Prose Fiction . . . 1475-1640* (Cambridge, Mass.: M.I.T., 1954) and Charles C. Mish's *English Prose Fiction, 1600-1700* (Charlottesville: Bibliographical Soc. of the Univ. of Virginia, 1952). The latter may be of some use to scholars who want the chronological approach to *all* prose fiction printed *in English* before 1660 with their library locations and *STC* or Wing numbers.

Background reading

J325. Krapp, George P. *The Rise of English Literary Prose.* New York: Ungar, 1963, c1915. 551pp. Paperback. PR767.K7   828.109

A most satisfying book that traces the birth of prose in Chaucer and Rolle to Wyclyf, Renaissance courtiers like Sidney, and the serious, dutiful, methodical Bacon.

DRAMA

Surveys

*J328. *Revels History of Drama in English.* London: Methuen, 1975–83.

> Vol. 2, 1500–1576. Ed. Thomas W. Craik. 1981. 344pp.
> Vol. 3, 1576–1613. Ed. J. Leeds Barroll. 1975. 525pp. PR625.R442 822'.009
> Vol. 4, 1613–1660. Ed. Philip Edwards. 1982. 337pp.

An examination of the social and literary context, the companies and their actors, the plays and playwrights, and the physical development of the playhouse itself. Excellent organization, selective bibliography, lavish illustrations, chronology of events, table of court performances, calendar of plays. This impeccably fine scholarship supplements the volumes by Chambers (J331) and Wickham (J329). Use all of these sources in conjunction with Harbage's *Annals* (J338). See the main entry (G114) for information on the other volumes in this series.

*J329.   Wickham, Glynne W. *Early English Stages, 1300-1660.* 3 vols. in 4. New York: Columbia Univ. Press, 1959-80. Vol. 1, 1300-1576, 2nd ed. (1980, c1959); vol. 2, 1576-1660, pt. 1 (1962) and pt. 2(1972); vol. 3 (1980). PN2587.W53   792'.0941

A historical survey that emphasizes the development of theatrical drama from its first vestiges in festivals and other celebrations of the Middle Ages. It discusses saints' plays, moral interludes, stage conventions, court influence, gamehouses, auditoriums, and all other conditions of theatrical presentation. A worthy supplement to Chambers' respected *Mediaeval Stage* (J278) and *Elizabethan Stage* (J331). See also Wickham's more concise survey *The Medieval Theatre* (J279).

J330.   Wilson, Frank P. *The English Drama, 1485-1585.* Vol. 4, pt. 1 of OHEL (J174). New York: Oxford Univ. Press, 1968. 244pp. PR641.W58   822'.2'09

A reliable and readable survey of events in pre-Shakespearian theater: morality plays, masques, interludes, pageants, comedies, and tragedies. Bibliographies of general subjects and specific authors (pp. 202-37). Chronological table (pp. 174-201).

*J331.   Chambers, Sir Edmund K. *The Elizabethan Stage.* 4 vols. Oxford: Clarendon, 1951, c1923. PN2589.C4   792.0942

A continuation of the author's *Mediaeval Stage* (J278), this describes the relationship of drama and the Elizabethan court, the cultural and religious position of the players in London, the companies (eleven made up of boys, twenty-four of adults, and three international), the sixteen public and two private theaters, and the staging, printing, and content of the plays as they related to the history of drama. Several appendixes treat specific subjects such as Lost Plays, Court Payments, and Plague Records. Fun browsing.

Indexes to plays, persons, places, and subjects. For additional information on this subject, see the more recent surveys (J329 and J328).

*J332.   Bentley, Gerald Eades. *The Jacobean and Caroline Stage.* 7 vols. Oxford: Clarendon, 1941-68. PN2592.B4   792.0942

This indispensable survey was designed to extend the coverage of Chambers' *The Elizabethan Stage* (J331), which ends at 1616, to the Commonwealth's closing of the theaters in 1642. It explains and analyzes the history of the most important dramatic companies, the lives of the actors, the plays and playwrights, and the theater buildings. Analytical index for all seven volumes. Chronology.

J333.   *The English Drama, 1585-1642.* Vol. 4, pt. 2 of OHEL (J174). In preparation.

Basic guides

J334.   Ribner, Irving, and Clifford C. Huffman. *Tudor and Stuart Drama*.
2nd ed. Goldentree Bibliographies (W1291). Arlington Heights. Ill.:
AHM, 1978. 121pp. Paperback. Z2014.D7.R5   [PR651]   016.822'3
    A convenient bibliography of 2,274 basic reference works: guides, an-
thologies, surveys of dramatic companies and theaters, critical and historical
studies on moralities, interludes, the masque, comedy, tragedy, and twenty-
two major dramatists, including Dekker, Ford, Beaumont, Fletcher, Jonson, Kyd,
Marlowe, and Webster. This edition has no asterisks to indicate the most helpful
titles, however, and coverage extends only through 1975.

J335.   *English Drama to 1660 (excluding Shakespeare): A Guide to Information Sources*. Ed. F. Elaine Penninger. Vol. 5 of Gale Information Guide
Library (A8). Detroit: Gale, 1976. 370pp. Z2014.D7.P46   016.822'008
    Individual bibliographies of thirty-four authors of the period, with emphasis
on the scholarship of the past two decades. The citations are for books only—no
articles, dissertations, or foreign material.

J336.   Houle, Peter J. *The English Morality and Related Drama: A
Bibliographical Survey*. Hamden, Conn.: Archon, 1972. 195pp.
PR643.M7.H6   822'.051
    Facts about the original publications, their editions, characters, and length
as well as summaries and bibliographies of criticism for specific plays and general
studies. A helpful book for a subject that is not well covered elsewhere.

**J337.   Howard-Hill, Trevor H. *Shakespearian Bibliography and Textual
Criticism: A Bibliography*. Vol. 2 of *Index to British Literary
Bibliography* (C26). Oxford: Clarendon, 1971. 322pp. Z8811.H67
016.8223'3
    The intimidating mass of research on Shakespeare is finally organized into
manageable form. Arrangement is by general bibliographies and guides (from
an 1884 list on the Bacon–Shakespeare controversy to a 1969 *Reading Guide*),
library catalogs, research on the quartos and folios, handwriting, collected emendations, individual titles (119 titles on Hamlet's "solid flesh"), apocrypha, and
poetry.
    The second half of the book is a supplement to the previously published
Bibliography of British Literary Bibliographies (C26), which is vol. 1 of the index cited above. It adds a few inadvertently omitted titles and all recent
bibliographies to the end of 1969 for subject, form, period (for example, the
Oxford Movement), and individual authors (such as Stathis' *Bibliography of
Swift Studies*, 1967). Detailed indexes, occasional brief annotations. A valuable,
scholarly book.

Bibliographies of primary works

**J338. Harbage, Alfred. *Annals of English Drama, 975–1700: An Analytical Record of All Plays, Extant or Lost, Chronologically Arranged and Indexed by Authors, Titles, Dramatic Companies, etc.* Rev. Samuel Schoenbaum. London: Methuen, 1964. 321pp. Supplements, 1966 and 1970 (Evanston, Ill.: Northwestern Univ.). Z2014.D7.H25

An essential tool for students who are interested in English plays written before the Restoration. Titles are arranged in tables, first by century and then by year, with information on the first performance, the company, original and latest edition, and numerous indexes that provide a variety of ways to get at the facts.

**J339. Greg, Walter Wilson. *A Bibliography of the English Printed Drama to the Restoration.* 4 vols. London: Oxford Univ. Press, for the Bibliographical Soc., 1939–59; rpt. 1970. Z2014.D7.G78   016.822

The most important bibliography for drama of the period (up to 1700). Its purpose is to provide for each title a full bibliographical description according to McKerrow's specifications (W1065) and to locate copies in British and American libraries.

Arrangement is by the supposed date of the earliest surviving edition. Each entry has been given an identification number which is now used in most sales catalogs and all reference books. Vol. 1 contains a bibliography of all the plays entered in the *Stationers' Register* (J308) and descriptions of the plays written to 1616, nos. 1–349. Vol. 2 lists plays written 1617–89, nos. 350–836; vol. 3, collections, appendix, reference lists; vol. 4, introduction, additions, corrections, index of titles.

Vol. 3 contains an astonishing array of appendixes covering advertisements in these early books, their "Prefaces & Such," dedications, prologues, epilogues, and stationers' signs. A section entitled "Quorum fit mentio" includes people, titles, and "a few other things" that do not seem to fit anywhere else. "Notabilia" cites references to incidental items so fascinating that the editor felt compelled to call attention to them—the apologies rendered by a conscientious printer, for instance. Vol. 4 contains additions, corrections, an index of titles, and, most important, a 169-page introduction to all four volumes, the first of which had appeared twenty years earlier. An excellent editor, Greg recognized the necessity of learning through experience. He therefore chose to formulate his editorial policy during the process of encountering and solving his unique bibliographical problems. Only another bibliographer can be fully aware of the time and determination required to produce this monument.

Series

*J340. New Variorum Edition of Shakespeare. Ed. Horace H. Furness et al. Philadelphia: Lippincott, 1871–1928. New variorum editions and supplementary bibliographies: ed. James G. McManaway, Robert K. Turner, Jr., Richard Knowles. New York: MLA, 1929– . PR2753.F5 822.33.U3

As sponsor of a literary project that has been under way for over a century, the MLA is publishing new variorum editions of the Shakespeare plays that supersede the original Furness variorums prepared between 1871 and 1928. In fact, Furness is only one of as many as fifty editions used by contemporary editors as they collate all known versions of each play and prepare their massive commentary. The MLA editions are reprints of either the Quartos or the First Folio of 1623 with slight modifications for ease in reading. They add extensive textual notes that explain all departures from that text in subsequent editions, a running commentary on the language, and interpretations of the criticism as it has appeared down through the centuries. The famed appendixes cumulate studies and facts on every conceivable point of interest: the sources of the plots, the date of composition, all the important characters (Falstaff is given fifty pages), the history of performances, even the music. The new variorum edition of *As You Like It*, for instance, is over seven hundred pages long, with a four-hundred-page appendix and a thirty-page bibliography for a play that in itself usually consumes a scant three dozen pages. The new variorum edition of *Measure for Measure* was completed in 1980, and twenty others are in progress. The MLA also occasionally publishes supplementary updated bibliographies for earlier volumes of the variorum edition. A worthy project, admirably executed.

J341.   Plays by Renaissance and Restoration Dramatists. Ed. Graham Storey. New York: Cambridge Univ. Press, 1978–   .

Readability and accuracy are the keynotes of these editions of the plays of Middleton, Massinger, Tourneur, and other Renaissance and Restoration dramatists. The volumes are important to researchers because each one includes a long introduction that is factual and historical rather than critical, a brief biography of the author, a short critical bibliography, information about the manuscripts and editions used to prepare the final text, and an introductory note to each play that gives source material, a short stage history, and facts about various earlier editions. Students will find them easy to read because of the modern spelling and extensive notes.

J342.   Regents Renaissance Drama Series. Lincoln: Univ. of Nebraska Press, 1963–76.

An excellent series that was designed to "provide soundly edited texts, in modern spelling, of the more significant plays of the Elizabethan, Jacobean, and Caroline theatre" (Introd.). Forty-three titles were published: by Beaumont, Brome, Chapman, Fletcher and Shakespeare, Ford, Greene, Heywood, Jonson, Kyd, Lodge, Lyly, Marlowe, Marston, Massinger, Middleton, Rowley, Sackville and Norton, J. Shirley, Tourneur, Wager, and Webster.

All texts are based on new collations of sixteenth- and seventeenth-century texts, and all variants and substantive departures from the edition used as copy text are recorded at the bottom of every page. (See the Glossary in this guide for explanations of these terms.) The editors had the student in mind when they normalized and modernized the spelling and punctuation, and they have provided emendations and explanatory notes where needed. The introduction expounds on sources, stage history, and facts about the text. Every title includes a chronology of the author's life and works interspersed with the important political and literary events of the time. The result is an accurate, readable text that students will read with pleasure. In most library card catalogs these editions are filed by author and title, not by series. Complete listing of titles may sometimes be found in *PTLA* (W1172) under University of Nebraska Press. Indexed in *MLAIB* (D31).

See also

Regents Critics Series (W1363)
Regents Restoration Drama Series (J402)

Criticism

*J343.   *The Predecessors of Shakespeare: A Survey and Bibliography of Recent Studies in English Renaissance Drama.* Ed. Terence P. Logan and Denzell S. Smith. Lincoln: Univ. of Nebraska Press, 1973. 348pp. Z2014.D7.L83   [PR646]   016.822'3'09

An excellent place to begin a study of Renaissance drama from 1580 to 1593. The authors provide brief facts about the life of Marlowe, Greene, Kyd, Nashe, Lyly, Peele, and Lodge as well as a résumé of stage history, editions, dating and authorship problems, textual and canon problems, an analysis of the more important critical and biographical works, and a lengthy bibliography for each author and play.

The format deserves comment. The arrangement of titles, subjects, and text permits unusually easy reading. The different sizes of type aid in the quick location of material, and the text seems to be entirely free of printing errors. A well-written, carefully produced work.

This and the next three titles (J344–46) by the same editors should be used to update information in Chambers' *Elizabethan Stage* (J331) and Bentley's *Jacobean and Caroline Stage* (J332). They are of course much more comprehensive than the slim but handy Goldentree bibliography by Ribner (J334) and more helpful in historical and evaluative problems than the Gale Library enumerative bibliography by Penninger (J335).

*J344.   *Popular School: A Survey and Bibliography of Recent Studies in English Renaissance Drama.* Ed. Terence P. Logan and Denzell S. Smith. Lincoln: Univ. of Nebraska Press, 1975. 299pp. Z2014.D7.L82   [PR651] 016.822'3'09

Just as fine a bit of research, in every way, as the editors' earlier *Predecessors of Shakespeare* (J343). Here the bibliographical essays survey the scholarship— past, present, and future—on Dekker, Middleton, Webster, Heywood, Munday, Drayton, and numerous other minor authors and anonymous plays of the *public* theater between 1593 and 1616. They select the best editions and biographies, place the author in historical perspective, evaluate the criticism up to the 1970s, and suggest areas that need further investigation. They even supply a list of books and articles at the end of each chapter so that the student does not have to do the preliminary spadework in research. A well-conceived, well-executed project. See also J345–46.

*J345. *New Intellectuals: A Survey and Bibliography of Recent Studies in English Renaissance Drama.* Ed. Terence P. Logan and Denzell S. Smith. Lincoln: Univ. of Nebraska Press, 1977. 370pp. Z2014.D7.L817 [PR671] 016.822'3

The third in the series by these editors (see *Predecessors of Shakespeare*, J343; *Popular School,* J344; *Later Jacobean and Caroline Dramatists,* J346). Several noted scholars survey the past, present, and possibilities for future research on Jonson, Chapman, Marston, Tourneur, Daniel, and several minor authors and anonymous plays of the *private* theater between 1593 and 1616. The scholars evaluate all important scholarship on each author and then list critical articles and books, which readers can obtain for their own interests. As in the other three volumes, indexes are provided for the people and plays mentioned in the text. Reviewers have not yet found a significant error in these excellent surveys.

*J346. *Later Jacobean and Caroline Dramatists: A Survey and Bibliography of Recent Studies in English Renaissance Drama.* Ed. Terence P. Logan and Denzell S. Smith. Lincoln: Univ. of Nebraska Press, 1978. 279pp. Z2014.D7.L816 [PR671] 016.822'3'09

This, the fourth in the series by these editors, is a review of research on plays and playwrights of both popular and private theaters for the period from 1616 to 1642. Summarizing and evaluating all scholarship on dramatists from Beaumont and Fletcher to Brome and Davenant, it supplements the groundwork in Bentley's *Jacobean and Caroline Stage* (J332), Greg's *Bibliography of the English Printed Drama* (J339), and Harbage's *Annals of English Drama, 975-1700* (J338).

Renaissance scholars should be equally familiar with three other books prepared by the same editors: *The Predecessors of Shakespeare* (J343), *The New Intellectuals* (J345), and *The Popular School* (J344). Do not overlook the chapter entitled "Other Dramatists" in all four of these books. Here the editors examine and evaluate, title by title, the critical books, editions, and articles on dozens of minor authors who simply are not mentioned elsewhere. Top-notch scholarship.

J347. *Caroline Drama: A Bibliographic History of Criticism.* Ed. Rachel Fordyce. Boston: Hall, 1978. 203pp. Z2014.D7.F67 [PR671] 822'.5'09

The careful descriptions and astute comments for each of the 180 books and articles on Jonson, Ford, Massinger, Shirley, and other Caroline dramatists deserve praise, even though the scope overlaps somewhat with that of other titles in this section. Students must remember that the only way to locate material in the book is through the subject, title, and name indexes because arrangement is simply by "Major" or "Minor" dramatists and by "Individual Studies and Comprehensive Works." This and the fact that it is alphabetized by critic rather than dramatist may discourage the less-than-ardent student.

J348. Bergeron, David M. *Twentieth-Century Criticism of English Masques, Pageants, and Entertainments: 1558-1642.* Checklists in the Humanities and Education. San Antonio: Trinity Univ. Press, 1972. 67pp.

Z2014.D7.B44   016.822'3
An example of the highly specialized reference book that became commonplace in the 1970s. Before signing up for a class or choosing a subject for a paper, every student should see if the library has a guide similar to this that contains both facts and advice on good research topics and procedures. This checklist covers scholarship on every facet of Jonson's masques, for instance, from the historical background to the actual staging.

See also

Bergquist (G113)
English Tragedy, 1370-1600: Fifty Years of Criticism (J213)
Stratman, *Bibliography of English Printed Tragedy, 1565-1900* (J209)
Studies in English Literature (J320), Spring issue, Elizabethan and Jacobean Drama
Wells, *Three Centuries* (G112)
Year's Wk. Eng. Stud. (D33), English Drama: 1550-1660

Periodicals

J349.   *Research Opportunities in Renaissance Drama (RORD)*. Lawrence: Univ. of Kansas, 1956- . Annual. Former title, 1956-64: *Opportunities for Research in Renaissance Drama*. PR621.M75   822'.2'09
Scholarly articles and occasional checklists of current projects, sources, lost plays, primary and secondary scholarship, and other subjects pertaining to drama. A medieval supplement in each issue includes articles, news, and bibliographies. An index to the bibliographies and to current projects mentioned in vols. 1–16 (1956–73) appears in vol. 17.
Indexed in *ABELL* (D32), *MLAIB* (D31).

J350.   *Renaissance Drama (RenD)*. Evanston: Northwestern Univ. Press, 1969- . Annual. PN2171.R4   809.2
Coverage extends to all nationalities and to precursors as well as imitators of Renaissance theories and themes. This includes stagecraft, the audience, pageants and celebrations, dramatic techniques, modern revivals, and political drama.
Indexed in *ABELL* (D32), *Arts and Hum. Cit. Ind.* (F47), *MLAIB* (D31).

See also: Periodicals listed in J311-21 for additional information on Renaissance drama.

POETRY

Criticism

J355.   Berry, Lloyd E., comp. *A Bibliography of Studies in Metaphysical Poetry, 1939-1960*. Madison: Univ. of Wisconsin Press, 1964. 99pp. Z2014.P7.B4   016.821'409
A guide to general studies and important metaphysical poets of the seventeenth century such as Donne, Marvell, Vaughan, George Herbert, Crashaw, and Traherne. Chronological arrangement facilitates the study of trends, but

there are no annotations and no subject index, so evaluation is sometimes difficult. Secondary author index.

The early copyright date is an obvious weakness, but students trained in research know several other sources that contain more recent scholarship: the long-awaited Goldentree Bibliography on the seventeenth century by Barker (J302), the fine review of research on Donne, Herbert, and Marvell in Dyson (J216), entries on Marvell and Donne in the excellent bibliography in *PQ* (H154), and of course the annual bibliographies (D31-33).

Background reading for poetry

J356.   Martz, Louis L. *The Poetry of Meditation: A Study in English Religious Literature of the Seventeenth Century*. Rev. ed. New Haven: Yale Univ. Press, 1962, c1954; rpt. 1978. 375pp. Paperback.   PR549.R4.M3 821.309

The title refers, not unexpectedly, to the poetry of Southwell, Donne, Herbert, Crashaw, and a dozen lesser poets, but the author makes a notable contribution by relating their approach and form to that of Hopkins, Yeats, and Eliot. Martz's affection for the poem and the poet is apparent. He is a pleasure to read.

Background reading for the Renaissance era

*J357.   Tillyard, Eustace M. W. *The Elizabethan World Picture*. London: Chatto, 1943. 108pp. Paperback. PR428.P5.T5   820.903

Contains more important information in its one hundred pages than any other book in the field of literary criticism. Essential reading for the Renaissance era.

Additional reference sources for Renaissance literature

English Renaissance Poetry (J215)
Lives of the Stuart Age (W1144)
Lives of the Tudor Age (W1144)
Renaissance Spain in Its Literary Relations with England and France: A Critical Bibliography (T1012)

Restoration and Eighteenth-Century Literature

Surveys

J360.   Butt, John E., and Geoffrey Carnall. *The Mid-Eighteenth Century*. Vol. 8 of OHEL (J174). New York: Oxford Univ. Press, 1979. 712pp. PR441.B3   820'.9'006

This volume of the respected Oxford History of English Literature surveys a period remarkable for its experiments in poetry, prose, history, and biography. Coverage extends beyond the strictly literary to Hume and Smith, nonfiction prose is discussed thoroughly, and an entire chapter is given to Samuel Johnson.

Alert students will use the extensive bibliography (127pp.), which is up to date, judiciously selective, and prepared by two eminent scholars.

J361.   Dobrée, Bonamy. *English Literature in the Early Eighteenth Century,*
1700-1740. Vol. 7 of OHEL (J174). Oxford: Clarendon, 1959; rpt. 1977.
701pp. PR445.D6   820.903
Dobrée discusses not only literature but also the cultural, social, and philosophical background that influenced the authors with whom he is concerned: Defoe, Swift, Pope, Steele, Arbuthnot, Thomson, and others. Bibliographies (pp. 586–696). Chronological table (pp. 570–85). Excellent index of critics, subjects, and all literary figures mentioned in the text.

J362.   Sutherland, James R. *English Literature of the Late Seventeenth Century.* Vol. 6 of OHEL (J174). New York: Oxford Univ. Press, 1969.
589pp. PR437.S9   820.9'004
Recommended background reading, like the others in this series, with ample information on writers of all genres and an examination of the intellectual and cultural crosscurrents that produced them. Bibliographies (pp. 442–578). Chronological table (pp. 418–41).

Basic guides

*J363.   *New Cambridge Bibliography of English Literature* (*New CBEL*). Ed.
George Watson. Vol. 2, 1600–1800. Cambridge, Eng.: Cambridge
Univ. Press, 1971. 2092 cols. Z2011.N45   [PR83]   016.82
Based on vol. 2 of the 1940 edition of the *CBEL* and the 1957 supplement but revised to cover primary and secondary materials of all established authors of the British Isles between 1660 and 1800 from Butler, Locke, Defoe, Dryden, and Swift to Johnson, Chatterton, Blake, Sterne, Wollstonecraft, and Burns. The general sections include items on literary theory, relations with the Continent (French, German, Shakespearian), medieval influences, book production, histories and surveys, religion, education, and Scottish literature. The author sections list bibliographies, primary and secondary material in chronological order, translations, and occasional notes on location of manuscripts. For a description of the complete edition, see *New CBEL* (J175).

J364.   *Eighteenth Century: Johnson through Burns.* Ed. Donald F. Bond.
Goldentree Bibliographies (W1291). Northbrook, Ill.: AHM, 1975.
184pp. Paperback. Z2013.B63   [PR441]   016.82'09'006
This aims for usefulness, like the others in the series, so it marks with asterisks the important sources, provides excellent subject and author indexes, and groups information for research on Romanticism, the genres, language, literary criticism, and scholarship on one hundred authors from Addison to Young.

J365.   Bond, Donald F. *The Age of Dryden.* Goldentree Bibliographies
(W1291). New York: Appleton (Meredith), 1970. 103pp.
Z2012.B74   016.8209'004
Like all the other Goldentree Bibliographies this is selective, with emphasis

on the best scholarship. After listing general surveys, historical studies, and literary criticism, the editor provides information on the best editions and criticism on Dryden (fourteen titles on "Mac Flecknoe"), thirteen poets in his circle (including John Wilmot and Nahum Tate), twenty dramatists (such as Behn, Congreve, Etherege, Davenant, Shadwell, and Wycherley), philosophers such as Hobbes and Locke, religious reformers including Bunyan and Penn, and prose writers like Brown and Pepys. No annotations, but asterisks indicate the most important contributions. For more extensive research, the editor suggests vol. 2 of the *New CBEL* (J363), the *DNB* (W1086), the annual bibliographies (D31–33), *PQ* (H154), and the *Johnsonian News Letter* (J382). It can easily be brought up to date with Lund (J369).

*J366.   Hanford, James H., and William A. McQueen. *Milton.* 2nd ed. Goldentree Bibliographies (W1291). Northbrook, Ill.: AHM, 1979. 111pp. Paperback. Z8578.H35 [PR3578]   016.828

The Milton scholar should start here. Scope ranges from a list of the editions published in Milton's lifetime to important editions of individual works; numerous critical articles and books on "Lycidas," the Paradises, and *Samson Agonistes*; information on prose works, prosody, imagery, source studies, theology, illustrations, and Milton's influence in his own and following eras. Selective, inexpensive, convenient.

J367.   Tobin, James E. *Eighteenth Century English Literature and Its Cultural Background: A Bibliography.* New York: Fordham Univ. Press, 1939; rpt. New York: Biblo and Tannen, 1967. 190pp. Z2013.T62 016.8209'006

About 8,500 titles on historical background, social thought, criticism, genre, bibliographical aids, and bibliographies by and about 169 individual authors. The entries are not annotated, and the book is old, but it is occasionally helpful. Arrangement is by subject, and then alphabetically by the author of the critical work.

J368.   Sachse, William L. *Restoration England: 1660–1689.* Cambridge, Eng.: Cambridge Univ. Press, 1971. 115pp. Conference on British Studies. Z2018.S3   016.9142'03'66

This comprehensive bibliography of Restoration England covers scholarly political, economic, social, and intellectual subjects.

J369.   Lund, Roger D. *Restoration and Early Eighteenth-Century English Literature, 1660–1740: A Selected Bibliography of Resource Materials.* New York: MLA, 1980. 42pp. Z2012.L88 [PR43]   016.82

A pamphlet designed especially for the Restoration and eighteenth-century scholar, suitably slim for both pocket and pocketbook, and focused solely on those reference sources essential for extended research. It lists (but does not annotate) those journals and books that have proved themselves in the study of fiction, drama, poetry, literary criticism, the arts, biography, religion, translation, and 177 individual authors from Addison to Wycherley. The two established guides for this era, *The Age of Dryden* (J365) and *The Eighteenth Century* (J364) of course contain much more information, but they both need the updating that Lund offers. This is an exemplary first volume in the MLA's new series entitled Selected Bibliographies in Language and Literature (ed. Walter S. Achtert).

Bibliographies of primary works

**J370. Wing, Donald, ed. *Short-Title Catalogue of Books Printed in England, Scotland, Ireland, Wales, and British America and of English Books Printed in Other Countries 1641-1700* (Wing). 2nd ed. New York: MLA, 1972- . Vol. 1 (1972), 642pp.; vol. 2, ed. Timothy J. Crist (1982), 690pp.; vol. 3 projected for 1985. Z2002.W5   015.42

A catalog giving concise bibliographical information on all extant editions that are (1) known to have been published between 1641 and 1700 in the specified countries and (2) known to be owned in the United States and Great Britain by any of 327 libraries for Wing's first edition or by about 420 libraries for the second edition.

Wing's project is a continuation of Pollard and Redgrave's *Short-Title Catalogue . . . 1475-1640* (J306). Because it is not concerned with pamphlets, periodicals, or any books other than those actually located in the specified libraries, students must keep in mind that omissions are inevitable. Accuracy is high, however, for the editors personally examined about ninety percent of the titles of the first edition, and the second edition is making thousands of additions and corrections, some of which were published in 1976-78 in *Studies in Bibliography* (W1076) for the edification of scholars.

Arrangement is alphabetical by author, anonymous title, and a few subjects. For a title index to Wing's first edition, see J307. Each entry is numbered consecutively within the letter of the alphabet. These numbers are used internationally by rare-book dealers, who tend to establish prices according to Wing's indication of ownership in spite of his protests that they are misreading his statements. The second edition retains these important numbers wherever possible, adding a distinguishing letter when it is necessary to insert an addition, or placing "Entry cancelled" after a number when the item has been withdrawn for some reason. John Bunyan's *The Water of Life*, therefore, has the same number in both editions (B5607), but the second edition locates copies in two additional libraries in the United States. About eight percent of the numbers in vol. 1 of the second edition were reassigned, however, so readers may need to consult vol. 2 for an appendix that clarifies the numbering problems in vol. 1.

Each entry cites the publisher, date, size, and present location in not more than five libraries in the British Isles and five elsewhere (British before the semicolon; elsewhere, after). The number of editions is, of course, some indication of the work's popularity (Dryden's "Absalom and Achitophel" went through five editions in two years). The second edition of Wing tries to locate books in London, Oxford, Cambridge, Scotland, Ireland, and five widely spaced locations in the United States, Canada, Australia, and other countries for the convenience of scholars. It is twenty percent larger than the first edition, with over one thousand new entries under the letter *A* alone for a total of 120,000 titles. A progress report for the edition may be found in *Literary Research Newsletter*, 4 (1979), 67-72 (W1421). A short-title catalog for the eighteenth century is also in preparation (J373).

All these titles are or soon will be on microfilm. Many libraries enter the microfilm reel number in the margin so that students can go directly to the files to read the work (see W1439).

J371.   Wing, Donald. *A Gallery of Ghosts: Books Published between 1641-1700 Not Found in the Short-Title Catalogue.* New York: MLA, 1967. 225pp. Z2002.W5   015.42

Five thousand entries for books that Wing believed had once existed and might perhaps still survive because they had been cited in various sources such as dealers' catalogs but that were not held by the libraries he consulted for the first edition of the *STC 1641-1700* (J370). He published *A Gallery of Ghosts* in the hope that the ghostly copies would be located before the second edition of his catalog was published. He was successful, for hundreds of these titles have since been reported as held by cooperating libraries and—equally important— hundreds more have been proved legitimate "ghosts."

J372.   Morrison, Paul G. *Index of Printers, Publishers, and Booksellers in Donald Wing's Short-Title Catalogue.* Charlottesville: Univ. of Virginia Press, 1955. 217pp. Z2002.W5   015.42

Eighty thousand items from Wing's first edition of the *STC 1641-1700* (J370). This is essential for the student interested in the history of the book, printing process, tracing of editions, and location of anonymous authors.

J373.   *Eighteenth-Century Short-Title Catalogue (ESTC).* London: British Library; Baton Rouge: Louisiana State Univ. In preparation.

A few members of the American Society for Eighteenth-Century Studies initiated this monumental undertaking, which will, many years hence, describe and locate in British and American libraries all available books printed in the eighteenth century in English throughout the world and in any language in Great Britain and its colonies. Two newsletters, *Facsimile* (New York) and *Factotum* (London), will keep scholars apprised of the project's progress.

A 1979 grant enables LSU to acquire information on and store available copies of all North American and Caribbean library holdings of eighteenth-century books published in English. As a first step, all cooperating libraries must report their eighteenth-century holdings to LSU. This is the largest bibliographic project ever attempted. By 1985, 750,000 titles will be available on machine-readable tape or microfiche so that eighteenth-century scholars will be able to do extensive research in their own libraries, using computer terminals.

See also

Stationers' Register 1710-1746 (J308)

Annual bibliographies

*J374.   *Eighteenth Century: A Current Bibliography for [———].* New York: AMS, 1976 (n.s., vol. 1)– . Annual.   Z5579.6.E36 [CB411] 016.909

A continuation of the famous annual bibliography of Restoration and eighteenth-century scholarship that appeared in *PQ* (H154) from 1926 to 1975. In 1971, in cooperation with the American Society for Eighteenth-Century Studies, the bibliography expanded to include comparative and interdisciplinary studies. In 1972 the amount of annotation and the number of reviews increased. Since 1975 *PQ* has featured only annual essay reviews of the previous year's scholarship, and the critically annotated bibliography has been produced as the separate publication described here. The first volume, which appeared in 1978, covers material published in 1976 on the fine arts, philosophy, religion, social and economic history, literary criticism, music, bibliography, and individual authors in Europe and North America during the eighteenth century. This is an exemplary bibliography in both form and scholarship, its unique contribution being the excellent evaluative annotations and exceptionally long, scholarly book reviews. They have proved so important to researchers that they are indexed by *Index to Bk. Rev. Hum.* (W1560). Rumors persist, however, that the bibliography may cease because of overlap with the *MLAIB* (D31).

*J375.   *English Literature, 1660-1800: A Bibliography of Modern Studies.* 6 vols. Princeton: Princeton Univ. Press, 1950–72. Z2011.E62   016.82

A compilation and reproduction of the bibliographies that appeared originally as an annual feature (1926–70) in *PQ* (H154) here reprinted (but not cumulated) for the convenience of scholars. Students who are interested in tracing trends in criticism (such as the rise and fall of interest in Pope) will be glad that the chronological arrangement has been retained. Those students who need to locate scholarship on a specific individual or title will consult vol. 2 for a cumulative index to vols. 1 and 2 (1926–50), vol. 4 for a cumulative index to vols. 3 and 4 (1951–60), vol. 6 for a cumulative index to vols. 5 and 6 (1961–70).

Coverage includes political and social background, philosophy, science, religion, literary history and criticism, individual authors, and Continental background. Critical authors are listed alphabetically under each subject heading. The unusually complete index records names of authors (with occasional titles), editors, reviewers, even names and subjects mentioned significantly in the reviews and annotations. A bibliography of eighteenth-century studies for 1900–24 is in preparation.

See also

> *ABELL* (D32) has sections on both the seventeenth century and the eighteenth century.
> *MLAIB* (D31) has a section on the eighteenth century.
> *Year's Wk. Eng. Stud.* (D33) has an annual review of research on Milton, the later seventeenth century, and the eighteenth century.

Students should also check the appropriate abstracting services (E38–43) and indexing services (F45–53) for recent publications.

Dictionaries

*J376.   Johnson, Samuel. *A Dictionary of the English Language: In Which the Words are Deduced from Their Originals, and Illustrated in Their Different Significations, by Examples from the Best Writers. To Which are Prefixed, a History of the Language, and an English Grammar.* 2 vols. London: Strahan, 1755; rpt. New York: AMS, 1967. PE1620.J6 423

Johnson explains his approach and purpose in a long preface and then instructs his readers in "The History of the English Language" and "A Grammar of the English Tongue." These selections are frequently anthologized because of their historical interest and the rare wit and candor that produced them.

Each entry indicates the stress of the word, the part of speech, derivation, and various meanings, with quotations from Johnson's own broad range of readings, both contemporary and Renaissance. His concise definitions reflect the atmosphere and learning of his day as well as his own personality and personal prejudices and, as can be expected, they are often prescriptive rather than descriptive. Students will be particularly amused by his entries for oats, patron, tarantula, network, Whig, Tory, lexicographer, and pragmatic.

Periodicals

J379.   *Eighteenth Century: A Journal of Theory and Interpretation (ECent).* Lubbock: Texas Technological Univ., 1979– . 3/yr. Former titles: 1959–Spring 1967, *Burke Newsletter;* Fall 1967–78, *Studies in Burke and His Time.* DA506.B9.B86   941.07'3'0924

Specializes in modern critical and historical theory, review essays, and bibliographical surveys of the period from 1660 to 1800. Cumulative index every five years (vols. 20–24, 1979–83).

Indexed in *ABELL* (D32), *Abst. Eng. Stud.* (E38), *Am. Hum. Ind.* (P738), *Arts and Hum. Cit. Ind.* (F47), *MLAIB* (D31).

J380.   *Eighteenth-Century Life (ECLife).* Williamsburg, Va.: Coll. of William and Mary, 1974– . Quarterly. HN1.E42   309.1'03

Devoted to all aspects of Restoration and eighteenth-century culture and society from interdisciplinary perspectives. Occasional special issues cover such subjects as pamphlets and pamphleteers in the eighteenth century (1978).

Indexed in *ABELL* (D32), *Arts and Hum. Cit. Ind.* (F47), *MLAIB* (D31), *Romantic Movement: A . . . Bibliography* (J443).

J381.   *Eighteenth-Century Studies: An Interdisciplinary Journal (ECS).* Columbus, Ohio: American Soc. for Eighteenth-Century Studies, 1967– . Quarterly. NX452.E54   700.5

Articles on British, American, Continental, and comparative literature and the relationship between literature and the arts. This journal is of particular importance because interdisciplinary periodicals are relatively scarce. Lengthy book reviews, reports from the American and international societies for eighteenth-century studies, and occasional illustrations. Students should note that "eighteenth century" is interpreted loosely. Coverage of English literature, for instance,

begins at 1660. No cumulative index as yet, which is unfortunate.
Indexed in *ABELL* (D32), *Abst. Eng. Stud.* (E38), *Arts and Hum. Cit. Ind.* (F47), *Current Bk. Rev. Cit.* (W1564), *Hum. Ind.* (F45), *Index to Bk. Rev. Hum.* (W1560), *MLAIB* (D31), *Romantic Movement: A . . . Bibliography* (J443).

*J382. *Johnsonian News Letter (JNL).* New York: Columbia Univ., 1940–   . Quarterly. PR1.J64
This small but important periodical reports on scholarship concerning Samuel Johnson, his age, and contemporaries such as Smollett, Wesley, Crabbe, and Cowper. It contains short news notes on latest editions, bibliographies, auctions, critical works, a brief listing of recent scholarship, works in progress, and "Conferences, Conferences." Subject index to vols. 1–10, 11–15, 16–20, 21–25, etc.
Indexed in *ABELL* (D32), *MLAIB* (D31), *Romantic Movement: A . . . Bibliography* (J443).

J383. *Restoration: Studies in English Literary Culture, 1660–1700.* Knoxville: Univ. of Tennessee, 1977–   . 2/yr. PR437.R47
Critical articles, reviews, news and notes, an annotated bibliography on all aspects of English and American Restoration study including individual authors, and an important survey of "Essential Studies" in specific fields such as Restoration libertine court poetry or prose fiction.

*J384. *Scriblerian and the Kit-Cats.* Philadelphia: Temple Univ., 1972–   . 2/yr. Former title, 1968–71: *The Scriblerian: A Newsletter Devoted to Pope, Swift, and Their Circle.* PR445.S3   820.9'005'05
Essential for any student of eighteenth-century literature because of its convenient accumulation of international activities and scholarship. The section entitled "Scribleriana" includes queries, news on recent publications, notes on meetings, work in progress, and activities of members. Every issue contains numerous book reviews and annotated lists of foreign and American scholarship concerning Pope, Swift, Addison, Steele, Congreve, Gay, Arbuthnot, Bolingbroke, and their circle. See also W1484 (Greene, Donald J.).
The subject and critic index, published every fifth year (1969–73, 1973–78), is actually a thorough, current bibliography of all Restoration and early eighteenth-century English literature. In 1979 it expanded to include reviews of scholarship on Defoe, Richardson, Fielding, Mrs. Manley, and others.
Indexed in *ABELL* (D32), *Abst. Eng. Stud.* (E38), *Am. Hum. Ind.* (P738), *Arts and Hum. Cit. Ind.* (F47), *Index to Bk. Rev. Hum.* (W1560), *MLAIB* (D31).

See also
Philological Quarterly (H154)
Studies in English Literature, 1500–1900 (J320), Summer issue, Restoration and Eighteenth Century, an indispensable review essay of most of the important scholarship, new editions, critical articles, and books published during the preceding year

FICTION

Basic guides

J386.   *English Fiction, 1660–1800: A Guide to Information Sources.* Ed. Jerry
C. Beasley. Vol. 14 of Gale Information Guide Library (A8). Detroit:
Gale, 1978. 313pp. Z2014.F5.B42   [PR851]   016.823
Entries on twenty-nine authors of the period from the Fieldings (Henry and
Sarah) to Charlotte Smith and Walpole, with discerning evaluations. Beginning
students would have appreciated the guidance of a few more cross-references.

*J387.   *Eighteenth-Century Gothic Novel: An Annotated Bibliography of
Criticism and Important Texts.* Ed. Dan J. McNutt. New York: Garland,
1975. 330pp. Z2014.F5.M3   [PR858.T3]   016.823'03
This bibliography of the eighteenth-century Gothic novel is particularly interesting because it assembles material explaining the background of the genre
and its complex relationship with the other arts, religion, the Continent, and
twentieth-century film and literature. Sections are given to Walpole, Reeve,
Smith, Radcliffe, Lewis, and Beckford. In a second volume now under way, the
author will cover Brown, Mary Shelley, Polidori, and Maturin. See also G81–82.

J387.1   Spector, Robert D. *The English Gothic: A Bibliographic Guide to
Writers from Horace Walpole to Mary Shelley.* Westport, Conn.: Greenwood, 1983. 320pp. Z2014.H67   [PR830.T3]   016.823'0872'09
A readable history of the early Gothic novel, and a guide to the most useful
commentary, the best editions, and the most reliable bibliographies.

Bibliographies of primary works

J388.   McBurney, William H. *A Checklist of English Prose Fiction, 1700–39.*
Cambridge, Mass.: Harvard Univ. Press, 1960. 154pp. Z2014.F4.M3
016.8235
Useful for studies concerning early novelists and the development of the
English novel, with a chronological list of four hundred titles (including English
translations of Continental novels) with original spelling, pages, size, price, and
the library call number of at least one extant copy. Index by author, publisher,
bookseller, translator, printer, and title (including anonymous works).

J389.   Beasley, Jerry C. *A Checklist of Prose Fiction Published in England,
1740–1749.* Charlottesville: Univ. Press of Virginia, 1972. 213pp.
Z2014.F4.B37   016.823'5'08
This well-executed bibliography does justice to the remarkable decade
1740–50 that produced novels by Richardson, Fielding, Smollett, and a host
of others. The remaining fifty years of eighteenth-century fiction have also been
cataloged, but most reviewers agree that another edition is in order because of
the numerous oversights in Leonard Orr's *A Catalogue Checklist of English Prose
Fiction, 1750–1800* (Troy, N.Y.: Whitston, 1979; 204pp.).

J390.   Block, Andrew. *English Novel, 1740-1850: A Catalogue including Prose Romances, Short Stories, and Translations of Foreign Fiction.* Rev. ed. London: Dawsons, 1961. 349pp. Z2014.F4.B6   016.823

In this questionably accurate catalog of novels, short stories, and translations of foreign fiction, reviewers have noted serious omissions, incomplete entries, inaccurate bibliographies, confusion of names and pseudonyms, and failure to locate all editions in libraries. Because the *New CBEL* (J363, J415) does not attempt to be comprehensive in minor fiction, the student still has no one authoritative source to consult.

Arranged alphabetically by author, translator, and anonymous and pseudonymous title, and then by title so that the science fiction devotee who happens to be reading *Frankenstein* can look up Mary Wollstonecraft Shelley and find out what other books she wrote, and the Goethe admirer can note the persistent popularity of *The Sorrows of Young Werther.*

J391.   Mayo, Robert D. *The English Novel in the Magazines, 1740-1815, with a Catalogue of 1375 Magazine Novels and Novelettes.* Evanston, Ill.: Northwestern Univ. Press, 1962. 695pp. PR851.M37

A scholarly, well-documented study with notes, glossary, chronological index, and a 250-page alphabetical catalog of titles, names of authors, editors, translators, and periodicals that feature long prose fiction. The theories and practices of both periodicals and authors are examined and illustrated. An excellent source of reliable information.

J392.   Streeter, Harold W. *The Eighteenth Century English Novel in French Translation: A Bibliographical Study.* New York: Blom, 1936; reissue 1970. 256pp. PR851.S7   016.823'5

This examination of comparative literature begins in the seventeenth century and goes through Defoe, Rousseau, Swift, Smollett, Fielding, Richardson, Sterne, Radcliffe, Lewis, and many others. It also discusses types of novel such as satirical, moral, philosophical, and sentimental. The bibliography lists 520 titles.

Background reading for fiction

J393.   McKillop, Alan D. *Early Masters of English Fiction.* Lawrence: Univ. Press of Kansas, 1956; rpt. 1979. 233pp. PR851.M33   823'.5'09

In his critical survey of novels by Defoe, Richardson, Fielding, Smollett, and Sterne, McKillop considers both cultural background and biography as he analyzes character, theme, and plot, thereby producing an excellent overview of prose in the eighteenth century.

J394.   Skilton, David. *The English Novel: Defoe to the Victorians.* New York: Harper, 1977. 200pp. PR821.S54   823'.03

This fine contribution to the field has acquired a reputation for reliable background information on Defoe, Richardson, Fielding, Sterne, Austen, Monk Lewis, Moore, Scott, Dickens, the Brontës, Hardy, Gissing, James, and others.

It also contains discussions of quixotic and picaresque fiction and the Gothic and Romantic influences. Bibliography and index.

J395.   Watt, Ian P. *Rise of the Novel: Studies in Defoe, Richardson, and Fielding*. Berkeley: Univ. of California Press, 1957. 319pp. Paperback. PR851.W3   823.09

Still on the required reading list, this is concerned with concepts like realism, the reading public, and their relation to the rise of the novel in the eighteenth century.

See also

    Plots and Characters in the Fiction of Eighteenth-Century English Authors (W1590)

DRAMA

Surveys

*J397.   *Revels History of Drama in English*. Ed. John C. Loftis et al. Vol. 5, 1660–1750. London: Methuen, 1977. 331pp. PR625.R442   822'.009

Social and historical background, type of drama (political, Spanish, romance, social comedy), the influence of the monarchs, the audience, the rise and fall of theaters and their companies, and the dramatists themselves, from Shadwell to Gay, from Aphra Behn to Otway. Illustrations, bibliography, and index. Use this with Harbage's *Annals of English Drama, 975–1700* (J338). For coverage of late eighteenth-century drama, see J425. See the main entry (G114) for information on the other volumes in this survey.

J398.   Hume, Robert D. *The Development of English Drama in the Late Seventeenth Century*. New York: Oxford Univ. Press, 1976. 554pp. PR691.H8   822'.4'09

Choice (W1557) says this is "The best historical and critical survey of the subject we have ever had." Five hundred plays are surveyed chronologically within their political and social backgrounds. Important—and good reading as well.

Basic guides

*J399.   *English Drama, 1660–1800: A Guide to Information Sources*. Ed. Frederick M. Link. Vol. 9 of Gale Information Guide Library (A8). Detroit: Gale, 1976. 374pp. Z2014.D7.L55   [PR701]   016.822

Reviewers give highest praise to this bibliography, saying it is one of the best in the Gale series. It provides information on background materials and research on 155 dramatists including Dryden, Congreve, and Sheridan. Accurate, complete, and discerning.

Bibliographies of primary works

**J400.   *The London Stage, 1660–1800: A Calendar of Plays, Entertainments & Afterpieces, Together with Casts, Box-Receipts, and Contemporary Comment, compiled from the Playbills, Newspapers and Theatrical*

Diaries of the Period. Ed. William Van Lennep, Emmett L. Avery, Arthur H. Scouten, George W. Stone, and C. Beecher Hogan. 11 vols. Carbondale: Southern Illinois Univ. Press, 1965–69. Index, 1979. PN1582.G72.L65   792'.09421

The eleven volumes appear in five parts: part 1: 1660–1700 in 1 vol.; part 2: 1700–1729 in 2 vols.; part 3: 1729–1747 in 2 vols.; part 4: 1747–1776 in 3 vols.; and part 5: 1776–1800 in 3 vols. Each volume contains the names of all the plays and related performances presented in London on a given day (such as Dryden's "Song for St. Cecilia's Day," 22 Nov. 1687) with as much relevant information on the event as could be gathered.

This is the definitive study in Restoration and eighteenth-century theater, the culmination of forty years of scholarship. The chronological entries themselves are interesting reading because they include scholarly comments as well as pertinent excerpts from the diary of Samuel Pepys, who apparently was hard to please. Facts and figures are provided on financing, management, costumes, size and response of audience, licensing, scenery, ticket prices, and playhouses. The long, critical introductions to each chronological section are exceptionally valuable and are now available individually in paperback. Each annual season is prefaced with an introduction; and each volume contains an index of dramatists, composers, subjects, farces, titles of songs and plays, pantomimes, operas, oratorios, critics, dances, and entertainments. The main index to the eleven volumes vastly increases the coverage, with 25,000 entries and 500,000 references to all names and titles mentioned in the text.

Since all eleven volumes have been converted to computer tape, the London Stage Information Bank is now receiving queries concerning the identification of characters mentioned casually in eighteenth-century literature, the location of quotations, and the roles and real names of the casts. The exhaustive index will encourage scholarly studies on, for example, eighteenth-century theatrical dance, the rise of melodrama, biographical studies of actors, and command performances as a reflection of royal patronage of drama. This is the source to use if the student wants to find out the first-night response to John Gay's *The Beggar's Opera*, the titles of plays that were running concurrently on 6 June 1718, or contemporary opinion of Goldsmith's *She Stoops to Conquer*. See also *London Stage, 1800–1900* (J428), *London Stage, 1890–1899* (J487), *London Stage, 1900–1909* (J553), and *London Stage, 1910–1919* (J553).

Criticism

*J401. *Restoration and Eighteenth Century Theatre Research: A Bibliographical Guide, 1900–1968.* Ed. Carl J. Stratman et al. Carbondale: Southern Illinois Univ. Press, 1971. 811pp. Z2014.D7.S854   016.822'5'09

A cumulation of over six thousand annotated subject entries on all phases of drama and the theater during the Restoration and eighteenth century. Authors (such as Milton, Johnson, Dryden, Fielding), the influence of Shakespeare, actors, musicians, audiences, scenery, type characters, and about 780 other subject headings are arranged alphabetically with the critical works or editions listed chronologically under each entry. Accurate, comprehensive work is ensured with Stratman's name on the title page and an editorial staff that examined eighty-two percent of the titles before writing the descriptive (not evaluative) annotations. The index includes all names and subjects but not, unfortunately, the titles of plays.

Since the cutoff date is 1967, students will have to go to the journal of the same name for current annual bibliographies (J403). Stratman has superseded his own earlier cumulation of bibliographies from the 1961–68 issues of that journal because he includes them in this volume and extends coverage back to 1900 and over into many other sources.

Series

J402.   Regents Restoration Drama Series. Lincoln: Univ. of Nebraska Press, 1965–81.

A series of special editions of plays written between 1660 and 1737. Thirty-five are currently in print: by Behn, Centlivre, Cibber, Congreve, Crowne, Dryden, Etherege, Farquhar, Fielding, Gay, N. Lee, Lillo, Otway, Rowe, Shadwell, Southerne, Steele, Tate, Vanbrugh, and Wycherley. The editors explain in the introductions that they have made new collations of the sixteenth- and seventeenth-century texts, standardized and modernized the spelling, noted the variant substantive readings, added textual notes, and bracketed the additions they feel are necessary for the copy text stage directions. (See the Glossary in this guide for explanations of these terms.)

The complete list of titles can usually be found in *PTLA* (W1172) under University of Nebraska. Libraries either add author cards to the catalog or insert a unit card for Regents Restoration Drama Series and write in each title as it is purchased.

Indexed in *MLAIB* (D31).

Periodicals

J403.   *Restoration and 18th Century Theatre Research (RECTR)*. Chicago: Loyola Univ., 1962–78, 1981– . 2/yr. Former title, 1962–May 1963: *17th and 18th Century Theatre Research*. PN2592.R46

Critical studies, occasional book notices or reviews, news and notes of research in progress, and each November since 1962 a bibliography of research for the previous year. Those for 1961–68 have been incorporated into Stratman's bibliography of drama scholarship for 1900–68 (J401).

Indexed in *ABELL* (D32), *Am. Hum. Ind.* (P738), *Arts and Hum. Cit. Ind.* (F47), *MLAIB* (D31).

Background reading for drama

J404.   Loftis, John C. *Politics of Drama in Augustan England*. Oxford: Clarendon, 1963. 173pp. PR714.P6.L6   822.509

This well-argued thesis maintains that politics of the eighteenth century influenced the form and themes of its comedy and tragedy, the fate of its theaters and productions, and the taste of its audiences.

J405.1   Sherbo, Arthur. *English Sentimental Drama*. East Lansing: Michigan
State Univ. Press, 1957. 181pp. PR635.S4.S5   822.09
   A play-by-play scrutiny of sentimental drama as a genre—its language, tone,
subject matter, exaggerations, delusions, illusions, popularity, and faults.

POETRY

Bibliographies of primary works

**J408.   Foxon, David F. *English Verse, 1701-1750: A Catalogue of Separately
Printed Poems with Notes on Contemporary Collected Editions*. 2 vols.
London: Cambridge Univ. Press, 1975. Z2014.P7.F69 [PR551]
016.821
   This catalog has rapidly gained the respect and confidence of scholars, who
now refer to "Foxon" as they do to "Wing" (J370). Foxon identifies poetry
written during the first half of the eighteenth century, just as McBurney (J388)
and Beasley (J389) identify fiction of that era. Expertly prepared by an editor
with many years' experience in the British Library, it includes all information
he thought might be of interest and value in identifying each work. The catalog
is arranged alphabetically by author or first word of the title, with an excellent
introduction and excellent indexes (chronological, subject, first line, printers,
and booksellers).

*J409.   *Variorum Commentary on the Poems of John Milton*. Ed. Douglas Bush
et al. 7 vols. New York: Columbia Univ. Press, 1970– . Vol. 1, 1970;
vol. 2 (3 pts.), 1972; vol. 3, in preparation; vol. 4, 1975. PR3593.V3
821'.4
   An example of excellence. This is the type of research aid that all literature
and methods of research professors should encourage their students to consult.
Using the accepted text of the Columbia edition of Milton's works as a basis,
it contributes a wealth of information that will increase the understanding and
appreciation of the poetry, which is what "research" is all about. As a variorum
commentary, it explains the history and meaning of individual words and general
ideas, and it cites all possible interpretations as they might have been influenced
by the literary background or the language itself. For example, in the eighty
pages given to "On the Morning of Christ's Nativity," the student can find
one section on the dating and circumstances of the composition, another on
literary sources and the ode form, a chronological survey of all criticism on the
poem between 1918 and 1969, and a line-by-line analysis of the allusions and
language with comparisons to other odes and references to published criticism
for each line. The benefits from exposure to such scholarship are obvious, and
yet many, many professors want nothing more from their students than an emo-
tional "reaction" to the poem itself.

J409.1   *English Poetry, 1660-1800: A Guide to Information Sources*. Ed.
Donald C. Mell. Vol. 40 of Gale Information Guide Library (A8).
Detroit: Gale, 1982. 501pp. Z2014.P7.M44 [PR551]   016.821
   Another competent volume in the Gale series. This expands on and up-
dates the poetry sections of some of the basic guides cited earlier in this section.

See also

From Dryden to Cowper (J215)

Background reading for Restoration and eighteenth-century literature

J410.   Geduld, Harry M. *Prince of Publishers: A Study of the Work and Career of Jacob Tonson.* Bloomington: Indiana Univ. Press, 1969. 245pp. AS36.I385 no.66   655.4'24

Much more than simply a biography of Tonson, the eighteenth-century publisher of Dryden, Milton, Shakespeare, and the classics. Geduld assembles anecdotes about the Kit-Cat Club members, records the agreements and disagreements between author and publisher, and mentions a host of memorable names and events for a realistic recreation of the era when the business of publishing became an art.

J411.   Greene, Donald J. *The Age of Exuberance: Backgrounds to English Eighteenth-Century Literature.* New York: Random, 1970. 184pp. Paperback. DA380.G7   914.2'03'7

Greene's book is perfect for the supplementary reading list in a survey of English literature course because of its practical study aids. Students are grateful for brief chronologies at the beginning of each chapter and the special sections on such subjects as the church, art, music, sculpture, painting, the business community, empiricism, and deism. The discussions cover events from about 1660 to 1780.

J412.   Loftis, John C. *Comedy and Society from Congreve to Fielding.* Stanford, Calif.: Stanford Univ. Press, 1959; rpt. New York: AMS, 1979. 154pp. PR714.C6.L6   822'.052

A convincing explanation of the interaction between the emerging middle class and the theater of the early eighteenth century, with summaries and analyses of numerous plays.

Additional reference sources for the eighteenth century

Biographical Dictionary of Actors . . . in London, 1660–1800 (W1141)
Dictionary of Women Writers, 1660–1800 (W1641)
Greene, Donald J. (W1484)
Lives of the Georgian Age (W1144)
Microtext: Wells, *Three Centuries* (G112); Bergquist, *Three Centuries . . . : A Checklist* (G113)
Regents Critics Series (W1363)
Regents Renaissance Drama Series (J342)
Stratman, *Bibliography of English Printed Tragedy* (J209)

Nineteenth-Century English Literature

Basic guides

*J415. *New Cambridge Bibliography of English Literature (New CBEL)*. Ed.
George Watson. Vol. 3, 1800–1900. Cambridge, Eng.: Cambridge
Univ. Press, 1969. 1956 cols. Z2011.N45 [PR83] 016.82

A revision of both vol. 3 of the original *CBEL* of 1940 and the supplement
of 1957. Coverage extends from literary history and literary relations with individual European countries to Wordsworth, Coleridge, and dozens of Romantic authors, through the novelists (Scott to Kipling), dramatists, prose critics
(Lamb to Pater), historians (Macaulay, Froude), evangelicals, educators,
newspapers and magazines, and Anglo-Irish literature to Yeats and Synge.

This would be the appropriate starting place for research on Southey, for
instance, or for information on the scope and frequency of translations of Byron
during the nineteenth century, or for an authoritative statement on the best
editions and biographies of Austen. Its aim, in fact, is "to represent the whole
of English studies . . . in primary and secondary materials." The analytical table
of contents furnishes quick indication of the work's scope. The index is to primary
authors and certain subject headings. Students would be wise to begin their
research, however, with the main cumulative index to all four volumes which
was completed in 1979, for it analyzes the contents much more thoroughly. For
a description of the complete edition, see *New CBEL* (J175).

Annual bibliographies that will update the preceding work

ABELL (D32) is the most comprehensive, with 2,535 entries in 1977.

MLAIB (D31) has 1,517 entries in its 1980 section on the nineteenth century.

Year's Wk. Eng. Stud. (D33) has a ninety-page review of research in 1977
on the nineteenth century.

Students should also consult the appropriate abstracting services (E38–43) and
indexing services (F45–53) for recent publications.

Indexes

*J416. *Poole's Index to Periodical Literature, 1802–1906*. New York: Smith,
1882–1908. Vol. 1: 1802–1881, with supplements (vols. 2–6,
1882–1906). AI3.P7 016.05

An alphabetical subject index to about 470 nineteenth-century periodicals
in English, with a few title entries for poems and stories. Subject headings are
capricious, however, so students must approach the contents with more than
a little determination and imagination.

William F. Poole was a student at Yale when he started this, the first
periodical index, but from his 154-page beginning it went through another half
century of editions and supplements and eventually indexed 12,241 volumes
and cited 590,000 articles. It was the only index to nineteenth-century periodicals
until the publication of the *Wellesley Index to Victorian Periodicals, 1824–1900*
(J466), which, although more accurate, indexes only about fifty periodicals.

As an index to periodical literature, *Poole's* holds a wealth of possibilities. Students might want to locate the periodical installments of *Great Expectations*, a nineteenth-century review of Hardy's *Tess*, an early article on Hardy's women, the wealth of nineteenth-century periodical literature dealing with Shelley, or verification of the statement that Byron's *Manfred* received no critical attention at all in the 470 periodicals indexed by Poole. Because entries indicate only the volume number, students must consult a master chart to ascertain the date.

Book reviews may be listed under the author of the book, the subject, the title, or "Recent Books," but all critical articles are found under the subject— "Nature" or "Wordsworth," for example. For public response to Darwin, the student might have to look under "Species, Origin of," but contemporary opinion of Oscar Wilde would be found under W. Some of this confusion has been alleviated by the publication of J417.

J417.   *Cumulative Author Index for* Poole's Index to Periodical Literature 1802–1906. Ed. C. Edward Wall. Ann Arbor, Mich.: Pierian, 1971. 488pp. AI3.W3   050

This, the first attempt to make Poole's information readily available to scholars, is a computer-produced index to over 300,000 names found in the multivolume index, which itself was arranged only according to subject. Included are such names as Dumas, Scott, Poe, Huxley, Chekhov, Tolstoy, Twain (and Clemens, with no cross-references), Veblen, Hardy, and Brandeis, so comparative and interdisciplinary studies as well as literary research should benefit. The master date chart in *Poole's Index* is not difficult to use, but students may prefer to consult J418.

J418.   Bell, Marion V., and Jean C. Bacon. Poole's Index: *Date and Volume Key.* Monograph no. 19. Chicago: Assn. of Coll. and Research Libraries, 1957. 61pp. AI3.P7   016.05

J419.   *Palmer's Index to the Times Newspaper, 1790–1941.* London: Palmer, 1868–1941. Quarterly. AI21.T5

One urgent need in nineteenth-century bibliographic control is a cumulative index to the *London Times*, for *Palmer's Index* (later called *The Official Index* and *The Times Index*) was issued quarterly and of course requires a time-consuming search in its alphabetical subject arrangement. Subject headings are interesting (Accidents, Bankruptcies, Deaths, Duels, Fires, Inquests, Murders, Publications, Books or Reviews), but because they are not always consistent from one issue or one decade to the next, cumulation will be extremely difficult. In spite of the problems, the index undoubtedly contains invaluable information that will eventually be extracted by some determined scholar with access to a computer. Entries can be found, for instance, that lead to contemporary responses to Byron's death in 1824 and to Henry James's birthday celebrations.

Periodicals—Reference books

J420.   Madden, Lionel, and Diana Dixon. *The Nineteenth-Century Periodical Press in Britain: A Bibliography of Modern Studies, 1901–1971.* Supplement to *Victorian Periodicals Newsletter* (J473), Sept. 1975. 76pp. New York: Garland, 1976. 280pp. Z6956.G6.M3   [PN5117]   016.072

Nineteenth-century authors who were connected in any way with periodicals may be listed here. William Hazlitt's connection with *Blackwood's* and the *Edinburgh Review*, Swinburne's with the *Spectator*, Dickens as journalist and serialist (ninety entries), Matthew Arnold as drama critic—these and many other familiar names are to be found in the contributor-editor index. Other indexes list bibliographies and surveys of the nineteenth-century periodical in general, as well as specific studies of each individual periodical. This highly specialized work with 2,600 annotated entries will, in spite of numerous minor errors, permit extensive research in a relatively new field.

Criticism

J421.   *Nineteenth-Century Literary Criticism*. Ed. Laurie L. Harris. Detroit: Gale, 1981– . In progress (vol. 6, 1984). PN761.N5   809'.04

Each volume contains excerpts from a wide range of nineteenth-century criticism on thirty authors who lived between 1800 and 1900, with birth and death dates, brief biographical information, a list of principal works, and an annotated checklist of criticism.

FICTION

Periodicals

*J422.   *Nineteenth-Century Fiction (NCF)*. Berkeley: Univ. of California Press, 1949– . Quarterly. PR873.T76   823.809

Established in 1945 as the *Trollopian* and expanded four years later, because of obvious need, to include the whole century. The articles and news notes are concerned with English and American authors such as Poe, Trollope, Melville, Twain, Austen, and the Brontës. The excellent book reviews treat English and American fiction in alternate issues. The absence of bibliographies is regrettable, but a fine cumulative index to vols. 1–30 (1945–76) leads to authors, subjects, and book reviews (1977; 196pp.).

Indexed in *ABELL* (D32), *Abst. Eng. Stud.* (E38), *America* (E43), *Arts and Hum. Cit. Ind.* (F47), *Current Bk. Rev. Cit.* (W1564), *Hist. Abst.* (E43), *Hum. Ind.* (F45), *Index to Bk. Rev. Hum.* (W1560), *MLAIB* (D31), *Romantic Movement: A . . . Bibliography* (J443).

See also

British Short Fiction in the Nineteenth Century (G75)

PROSE

Basic guides

J423.   *English Prose and Criticism in the Nineteenth Century: A Guide to Information Sources*. Ed. Harris W. Wilson and Diana Long Hoeveler.

Vol. 18 of Gale Information Guide Library (A8). Detroit: Gale, 1979. 437pp. Z2014.P795.W54 016.08

A carefully selected list of surveys, histories, background studies, and primary and secondary material for thirty-four authors including Arnold, Bentham, Carlyle, Coleridge, De Quincey, Lamb, Mill, Stevenson, Macaulay, Darwin, and Huxley.

DRAMA

Surveys

*J425.   *Revels History of Drama in English*. Ed. Michael R. Booth et al. Vol. 6, 1750–1880. London: Methuen, 1975. 304pp. PR625.R44   822'.009

A descriptive guide to London theaters of the era, with an interesting chapter on the demands of the audience and eminently readable chapters on the problems of law and copyrights, stage machinery, the Garrick era, wars, players, and playwrights, from the Licensing Act of 1737 to Strindberg's first play in 1881. Numerous illustrations, index. See the main entry (G114) for information on other volumes in this survey.

Basic guides

J426.   *English Drama and Theatre, 1800–1900: A Guide to Information Sources*. Ed. Leonard W. Conolly and J. Peter Wearing. Vol. 12 of Gale Information Guide Library (A8). Detroit: Gale, 1978. 508pp. Z2014.D7.C72 [PR721] 016.822'7'08

The definitive bibliography for this subject and century, with three thousand entries, mostly annotated, by and about 110 dramatists and all aspects of the drama—history, theaters, critics, costume, and much more. Remember that this is limited to English and Scottish (not Irish) authors and to those who published during the century. Use this with Arnott and Robinson's *English Theatrical Literature* (J210), and keep it up to date with the annual bibliography in *Nineteenth-Century Theatre Research* (J430).

Bibliographies of primary works

J427.   *Nineteenth- and Twentieth-Century Drama: A Selective Bibliography of English Language Works*. Ed. Lawrence S. Thompson. Boston: Hall, 1975. 456pp. Z2014.D7.T5 [PR721] 016.822'008

This bibliography lists all the major drama in English of these two centuries: 3,209 entries, with author, title, subject, and illustrator indexes. The volume locates hitherto unknown or inaccessible titles and provides information about purchasing copies from the General Microfilm Company.

J428.   *London Stage, 1800–1900: A Documentary Record and Calendar of Performances*. Ed. Joseph Donohue and James Ellis. In preparation.

This will include a calendar of performances, a directory of London theaters and music halls, a register of production statistics, a checklist of theatrical periodicals, a locator list and survey of theater archives, a bibliography of the drama itself, and information on theatrical personnel. See also *London Stage,*

1890-1899 (J487), *London Stage, 1900-1909* (J553), *London Stage, 1910-1919* (J553), and *London Stage, 1660-1800* (J400).

Microtext

J429.   Freedley, George, and Allardyce Nicoll. *English and American Plays of the Nineteenth Century.* New York: Readex Microprint, 1965– . In progress.

An ambitious project to provide microprint reproductions of early editions of every available nineteenth-century play. It is an astonishing collection that most large university libraries will own because they are unable (or do not want) to purchase the rare and costly printed books. The 6" by 9" microprint cards are made of paper guaranteed to last for three hundred years and are generally arranged alphabetically by author in the microprint boxes. Most libraries own microprint readers. Students should learn to operate them. The plays are also being cataloged for availability on OCLC (see Glossary).

This is an excellent source for obscure titles or authors. Freedley and Nicoll had intended to microprint all 25,000 plays written during the nineteenth century, but they were able to process only about 4,500. Their work is being continued by James Ellis and Joseph Donohue (see also J428). For a description of the recently completed index to the American drama titles, see P801. For information on microprints of earlier drama, see G112–13.

Periodicals

J430.   *Nineteenth-Century Theatre Research* (*NCTR*). Edmonton: Univ. of Alberta, 1974– . 2/yr. PN1851.N55   792.0942

Features book reviews, an annual bibliography, research in progress, notes and queries, and news of professional and student productions.

Indexed in *ABELL* (D32), *Abst. Eng. Stud.* (E38), *Am. Hum. Ind.* (P738), *Arts and Hum. Cit. Ind.* (F47), *MLAIB* (D31).

Background reading for nineteenth-century English literature

For background reading related solely to the Romantic era, see J449–52. For background reading related solely to the Victorian era, see J481–84, J486, J491–92, J495–504.

J432.   Altick, Richard D. *The English Common Reader: A Social History of the Mass Reading Public, 1800-1900.* Chicago: Univ. of Chicago Press, 1957. 430pp. Z1003.A57   028.9

This survey examines facts and draws conclusions about the literate world of the Victorian reader, with its thousands of periodicals, its Useful Knowledge Society, yellow-backs, the range of best-sellers from *Self-Help* to *Uncle Tom's Cabin*, and an eight-year-old boy who enjoyed the Apocrypha as much as *Arabian Nights* but found *Rasselas* dull. Good reading, with all the essential information about the social upheavals of the nineteenth century and the emergence of the common person as a reader.

J433.   Kermode, Frank. *The Romantic Image*. New York: Vintage, 1964,
c1957. 171pp. PN1111.K4   808.1
Kermode offers an explanation of "romantic" ideas as they developed in
the nineteenth century and the ways they are used, abused, unused, and mis-
used in the twentieth. The style will not appeal to everyone, but the ideas are
important.

Additional reference sources for the nineteenth century

J433.1   *British Manuscript Diaries* (W1056)
Nineteenth Century Short Title Catalogue. 5 vols. Newcastle upon
Tyne: Avero Publications, 1984–   . In progress.
Studies in English Literature, 1500-1900 (J320), Autumn issue

Romantic Literature

Surveys

J434.   Renwick, William L. *English Literature, 1789-1815*. Vol. 9 of OHEL
(J174). Oxford: Clarendon, 1963. 293pp. PR447.R4   820.903
A survey of the social and cultural influences that produced such authors
as Radcliffe, Crabbe, Darwin, Wordsworth, Austen, Blake, and Scott. Reviewers
are not so enthusiastic about this volume in the OHEL series as they are about
the one by Bush (J300), for instance. Nevertheless, research students will want
to read and consider its conclusions. Bibliographies (pp. 254–89). Chronological
table (pp. 242–53).

J435.   Jack, Ian R. *English Literature, 1815-1832*. Vol. 10 of OHEL (J174).
Oxford: Clarendon, 1963. 643pp. PR457.J24
The tenth volume in the OHEL series is useful for background informa-
tion. This one is concerned with Keats, Shelley, Byron, Hazlitt, Lamb, De
Quincey, Scott, Peacock, Leigh Hunt, and numerous minor authors.
Bibliographies (pp. 452–631). Chronological table (pp. 440–57).

*J436.   Jackson, James R. de J. *Poetry of the Romantic Period*. Vol. 4 of
Routledge History of English Poetry (J215). Boston: Routledge, 1980.
352pp. PR502.R58 [PR571]   821'.009
Reviewers have expressed gratitude for the extensive treatment of minor
poets, discovering in the new background a greater understanding of the major
authors. Jackson himself says he has written "a history of poems rather than
of poets." Excellent comprehensive chronological table.

Basic guides

*J437.   Jordan, Frank, Jr., ed. *The English Romantic Poets: A Review of
Research and Criticism*. 3rd ed. New York: MLA, 1972. 480pp. Paper-
back. 4th ed. projected for 1985. PR590.J6   016.821'7'09
The 1972 edition was most welcome, for the 1956 copyright date of the

previous review of research by Thomas M. Raysor limited its value severely. The edition announced for 1983 is cause for celebration. The current volume is still essential, however, because the essays on Wordsworth, Coleridge, Byron, Shelley, Keats, and, of special value, the Romantic movement were written by authorities who describe and evaluate all the important bibliographies, editions, biographies, and studies up to 1971. Index of editors and critical authors only. An index of all proper names mentioned in the text would have permitted the student to locate a wealth of material on the interaction of people and ideas throughout the whole era.

J438.   Houtchens, Carolyn W., and Lawrence H. Houtchens. *The English Romantic Poets and Essayists: A Review of Research and Criticism*. Rev. ed. New York: New York Univ. Press, for MLA, 1966. 395pp. PR590.H6   820.9007

Essays by noted scholars such as Frye, Schneider, and Nurmi evaluate the scholarship on Blake, Lamb, Hazlitt, Scott, Southey, Campbell, Moore, Landor, De Quincey, and Carlyle. Each important biography, bibliography, edition, and critical work is analyzed for its contributions and weaknesses. This answers such questions as "Which edition of Hunt's autobiography includes a good critical essay evaluating the man himself?" and "What has already been written on Blake's poem 'Holy Thursday'?"

Every student should read this review of research before embarking on the study of the Romantic period, for it selects the best critics, editors, and titles, shows the relationship between all the literary figures of the early nineteenth century, and in addition, makes pleasant reading. The proper name index provides access to all the important names mentioned in the text. Be on the alert for a new edition.

J439.   Fogle, Richard H. *Romantic Poets and Prose Writers*. Goldentree Bibliographies (W1291). New York: Appleton (Meredith), 1967. 87pp. Paperback. Z2013.F6   016.8208'008

A particularly well-organized guide to the scholarship on fourteen Romantic authors including Blake, Byron, Coleridge, Scott, Shelley, Wordsworth, and others. Outstanding feature—separate entries for many individual poems such as "The Rime of the Ancient Mariner" and fiction such as the Waverley novels, with their critical works so the student will not have to scan many pages looking for pertinent-sounding titles. Important scholarship is marked with asterisks, and there is a proper name index. This is still a convenient source because of its size and selectivity, but Reiman's *Guide* (J440) is, of course, much more up to date for research information on the poets, and Wilson and Hoeveler's (J423) is more comprehensive and recent for prose.

*J440.   *English Romantic Poetry, 1800-1835: A Guide to Information Sources*. Ed. Donald H. Reiman. Vol. 27 of Gale Information Guide Library (A8). Detroit: Gale, 1979. 294pp. Z2014.P7.R46 [PR590] 016.821'7'09

This scholarly production will be of measurable value to all students. It has annotations that evaluate and compare, symbols that indicate titles appropriate for beginning or advanced students, long sections on background studies, and lists of works by and about the five major Romantics (Wordsworth, Coleridge, Byron, Keats, and Shelley) and twelve minor poets. One of the best edited volumes of this series.

Criticism

J441.   *Romantics Reviewed: Contemporary Reviews of British Romantic Writers.* Ed. Donald H. Reiman. 9 vols. New York: Garland, 1972. PR590.R43   821'.7'09

Facsimiles of every significant review written between 1793 and 1824 of the five major Romantics, plus many reviews for the lesser figures, totaling almost one thousand articles from over one hundred periodicals. Research in early periodicals is usually tedious, expensive, and unsuccessful. This nine-volume set should encourage students to investigate the unusual effect that reviewers had on the Romantics during these years and to question the power of editors, periodicals, and headlines.

J442.   *Literary Reviews in British Periodicals . . . with a Supplementary List of General (Non-Review) Articles on Literary Subjects: A Bibliography.* Ed. William S. Ward. 4 vols. New York: Garland, 1972–79.

1789–1797. 1979. Z2013.W36   [PR442]   016.820'9'006
1798–1820. 2 vols. 1972. Z2013.W36   016.809'034
1821–26. 1977. Z2013.W36   [PR453]   016.809'034

Reprints of thirty thousand reviews of the poetry, novels, and essays of both British and American authors during this era. The author's reputation, the critic's bias, the reader's preference are clearly visible. An interesting project that greatly facilitates research in that era. A welcome, useful project.

Annual bibliographies

*J443.   *Romantic Movement: A Selective and Critical Bibliography for [———].* New York: Garland, 1979–   . Annual. Z6514.R7.R76   [PE1.E53]

Master Cumulated Index, 1972: The Romantic Movement Bibliography, 1937–1970. Ed. Aubrey C. Elkins, Jr., and Lorne J. Forstner. Foreword by David V. Erdman. 7 vols. Ann Arbor, Mich.: Pierian, 1971. Z6514.R7.R65   016.809'894

This annual bibliography appeared as a September supplement to *ELN* (J186) from 1964 through 1978 and before that in *PQ* (1950–63, H154) and *ELH* (1936–49, H144). There were no cumulative indexes to any of these three bibliographies, so access to the material was cumbersome until the publication of the seven-volume Master Cumulated Index in 1971. This retains the chronological arrangement of all bibliographies in *ELH*, *PQ*, and *ELN* from 1937 to 1970 with their abstracts and book review citations, but the author-main entry-reviewer index and subject index in vol. 7 give the student several ways to locate entries in the other six volumes. It is still, however, a long, long search for any one specific article in, for instance, the list of two hundred entries for Shelley.

A title index with a list of criticism for each poem would certainly have been a good editorial decision.

The scope of the annual bibliography is broad: English, French, German, Italian, and Spanish Romanticism extending frequently beyond the years 1789 to 1837. It is the source to consult, for example, when looking for information on comparative literature studies linking Keats and Yeats, or for Romantic tendencies in Milton. It selects only the most scholarly books and the most outstanding articles from 460 journals. The descriptive, evaluative annotations and book reviews, in addition to the notations of current book reviews that can be found in other sources, are great timesavers.

Arrangement is first by country, then by general studies and literary criticism. and finally alphabetically by literary author and critic. No American literature is covered except in its relationship to English studies.

Periodicals

*J444.   *Keats-Shelley Journal (K-SJ)*. New York: Keats-Shelley Journal Assn.,
         1952– . Annual. PR4836.A145   821.705

An important source of information on the Romantic period, with a cumulative index for vols. 1–10 (1952–61), in vol. 10. The journal includes scholarly articles, long book reviews, news of meetings, acquisitions, queries, unpublished letters, and—of greatest interest—a comprehensive, international bibliography of books, articles, dissertations, and phonorecords concerned with the Romantic era and all early Romantic poets, not just Keats and Shelley. Annotations and references to current book reviews are included for important titles.

Arrangement is alphabetical by major author (Byron, Hazlitt, Hunt, Keats, and Shelley). The index to titles and proper names expands the accessibility considerably because it lists Blake, Wordsworth, Coleridge, Lamb, Fanny Brawne, *Blackwood's Magazine*, critics, and other subjects referred to in the entries.

Indexed in *ABELL* (D32), *Arts and Hum. Cit. Ind.* (F47), *Current Bk. Rev. Cit.* (W1564), *Hum. Ind.* (F45), *MLAIB* (D31), *Romantic Movement: A . . . Bibliography* (J443), *Year's Wk. Eng. Stud.* (D33).

The bibliography has been published as a separate issue since 1968. The first twenty-four bibliographies have been reprinted in their original chronological order so that students can trace trends in criticism. The indexes to titles and proper names provide easy access to all issues in the compilations:

> *Keats, Shelley, Byron, Hunt and Their Circles: A Bibliography, 1950-62.*
> Ed. David B. Green and Edwin G. Wilson. Lincoln: Univ. of Nebraska
> Press, 1964. 323pp. Z2013.K4   016.821'7'09
> *Keats, Shelley, Byron, Hunt and Their Circles: A Bibliography, July 1,
> 1962-December 31, 1974.* Ed. Robert A. Hartley. Lincoln: Univ. of
> Nebraska Press, 1978. 487pp. Z2013.K42 [PR457] 016.821'7'09

*J445.   *Wordsworth Circle (WC; TWC)*. Philadelphia: Temple Univ., 1970– .
         Quarterly. PR1.W67   820'.9'14

A small periodical containing articles, notes and queries, abstracts of new books, information on research in progress, auctions, and other news. Its scope extends beyond Wordsworth to Coleridge, Hazlitt, De Quincey, Lamb, Southey,

and many other writers of the Romantic period. There are no bibliographies and no cumulative indexes as yet, however, so the student will have to scan the issues for information until the contents are indexed by the services listed below.
Indexed in *ABELL* (D32), *Abst. Eng. Stud.* (E38), *Am. Hum. Ind.* (P738), *Arts and Hum. Cit. Ind.* (F47), *MLAIB* (D31).

J446.   *Studies in Romanticism (SIR).* Boston, Mass.: Boston Univ., 1961–   .
Quarterly. PN751.S8   809.91'4
A good periodical for scholarly articles and long book reviews, but there are no bibliographies and no cumulative index, so its value as a research tool is limited. It does, however, extend its scope to comparative and interdisciplinary studies including German Romanticism, Romanticism and history, psychoanalysis, and structuralism. It occasionally publishes issues on special subjects such as Keats or Romanticism and modern poetry.
Indexed in *ABELL* (D32), *Abst. Eng. Stud.* (E38), *Arts and Hum. Cit. Ind.* (F47), *Current Bk. Rev. Cit.* (W1564), *Hum. Ind.* (F45), *Index to Bk. Rev. Hum.* (W1560), *MLAIB* (D31), *Romantic Movement: A . . . Bibliography* (J443).

J447.   *Editing the Romantics Newsletter.* Newark: Univ. of Delaware, 1978–   .
Editor's notes concerning the policies and problems involved in editing the Romantics, queries and answers, and news notes. See Textual Criticism (W1610–23).

Background reading for the Romantic era

*J449.   Abrams, Meyer H. *The Mirror and the Lamp: Romantic Theory and the Critical Tradition.* New York: Norton, 1953. 406pp. Paperback. PN769.R7.A2   801
Essential for understanding Shelley, Keats, Wordsworth, Coleridge, and others concerned with Romantic poetry and criticism.

J450.   Bloom, Harold. *The Visionary Company: A Reading of English Romantic Poetry.* Rev. ed. Ithaca: Cornell Univ. Press, 1971. 477pp. PR590.B39   821'.7'09
The definitive statement on the nature of Romanticism.

J451.   Bowra, Sir Cecil M. *The Romantic Imagination.* New York: Oxford Univ. Press, 1969, c1949. 306pp. Paperback. PR590.B6   821.709
This study of Romanticism as a historical movement from imagination to reality has become a classic. The traditional Romantics are discussed—Blake, Coleridge, Wordsworth, Shelley, Keats, Byron—and then others who modified their conception of Romanticism such as Poe, Swinburne, and the Rossettis. Students should put this on their required browsing list.

*J452.   Lowes, John Livingston. *The Road to Xanadu: A Study in the Ways of the Imagination.* Rev. ed. Boston: Houghton, 1927. 339pp. Paper-

back. PR4484.L6   821
An exploration of Coleridge's mind in the process of creating "The Rime of the Ancient Mariner" and "Kubla Khan." This is a study of the imagination that perhaps reveals as much of the critic as it does of the poet.

Victorian Literature

Surveys

J455.   *Transitional Age of British Literature, 1880-1920.* Ed. Edward S. Lauterbach and W. Eugene Davis. Troy, N.Y.: Whitston, 1973. 323pp. Z2013.L38   016.82'09'008
The publisher has produced another quality research aid, this one beginning with four essays showing the important trends in fiction, poetry, drama, and prose during the transition between the nineteenth and twentieth centuries. Works, letters, autobiographies, biographies, bibliographies, and critical studies are listed for about 170 major and minor authors including Bennett, Beerbohm, Beardsley, Graham, Gregory, Owen, Strachey, Saintsbury, and a certain Joseph Leopold Ford Hermann Madox Hueffer.

J456.   *The Mid-Nineteenth Century.* Vol. 11 of OHEL (J174). In preparation.

Basic guides

J457.   Altholz, Joseph L. *Victorian England: 1837-1901.* Cambridge, Eng.: Cambridge Univ. Press, 1970. Conference on British Studies. 100pp. Z2019.A56   016.9142'03'81
This selective bibliography of scholarly books might be useful in interdisciplinary studies of nineteenth-century England. Sections on handbooks, surveys, politics, social problems, agriculture, science, religion, and history of the fine arts. Index of authors, editors, and translators.

*J458.   Freeman, Ronald E. *Bibliographies of Studies in Victorian Literature for the Ten Years 1965-1974.* New York: AMS, 1980. 730pp. Z2013.B592   [PR461]   016.820'9'008
This continuation of the bibliographies compiled by Slack, Wright, and Templeman (J459-61) has been thoroughly indexed (120pp.) by author, scholar, and subject to make the entries easily accessible to readers. Furthermore, the coverage of journals has been greatly enlarged so that the number of entries (18,000) is almost double that of Slack's volume for 1955-64. Students will be grateful for the time and care expended on this index to criticism of Victorian literature.

*J459.   Slack, Robert C., ed. *Bibliographies of Studies in Victorian Literature, 1955-64.* Urbana: Univ. of Illinois Press, 1967. 461pp. Z2013.B59
A reproduction of the annual Victorian bibliographies as they originally appeared in *MP* for 1956-57 (H150) and in *VS* for 1958-65 (J470); a sequel to the earlier compilations of Templeman (J461) and Wright (J460); continued

by Freeman (J458).

The bibliography contains 7,900 entries, not including book reviews. In an interesting introductory analysis of the type and number of critical works, the editor finds that Dickens received the most attention during these years, and students will be able to draw their own conclusions as to trends in scholarship. The subject and proper name index provides easy access to the contents of many titles. The original periodical pagination is retained at the top of the page for easy cross-reference; continuous pagination is at the bottom.

J460.   Wright, Austin. *Bibliographies of Studies in Victorian Literature for the Ten Years 1945-54.* Urbana: Univ. of Illinois Press, 1956. 310pp. Z2013.W77

This sequel to the bibliography by Templeman (J461) for the years 1932-44 is continued by Slack (J459) and Freeman (J458). Wright's volume contains chronological reproductions of the annotated, alphabetical lists that were originally published annually in the May issue of *MP* (H150) as a project of the MLA. A cumulative author index facilitates search.

J461.   Templeman, William D. *Bibliographies of Studies in Victorian Literature for the Thirteen Years 1932-44.* Urbana: Univ. of Illinois Press, 1945. 450pp. Z2013.T4   016.82'09'008

Reproductions of the annual Victorian bibliographies that appeared in *MP* (H150) from 1932 to 1944. Sequels are the bibliographies by Wright (J460), Slack (J459), and Freeman (J458). Each bibliography has four sections: Bibliographical Material, Environment, Movements of Ideas, and Individual Authors. Templeman, Wright, and Slack warn that only "noteworthy" publications are included and that, for comprehensive research, the students must consult other bibliographies such as *VS* (J470), Faverty (J488), Stevenson (J478), and the annual bibliographies (D31-33).

J462.   Ehrsam, Theodore G., comp. *Bibliographies of Twelve Victorian Authors.* New York: Wilson, 1936; rpt. Octagon, 1968. 362pp. Z2013.E33   016.8209'008

In spite of the 1936 copyright date, this work might still help the student doing extensive research on Arnold, Browning, Clough, FitzGerald, Hardy, Kipling, Morris, Rossetti, Tennyson, Stevenson, and Swinburne.

Ehrsam examined two hundred sources for this compilation. Unfortunately, it is difficult to use, for it is arranged by author of the critical article or book, and the user must scan each entry for hints as to the subject matter. It has one interesting feature, however: Listed under each literary author are individual works with their reviews. Matthew Arnold's *Essays in Criticism* (c1865), for instance, is accompanied by citations for twenty-two reviews from contemporary periodicals and newspapers. That feature alone makes this an important source for anyone doing research on either Victorian literary criticism or the initial response to any of the cited authors.

J463.   *Primary Sources for Victorian Studies.* Ed. Richard Storey and Lionel Madden. London: Phillimore, 1977. 81pp. Z2019.S86 [DA550]

016.941081
This guide explains how to go about locating and using unpublished material—manuscripts, personal papers, archives, public records, and repositories. Practical and orderly.

Annual bibliographies

*J464.   *Annual Bibliography of Victorian Studies.* Edmonton: Univ. of Alberta, 1981– . Annual. Z2019.A64   016.820'9'008

An online bibliographic data base that provides information on Victorian research in the humanities, sciences, and social sciences published during the past ten years. Several notable features for the researcher: (1) It provides a variety of approaches—by author, coauthor, editor, compiler, translator, annotator, illustrator, reviewer, title, and subject (8,000 key words). (2) It lists books, articles, dissertations, reviews, and works in progress. (3) It claims to be more interdisciplinary in scope and to cover more subject journals (two hundred) than other bibliographies. (4) It is annotated. (5) Five-year cumulated indexes facilitate access to the contents (the index for 1976–80 was compiled in 1982).

The first three volumes, for the years 1977, 1978, and 1979, were published in 1981. Those for 1976, 1980, and 1981 were completed in 1982. The 1973–75 and 1982 volumes are scheduled to appear in early spring 1983. The 1971–72 volumes are in preparation.

Dissertations

J465.   Altick, Richard D., and William R. Matthews, comps. *Guide to Doctoral Dissertations in Victorian Literature, 1886-1958.* Urbana: Univ. of Illinois Press, 1960; rpt. Westport, Conn.: Greenwood, 1973. 119pp. Z2013.A4   016.82'09'008.

Because this guide covers America, Austria, Switzerland, France, and other foreign countries, it may provide information that does not appear in any other source. The first eight sections list general topics such as fiction, drama, poetry, literary criticism, periodicals, the influence of foreign authors on the Victorians and vice versa, movements, and themes. The ninth section is an alphabetical list of Victorian authors with pertinent dissertations under each name by author, title, university, and year. Entries W1211–15 in this guide provide more recent information.

Indexes

*J466.   *Wellesley Index to Victorian Periodicals, 1824-1900: Tables of Contents and Identification of Contributors with Bibliographies of Their Articles and Stories.* Ed. Walter E. Houghton and Esther R. Houghton. Toronto: Univ. of Toronto Press, 1966– . Vol. 1 (1966); vol. 2 (1972); vol. 3 (1979); vol. 4 projected for 1984; vol. 5, cumulated index to bibliographies of contributors, projected for 1985. Z2005.H6   [AI3.W45]   052

This ambitious project, which has been under way at Wellesley College for over twenty years, indexes the contents of about fifty of the more important nineteenth-century monthly and quarterly periodicals. Introductions explain the history and problems connected with each periodical, and several references are cited for further study. Each issue is analyzed chronologically by title of the material (excluding poetry). Explanations are given for the identification of pseudonyms, authorship, and the source used to establish authorship.

Scanning the subject matter in these titles provides clues as to what people were thinking and reading during every month of the century, but the most important contribution of this work is unquestionably the identification of the authors, for ninety-seven percent of the articles in Victorian periodicals before 1870 were anonymous. Thackeray, for instance, displayed his characteristic wit when he coined such pseudonyms as Michael Angelo Titmarsh, Charles Yellowplush, and George Savage Fitz-boodle. On the other hand, one of the few women who did not use a pseudonym in this prim Victorian era was, believe it or not, one Jane Sexey.

When vol. 4 is published, the invaluable author-contributor indexes of the four volumes will together contain the names of about twelve thousand writers. About ninety thousand articles will have been read, and most of their authors will have been identified, thus undoubtedly enlarging many existing bibliographies of Victorian authors. Charlotte Brontë, Scott, Stevenson, Thackeray, Patmore, Pater, Mill, George Eliot, Hardy, and Francis Jeffrey are only a few of the important names already identified.

The indexes of initials and pseudonyms, which will surely help provide access to these authors' works in other publications, are the first ever compiled for English periodicals. Halkett and Laing's *Dictionary of Anonymous and Pseudonymous English Literature* (W1033), it must be remembered, covers only books and pamphlets. There are also abbreviation and short-title indexes in each volume. Subject indexes are not planned because of the cost. The price of each volume is $125.

Students looking for research projects and a lifetime occupation need only consider that an additional 12,400 nineteenth-century periodicals remain to be indexed (720 of these in London in the year 1864 alone).

J467.   *Waterloo Directory of Victorian Periodicals, 1824-1900.* Ed. Michael Wolff. Phase I. Waterloo, Ont.: Wilfrid Laurier Univ. Press, for the Univ. of Waterloo, 1976. 1187pp. Z6945.W38

An attempt to list all newspapers and periodical titles published in the British Isles between 1824 and 1900. It contains 29,000 entries with complete bibliographical information, but errors abound. Phase II will augment and correct this material, the aim being to make it readily available to scholars interested in the journal phenomenon of the Victorian period. The subject guide that is now under way will probably produce good thesis subjects for those working with Dickens, Newman, the Pre-Raphaelites, and others who figured large in the periodical world of the nineteenth century. See the *Wellesley Index* (J466), which analyzes the contents of about fifty Victorian periodicals.

J468.   *Nineteenth Century Readers' Guide to Periodical Literature, 1890-99, with Supplementary Indexing, 1900-22.* 2 vols. New York: Wilson,

1944. AI3.R47   050

Some titles that appear in *Poole's Index* (J416) will be found here also, but many additional titles can be located only in this guide. It has both subject and author indexes and covers fifty-one of the most influential English and American periodicals of the century such as *Atlantic Monthly*, *Dial*, and *Living Age*.

Author entries are added to Poole's subject and title entries, subject headings are standardized, and book reviews are listed under the author of the work reviewed. For some periodicals, indexing extends beyond the above dates to 1888, when the *National Geographic* began publishing, and to 1922, when the titles were picked up by other indexes.

Periodicals

*J470.   *Victorian Studies: A Quarterly Journal of the Humanities, Arts, and Sciences (VS*; *Vict. Stud.*). Bloomington: Indiana Univ., 1957– .
        Quarterly. PR1.V5   820'9'008

The most prestigious periodical in the field, with scholarly articles, news notes, long book reviews, occasional illustrations, and a cumulative index for each year. Frequent special issues focus on one subject such as that in 1980 on Victorian imperialism, racism, and colonialism. Since 1958 the journal's outstanding feature has been an annual June bibliography of the previous year's scholarship. A project of the Victorian Literature Group of the MLA, the bibliography was previously, since 1932, published in *MP* (H150). It cites book reviews for important research and provides occasional annotations for noteworthy publications, including articles. It draws its information from about ninety periodicals, numerous books, and English and foreign language dissertations that are concerned with English Victorian literature. Pertinent works by and about transition figures such as Yeats, Conrad, Ford, Shaw, and Wells are also listed.

Because these bibliographies have been cumulated into four volumes by Freeman, Slack, Wright, and Templeman (J458–61), research in Victorian literature is unusually methodical and efficient. Students should be aware, however, that these bibliographies were not meant to be comprehensive, so they will have to consult other sources like the annual bibliographies *MLAIB* (D31), *Year's Wk. Eng. Stud.* (D33), and *ABELL* (D32).

Indexed in *ABELL* (D32), *Abst. Eng. Stud.* (E38), *Arts and Hum. Cit. Ind.* (F47), *Bk. Rev. Ind.* (W1559), *Current Bk. Rev. Cit.* (W1564), *Hum. Ind.* (F45), *Index to Bk. Rev. Hum.* (W1560), *MLAIB* (D31), *Romantic Movement: A . . . Bibliography* (J443).

J471.   *English Literature in Transition, 1880–1920 (ELT*). Tempe: Arizona State Univ., 1963– . Quarterly. Former title, 1957–62: *English Fiction in Transition*. PR1.E55

The best periodical for research in this era because of its specialized articles, current news on research completed, book reviews, and reports of work in progress. Issue no. 1 of the annual volumes from 1956 to 1974 listed the names of authors for whom the editors solicited annotated bibliographies. Since 1975, *ELT*'s outstanding feature has been the bibliographical essays on individual transition figures such as Henry Arthur Jones, John Gray, and R. B. Cunninghame Graham. This is usually the only source for such highly specialized information. The news notes may give some aspiring young author an idea, too. One item reported the sponsoring of Makers of the Nineties Series by the Eighteen Nineties Society, with monographs planned for Harland, Horne, Moore, and others. Analytical index for 1957–72 (vols. 1–15).

Indexed in *ABELL* (D32), *Abst. Eng. Stud.* (E38), *Arts and Hum. Cit. Ind.* (F47), *Hum. Ind.* (F45), *Index to Bk. Rev. Hum.* (W1560), *MLAIB* (D31).

J472.   *Victorian Newsletter (VN)*. Bowling Green: Western Kentucky Univ., 1952–   . 2/yr. PR1.V48

Short scholarly articles, reviews of important books, a selected, annotated list of the most recent publications in the field, news of Victorian activities and research projects in progress.

Indexed in *ABELL* (D32), *Abst. Eng. Stud.* (E38), *Am. Hum. Ind.* (P738), *Arts and Hum. Cit. Ind.* (F47), *MLAIB* (D31), *Romantic Movement: A . . . Bibliography* (J443).

J473.   *Victorian Periodicals Review (VPR)*. Toronto: Univ. of Toronto, 1979–   . Quarterly. Research Soc. for Victorian Periodicals. Former title, 1968–79: *Victorian Periodicals Newsletter*. PN5124   052

One of many current projects concerned with organizing the mass of nineteenth-century periodical literature. The subject bibliographies should inspire a horde of research projects, and the book review and work in progress sections are important sources for current information. United Kingdom and United States research on Victorian periodicals is chronicled in the annual checklist of scholarship and criticism, with the time span in some cases extending from 1800 to 1914.

Indexed in *ABELL* (D32), *Am. Hum. Ind.* (P738), *MLAIB* (D31).

J474.   *Victorian Studies Bulletin (VSB)*. Garden City, N.Y.: Nassau Community Coll., 1977–   . Northeast Victorian Studies Assn. PR461.A1.V7

This interdisciplinary publication aims to keep scholars informed on exhibitions, conferences, publications, research in progress, news, grants, summer programs, and research problems.

Indexed in *ABELL* (D32).

Periodicals—Background reading

J475.   *Victorian Periodicals: A Guide to Research*. Ed. J. Don Vann and Rosemary T. VanArsdel. New York: MLA, 1978. 188pp. Paperback. PN5124.P4.V5   052

Why read Victorian periodicals? Over seventy-five percent of all nineteenth-century periodical literature was unsigned. Is it possible to find out who wrote all this material? How can we locate articles on specific subjects? Where can students find reliable information on editors, contributors, and the journals themselves? These and other problems concerning Victorian periodicals are answered in this collection of essays written by specialists in the field. A valuable contribution to an area that only recently, since the publication of the *Wellesley Index* (J466), has been given the scholarly attention it deserves.

FICTION

Basic guides

*J477.   Ford, George H., ed. *Victorian Fiction: A Second Guide to Research*. New York: MLA, 1978. 401pp. Paperback. PR871.V5   823'.8'09

The most recent of the surveys of research that all scholars hope to find in their field. Because this surveys and evaluates only that scholarship published between 1963 and 1974, it must be used in conjunction with the first edition (J478). Complete coverage is given to Stevenson and Butler, who have been added to the original fifteen novelists, and all other information has been revised and updated. Every book and important article is measured for its original ideas, compared with existing theories, and used as a sounding board for other possible research projects. Bibliographies, biographies, critical editions, and individual novels are evaluated one by one. This is a worthy project for which all Victorian scholars are grateful. Victorian fiction, with its forty thousand novels, needs all the help it can get, as more than one critic has noted. Students can obtain more recent information in *Nineteenth-Century Fiction* (J422), *Victorian Studies* (J470), and the annual bibliographies (D31–33).

*J478.   Stevenson, Lionel, ed. *Victorian Fiction: A Guide to Research*. Cambridge, Mass.: Harvard Univ. Press, 1964; rpt. New York: MLA, 1980. 440pp. PR871.V5   823'.8'09

The 1956 publication of *The Victorian Poets* by Faverty (J488) was so well received that MLA decided to sponsor a companion volume for fiction. This is a collection of bibliographical essays by noted scholars evaluating the research on Disraeli, Bulwer-Lytton, Dickens, Thackeray, Trollope, the Brontës, Gaskell, Kingsley, Collins, Reade, George Eliot, Meredith, Hardy, Moore, and Gissing. The bibliographies of each author are cited and criticized, the various editions and critical works summarized and recommended or refuted. Students should consult this invaluable guide to quick and efficient research if they want to locate, for example, major studies on Hardy's *The Return of the Native* up to 1963. For scholarship after that date, they should go to Ford's *Second Guide* (J477).

J479.   Watt, Ian P. *The British Novel: Scott through Hardy*. Goldentree Bibliographies (W1291). New York: Appleton (Meredith), 1973. 134pp. Paperback. Z2014.F5.W37   016.823'03

Victorian literature students are still loyal to this accumulation of research on eighty novelists. They find it a convenient brief guide to scholarship on major Victorian authors such as Dickens, Disraeli, Eliot, Pater, and Thackeray as well as a valuable, relatively comprehensive guide to critical works on lesser figures who are often difficult to locate—Ainsworth, MacDonald, Yonge, and many others.

Bibliographies of primary works

J480.   Sadleir, Michael. *XIX Century Fiction: A Bibliographical Record Based on His Own Collection*. 2 vols. London: Constable, 1951; rpt. New York: Cooper Square, 1969. Z2014.F4.S16   016.823'8

Sadleir was, in his own term, a bibliomaniac. He devoted his life to satisfying his love of books and relates in the preface to this collection the fascinating tale of his collecting adventures. The hand of a real book lover can be seen throughout both volumes, with their delightful informal essays on various types of novels. Often an entry has paragraphs explaining the book's provenance and the anecdotes that made it particularly memorable to Sadleir. In describing a first edition of Mrs. Gaskell's *Cranford*, for example, he rebukes an unknown binder for shifting a back flyleaf to the front and writes "This sort of tinkering-about is just silly" (vol. 1, p. 136).

Victorian literature students will find this a joy for browsing and a gold mine for facts, but they must remember that it is not comprehensive and reflects only Sadleir's personal preferences. It is still the only truly descriptive bibliography of Victorian fiction. Sadleir's collection is now at the University of California at Los Angeles.

Background reading for Victorian fiction

J481.   Buckley, Jerome H., ed. *Worlds of Victorian Fiction*. Cambridge, Mass.: Harvard Univ. Press, 1975. 416pp. PR873.W6   823'.8'09

A collection of significant essays by J. Hillis Miller, Harry Levin, Melvyn Haberman, and other scholars.

*J482.   Karl, Frederick R. *Reader's Guide to the Nineteenth Century British Novel*. Rev. ed. New York: Octagon, 1975. 374pp. Paperback. Original hardcover title: *An Age of Fiction*. PR861.K3   823'.8'09

If the need is for an enthusiastic, readable examination of the development of realism in the novel, the solution is here. This book's subject is not journalism, not sentimentalism, not character analysis, not entertainment, but realism, a serious vehicle for "questioning existing standards and for creating social equality" (p. 17). Austen, Dickens, Thackeray, Eliot, Meredith, Hardy, and many other novelists are discussed in detail. Karl has also written guides to the eighteenth-century and contemporary American and English novel. They all are reliable.

J483.   Watt, Ian P., ed. *The Victorian Novel: Modern Essays in Criticism*. London: Oxford Univ. Press, 1971. 485pp. Paperback. PR873.W3   823'.03

Critics agree that this collection of thirty-one essays contains most of the worthy statements on Victorian fiction.

Additional reference sources for information on Victorian fiction

J484.   Allen, *English Novel* (J196)
Baker, *History of the English Novel* (J197)
Dickens Studies Annual: Essays on Victorian Fiction. New York: AMS Press, 1980– .

Skilton, *English Novel: Defoe to the Victorians* (J394)
Stevenson, *History of the English Novel* (J198)
Wagenknecht, *Cavalcade of the English Novel* (J199)

PROSE

Basic guides

*J485.   DeLaura, David J. *Victorian Prose: A Guide to Research*. New York:
MLA, 1973. 576pp. Paperback. PR785.D4   820'.9'008

Summarizes and criticizes modern studies on Carlyle, Macaulay, Newman,
Mill, Ruskin, Arnold, and Pater, and devotes chapters to such broad subjects
as the Oxford Movement and Victorian religion. A comprehensive, reliable work.

See also

Buckley, *Victorian Poets and Prose Writers* (J489)
English Prose and Criticism in the Nineteenth Century (J423)

Background reading

J486.   Levine, George L., and William Madden. *The Art of Victorian Prose*.
New York: Oxford Univ. Press, 1968. 378pp. PR783.L4   828'.8'08

Essays on the structure and style of Mill, Arnold, Carlyle, Macaulay, Darwin, Ruskin, Pater, Victorian oratory, rhetoric, and linguistic and psychoanalytic
features. Still the best assessment of this subject.

DRAMA

Bibliographies of primary works

J487.   Wearing, J. Peter. *London Stage, 1890–1899: A Calendar of Plays and
Players*. 2 vols. Metuchen, N.J.: Scarecrow, 1976. PN2596.L6.W37
792'.09421'2

The first of a series that will document day-by-day performances and accumulate all information on plays performed from 1890 to the present. It is
similar in design to the revered *London Stage, 1660–1800* (J400) but not so exquisitely wrought. See also *London Stage, 1800–1900* (J428), *London Stage,
1900–1909* (J553), and *London Stage, 1910–1919* (J553).

POETRY

Basic guides

*J488.   Faverty, Frederic E., ed. *The Victorian Poets: A Guide to Research*. 2nd
ed.   Cambridge, Mass.: Harvard Univ. Press, 1968. MLA. 433pp.
PR593.F3   821'.8'09

This MLA project still provides—up to its own copyright date—a selective,
reliable appraisal of twentieth-century research on the Victorian poets. Authorities
such as Buckley, Pick, and Stevenson explain and evaluate the general materials
useful for this period and then analyze the scholarship on Tennyson, the Brownings, Arnold, Swinburne, the Pre-Raphaelites, Hopkins, and other Victorian

poets. Research students who find their subject in this book are fortunate, for their first task—the collection and appraisal of sources—is presented to them in compact, readable form. Whether they need a good biography on Clough, verification of FitzGerald's study of the Persian language, or the best works on Hardy as a poet, this is the source to use. Be on the alert for a third edition.

J489.   Buckley, Jerome H. *Victorian Poets and Prose Writers*. 2nd ed. Golden-tree Bibliographies (W1291). Arlington Heights, Ill.: AHM, 1978. 96pp. Paperback. Z2013.B8   016.8209'008
A bibliography of Victorian social and political background material, general studies in intellectual and literary history, and essays on thirty-two individual authors including Arnold, the Brownings, Hardy, Hopkins, Newman, Ruskin, Tennyson, Wilde, and many minor writers. Because the list is intended as a guide to scholarship for students, only the best titles are included, the most important are marked with asterisks, and paperback editions are noted.

Periodicals

*J490.   *Victorian Poetry: A Critical Journal of Victorian Literature* (*VP*). Morgan-town: West Virginia Univ., 1963–   . Quarterly. PR500.V5   821.005
Articles, news items, long, critical book reviews, and an important annual bibliography on the year's work in Victorian poetry.
Indexed in *ABELL* (D32), *Abst. Eng. Stud.* (E38), *Arts and Hum. Cit. Ind.* (F47), *Current Bk. Rev. Cit.* (W1564), *Hum. Ind.* (F45), *Index to Bk. Rev. Hum.* (W1560), *MLAIB* (D31), *Romantic Movement: A . . . Bibliography* (J443).

Background reading for poetry

J491.   Johnson, Edward D. H. *The Alien Vision of Victorian Poetry: Sources of the Poetic Imagination in Tennyson, Browning, and Arnold*. Princeton: Princeton Univ. Press, 1952. 224pp. Paperback. PR593   821.809
A study of the problems—social, religious, aesthetic, and intellectual—that the Victorian poet faced.

J492.   Langbaum, Robert W. *The Poetry of Experience: The Dramatic Monologue in Modern Literary Tradition*. London: Chatto and Windus, 1957. 246pp. PR509.M6.L3
Controversial, but poetry lovers will find his arguments compelling.

See also

Critical History of Victorian Poetry (J215)
Pinto, *Crisis in English Poetry, 1880-1940* (J576)

Background reading for the Victorian era

J495.   Baker, Joseph E., ed. *The Reinterpretation of Victorian Literature*. New York: Russell, 1962, c1950. 236pp. MLA. PR732.B3   820.903
A collection of worthy conclusions by such authorities as Howard Mumford Jones and Norman Foerster.

J496.   Buckley, Jerome H. *The Victorian Temper: A Study in Literary Culture.*
Cambridge, Mass.: Harvard Univ. Press, 1951. 282pp. Paperback.
PR461.B75   820.903
Traces currents of thought through seventy years, with many examples from
minor authors.

J497.   Carter, John, and Graham Pollard. *An Enquiry into the Nature of Certain Nineteenth Century Pamphlets.* London: Constable, 1934. 2nd
ed. 2 vols. Berkeley, Calif.: Scolar, 1984. Z1024.C32   098'.3
Scandal! The Victorian literature student will soon become familiar with
the names of these authors and of the bibliophile they exposed as a forger,
Thomas J. Wise. The story of their investigation—and the results—will make
every literature student a more careful researcher.The second edition consists
of two volumes: an enlarged, corrected text of the *Enquiry* and *A Sequel* bringing the affair up to date (ed. Nicolas Barker and John Collins).

*J498.   Houghton, Walter E. *The Victorian Frame of Mind.* New Haven: Yale
Univ. Press, 1957. 467pp. Paperback. DA533.H85   942.081
Good leisure reading that defends the humanity of the much-maligned
Victorian.

J499.   Miller, Joseph Hillis. *The Disappearance of God: Five Nineteenth-
Century Writers.* Cambridge, Mass.: Belknap, 1963. 367pp.
PR469.R4.M5   820.93
Brilliant, convincing analyses of De Quincey, Robert Browning, Emily
Brontë, Matthew Arnold, and Gerard Manley Hopkins.

J500.   Schneewind, Jerome B. *Backgrounds of English Victorian Literature.*
New York: Random, 1970. 160pp. Paperback. DA550.S33
914.2'03'81
Still one of the best surveys of the Victorian period.

J501.   Willey, Basil. *Nineteenth Century Studies: Coleridge to Matthew Arnold.* New York: Columbia Univ. Press, 1949. 287pp. Paperback.
B1561.W52   192
Studies of Coleridge, Arnold, Newman, Carlyle, Bentham, Mill, Comte,
and Eliot, especially as they reflected the pressures of nineteenth-century religious
and moral ideas.

J502.   ———. *More Nineteenth Century Studies: A Group of Honest
Doubters.* New York: Columbia Univ. Press, 1956. 304pp. Paperback.
B1561.W5   192
Studies on Newman, Tennyson, Froude, and numerous minor figures and
major ideas of the nineteenth century.

J503.   Wilson, Edmund. *Axel's Castle: A Study in the Imaginative Literature
of 1870–1930.* New York: Scribners, 1931. 319pp. Paperback.
PN771.W55   809'.91'5
A study of the rebellious Romantic movement, which first emphasized the

individual and finally led us into symbolism as it is seen in Poe, Mallarmé, Yeats, Valéry, Eliot, Proust, Joyce, Stein, and Rimbaud.

*J504.   Young, George M. *Portrait of an Age: Victorian England.* Annotated by George K. Clark. 2nd ed. New York: Oxford Univ. Press, 1977. 416pp. DA550.Y6   942.081
Young's classic was first published in 1936 and revised in a second edition in 1953. Here the work is fully annotated, with identification of all quotations and allusions. It is still one of the most treasured evaluations of the Victorian period, mainly because, as the author himself said, he could "not only write but think Victorian." Young is witty, factual, and convincing, because he realizes that "The real, central theme of History is not what happened, but what people felt about it when it was happening" (Preface).

See also
   Lives of the Victorian Age (W1144)

Twentieth-Century English Literature

Because of mutual interests and author mobility, many works listed in this section contain information not only on English literature but also on American, Continental, and other literatures. Efficiency required that titles with overlapping interests be located in one place, and this section seemed the most accommodating. Those titles devoted solely to American or other literatures are found in their respective sections.

Surveys
J510.   Stewart, John I. M. *Eight Modern Writers.* Vol. 12 of OHEL (J174). Oxford: Clarendon, 1963. 704pp. Paperback. PR461.S8   820.904
Lucid, readable studies of Hardy, James, Shaw, Conrad, Kipling, Yeats, Joyce, and Lawrence as these writers functioned within the social and political turbulence of the early twentieth century. It is interesting to note that this survey includes three authors born in Ireland, one in America, one in Poland, and one in India. Particularly helpful to research students is the bibliography in the back of the book (pp. 629–94) in which Stewart evaluates each author's works and the editions, biographies, and critical studies as they have appeared over the decades. There is also a good chronological table (1880–1941, pp. 596–627) that correlates public events with literature and the arts. A proper name and title index provides easy access to the contents. To bring the information partly up to date, see Perkins for poetry (J568), *Revels* for drama (J549), the fiction guides by Rice (J535) and Wiley (J537), and Pownall (J519).

Basic guides
*J511.   *New Cambridge Bibliography of English Literature.* Ed. Ian R. Willison. Vol. 4: 1900–1950. New York: Cambridge Univ. Press, 1972. 1414 cols. Z2011.N45   [PR83]   016.82
This is still the single most comprehensive source for the first half of the

twentieth century. Its title, editor, and scope make it indispensable. Arrangement is by genre, and it includes general studies as well as books by and about individual authors. See the main entry (J175) for a full description.

J512. **Twentieth Century British Literature: A Reference Guide and Bibliography.** Ed. Ruth Z. Temple and Martin Tucker. New York: Ungar, 1968. 261pp. Z2013.3.T4   016.82

An aging guide with descriptive, evaluative annotations to important books that still might assist the student of twentieth-century literature. Part 1 includes bibliographies, sources for biographical information, background studies in history and literary history, a much-needed bibliography of autobiographies and diaries, essay collections, and titles concerned with literary criticism, drama, the contemporary novel, and poetry. Part 2 contains an alphabetical list of about four hundred authors and their works, with only an occasional one or two titles of criticism. These author bibliographies are in chronological order, and genre is indicated, but they are sometimes selective, so they are of limited value. Most scholars will prefer to use Mellown's more recent and more comprehensive works for author bibliographies (J513-14). An analytical index to Part 1 cites further studies pertaining to all authors listed in Part 2, so the book does, in this way, give access to some critical works.

"British" here means English, Irish, Welsh, and Scottish. "Twentieth century" includes Hopkins (died 1889), Samuel Butler, James, Conrad, and Wilfred Owen as well as John Osborne, Dorothy Sayers, Nevil Shute, and George Orwell. A second edition will probably not be attempted because of the great proliferation of more specialized genre bibliographies such as *English Drama, 1900-1950* (J552), *English Fiction, 1900-1950* (J535), *Irish Literature* (K583), *Anglo-Irish Literature* (K581), and a host of others.

Bibliographies of primary works

J513. **Descriptive Catalogue of the Bibliographies of 20th Century British Writers.** Ed. Elgin W. Mellown. Troy, N.Y.: Whitston, 1972. 446pp. Z2011.A1.M43   016.01682'08'0091

Current bibliographies on modern authors are hard to find. This compilation on nonliterary writers and Mellown's more recent work on British poets, novelists, and dramatists (J514) are good places to begin any research project, and they both can be updated by *Bibliographic Index* (C28). Students should look first in their library card catalog for volumes containing primary or secondary material on their assigned authors, and then they should look here to locate additional author bibliographies in periodicals, parts of books, or books that their library may not own. They will discover that hundreds have already been compiled on modern essayists and critics such as Harold Pinter, Katherine Mansfield, Frank Leavis, A. E. Housman, Virginia Woolf, and H. R. Haggard. Some of the information has of course been superseded by Mellown's second compilation that is described in the following entry.

See Howard-Hill (C26) for bibliographies on earlier writers. See also Author Bibliographies (W1053-55) for additional ways to locate this type of research aid.

*J514.   *Descriptive Catalogue of the Bibliographies of Twentieth Century British Poets, Novelists, and Dramatists.* Ed. Elgin W. Mellown. 2nd ed. Troy, N.Y.: Whitston, 1978. 414pp. Z2011.A1.M43

Students must consult Mellown's first catalog (J513) for bibliographies of nonliterary authors, but this is an exceptionally well-done, up-to-date edition that adds dozens of titles for authors in the field of poetry, fiction, and drama. Most reviewers rate this as an excellent guide to reliable bibliographical information.

Criticism

J515.   *Twentieth-Century Literary Criticism: Excerpts from Criticism of the Works of Novelists, Poets, Playwrights, Short Story Writers, and Other Creative Writers, 1900–1960.* Ed. Dedria Bryfonski, Phyllis Carmel Mendelson, and Sharon K. Hall. Detroit: Gale, 1978–   . In progress (vol. 13, 1984). PN771.G27   809'.04

Like *Contemporary Literary Criticism* (J516), this specializes in providing *long* excerpts from the *best* available criticism, but here the interest is solely in the great international novelists, poets, and playwrights who published between 1900 and 1960. The editors deliberately include some early excerpts to indicate the author's initial reception and some current excerpts for the historical perspective. The coverage is wide: vol. 1 includes criticism on Agee, Aleichem, Benchley, Bierce, Cary, Chesterton, Gibran, Lady Gregory, Rilke, Stein, Strindberg, Woolf, Zola, and about fifty others. Each volume contains a cumulative index of authors and critics appearing in the previous volumes, and vol. 3 includes the names of authors who will be included in future volumes. Beginning with vol. 4, author portraits accompany each entry. For a general idea of the author's reputation and for an overview of trends in literary criticism, this is a great timesaver that will at the same time encourage students to go to the original sources.

J516.   *Contemporary Literary Criticism: Excerpts from Criticism of the Works of Today's Novelists, Poets, Playwrights and Other Creative Writers.* Ed. Sharon R. Gunton. Detroit: Gale, 1973–   . 2/yr. (vol. 28, 1984). PN771.C59   809'.04

The contents: key excerpts from reviews and criticism in about one hundred periodicals and numerous books published during the past twenty-five years. Each successive volume focuses on about two hundred world-famous authors, songwriters, screenwriters, and other creative writers who are now living or who died after 1960, including Brautigan, Murdoch, Castaneda, Heinlein, Roethke, Berryman, Borges, Lessing, Pomerance, Didion, Oates, Achebe, Christie, Genet, Snyder, O'Brien, Leary, and Bowen. Each new volume adds new criticism and authors. Special subjects such as young adult literature, filmmakers, black authors, or feminist authors are also covered. Cumulative author and critic indexes provide easy access to all earlier volumes. The value of this splendid project of course increases with the publication of each new volume. A mixed bag, as one reviewer said, and a satisfying one.

J517.   *Library of Literary Criticism: Modern British Literature.* Ed. Ruth Z. Temple and Martin Tucker. 3 vols. New York: Ungar, 1966. Supplement, ed. Martin Tucker and Rita Stein (1975), 650pp. Supplement, ed. Denis Lane and Rita Stein (1984), 600pp. PR473.T4   820'.9'0091

Long extracts from reviews of about four hundred British and a few American authors who have become well known in the twentieth century. They include celebrities such as Conrad, Henry James, Hopkins, Auden, Lionel Trilling, Allen Tate, Evelyn Waugh, and a host of lesser players. This is a convenient way to get an overview of how authors and critics interpret the work of their fellow artists. It is also brimming with ideas for further research. The supplement is important for the criticism assembled on forty-nine "new" authors such as Bolt, Drabble, Fowles, Moore, Rhys, and Storey.

Moulton's original and successful *Library of Literary Criticism* (W1359), which first appeared in 1901–05, was the inspiration for this work. See also *Modern Romance Literatures* (Q887), *Modern American Literature* (P732), *Modern German Literature* (Q921), *Critical Temper* (W1358), *Modern Slavic Literatures* (Q942), *Modern Latin American Literature* (R992), *Modern Black Writers* (P845), *Modern Commonwealth Literature* (N646), *Modern French Literature* (Q910), and *Major Modern Dramatists* (J558).

J518.   *Survey of Contemporary Literature: Updated Reprints of 2300 Essay-Reviews from Masterplots Annuals, 1954–1976.* Ed. Frank N. Magill. 12 vols. Englewood Cliffs, N.J.: Salem, 1977. PN44.M34   809'.04

Artistic merit, not popularity, was the criterion for selecting these one hundred best books each year since 1954 (see W1591). They represent the second phase of the Southern renaissance; the Jewish urban novel; the "beat" novel; black humor; the Angry Young Men; novels by Cheever, Golding, Barth, Bellow, Pasternak, Camus, Malamud, Snow, Solzhenitsyn, Koestler, Adams, Dickey; letters (by Boswell and Shaw); plays (by Albee and O'Casey); poetry (Berryman); histories; biographies and autobiographies; essays; and works on current affairs.

Entries give date, publisher, number of pages, price, genre, setting and time of action, characters, a one-sentence explanation of the theme, a three- to four-page summary and evaluation, and recommendations for further study including both criticism and reviews. This is not scholarly, but there isn't time to read everything. This may be all that busy students will need to keep them in touch with peripheral titles.

Arranged alphabetically by title with a complete author index in vol. 12.

*J519.   *Articles on Twentieth-Century Literature: An Annotated Bibliography, 1954–70.* Subtitle: *An Expanded Cumulation of "Current Bibliography" in the Journal* Twentieth Century Literature. *Volume One to Volume Sixteen, 1955–1970.* Ed. David E. Pownall. 7 vols. Millwood, N.Y.: Kraus, 1973–80. Z6519.P66   016.809'04

One of the best things to come out of the previous decade's flurry of reference publications—a superb aid to the busy scholar. This, the first comprehensive gathering of critical articles on literature of this century, cumulates all the excellent bibliographies that appeared in every issue of *Twentieth Cen-*

tury Literature (J528). It also corrects them and adds ten thousand titles from other sources. Whether students have time to consult only one source or whether they are doing extensive research on a twentieth-century author, they should start here—at least, until the title described in the following entry (J520) is completed and scholars have an opportunity to compare coverage.

The scope of this work is enormous. Its brief annotations summarize more than 22,000 articles concerned with major international authors of the twentieth century. Joyce, Faulkner, and Henry James each have five hundred articles listed, and Auden, Gide, García Lorca, and E. M. Forster have over one hundred apiece. This is a source that undoubtedly contains items not included in Adelman and Dworkin (J542, J555), Leary (P727), Gerstenberger and Hendrick (P786), Eddleman (P804), Palmer and Dyson (J202), Palmer (Q897), and other bibliographies concerned wholly or partly with the twentieth century. The editors claim that this work cites at least four thousand titles omitted from *MLAIB* (D31).

J520.   *Bibliography of Articles on English Literature Published in Periodicals between 1925 and 1975* (proposed title). 17 vols. Dallas: New London Press, 1980–   . *Part 1: Old English* (1980). In progress.

If this massive accumulation of information about critical articles on English literature lives up to its prepublication description, it will be a most welcome contribution to literary research. The seventeen volumes will be issued in eight parts, each having an individual author index which will ultimately be cumulated. The bibliography itself is organized by subject. The set will of course not be complete for several years.

See also

   Contemporary Literary Critics (W1360)
   English Literature in Transition, 1880–1920 (J471), scholarship on early twentieth-century authors
   Post-Symbolist Bibliography (T1011)
   Somer and Cooper, *American and British Literature, 1945–1975* (B20)

Annual bibliographies that will update the preceding works

   ABELL (D32) has 5,668 entries on the twentieth century in the 1980 volume.
   MLAIB (D31) has 1,677 entries in 1980.
   Year's Wk. Eng. Stud. (D33) has a review of research that includes chapters on twentieth-century English and American scholarship.

See also appropriate abstracting services (E38–43) and indexing services (F45–53).

Interviews

J521.   *Conversations with Writers.* Ed. Matthew J. Bruccoli, C. E. Frazer Clark, Jr., and Richard Layman. 2 vols. Detroit: Gale, 1977–78. PS129.C57 810.9'005

Interviews with Brendan Gill, James Dickey, Thomas Tryon, and others suggest new approaches and new insights for literary critics.

Identification problems

*J523. *Encyclopedia of World Literature in the 20th Century.* Ed. Leonard G.
Klein. 2nd ed. 4 vols. New York: Ungar, 1981–84. PN774.L433   803

An international survey of the major authors and aspects of twentieth-
century literature. The 1,700 articles on individuals include portraits and signed
biographical and bibliographical information on international figures such as
Achebe, Arrabal, Brecht, Camus, Cocteau, Colette, Eliot, Empson, Freud, Ted
Hughes, Lukács, O'Connor, and Wesker. Broad subject areas such as Black
Humor, Fantasy, Phenomenology and Literature, and Science Fiction receive
full discussions with examples of titles and authors. Coverage ranges from literary
movements (Expressionism, Futurism), major genres (the essay), and literary
criticism to movements in ideas (Christianity, Existentialism). The 150 survey
articles on national literatures include Asia, Spanish America, and Africa, the
latter having a section on South African literature that is divided into nine parts:
English, Afrikaans, and seven native languages.

This is a good starting point for identifying unfamiliar authors, placing their
works in twentieth-century trends, finding a brief essay on their influence, reading
critical comments by contemporaries, and locating sources to consult for more
thorough investigation. This work has no title entries because its focus is on ideas,
trends, and the twentieth-century writers, whether living or dead, who have contributed to them. A unique, impressive, attractive work.

J524. *Twentieth Century Writing: A Reader's Guide to Contemporary
Literature.* Ed. Kenneth R. Richardson. London: Newnes, 1969. 751pp.
PN771.R5   809'.04

This encyclopedia of biographical and bibliographical information on twelve
hundred leading twentieth-century authors, from avant-garde poets to mystery
writers, covers the literature of Africa, Latin America, the Continent, and Russia
as well as Great Britain and the United States.

Arrangement is alphabetical by author, and the entries are signed. The index of English titles and the list of principal entries by countries help students
to identify this century's leading Irish or Spanish authors and to evaluate the
literary output of South, West, Central, and East Africa. It leads to answers for
such questions as "What sort of work does Lawrence Durrell do?" "Just who
was Cavafy?" "What are Ionesco's plays all about?" and "Why is Sartre so
important?"

*J525. *Longman Companion to Twentieth Century Literature.* Ed. Alfred C.
Ward. 3rd ed. London: Longman, 1981. 598pp. PN771.W28   803

A respected handbook that emphasizes English and Scottish twentieth-
century writers, but includes some from the Commonwealth, America, and
Europe. Entries on fictional characters, plot summaries, pseudonyms, literary
terms, copyright laws, literary societies—in other words, this is a *Reader's Encyclopedia* (W1402) for the twentieth century.

See also

Biography (W1126–30) and other biographical dictionaries in specific areas

Series

J526.   Columbia Essays on Modern Writers. New York: Columbia Univ. Press, 1978– .

Small booklets (about fifty pages) that are adequate introductions for students who do not have the need, time, or interest to do more extensive research. As with all series, the quality varies, but most are accurate and interesting.

Jean Anouilh
Guillaume Apollinaire
W. H. Auden
Marcel Ayme
Arnold Bennett
Jorge Luis Borges
Bertolt Brecht
Hermann Broch
Albert Camus
Joyce Cary
Constantine Cavafy
Louis Ferdinand Céline
Jean Cocteau
Ivy Compton-Burnett
Joseph Conrad
Norman Douglas
Lawrence Durrell
William Empson
Ronald Firbank
Ford Madox Ford
E. M. Forster
Jean Genet
Stefan George
William Golding
Robert Graves

Henry Green
Graham Greene
Christopher Isherwood
Nikos Kazantzakis
Pär Lagerkvist
Malcolm Lowry
André Malraux
Eugenio Montale
Alberto Moravia
Iris Murdoch
Sean O'Casey
John Osborne
Luigi Pirandello
Raymond Queneau
Alain Robbe-Grillet
C. P. Snow
Muriel Spark
Georg Trakl
Anthony Trollope
Miguel de Unamuno
Guiseppe Ungaretti
Evelyn Waugh
Virginia Woolf
Émile Zola

J527.   Modern Writers Series. New York: Barnes and Noble, 1973– .

Special studies of writers such as Plath, Solzhenitsyn, Pinter, Borges, Thom Gunn and Ted Hughes, Lowell, Grass, and George Mackay Brown.

Periodicals

*J528.   *Twentieth Century Literature: A Scholarly and Critical Journal (TCL).* Hempstead, N.Y.: Hofstra Univ., 1955– .   Quarterly.   PN2.T8 809.04

Two outstanding research aids: (1) the annotated, critical, comprehensive "Current Bibliography" that appears in every issue, and (2) its occasional special bibliographies for authors such as Evelyn Waugh, Edward Albee, Theodore Roethke, and John Dos Passos and for subjects such as West Indian fiction. The periodical is small (only three or four articles), but its interests include English,

American, and Continental fiction, so it is important. In addition to the table of contents for each annual volume, an outstanding cumulative index covers its first sixteen years of scholarship (*Articles on Twentieth-Century Literature*, J519).

Indexed in *ABELL* (D32), *Abst. Eng. Stud.* (E38), *Arts and Hum. Cit. Ind.* (F47), *Hum. Ind.* (F45), *MLAIB* (D31).

J529. *Contemporary Literature (ConL)*. Madison: Univ. of Wisconsin Press, 1968– . Quarterly. Former title, 1960–68: *Wisconsin Studies in Contemporary Literature*. PN2.W55   809.04

Covers English, American, and Continental literature of the twentieth century, including such authors as Brecht, Auden, Brooks, MacNeice, Olson, Fowles, Singer, Patrick White, Beckett, Roth, and Ibsen. About half the periodical is devoted to sharply critical book reviews, so it is an important source for an accurate evaluation of contemporary literature. An occasional special number is devoted to Nabokov, Hemingway, H. D., the Objectivist Poet, Art and Literature, Structuralism, and other timely subjects. A two-year cumulative index appears every other year in the autumn.

Indexed in *ABELL* (D32), *Abst. Eng. Stud.* (E38), *Arts and Hum. Cit. Ind.* (F47), *Current Bk. Rev. Cit.* (W1564), *Hum. Ind.* (F45), *Index to Bk. Rev. Hum.* (W1560), *MLAIB* (D31).

*J530. *Journal of Modern Literature (JML)*. Philadelphia: Temple Univ., 1970– . Quarterly. PN2.J6   809'.04

Scholarly articles and book reviews concerned with all twentieth-century literature, so students will find studies of Conrad, Pound, and Joyce as well as of Hemingway, O'Hara, and O'Connor. Two outstanding research features: (1) occasional special issues containing several articles and an excellent bibliography of works by and about selected authors such as Cummings (April 1979), and (2) an annual international bibliography of English language scholarship on modernist writers (1885–1950) that emphasizes Anglo-Americans. It includes information on books, articles, dissertations, a special section on Film as Literature, and news on symposia, library holdings, conferences, and sales. Some annotations and an author and critic index. A fine publication, intellectually and aesthetically, with striking illustrations, large print, wide margins, and heavy paper—a pleasure to handle and read.

Indexed in *ABELL* (D32), *Arts and Hum. Cit. Ind.* (F47), *Film Literature Ind.* (W1252), *Hum. Ind.* (F45), *Index to Bk. Rev. Hum.* (W1560), *MLAIB* (D31).

J531. *Modern British Literature (MBL)*. Butler, Pa.: Slippery Rock State Coll., 1976– . 2/yr. PR1149.M68

Short articles and notes on British and Irish literature from the late nineteenth century to the present, with emphasis on the "modernism" of both major and minor authors including Yeats, Shaw, Owen, Larkin, Behan, Aldington, Woolf, Greene, Gosse, and others.

Indexed in *Am. Hum. Ind.* (P738), *MLAIB* (D31).

J532.   *Notes on Contemporary Literature (NConL)*. Carrollton, Ga.: n.p. (550 North White St.), 1971–   . PN771.N91

Features short articles on post–World War II prose fiction, drama, and poetry.

Indexed in *ABELL* (D32), *Abst. Eng. Stud.* (E38), *MLAIB* (D31).

Periodicals—Reference books

J533.   *English Literary Journal, 1900–1950*. Ed. Michael N. Stanton. Detroit: Gale, 1981. 119pp.

Gerstenberger and Hendrick (W1475), Contemporary Literature

FICTION

Basic guides

J535.   *English Fiction, 1900–1950: A Guide to Information Sources.* Ed. Thomas J. Rice. 2 vols. Vol. 20 of Gale Information Guide Library (A8). Detroit: Gale, 1979–83. Vol. 1 (1979), 598pp. Vol. 2 (1983), 501pp. Z2014.F4.R5   [PR881]   016.823'9

A guide to primary and secondary material concerning the life and works of about thirty-five authors who lived during the first half of the twentieth century. Vol. 1 lists bibliographies, histories, genre studies, and other general works, and then works by and about individual authors from Richard Aldington through Aldous Huxley. Vol. 2 contains author bibliographies for James Joyce through Virginia Woolf. Asterisks indicate items of special importance. Annotations are very brief, however, and the choice of authors has been questioned.

*J536.   *Contemporary Fiction in America and England, 1950–1970: A Guide to Information Sources.* Ed. Alfred F. Rosa and Paul A. Eschholz. Vol. 10 of Gale Information Guide Library (A8). Detroit: Gale 1976. 454pp. Z1231.F4.R57   [PS379]   016.823'9'1408

The most popular course on many campuses is the contemporary novel. Here is a remarkably thorough, accurate accumulation of entries on scholarship concerning 136 authors such as Boyle, Burgess, Knowles, Achebe, Greene, Warren (8pp.), and Bellow (8pp.). Of equal value is the separate section on thirty-six journals devoted to contemporary literature. Name index.

J537.   Wiley, Paul L. *British Novel: Conrad to the Present.* Goldentree Bibliographies (W1291). Northbrook, Ill.: AHM, 1973. 137pp. Paperback. Z2014.F55.W54   016.823'03

Another convenient bibliography in the popular Goldentree series is this guide to the works and criticism of forty English novelists from Galsworthy to Waugh. Its special contribution is generally unavailable information on minor authors like Firbank, Garnett, Henry Green, Hanley, Hartley, Rose Macaulay, Powell, Dorothy Richardson, and Angus Wilson. Asterisks mark important works.

Bibliographies of primary works

J538.   Bufkin, Ernest C. *The Twentieth-Century Novel in English: A Checklist.*

Athens: Univ. of Georgia Press, 1967.   138pp.   Z2014.F5.B93
016.823'91208

Who wrote what? All major and many minor twentieth-century writers in English through 1966 are listed here with the titles of most, but not all, of their novels and novelettes. The word "novel" is interpreted loosely, for Beckett's fourteen-page *Imagination Dead Imagine* is included.

Arrangement is alphabetical by author; no criticism is included. Convenient for quick information on such modern authors as McCullers, Mailer, and Malamud but inferior to Stanton (J539) in all matters bibliographical for his seventeen novelists. Here, Iris Murdoch is given one-third of a page for ten of her novels. In Stanton she is given fifty pages and 507 entries for all of her works and their criticism (including her eighteen novels).

*J539.   Stanton, Robert J. *Bibliography of Modern British Novelists.* 2 vols. Troy, N.Y.: Whitston, 1978. PR884.S74

The most efficient source for material on seventeen contemporary British novelists from Margaret Drabble to Jean Rhys. It includes a list of all their writings (not just their novels) and entries for all criticism, interviews, biographical studies, and reviews. Thorough. A pleasure to use. Timesavers like this are the best possible argument for scheduling methods of research courses and for encouraging the habit of research. Students who do not know of the existence of these gold mines are handicapped before they begin.

Criticism

J540.   *Twentieth-Century English Novel: An Annotated Bibliography of General Criticism.* Ed. A. F. Cassis. New York: Garland, 1977. 413pp. Z2014.F5.C35   [PR881]   016.823'9'109

Start at the *back* of this book to make the best use of it. The author index shows that Lawrence Durrell is mentioned in sixty entries; the recurring topics and themes index, that "prose style" has forty entries and "epiphany," five. This is the only reference source that analyzes the contents of 2,800 *general* studies, including dissertations. Note that it is not concerned with individual authors except as they are cited in surveys and other general works. The annotations are descriptive and thorough. A very helpful book for this problem area.

*J541.   Drescher, Horst W., and Bernd Kahrmann. *The Contemporary English Novel: An Annotated Bibliography of Secondary Sources.* New York: International Publications Service, 1973. 204pp. Z2014.F5.D74 016.823'9'109

Two important features: (1) It emphasizes *international* research, with many entries on European scholarship and special strength in European reviews, and (2) it emphasizes individual author bibliographies rather than general studies or general reference works. The first of its kind, and a very good beginning.

*J542.   Adelman, Irving, and Rita Dworkin. *The Contemporary Novel: A Checklist of Critical Literature on the British and American Novel since*

1945. Metuchen, N.J.: Scarecrow, 1972. 614pp. Z1231.F4.A34
016.823'03

A bibliography of criticism gleaned from about six hundred books and four hundred periodicals on works by Agee, Dos Passos, Faulkner, Kerouac, O'Connor, and 180 other novelists who wrote and published between 1945 and 1970. The entries are alphabetical by author and then by title, with critical works listed chronologically under each title. Students will find additional information in the more recent guides by Rosa and Eschholz (J536), Somer and Cooper (B20), and, of course, in the Annual Bibliographies (D31–33).

Periodicals

*J544.   *Modern Fiction Studies* (*MFS*). West Lafayette, Ind.: Purdue Univ.,
1955– . Quarterly. PS379.M55   809.3

Broad scope, progressive viewpoints, emphasis on technique, and good scholarship are the outstanding features of this excellent periodical, which is devoted to criticism, research, and bibliography of American, English, and European fiction since 1880.

Summer and Winter issues include a variety of articles, news notes, and a lengthy review section entitled "Recent Books on Modern Fiction." Spring and Autumn issues are devoted to individual authors. These special issues often contain the best available cumulation of research. The Katherine Mansfield issue of Autumn 1978, for example, features ten articles and a bibliography, and the James Joyce issue of Spring 1969 offers nine articles and a bibliography that contains separate listings for each episode of *Ulysses*. Other special issues focus on Iris Murdoch, German Fiction, Modern Canadian Fiction, the Modern French Novel, Howells, Mailer, Kafka, Dostoevsky, Svevo, Borges, Updike, Lessing, and Dos Passos.

A commendable editorial decision: The annual subject and author indexes for vols. 1–20 have been cumulated. Researchers now need consult only one source to locate all critical articles, notes, and book reviews published from 1955 through 1975. Another convenience: Lists of past and future special issues are posted in the back of each annual volume.

Indexed in *ABELL* (D32), *Abst. Eng. Stud.* (E38), *Arts and Hum. Cit. Ind.* (F47), *Current Bk. Rev. Cit.* (W1564), *Hum. Ind.* (F45), *Index to Bk. Rev. Hum.* (W1560), *MLAIB* (D31), *Romantic Movement: A . . . Bibliography* (J443).

*J545.   *Critique: Studies in Modern Fiction* (*Crit*). Atlanta: Georgia Inst. of
Technology, 1956– . 3/yr. PN3503.C7   809.3

The best periodical for very contemporary, avant-garde English and American authors. *Critique* deals with dozens of minor writers as well as Lessing, Heller, Oates, Crews, Nabokov, Bowen, Malamud, Barth, and Singer. Special issues focus on such subjects as Contemporary African Fiction, Nordic Fiction, Bellow, Cozzens, Styron, and Allen Tate, with bibliographies. Cumulative index for vols. 1–20 (1956–78) in vol. 20, no. 3 (April 1979).

Indexed in *ABELL* (D32), *Abst. Eng. Stud.* (E38), *Arts and Hum. Cit. Ind.* (F47), *Bk. Rev. Ind.* (W1559), *Current Bk. Rev. Cit.* (W1564), *Hum. Ind.* (F45), *MLAIB* (D31).

Background reading for fiction

J546. Allen, Walter. *The Modern Novel in Britain and the United States.* New York: Dutton, 1964. 346pp. Paperback. PR881.A4 823.9109

Allen's subject is the novel since the 1920s—the English novel and its preoccupation with class, the American novel with its solitary hero at odds with society. Joyce, Salinger, Woolf, Wyndham Lewis, Garnett, Rebecca West, Styron, Ellison, Gold, and hundreds of major and minor authors and titles are discussed, compared, contrasted, and evaluated. An excellent way to learn a lot in a short time.

J547. Beach, Joseph W. *The Twentieth Century Novel: Studies in Technique.* New York: Appleton, 1932. 569pp. PN3503.B4

Beach examines the mechanics of twentieth-century prose fiction as it has evolved from dozens of major and minor novelists including Fielding, Hugo, Cabell, and Dostoevsky. This includes structure, the unities, dialogue, point of view, themes, the use of such -isms as realism, imagism, and impressionism. Good reading.

J548. Edel, Leon. *The Modern Psychological Novel.* Rev., enl. Gloucester, Mass.: Peter Smith, 1972, c1955. 210pp. Paperback. PN3448.P8.E3 808.93

Plain style and convincing argument characterize this analysis of stream of consciousness as it appears in the works of Joyce, Proust, and other modern novelists.

See also

Contemporary Novelists (W1130)
Gothic Novels of the Twentieth Century (G81)
Twentieth-Century Romance and Gothic Writers (W1130)
Weinstein, *Vision and Response in Modern Fiction* (T1022)

DRAMA

Surveys

*J549. *Revels History of Drama in English.* Ed. Hugh Hunt et al. Vol. 7: 1880 to the Present Day. New York: Barnes and Noble, 1978. 298pp. PR625.R442 822'.009

Like the other valuable surveys in this series, this focuses on the growth of the theater in all its aspects: the theater buildings, actors, companies, audience, and social background. Admirably prepared, with fine illustrations, annotated bibliography, index, and extensive chronological table of plays and dramatists, including Shaw, Synge, O'Casey, Beckett, Osborne, and Pinter. The chronology should be used to supplement Nicoll's *History of English Drama, 1660-1900* (J208), the *Annals of English Literature, 1475-1950* (J176), and Rogal's *Chronological Outline of British Literature* (J177). See the main entry (G114) for information on the other volumes in this series.

J550. *English Drama, 1900-1930: The Beginnings of the Modern Period.* Ed.

Allardyce Nicoll. Cambridge, Eng.: Cambridge Univ. Press, 1973. 1083pp. PR721.N45   016.822'9'1209

The first half of this monumental compilation evaluates hundreds of plays in a category arrangement (London's West End, Melodrama, Regional Drama, Musical Comedy) ranging from Shaw to Coward; the second half is a checklist of plays arranged alphabetically by author. There is even an index of names mentioned in the comments. An especially good bibliographer prepared this text.

Basic guides

J551.   *Modern British Drama.* Ed. Charles A. Carpenter. Goldentree Bibliographies (W1291). Arlington Heights, Ill.: AHM, 1979. 120pp. Paperback. Z2014.D7.C3 [PR736]   016.822'91

Selective, convenient, well organized, and accurate. Suitable for preliminary research on over fifty English, Irish, Scottish, and Welsh dramatists from the mid–nineteenth century to Storey and Pinter, but students will wish there were annotations to help them select the essential titles.

J552.   *English Drama, 1900-1950: A Guide to Information Sources.* Ed. Edward H. Mikhail. Vol. 11 of Gale Information Guide Library (A8). Detroit: Gale, 1977. 328pp. Z2014.D7.M545 [PR736]   016.822'9'1

Scholarship on seventy-nine playwrights of the period, including Auden, Bennett, Eliot, Galsworthy, O'Casey, Shaw, Synge, and Yeats.

See also

Modern Drama in America and England, 1950-1970 (P797)

Bibliographies of primary works

J553.   *London Stage, 1900-1909: A Calendar of Plays and Players.* Ed. J. Peter Wearing. 2 vols. Metuchen, N.J.: Scarecrow, 1981. PN2596.L6.W38 792'.09421'2

A list of almost three thousand plays performed in thirty-five different London theaters in the first decade of the twentieth century. Because it is arranged chronologically and provided with all the production facts, it allows students to follow the careers of such artists as Wilde, Galsworthy, Yeats, Synge, Tree, and Pinero. An important contribution to modern theater research, this should be used with *London Stage, 1890-1899* (J487) and *London Stage, 1910-1919* (2 vols., 1982). The 1920-29 volume is in preparation.

Criticism

*J554.   *Dramatic Criticism Index: A Bibliography of Commentaries on Playwrights from Ibsen to the Avant-Garde.* Ed. Paul F. Breed and Florence M. Sniderman. Detroit: Gale, 1972. 1022pp. Z5781.B8 016.8.092'04

Lists about twelve thousand critical articles, essays, and books on individual plays by over three hundred American and foreign twentieth-century playwrights such as Pirandello, Arrabal, Hansberry, Lady Gregory, Beckett, and Weiss. Arranged alphabetically by playwright, with title and critic name indexes. The editors gleaned material from international sources—630 monographs and 200 periodicals. Entries range from one title on Hemingway to fifty pages for Shaw, with concentration on criticism rather than on reviews.

In spite of its copyright date, this is still a useful source. Eddleman (P804), published in 1979, has been much more successful in listing a greater number of both the authors' plays and the criticism about those plays, but Breed includes the major foreign dramatists, many minor dramatists, and general studies, all of which Eddleman omits. Use both for extensive research.

J555.   Adelman, Irving, and Rita Dworkin. *Modern Drama: A Checklist of Critical Literature on 20th Century Plays.* Metuchen, N.J.: Scarecrow, 1967. 370pp. Z5781.A35   016.809'2'04

Eddleman (P804) supersedes this in his coverage of American dramatists, but this is still useful for some foreign authors who are not found in Breed (J554). Gorki, for instance, is given much better coverage in Adelman and Dworkin, but Eddleman has located seventeen critical works for Inge's *Bus Stop*, while Adelman provides only two entries and Breed only three. This is not a comprehensive source, but it is valuable because it is selective on the basis of literary merit. It indexes about three hundred periodicals, books, newspapers, and some play reviews and covers English, American, and Continental authors such as Shaw, O'Neill, Eliot, Chekhov, Capote, Inge, Strindberg, Ibsen, Anouilh, and Ionesco.

Arrangement is alphabetical by author, with entries under specific titles but no annotations. An important aid for further research is the listing of bibliographies, when available, at the end of the author entries. Subdivision of titles and articles is not well defined on the page, however.

*J556.   *Twenty Modern British Playwrights: A Bibliography, 1956–1976.* Ed. Kimball King. New York: Garland, 1977. 289pp. Z2014.D7.K47 [PR736]   016.822'9'1

An assignment on contemporary authors is frequently unexpectedly difficult because indexers and bibliographers have not had time to collect the material and put it in order. Here is an eminently convenient source for critical books, articles, and bibliographies on Arden, Bolt, Bond, Osborne, Pinter, the Shaffers, Stoppard, Storey, Wesker, and other moderns. A real timesaver.

J557.   *Contemporary British Drama, 1950–1976: An Annotated Critical Bibliography.* Ed. Edward H. Mikhail. Totowa, N.J.: Rowman, 1976. 147pp. Z2014.D7.M55   [PR736]   016.822'9'14

An important era, a popular subject—but how does one locate helpful titles in a reference source that divides its material into simply "Books" and "Periodical Titles" and neglects to provide a subject or name index? How does one separate the scholarly from the popular when the "annotation" consists of the briefest of descriptive phrases? This may contain helpful information, but in spite of its 1976 copyright date, it lists few books published in the 1970s, omitting the *Humanities Index* (which took over from the *Social Sciences and Humanities Index* in 1974), *Dramatic Criticism Index* (published in 1972), *Contemporary Dramatists* (1974), and many other sources essential for good research procedure.

J558.   *Library of Literary Criticism: Major Modern Dramatists.* Ed. Rita Stein et al. 2 vols. New York: Ungar, 1983– . Vol. 1 (1983), 500pp.

Excerpts from international criticism, much of it newly translated, on important dramatists of Europe and America since Ibsen. A quick way to find out which critical books and articles are worth reading.

Theater

J559.   Salem, James M., ed. *A Guide to Critical Reviews: British and Continental Drama from Ibsen to Pinter.* Metuchen, N.J.: Scarecrow, 1968. 309pp. Z5782.S34   016.809'2

An index to critical reviews (not scholarly studies) of modern British and Continental plays produced in New York between 1909 and 1966. Off-Broadway productions are included after 1961. Salem's book is particularly important because it includes French drama, which is of great interest now and is not well covered elsewhere.

Arranged alphabetically by author and then by title, with information about where and when the play opened, and a list of reviews from American and Canadian newspapers. The student can take numerous approaches to the subject through several indexes: dramatists (with nationality and dates), number of performances, dramatists with the greatest number of performances, awards, authors, adaptors, translators, and titles. See four other volumes in this series by Salem: *The Musical* (P806), *The Screenplay* (W1242), *American Drama 1909–1969* (P805), and *Foreign Drama* (R969).

Summaries

J560.   *Twentieth Century Plays in Synopsis.* Ed. Evert Sprinchorn. New York: Crowell, 1965. 493pp. PN6112.5.S68   808.2

Long summaries of about two hundred plays by sixty-three twentieth-century English, American, and Continental authors. It includes, for instance, a four-page summary of Albee's *Who's Afraid of Virginia Woolf*, six plays by Bertolt Brecht summarized in fifteen pages, and eight plays by Strindberg in thirty pages. The editor has written a helpful introduction entitled "The Decline and Disappearance of Plot," and at the back of the book are biographical notes on the playwrights. Title index.

Identification problems

*J561.   *Crowell's Handbook of Contemporary Drama.* Ed. Michael Anderson et al. New York: Crowell, 1971. 505pp. PN1861.C7   809.2'04

The scope is indicated by the first entry in this sorely needed encyclopedia—a summary of the history, titles, authors, -isms, and current (1970s) interpretation of the "absurd" elements in literature. Reference books on contemporary thought are hard to come by. This one concentrates on written drama in Europe (from Norway to Czechoslovakia and Russia) and the Americas since World War II. Historical perspective, biographical facts, and evaluation of individual titles by important dramatists should please the younger generation. Long discussions of Fernando Arrabal, Günter Grass, the Soviet Union and its political influence on the arts, the innovations of Harold Pinter, John Osborne, the Angry Young

Men, and hundreds more. Title, subject, and author entries, with occasional suggestions for further study. A second edition would be most appreciated.

Periodicals

*J563. *Modern Drama* (*MD*). Toronto: Univ. of Toronto, 1958– . Quarterly. PN1861 809.2'005

In spite of the title, this periodical includes articles on Strindberg and Wilde as well as on Albee, Beckett, and Ionesco. It covers English, American, Continental, and world literature and features long, scholarly book reviews and special issues on such subjects as German drama since World War II, George Bernard Shaw, and classical myth in modern drama. A selective, enumerative bibliography appeared annually from 1960 to 1968, when it lapsed until 1972–73. The lack of an annual or cumulative index makes the journal somewhat difficult to use.

Indexed in *ABELL* (D32), *Abst. Eng. Stud.* (E38), *Arts and Hum. Cit. Ind.* (F47), *Current Bk. Rev. Cit.* (W1564), *Film Literature Ind.* (W1252), *Hum. Ind.* (F45), *Index to Bk. Rev. Hum.* (W1560), *MLAIB* (D31), *Year's Wk. Eng. Stud.* (D33).

J564. *tdr: the drama review*. New York: New York Univ., 1972– . Quarterly.
Former titles, 1955–71: *Tulane Drama Review* and *Carleton Drama Review*. PN2000.D68 792'.09

Emphasizes the popular theater, not literary drama. From 1958 to 1966 it featured an annual, selective, enumerative bibliography arranged by subject (new editions of plays, criticism, history, movies, production, for example). Since then it has specialized in issues devoted to one subject for which it provides an extensive bibliography: Film (Winter 1966), Bertolt Brecht (Fall 1967), Black Theater (Summer 1967), Theater and Therapy (1976), Structuralist Performance (1979), and Italian Theater (1978).

Indexed in *ABELL* (D32), *Abst. Eng. Stud.* (E38), *MLAIB* (D31), *Year's Wk. Eng. Stud.* (D33).

Background reading for drama

J565. Brustein, Robert S. *The Theatre of Revolt: An Approach to the Modern Drama*. Boston: Little, 1962. 435pp. Paperback. PN2189.B7 809.2

Values have changed. Brustein studies the positive and negative aspects of this change in Ibsen, Strindberg, Chekhov, Shaw, Brecht, Pirandello, O'Neill, and Genet. This is a landmark in dramatic criticism. The author's response to and reservations about the theater of the 1970s appear in a later volume that has received excellent reviews: *Critical Moments: Reflections on Theatre and Society, 1973-1979* (New York: Random, 1980; 232pp.). PN2266.B718 792'.0973

Additional reference sources

Contemporary Dramatists (W1128)
London Stage, 1900-1909 and *1910-1919* (J553)
Who's Who in the Theatre (W1098)
Who Was Who in the Theatre (W1110)

POETRY

Surveys

*J568.   Perkins, David. *A History of Modern Poetry from the 1890s to the High Modernist Mode*. Cambridge, Mass.: Belknap, 1976– . Vol. 1 (1976), 623pp. Vol. 2, *From the 1920s to the Present*, projected for 1985. PR610.P4   821'.009

Extraordinarily fine reading. Perkins sees both the forest and the trees, the interaction between major and minor poets, the inscape of each poem, the relation of poetry to other arts, the complexity of contradictory pressures in the nineteenth century. He understands poetry and poetry-makers, and he has the gift of prose. His work is survey and explication, obviously a labor of love that he expresses with a sincere, sympathetic, even witty voice. Vol. 1 covers 130 poets from Meynell and Thompson to Blunden, Masters, Toomer, Eliot, and Stevens. An exemplary literary history, the kind of book every critic would like to write.

Basic guides

*J569.   *Modern Poetry*. Ed. Charles F. Altieri. Goldentree Bibliographies (W1291). Arlington Heights, Ill.: AHM, 1979. 129pp. Z1231.P7.A45 [PS323.5.A1.A5]   016.821'91409

Poetry lovers have been waiting for this for years. They will be pleased to find that it supplies primary and secondary works for fifty-six poets who have exerted some influence or aroused substantial critical interest such as Williams, Eliot, Frost, Stevens, Logan, MacNeice, Tate, Betjeman, Hart Crane, Yeats, and Ashbery. Coverage extends only to the mid-1970s, however, so a second edition is already in order.

J570.   *English Poetry, 1900–1950*. Ed. Emily Ann Anderson. Vol. 33 of Gale Information Guide Library (A8). Detroit: Gale, 1981. 460pp. Z2014.P7.A54   016.821'52

Betjeman, Empson, Comfort, Hopkins, Housman, Muir, Owen, Raine, Watkins, and many other early twentieth-century poets are listed here with their primary works and selected criticism. Annotations; author, title, and subject index.

Periodicals

J571.   *Parnassus: Poetry in Review*. New York: Stanley Lewis, 1972– . 2/yr. PN6099.6.P36   809.1'009

This important periodical publishes long reviews of recently published works by contemporary poets including Berryman, Valéry, Levertov, and Auden.

Indexed in *Am. Hum. Ind.* (P738), *Arts and Hum. Cit. Ind.* (F47), *Index to Bk. Rev. Hum.* (W1560), *MLAIB* (D31).

J572.   *Modern Poetry Studies (MPS)*. Buffalo, N.Y.: n.p. (207 Delaware Ave.), 1970– . 3/yr. PS301.M58

Traditional, dependable, and encouraging, this journal is devoted to the analysis and explication of modern poetry and to the publication of original poems, with occasional special issues devoted to one poet. Emphasis is on American authors, but English and European poets are included as well: Elizabeth Bishop, Margaret Atwood, several Hungarian poets, Stafford, Rosenthal, and hundreds more.

Indexed in *ABELL* (D32), *Arts and Hum. Cit. Ind.* (F47), *Current Bk. Rev. Cit.* (W1564), *Hum. Ind.* (F45), *Index to Bk. Rev. Hum.* (W1560), *MLAIB* (D31).

Background reading for poetry

*J573.   Deutsch, Babette. *Poetry in Our Time: A Critical Survey of Poetry in the English-Speaking World, 1900–1960.* 2nd ed. Westport, Conn.: Greenwood, 1975. 457pp. PR610.D4   821'.9'109
Finely wrought in both perception and style.

J574.   Leavis, Frank R. *New Bearings in English Poetry: A Study of the Contemporary Situation.* New ed. New York: Stewart, 1950, c1932. 238pp. Paperback. PR601.L4   821.9109
A competent, exacting, provocative dissection of the makings of modern English poetry, especially that of Hopkins, Pound, and Eliot.

J575.   Miller, Joseph Hillis. *Poets of Reality: Six Twentieth-Century Writers.* Cambridge, Mass.: Belknap, 1965. 369pp. PR601.M5   821.00912
Important ideas about the hazardous transition from nineteenth-century doubt to twentieth-century acceptance of realism, with special emphasis on the poetry of Conrad, Yeats, Eliot, Dylan Thomas, Stevens, and William Carlos Williams.

J576.   Pinto, Vivian de Sola. *Crisis in English Poetry, 1880–1940.* 5th ed. London: Hutchinson, 1967. 203pp. PR601.P5   821'.9'109
Fine interpretations of Hardy and Housman, Hopkins and Bridges, Yeats and Synge, the Imagists, Eliot, and others. The author feels that poetry has survived the crisis of conflict between the traditionalists and the modernists.

J577.   Rosenthal, Macha L. *The Modern Poets: A Critical Introduction.* London: Oxford Univ. Press, 1975, c1960. 288pp. PR601.R6   821.9109
Written by a man who wants his readers to enjoy poetry, a sound, sensible approach that encourages curiosity and produces sensitivity. Hundreds of references to poems and poets.

See also

Contemporary Poetry in America and England, 1950–1975 (A8)
Contemporary Poets (W1129)
International Who's Who in Poetry (W1101)
Twentieth Century in English Poetry (J215)
Wilson, Axel's Castle (J503)

K

Irish Literature

Bibliographies of bibliographies

*K580. Eager, Alan R. *A Guide to Irish Bibliographical Material: A Bibliography of Irish Bibliographies and Sources of Information.* 2nd ed. Westport, Conn.: Greenwood, 1980. 560pp. Z2031.E16   016.0169415

The long-awaited second edition cites 9,500 titles in libraries and collections in Ireland, England, and the United States. Researchers are grateful that it lists not only book-length bibliographies but also shorter lists in books and periodicals. Excellent subject coverage and clear arrangement are the most valuable features, and both are important to the struggling scholar. Bibliographies are listed on Irish periodicals, incunabula, censorship, folklore, printing, work in progress, numismatics, science, church history (by sect and order), the Irish abroad, and dozens of other areas, including all forms of literature such as drama, poetry, fiction, biography, and Gaelic. No annotations, but the detailed arrangement will benefit anyone interested in any facet of Irish studies. The author index contains critics' names only, but the subject index includes such entries as *Finnegans Wake*, Famine, Galway, Jonathan Swift, Young Irelanders, and the Cuala Press.

Basic guides

*K581. Finneran, Richard J., ed. *Anglo-Irish Literature: A Review of Research.* New York: MLA, 1976. 596pp. Paperback. Supplement, 1983: *Recent Research on Anglo-Irish Writers.* 361pp. PR8712.A5   820'.9

No other source covers this territory in this way. As a review of research it collects evaluations by experienced scholars of the international research on Wilde, Moore, Shaw, Yeats, Synge, Joyce, Lady Gregory, A.E., Gogarty, Stephens, O'Casey, modern drama, and the Irish Literary Revival. The inclusion of both a list of 180 journals and a detailed name index was a good editorial decision. Reviewers agree that this is an outstanding reference book. The next edition will replace the present two volumes, include a new chapter on Beckett, and appear in 1988.

*K582. McKenna, Brian, ed. *Irish Literature, 1800-1875: A Guide to*

Information Sources. Vol. 13 of Gale Information Guide Library (A8). Detroit: Gale, 1978. 388pp. Z2037.M235   [PR8750]   016.82

A fine introductory guide to scholarship relating to one hundred nineteenth-century Irish authors who wrote in English and who, in many cases, are not researched elsewhere. For the minor authors, this may be definitive; only the most extensive research in major authors will require additional sources.

K583.   McKenna, Brian, ed. *Irish Literature, 1876–1950: A Guide to Information Sources.* Detroit: Gale. In preparation.

See A8 for a full annotation on this series.

K584.   *Bibliography of Modern Irish and Anglo-Irish Literature.* Ed. Frank L. Kersnowski, Cary W. Spinks, and Laird Loomis. San Antonio: Trinity Univ. Press, 1976. 157pp. Z2037.K47   016'.82

Strictly limited to the most important works by and about the most popular Irish authors from 1878 to 1973, approximately sixty in all, including Bowen, Cary, Colum, Dunsany, Graves, Lady Gregory, and Hyde. No annotations, no indexes, and no entries for critical articles, but the lists of selected critical books are of some help. Most students will probably prefer to use McKenna (K583) when it is published because of his excellent reputation in matters bibliographical.

K585.   Harmon, Maurice, ed. *Select Bibliography for the Study of Anglo-Irish Literature and Its Backgrounds: An Irish Studies Handbook.* Port Credit, Ont.: Meany, 1977. 187pp. Z2037.H32   [PR8711]   016.82'08'09415

The literary maps and forty-page chronology from 1765 to 1976 of literary works and world events are definite assets, but the lack of a subject index, the insufficient cross-references, and the omission of outstanding authors such as Lady Gregory, MacNeice, and Behan certainly limit the usefulness of this highly selective bibliography.

Bibliographies of primary works

K587.   *Modern Irish Literature, 1800–1967: A Reader's Guide.* Ed. Maurice Harmon. Chester Springs, Pa.: Dufour, 1967. 71pp. Z2037.H3   016.82

When the author wrote this, his "main intention was to open up the whole of modern Irish literature for study and exploration" (p. 9). His efforts coincided with a surge of interest by scholars in Irish literature and by publishers in the bibliography as an economically profitable vehicle. The result has been a bevy of fine reference works that supersede Harmon's original work, especially those by McKenna (K582–83), Finneran (K581), and Eager (K580).

Library collections

K588.   Guide to Irish Resources in North America. In preparation, 1979–   . American Committee for Irish Studies.

This guide will describe and locate North American collections of manuscripts, books, periodicals, and other material relating to everything Irish, including literature, art, history, music, and the Irish abroad. The committee's first task is to obtain from every public and private library in America a list of their Irish holdings. This will be many years in the making.

See also

> *British and Irish Library Resources* (W1314)
> *Index of English Literary Manuscripts* (W1318)

Series

K589.   Irish Writers' Series. Ed. James F. Carens. Lewisburg, Pa.: Bucknell Univ. Press, 1971–78. Paperback.

Respected critics such as Hazard Adams, D. E. S. Maxwell, and Daniel Casey have contributed to this well-received series of biographical-critical monographs on the following nineteenth- and twentieth-century Irish authors:

William Allingham	John Montague
Elizabeth Bowen	Brian Moore
Paul Vincent Carroll	Iris Murdoch
Daniel Corkery	Edna O'Brien
Thomas Davis	Sean O'Casey
Maria Edgeworth	Frank O'Connor
Samuel Ferguson	Peadar O'Donnell
George Fitzmaurice	Eimar O'Duffy
Brian Friel	Liam O'Flaherty
Oliver St. John Gogarty	Standish O'Grady
Lady Gregory	Seumas O'Kelly
Seamus Heaney	W. R. Rodgers
Douglas Hyde	George Russell (A.E.)
Patrick Kavanagh	Somerville and Ross
Bendedict Kiely	Francis Stuart
Mary Lavin	J. M. Synge
Joseph Sheridan Le Fanu	Katharine Tynan
James Clarence Mangan	Mervyn Wall
Charles Robert Maturin	John Butler Yeats
Susan L. Mitchell	

Identification problems

*K590.   *Dictionary of Irish Biography*. Ed. Henry Boylan. New York: Harper, 1978. 385pp. CT862.B69 920'.0415

The first scholarly, comprehensive biographical dictionary in fifty years, with one thousand entries covering thirteen centuries and five continents. Perhaps its most significant revelation to readers of this IRA-ridden decade is the reality, as one critic noted, of Ireland's stormy history, with its confusion of heroes and antiheroes; its Colum, Gogarty, Moore, and Swift; its Pearse and Saint Patrick; its Edmund Burke and John O'Leary. Fascinating but discouraging.

K591.   *Dictionary of Irish Writers*. Ed. Brian T. Cleeve. 3 vols. Cork, Ireland: Mercier, 1967–71. PR8727.C5 820.9'9415

Three neat little volumes (399pp. in toto) divided into fiction, nonfiction, and writers in the Irish language. They contain brief biographical sketches (no more than a page) of hundreds of Irish authors, many of whom are difficult if not impossible to locate elsewhere, even in Boylan (K590). Coverage extends from Eriugena (Johannes Scotus) to Douglas Hyde and Frank O'Connor, with a great many facts packed into very little space. It identifies the controversial Margaret Cusack, for instance, while neither the *DNB* (W1086) nor Allibone (W1125) acknowledges her existence. And it surveys briefly the life and works of John Wilson Croker, giving him much more space than does Allibone but much less than the ten-page essay in the *DNB*. Not as comprehensive or as up to date as Hogan (K592) but still useful.

*K592. *Dictionary of Irish Literature*. Ed. Robert Hogan. Westport, Conn.: Greenwood, 1979. 815pp. PR8706.D5   820'.9'9415
   Biographical-critical essays on five hundred authors of Irish extraction, an introduction linking Irish history to its literature, and, most important, up-to-date bibliographies that constitute one-third of the book and that list chronologically the significant primary and secondary works. Witty, earnest, energetic prose, a delight to read. One word of caution: Begin with the index because it includes names mentioned in the text even though they are not important enough to warrant entries of their own.

Periodicals

K593. *Éire-Ireland: A Journal of Irish Studies*. St. Paul, Minn.: Irish American Cultural Inst., 1966– . Quarterly. DA900.E37   AP2.E35
   Articles and news on historical and cultural activities.
   Indexed in *ABELL* (D32), *Abst. Eng. Stud.* (E38), *Am. Hum. Ind.* (P738), *Arts and Hum. Cit. Ind.* (F47), *Index to Bk. Rev. Hum.* (W1560), *MLAIB* (D31).

*K594. *Hermathena: A Dublin University Review*. Dublin: Univ. Press, 1873– . Quarterly. AS121.H5
   Articles on Donne's death, Swift's library, Synge's notebooks, modern language teaching, *Othello*, Austin Clarke, and any other subject with an Irish orientation. Reviews.
   Indexed in *Arts and Hum. Cit. Ind.* (F47), *Brit. Hum. Ind.* (F49), *MLAIB* (D31).

K595. *Irish Renaissance Annual*. Newark: Univ. of Delaware Press, 1980– . Annual. PR8753.I7   820'.9'00912
   Interested in literary figures and events connected with the Irish political and social rebellion of 1916 and with Ireland's independence.

*K596. *Irish University Review: A Journal of Irish Studies (IUR)*. Dublin: University Coll., 1970– . 2/yr. LH5.I68
   The only source concerned with modern Irish literature in its totality: original short stories, plays, and poems; articles about the context of that literature—folklore, history, politics; book reviews; special issues on contemporary writers such as Brian Coffey and Austin Clarke; annual international bibliography of

publications by and about Irish writers.
Indexed in *Arts and Hum. Cit. Ind.* (F47), *MLAIB* (D31).

*K597. Journal of Irish Literature (JIL). Newark, Del.: Proscenium, 1972– .
3/yr. PR8700.J68
Each issue is devoted to a specific subject such as Paul Vincent Carroll,
Juanita Casey, or the Listowel Writers. It features unpublished material, inter-
views, reminiscences, and an annual bibliography of critical studies.
Indexed in *ABELL* (D32), *Am. Hum. Ind.* (P738), *Arts and Hum. Cit.
Ind.* (F47), *Index to Bk. Rev. Hum.* (W1560), *MLAIB* (D31).

K598.   *Studies: An Irish Quarterly Review of Letters, Philosophy, and Science.*
Dublin: University Coll., 1912– . 3/yr. AP4.S78   052
Articles concerning Yeats, Synge, Joyce, Newman's Catholic University in
Dublin, the fictional Irishman, George Moore, and all Irish lore and lyrics. A
regular report on film and book reviews. Index to vols. 1–50 (1912–61).
Indexed in *ABELL* (D32), *Abst. Eng. Stud.* (E38), *MLAIB* (D31).

Author newsletters, journals, and other serial publications devoted to individual Irish authors

K600.   Additional author newsletters are listed in this guide for American
(P777), English (J195), Continental (Q893), Canadian (N685), Scottish
(L627), and Welsh (M640) authors. For full bibliographical information and
descriptive annotations of these and other periodicals concerned with one person, see *Author Newsletters and Journals* (W1476) and its annual supplement
in *Serials Review* (W1482).

Burke, Edmund
  Burke Newsletter, 1959–67.
  Studies in Burke and His Time, 1967–78
  (superseded by *Eighteenth Century*,
  J379).
Carleton, William
  Carleton Newsletter, 1970–75.
Joyce, James
  James Joyce Broadsheet, 1980– .
  James Joyce Quarterly, 1963– .
  James Joyce Review, 1957–59.
  A Wake Newslitter, 1962– .
O'Casey, Sean
  Sean O'Casey Review, 1974– .

Shaw, George Bernard
  Bernard Shaw Society Journal, 1976– .
  Independent Shavian, 1962– .
  Shavian, 1953– .
  *Shaw: The Annual Bulletin of Ber-
  nard Shaw Studies*, 1981– .
  Shaw Bulletin, 1951–58.
  Shaw Newsletter, 1976– .
  Shaw Review, 1959–80.
Yeats, William Butler
  New Yeats Papers, 1971– .
  T. S. Eliot Review, 1975–77.
  Yeats Annual, 1981– .
  Yeats Studies, 1971–72.
  Yeats Studies Series, 1975– .
  Yeats-Eliot Review, 1978– .

FICTION

Surveys

K601.   Cronin, John. *Anglo-Irish Novel*. Totowa, N.J.: Barnes and Noble, 1980– . Vol. 1, *Nineteenth Century*. 157pp. PR8797.C7 823'.009'9415

A survey of the major novels by Edgeworth, Banim, Griffin, Carleton, Kickham, Moore, and Somerville and Ross, with brief biographical sketches and selected bibliographies of primary and secondary works.

K602.   Kiely, Benedict. *Modern Irish Fiction: A Critique*. Dublin: Golden Eagle, 1950. 179pp. 823.4

A well-known Irish storyteller offers frank (Irish) opinions on fifty contemporaries.

Basic guides

K603.   *Ireland in Fiction: A Guide to Irish Novels, Tales, Romances, and Folklore*. Ed. Stephen J. Brown, S.J. Vol. 1. 2nd ed. New York: Barnes and Noble, 1919; rpt. 1968. Z2039.F4.B8   016.823

No other source provides this inaccessible material: summaries of nineteenth-century Irish fiction; brief biographies of authors such as Emily Lawless, John Gamble, Dorothea Conyers, and Lady Morgan; indexes of publishers and series, historical fiction, Gaelic epic and romance, clerical life, humorous books, fiction in periodicals, titles and subjects. Vol. 2 is in preparation.

DRAMA

Surveys

*K604.   *Modern Irish Drama: A Documentary History*. Ed. Robert Goode Hogan and James Kilroy. Dublin: Dolmen, 1975– . In progress. PR8789.H62 792'.09415

This multivolume set will compile and preserve all basic information on Irish twentieth-century theater, including such elusive material as cast lists of important first productions. Students will undoubtedly find new approaches here for their papers and dissertations.

Vol. 1: *The Irish Literary Theatre, 1899–1901*. 1975. 164pp.
Vol. 2: *Laying the Foundations, 1902–1904*. 1976. 164pp.
Vol. 3: *The Abbey Theatre: The Years of Synge, 1905–1909*. 1978. 385pp.
Vol. 4: *The Rise of the Realists, 1910–1915*. 1979. 532pp.

Basic guides

K605.   *Ten Modern Irish Playwrights: A Comprehensive Annotated Bibliography*. Ed. Kimball King. New York: Garland, 1979. 105pp.

Z2039.D7.K56   016.822'9'1408.

A selective (incomplete) bibliography of the works and criticism of ten cultural descendants of the Abbey Theatre group: Behan, Boyd, Douglas, Friel, Keane, Kilroy, Leonard, McKenna, Murphy, and O'Brien.

K606.   *Bibliography of Modern Irish Drama, 1899-1970.* Ed. Edward H. Mikhail. Seattle: Univ. of Washington Press, 1972. 51pp. Z2039.D7.M53   016.792'09415

The first bibliography of *general* studies of Irish drama written in the twentieth century, and, therefore, valuable for its charting of stylistic trends, popularity of the Irish theater, and treatment of controversial subjects. It includes six hundred entries of books, periodical articles, and unpublished material. No subject or title indexes, however, no annotations, and no way to distinguish the important from the less helpful.

Background reading for Irish literature

K607.   Cahill, Susan, and Thomas Cahill. *A Literary Guide to Ireland.* New York: Scribners, 1973. 333pp. Paperback. PR8731.C3   914.15'04

This unique travel companion blends Irish myth, history, and literature with the lairs and byways of Beckett, Lady Gregory, Joyce, O'Casey, O'Faoláin, Shaw, Swift, Synge, Yeats, and many other currently popular authors.

K608.   Casey, Daniel J., and Robert E. Rhodes, eds. *Views of the Irish Peasantry, 1800-1916.* Hamden, Conn.: Shoe String, 1977. 225pp. HD625.V53   301.44'43'09415

Essays by Irish and American scholars explain the customs, folklore, living conditions, traditional songs, literature, oral tradition, and religion of the common folk of Ireland. Students of Yeats, Carleton, O'Casey, O'Neill, Joyce, Goldsmith, and other Irish writers should read this in spite of the occasional errors of omission and commission.

K609.   Farren, Robert (Roibeard O'Farachain). *The Course of Irish Verse in English.* London: Sheed and Ward, 1948. 171pp. PR8765.03

One of the three best books on Irish literature, Hyde (K611) and Flower (K610) being the other two.

K610.   Flower, Robin. *The Irish Tradition.* Oxford: Clarendon, 1947. 173pp. PB1322.F5   891.6209

A noted scholar offers interpretations of early Irish literature.

*K611.   Hyde, Douglas. *A Literary History of Ireland from the Earliest Times to the Present Day.* New ed. London: Benn, 1967, c1899. 654pp. Paperback. PB1306.H8   820'.9

Probably the most influential book on Irish literature. Required reading.

K612.   Mercier, Vivian. *Irish Comic Tradition.* New York: Oxford Univ. Press, 1962. 258pp. PB1307.M45

Mercier has written a scholarly and important book about a pleasant subject, but the work is sometimes not convincing, according to the critics.

K613.   Moody, Theodore W., and Francis X. Martin. *The Course of Irish History*. Cork, Ireland: Mercier, 1967. 404pp. Paperback. DA912.M6   941.5
Fine prose and a fair representation of the facts. Good background reading. Bibliography (pp. 349–67). A ten-volume *New History of Ireland* edited by Moody, Martin, and F. J. Byrne will soon be completed (New York: Oxford Univ. Press, 1976–   ; vols. 1–9, 1976–83).

K614.   O'Connor, Frank (Michael O'Donovan). *A Short History of Irish Literature: A Backward Look*. New York: Putnam, 1967. 264pp. PB1306.03   820.9
A lively, appealing account by a lively, appealing author. Essential.

K615.   Power, Patrick C. *Literary History of Ireland*. Dublin: Mercier, 1969. 192pp. Paperback. PR8711.P6   820.9'94'15
Easy background reading.

Additional reference sources

British and Irish Authors Series (J182)
MLAIB (D31), vol. 1, Celtic Literatures
Modern British Literature (J531)
Myers (W1122), geographical and chronological index to authors, pp. 964–65
New CBEL, vol. 1 (J227), Irish Writers, cols. 341–44; vol. 3 (J415), Anglo-Irish Literature, cols. 1885–1948; vol. 5 (J175), index, Ireland
Twayne's English Authors Series (J181), Irish writers
Year's Wk. Mod. Lang. Stud. (W1328)

L

Scottish Literature

Basic sources

*L620. *Annual Bibliography of Scottish Literature*. Stirling, Scotland: Bibliotheck, 1969– . Annual. Z2057.A55

Previously published, 1956–68, in *Bibliotheck* (L622), this developed in size and stature to become an independent supplement in its own right. It is an excellent international bibliography of scholarship that includes reviews, folk literature, ballads, and all aspects of Scottish literary culture. Author and critic indexes.

Periodicals

*L622. *Bibliotheck: A Scottish Journal of Bibliography and Allied Topics*. Stirling, Scotland: Univ. Library, 1956– . 3/yr. and bibliographical supplement. Z2054.B58

Articles, reviews, and from 1956 to 1968 an annual bibliography of Scottish literature that is now published separately (L620). Index to vols. 1–10 (1956–80).

Indexed in *ABELL* (D32), *Abst. Eng. Stud.* (E38), *MLAIB* (D31).

*L623. *Scottish Literary Journal: A Review of Studies in Scottish Language and Literature*. Old Aberdeen: Univ. of Aberdeen, 1974– . 2/yr. Assn. for Scottish Literary Studies. Former title, 1970–74: *Scottish Literary News*. PR8514.S3   820'.8'09411

Scholarly criticism, numerous brief reviews, notes, and occasional poems; an annual checklist of the year's creative writing, with reviews, in the Fall supplement; occasional long essay reviews on various titles selected from the annual bibliography (L620) published by *Bibliotheck* (L622); and since 1975 a list of the year's work on medieval literary and linguistic studies.

Indexed in *ABELL* (D32), *Arts and Hum. Cit. Ind.* (F47), *MLAIB* (D31).

L624. *Scottish Studies (ScS)*. Edinburgh: Univ. of Edinburgh, 1957– .

Annual. AS121.S43

This publication focuses on Scottish traditional life and cultural history, with studies of manuscripts, lyric songs, courtly poems, identification problems, bards, and folk dances. The literature student needs to know that it features an annual bibliography of Scottish studies covering a wide range of research including folklore, history, and literature. Index to vols. 1–10 (1957–66) in vol. 10. Essential for the field.

Indexed in *Arts and Hum. Cit. Ind.* (F47), *Brit. Hum. Ind.* (F49), *Index to Bk. Rev. Hum.* (W1560), *MLAIB* (D31).

L625.   *Studies in Scottish Literature* (*SSL*). Columbia: Univ. of South Carolina Press, 1963–75, 1978–80. Annual. PR8500.S8   820'.9'411

Articles on current interests such as the state of Scottish poetry in 1973, and on historical problems such as the hymns of Martin Luther in Scottish hymnals, stanza form in Burns, and Scott's novels. Book reviews. International contributors.

Indexed in *ABELL* (D32), *Abst. Eng. Stud.* (E38), *Am. Hum. Ind.* (P738), *Arts and Hum. Cit. Ind.* (F47), *Index to Bk. Rev. Hum.* (W1560), *MLAIB* (D31).

Author newsletters, journals, and other serial publications devoted to individual Scottish authors

L627.   Additional author newsletters are listed in this guide for American (P777), English (J195), Continental (Q893), Canadian (N685), Irish (K600), and Welsh (M640) authors. For full bibliographical information and descriptive annotations of these and other periodicals concerned with one person, see *Author Newsletters and Journals* (W1476) and its annual supplement in *Serials Review* (W1482).

Burns, Robert
  Burns Chronicle, 1892– .
Carlyle, Thomas
  Carlyle Newsletter, 1979– .
  Occasional Papers, 1965– .
  Thomas Green Lectures, 1959– .

Hume, David
  Hume Studies, 1975– .
Scott, Sir Walter
  Sir Walter Scott Quarterly, 1927–28.

Background reading

L629.   Hart, Francis R. *The Scottish Novel from Smollett to Spark*. Cambridge, Mass.: Harvard Univ. Press, 1978. 442pp. PR8597.H37   823'.03

Two centuries of Scottish fiction surveyed in the works of Scott, Galt, George MacDonald, Stevenson, Gunn, Jane Duncan, Muriel Spark, Eric Linklater, Compton MacKenzie, and about forty other novelists. No other reference work covers this material so thoroughly and so accurately. Title in England: *The Scottish Novel: A Critical Survey*.

Additional reference sources

L630.   *Companion to Scottish Literature*. Ed. Trevor Royle. Detroit: Gale,
1983. 322pp. PR8506.R69

Longman Companion to Twentieth Century Literature (J525)

MLAIB (D31), vol. 1, Celtic Literatures

Myers (W1122), geographical and chronological index to authors,
pp. 966–68

New CBEL (J227 and J363), vols. 1 and 2, Scottish literature. Vols. 3
and 4 do not have a special section for Scotland; authors are arranged
by genre

Scottish Literature in English and Scots. Ed. William R. Aitken. Detroit:
Gale, 1982. 421pp.

Year's Wk. Mod. Lang. Stud. (W1328)

M

Welsh Literature

Surveys

*M631. Jarman, Alfred O. H., and Gwilym Rees Hughes, eds. *Guide to Welsh Literature*. Swansea, Wales: Christopher Davies, 1976– . Vol. 1, 295pp.; vol. 2 (1980), 400pp. In progress. PB2206.G8   891'.6'6'09

Vol. 1 covers Welsh literature from its beginnings to the fourteenth century, and vol. 2 from the thirteenth to the sixteenth, with discussions of all aspects of literature, including authors, poems, tales, romances, ballads, sagas, and historical background. Bibliographies at the end of each chapter, and many English translations. Especially welcome because it seems to be directed toward the student who does not speak Welsh.

*M632. Parry, Thomas. *History of Welsh Literature*. Trans. Harold Idris Bell. London: Oxford Univ. Press, 1955; corrected rpt. 1970. 534pp. PB2206.P33   820.9

This scholarly classic is still revered and still used.

Basic guides

M634.   *Bibliography of Anglo-Welsh Literature, 1900-65*. Ed. Brynmor Jones. Monmouth, Wales: Library Assn., 1970. 139pp. Z2013.3.J64 016.8209'0091

A selective primary and secondary bibliography for Welsh writers of the twentieth century with brief descriptions of the titles and their various editions. Helpful for studies of Kingsley Amis, Dylan Thomas, William Henry Davies, Arthur Machen, Vernon Watkins, John Cowper Powys, and many authors who are not included in the larger bibliographies. The relevant volumes of the Writers of Wales series (M636) supersede this, of course.

Series

M636.   Writers of Wales. Cardiff: Univ. of Wales Press, for the Welsh Arts

Council, 1970–   .

A series of critical studies on important Welsh authors and subjects. Most are about one hundred pages long and include bibliographies of works by and about the author.

Cynan
Idris Davies
Rhys Davies
W. H. Davies
John Dyer
Caradoc Evans
Folk Poets
Geraint Goodwin
Ann Griffiths
W. J. Gruffydd
Dafydd ap Gwilym
Richard Hughes
T. Rowland Hughes
Introduction to Welsh Literature
Emrys ap Iwan
R. T. Jenkins
David Jones
Glyn Jones
Jack Jones

T. H. Jones
Thomas Gwynn Jones
Alun Lewis
Saunders Lewis
The Mabinogi
Iolo Morganwg
T. H. Parry-Williams
Poets of the Welsh Princes
John Cowper Powys
Allen Raine
Kate Roberts
Dylan Thomas
Edward Thomas
Gwyn Thomas
R. S. Thomas
Vernon Watkins
D. J. Williams
Emlyn Williams
Waldo Williams

Periodicals

M638.   *Anglo-Welsh Review (AWR)*. Tenby, Dyfed, Wales: H. G. Walters, 1949–   . 2/yr. PR8901.A52

The best source for current, reliable information on Welsh literature, with critical, historical, and biographical articles, original poetry and fiction, reviews, and an abundance of news, notes, and letters.

Indexed in *ABELL* (D32), *Arts and Hum. Cit. Ind.* (F47), *MLAIB* (D31).

Author newsletters, journals, and other serial publications devoted to individual Welsh authors

M640.   Additional author newsletters are listed in this guide for American (P777), English (J195), Continental (Q893), Canadian (N685), Irish (K600), and Scottish (L627) authors. For full bibliographical information and descriptive annotations of these and other periodicals concerned with one person, see *Author Newsletters and Journals* (W1476) and its annual supplement in *Serials Review* (W1482).

Machen, Arthur
   AMS Occasional, 1965–?.
   Arthur Machen Journal, 1963–?.

Additional reference sources

MLAIB (D31), vol. 1, Celtic literatures
Myers (W1122), geographical and chronological index to authors, p. 968
New CBEL (J175), vol. 5, index, Wales
Year's Wk. Mod. Lang. Stud. (W1328)

N

Commonwealth Literature

General

Criticism

*N645. *Critical Writings on Commonwealth Literatures: A Selective Bibliography to 1970, with a List of Theses and Dissertations.* Comp. William H. New. University Park: Pennsylvania State Univ. Press, 1975. 333pp. Z2000.9.N48   016.82'09

The best available cumulation of research completed up to 1970 on authors from East and West Africa, Australia, Canada, New Zealand, South Africa, Rhodesia, India, Pakistan, Ceylon, Malaysia, Singapore, the Philippines, and the West Indies. The coverage is remarkable—6,576 entries for books and articles from eight hundred periodicals concerned with such authors as Thomas Chandler Haliburton (Canada), Patrick White (Australia), Roy Campbell (South Africa), Tagore (India), and hundreds more. Be on the alert for a supplement locating research completed during the 1970s.

N646. *A Library of Literary Criticism: Modern Commonwealth Literature.* Ed. John H. Ferres and Martin Tucker. New York: Ungar, 1977. 561pp. PR9080.M6   820'.9

The sudden proliferation of worthy authors from Commonwealth countries, both those who write in English and those who write in their own language and are translated into English, makes this an unexpectedly but deservedly popular source. Much of the criticism on these widely scattered 150 authors would not otherwise be easily available, of course. Arrangement is by country (Africa, Australia, Canada, the Caribbean, India, New Zealand) and then by author. Both favorable and unfavorable criticism is included, and both new and seasoned authors are represented: Patrick White, Edmund Wilson, Morley Callaghan, Narayan, Davies, Ashton-Warner, Paton, Richler, Roy, and dozens more. Remarkably up to date. Almost all the authors are still living, and native criticism is included wherever possible.

Indexes

N647.   *Index to Commonwealth Little Magazines.* Ed. Stephen H. Goode.
Troy, N.Y.: Whitston, 1965–   . Every two years. AI3.I48   051

Important because most of the thirty-four titles analyzed from England,
Ireland, Scotland, Australia, Africa, and other Commonwealth countries (except Canada) are not indexed elsewhere. The subject headings and indexing
policy are sometimes baffling, but when the editor fulfills his intentions of adding more periodicals and extending coverage back to 1900, the index will open
up whole new fields of literature and criticism. It has great promise, therefore,
of becoming an important and popular reference work. Entries for authors and
subjects, with an uncommon and highly desirable research aid—citations for
reviews of the works.

A few Commonwealth magazines are also indexed by the *Comprehensive
Index to English-Language Little Magazines, 1890-1970* (W1427) and Goode's
Index to American Little Magazines (W1428).

Periodicals

N649.   *Ariel: A Review of International English Literature (ArielE).* Calgary,
Alta.: Univ. of Calgary, 1970–   . Quarterly. Former title, 1960–67:
Review of English Literature. PR1.R352   820.9

Ariel covers English, Canadian, Irish, Indian, West Indian, and other Commonwealth authors, including Derek Walcott, Jean Rhys, Cary, Wycherley, and
Conrad. Even Pynchon, Emerson, and Franklin are subjects of source and
influence studies. A large part of each issue is given to original poetry.

Indexed in *ABELL* (D32), *Arts and Hum. Cit. Ind.* (F47), *Brit. Hum. Ind.*
(F49), *Current Bk. Rev. Cit.* (W1564), *Hum. Ind.* (F45), *MLAIB* (D31).

*N650.   *Journal of Commonwealth Literature (JCL).* London: Oxford Univ.
Press, for the Univ. of Leeds, 1965–   . 3/yr. PR1.J67   820.05

Critical articles, reviews, and annual bibliographies compiled with brief but
important evaluative introductions by editors in Africa, Australia, India, New
Zealand, Pakistan, Canada, and all Commonwealth and former Commonwealth
countries.

Indexed in *ABELL* (D32), *Abst. Eng. Stud.* (E38), *Arts and Hum. Cit. Ind.*
(F47), *Brit. Hum. Ind.* (F49), *Hum. Ind.* (F45), *MLAIB* (D31).

Works in progress

N652.   *Bibliography of Commonwealth Literature.* A gigantic project sponsored by a few courageous members of the MLA. It will probably be
many years in the making.

Additional reference sources

ABELL (D32) has international coverage
Brit. Hum. Ind. (F49) indexes a few Australian, Scottish, and Welsh
journals
English Studies (H145)

Longman Companion to Twentieth Century Literature (J525)
McNamee, *Dissertations* (W1212), Empire Literature includes dissertations on Ireland, Scotland, Wales, Australia, and Canada
MLAIB (D31), vol. 1, English II
Twayne's World Authors Series (R957)
World Literature
   Black African Literature in English (R972)
   Black African Literature in English since 1952 (R974)
   Reader's Guide to African Literature (R973)
   WLWE (R960)
   Year's Work in English Studies (D33), international coverage

Australian Literature

Surveys

*N653. *Oxford History of Australian Literature.* Ed. Leonie Kramer. New York: Oxford Univ. Press, 1981. 456pp. PR9604.K73

The only up-to-date survey that traces the development of Australian literature from 1788 to the present day, with special sections on fiction, drama, and poetry. For quick consultation, this offers brief evaluations of the major reference tools; information on manuscript depositories; specialized bibliographies on specific areas including genres, dictionaries, encyclopedias, histories, and periodicals; research sources for about seventy authors including Slessor, White, Brennan, Furphy, Lawson, Lindsay, Richardson, Stow, Stewart, McAuley, and Campbell.

Basic guides

*N654. *Australian Literature: A Reference Guide.* Ed. Fred Lock and Alan Lawson. 2nd ed. New York: Oxford Univ. Press, 1980. 120pp. Paperback. Z4011.L6 [PR9604.3] 016.82

A concisely annotated guide with good coverage of general books and bibliographies but slim notice of criticism for the forty individual authors. Some valuable features, however—for instance, the descriptions of manuscript holdings in the more important Australian libraries. The first edition was especially important because it was the first convenient, comprehensive guide to Australian literature since the highly respected volume by E. Morris Miller and Frederick T. Macartney in 1956 (Sydney: Angus and Robertson; 501pp.). Since then, it has been partially superseded by those bibliographies that focus on specific genres or eras (see N655–57). All these are of course brought up to date by the annual bibliography in *Australian Literary Studies* (N660).

N655. *Australian Literature to 1900: A Guide to Information Sources.* Ed. Barry G. Andrews and William H. Wilde. Vol. 22 of Gale Information Guide

Library (A8). Detroit: Gale, 1979. 472pp. Z4021.A54 [PR9604.3] 016.82

A well-researched, well-prepared guide to works by and about sixty-six Australian authors (including Trollope!) whose work was published before 1900 and to nineteenth-century journals, newspapers, language, and other subjects of interest to the literature major. Students will certainly welcome the evaluations of the authors' contributions to their nation's literature and the comments on the merit of the critical work.

N656.   *Modern Australian Poetry, 1920-1970: A Guide to Information Sources.* Ed. Herbert C. Jaffa. Vol. 24 of Gale Information Guide Library (A8). Detroit: Gale, 1979. 241pp. Z4024.P7.J34 [PR9610.5] 821

Reviewers agree: The work is erudite and judicious; the subject, rich and vital. This is a thoughtfully prepared bibliography. One long section has primary and secondary works for individual authors, including Slessor, FitzGerald, Hope, Stewart, Wright, and McAuley. Other sections cover schools, movements, and general reference tools.

N657.   *Modern Australian Prose, 1901-1975: A Guide to Information Sources.* Ed. Arthur Grove Day. Vol. 32 of Gale Information Guide Library (A8). Detroit: Gale, 1980. 425pp. Z4011.D38 [PR9604.3] 016.82

Important especially for the biographical information and lists of works by and about fifty twentieth-century authors who either lived in or wrote about Australia. Includes entries for reference works, periodicals, surveys, and nonfiction.

Book reviews

N658.   *Index to Australian Book Reviews.* Adelaide: Libraries Board of South Australia, 1965– . 4/yr.

An index of reviews found in Australian periodicals, with emphasis on literature, the humanities, and social sciences. The last issue is cumulative for the year.

Library collections

N659.   Downs, Robert B. *Australian and New Zealand Library Resources.* New York: Mansell, 1979. 164pp. Z870.A1.D6   026.000994

A guide to library catalogs and other descriptors of special collections in Australian and New Zealand libraries. For further information, see two other guides by Downs to library catalogs of the United States (W1313) and British and Irish libraries (W1314).

Periodicals

*N660.   *Australian Literary Studies (ALS).* Hobart, Australia: Univ. of Tasmania, 1963– . 2/yr. PR9400.A86   820.9

The only journal devoted exclusively to the scholarly study of Australian literature. Articles on Australian writers, bibliographic essays commenting on primary and secondary works, reviews, notes, regular reports of research in progress, and, most important, an annual bibliography of studies in Australian literature, including reviews.

Indexed in *ABELL* (D32), *Abst. Eng. Stud.* (E38), *Arts and Hum. Cit. Ind.* (F47), *Index to Bk. Rev. Hum.* (W1560), *MLAIB* (D31).

Additional reference sources for information on Australian literature

N661.　*Australian National Bibliography* (D36)
　　　McNamee, *Dissertations* (W1212)
　　　MLAIB (D31), vol. 1, General II, Australia
　　　Nicoll, *World Drama* (R965)
　　　Reference Services Review, 6, no. 2 (1978), 33–39; 7, no. 2 (1979),
　　　　3–11. See *RSR* (W1569.1)
　　　Twayne's World Authors Series (R957), Australia

Canadian Literature

Surveys

*N662.　*Literary History of Canada: Canadian Literature in English*. Ed. Carl
　　　F. Klinck. 2nd ed. 3 vols. Toronto: Univ. of Toronto Press, 1976, c1965.
　　　Paperback. PR9184.3.K5　810'.9'005

Similar in scheme to *The Literary History of the United States* (P701), this examines significant authors and movements that have contributed to the history of Canada, from New Found Lands and Haliburton, adventure stories inspired by explorations and gold strikes, to scholars of the twentieth century like F. E. L. Priestley. The essays are written by recognized authorities (including Northrop Frye) and together serve to illustrate the unexpectedly long history and growing importance of Canadian literature. Vol. 3 covers activities from 1960 to 1973. Long bibliographies and an analytical index.

Basic guides

**N663.　*Canadian Reference Sources: A Selective Guide*. Ed. Dorothy E. Ryder.
　　　Ottawa: Canadian Library Assn., 1973. 185pp. Supplement, 1975.
　　　121pp. Z1365.R8　[F1008]　011.02'0971

The officially recognized source for advice on Canadian and French-Canadian reference material. It ranks with Sheehy (A5) and Walford (A6) for American and English works. The brief section on literature in the main volume is greatly improved in the supplement, which adds information on authors such as Haliburton, Knister, Leclerc, and Roy. The annotations describe carefully but seldom evaluate. Some students will wish they did. The editor brings her book up to date in *Reference Services Review*, 6, no. 4 (1978), 11–14. See *RSR* (W1569.1).

N664.　Moyles, Robert G., ed. *English-Canadian Literature to 1900: A Guide
　　　to Information Sources*. Vol. 6 of Gale Information Guide Library (A8).

Detroit: Gale, 1976. 346pp. Z1375.M68   [PR9184.3]   016.81'08

The size of the book dispels the belief that there was no early Canadian literature. This lists hundreds of historical novels and romances by De Mille and Oxley, poems by Carman and Lampman, humor by Haliburton, realistic animal stories by Roberts, representative nineteenth-century journals, and a surprising number of critical studies on forty-six Canadian writers. Only the section on travel literature is well annotated, however; the reference books are given brief comments, and the remainder no explanation at all. Author and title indexes.

*N665. *Checklist of Canadian Literature and Background Materials, 1628-1960.*
    Ed. Reginald E. Watters. 2nd ed. Toronto: Univ. of Toronto Press, 1972.
    1084pp. Z1375.W3   013'.971

This is one of the most ambitious reference works in Canadian literature. It aims to provide all basic publishing facts on the poetry, drama, and fiction of English-speaking Canada plus the related biographies, literary criticism, religious works, and histories that might be helpful in the interpretation of six-teen thousand books by seven thousand authors. It is arranged by genre, so students interested in that approach will find it most useful. Authors are ar-ranged alphabetically in each genre section. It is easy to ascertain, for instance, that Frederick John Niven wrote poetry, fiction, biography, and travel literature. The first half of the book is a checklist of the original works; the second half, a selective listing of the studies of the environment that produced those works. Used with Moyles (N664), Stevens (N691), Gnarowski (N666), and current bibliographies, this could easily produce a well-researched paper for any in-dustrious student.

*N666. Gnarowski, Michael, ed. *Concise Bibliography of English-Canadian
    Literature.* Rev. ed. Toronto: McClelland and Stewart, 1978. 145pp.
    Z1375.G53   [PR9184.3]   016.81'08

The editor wanted this to be a "manageable, practical, handy" checklist to immediately available works by and about Canadian authors—and it is. Eminently so. Morley Callaghan, for instance, has fourteen novels listed (with their reviews), three collections of short stories (with their reviews), an autobiography and a travel book (with their reviews!), and two articles. This is followed by a list of twenty-three books and articles containing criticism about his life and works. Jean Laurence, Irving Layton, Stephen Leacock, and Hugh MacLennan are given even more space. Students will find this up to date and easy to use. It will be all that undergraduates will need, and a good starting point for anyone else working with the major (not minor) Canadian authors.

N667. *Canadian Literature: A Guide to Reference Sources.* Ed. Lillian Rider.
    2nd ed. Montreal: McLennan Library, McGill Univ., 1982. 28pp. ERIC
    no.: ED 096 942.   Z1375.M3   [PR9184.3]   016.81   Former title:
    A Student's Guide to Reference Sources in Canadian Literature.

A real student's guide that covers English, French, and American elements in Canadian literature. Its descriptions of handbooks, biographical dictionaries, histories, and general and specialized bibliographies make this especially helpful to students who need help in deciding which book to use. See the Index for additional titles in the McGill series. For information on purchasing copies, see ERIC, in the Glossary of this guide.

N668. *On Canadian Literature, 1806–1960: A Checklist of Articles, Books, and Theses on English-Canadian Literature, Its Authors, and Language.* Ed. Reginald E. Watters and Inglis F. Bell. Toronto: Univ. of Toronto Press, 1966; corrected rpt. 1973. 165pp. Z1375.W33 016.8109

The terminal date for the contents of this book is 1960, but it is still a pleasure to use. Thorough, reliable, and well arranged, with numerous general studies listed for such subjects as drama, fiction, poetry, songs, regionalism, publishing, and periodicals. Another section lists critical books and articles for individual authors like Haliburton (Sam Slick), Lampman (nature poet), Leacock (satirist), and Seton (animal stories). For research on authors it is of course superseded by Gnarowski (N666). The annual bibliographies in *Canadian Literature* (N676, for the years 1959 to 1971) and *Journal of Canadian Fiction* (N688, since 1972) will provide more recent information for the other subjects.

*N669. Lecker, Robert, and Jack David, eds. *The Annotated Bibliography of Canada's Major Authors.* 10 vols. Downsview, Ont.: ECW Press, 1979– . In progress (vol. 5, 1984). Z1375.L43 [PR9184.3] 016.81

Five fiction writers are the subject of the first volume of this unique bibliographical effort: Margaret Atwood, Margaret Laurence, Hugh MacLennan, Mordecai Richler, and Gabrielle Roy. Vol. 2 supplies information on five poets: Margaret Atwood, Leonard Cohen, Archibald Lampman, E. J. Pratt, and Al Purdy. Vol. 3 covers Ernest Buckler, Robertson Davies, Raymond Knister, W. O. Mitchell, and Sinclair Ross. Of the projected ten volumes, five are devoted to fictionists and five to poets. Lists of every version of their complete works and all criticism—including reviews, interviews, and awards—are arranged chronologically to show how the work has been received by the public. Updating supplements will be produced periodically. This will of course be the place to begin any research on the projected fifty French- and English-Canadian authors of the nineteenth and twentieth centuries. The reviewers are unanimous: This is quality bibliography.

N669.1 *Bibliography of Canadian Folklore in English.* Ed. Edith Fowke and Carole Henderson Carpenter. Toronto: Univ. of Toronto Press, 1981. 272pp. Z5984.C2.F68 016.390'00971

A surprising mass of research material through 1979 arranged first by genre (folktales, folk speech, superstitions, customs, etc.), then by ethnic group, and then by type of reference work (periodicals, articles, films, biographies, dissertations). Annotations and an index of authors and editors. A valuable contribution to Canadian literature.

Identification problems

N670. *Oxford Companion to Canadian Literature.* Ed. William Toye. New York: Oxford Univ. Press, 1984. 864pp.

Entries on the entire history of Canadian literature including French-

Canadian, Indian, regional surveys, period surveys, humor, satire, criticism, literary magazines, publishers, poets, dramatists, novelists, and writers such as Stephen Leacock and Northrop Frye. A most welcome addition to the Oxford Companion series (see Index).

*N671. *Dictionary of Canadian Biography* (*DCB*). Ed. George W. Brown. Toronto: Univ. of Toronto Press, 1966– . In progress (projected completion date, 2000). F1005.D49 920.071

Equal in policy, format, and scholarship to the *DAB* (W1087) and *DNB* (W1086), with signed biographical entries and copious bibliographies for further study.

Vol. 1: 1000–1700	Vol. 5: 1801–1820
Vol. 2: 1701–1740	Vol. 9: 1861–1870
Vol. 3: 1741–1770	Vol. 10: 1871–1880
Vol. 4: 1771–1800	Vol. 11: 1881–1890, with regional index
Index, vols. 1–4	

This most worthy and appreciated project was made possible by the bequest of a man who loved his country. The chronological arrangement by date of death has two advantages: It permits the editors to do intensive research in one area while writing on individual subjects, and it permits the reader to see, in one convenient volume, the interrelationship of contemporaries and society. The unusual tale will be found here, the background figure, the forgotten hero. Vol. 1, for instance, contains information on sixty-five Indians and fifty-nine Maritime explorers. The index to vols. 1–4 lists all persons mentioned in the articles as well as all biographees, and it arranges the biographees by occupation and geography to facilitate research. Cumulative indexes and cross-references to other volumes. A French edition is being prepared. The reviews are unanimous: "a wealth of new information."

Book reviews

N672. *Canadian Book Review Annual.* Toronto: Peter Martin, 1975– . Annual. F1001.C224 028.1

Book reviews of English-language books published in Canada, with good author, title, and subject indexes. Coverage extends to reference books, the humanities, literature (fiction and nonfiction), folklore, mythology, children's literature, linguistics, film, and television.

Indexes

N673. *Canadian Essay and Literature Index* (*Can. Ess. Lit. Ind.*). Toronto: Univ. of Toronto Press, 1973–75. Annual.   AI3.C238 016.81'08'08112

This author-title-subject index covered over fifty Canadian periodicals and almost one hundred anthologies published during the previous year, most of which are not indexed elsewhere. Reviews are listed only under the book's author. Researchers hope this will be revived.

N674.   *Canadian Periodical Index: An Author and Subject Index (Can. Per. Ind.).* Ottawa, Ont.: Canadian Library Assn., 1964– . Monthly, with annual and five-year cumulations. Former titles, 1928–47: *Canadian Periodical Index and Documentary Films*; 1948–63: *Canadian Index to Periodicals.* AI3   016.051

Indexes Canadian-related material on all disciplines found in 113 English and French periodicals including the *Journal of Canadian Fiction* (N688) and *Dalhousie Review* (N678). Literature students should note that book reviews are found under *B* and poems and short stories under *P* and *S*. Cumulative index, 1948–59.

Periodicals

*N676.   *Canadian Literature: A Quarterly of Criticism and Review (CanL).* Vancouver: Univ. of British Columbia, 1959– . Quarterly. PS8061

The oldest journal devoted entirely to writing in Canada. Lively criticism of Canadian authors; reviews of current works; original poetry; unannotated annual bibliography (1959–71) of English-Canadian and French-Canadian creative and critical works, including theses, that updated the basic bibliography of criticism found in *On Canadian Literature* (N668). This annual bibliography was transferred to *Journal of Canadian Fiction* (N688) in 1972. Text in both English and French. Title in French: *Littérature Canadienne.*

Indexed in *ABELL* (D32), *Abst. Eng. Stud.* (E38), *Am. Hum. Ind.* (P738), *Arts and Hum. Cit. Ind.* (F47), *Current Bk. Rev. Cit.* (W1564), *Hum. Ind.* (F45), *Index to Bk. Rev. Hum.* (W1560), *MLAIB* (D31).

N677.   *Canadian Review of Comparative Literature (CRCL).* Toronto: Univ. of Toronto Press, 1974– . Annual. PN851.C35

Designed for literary scholars whose studies transcend national boundaries, with numerous abstracts of articles from international journals.

Indexed in *ABELL* (D32), *Arts and Hum. Cit. Ind.* (F47), *Index to Bk. Rev. Hum.* (W1560), *MLAIB* (D31).

N678.   *Dalhousie Review (DR).* Halifax, N.S.: Dalhousie Univ. Press, 1921– . Quarterly. Z1375.W33   [PS8001]

Scholarly articles and reviews on literature, philosophy, political science, and history, with a slight preference for Canadian subjects and contributors. A recent issue contained articles on themes, influences, and novelists and a review of the latest scholarship on poetry.

Indexed in *ABELL* (D32), *Arts and Hum. Cit. Ind.* (F47), *Index to Bk. Rev. Hum.* (W1560), *MLAIB* (D31).

N679.   *Essays on Canadian Writing: A Quarterly of Criticism (ECW).* Downsview, Ont.: York Univ., 1974– . Quarterly. PS8043   810.9

Articles, interviews, and bibliographies on Margaret Atwood, Gallant,

Lampman, bpNichol, and others; annual bibliography of Canadian literature. Index for nos. 1–12 (1974–78), 1978.

> Indexed in *ABELL* (D32), *Am. Hum. Ind.* (P738), *MLAIB* (D31).

N680.   *Studies in Canadian Literature (SCL)*. Fredericton: Univ. of New Brunswick, 1976–   . 2/yr. PS8071   810'.9

Articles and notes, but no reviews, on Malcolm Lowry, Saul Bellow (born in Canada), Margaret Atwood, and others.

> Indexed in *ABELL* (D32), *Abst. Eng. Stud.* (E38), *Am. Hum. Ind.* (P738), *Arts and Hum. Cit. Ind.* (F47), *MLAIB* (D31).

N681.   *Tamarack Review (TamR)*. Toronto: n.p. (P.O. Box 500, Terminal A), 1956–   . Quarterly. AP5.T3

One of the earliest periodicals to devote itself to Canadian literature: poetry, fiction, reviews. Index to nos. 1–20 (1950–61) in no. 21; index to nos. 21–41 (1961–66) in no. 42.

> Indexed in *Arts and Hum. Cit. Ind.* (F47), *Can. Per. Ind.* (N674), *Index to Bk. Rev. Hum.* (W1560), *MLAIB* (D31).

N682.   *West Coast Review: A Quarterly Magazine of the Arts (WCR)*. Burnaby, B.C.: Simon Fraser Univ., 1965–   . Quarterly. AP2.W395 PS8001

This low-key but solid influence on contemporary literature publishes short stories, poetry, critical articles, scholarly book reviews, and bibliographies on avant-garde literature. Its fine reputation attracts contributors like Günter Grass.

> Indexed in *ABELL* (D32), *Abst. Eng. Stud.* (E38), *Am. Hum. Ind.* (P738), *Bk. Rev. Ind.* (W1559), *Index to Bk. Rev. Hum.* (W1560), *Index to Lit. Mag.* (W1429), *MLAIB* (D31).

*N683.   *University of Toronto Quarterly: A Canadian Journal of the Humanities (UTQ)*. Toronto: Univ. of Toronto Press, 1932–   . Quarterly. AP5.U58 051.U582

An international cross-disciplinary journal with an annual bibliographical essay ("Letters in Canada") that surveys the year's scholarship in the humanities, social sciences, fiction, poetry, drama, and theater translations in French, English, and other languages. Author index to the books reviewed. In English and French.

> Indexed in *ABELL* (D32), *Arts and Hum. Cit. Ind.* (F47), *Current Bk. Rev. Cit.* (W1564), *Hum. Ind.* (F45), *Index to Bk. Rev. Hum.* (W1560), *MLAIB* (D31).

Author newsletters, journals, and other serial publications devoted to individual Canadian authors

N685.   Additional author newsletters are listed in this guide for American (P777), English (J195), Continental (Q893), Irish (K600), Scottish (L627), and Welsh (M640) authors. For full bibliographical information and descriptive annotations on these and other periodicals concerned with one person, see *Author Newsletters and Journals* (W1476).

Choquette, Robert
Cahiers du cercle Robert Choquette,
1956–64.

Seers, Eugène (Louis Dantin)
Cahiers Louis Dantin, 1962–?.

FICTION

Basic guides

N687. *Canadian Fiction: An Annotated Bibliography.* Ed. Margery Fee and
     Ruth Cawker. Toronto: Peter Martin, 1976. 170pp. Z1377.F4.F44
     [PR9192.2]   016.813

Written for teachers who need help in selecting titles for their courses, and
for students who are interested in Canadian literature but do not have time to
read everything. Brief summaries of the works, title and subject indexes for novels,
and title and author indexes for the short stories. This format accomplishes the
book's purpose: to provide a tool that will encourage the wider reading and
study of Canadian literature.

Periodicals

*N688. *Journal of Canadian Fiction (JCF; Jour. Can. Fict.).* Guelph, Ont.:
     Canada Council, 1972–   . Quarterly. PS8001   PR9100.J697

Short stories and critical essays, but important especially for the annual annotated bibliography it has featured since 1972 of all scholarship in all media
concerned with Canadian literature (the bibliography previously appeared in
Canadian Literature, N676). Occasional special issues such as the one in 1974
on early Canadian fiction. Name index. In English or French.

Indexed in *ABELL* (D32), *Abst. Eng. Stud.* (E38), *Am. Hum. Ind.* (P738),
Arts and Hum. Cit. Ind. (F47), *Can. Per. Ind.* (N674), *Index to Bk. Rev. Hum.*
(W1560), *MLAIB* (D31).

N689. *Canadian Fiction Magazine (CFM).* Vancouver: CFM, 1971–   . Quarter-
     ly. PS8001

The editor calls himself "a missionary in the Third World of Canadian letters." His journal is largely devoted to original stories, but a few critical articles
and reviews are included in each issue. Occasional cumulated indexes and special
issues on, for instance, the political novel or science fiction.

Indexed in *Abst. Pop. Cult.* (W1498), *Am. Hum. Ind.* (P738), *Can. Ess.
Lit. Ind.* (N673), *Can. Per. Ind.* (N674), *Jour. Can. Fict.* (N688), *MLAIB* (D31).

Additional reference sources for Canadian fiction

N690. Ferres, John H. "Criticism of Canadian Fiction since 1945: A Selective
     Checklist." *Modern Fiction Studies,* 22 (1976/77), 485–500. See *MFS*
     (J544).

POETRY

Basic guides

N691.   *Modern English-Canadian Poetry: A Guide to Information Sources.* Ed.
Peter Stevens. Volume 15 of Gale Information Guide Library (A8).
Detroit: Gale, 1978. 216pp. Z1377.P7.S79   [PR9184.3]   016.811'5

Broken down into three eras: 1900 to 1940, 1940 to 1960, and 1960 to
the copyright date, with annotations for the works and their criticism as well
as for all periodicals, biographical dictionaries, indexes, and other sources helpful
in researching twentieth-century Canadian poetry. Margaret Atwood, Dorothy
Livesay, Raymond Knister, E. J. Pratt, and dozens more receive fairly complete
treatment. The *Journal of Canadian Poetry* (N692) and the annual bibliography
in the *Journal of Canadian Fiction* (N688), which records scholarship on *all*
Canadian literature, bring it up to date. Watters' *Checklist* (N665) is more comprehensive in subject matter, of course, but it may contain some specific helpful
items in poetry. Students should also be on the alert for another book that is
currently in preparation: *Contemporary Canadian Poetry: A Critical Survey and
Bio-Bibliographical Guide*, ed. Richard Morgan and Bradley Hayden (Westport,
Conn.: Greenwood).

Periodicals

N692.   *Journal of Canadian Poetry.* Ottawa, Ont.: n.p. (Station F), 1978–   .
2/yr. PR9190.25.J68   C811'.009

Devoted to scholarly research and criticism of the poetry of Canada from
its origins to the present. Bibliographies.

Additional reference works for information on Canadian literature

N693.   *Abst. Eng. Stud.* (E38) indexes several Canadian literary periodicals
America (E43)
America in Fiction (P779)
American Doctoral Dissertations (W1213)
Am. Hum. Ind. (P738) indexes a few Canadian periodicals
Arts and Hum. Cit. Ind. (F47)
Canadian Diaries and Autobiographies (W1058)
*Canadian Writers and Their Works: Essays on Form, Context, and
Development.* 20 vols. Downsview, Ont.: ECW Press, York Univ.,
1982–   .
Canadiana (D36)
Commonwealth Literature (N645–95)
Contemporary Poets (W1129)
*Creative Canada: A Biographical Dictionary of Twentieth-Century
Creative and Performing Artists.* Toronto: Univ. of Toronto Press,
1971–   .
Dictionary of Literature in the English Language (W1122)
Index to Periodical Fiction in English, 1965–69 (G77)

McNamee, *Dissertations* (W1212)
MLAIB (D31), vol. 1, English II, Canada
Modern English-Canadian Prose. Ed. Helen Hoy. Detroit: Gale, 1983.
   605pp. Z1377.F4.H69   [PR9192.5]   016.818'508
Reference Guide to English, American, and Canadian Literature (B18)
Salem, *Foreign Drama* (R969)
Twayne's World Authors Series (R957), Canada
World Literature since 1945 (R950)

New Zealand Literature

Basic guides

*N694. *New Zealand Literature to 1977.* Ed. John E. P. Thomson. Vol 30 of
   Gale Information Guide Library (A8). Detroit: Gale, 1979. 272pp.
   Z4111.T45   [PR9624.3]   016.82
   The only guide to New Zealand literature, remarkably current and thorough.
It deals extensively with thirty-one major authors and, in a separate chapter,
summarizes the accomplishments of seventy-three lesser authors. It provides brief
biographical sketches and a selected list of each author's works, the more important biographies, and critical books and articles. The author annotates some
but not all of the entries. Author and title indexes.

Periodicals

*N695. *Landfall.* Christchurch, N.Z.: Caxton, 1947–   . Quarterly. AP7.L35
   052
   Focuses on the critical and creative literature of New Zealand.
   Indexed in *ABELL* (D32), *Abst. Eng. Stud.* (E38), *Arts and Hum. Cit. Ind.*
(F47), *Brit. Hum. Ind.* (F49), *Index to Bk. Rev. Hum.* (W1560), *MLAIB* (D31).

Additional reference sources

MLAIB (D31), vol. 1, English II, New Zealand
Twayne's World Authors Series (R957), New Zealand

P

American Literature

Many titles listed in Twentieth-Century English Literature (J510–77) also contain information on twentieth-century American literature, especially the periodicals and background-reading materials. This is true partly because of the mobility of the authors and partly because of the similarity in themes and style. Students should, therefore, consult both sections for complete coverage.

Surveys

**P700. *Guide to the Study of the United States of America: Representative Books Reflecting the Development of American Life and Thought.* Ed. Roy P. Basler. Washington, D.C.: Library of Congress, 1960. 1193pp. Supplement (1976), 526pp. Z1215.U53 [E156] 016.973

The final authority for information on publications that reflect our historical background. Unique features: (1) a point of view that is at once American, historical, and cross-disciplinary; (2) biographical sketches of major and minor American authors in all disciplines from literature and philosophy to American Indians, travel, folklore, and book production; (3) brief summaries of not "mere literature . . . but literature which preserves a record of American life"; and (4) material that is not easily found elsewhere. This is not a book you will read from cover to cover. Nor is it a book with recent information (the first volume covers publications through 1955; the supplement, from 1956 to 1965). It is, however, the only source that focuses on American culture in its totality and presents literature, almost incidentally, as both a contributor to and a result of that culture. Furthermore, the prose is American style at its finest. This is a literary history of which Americans can be proud.

*P701. *Literary History of the United States* (*LHUS*; Spiller). Ed. Robert E. Spiller. 4th ed. 2 vols. New York: Macmillan, 1974. PS88.L522 810.9

This is still required reading for anyone beginning the study of American literature, especially the early years, but there have been all too few revisions and additions since its first appearance in 1948. Students who need an evaluation of the contemporary literary scene will be obliged to look elsewhere, as in the highly respected *Harvard Guide to Contemporary American Writing* (P826).

Vol. 1 contains scholarly essays on the social, political, religious, and intellectual background, discussing not only authors but individual titles as they relate to the history and development of the country. Fewer than one hundred pages of this 1,556-page volume are given to post–World War II authors, so students must expect to find careful treatment of Emerson and Clemens, but relatively little on the Black Mountain or San Francisco poets of the 1950s. The material on Dickinson and Lanier has been rewritten, and Albee and Robert Lowell are now included, but there is scant mention of McCullers, Mailer, Malamud, Salinger, and Sexton. A table of authors identifies the author of each essay, and there is a title, subject, and author index for the whole volume as well as a bibliography for each section.

Vol. 2 contains selective, evaluative essay-style bibliographies of general and specific reference tools and problems, literary history and criticism, language, regionalism (for example, the Southwest), cultural background, and 207 individual authors. The editions and biographies of each author are cited and evaluated; critical works are listed for all important individual titles; library collections of papers and manuscripts are noted; and there are descriptions of the author bibliographies and checklists. As an updated bibliography, however, it is a severe disappointment because, while it brings together under one cover the bibliographies of 1948, 1959, and 1972, it does not cumulate them. It does, however, have a well-edited author-title-subject index for the whole volume. Even so, *LHUS* remains what critics have judged it to be—an example of outstanding scholarship of the 1940s.

Bibliographies of bibliographies

P702.   *Index to American Author Bibliographies.* Ed. Patricia P. Havlice. Metuchen, N.J.: Scarecrow, 1971. 204pp. Z1225.H37   016.01681

Because of its arrangement (one alphabet with 2,225 unannotated entries) and selectivity (limited to authors only and to scholarship in twenty-eight periodicals, not books), this is much easier for the average student to use than Nilon's *Bibliography of Bibliographies in American Literature* (C27). Unfortunately, it is too selective for our current needs (many author bibliographies are now produced in book form, which this does not cover) and at the same time too old to reflect the explosive increase in bibliographical material during the past decade. It does, however, list major authors, such as Richard Wright (with six bibliographies) and Hawthorne (with thirteen), as well as many minor authors who may not appear elsewhere, so it may still be useful to some students. Most will probably prefer to look for information on their authors in recently published bibliographies devoted to special areas, such as *American Drama to 1900* (P796) or, for the latest publications, in *Bibliographic Index* (C28) and *Bulletin of Bibliography* (C29). In every case, they might want to consider Brenni's evaluations (P716).

Basic guides

P704.   *Guide to American Literature from Its Beginnings through Walt Whit-man.* Ed. James T. Callow and Robert J. Reilly. New York: Barnes and Noble, 1976. 244pp. Paperback. PS92.C33   810'.9

   Guide to American Literature from Emily Dickinson to the Present. Ed. James T. Callow and Robert J. Reilly. New York: Barnes and Noble, 1977. 272pp. Paperback. PS203.C27   810'.9

   These attempt to do for American literature what Martin Day's history (J172) does for English literature—reduce the facts to manageable size. Aimed at the student who is just beginning to specialize in American literature, these guides summarize and interpret trends, titles, and contributions of individual authors. The chapter-by-chapter and author-by-author bibliographies are a commendable effort, but they do tend to overlook many bibliographical aids that appeared during the 1970s. A second edition can easily rectify this one weakness. Good for browsing, for use as a classroom text, and for last-minute reading before exams.

P705.   Gohdes, Clarence L., and Sanford E. Marovitz. *Bibliographical Guide to the Study of the Literature of the U.S.A.* 5th ed. Durham, N.C.: Duke Univ. Press, 1984. 300pp. Z1225.G6   016.81
   Particularly good for a subject (not author) approach in such areas as drama, fiction, religion, criticism, racial and religious minorities, historical and cultural trends through the centuries, regional literature, racial literature, folklore, biography, psychology, women's studies, technical procedures in research, and preparation of manuscripts. Two indexes—one by subject and another by author, editor, and compiler. Brief annotations and a list of major biographies.

P706.   *American Literature: A Study and Research Guide.* Ed. Lewis Leary. New York: St. Martin's, 1976. 185pp. Paperback. Z1224.L47   [PS88] 810.'9
   Undergraduates in American literature will appreciate several features of this book: the chapter discussing the slow development and appreciation of our national literature; the sections on twenty-eight prominent authors with evaluations of major critical studies; the sections on regional and ethnic literatures; the inclusion of L.C. numbers; the chapter that explains how to start, stop, document, and type a research paper; and the chapter discussing critical methods that range from the traditional to the modern, from biography to phenomenology. Quality selections and sage advice abound, but no contemporary authors are discussed.

P707.   Jones, Howard Mumford, and Richard M. Ludwig. *Guide to American Literature and Its Backgrounds since 1890.* 4th ed. Cambridge, Mass.: Harvard Univ. Press, 1972. 264pp. Paperback. Z1225.J65   016.81
   This unique subject, genre, and chronological arrangement frequently has answers for those who want to relate literature to reality. The first part includes

general histories; works concerned with social problems, music, and movies; literary history by genre; biography; a particularly fine list of magazines with descriptive and evaluative annotations; and a chronological summary of American and world history from 1890 to 1971. The second part supplies reading lists on specific subjects, such as the West, the Forces of Naturalism, the Impact of World War I, the New Method in the Historical Novel, the Cold War and the Moral Problem, and Science Fiction. Furthermore, an author index to the entire book relates specific titles and general ideas. The E. E. Cummings entry, for instance, refers the reader to bibliographies of the War Novels and the New Spirit in Fiction and Poetry that suggest comparisons with Faulkner, Fitzgerald, Hemingway, Aiken, Eliot, and Stevens. The short introductions summarizing the problems of each subject area and the occasional evaluative annotations are helpful to students looking for topics and to teachers seeking guidance in compiling lesson plans.

P708.   *Field Guide to the Study of American Literature.* Ed. Harold H. Kolb, Jr. Charlottesville: Univ. Press of Virginia, 1976. 136pp. Paperback. Z1225.K65 [PS88]   016.81

American literature students should definitely browse through the annotations for the 140 recommended titles in "Literary History and Criticism," but they will have trouble locating information in the rest of the book. Book reviewing sources are listed in various sections under "Bibliographies," and research on the novel is found in not one but several places. Students should also be aware that the "annotations" are most often quotations from the prefaces of the books.

P709.   Davis, Richard B. *American Literature through Bryant, 1585-1830.* Goldentree Bibliographies (W1291). New York: Appleton (Meredith), 1969. 135pp. Paperback. Z1225.D3   016.810'9

A convenient bibliography (up to its copyright date) of primary and secondary works on fifty-six major and minor authors in the Colonial period to 1763 (including Bradstreet, Taylor, and Wigglesworth), thirty-two authors of the Revolutionary period (such as Freneau, Paine, Weems), and thirty-six of the early national period (such as Webster, Brown, Irving). There are sections on periodicals, literary history, and cultural background, and under each author are cited the best biographies, bibliographies, and editions. This is especially useful for lesser figures who may have been overlooked in *LHUS* (P701). Some students may prefer to consult recently published bibliographies in specific areas, such as *American Drama to 1900* (P796).

P710.   Clark, Harry H. *American Literature: Poe through Garland.* Goldentree Bibliographies (W1291). New York: Appleton (Meredith), 1971. 148pp. Paperback. Z1227.C58   016.8108

Superseded in many areas by more specialized, recently published bibliographies in American fiction, drama, and poetry, but still a popular source because it is a convenient size and limited to authors who held a significant position in American literature between 1830 and 1914. It places special emphasis on social and literary criticism, history, and the short story. Bibliographies, editions, concordances, biographies, and critical studies are listed for twenty-one major authors including Twain, Crane, Dickinson, James, Melville, and twenty-three minor authors like Bierce, Harte, London, and Santayana. No annotations, and no asterisks to indicate the best scholarship.

P711.   Rubin, Louis D., Jr., ed. *A Bibliographical Guide to the Study of Southern Literature.* Baton Rouge: Louisiana State Univ. Press, 1969. 351pp. Appendix, ed. J. A. Leo Lemay. Z1225.R8   016.81

Designed to aid in the scholarly assessment of Southern literature, but not intended to be comprehensive, either in number of writers or in scope of the authors' work. Part 1 covers specific subjects, eras, and problems such as Antebellum Southern Writers, the South in Northern Eyes, Black Humor, Local Color, Folklore, the Civil War in Southern Literature, and Twentieth-Century Southern Drama. Each section contains a short introduction and a briefly annotated, selective bibliography of pertinent critical articles and books.

Part 2 is arranged alphabetically by 135 individual authors such as Faulkner, Jesse Stuart, Poe, Toomer, Ransom, and Jarrell, with evaluative introductions and selective bibliographies. The appendix adds sixty-eight more writers of the Colonial South. Students interested in the Southern Gothic school of writing can thus easily locate numerous bibliographies and studies of McCullers, O'Connor, Welty, Porter, and others.

Editors Rubin, Robert Bain, and Joseph M. Flora have prepared a companion piece to Rubin's guide entitled *Southern Writers: A Biographical Dictionary* (Baton Rouge: Louisiana State Univ. Press, 1979; 515pp.). This provides biographical sketches, commentary, and primary bibliographies for almost four hundred authors including Agee, Arnow, Barth, Bontemps, Haley, Hardwick, Harris, Heyward, Tate, Warren, Tom and Thomas Wolfe. Critics will be able to point out that several of their favorite minor authors have been overlooked, but this will probably be a favorite first source for basic information on Southern writers for several years. Another bibliography on this same subject by Jack D. Wages, *Seventy-Four Writers of the Colonial South* (Boston: Hall, 1979) is disappointing in both coverage and arrangement, but it may supplement Rubin in some areas. For more recent information, see *Mississippi Quarterly* (P755).

P712.   *Southwestern American Literature.* Ed. John Q. Anderson et al. Athens: Swallow, 1979. 445pp. Z1251.S8.A52   016.979

The first comprehensive list of works about the region, its characteristic genres, and four hundred of its authors. It is particularly useful for locating primary and secondary material on minor authors who are not recorded elsewhere. Reviewers have noticed omissions, but this is a fine first effort that can easily be perfected in the second edition. See also the periodical with the same title (P768). Would that it had an annual bibliography of criticism about Southwestern authors.

P712.1 Nemanic, Gerald C., ed. *A Bibliographical Guide to Midwestern Literature.* Iowa City: Univ. of Iowa Press, 1981. 380pp. Z1251.W5.B52 [PS273]   016.81'08'0977

A guide to Midwestern literature that organizes scattered bits and pieces of information concerning the writers and their works and at last makes this worthy segment of American culture accessible to the public. It lists bibliographies not only for 120 different authors but also for scholarship devoted to individual states, folklore, Indian and black literature, and other subjects characteristic of the area. Jessamyn West appears here with a brief summary of her unique accomplishments and the titles of the best primary and secondary works, as do Ruth Suckow, William Stafford, Rolvaag, Harriet Monroe, Algren, Masters, Kantor, and others whose works need to be researched and publicized.

P712.2 Etulain, Richard W. *Bibliographical Guide to the Study of Western American Literature*. Lincoln: Univ. of Nebraska Press, 1982. 317pp. Z1251.W5 [PS271] 016.81'09'978

Entries for over five thousand books concerned with four hundred authors, Western topics, and literature. See also W1130 and P772.

P712.3 *Fifty Western Writers: A Bio-Bibliographical Sourcebook*. Ed. Fred Erisman and Richard W. Etulain. Westport, Conn.: Greenwood, 1982. 562pp. PS271.F5 810'.9'978

From Cather and Kesey to Stafford and Suckow—two pages of biography, several pages on the major themes, a brief survey of the criticism, and a select bibliography. See also W1130 and P772.

P712.4 *American Writers before 1800: A Biographical and Critical Reference Guide*. Ed. James A. Levernier and Douglas M. Wilmes. 3 vols. Westport, Conn.: Greenwood, 1983. PS185.A4 810'.9'001

Biographical, bibliographical, and critical information on 780 early American writers. Three appendixes and a chronology.

Additional guides containing information on American literature

Altick and Wright, *Selective Bibliography* (B15), two pages on American literature, with many other relevant titles scattered throughout the book, but no cross-references leading readers to those titles.

Bateson and Meserole, *Guide to English and American Literature* (B17), a generous section on American literature, with delightful one-sentence annotations.

Kennedy and Sands, *Concise Bibliography for Students of English* (B19), a thirteen-page section on American literature, but no annotations.

Schweik and Riesner, *Reference Sources* (B16), a separate section on American literature and numerous relevant titles in other sections that are somewhat difficult to locate because there is no title index.

Somer and Cooper, *American and British Literature, 1945–1975* (B20), the best source for guidance in studying contemporary American literature.

Bibliographies of primary works

P713. Blanck, Jacob, ed. *Bibliography of American Literature*. New Haven: Yale Univ. Press, 1955– . In progress (6 vols. completed by 1980). Bibliographical Soc. of America. Z1225.B55 016.81

This project has been looking for a new editor since Jacob Blanck died.

It is an author bibliography covering only first editions of the belles lettres of three hundred significant authors who wrote between the Revolution and 1930. It is, therefore, a complement to Evans (P717) and Sabin (P718). The chronological entries describe binding, size, page numbering, illustrations, and library locations.

For some important authors, the editor provides a brief list of reprints, biographies, bibliographies, and critical works for further study. He does not include periodicals, later editions, or translations. A scholarly work that American literature students should know about, even if they use it only occasionally.

P714.   *First Printings of American Authors: Contributions toward Descriptive Checklists.* Ed. Matthew J. Bruccoli. 4 vols. Detroit: Gale, 1977–79. Supplement, vol. 5 (1984). Z1231.F5.F57   [PS88]   016.81

Book collectors, booksellers, and rare book librarians may find some use for this handsome bibliography of first American and English printings of novels, plays, essays, and poems by American authors. Its main purpose is to identify first printings (not first editions) of historically important authors such as Thomas Bulfinch, Booth Tarkington, Wilma Dykeman, and about 360 others. It also supplies information on other bibliographies and biographies in the field and contains about two thousand facsimiles of title pages, dust jackets, and bindings. Cumulative index in vol. 4. The editors are accurate in their subtitle: This is a "contribution" toward that final, definitive American bibliography (see also Wright, P778).

P715.   *Literary Writings in America: A Bibliography.* Ed. Edward H. O'Neill. 8 vols. Millwood, N.Y.: KTO, 1977. Z1225.L58   [PS88]   016.81

A government program that really worked, even though it was forty years in the making. During the depression years of 1938 to 1942, this WPA project put fifty scholars to work locating materials and making a card file for over 200,000 titles by and about 600 major and minor American authors. They found material in 2,600 periodicals and books published between 1850 and 1942, years that had never before been adequately indexed. It is, therefore, a unique contribution to American history, especially for a host of minor writers who have no other published bibliographies and for specialized material such as the book review, which is usually overlooked by indexing sources. Arrangement is alphabetical by author. A valuable source in spite of its numerous errors. See Wells (P743) for similar coverage of earlier periodicals.

*P716.   *Bibliographic Control of American Literature, 1920–1975.* Ed. Vito J. Brenni. Metuchen, N.J.: Scarecrow, 1979. 218pp. Z1224.5.B73 [PS221]   016.810'8'0052

An important historical, comparative study of the merits and demerits of existing bibliographies of many twentieth-century American authors. This examines and evaluates the lists of their novels, short stories, poems, plays, and regional literature as they appear in books, parts of books, and periodicals. In the back of the book is a list of the 717 bibliographies discussed in the text. Many ideas here for research projects and prospective editors. Essential browsing for all American literature scholars, who should consider the evaluations even though they may not agree with them. They will regret the omissions and the cutoff date of 1975, but still, this is a commendable first effort.

National bibliographies

—for verification or identification problems that the *NUC* (B10–11) or the *L. C. Catalog* (B12) may not be able to solve.

**P717. Evans, Charles. *American Bibliography: A Chronological Dictionary of All Books, Pamphlets and Periodical Publications Printed in the United States of America from the Genesis of Printing in 1639 down to and including the Year 1820, with Bibliographical and Biographical Notes.* 14 vols. Chicago: Blakely, for Evans, 1903–34 (vols. 1–12); Worcester, Mass.: American Antiquarian Soc., 1955–59 (vols. 13–14). Z1215.E923 015.73

Scholars interested in America's earliest printed books will use this as their basic research aid. Incredibly, it is the work of one man, a painstaking scholar who copied all the information from each title page, named a library that owned a copy of the book, and like many an editor before and after him, found delight in noting outstanding bits of booklore (in 1664, five hundred copies of the Song of David were printed in the Massachusetts Indian language, and in 1903 the Bay Psalm Book could be purchased for $1,200).

In spite of the title, Evans unfortunately was able to complete his work only through the letter *M* of 1799 (12 vols.). The following outline illustrates the careful planning of determined scholars to extend and perfect his original concept of an American bibliography:

.1   Shipton, Clifford K. (vol. 13, 1955). Shipton started with the letter *N* and completed through the year 1800, with author and subject indexes. Z1215.E923

.2   Bristol, Roger P. (vol. 14, 1959). Bristol prepared a cumulated author-title index for the whole thirteen volumes including pseudonyms and dates for the authors, a boon in biographical searches because many minor authors are extremely difficult to identify. Z1215.E923

.3   ———. Bristol then compiled an index of printers, publishers, and booksellers to the whole work (Charlottesville: Bibliographical Soc. of the Univ. of Virginia, 1961; 172pp). Z1215.E9233

.4   Shipton, Clifford K., and James E. Mooney. *National Index of American Imprints through 1800: The Short-Title Evans.* 2 vols. Worcester, Mass.: American Antiquarian Soc., 1969. Z1215.S495   015'.73

The Early American Imprints Project, sponsored by Readex Microprint and the AAS, plans to reproduce the text of all nonserial items in Evans through 1819. In preparation for this, the *National Index* incorporates Evans' original 39,162 items with the tens of thousands of corrections found during the ensuing fifty years. It admittedly still contains countless errors and inconsistencies, but it is a significant step toward that ultimate goal of a definitive American bibliography. The Imprints Project was given a Mellon Foundation grant in 1979 and expects to complete its work in 1982.

.5   Bristol, Roger P.   Bristol edited a supplement to the original thirteen

volumes (Charlottesville: Univ. Press of Virginia, 1970; 636pp.). This
adds about 11,200 entries to the original Evans-Shipton total of 39,162.
Z1215.E923

.6 ———. Bristol then prepared an index to his supplement (Charlottesville: Univ. Press of Virginia, 1971; 191pp.). This completes the work
started by Evans seventy years earlier. New entries and corrections such
as are found in the following title will of course have to be added from
time to time. Z1215.E92334

.7 ———. *American Bibliographical Notes: Additions and Corrections to
Evans and Bristol's Supplement.* Worcester, Mass.: American Antiquarian Soc., 1974. Reprint from the proceedings of the AAS.

.8 Shaw, Ralph R., and Richard H. Shoemaker. *American Bibliography:
A Preliminary Checklist for 1801-1819.* 22 vols. New York: Scarecrow,
1958-66. Z1215.S48
This extends coverage twenty years, one volume for each year, with library
symbols and author and title indexes. Printers, publishers, and booksellers index, geographical index (1983; 457pp.).

.9 Shoemaker, Richard H. *Checklist of American Imprints for 1820-1829.*
10 vols. Metuchen, N.J.: Scarecrow, 1964-71. Z1215.S55
This extends coverage ten more years, one volume for each year. It greatly
enlarges an earlier, much less comprehensive, but nevertheless heroic, work on
the same period by Orville A. Roorbach, *Bibliotheca Americana . . . 1820-61*
(New York: Roorbach, 1852-61; 4 vols.).

.10 Cooper, M. Frances. Cooper, who assisted in the preparation of the
volumes for 1826-29 of the previous entry, prepared for the whole ten
years a title index (Metuchen, N.J.: Scarecrow, 1972; 556pp.) and an
author index (1973; 172pp.), with pseudonyms and corrections.
Z1215.S5

.11 ———. Cooper continued the project with a checklist of American imprints for the year 1830 (Scarecrow, 1972; 493pp.). Z1215.S5

.12 Bruntjen, Scott, and Carol Rinderknecht Bruntjen. *Checklist of
American Imprints for 1831-* . Metuchen, N.J.: Scarecrow, 1975- .
429pp. Z1215.S553
The current editors of the project state clearly that their undertaking (one
volume a year) is only the first step toward a definitive American bibliography
for the period. They are aware of numerous inaccuracies because their work is
based on thousands of slips of paper prepared by a WPA bibliographical program of the 1930s and 1940s. They also know that their work is significantly
increasing the scope of known American publishing, and they hope it will soon
be corrected and supplemented.
The volume for 1832 contains 523 pages (1977), that for 1833, 478 pages
(1979), and that for 1834, 644 pages (1982). They, too, are arranged by author
with birth and death dates, title of the book, place of publication and publisher,
date of publication, number of pages, and names of one or more libraries owning a copy. The series, when completed, will cover the period 1820-75.

.13 Kelly, James. *The American Catalogue of Books (Original and Reprints)
Published in the United States from Jan., 1861, to Jan. [1871], with
Date of Publication, Size, Price, and Publisher's Name.* 2 vols. New
York: Wiley, 1866–71. Z1215.A3   015.73

Kelly continued Roorbach's work (see no. 9). Both projects are incomplete
and inaccurate, but they were the necessary first steps for which present editors
and scholars are grateful.

.14 *American Catalogue . . . Author and Title Entries of Books in Print
and for Sale . . . 1876.* Ed. Frederick Leypoldt. 8 vols. in 13. New
York: Armstrong, 1880. Z1215.A52

Leypoldt undertook this work with reluctance, but with Roorbach dead and
Kelly disheartened, there was no one else willing to tackle this unimaginably
disorganized mass of material. Put quite simply, this resembles our current *Books
in Print* (W1170), even to the list of publishers and the author-title and subject
indexes. Various publishers and editors carried the work forward under this title
through 1910.

.15 *United States Catalog: Books in Print, 1899–1928.* 4th ed. New York:
Wilson, 1928. Z1219.M78

This became a record of all books published in the United States and the
chief importations, arranged by author, title, and subject. It thus was the first
step toward our current *CBI* (D35), which actually was the title given the *U.S.
Catalog*'s supplements that were published irregularly beginning in 1902.

.16 *Cumulative Book Index: A World List of Books in the English Language*
(see D35 for a full annotation).

This originally began publication in 1902 in the form of supplements to
the *U.S. Catalog* (see P717.15). It thus both continues and expands on the work
of the previous century.

.17 *Publishers Weekly: The Book Industry Journal.* New York: Bowker,
1872–   . Weekly.

This catch-all for news, advertisements, announcements, articles, and interviews concerning new publications amounts to five thousand reviews a year
(fifty a week for literature). They are the earliest available reviews because they
always precede the publication date. Until 1974 this featured a list of the week's
publications in the United States (see P717.18).

.18 *Weekly Record.* New York: Bowker, 1876–   . Weekly.

Since 1974 this has included a list of American and foreign titles published
and distributed in the United States. This, the most up-to-date report available,
gives complete publishing information, brief descriptions, Dewey numbers, L.C.
Catalog numbers, and subject headings. About three hundred literature titles
appear in every issue. The issues cumulate into the monthly *American Book
Publishing Record* (New York: Bowker, 1950–   ), for which there is a title and
author index. These in turn cumulate into annual and five-year volumes, which
themselves were cumulated in 1979 into a set covering the years 1950–77 and, in
1980, into a massive fifteen-volume set covering the years 1876–1949.

.19 *Forthcoming Books.* New York: Bowker, 1966– . 6/yr.
Lists all books published since the last annual *Books in Print* (W1170) and all books scheduled to be published in the next five months.

**P718. Sabin, Joseph. *Bibliotheca Americana: A Dictionary of Books Relating to America from Its Discovery to the Present Time.* 29 vols. New York: Sabin, 1868–1936. Bibliographical Soc. of America. Z1201.S22   015.73
One of the first major efforts to bring order to the mass of materials about America, no matter where it was published. Students interested in historical studies will find author, anonymous title, and subject entries such as "Blue Laws Revived" (ca. 1806); Worcester, Mass., Executions for burglary (1786); and a Young Men's Temperance Convention in 1834. Alphabetically arranged, with delightful annotations, authors' dates, and, in many cases, names of libraries owning copies, but no index.
Two new publications are making the contents more accessible. John E. Molnar's *Author-Title Index to Joseph Sabin's Dictionary of Books Relating to America* (Metuchen, N.J.: Scarecrow, 1974; 3 vols.) identifies many anonymous and pseudonymous works. Lawrence S. Thompson's *New Sabin* (Troy, N.Y.: Whitston) contains additions, corrections, an excellent multi-access index, and a cumulative index with every fifth volume. Latin American and Canadian material is also found here. This continuing project so far has produced nine volumes (1974–84) and has indexed about 30,000 of Sabin's 106,000 items.
John E. Alden is now preparing a chronological guide to writings on the Americas published in Europe before 1801. The eight-volume project is expected to be completed by 1984: *European Americana* (New York: Readex, 1980–).

Series

*P720. Twayne's U.S. Authors Series (TUSAS). Boston: Twayne, 1961– .
These introductory studies are especially suitable for the busy undergraduate who knows almost nothing about an author, for they are readable, simplified, and relatively brief (100–200pp). They include a chronology, biographical information, analyses of themes and style, interpretations of the more important individual works, footnotes, a selective bibliography, and a helpful index. Furthermore, they are often the only work available on minor or newly recognized authors. Students should remember, however, that the quality of the scholarship varies. By 1984, over 450 had been published.
See also Twayne's English Authors Series (J181) and World Authors Series (R957). All studies in the Twayne Series are more comprehensive than the small pamphlets published by the University of Minnesota (P721) and the British Book News (J180).

Henry Adams, by F. Bishop	293	Horatio Alger, Jr., by G. Scharnhorst	363
George Ade, by L. Coyle	63	Nelson Algren, by M. H. Cox	249
James Agee, by V. Kramer	252	James Lane Allen, by W. K. Bottorff	56
Conrad Aiken, by F. J. Hoffman	17	A. R. Ammons, by A. Holder	303
Edward Albee, by R. E. Amacher	141	Maxwell Anderson, by A. S. Shivers	279
Louisa May Alcott, by R. K.		Robert Anderson, by T. P. Adler	300
MacDonald	457	Sherwood Anderson, by R. Burbank	65
Thomas Bailey Aldrich,			
by C. E. Samuels	94		

THE NATIONAL BIBLIOGRAPHY OF THE UNITED STATES

A CHRONOLOGICAL TABLE

P717.	Evans (vols. 1–12), 1903–34	1639——1799
P717.1	Shipton (vol. 13), 1955	1799-1800
P717.2	Bristol (vol. 14, author-title index for vols. 1–13), 1959	1639——1800
P717.3	Bristol (index of printers, publishers, and booksellers), 1961	1639——1800
P717.4	Shipton and Mooney (*Short-Title Evans*), 1969	1639——1800
P717.5	Bristol (supplement), 1970	1639——1800
P717.6	Bristol (index to supplement), 1971	1639——1800
P717.7	Additions to Evans, 1974	1639——1800
P717.8	Shaw and Shoemaker, 22 vols., with author and title indexes, 1958–66	1801-19
P717.9	Roorbach, 4 vols., 1852–61	1820——61
P717.9	Shoemaker, 10 vols., 1964–71	1820-29
P717.10	Cooper (title index for Shoemaker, vols. 1–10), 1972	1820-29
P717.10	Cooper (author index for Shoemaker, vols. 1–10), 1973	1820-29
P717.11	Cooper (imprints for 1830), 1972	1830
P717.12	Bruntjen (imprints for 1831–), 1975–	1831-34....[1875]
P717.13	Kelly, 1866–71	1861——71
P717.14	*American Catalogue*, 1880–1910	1876——1910
P717.15	*U. S. Catalog*, 1899–1928	1899–1928
P717.16	*Cumulative Book Index*, 1928–	1902-28
P717.17	*Publishers Weekly*, 1872–1973	1872————1973
P717.18	*Weekly Record*, 1974–	1974
P717.19	*Forthcoming Books*, 1966–	1966

*P721.   Minnesota. University. Pamphlets on American Writers. Ed. Leonard Unger and George T. Wright. Minneapolis: Univ. of Minnesota Press, 1959–72. Supplements. Paperback. PS129.A55

Brief fifty-page studies that undergraduates will find useful for background information of the simplest kind. They are similar in purpose and scope to the bibliographical series of supplements to English writers published by British Book News (J180) and, like those, often treat relatively obscure or contemporary authors on whom it is difficult to find information elsewhere. Quality of scholarship varies, but the biographical sketch, analysis of style, interpretation of specific titles, and selective bibliography are frequently helpful. Some of the critics are noted scholars, including Gassner (O'Neill), Spiller (Cooper), Miles (Emerson), Leary (Irving), Edel (James), Allen (James), Holman (Marquand), and Asselineau (Poe).

The first ninety-seven titles are available in a four-volume revised edition entitled *American Writers* (New York: Scribners, 1974). The supplements (2 vols., 1979; 2 vols., 1981) add over fifty authors including Rich, Cheever, Oates, and E. B. White.

P722.   Serif Series. Ed. William White. Kent, Ohio: Kent State Univ. Press, 1968–   .

Students who are wise in the ways of research know that their first step is to find out whether basic information on their subject has already been assembled in one reference book. If they are working, therefore, on a currently popular author, they should certainly check this reliable series of bibliographies and checklists of works by and about individual authors (mainly American) and a few timely subjects.

Louis Adamic	Wilfred Owen
Kingsley Amis	Published Screenplays
Isaac Asimov	Edwin Arlington Robinson
Samuel Beckett	Theodore Roethke (2)
Raymond Chandler	Jean-Paul Sartre
James Gould Cozzens	Science Fiction Criticism
Robert Creeley	Upton Sinclair
Emily Dickinson	Gertrude Stein
Theodore Dreiser	Edward Taylor
John Gould Fletcher	J. R. R. Tolkien
Erle Stanley Gardner	John Updike
Graham Greene	Nathanael West
Dashiell Hammett	Walt Whitman
Robert G. Ingersoll	Richard Wilbur
C. S. Lewis	Charles Williams
Archibald MacLeish	Thomas Wolfe
Bernard Malamud	Year's Scholarship in Science Fiction and
Thomas Merton	Fantasy
Anaïs Nin	

P723.   American Authors Logs Series. Boston: Hall, 1979–   . In preparation.
    Scholarly chronologies of the lives of major American authors such as Hawthorne, Poe, Whitman, with excerpts from contemporary documents.

P724.   American Critical Tradition Series. Ed. M. Thomas Inge. New York: Burt Franklin, 1972–   . In progress.
    This series specializes in ferreting out all criticism printed during an author's lifetime in newspapers, reviews, articles, and books. When students read this collection of reprints, excerpts, and summaries, they can judge the relation of the authors to their cultural milieu. About thirty volumes are planned for Cabell, Cather, Crane, Cummings, Dos Passos, Dreiser, Faulkner, Fitzgerald, Frost, Glasgow, Hemingway, Hughes, London, Melville, Norris, O'Neill, Pound, Steinbeck, Twain, Wharton, Whitman, Williams, Wolfe, Wright, and others.

P725.   Critical Essays on American Literature. Ed. James Nagel. Boston: Hall, 1979–   . In progress.
    The most important criticism and the best reviews are collected here in one convenient volume so that students can grasp with ease the growth and trends of scholarship on their favorite author. Each introduction presents an overview of research accomplishments and suggests areas that require further attention. Prediction: Every important American and English writer will soon be the subject of a volume like this.

Henry Adams	George Washington Cable
American Transcendentalism	Erskine Caldwell
Sherwood Anderson	John Cheever
John Barth	Hart Crane
Saul Bellow	John W. De Forest
Ambrose Bierce	Theodore Dreiser
Charles Brockden Brown	Jonathan Edwards

William Faulkner
Harold Frederic
Robert Frost
Margaret Fuller
Hamlin Garland
Joel Chandler Harris
Henry James
Herman Melville
Arthur Miller
Frank Norris
Joyce Carol Oates

Thomas Pynchon
Wallace Stegner
Harriet Beecher Stowe
William Styron
Edward Taylor
Mark Twain
John Updike
Robert Penn Warren
Western American Novel
Phillis Wheatley
John Greenleaf Whittier
Richard Wright

See also

G. K. Hall Reference Guides (W1055)
Pittsburgh Series in Bibliography (W1616)

Criticism

P727.   *Articles on American Literature, 1900-50* (Leary). Ed. Lewis Leary.
Durham, N.C.: Duke Univ. Press, 1954. 437pp. Supplement, 1950–67
(1970), 751pp. Supplement, 1968–75 (1979), 745pp. 3rd supplement
in preparation. Z1225.L49   016.81

These three volumes will save the student many hours of research time and
illustrate the extent to which publishers have responded in the past few years
to the researcher's demand for highly specialized reference works. The main
volume of 1954 began as a compilation of scholarship from the quarterly checklist
in *Am. Lit.* (P744), the annual lists in *MLAIB* (D31), many standard
bibliographies, and about 140 other journals, especially those appearing before
1929, when *Am. Lit.* began publication. The 1979 volume greatly expands
coverage by indexing eleven hundred periodicals and bringing the scholarship
up to 1975. "Serial Bibliographies," for instance, provides information about
the annual bibliography of criticism on prose fiction in *JEGP* (Q924) and the
annual bibliography on Midwestern literature in *Midamerica* (P754). "Special
Bibliographies" cites the checklist appearing in *Early American Literature* (P751)
of Americana found in the *STC 1475-1640* (J306). This efficiency makes "Leary"
one of the most popular books in American literary research. And because of
its cumulative format, it is even easier to use than the *MLAIB.*

Arrangement is alphabetical by literary and then by critical author, with
no annotations. As an example of its comprehensiveness, almost one hundred
entries are cited for Cooper and over 250 for Hawthorne in the main volume.
The first supplement adds 120 and 600 respectively; the second supplement,
87 and 800. The subject and genre sections include bibliographies ranging from
regionalism and literary history to Afro-American literature, printing, religion,
foreign influences, literary societies, and theater. More recent information can
be located in the annual volumes of *Am. Lit. Schol.* (P734) and the other Annual Bibliographies (D31–33).

*P728.   Bryer, Jackson R., ed. *Sixteen Modern American Authors: A Survey
of Research and Criticism.* Durham, N.C.: Duke Univ. Press, 1973.
673pp. Paperback. Supplement in preparation. PS221.F45   810'.9'0052

A welcome revision of the first edition (*Fifteen Modern American Authors,* c1969), which itself was inspired by the success of Stovall's *Eight American Authors* (see P730). Noted scholars evaluate the bibliographies, editions, manuscripts, letters, biographies, and critical studies completed through 1971–73 on Sherwood Anderson, Cather, Hart Crane, Dreiser, Eliot, Faulkner, Fitzgerald, Frost, Hemingway, O'Neill, Pound, E. A. Robinson, Steinbeck, Stevens, Williams, and Wolfe. The introduction illustrates the explosion of interest in American literature by comparing figures in *MLAIB* (D31). In 1951 there were 240 entries on nineteenth-century American literature and 135 on twentieth-century, while 1966 showed 544 on the nineteenth and 844 on the twentieth. By 1979 these figures had increased to 924 and 2,514 entries, respectively. The survey needs to be updated, of course, but it is still the most helpful source for its stated area. See *Am. Lit. Schol.* (P734) and the Annual Bibliographies (D31–33) for more recent scholarship.

*P729.   Rees, Robert A., and Earl N. Harbert, eds. *Fifteen American Authors before 1900: Bibliographic Essays on Research and Criticism*. Rev. ed. Madison: Univ. of Wisconsin Press, 1984. 560pp. PS201.R38   016.8109
    Another title inspired by the success of Stovall's original *Eight American Authors* (see P730). This review of research includes chapters surveying the literature of the Old South and the New South as well as chapters on pivotal authors of pre-1900 America: Henry Adams, Bryant, Cooper, Crane, Dickinson, Jonathan Edwards, Franklin, Oliver Wendell Holmes, Howells, Irving, Longfellow, Lowell, Norris, Edward Taylor, and Whittier. The revision of 1984 gives today's scholars what they need, a survey that selects the best scholarship from the mass of mediocrity and explains how it can be used for constructive purposes.

*P730.   Woodress, James L., ed. *Eight American Authors: A Review of Research and Criticism*. Rev. ed. New York: Norton, 1971. 392pp. Paperback. PS201.E4   810'.9'003
    A thorough revision of Floyd Stovall's long-respected *Eight American Authors* (New York: MLA, 1956; rpt. with bibliographical supplement, New York: Norton, 1963). The same literary authors are examined (Poe, Emerson, Hawthorne, Thoreau, Melville, Whitman, Twain, and James), but special attention is given to the more recent bibliographies, editions, biographies, and critical studies. Five critics revised their own essays (Hubbell, Stovall, Blair, Leary, Clark); Wright, Asselineau, and Gale took the place of Williams, Thorp, and Spiller. The merit of the evaluations and recommendations is well established.

P731.   Gross, Theodore L., and Stanley Wertheim. *Hawthorne, Melville, Stephen Crane: A Critical Bibliography*. New York: Macmillan, 1971. 301pp. Z1225.G76   016.813'3'09
    An excellent example of the type of reference book that is designed to conserve students' time and energy—if they are aware of its existence. It is an exhaustive analysis of critical and editorial scholarship with an introduction and brief chronology for each author. It reviews the best bibliographies, editions, biographies, and criticism. It even discusses criticism for specific titles such as *The Scarlet Letter*, *Moby-Dick*, and *The Red Badge of Courage*. And then, with

a commendable editorial touch, it includes a bibliographical index arranged alphabetically with entry numbers so readers can refer back to the text for the editors'comments on each of the books. If students want guidance in selecting a biography of Stephen Crane, for instance, they will find six titles compared and analyzed here, with a concluding statement that Stallman's will probably be the definitive work for many years.

P732.   *Library of Literary Criticism: Modern American Literature*. Ed. Dorothy Nyren Curley, Maurice Kramer, and Elaine F. Kramer. 4th ed. 3 vols. New York: Ungar, 1973. Supplement (1976), 605pp. PS221.C8 810.9'005
Excerpts from critical articles and books written by the contemporaries of about three hundred twentieth-century authors. This includes Robert Penn Warren's criticism of Saul Bellow, John Gassner's comments on Arthur Miller, and John Ciardi's on Countee Cullen. Admittedly a "popular" source, it is nonetheless useful for background material or a quick overview of an author's reputation in his own day, such as Sherwood Anderson's when he wrote *Winesburg, Ohio*.

A few nineteenth-century authors and critics are included, most notably Higginson's response to Emily Dickinson and her work. The supplement includes important updating on such authors as Nemerov and Singer. More important, it has added entries for about fifty contemporary popular authors (Oates, Reed, Gardner, Plath) and rediscovered authors (Vonnegut, Gordon, J. W. Johnson, Charles Olson, Toomer). Arrangement is alphabetical by the literary author; critics can be located through the index.

P733.   *American Literary Criticism*. Ed. John W. Rathbun. 3 vols.: 1800–1860, 1860–1905, 1905–1965. Nos. 339–41 of TUSAS (P720). Boston: Twayne, 1979. PN99.U5.R37   801'.95'0973
Traces the growth of literary criticism in America from the beginnings to 1965, with discussions of the contributions of Poe, Emerson, Henry James, Santayana, the New Humanists, the Marxists, the Chicago school, the myth critics, and the theories of idealism, realism, and naturalism. Readable and convincing.

P733.1   *Articles on American and British Literature: An Index to Selected Periodicals, 1950–1977*. Ed. Larry B. Corse and Sandra B. Corse. Athens: Ohio Univ. Press, 1981. 450pp.
Designed specifically for undergraduates in small universities that have limited collections of periodicals. This is a quick, convenient source that specializes in locating random critical passages within articles of a more general nature. It covers only forty-seven periodicals but may contain enough information for students who do not have the resources or the time for extensive research projects.

Annual bibliographies
—for bringing all standard American literature bibliographies up to date.

*P734.   *American Literary Scholarship (AmLS; Am. Lit. Schol.)*. Ed. James L.

Woodress and J. Albert Robbins. Durham, N.C.: Duke Univ. Press, 1963–   . Annual. PS3.A47   016.81

An indispensable critical survey of the year's scholarship in American literature, with each chapter written by an authority in the field. Students will be grateful to find that it is readable as well as reliable in its selection of only the most outstanding or controversial titles. Publication of the latest volume, however, will always be one or two years behind the current date because of the time required for selection and appraisal of the titles.

Arrangement is by author and genre, with entries, for instance, under both Melville and Nineteenth-Century Literature, both Faulkner and Fiction—1930's to the 1950's. Important individual titles, such as Melville's *Moby-Dick*, are discussed separately. Students should consult the sections surveying black literature and foreign scholarship (French, German, Italian, Japanese, and others) if they are interested in those fields. These are the most convenient surveys available. In 1977 the editors initiated a "Bibliographical Addendum" with brief descriptions and comments on the latest reference books (see also W1568–69.1). Author index, subject index. All in all, students will not find a more helpful annual guide to new research material in American literature. Indexed in *Am. Hum. Ind.* (P738), *MLAIB* (D31).

See also

ABELL (D32) has excellent coverage of American scholarship, but English and American works are arranged in one alphabet, so students have to search out their own authors and subjects.

MLAIB (D31) has a long section on American literature that is arranged chronologically and then alphabetically, 4,251 entries in 1980.

Year's Wk. Eng. Stud. (D33) has two chapters on American literature: Pre-1900, and the Twentieth Century.

Identification problems

P736.   Oxford Companion to American Literature. Ed. James D. Hart. 5th ed. New York: Oxford Univ. Press, 1983. 896pp. PS21.H3   810.9

Every lover of American literature should have this book, for it includes short biographies and bibliographies of American authors, summaries of a thousand important American works, definitions and outlines of movements, awards, literary publications, literary terms with historical significance (such as stream of consciousness), and any person or subject that has had any relationship with American literature, including Charles Dickens' tour of the United States, Hester Prynne, *Uncle Tom's Cabin*, and the Quakers.

Of great value is the chronological index of literary and social history from 1577 to 1982 in which the student can examine, for instance, contemporary events at the time Twain was writing.

Dissertations

P737.   *Dissertations in American Literature, 1891–1966.* Ed. James L. Woodress. 3rd ed. Durham, N.C.: Duke Univ. Press, 1968. 185pp.

Z1225.W8   016.8109

This is the only comprehensive source that includes information on all dissertations ever written, from the beginnings to 1966, on American literature in English, French, and German. It lists 4,700 titles, first for individual literary authors in alphabetical order and then for periods of historical significance (Civil War), genres (drama, with fourteen subdivisions), and numerous fields related to literature such as education, theater, medicine, libraries, periodicals, and philosophy. Under Holmes, for instance, are listed titles on his novels and his theories of determinism, free will, responsibility, and the impact of science on religion.

Entries include the title, author, institution, and year of publication. Omission of date indicates that the dissertation is in progress. Students should also consult the *DA* and *DAI* (W1214) for possible oversights by Woodress, but these two sources will not include all his entries because at that time they gathered information from only about 150 cooperating institutions. Even the *Comprehensive Dissertation Index* (W1211) focuses mainly on United States institutions. Woodress' introduction calls attention to the Germans' continued interest in American literature over the years, to the slight French interest, and to the increasing interest of British students during the 1960s.

See also

American Dissertations on the Drama and the Theatre (P810)
McNamee, *Dissertations in English and American Literature* (W1212)

Abstracting and indexing services
—for updating the preceding works.

*P738.   *American Humanities Index*. Troy, N.Y.: Whitston, 1975–   . Quarterly, with annual cumulations. AI3.A278   016.051

Important for literature students because ninety percent of the three hundred critical and creative periodicals it indexes are not indexed elsewhere. The small author newsletter and the little magazine are well covered here. So are regional publications like *Western American Literature*, *Great Lakes Review*, *Canadian Fiction*, and certain scholarly periodicals such as the *Kenyon Review*, *Yale Italian Studies*, and others that have cross-disciplinary interests in the arts and humanities. Subject and author entries, with reviews listed under reviewer, author, and subject. This index becomes more valuable every year. Vol. 4 for 1978, for instance, contains 377 pages of double columns and small print, with subject headings such as Jewish Studies, Poems, Publishers, Semiotics, Seventeenth Century, Stories, Women's Studies, and every author who has been the subject of a scholarly article. It overlaps to some extent with *MLAIB* (D31) but not with *Hum. Ind.* (F45).

See also

Abstracts of English Studies (E38)
—and other abstracting services (E39–43) and indexing services (F45–53)

Periodicals—Reference books

P740.   *Literary Journal in America, 1900-1950: A Guide to Information Sources.* Ed. Edward E. Chielens. Vol. 16 of Gale Information Guide Library (A8). Detroit: Gale, 1977. 186pp. Z6951.C572   [PN4877] 016.051

Favorable reviews for this guide to one hundred literary periodicals, little magazines (W1423-30), and regional publications, with entries for both general and specific studies.

P741.   *Literary Journal in America to 1900: A Guide to Information Sources.* Ed. Edward E. Chielens. Vol. 3 of Gale Information Guide Library (A8). Detroit: Gale, 1975. 197pp. Z6951.C57   [PN4877]   016.81'05

A valuable guide to histories, regional studies, individual periodicals, and general surveys of the early literary journal in America. Author, editor, subject, and title indexes.

P742.   Kribbs, Jayne K. *An Annotated Bibliography of American Literary Periodicals, 1741-1850.* Boston: Hall, 1977. 285pp. Z1219.K75   [PS1] 016.81'05

Careful, finely detailed descriptions of the contents of 940 early American periodicals, with current location in two libraries, and five indexes for easy access (chronological, geographical, names, editors and publishers, and titles of tales, novels, and drama). Particularly useful for studies in the fiction, biography, travel literature, essays, and reviews of the period.

Periodicals—Retrospective indexes

P743.   *Literary Index to American Magazines, 1815-65.* Ed. Daniel A. Wells. Metuchen, N.J.: Scarecrow, 1980. 218pp. Z6513.W44   [PN523] 051'.01'6

An index to twenty-five important magazines including the *American Quarterly* and the *Southern Quarterly.* Students will now be able to judge for themselves how the nineteenth-century reader viewed such subjects as women's rights, copyright, and the poetry of Wordsworth. Four hundred entries for names and titles, with biographical information, details about serialized works, citations for reviews, and lists of magazine contents.

This overlaps somewhat with the *Index to Early American Periodicals to 1850* (New York: Readex Microprint, 1962), which provides access to the contents of 340 periodicals of early America, with separate sections for fiction, poetry, book reviews, and subjects such as Indians, slavery, the army, and the theater. The latter is, however, a WPA project of the depression with certain predictable faults in execution, so it must be used with determination and caution. See O'Neill (P715) for similar coverage of later periodicals.

Periodicals

*P744.   *American Literature: A Journal of Literary History, Criticism, and Bibliography* (AL; Am. Lit.). Durham, N.C.: Duke Univ. Press,

1929– . Quarterly. PS1.A6   810.5

The most important periodical in this field. It has comprehensive coverage (over five hundred periodicals) and its approach tends to be traditional and historical.

In addition to critical articles, every issue contains long, signed book reviews; "Brief Mention" of new major editions, bibliographies, guides, and additions to series; and, since March 1982, "A Select, Annotated List of Current Articles on American Literature" that cites only "exemplary contributions to scholarship" and then lists the full contents of special issues devoted to specific authors or subjects. Through January 1982, each bound annual volume had a cumulative index of primary and secondary authors for both articles and book reviews. An indispensable feature is the analytical index, a separately bound volume that indexes by author and subject all the articles and book reviews published in *AL* in vols. 1–30 (1929–59). An index for 1960–80 would certainly be appreciated. Another approach to the contents is through Leary's *Articles on American Literature, 1900–50* and its three supplements (P727).

Indexed in *ABELL* (D32), *Abst. Eng. Stud.* (E38), *Arts and Hum. Cit. Ind.* (F47), *Bk. Rev. Dig.* (W1558), *Bk. Rev. Ind.* (W1559), *Curr. Bk. Rev. Cit.* (W1564), *Hum. Ind.* (F45), *Index to Bk. Rev. Hum.* (W1560), *MLAIB* (D31), *Romantic Movement: A . . . Bibliography* (J443).

P745. *American Quarterly (AQ).* Philadelphia: Univ. of Pennsylvania, 1949– . 5/yr. Official publication of American Studies Assn. AP2.A3985   051

AQ stresses the influence and background of environmental trends in literature. It is interested in studies such as "The Puritan Structure of Edward Taylor's Poetry" and "Frost and the American View of Nature." The annual, annotated, interdisciplinary subject bibliography of current "Articles in American Studies," which includes dissertations, ceased in 1973. (Partial cumulation: *Articles in American Studies, 1954–1968: A Cumulation of the Annual Bibliographies from* American Quarterly. Ed. Hennig Cohen. 2 vols. Ann Arbor: Pierian, 1972.) This was replaced by an annual, enumerative bibliography, "American Studies Research in Progress," and a bibliographical survey in which several essays survey the completed scholarship in such fields as Women's Studies, Autobiographies, American Drama (1918–1940), and Afro-American Theater.

Indexed in *ABELL* (D32), *Abst. Eng. Stud.* (E38), *Arts and Hum. Cit. Ind.* (F47), *Current Bk. Rev. Cit.* (W1564), *Hum. Ind.* (F45), *MLAIB* (D31).

Specialized periodicals

Most American literary periodicals produced by university presses prefer, for pragmatic (i.e., economic) as well as intellectual reasons, to specialize in their own regional literature or in specific subjects that reflect their library holdings or faculty interests. The few titles described below have been selected to illustrate a gratifying variety of geographical and literary interests. For a comprehensive list, see the *MLA Directory of Periodicals* (W1474) and others described in the sections on Periodicals (W1474–84) and Little Magazines (W1423–30).

P746. *American Humor: An Interdisciplinary Newsletter (AHumor).* Rich-

mond: Virginia Commonwealth Univ., 1974–   . 2/yr. American
Humor Studies Assn. PS430.A43.

Articles of regional or linguistic interest such as New England humor or
black American humor, and a helpful annotated checklist of criticism on
American humor as it appears in literature, the film, folklore, drama, art, popular
culture, education, and other disciplines.

Indexed in *ABELL* (D32), *MLAIB* (D31).

*P747. *American Literary Realism, 1870–1910 (ALR)*. Arlington: Univ. of
Texas, 1967–   . 2/yr. PS228.R3.A522

The bibliographers' exemplum because it specializes in annotated checklists,
reference guides, critical bibliographies, and surveys of dissertations. Articles,
news notes, and book reviews focus on Harold Frederic, Bonner, Twain, Bierce,
Cather, Howells, James, Norris, Garland, and other "realists" in American
literature.

Annual index. Cumulated index to vols. 1–10 in vol. 10, no. 4. Occasional
special issues such as that for Utopian literature and the 139-page bibliography
in 1969 of critical works on William Dean Howells.

Indexed in *ABELL* (D32), *Am. Hum. Ind.* (P738), *Arts and Hum. Cit.
Ind.* (F47), *Index to Bk. Rev. Hum.* (W1560), *MLAIB* (D31).

*P748. *American Speech: A Quarterly of Linguistic Usage (AS)*. University:
Univ. of Alabama Press, 1925–   . Quarterly. American Dialect Soc.
PE2801.A6.

Emphasis is on current usage of the English language in the Western
Hemisphere and in other parts of the world as well. Contents range from a line-
by-line scrutiny of several dictionaries to yet another consideration of "good"
English. The brief notes are amusing: "Zori" has several synonyms including
"thongs," "flip-flops," and "go-aheads," the last because they are impossible
to negotiate backwards. A readable linguistics publication (rare species).

Indexed in *Abst. Eng. Stud.* (E38), *Arts and Hum. Cit. Ind.* (F47), *Hum.
Ind.* (F45), *Index to Bk. Rev. Hum.* (W1560), *Language and Lang. Beh. Abst.*
(W1332), *MLAIB* (D31).

P749.   *ATQ: American Transcendental Quarterly, Journal of New England
Writers (ATQ)*. Kingston: Univ. of Rhode Island, 1969–   . Quarterly. PS243.A55

Focus is on Emerson, Hawthorne, Melville, Whitman, Thoreau, and their
circle. Occasional issues feature such subjects as unrecognized female writers of
nineteenth-century New England. The supplements include memoirs, reproductions of contemporary articles, and other elusive or pertinent material.

Indexed in *ABELL* (D32), *Abst. Eng. Stud.* (E38), *Am. Hum. Ind.* (P738),
Arts and Hum. Cit. Ind. (F47), *MLAIB* (D31).

P750.   *California Quarterly: A Journal of Literature, Reviews, and Translation*.
Davis: Univ. of California, 1971–   . 3/yr. NX1.C34   700'.5

Critical articles, original poetry, news, and reviews.

Indexed in *Am. Hum. Ind.* (P738), *Index of Am. Per. Verse* (P818).

P751.   *Early American Literature (EAL)*. Amherst: Univ. of Massachusetts, 1966–   . MLA Early American Literature Division. PS1.E12.
The only periodical concerned with American literature of the seventeenth and eighteenth centuries, although *Seventeenth-Century News* (J314) has occasional items pertaining to American activities during this era. In addition to short articles, *EAL* has book reviews, occasional author checklists, news notes, reports on dissertations, works in progress, and completed research.
Indexed in *ABELL* (D32), *Am. Hum. Ind.* (P738), *Arts and Hum. Cit. Ind.* (F47), *Hum. Ind.* (F45), *Index to Bk. Rev. Hum.* (W1560), *MLAIB* (D31), *Religion Index One: Periodicals* (F53).

P752.   *Great Lakes Review: A Journal of Midwest Culture (GLR)*. Mt. Pleasant: Central Michigan Univ., 1974–   . 2/yr. PS273.G73   810'.8'0977
Critical articles and regional bibliographies focus on Midwestern authors and folklore but extend occasionally outside the realm of literature to native cultures. Recent issues contained reviews concerning Farrell, Masters, Roethke, and Sherwood Anderson, an article on Oates, and a bibliography of literary works focusing on Chicago.
Indexed in *ABELL* (D32), *Am. Hum. Ind.* (P738), *Arts and Hum. Cit. Ind.* (F47), *MLAIB* (D31).

P753.   *MELUS*. Los Angeles: Univ. of Southern California, 1978–   . Quarterly. Soc. for the Study of the Multi-Ethnic Literature of the United States.
Interested in articles on forgotten literatures, explication de texte, comparative studies, and the impact of ethnic diversity on American literature.
Indexed in *Am. Hum. Ind.* (P738), *Arts and Hum. Cit. Ind.* (F47), *Hum. Ind.* (F45), *MLAIB* (D31).

P754.   *Midamerica: The Yearbook of the Society for the Study of Midwestern Literature*. East Lansing: Michigan State Univ. 1974–   . Annual. PS251.M53
Critical articles and an annual bibliography of studies in Midwestern literature.
Indexed in *ABELL* (D32), *MLAIB* (D31).

*P755.   *Mississippi Quarterly: The Journal of Southern Culture (MissQ)*. State College: Mississippi State Univ., 1947–   . Quarterly. AS30.M58.A2
Articles, notes, and an annual checklist of scholarship on Southern literature. See below for a description of the conflated bibliographies for 1968–75.
Indexed in *ABELL* (D32), *Abst. Eng. Stud.* (E38), *Am. Hum. Ind.* (P738), *Arts and Hum. Cit. Ind.* (F47), *Hist. Abst.* (E43), *Hum. Ind.* (F45), *MLAIB* (D31), *Soc. Abst.* (E40).

Southern Literature, 1968–1975: A Checklist of Scholarship. Ed. Jerry T. Williams. Boston: Hall, 1978. 256pp. Soc. for the Study of Southern Literature. Z1225.S63 [PS261]   016.81
This conflates the first eight annual checklists from the *Mississippi Quarterly* (see above) with some additional entries. It should be considered

a supplement to Rubin's guide to Southern literature (P711). The same information can be found in *MLAIB* (D31), but this one-volume compilation of scholarship on 250 writers is slightly more convenient. It is regrettable, however, that the information was not cumulated into one alphabetical arrangement. Annotations are sparse; a few cross-references.

P756.   *New England Quarterly: A Historical Review of New England Life and Letters (NEQ)*. Boston: Northeastern Univ., 1928–   . Quarterly. F1.N62   974.005

Articles on Dickinson's names, Twain's Connecticut conscience, Amy Lowell and the *Atlantic Monthly*, and similar Yankee subjects. Annual index. Bibliography of New England, 1928–66.

Indexed in *ABELL* (D32), *Arts and Hum. Cit. Ind.* (F47), *Bk. Rev. Dig.* (W1558), *Bk. Rev. Ind.* (W1559), *Current Bk. Rev. Cit.* (W1564), *Hum. Ind.* (F45), *Index to Bk. Rev. Hum.* (W1560), *MLAIB* (D31), *Romantic Movement: A . . . Bibliography* (J443).

P757.   *Northwest Review (NWR)*. Eugene: Univ. of Oregon, 1957–   . 3/yr. AP2.N855   051.N878

Articles, notes, and reviews. Cumulative index for vols. 1–5 and 6–10.

Indexed in *Am. Hum. Ind.* (P738), *Index to Bk. Rev. Hum.* (W1560), *Year's Wk. Eng. Stud.* (D33).

P758.   *Notes on Mississippi Writers (NMW)*. Hattiesburg: Univ. of Southern Mississippi, 1968–   . 3/yr. PS266.M7.N67   810'.99762

Articles, notes, and an annual bibliography.

Indexed in *ABELL* (D32), *Abst. Eng. Stud.* (E38), *MLAIB* (D31).

P759.   *Notes on Modern American Literature (NMAL)*. Jamaica, N.Y.: St. John's Univ., 1977–   . Quarterly. PS221.N67

Concerned with literature written since the year 1900: explications, comments on sources, comparisons, and notes on the lives of Berryman, Snyder, Sexton, Porter, Oates, Hawkes, Wilbur, Peter Taylor, Bellow, Shapiro, and others. Annual index.

Indexed in *MLAIB* (D31).

P760.   *Proof: The Yearbook of American Bibliographical and Textual Studies*. Columbia: Univ. of South Carolina Press, 1971–77 (vols. 1–5). Annual. Z1007.P766

Highly specialized, and valuable because it was the only periodical concerned solely with problems of the text. It inquired into such problems as Melville's final intentions in his unfinished manuscripts, the editorial policy of the Centenary Edition of Hawthorne's works, copyright complications, computer possibilities, and modern textual editing. The academic world needs to have this periodical revived.

Indexed in *ABELL* (D32), *Am. Hum. Ind.* (P738), *MLAIB* (D31).

P761.   *Resources for American Literary Study (RALS)*. College Park: Univ. of

Maryland, 1971– . 2/yr. Z1225.R46   016.81

Interested in editorial problems of bibliography and research in American literature. The range is wide—from a review of research on William Carlos Williams to bibliographies on specific subjects such as Faulkner's *The Sound and the Fury* and James's *The Bostonians*, a list of new acquisitions, accounts of special collections in libraries, and newly edited or unpublished primary materials including manuscripts. The checklists of critical and biographical scholarship are sometimes annotated (as for "Early American Gallows Literature"), and the bibliographical essays may be on trends, genres, or authors such as Cotton Mather. In 1980 the editors initiated a series of bibliographical articles updating the G. K. Hall Reference Guide Series (W1055) beginning with Roger Williams, Anderson-Behrman, Norris, Wolfe, Seventeenth-Century American Poetry, Garland-Fuller, Porter-McCullers, Irving, Wharton-Chopin, and Welty.

Indexed in *ABELL* (D32), *Am. Hum. Ind.* (P738), *Arts and Hum. Cit. Ind.* (F47), *MLAIB* (D31).

*P762. *Sewanee Review* (*SR*). Sewanee, Tenn.: Univ. of the South, 1892– . Quarterly. AP2.S5

The oldest literary periodical in the United States, with original fiction and poetry, critical articles, book reviews, and letters. Editorial policy encourages contributions from new talent as well as from international scholars. Special attention is given to Southern literature. Cumulative index for vols. 1–10 (1892–1902) and vols. 51–87 (1943–79).

Indexed in *ABELL* (D32), *Abst. Eng. Stud.* (E38), *Arts and Hum. Cit. Ind.* (F47), *Bk. Rev. Ind.* (W1559), *Current Bk. Rev. Cit.* (W1564), *Current Contents* (F47), *Hum. Ind.* (F45), *Index to Bk. Rev. Hum.* (W1560), *MLAIB* (D31).

P763.   *South Carolina Review* (*SCR*). Greenville: Furman Univ., 1968– . 2/yr. PS558.S6.S67   810'.8'0054

Articles, notes, and occasional special issues such as that for Fall 1979, which focuses on the literary year 1929.

Indexed in *ABELL* (D32), *Abst. Eng. Stud.* (E38), *Am. Hum. Ind.* (P738), *Index to Bk. Rev. Hum.* (W1560), *MLAIB* (D31).

P764.   *South Dakota Review* (*SDR*). Vermillion: Univ. of South Dakota, 1963– . Quarterly. AP2.S713

Criticism, poetry, and fiction by contemporary American authors.

Indexed in *ABELL* (D32), *Abst. Eng. Stud.* (E38), *Am. Hum. Ind.* (P738), *Arts and Hum. Cit. Ind.* (F47), *MLAIB* (D31).

P765.   *Southern Literary Journal* (*SLJ*). Chapel Hill: Univ. of North Carolina, 1968– . 2/yr. PS261.S527   810.9'975

Essays on Faulkner, Caldwell, Simms, Adams, Aiken, and other Southern writers. Reviews, but no news or notes. Index in every second volume.

Indexed in *ABELL* (D32), *Arts and Hum. Cit. Ind.* (F47), *Hum. Ind.* (F45), *Index to Bk. Rev. Hum.* (W1560), *MLAIB* (D31).

P766.   *Southern Review (SoR)*. Baton Rouge: Louisiana State Univ., 1935–42, 1965– . Quarterly. AP2.S8555   051

The coverage of criticism, poetry, and fiction is gradually expanding beyond Southern literataure to traditionally and historically important English and Continental works. Occasional special issues on such subjects as *Writing in the South* or a tribute to Yvor Winters.

Indexed in *ABELL* (D32), *Abst. Eng. Stud.* (E38), *Arts and Hum. Cit. Ind.* (F47), *Bk. Rev. Ind.* (W1559), *Hum. Ind.* (F45), *Index to Bk. Rev. Hum.* (W1560), *MLAIB* (D31).

*P767.   *Southwest Review (SWR)*. Dallas: Southern Methodist Univ. Press, 1915– . Quarterly. AP2.S7

Fiction and poetry, with occasional interviews and critical essays that focus on contemporary works. Annual index.

Indexed in *ABELL* (D32), *Abst. Eng. Stud.* (E38), *Abst. Pop. Cult.* (W1498), *America* (E43), *Bk. Rev. Ind.* (W1559), *Hist. Abst.* (E43), *Hum. Ind.* (F45), *Index to Bk. Rev. Hum.* (W1560), *MLAIB* (D31).

P768.   *Southwestern American Literature (SwAL)*. Denton: North Texas State Univ., 1971– . 9/yr. PS277.S68

Fiction, poetry, and criticism. Ideally, it would have an annual bibliography that would update Anderson's book-length bibliography with the same title (P712).

Indexed in *ABELL* (D32), *Am. Hum. Ind.* (P738), *MLAIB* (D31).

P769.   *Studies in American Humor (StAH)*. San Marcos: Southwestern Texas State Univ., 1974–76. 3/yr. PS430.S88

Articles, reviews, notes, and queries on the study and explication of American humor. Occasional checklists and bibliographies. Temporarily suspended.

Indexed in *ABELL* (D32), *Am. Hum. Ind.* (P738), *MLAIB* (D31).

P770.   *Studies in the American Renaissance (SAR)*. Boston: Hall, 1977– . Annual. PS201.S86   810'.9'003

Collections of essays on the lives and works of mid-nineteenth century American authors such as Fuller, Alcott, Briggs, Poe, Cranch, and Stowe; previously unpublished papers; primary and secondary bibliographies; accounts of publishing houses; and other material focusing on the years 1830–60.

Indexed in *ABELL* (D32), *Am. Hum. Ind.* (P738), *MLAIB* (D31), *Religion Index One: Periodicals* (F53).

P771.   *Studies in the Literary Imagination (SLitI)*. Atlanta: Georgia State Univ., 1968– . 2/yr. PR1.S84

Long studies on controversial subjects such as Yeats and the occult, the Inklings (Lewis, Williams, Tolkien), Conrad Aiken as man-of-letters, and women (authors, literary characters, critics, social leaders). It is free to libraries.

Indexed in *ABELL* (D32), *Am. Hum. Ind.* (P738), *Arts and Hum. Cit. Ind.* (F47), *Hum. Ind.* (F45), *MLAIB* (D31), *Year's Wk. Eng. Stud.* (D33).

*P772. *Western American Literature* (*WAL*). Logan: Utah State Univ., 1966–   . Quarterly. PS271.W46   810.9'978

The only periodical devoted to literature of the West, with articles on such authors as Cather, Sandoz, Momaday, London, Arms, and Kroetsch. Especially important are the annual bibliographies of studies in Western American literature, including the work of American Indians, and the lists of dissertations and theses. See also P712–12.3 and W1130.

Indexed in *ABELL* (D32), *Am. Hum. Ind.* (P738), *Arts and Hum. Cit. Ind.* (F47), *Film Literature Ind.* (W1252), *Index to Bk. Rev. Hum.* (W1560), *MLAIB* (D31).

Periodicals—English and American literature

P776.   The section entitled Periodicals—General (H140–57) describes publications that are interested in the literature of nations in various parts of the world. The following periodicals, on the other hand, generally feature articles, news, and criticism on both English and American literature. Full annotations are in the main entry:

> *Contemporary Literature* (J529)
> *Critique* (J545)
> *Journal of Modern Literature* (J530)
> *Modern Drama* (J563)
> *Modern Fiction Studies* (J544)
> *Modern Poetry Studies* (J572)
> *Nineteenth-Century Fiction* (J422)
> *Notes on Contemporary Literature* (J532)
> *Parnassus* (J571)
> *Seventeenth-Century News* (J314)
> *Studies in Short Fiction* (G80)
> *tdr* (J564)
> *Twentieth Century Literature* (J528)

Author newsletters, journals, and other serial publications devoted to individual American authors

P777.   Additional author newsletters are listed in this guide for English (J195), Canadian (N685), Continental (Q893), Irish (K600), Scottish (L627), and Welsh (M640) authors. For full bibliographical information on these and other periodicals concerned with one person, see *Author Newsletters and Journals* (W1476) and its annual supplement in *Serials Review* (W1482).

Alger, Horatio
 The Newsboy, 1962–   .
Anderson, Sherwood
 Winesburg Eagle, 1975–   .
Asimov, Isaac
 Isaac Asimov's Science Fiction, 1977–   .

Barbieri, Cesare
 Cesare Barbieri Courier, 1958–   .
Baum, Frank
 Baum Bugle, 1957–   .
Berryman, John
 John Berryman Studies, 1975–77.

Brand, Max. See Faust, Frederick.
Burroughs, Edgar Rice
 Barsodmian, 1952– .
 Burroughs Bibliophile, 1964– .
 Burroughs Bulletin, 1947– .
 Burroughsiana, 1975– .
 ERBania, 1956– .
 ERB-dom and the Fantasy Collector,
  1960– .
 ERBivore, 1967– .
 Fantastic World, 1976– .
 Gridley Wave, 1959– .

Cabell, James Branch
 The Cabellian, 1968–72.
 Kalki: Studies in James Branch Cabell,
  1965– .
Cather, Willa
 Newsletter, 1957– .
Chaney, William H.
 Chaney Chronicle, 1972– .
Chopin, Kate
 Kate Chopin Newsletter, 1975–77.
Clemens, Samuel L. (Mark Twain)
 Mark Twain Journal, 1954– .
 Mark Twain Memorial Newsletter,
  1955– .
 Mark Twain Quarterly, 1936–53.
 Mark Twain Society Bulletin, 1978– .
 The Twainian, 1939– .
Collier, John
 Presenting Moonshine, 1969– .
Crane, Hart
 Hart Crane Newsletter, 1977–80.
Crane, Stephen
 Stephen Crane Newsletter, 1966–70.
Crawford, Francis Marion
 Romantist, 1977– .
Curwood, James Oliver
 Curwood Collector, 1972– .

Derleth, August
 August Derleth Society Newsletter,
  1977– .
Dewey, John
 Dewey Newsletter, 1967– .
 Studies in Educational Theory, 1963–71.
Dickinson, Emily
 Dickinson Studies, 1979– .
 Emily Dickinson Bulletin, 1968–78.
Dreiser, Theodore
 Dreiser Newsletter, 1970– .

Eliot, T. S.
 T. S. Eliot Newsletter, 1974.
 T. S. Eliot Review, 1975–77.

Emerson, Ralph Waldo
 *ESQ: A Journal of the American
  Renaissance*, 1969– .
 Emerson Society Quarterly, 1955–68.

Faulkner, William
 Faulkner Concordance Newsletter,
  1972–76.
 *Faulkner Newsletter and Yoknapatawpha
  Review*, 1981– .
 Faulkner Studies (Miami), 1978– .
Faust, Frederick (Max Brand)
 Faust Collector, 1969– .
Fitzgerald, F. Scott
 Fitzgerald/Hemingway Annual, 1969– .
 Fitzgerald Newsletter, 1958–68.
Frederic, Harold
 Frederic Herald, 1967–70.
Frost, Robert
 Robert Frost Newsletter, 1977– .

George, Henry
 Henry George News, 1943– .
Glasgow, Ellen
 Ellen Glasgow Newsletter, 1974– .
Grey, Zane
 Zane Grey Collector, 1968–75.

Hartmann, Sadakichi
 Sadakichi Hartmann Newsletter,
  1969–75.
Hawthorne, Nathaniel
 Nathaniel Hawthorne Journal, 1971– .
 Nathaniel Hawthorne Society Newsletter,
  1975– .
Hemingway, Ernest
 Fitzgerald/Hemingway Annual, 1969– .
 Hemingway Notes, 1971–74; 1979–81.
 Hemingway Review, 1981– .
Higginson, Thomas Wentworth
 Higginson Journal of Poetry, 1971– .
Howard, Robert E.
 Amra, 1956– .
 Howard Collector, 1961–73.
Howells, William Dean
 Howells Sentinel, 1951– .

Irving, Washington
 Sketch Book, 1954.

James, Henry
 Henry James Review, 1979– .
Jeffers, Robinson
 Robinson Jeffers Newsletter, 1962– .

Kerouac, Jack
 Moody Street Irregulars, 1978– .

Lewis, Sinclair
  Sinclair Lewis Newsletter, 1969–76.
Lindsay, Vachel
  Vachel Lindsay Association, 1946– .
London, Jack
  Jack London Newsletter, 1967– .
  London Collector, 1970– .
  What's New about London, Jack?
  1971– .

MacDonald, John D.
  JDM Bibliophile, 1965– .
Markham, Edwin
  Markham Review, 1968– .
Melville, Herman
  *Extract (An Occasional Newsletter of the
  Melville Society),* 1969– .
  Melville Annual, 1965–68.
  Melville Society Newsletter, 1945–60.
  Special Publications, 1973– .
Mencken, Henry Louis
  Menckeniana, 1962– .
Miller, Henry
  Henry Miller Literary Society Newsletter,
  1958–63.
Moore, Marianne
  Marianne Moore Newsletter, 1977– .
Morley, Christopher
  Christopher Morley Knothole Association.
  Annual Letter, 1961– .

Nin, Anaïs
  *Under the Sign of Pisces: Anaïs Nin and
  Her Circle,* 1970– .
Nock, Albert Jay
  Nockian Society, 1963– .

Oates, Joyce Carol
  Joyce Carol Oates Newsletter, 1978–79.
O'Connor, Flannery
  Flannery O'Connor Bulletin, 1972– .
O'Hara, John
  John O'Hara Journal, 1978– .
Olson, Charles J.
  Olson, 1974–79.
O'Neill, Eugene
  Eugene O'Neill Newsletter, 1977– .

Peirce, Charles S.
  Charles S. Peirce Newsletter, 1973– .
  Transactions of the C. S. Peirce Society,
  1965– .
Poe, Edgar Allan
  Poe Messenger, 1970– .
  Poe Newsletter, 1968–70.
  Poe Studies, 1968– .
  Poe Studies Association Newsletter,
  1973– .

Pound, Ezra
  Anagogic and Paideumic Review,
  1959– .
  Paideuma, 1972– .
  Pound Lectures in the Humanities,
  1974– .
  Pound Newsletter, 1954–56.
Pynchon, Thomas
  Pynchon Newsletter, 1981– .
  Pynchon Notes, 1979– .

Rand, Ayn
  Ayn Rand Letter, 1971–76.
Riley, James Whitcomb
  Riley Memorial Association News,
  1958–?.

Sandoz, Mari (Suzette)
  Mari Sandoz Heritage, 1971– .
Sapir, Edward
  Monograph Series, 1977– .
Sinclair, Upton
  Uppie Speaks, 1977–79.
  Upton Sinclair Quarterly, 1980– .
Stein, Gertrude
  Lost Generation Journal, 1973– .
Steinbeck, John
  Report of the John Steinbeck
  Bibliographical Society, 1968– .
  Steinbeck Monograph Series, 1971– .
  Steinbeck Newsletter, 1968–69.
  Steinbeck Quarterly, 1969– .
Stevens, Wallace
  Wallace Stevens Journal, 1977– .
  Wallace Stevens Newsletter, 1969–71.
Stuart, Jesse
  Jesse Stuart Creative Writing Workshop,
  1970– .

Thoreau, Henry
  Bibliography of the Thoreau Society
  Bibliographies, 1941–69: A Cumula-
  tion and Index (ed. Walter Harding,
  1971)
  Concord Saunterer, 1966– .
  Newsletter, 1971– .
  Thoreau Journal Quarterly, 1969–81.
  Thoreau Quarterly, 1982– .
  Thoreau Society Booklet, 1942– .
  Thoreau Society Bulletin, 1941– .
Torsvan, Berick Traven (B. Traven)
  B. Traven Newsletter, 1975– .
Traven, B. See Torsvan, Berick Traven.
Twain, Mark. See Clemens, Samuel L.

Updike, John
  John Updike Newsletter, 1977– .

229

Welty, Eudora
  Eudora Welty Newsletter, 1977– .
Whitman, Walt
  Calamus, 1969– .
  Mickle Street Review, 1979– .
  *Walt Whitman Birthplace Association
    Newsletter*, 1961– .
  Walt Whitman Birthplace Bulletin,
    1957–61.
  Walt Whitman Foundation Bulletin,
    1948–55.
  Walt Whitman Newsletter, 1955–58.
  Walt Whitman Review, 1959– .
Whittier, John Greenleaf
  Whittier Newsletter, 1966– .

Williams, Tennessee
  Tennessee Williams Newsletter, 1979–80.
  Tennessee Williams Review, 1981– .
Williams, William Carlos
  William Carlos Williams Newsletter,
    1975–79.
  William Carlos Williams Review,
    1980– .
Wister, Owen
  Owen Wister Review, 1978– .
Wolfe, Thomas
  Thomas Wolfe Newsletter, 1977–80.
  Thomas Wolfe Review, 1981– .

Some of these publications on individual authors have cumulated indexes, such as the relatively brief five-year cumulations for the *Johnsonian News Letter* (J382) or the lengthier cumulation for the Thoreau Society cited above. Every time students use a periodical, they should look for cumulations like these because they bring research time down to a minimum. Editors generally feature them at five- or ten-year intervals, and "Cumulated Index" is usually printed on the spine of the book so the library browser can bypass all the individual indexes and consult only the one cumulation. The creative, experienced researcher makes good use of shortcuts such as this; the beginner doesn't know they exist. They are an integral feature in that deplored graduate course entitled Methods of Research, which most graduates are reluctant to take and many professors believe consumes too much time.

FICTION

Bibliographies of primary works

P778.   Wright, Lyle H., ed. *American Fiction, [———]: A Contribution toward a Bibliography*. San Marino, Calif.: Huntington Library, 1957– . Available on microfilm. Z1213.F4.W9   016.813'2

> Vol. 1: 1774–1850. 2nd ed. 1969. 411pp.
> Vol. 2: 1851–1875. Corrected ed. 1965. 438pp.
> Vol. 3: 1876–1900, records only first editions. 1966. 683pp.
> Vol. 5: 1906–1910. 1982.

Valuable for students who are specializing in fiction and who need verification of author bibliographies or specific editions of books. This includes information on almost eleven thousand novels, tall tales, romances, travels, sentimental novels, books on slavery, fictitious biographies, short stories, and other forms of fiction. Entries are by author only, but title and chronological indexes offer other ways to locate material. Entries include title, date, size, description, illustrations, format, notes, cross-references, list of contents, and location in about twenty American libraries. Pseudonyms are cross-referenced. Cumulative author index to the microfilm collection (New Haven, Conn.: Research Publications, 1974; 416pp.).

Specialized bibliographies

Specialized bibliographies of primary works are excellent for research projects on one specific area. For example:

P779.   *America in Fiction.* Ed. Otis W. Coan and Richard G. Lillard. 5th ed. Palo Alto: Pacific, 1967. 232pp. Z1361.C6.C6   016.813'00
   An annotated subject guide to novels about life in the United States, Canada, and Mexico, with sections on Pioneering, Farm and Village, Industrial America, Politics and Public Institutions, Religion, Minority Ethnic Groups, and many other subjects. Be on the alert for a sixth edition.

P780.   *Illinois! Illinois!: An Annotated Bibliography of Fiction.* Ed. Thomas L. Kilpatrick and Patsy-Rose Hoshiko. Metuchen, N.J.: Scarecrow, 1979. 617pp. Z1277.K54   [PS374.I45]   016.813'008'032
   Summaries of over fifteen hundred novels and short stories are arranged in chronological sections and followed by citations for book reviews. Excellent indexes for author/title and subject/place name, making it possible for students to turn immediately to fiction on the Chippewa Indians, Crime, French in Illinois, Mississippi River, or Small-Town Life. It is equally easy to see the coverage given such Midwesterners as George Ade (28 summaries), Henry K. Webster (13), Sherwood Anderson (5), Theodore Dreiser (4), Booth Tarkington (4), and Eunice Tietjens (2). Every state needs a bibliographical record like this. It is a historical, academic, and cultural asset.

See also
   Dickinson's American Historical Fiction (G84)

Basic guides

P781.   *American Fiction to 1900: A Guide to Information Sources.* Ed. David K. Kirby. Vol. 4 of Gale Information Guide Library (A8). Detroit: Gale, 1975. 296pp. Z1231.F4.K57   [PS368]   016.813'008
   A survey of scholarship on forty-one authors of the period from Melville and Twain to James Lane Allen, Edward Bellamy, Weir Mitchell, Stowe, Thompson, Tourgee, and Woolson. Remarkably comprehensive, with entries for general studies, bibliographies, primary works including letters, biographies, critical articles and books, all briefly annotated. Stephen Crane, for instance, is given about ten pages, whereas Gerstenberger and Hendrick give him only six pages (P786), and Holman only three (P783). Index for titles and all names.

P782.   *American Fiction, 1900–1950: A Guide to Information Sources.* Ed. James L. Woodress. Vol. 1 of the Gale Information Guide Library (A8). Detroit: Gale, 1974. 260pp.   Z1231.F4.W64   016.813'03
   Bibliographical essays with brief, one-sentence comments about post–World War II scholarship (1950–73) on forty-four writers, including Wister, E. M. Roberts, Farrell, Chandler, B. Traven, and others of greater stature. The reliable evaluations make this useful as a general survey of scholarly activities, but it does not attempt to be comprehensive and so is not adequate for extensive research.

P783.   Holman, Clarence Hugh, ed., and Janis Richardi, asst. *The American Novel through Henry James.* 2nd ed. Goldentree Bibliographies (W1291). Arlington Heights: AHM, 1979. 177pp. Paperback. Z1231.F4.H6   016.813

A selective bibliography of (1) general works on such subjects as American Literary History, American Publishing, the Novel as Form, Histories of the American Novel, and special studies arranged by period, genre, theme, and subject, and (2) individual bibliographies for thirty-eight novelists, which list their works, relevant bibliographies, biographies, and critical books and articles. The important works carry asterisks, and the occasional comments are of measurable assistance to beginning students faced with the problem of selecting the most trustworthy titles from the three thousand entries.

These Goldentree bibliographies are convenient to have on the desk at home so that time spent in aimless search in the library can be kept to a minimum. This is the source to use if, for instance, students need some articles and books for background reading on the beginnings of the American novel, or if they want to know whether there is a definitive edition of Theodore Dreiser's works or whether any studies have been made of lesser writers such as Brackenridge, Eggleston, and Tourgee. This volume overlaps to some extent with Kirby (P781) but is less expensive. Students must use both books for extensive research.

P784.   Nevius, Blake, comp. *The American Novel: Sinclair Lewis to the Present.* Goldentree Bibliographies (W1291). New York: Appleton (Meredith), 1970. 126pp. Paperback. Z1231.F4.N4   016.813'5'209

Special studies by period, theme, and subject are listed first, including Bibliographies, American Literary History, the Novel as a Form, Histories of the American Novel, and Collections. This section is followed by selective bibliographies on forty-eight contemporary American novelists from Conrad Aiken to Wilder, Wolfe, and Wright. The entries are arranged alphabetically by editor or critic under each major author. Texts, biographies, and bibliographies are listed as well as critical articles and books. An inexpensive, up-to-date, and convenient guide to the literature. Very few listings for individual titles, however, so a page-by-page search is sometimes necessary. This would be a good source for a bibliography of Jack Kerouac or a biography of Carson McCullers, but if students want something on *For Whom the Bell Tolls,* they will have to scan seven pages of Hemingway criticism. More recent and more comprehensive information can be found in *American Fiction, 1900-1950* (P782) and *Contemporary Fiction in America and England, 1950-1970* (J536).

See also

Contemporary Fiction in America and England, 1950-1970 (J536)

Criticism

*P786.   Gerstenberger, Donna L., and George Hendrick. Vol. 1: *The American Novel 1789-1959: A Checklist of Twentieth-Century Criticism.* Denver: Swallow, 1961. 333pp. Vol. 2: *The American Novel: A Checklist of Twentieth-Century Criticism on Novels Written since 1789; Criticism*

Written 1960–68. Chicago: Swallow, 1970. 459pp. Z1231.F4.G4
016.813'03

Assignment: Has critical response to Cooper's novels undergone any significant change during the twentieth century? How was Fitzgerald's *Great Gatsby* received immediately after its publication? Recommended research procedure: Use both this book and the appropriate volume of more recent research lists such as Kirby (P781), Woodress (P782), or Holman (P783).

The first part of vol. 1 lists selected critical works about individual authors, individual titles, general studies, and bibliographies; the second part includes criticism of the American novel as a genre, with subdivisions by centuries. The approximately 675 books and ninety periodicals that were used as sources are listed in the back of the book. Efficient libraries will see that the call number is written beside each title.

The scope of vol. 2 is increased to 150 journals and some works overlooked in the first volume. In the first section individual authors are listed alphabetically with subentries for individual titles (twenty-three critical works are listed for Porter's *Ship of Fools*). Most important, this volume lists bibliographies published either separately or as parts of books by and about authors such as Faulkner, who has nineteen bibliographies. No annotations; no book reviews except long review articles from sources like the *New York Times Book Review* and *Saturday Review*; no short fiction except for a few titles like Melville's *Billy Budd* (see G77.1, G78, and others in the Short Story section of this guide).

P787.   Eichelberger, Clayton L. *A Guide to Critical Reviews of U. S. Fiction, 1870–1910.* Metuchen, N.J.: Scarecrow, 1971. 415pp. Vol. 2 (1974), 351pp. Z1225.E35   016.813'4'09

A bibliography of critical material from thirty periodicals on major and minor writers such as Thomas Nelson Page (three columns), Sarah Orne Jewett (more than three), George Washington Cable (three), and Bret Harte (nine). Particularly good for minor writers because the editors consulted many lesser-known periodicals such as *Cottage-Hearth*, *Bystander*, *Overland Monthly*, *Godey's Lady's Book*, and *Poet Lore*. Appendix of anonymous and pseudonymous titles. Title index. Vol. 2 covers ten more journals and brings the total number of reviews to over twenty thousand—a "preliminary and tentative" list, according to the author.

See also

Weixlmann, *American Short-Fiction Criticism* (G77.1)

Periodicals

P788.   *Studies in American Fiction (SAF)*. Boston: Northeastern Univ., 1973– . 2/yr. PS370.S87   813'.009

SAF publishes articles, notes, and reviews concerning the scholarly investigation of the fiction of the United States from Cooper to Cather, Poe to Dickey, Popular Culture to Women's Studies.

Indexed in *ABELL* (D32), *Abst. Eng. Stud.* (E38), *Am. Hum. Ind.* (P738), *Arts and Hum. Cit. Ind.* (F47), *Index to Bk. Rev. Hum.* (W1560), *MLAIB* (D31).

Background reading for fiction

P789.   Karl, Frederick R. *American Fictions, 1940–1980: A Comprehensive History and Critical Evaluation.* New York: Harper, 1983. 864pp. PS379.K24   813'.54'09

A wise, timely evaluation of recent American novels, written by an experienced, respected critic. Bibliography and index.

P790.   Quinn, Arthur H. *American Fiction: An Historical and Critical Survey.* New York: Appleton, 1936. 805pp. PS371.Q5   813.09

Quinn examines the American novel and short story as artistic forms that arise from and are influenced by American life. He analyzes and summarizes the work of Franklin, Brown, Irving, Cooper, Poe, Hawthorne, Melville, Harte, Howells, James, Jewett, Harris, Crawford, Hearn, Wharton, Liberals and Radicals, the Realists, Southern Literature, and many other topics and authors. An especially good book for students beginning the study of American literature because of Quinn's forthright judgments: Dreiser is sometimes "irritating," and Garland can be "melodramatic."

P791.   Wagenknecht, Edward C. *The Cavalcade of the American Novel.* New York: Holt, 1952. 575pp. PS371.W3   813.09

Still a valid appraisal of the development of the American novel from *Charlotte Temple* (1790) and its 160 editions to the post–World War II generation.

PROSE

Basic guides

P792.   *American Prose and Criticism, 1900–1950.* Ed. Peter A. Brier and Anthony Arthur. Vol. 35 of Gale Information Guide Library (A8). Detroit: Gale, 1981. 260pp. Z1231.P8.B74   [PS362]   016.81'08'0052

This is similar in structure and purpose to P793.

P793.   *American Prose and Criticism to 1820: A Guide to Information Sources.* Ed. Donald Yannella and John H. Roch. Vol. 26 of Gale Information Guide Library (A8). Detroit: Gale, 1979. 653pp. Z1231.P8.Y3 [PS367]   016.818'08

Indisputable testimony that culture, literacy, and intellectual curiosity abounded in Colonial and Revolutionary America. About a thousand books of a general nature are listed and annotated, and then 140 authors are presented with annotations for their primary works and related criticism. A tidy, enlightening, convenient reference work. See also its companion volume, *American Prose and Criticism, 1820–1900,* ed. Elinore H. Partridge (Detroit: Gale, 1983; 575pp.). Z1231.P8.P37   [PS368]   016.818'08

DRAMA AND THEATER

Because drama (written) and theater (stage) overlap so extensively in the reference books for American literature, they are treated as one subject in the following entries.

Surveys

*P794.   *Revels History of Drama in English*. Ed. Travis Bogard et al. Vol. 8,
    American Drama. London: Methuen, 1977. 324pp. Paperback.
    PS623.B6

This encyclopedia of information emphasizes the range of American drama.
Of special note is the chronological table of historical and theatrical events beginning with the first professional performance in 1703 and ending with the death
of Thornton Wilder in 1975. The survey contains bizarre tales of travelling companies in the early 1800s, explains the development of theater guilds and stock
characters, discusses today's trends, and comments on all the famous actors and
authors, including Julia Marlowe, Mrs. Fiske, O'Neill and his wharf in Prov-
incetown, Lunt and Fontanne, Hellman, and the Le Galliennes. Bibliography
and index. See the main entry (G114) for information on the other volumes.

Basic guides

P795.   Long, E. Hudson. *American Drama from Its Beginnings to the Pres-
    ent*. Goldentree Bibliographies (W1291). New York: Appleton
    (Meredith), 1970. 78pp. Z1231.D7.L64   016.812

Students may still prefer this because it includes only the best titles and
emphasizes work published since 1900. It is not, however, as suitable as Eddleman (P804) for extensive research on dramatists and their plays because he
is much more comprehensive and up to date. Long's cutoff date for critical works
seems to be the early 1960s. And both Meserve (P796) and Larson (P798) provide much more information on theater history before 1900. Arrangement is
by subject (special theatrical groups, chronological period, region, genre, theme)
and then alphabetical by fifty-two major and minor American dramatists such
as Albee, Eliot, Inge, MacLeish, O'Neill, and Tyler. There is a long section on
Tennessee Williams, for instance, but nothing on LeRoi Jones because he is included in the Goldentree Bibliography on Afro-American literature (P838).
Critical works are arranged chronologically to permit the study of trends. Index
of critics' names; numerous cross-references. Important works are marked with
an asterisk, and paperback editions are noted.

P796.   Meserve, Walter J. *American Drama to 1900: A Guide to Information
    Sources*. Vol. 28 of Gale Information Guide Library (A8). Detroit: Gale,
    1980. 254pp. Z1231.D7.M45   016.812

The best guide to American drama written before 1900. The author, a noted
authority in the field, does not attempt to include information on staged theater,
which is well covered by reference books described elsewhere in this section. He
provides a brief survey, a list of general studies, and briefly annotated
bibliographies for over thirty authors such as Belasco, Howard, Clemens, Henry
James, Herne, and Payne. Author, subject, and title index to the fifteen hundred entries.

P797.   Harris, Richard H. *Modern Drama in America and England, 1950-1970:
    A Guide to Information Sources*. Vol. 34 of Gale Information Guide

Library (A8). Detroit: Gale, 1981. 606pp. Z1231.D7.H36 [PS351]
016.822'914
Fortunate is the student who discovers this remarkably up-to-date guide
to works by and about 225 modern dramatists. A timely guide to a timely subject.

*P798. *American Regional Theatre History to 1900: A Bibliography*. Ed. Carl
F. W. Larson. Metuchen, N.J.: Scarecrow, 1979. 200pp. Z5781.L34
[PN2221]   016.792'0973
This corrects and updates Stratman's bibliography (P799), provides more
information on the American regional theater before 1900 than Gohdes (P800),
and is more comprehensive than Wilmeth's *American Stage to World War I*
(W1470.4). As source material it cites books, articles, dissertations, newspaper
clippings, local histories, and manuscripts of the twentieth century only, so
students will have to consult other sources for early criticism. The arrangement
by state, city, and then date is especially helpful in regional and historical studies.

P799. Stratman, Carl J., C.S.V. *Bibliography of the American Theatre, excluding New York City*. Chicago: Loyola Univ. Press, 1965. 397pp.
Z1231.D758   016.7920973
An inclusive list of 3,856 books and periodical articles on all phases of the
history and development of the American theater and stage. Arranged by state
and city. It has been superseded by Larson (P798) in most but not all areas.

P800. Gohdes, Clarence L. *Literature and Theater of the States and Regions
of the U.S.A.: An Historical Bibliography*. Durham, N.C.: Duke Univ.
Press, 1967. 276pp. Z1225.G63   016.8109
Lists anthologies, chapters of books, periodical articles, monographs, and
pamphlets that might assist in the study of American theater. Arrangement is
alphabetical by state and geographical area, so it is easy, for instance, to locate
material on Atlanta's regional theater. There is no index and no individual author
listing, so unless students need an area approach, search is difficult. This has
been superseded by Larson (P798) for information on American regional theater
before 1900.

Microtext

P801. *Nineteenth-Century American Drama: A Finding Guide*. Ed. Donald
L. Hixon and Don A. Hennessee. Metuchen, N.J.: Scarecrow, 1977.
579pp. PS632.H57   016.812
A locator guide to the Readex microprints of the American works in Freedley
and Nicoll's *English and American Plays of the Nineteenth Century* (J429). The
important appendixes enable scholars to make special studies of plays in series,
ethnic and racial characters, or specific subjects such as Quakers, North American
Indians, or the women's movement.

See also
Wells, *Three Centuries* (G112)
Bergquist, *Three Centuries . . . : A Checklist* (G113)

Bibliographies of primary works

P802. *Documents of American Theater History.* Ed. William C. Young. Chicago: American Library Assn., 1973. NA6830.Y68   792'.0973

Vol. 1: *Famous American Playhouses, 1716-1899.* 327pp.
Vol. 2: *Famous American Playhouses, 1900-1971.* 297pp.

Diaries, letters, newspaper clippings, and eyewitness accounts on actors, designers, directors, playwrights, and major events in American theater history.

P803.   Stratman, Carl J., C.S.V. *American Theatrical Periodicals, 1798-1967: A Bibliographical Guide.* Durham, N.C.: Duke Univ. Press, 1970. 133pp. Z6935.S75   016.7902
This chronological list of about seven hundred American theatrical periodicals gives complete publishing information and uses symbols to denote libraries in which they can be found.

Criticism

*P804. Eddleman, Floyd E., ed. *American Drama Criticism: Interpretations, 1890-1977.* 2nd ed. Hamden, Conn.: Shoe String, 1979. 488pp. Supplement 1 (1984), 168pp. Z1231.D7.P3   [PS332]   016.792'0973
A checklist of critical books and articles in many popular and some scholarly periodicals concerning American stage plays, including a few musicals, of all centuries. Limitations: It treats United States authors and a few Canadians and Caribbeans, but it has no biographical studies, no interviews, no author bibliographies, and no general works (see Breed, J554, for broader but less thorough coverage). It is admittedly not selective according to quality of the work; rather it draws many of its entries from *Theatre Arts, New Yorker, Newsweek, Saturday Review,* and easily available sources, a method that does have its merits for certain student projects. The 1979 edition consolidates all three previous volumes and adds new material through 1977; the supplement updates the criticism to 1982. Students can now easily make chronological surveys of the criticism of James's plays, find reviews of Neil Simon's *Sunshine Boys* (1972) and Albee's *Seascape* (1975), locate information on plays by women and blacks, and do research on off-Broadway groups. Students will be grateful for the great variety of research possibilities. The entry on Kingsley, for instance, lists dozens of critical works for all ten of his plays including seventeen for *Darkness at Noon* (based on Koestler's novel). In Long (P795) the complete listing for Kingsley consists of only nine general titles. And Eddleman lists over four hundred critical works on Albee, while Breed (J554) lists fewer than two hundred.
Arrangement is alphabetical by author and then by title, with an index by title, playwright, and critic, but no annotations. Loyal drama buffs will always remember that Helen H. Palmer and Anne J. Dyson were the editors of the pioneering first edition.

P805.   Salem, James M., ed. *A Guide to Critical Reviews: Part I: American Drama, 1909-1969.* 2nd ed. Metuchen, N.J.: Scarecrow, 1973. 591pp.

3rd ed. in preparation. Z5782.S342   016.809'2

A bibliography of critical reviews (not scholarly examinations) of plays that have appeared on the New York stage. The editors recommend that students may want to go to Leary (P727), *MLAIB* (D31), *Am. Lit.* (P744), *Modern Drama* (J555), *Theatre Journal* (G118), and other sources for coverage of scholarly periodicals and books.

Arrangement is alphabetical first by author then by title of the play, then by title of the periodical (American and Canadian) and newspaper (*New York Times* and others covered by the *New York Theatre Critics' Reviews*, P807). The virtue of Salem is that he draws all these sources into one alphabetical arrangement.

The second edition provides review information on 290 dramatists and 1,700 plays, including hits such as *The Odd Couple* by Neil Simon and Gibson's *Miracle Worker*. Students might want, for instance, to evaluate the reception of O'Neill's *Emperor Jones* over a period of forty-three years, or to compare the critics' response to O'Neill's *Anna Christie* in 1921 with their comments in 1952, or to note the reception of Williams' *Glass Menagerie* when it was first produced in New York in 1945. Title indexes. Be on the alert for a third edition.

See four other volumes in this series by Salem: *The Musical* (P806), *British and Continental Drama* (J559), *The Screenplay* (W1242), and *Foreign Drama, 1909-1977* (R969).

P806.   ———. *Guide to Critical Reviews: Part II: The Musical, 1909-1974.* 2nd ed. Metuchen, N.J.: Scarecrow, 1976. 611pp. Z5782.S342 016.809'2

This bibliography of reviews (not scholarly studies) of Broadway musicals from the Ziegfeld Follies in 1910 to *Raisin* and *Candide* in 1974 is a good place to start even though it does not pretend to be exhaustive. Arranged alphabetically by title of the musical, with statistics on author, performances, dates, costumes, and choreographer. Under each title are listed reviews that may be found in American and Canadian periodicals and newspapers. It has one outstanding feature: It provides various ways to approach the subject through the numerous indexes of long-run musicals (*The Fantasticks*), award winners, authors, titles, composers, lyricists, directors, designers, choreographers, original works and their authors.

See also four other volumes in this series by Salem: *American Drama, 1909-1969* (P805), *British and Continental Drama* (J559), *The Screenplay* (W1242), and *Foreign Drama, 1909-1977* (R969).

P807.   *New York Theatre Critics' Reviews.* New York: Critics' Theatre Reviews, 1940–   . Irregular, with the theater season. PN2000.N76   792

A photographic reproduction of reviews of Broadway and off-Broadway plays as they appeared in six papers (*New York Times, New York Daily News, Wall Street Journal, New York Post, Women's Wear Daily, Christian Science Monitor*), in two periodicals (*Time* and *Newsweek*), and as broadcast on two television stations (WABC-TV, WCBS-TV). Each issue includes a list of premières offered that year as well as a list of current productions that opened in previous years so the student can refer to the proper volume for additional reviews. Students of contemporary drama—or professors who plan to go to MLA meetings in New York—may be interested in reading that Clive Barnes admires the "defiant difference" of Joseph Papp's production of *The Pirates of Penzance* and that praise for *Da* is unanimous. A new feature: four off-Broadway supplements a year.

Annual bound volumes feature year-end indexes of authors, actors, actresses, producers, stage directors, scenic designers, costume designers, dance directors, composers, and lyricists. The cumulative indexes covering 1940–60 and 1961–72 are arranged alphabetically by title.

Indexed in *Arts and Hum. Cit. Ind.* (F47).

P808.   *New York Times Theater Reviews, 1870–1978.* New York: Arno, 1980.
20 vols., with index (3 vols.). PN1581.N38   792'.09747'1

All the reviews in the *Times* since 1870 are reproduced here chronologically with indexes by name, title, and production company, and additional information on awards and statistics. Use this in conjunction with Salem's two guides (P805–06) and the *New York Theatre Critics' Reviews* (P807).

P809.   *Ten Modern American Playwrights: An Annotated Bibliography.* Ed.
Kimball King. New York: Garland, 1982. 260pp. Z1231.D7.K56
[PS351]   016.812'54

Current scholarship on dramatists currently in the news—Edward Albee, Amiri Baraka (LeRoi Jones), Ed Bullins, Jack Gelber, Arthur Kopit, David Mamet, David Rabe, Sam Shepard, Neil Simon, and Lanford Wilson. This guide lists all their plays and related criticism—convenient and timely.

Dissertations

P810.   *American Dissertations on the Drama and the Theatre: A Bibliography.*
Ed. Fredric M. Litto. Kent, Ohio: Kent State Univ. Press, 1969. 519pp.
Z5781.L56   016.8092

This early computer-produced bibliography lists 4,500 authors from forty-five countries, subjects from several centuries B.C. to 1969, topics from performance to stagecraft, history, and criticism. Besides the bibliography there is an author, keyword-in-context, and subject index, so access is easy. A thorough search for completed scholarship in this field would have to extend to *Dissertations in American Literature, 1891–1966* (P737), *Guide to Doctoral Dissertations in Victorian Literature* (J465), and Dissertations (W1211–15).

Periodicals

P812.   *Theatre Survey* (*ThS*). Albany: State Univ. of New York, 1960– . 2/yr.
American Soc. for Theatre Research. PN2000.T716   792'.05

Articles and notes on theater history only, not on current productions.
Indexed in *ABELL* (D32), *Arts and Hum. Cit. Ind.* (F47), *MLAIB* (D31).

See also

American and British Theatrical Biography (W1138)
American Stage to World War I (W1470.4)
American Women Dramatists (W1647.1)

Contemporary American Theater Critics (W1142)
Gohdes (P705), Section 23, ninety-three titles on American drama
National Playwrights Directory (W1140)
Notable Names in the American Theatre (W1139)

POETRY

Surveys

*P814. *Crowell's Handbook of Contemporary American Poetry.* Ed. Karl
Malkoff. New York: Crowell, 1973. 338pp. PS323.5.M3   811'.5'409
This is first a guide to the appreciation of the poetry; it is only incidentally
a source of biographical and bibliographical information. Unlike most handbooks, this can be read from cover to cover. It has long discussions of such poets
as Hecht, Olson, Baraka, and Rich, a few broad subject entries, and an important, very important, survey of poetic history from Imagism and projective verse
to the confessional poets. "Contemporary" means 1940 to the early 1970s.

Basic guides

*P815. *A Bibliographical Guide to the Literature of Contemporary American
Poetry, 1970–1975.* Ed. Phillis Gershator. Metuchen, N.J.: Scarecrow,
1976. 124pp. Z1231.P7.G47   [PS325]   016.811'5'4
This unexpectedly readable book focuses solely on contemporary American
poetry *as a genre* or as it appears in works of ethnic, regional, or topical interest.
It is not concerned with works by and about individual poets. It provides information on the poetry itself as well as on works of criticism written between 1970
and 1975. It has discerning annotations, author and book title indexes, and a
topical guide. Professors preparing lesson plans and students writing papers
should consult this; aspiring poets probably should consult it, also.

Series

P817. Introductions to Twentieth-Century American Poetry. New York: Columbia Univ. Press, 1977– . Alternate title: Columbia Introductions
to Twentieth-Century American Poetry. In progress.
Here is a good starting point for material that is not well covered elsewhere.
Volumes published so far include

John Ashbery, by David Shapiro
John Berryman, by Joel Conarroe
Robert Bly, by Howard Nelson
Hart Crane, by Herbert A. Leibowitz
E. E. Cummings, by Rushworth M. Kidder
Langston Hughes, by Onwuchekwa Jemie

Robert Lowell, by Mark Rudman
James Merrill, by Judith Moffett
Marianne Moore, by George W. Nitchie
Ezra Pound, by Bernetta Quinn
Theodore Roethke, by Karl Malkoff
Wallace Stevens, by Susan Weston

Indexes

P818.   *Index of American Periodical Verse.* Metuchen, N.J.: Scarecrow,
1971– . Annual. Z1231.P7.I47   016.811'5'4
This annual publication now indexes two hundred American popular and
little magazines (W1423–30) for recently published poetry by about four thousand international poets, including Stafford, Bishop, Bronk, Goldbarth, and
Harper. Its coverage and, therefore, its value should increase every year, but

reviewers have suggested that the editors should cease indexing periodicals that are already indexed elsewhere and pick up those periodicals that have no indexing service at all. Earlier poems may be located in *Contemporary American Poetry: A Checklist* (Metuchen, N.J.: Scarecrow, 1975; 179pp.), which covers about eleven hundred poets who published in the 1950s and 1960s, or in *Contemporary Poets in American Anthologies, 1960-1977* (Metuchen, N.J.: Scarecrow, 1978; 236pp.).

Periodicals

*P821.   *American Poetry Review (APR)*. Philadelphia: Temple Univ., 1972–   .
6/yr. PS580.A44

A tabloid in format (like *Rolling Stone*) that puts poetry in headlines, where it finally gets the attention it deserves. *APR* is aggressive in subject matter, lively in prose style, and hospitable in printing criticism, poems, and translations from all over the world. Some of its regular contributors are among today's best American authors. Circulation: 30,000.

Indexed in *ABELL* (D32), *Abst. Eng. Stud.* (E38), *Am. Hum. Ind.* (P738), *Arts and Hum. Cit. Ind.* (F47), *Bk. Rev. Ind.* (W1559), *Index to Bk. Rev. Hum.* (W1560), *MLAIB* (D31).

*P822.   *Poetry*. Chicago: n.p. (601 S. Morgan St.), 1912–   . Monthly. Modern
Poetry Assn. PS301.P6   811'.005

Affectionately and respectfully referred to as an American institution. It has earned its reputation by criticizing wisely and honestly, by daring to publish the unknown as well as the known, and by promoting the cause of many, many young poets who have ultimately become our best authors. Circulation: 9,000.

Indexed in *ABELL* (D32), *Arts and Hum. Cit. Ind.* (F47), *Bk. Rev. Dig.* (W1558), *Current Bk. Rev. Cit.* (W1564), *Index to Bk. Rev. Hum.* (W1560), *Readers' Gd.* (F48).

See also

—appropriate titles for poetry in other sections of American and English literature

Author Newsletters and Journals (P777)
Bibliographies and Guides (P702-12.1)
Contemporary Poetry in America and England, 1950-1975 (A8)
Criticism (P727-33.1)
Modern Poetry Studies (J572), numerous articles on American poets
Poetry by American Women (W1648)
Series (P720-25)

Recordings

P824.   *Poet's Voice*. Ed. Stratis Haviaras. Cambridge, Mass.: Harvard Univ.
Press, 1978. PS615.P64

A rare oportunity to hear poems read and discussed by their own creators: Auden, Berryman, Eliot, Frost, Jarrell, Jeffers, Lowell, Moore, Plath, Pound, Roethke, Stevens, and Williams. The recordings of about 130 poems and their commentary were made at Harvard between 1933 and 1970.

Background reading for American literature

P826.   Hoffman, Daniel, ed. *Harvard Guide to Contemporary American Writing.* Cambridge, Mass.: Belknap, 1979. 618pp. Paperback. PS221.H357   810.9'0054

Reliable background reading for students interested in fiction, poetry, drama, and literary criticism from World War II to the late 1970s. Janeway on Women's Literature, Simpson on Southern Fiction, Braudy on the realists and naturalists, and seven other critical surveys of contemporary ideas and their interpreters. Certainly a desirable addendum to the fine but dated *Literary History of the United States* (P701).

P827.   Horton, Rod W., and Herbert W. Edwards. *Backgrounds of American Literary Thought.* 3rd ed. Englewood Cliffs, N.J.: Prentice-Hall, 1974. 630pp. PS88.H6   917.3'03

Commonsense background reading that pulls everything together from "Puritanism to Babbittry and Freudianism," as one reviewer aptly noted.

P828.   Matthiessen, Francis O. *American Renaissance: Art and Expression in the Age of Emerson and Whitman.* London: Oxford Univ. Press, 1941. 678pp. Paperback. PS201.M3   810.9'003

Matthiessen is on all the reading lists, but students must remember that his book is concerned with the background of the literature, the influence of tradition, the impact of American democratic ideas, the surge of spiritualism and individualism. He focuses mainly on Hawthorne, Melville, and Whitman, but his references and research are so panoramic that his work has become important to anyone interested in any area of American literature.

*P829.   Spiller, Robert E. *The Cycle of American Literature: An Essay in Historical Criticism.* New York: Macmillan, 1955. 318pp. Paperback. PS88.S6   810.9

The author aptly describes this as a "distillation" of the corporate knowledge that produced the *Literary History of the United States* (P701). He begins with Edwards, ends with Faulkner, and discusses every important author and idea in the intervening two centuries. Unquestionably the best choice for a judicious appraisal of American literature during that period.

Additional scholars who have written reliable criticism on American literature are Beard, Van Wyck Brooks, Charvat, Commager, Foerster, Hicks, Hubbell, Lerner, Perry Miller, Parrington, Schneider, Snell, Tyler, Van Doren, Wilson.

Additional reference sources containing information on American literature

P830.   *American Book-Prices Current* (W1162)
American Folklore: A Bibliography (W1271)
American Literary Manuscripts (W1317)
Articles on Twentieth-Century Literature (J519)
Ash, *Subject Collections* (W1315)

Blumenthal, *Printed Book in America* (W1068)
Book Collecting (W1153–69), selected titles
Center for Editions of American Authors (W1177)
Center for Scholarly Editions (W1179)
Contemporary Literary Criticism (J516)
Dictionary of American Biography (W1087)
Dictionary of Literary Biography (W1121)
Directory of Archives (W1319)
Downs, *American Library Resources* (W1313)
Early American Proverbs (W1533)
Encyclopedia of World Literature in the 20th Century (J523)
Jewish Writers of North America (A8.1)
Journal of American Folklore (W1278)
*Literary History of the South. Ed. Louis D. Rubin, Jr., et al. Baton
  Rouge: Louisiana State Univ. Press. Projected for 1985.
Longman Companion to Twentieth Century Literature (J525)
Magill, *Masterplots* (W1591)
Notable American Women (W1088)
Publishers and Publishing (W1514–25)
Twentieth-Century Literary Criticism (J515)
Twentieth Century Writing (J524)
Webster's American Biographies (W1083)
Webster's Guide to American History (W1295)
Whiting, *Early American Proverbs* (W1533)
Women's Studies (W1629–32, 1634–35, 1640–41, 1644–49)

Afro-American Literature

Surveys

P835.   *Afro-American Literature: The Reconstruction of Instruction*. Ed. Dexter
        Fisher and Robert B. Stepto. New York: MLA, 1979. 256pp.
        PS153.N5.A35   810'.9'8960

   A collection of essays on the place of Afro-American literature in literary
history, the characteristics and contributions of black imaginative language, the
elements of Afro-American folklore, and ways to approach the literature.

Basic guides

*P836. *Black American Writers: Bibliographical Essays*. Ed. M. Thomas Inge,
        Maurice Duke, and Jackson R. Bryer. 2 vols. New York: St. Martin's,
        1978. PS153.N5.B55   016.810'9'896073

   This, like *American Literary Scholarship* (P734), is a collection of essays by
specialists who have surveyed existing research material and evaluated it for those
students who want guidance in selecting reliable critics and criticism. It examines
topics such as slave narratives or the Harlem Renaissance and then considers the
state of completed research on twenty-four authors, such as Wright, Hughes,
Ellison, Baraka, Brown, Chesnutt, Griggs, Harper, and Bontemps. There is some
overlapping with other sources described in this section, but thorough scholars
will want to consult them all, anyway. It, for instance, updates Turner's *Afro-*

American Writers (P838) but does not replace it as a basic text for preliminary work. And for writers like Jupiter Hammon, the first black poet (published in 1761), it gives a brief biographical sketch, a bibliography of works, a description of manuscripts and letters, and an essay appraising the best biographies and critical works, with both complimentary and derogatory comments on the quality of the criticism. This is the kind of reference book that encourages mature judgment and good research papers.

P837.   *Afro-American Literature and Culture since World War II: A Guide to Information Sources.* Ed. Charles D. Peavy. Vol. 6 of American Studies Information Guide Series (A8.1). Detroit: Gale, 1979. 302pp. Z1229.N39.P4   [PS153.N5]   016.810'8'0896
Two useful main sections. One is arranged by broad subject (Poetry, Prison Writing, Religion, Theater, Women), with an annotated bibliography of books and articles; the other is by individual author (Brooks, Cain, Danner, Demby, Reed, and about fifty others) with a list of books and articles by and about the writer, including interviews and biographical works. Author, title, and subject indexes. A commendable contribution to the field.

*P838.   Turner, Darwin T. *Afro-American Writers.* Goldentree Bibliographies (W1291). New York: Appleton (Meredith), 1970. 117pp. Paperback. Z1361.N39.T78   016.8108'091'7496
One of the most convenient and most welcome of the Goldentree Bibliographies, but for serious research it has been superseded by *Black American Writers* (P836) and the specialized bibliographies for fiction (P856–59), drama (P860–64), and poetry (P867–70). Focus is on 136 black authors of drama, fiction, and poetry who have been significant in American literature, from Phillis Wheatley of the eighteenth century to Gordon Parks of the 1970s. All relevant primary works are listed, and all scholarship about these authors if it relates to the literature, historical and sociological background, arts, journalism, and folklore. A separate section of selected criticism on Africans and Afro-Americans as characters in literature contains studies of the black in works by Faulkner, O'Neill, Simms, G. W. Cable, Twain, Stowe, Melville, Whitman, Harris, Trollope, Carlyle, Mill, and many more. Students, therefore, can get at the subject from two directions. Outstanding scholarship is marked with asterisks.

Library collections

P841.   Schatz, Walter. *Directory of Afro-American Resources.* New York: Bowker, 1970. 485pp. Z1361.N39.R3   917.3'06'96073
Similar in concept and scope to Downs's *American Library Resources* (W1313) and Ash's *Subject Collections* (W1315), this describes over five thousand collections of various aspects of Afro-American culture at over two thousand libraries. Arrangement is geographical.

P842.   *Black American Writers, 1773–1949: A Bibliography and Union List.* Comp. Geraldine O. Matthews et al. Boston: Hall, 1975. 221pp.

Z1361.N39.M35   [E185]   016.9173'06'96073
A union catalog with clearly defined limitations. It locates the writings of sixteen hundred black authors that are presently owned by sixty libraries in North Carolina, South Carolina, Georgia, Alabama, and Tennessee. No effort has been made to compile complete bibliographies for these authors. Hughes and Hurston, for instance, are listed with only three titles each. Birth and death dates are provided, a useful identification aid for obscure authors who are cited here for the first time. Arranged by broad subject (fifty-two pages on literature) with an author index.

**P843. *Dictionary Catalog of the Schomburg Collection of Negro Literature and History*. New York Public Library. 9 vols. Boston: Hall, 1962. First supplement of 2 vols., 1967. Second supplement of 4 vols., 1972. Annual supplements since 1973. Z881.N592.S35   016.96
One of the most important sources in the world for the study of the life and culture of the black race. The Schomburg Center for Research in Black Culture is interested in anything concerning peoples of African descent including books by and about them, art, folklore, biography, literature, music, and all disciplines. The annual supplements are published under the title *Bibliographic Guide to Black Studies*.

Criticism

P845.   *Library of Literary Criticism: Modern Black Writers*. Ed. Michael Popkin. New York: Ungar, 1978. 540pp. Paperback. PN841.M58   809'.889'6
Important because it offers an unprecedented opportunity to examine cross-cultural viewpoints. By means of excerpts from criticism, this surveys the lives and works of eighty black novelists, poets, and dramatists from the United States, Africa, and the Caribbean, with half of the critics being white and the other half black, some from Africa and some from America. If the excerpt seems pertinent or promising, students can then read the entire article or book (the citation is provided at the end of each entry). Index to critics. List of authors by country.

Identification problems

P846.   *Black Plots and Black Characters: A Handbook for Afro-American Literature*. Ed. Robert L. Southgate. Syracuse, N.Y.: Gaylord, 1979. 456pp. PS153.N5.S65   810'.9'896073
Five important features, any one of which would make this a useful book for beginning students: (1) The first half contains summaries and comments on novels, plays, speeches, ballads, folktales, and long poems, mainly written by blacks about blacks; (2) a "short companion" section contains alphabetically arranged entries on people, places, organizations, publications, events, and terms important in the black literary and historical movement; (3) the third section is a bibliography of selected works by and about black authors; (4) the fourth, a list of works about literary and historical subjects; and (5) the fifth, a chronological index of historical and literary events from 1526 to the present. A good starting point.

Indexes

*P847. *Index to Periodical Articles by and about Blacks.* Boston: Hall, 1973– .
Annual. AI3.04   Former title, 1965–72: *Index to Periodical Articles
by and about Negroes.*
This index to the contents of twenty-five black American periodicals lists
authors, titles, reviews, and subjects (such as Poems, Poetry—History and
Criticism, Women Poets, and Poets, American) in dictionary order. The 1979
volume contains information on three thousand articles, but the emphasis is
not on literature. Scholars wish the editors would expand their coverage. Cumulations for 1950–59 and 1960–70.

P848. *Index to Black American Literary Anthologies.* Ed. Jessamine Kallenbach. Boston: Hall, 1978. 219pp. Z1229.N39.K34 [PS153.N5]
016.8108'0896
Kallenbach locates the works of seventeen hundred black authors, works
that have in most instances been buried in anthologies. Important features: birth
and death dates, author-title index.

See also
Index to Black Poetry (P870)

Periodicals

P850. *Black American Literature Forum (BALF).* Terre Haute: Indiana State
Univ., 1976– . Quarterly. E185.5.H35   810'.9'896073   Former ti-
tle, 1967–76: *Negro American Literature Forum.*
Concerned with all areas of black literature: its interpretations, authors,
impact, and methods of teaching. Book reviews; news; art; poetry.
Indexed in *ABELL* (D32), *Am. Hum. Ind.* (P738), *Arts and Hum. Cit.
Ind.* (F47), *Film Literature Ind.* (W1252), *Hum. Ind.* (F45), *MLAIB* (D31).

P851. *Black Dialogue.* San Francisco: n.p. (1459 Waller St.), 1965– . Irregular.
Poems, fiction, critical articles, reviews, plays, and photographs. One of
the better periodicals in this area.
Indexed in *ABELL* (D32).

P852. *Obsidian: Black Literature in Review.* Detroit: Wayne State Univ.,
1975– . 3/yr. PR1110.B503   820'.8'0896
Articles, fiction, poetry, interviews, and an annotated annual bibliography
of scholarship. Index to vols. 1–2 in vol. 3.
Indexed in *ABELL* (D32), *Am. Hum. Ind.* (P738), *Arts and Hum. Cit.
Ind.* (F47), *MLAIB* (D31).

*P853. *Phylon: The Atlanta University Review of Race and Culture.* Atlanta:
Atlanta Univ., 1940– . Quarterly. E185.5.P5   325.260973
Scholarly articles on every phase of black life, including the historical and
the social aspects. This fine periodical also includes excellent book reviews, poetry,

and short stories.
Indexed in *ABELL* (D32), *Bk. Rev. Ind.* (W1559), *Current Ind. Jour. Ed.* (W1224), *Hum. Ind.* (F45), *Ind. to Per. by/about Blacks* (P847), *MLAIB* (D31).

P854.   *Studies in Black Literature*. Fredericksburg, Va.: Mary Washington Coll., 1970–77 (vols. 1–8). 3/yr. PS153.N5.S88   809
This periodical made a scholarly contribution to the study of black literature; its cessation is regretted. It contains articles on authors and their works, interviews, long book reviews, and checklists on, for instance, early Afro-American novelists (vol. 8, no. 1). Cumulated author and subject indexes, vols. 1–6 (1970–75) in vol. 8, no. 1 (Spring 1977).
Indexed in *ABELL* (D32), *Abst. Eng. Stud.* (E38), *Arts and Hum. Cit. Ind.* (F47), *MLAIB* (D31).

FICTION

Basic guides

P856.   *Afro-American Fiction, 1853–1976: A Guide to Information Sources*. Ed. Edward Margolies and David Bakish. Vol. 25 of Gale Information Guide Library (A8). Detroit: Gale, 1979. 161pp. Z1229.N39.M37 [PS374.N4]   016.813'008'0352
A historical essay, a checklist of primary material, and annotated bibliographies of secondary works for fifteen major Afro-American novelists including Toomer, Hurston, and Reed. Deemed excellent by most reviewers, this is currently the best source for information on these fifteen authors. It supersedes most previous reference works, overlapping somewhat with *Black American Fiction* (P857). Some errors and omissions have been noted, however, and the bibliographical treatment is not as professional as it should be.

*P857.   *Black American Fiction: A Bibliography*. Ed. Carol Fairbanks and Eugene A. Engeldinger. Metuchen, N.J.: Scarecrow, 1978. 351pp. Z1229.N39.F34   [PS153.N5]   016.813
A list of about six hundred major and minor black American authors of the nineteenth and twentieth centuries with the titles of their novels, short stories, biographies, criticism, and reviews. Convenient—everyone working in this field welcomes this source. Comprehensive—Chesnutt, for instance, has over eight pages of entries, and Hughes, nine. Easy to use—and most of the cited periodicals are available in large libraries. This supersedes all earlier titles. It is recommended especially for its twenty-five-page supplemental bibliography of books about black American writings.

Bibliographies of primary works

P859.   *Afro-American Novel, 1965–1975: A Descriptive Bibliography of Primary and Secondary Materials*. Ed. Helen R. Houston. Troy, N.Y.: Whitston, 1977. 214pp. Z1229.N39.H68   [PS153.N5]   813'.03
Lists works by and about fifty-six black American novelists, with a biographical sketch of each author, brief plot summaries, and references to favorable and

unfavorable reviews of the novels.

See also

Black Women Novelists (W1647)

DRAMA

Basic guides

P860.   *Black American Playwrights, 1800 to the Present: A Bibliography.* Ed.
Esther S. Arata and Nicholas J. Rotoli. Metuchen, N.J.: Scarecrow, 1976.
295pp. Z1229.N39.A7   [PS153.N5]   016.812'008

   More Black American Playwrights: A Bibliography. Ed. Esther S. Arata.
Metuchen, N.J.: Scarecrow, 1978. 335pp. Z1229.N39.A7   [PS153.N5]
016.812'008

   Students must use both volumes because the second corrects the weaknesses
of the first, providing supplementary information on two hundred dramatists
who were included in vol. 1 and adding about three hundred more, many of
whom are minor figures not covered elsewhere. Together they list plays, published
separately or in anthologies, as well as musicals, operas, criticism, reviews, television and radio scripts, and awards. And together they markedly improve accessibility to research in black American drama. They provide, for example, information on 1,550 titles (including several pages on Hughes), and they pointedly
refer to criticism that can be found in the popular books and periodicals that
are generally available in large libraries. The bibliographical information,
however, is not always complete, and obvious factual errors or omissions have
been noted.

*P861.   *Black Playwrights, 1823-1977: An Annotated Bibliography of Plays.*
Ed. James V. Hatch and OMANii Abdullah. New York: Bowker, 1977.
319pp. Z1231.D7.H37   [PS338.N4]   016.812'009'352
   This fine production is based on several earlier works. It is a comprehensive
and reliable source to 2,700 plays (including stage, film, television, and radio
scripts) by about nine hundred major and minor Afro-American and some Caribbean authors. It is alphabetically arranged by author with brief notes about the
plot, cast, length, and performance dates of each play so that directors can select
them for production. Several appendixes give more research guidance for agents,
dissertations, interviews, awards, and other fields of black drama and theater
arts. Bibliography and title index.

P862.   Hatch, James V. *Black Image on the American Stage: A Bibliography
of Plays and Musicals, 1770-1970.* New York: DBS Publications, 1970.
162pp. Z5784.N4.H35   016.812'008
   Hatch takes a chronological approach to over two thousand entries, including
the authors alphabetically under each decade, a bibliography of his sources, and
title and author indexes. Of interest are the unexpectedly large number of
pre-1800 plays and the suggested areas for further research. Because it is con-

cerned only with plays in which the action and plot focus on the black race, regardless of the race of the author, it is not superseded by Hatch's later work, *Black Playwrights, 1823-1977* (P861), which confines its scope to black authors and to factual information on the plays. Nor is it duplicated by *Black American Playwrights* and *More Black American Playwrights* (P860), which also cover only black dramatists but which contribute the added feature of information on criticism and reviews.

Periodicals

P864.   *Black Theatre: A Periodical of the Black Theatre Movement.* New York: New Lafayette, 1968– . 3/yr.

Interested in the activities of black theater workshops, with plays, interviews, interpretive articles, and reviews.

See also

Afro-American Poetry and Drama, 1760-1975 (P868)

POETRY

Surveys

*P866.   Wagner, Jean. *Black Poets of the United States: From Paul Laurence Dunbar to Langston Hughes.* Trans. Kenneth Douglas. Urbana: Univ. of Illinois Press, 1973, c1962. 561pp. Paperback. PS153.N5.W313 811'.009

This, the first and still one of the best full-length scholarly studies of Afro-American poetry, is faring very well indeed under the test of criticism and time. The author's thesis is that racial and religious feeling are interdependent in the poetry of such authors as Dunbar, Johnson, Hughes, Brown, McKay, Toomer, and Cullen. The book's excellent bibliography has been brought up to date first by the translator and then in a supplement to the Black Poetry section, 1962-73, by Keneth Kinnamon. A very fine, intellectually honest book.

Basic guides

P867.   Sherman, Joan. *Invisible Poets: Afro-Americans of the Nineteenth Century.* Urbana: Univ. of Illinois Press, 1974. 270pp. PS153.N5.S48 811'.009

A critical study of twenty-six "forgotten" black poets. It contains important bibliographical essays explaining the basic finding aids, periodicals, anthologies, and manuscripts for each author. This is an extremely thorough study of these poets up to its own copyright date.

*P868.   *Afro-American Poetry and Drama, 1760-1975: A Guide to Information Sources.* Ed. (Poetry) William P. French, Amritjit Singh, and Michel J. Fabre. Ed. (Drama) Geneviève E. Fabre. Vol. 17 of Gale Information Guide Library (A8). Detroit: Gale, 1979. 493pp. Z1229.N39.A37 [PS153.N5]   016.810'9'8960

This fine historical essay assesses contemporary black theater and lists bibliographies of general studies, biographies, and primary and secondary works for individual authors. It also has a poetry section covering two centuries of American and foreign-born black poets. This is the best source available ("outstanding," according to *Choice*, W1557). As a bibliography this supersedes most earlier works. As a convenient reference source, it also gives birth and death dates, provides a summary of each play, and in the poetry section includes appendixes of folk songs, blues, and spirituals. Author, title, and subject indexes.

Indexes

*P870.   *Index to Black Poetry*. Ed. Dorothy H. Chapman. Boston: Hall, 1974. 541pp. PS153.N5.C45   811'.008

Title, first-line, subject, and author arrangement for easy location of five thousand poems that previously were often either unknown or inaccessible in 130 books and anthologies. The first index of its kind and, therefore, valuable. The poetry is limited to that written by or about blacks from Blake to Dubois and Sanchez. Students who are familiar with Granger's (W1536) will feel comfortable with this because of the similar arrangement and intention. The author-title index will give them a general idea of the author's productivity, and the subject index will indicate the central concerns of the black race. Very well done indeed, even to the generous-size pages, wide margins, clear print, and flawless arrangement.

Additional reference sources for Afro-American literature

P870.1   African Literature (R972–82)
   Am. Lit. Schol. (P734)
   Black American Writers (W1131)
   Black Americans in Autobiography: An Annotated Bibliography. Ed.
      Russell C. Brignano. 2nd ed. Durham, N.C.: Duke Univ. Press, 1983.
   Black English (W1344)
   CLA Journal (H142)
   Living Black American Authors (W1133)
   MLAIB (D31), American Literature, subheading "Afro-American" in
      all subsections
   MELUS (P753)
   Selected Black American Authors (W1134)
   Who's Who among Black Americans (W1095)

American Indian Literature

Basic guides

P871.   Allen, Paula Gunn, ed. *Studies in American Indian Literature: Critical Essays and Course Designs*. New York: MLA, 1983. 384pp. PS153.I52.S8   810'.9'897

This collection of essays and course designs includes a survey of scholarship and an extensive bibliography.

P872.   *American Indian: Language and Literature*. Ed. Jack W. Marken. Goldentree Bibliographies (W1291). Arlington Heights, Ill.: AHM,

1978. 204pp. Z7118.M30   970.1
A welcome addition to the Goldentree Bibliographies, timely, selective, easy to use. It lists 3,600 books and articles in English and European languages that are concerned with American Indian literature and language. Arrangement is by region and American Indian group.

P873.   American Indian Bibliographical Series. Bloomington: Indiana Univ. Press, 1976– . Center for the History of the American Indian, Newberry Library. In progress (vol. 23, 1982).
A series of historical essays, recommended reference books, and scholarly bibliographies that serve as guides to the culture, tribes, history, and contemporary problems of the American Indian—Ojibwes, Navajos, Plains, Apaches, and many more.

P874.   *Indians of North and South America*. Ed. Carolyn E. Wolf and Karen R. Folk. Metuchen, N.J:. Scarecrow, 1977. 576pp. Z1209.W82 [E58]   016.97'0004'97
A few literature titles listed here may be of some help. Look in the index under Indian Literature, Indian Poetry, Indians in Literature, Folklore, Drama, and other subject headings. The title, series, subject, newspaper clipping, and tribe indexes are excellent.

Identification problems

*P875.   *Reference Encyclopedia of the American Indian*. Ed. Barry T. Klein. 2 vols. 3rd ed. Rye, N.Y.: Todd, 1978. E76.2.K4   973'.04'97
Brief information on Indian tribal councils, parks, museums, libraries, schools, periodicals (over 350!), college courses, and other areas of special interest. Vol. 2 is a "Who's Who" of prominent American Indian authors, anthropologists, tribal chiefs, curators, and non-Indians active in Indian affairs. Two important bibliographies: one alphabetically by title of three hundred books concerning Indians and one by subjects such as Alaska, Artists—American, and Indians of North America—Fiction. One reader's response: interest, amazement, pride.

P876.   *Indians of Today*. Ed. Marion E. Gridley. 4th ed. Chicago: Indian Council Fire Publications, 1971. 504pp. E89.G75   920.07
Biographical information on about four hundred outstanding American Indians. A vocation index and a geographical index would greatly expand the research possibilities.

Indexes

P877.   *Index to Literature on the American Indian*. San Francisco: American Indian Historical Soc., 1970– . Irregular. Z1209.I53   016.9701
An author-subject index to literature about the American Indian. It indexes about 250 scholarly (not popular) periodicals for material on language, literature, poetry, religion, women, and all social and cultural aspects of Indian life. The first four volumes were published in 1970, 1971, 1972, and 1973; the fifth volume will cover 1974–80.

P878.   *American Indian in Short Fiction: An Annotated Bibliography*. Ed.
Peter G. Beidler and Marion F. Egge. Metuchen, N.J.: Scarecrow, 1980.
203pp. Z1231.F4.B44 [PS374.I49]   016.813'03
Plot summaries for almost nine hundred short stories about American Indians. This fine contribution to American literature covers American publications of the past hundred years and serves as a supplement to *Short Story Index*
(G76) because it includes unanthologized stories. The indexes by tribe and subject should encourage interesting research projects because they indicate local
problems, general trends, and dramatic changes in attitude. Alphabetical by
writer, but no title index.

Periodicals

P880.   *ASAIL Newsletter*. Chinle, Ariz.: Navajo Community Coll.–Tsaile,
1974–79. 4–5/yr. PM151.A8716
This newsletter of the Association for Studies in American Indian Literatures
includes reviews, book lists, and other information helpful to teachers. Alternate address: Dept. of English, 602 Philosophy Hall, Columbia Univ., New York,
N.Y. 10027.

Additional reference sources for information on American Indian literature

P881.   *America* (E43)
Haas, Marilyn L. "A Basic Guide to Reference Sources for the Study
of the American Indian." *Reference Services Review*, 7, no. 3 (1979),
15–66. See *RSR* (W1569.1)
MELUS (P753)
Nineteenth-Century American Drama (P801)
Resources in Education (W1223)
Ryder, *Canadian Reference Sources* (N663)
Western American Literature (P772)

Q

Continental Literature

Rousseau, La Pléiade, Goethe, the *Decameron,* El Cid, the Golden Age of Spanish drama, the Russian novel, Sartre, Unamuno—allusions to these Continental literary movements, authors, and works are rife in English and American literature. Most students know that they can locate brief identifications for these references in their familiar Oxford Companions (see Index) or *Reader's Encyclopedia* (W1402). Frequently, however, they need more than a definition or a date. They need an explanation of the allusion to Francesca or Beatrice, Roland or Siegfried. They need a summary, perhaps, of the literary impact of eighteenth-century France, or a history of the development of the novel in Russia, a manageable survey of a nation's literature, or the European viewpoint of a single author. And, because most American students have neither the time nor training to handle foreign reference works, they prefer that this material be written expressly for the English-speaking reader. The books discussed in this section are only a few of the many that have been written to satisfy these needs. They have been selected because they are supportive in nature. They clarify, explain, summarize, distill, and survey. A few titles contain leads to sources that could be helpful in more extensive research, but most are "ready reference" material—concise, clear, in English, and available in most large libraries.

General

Basic sources

*Q884. *Columbia Dictionary of Modern European Literature.* Ed. Jean-Albert Bédé and William B. Edgerton. 2nd ed. New York: Columbia Univ. Press, 1980. 895pp. PN771.C575

A remarkably up-to-date dictionary with long entries on every phase of European literature from the symbolists of the late nineteenth century to authors who died in the 1970s. Its entry on Polish literature, for example, fills eleven double-column pages beginning with the "Young Poland" movement of a century ago and ending with the proliferation of poets in the 60s and 70s including Czeslaw Milosz and Witold Gombrowicz.

The five hundred international contributors have collected information on eighteen hundred authors who wrote in thirty-three languages. They cite the available translations, survey each of the national literatures, and maintain the high level of scholarship established by the first edition. This fine handbook will be both aid and inspiration to students who have questions about twentieth-century literature on the Continent.

Q885.   Pelican Guides to European Literature. *Modernism, 1890-1930.* Ed. Malcolm Bradbury and James McFarlane. Atlantic Highlands, N.J.: Humanities Press, 1978, c1976. 684pp. PN56.M54.M6   809'.04'1

Forbidding in size and print, but worth consulting. Written from a European, not a national, viewpoint, this discusses major figures and movements in their historical and intellectual context, including Tolstoy, Pérez Galdós, Zola, Darwin, Marx, and the realist novels of Stendhal. Especially useful are the chronology of events, the brief biographies of people mentioned in the text, and the bibliography of works on modernism arranged by country, -isms, and genre. Proper name and title index. Others that have been published so far in the series are *The Continental Renaissance, 1500-1600* and *The Age of Realism.*

See also

Malclès, *Les Sources du travail bibliographique* (A7)
Present State of Scholarship in Sixteenth-Century Literature (J305), Italian, French, Spanish, German, and Neo-Latin Renaissance literature

Series

Q886.   Writers from the Other Europe. New York: Penguin, 1979– Irregular.

Translations of works by writers whose books have been banned or censored for political reasons. This excellent series is our only access to such talented authors as Danilo Kiš, Milan Kundera, Bruno Schulz, and Jerzy Andrzejewski.

Criticism

Q887.   *Library of Literary Criticism: Modern Romance Literatures.* Ed. Dorothy Nyren Curley and Arthur Curley. New York: Ungar, 1967. 510pp. PN813.C8   879.9'09

Excerpts from critical books and periodicals about such twentieth-century writers in France, Italy, Spain, Portugal, Switzerland, Belgium, and Romania as Beckett, Cocteau, Giraudoux, Guareschi, Lampedusa, Rolland, Sagan, and Unamuno. Citations are given for each excerpt so that students can go find and read the complete work if they wish. They might, for instance, want to read more of what Cocteau, Eliot, and Stravinsky wrote about Paul Valéry. Index to critics.

Identification problems

Q888.   *Penguin Companion to European Literature.* New York: McGraw-Hill,

1969. 908pp. PN41.P43   809.8'94

Some of the other Penguin Companions fail to make a unique contribution to the literature, but this fills a need because it cumulates elusive information on such varied subjects as Icelandic Sagas, Old Bulgarian literature, *La Celestina*, Italian Futurism, and minor authors like Zoshchenko, the Russian humorist. Most entries also suggest titles for further study. And thanks must go to the farsighted editor who saw to it that lists of countries and their authors are included at the back of the book so that readers can pull together and compare the national literatures.

Additional sources that include information on Continental literature

Q889.   Alexander, Harriet Semmes. *English Language Criticism on the Foreign Novel, 1965-1980*. Athens: Ohio Univ. Press, 1983. 550pp.

Altick and Matthews, *Dissertations* (J465), Austrian, French, and Swiss *Am. Lit. Schol.* (P734)

Columbia Essays on Modern Writers (J526)

Comparative Literature (T1007-24)

Dictionary of the Middle Ages (J247)

Eighteenth Century: A Current Bibliography (J374)

Encyclopedia of World Literature in the 20th Century (J523)

European Authors, 1000-1900 (W1124.4)

European Writers. Ed. George Stade. 10 vols. New York: Scribners, 1983– . In progress (vols. 1-4, 1983-84).

Fisher, *Medieval Literature of Western Europe* (J255)

Hall, *Literary Criticism* (W1356)

Index Translationum (W1625)

International Medieval Bibliography (J263)

Longman Companion to Twentieth Century Literature (J525)

MLAIB (D31), vol. 2, French, German, Italian, Spanish, Portuguese, Romanian, Netherlandic, Modern Greek, East European, Scandinavian; vol. 3, Linguistics

Medieval Lyric (Q899)

Medieval Studies (J253)

Paetow's *Guide* and Boyce's *Supplement* (J254)

Philosopher's Index (W1489)

Romantic Movement: A . . . Bibliography (J443)

Summaries (W1589-92)

Twayne's World Authors Series (R957), authors from Austria, Denmark, France, Germany, Greece, Iceland, Italy, Netherlands, Norway, Poland, Spain, Sweden, Switzerland, and many other countries

Twentieth Century Writing (J524)

World Literature (R950-94.1)

Year's Work in Modern Language Studies (W1328)

Periodicals

*Q890. *MLN* (*Modern Language Notes*). Baltimore: Johns Hopkins Univ. Press, 1886– . 5/yr. PB1.M64   809

    Scholarly articles and reviews, with each issue focusing on one area: Italian (Jan.), Hispanic (March), German (April), French (May), and comparative (Dec.). Contents are written in the native language. Cumulative indexes for vols. 1–50 and 51–60.

    Indexed in *ABELL* (D32), *Arts and Hum. Cit. Ind.* (F47), *Hum. Ind.* (F45), *Index to Bk. Rev. Hum.* (W1560), *MLAIB* (D31).

Q891.   *Studies in Twentieth Century Literature* (*StTCL*). Lincoln: Kansas State Univ. and Univ. of Nebraska, 1976– . 2/yr. PN771.S78   809'.04

    The only periodical that specializes in twentieth-century Continental literature, especially French, German, Spanish, and Russian. Articles only.

    Indexed in *ABELL* (D32), *Am. Hum. Ind.* (P738), *Arts and Hum. Cit. Ind.* (F47), *MLAIB* (D31).

Periodicals interested in Continental, English, and American literature

Q892.   *Contemporary Literature* (J529)
    Diacritics (W1365)
    Eighteenth-Century Studies (J381)
    Essays in Literature (H147)
    Georgia Review (H148)
    Journal of English and Germanic Philology (Q924)
    Journal of Modern Literature (J530)
    Modern Drama (J563)
    Modern Fiction Studies (J544)
    Modern Language Quarterly (H149)
    Modern Philology (H150)
    New Literary History (W1306)
    PMLA (H152)
    Papers on Language and Literature (H153)
    Philological Quarterly (H154)
    Renaissance Quarterly (J313)
    Sader, *Comprehensive Index to English-Language Little Magazines* (W1427)
    Seventeenth-Century News (J314)
    Speculum (J265)
    Studies in Philology (J321)
    Studies in Romanticism (J446)
    Studies in Short Fiction (G80)
    Studies in the Novel (G66)
    Texas Studies in Literature and Language (H156)
    Twentieth Century Literature (J528)
    Western European Specialists Section Newsletter (H157)
    World Literature Today (R961)

Author newsletters, journals, and other serial publications devoted to individual Continental authors

Q893.   Additional author newsletters are listed in this guide for English (J195), American (P777), Irish (K600), Scottish (L627), and Welsh (M640) authors. For full bibliographical information on these and other periodicals devoted to a single individual, see *Author Newsletters and Journals* (W1476) and its annual supplement in *Serials Review* (W1482).

Alain. See Chartier, Émile Auguste.

Alain-Fournier (pseud. for Fournier, Henri-Alban). See Rivière, Jacques.

Ampère, André-Marie
Bulletin de la Société des Amis d'André-Marie Ampère, 1931–?.

Andersen, Hans Christian
Anderseniana, 1933– .

Apollinaire. See Kostrowitzky, Wilhelm.

Aristotle
Studia aristotelica, 1958– .

Arouet, François (Voltaire)
Bulletin de l'Institut Voltaire en Belgique, 1961– .
Studies on Voltaire and the Eighteenth Century, 1955– .

Baillon, André
Cahiers André Baillon, 1935–?.

Balzac, Honoré de
L'Année Balzacienne, 1960– .
Balzac à Saché, 1951– .
Balzac Bulletin, 1939–?.
Balzaciana, 1925–?.
Courrier Balzacien, 1948–50.
Études Balzaciennes, 1951–60.

Barbey d'Aurevilly, Jules
Cahiers Aurevilliens, 1935–39.

Barlach, Ernst
Ernst Barlach-Gesellschaft. *Den Mitgliedern*, 1961(?)– .
Jahresgabe, 1947–70(?).

Barrault, Jean-Louis. See Renaud, Madeleine.

Baty, Gaston
Cahiers Gaston Baty, 1963– .

Baudelaire, Charles
Bulletin Baudelairien, 1965– .
Cramérien, 1969– .
Études Baudelairiennes, 1969– .
Publications (Vanderbilt), 1972– .

Beckett, Samuel
Beckett Circle, 1978– .
Journal of Beckett Studies, 1976– .

Bergman, Hjalmar
Hjalmar Bergman Samfundet Arsbok, 1959– .

Bergson, Henri-Louis
Études Bergsoniennes, 1948– .

Bernanos, Georges
Bulletin de la Société des Amis de Georges Bernanos, 1961–69.
Courrier Georges Bernanos, 1969– .
Études Bernanosiennes, 1960– .
Société des Amis de Georges Bernanos.
Bulletin, 1949–60.

Bernardino da Siena, Saint
Bolletino di studi bernardiniani, 1935–44/50.

Beyle, Marie Henri (Stendhal)
Collection Stendhalienne, 1958– .
Études Stendhaliennes, 1931– .
Stendhal Club: Revue Trimestrielle, 1958– .

Bloch, Jean-Richard
Europe, 1923– .

Blondel, Maurice
Études Blondeliennes, 1951–54.

Bloy, Léon
Cahiers Léon-Bloy, 1924–39; 1952.

Blum, Léon
Bulletin de la Société des Amis de Léon Blum, 1966–73.
Bulletin des Amis de Léon Blum, 1952–66.
Cahiers Léon Blum, 1977– .

Blunck, Hans Friedrich
Hans Friedrich Blunck-Jahrbuch, 1963– .

Boccaccio, Giovanni
Boccaccio, 1974– .
Publications, 1971– .
Studi sul Boccaccio, 1963– .

Bosco, Henri
Bulletin du Centre Henri Bosco, 1971– .
Cahiers de l'Amitié Henri Bosco, 1972– .

Bossuet, Jacques-Bénigne
Bulletin des Amis de Bossuet, 1931–35; 1973(?)– .
Revue Bossuet, 1900–04.

Boutelleau, Jacques (Jacques Chardonne)
Cahiers Jacques Chardonne, 1971– .

Boylesve, René. See Tardiveau, René.

Brasillach, Robert
Amis de Robert Brasillach. *Bulletin*, 1950– .

Brasillach, Robert (continued)
  Cahiers, 1950– .
Brecht, Bertolt
  Brecht Heute, 1971–73.
  Brecht-Jahrbuch, 1974– .
Bremond, Henri
  Études Bremondiennes, 1967– .
Budé, Guillaume
  *Bulletin de l'Association Guillaume
  Budé*, 1923– .
  *Bulletin des Jeunes de l'Association
  Guillaume Budé*, 1960– .
Burckhardt, Jacob
  Jacob Burckhardt Studien, 1970– .
Busch, Wilhelm
  *Jahrbuch der Wilhelm-Busch-Gesell-
  schaft*, 1949–64.
  Wilhelm-Busch-Jahrbuch, 1964– .
Buzzati, Dino
  Cahiers Dino Buzzati, 1977– .

Calvin, John
  Cahiers Calvinistes, 1957– .
Camus, Albert
  Cahiers Albert Camus, 1971– .
Casanova de Seingalt, Jacques
  Casanova Gleanings, 1958– .
Cathlin, Léon
  Cahiers Léon Cathlin, 1957–60.
Céline, Louis-Ferdinand. See Destouches,
  Louis-Ferdinand.
Cervantes Saavedra, Miguel de
  Anales Cervantinos, 1951– .
Césaire, Aimé
  Cahiers Césairiens, 1974– .
Chardonne, Jacques. See Boutelleau,
  Jacques.
Chartier, Émile Auguste (Alain)
  Association des Amis d'Alain. *Bulletin*,
  1954– .
Chateaubriand
  Bulletin de la Société Chateaubriand,
  1955– .
  Grand Bulletin, 1930–37.
  Petit Bulletin, 1948–54.
Chénier, André
  Cahiers Roucher-André Chénier,
  1980– .
Cicero, Marcus Tullius
  Ciceroniana: Rivista di studi ciceroniani,
  1959–?.
Claudel, Paul
  Bulletin de la Société Paul Claudel,
  1958– .
  *Bulletin de la Société Paul Claudel du
  Japon*, 1968– .
  Cahier Canadien Claudel. Ottawa,
  1963– .

Claudel, Paul (continued)
  Cahiers Paul Claudel. Paris, 1959– .
  Claudel Newsletter, 1968–72.
  Claudel Studies, 1972– .
  Société Claudel en Belgique. *Bulletin
  Régional*, 1960– .
Cocteau, Jean
  Cahiers Jean Cocteau, 1969– .
Colette. See Jouvenal, Sidonie-Gabrielle de.
Constant, Benjamin
  Cahiers Benjamin Constant, 1955–69(?).
Courier, Paul-Louis
  Cahiers Paul-Louis Courier, 1968– .
  Publications, 1974– .
Cusanus, Nicolaus
  Buchreihe, 1964– .
  Kleine Schriften, 1963– .
  Mitteilungen und Forschungsbeiträge,
  1961– .

Daniélou, Cardinal Jean
  Bulletin, 1975– .
D'Annunzio, Gabriele
  Quaderni dannunziani, 1941–43;
  1955– .
Dante Alighieri
  L'Alighieri: Rassegno, 1960– .
  Annali dell'Istituto di Studi Danteschi,
  1967– .
  Annual Report of the Dante Society,
  1882–1965.
  *Bulletin de la Société d'Études Dan-
  tesque*, 1950– .
  Bollettino della Società Dantesca Italiana,
  1890–1921.
  Dante Studies, 1966– .
  Dantovskie Chtenia, 1968– .
  Deutsche Dante-Jahrbuch, 1920–25;
  1928– .
  Giornale dantesco, 1893–1915; 1921–27;
  1930–43.
  *Jahrbuch der deutschen Dante-Gesell-
  schaft*, 1867–77.
  Mitteilungsblatt, 1970(?)– .
  Nuove letture dantesche, 1966– .
  Nuovo giornale dantesco, 1917–21.
  Studi Danteschi, 1920–43; 1949– .
Degée, Olivier (Jean Tousseul)
  Cahiers Jean Tousseul, 1946– .
Delisle, Léopold
  Cahiers Léopold Delisle, 1947– .
Derleth, August
  Newsletter, 1977– .
Destouches, Louis-Ferdinand (Louis-
  Ferdinand Céline)
  Bulletin Célinien, 1982– .
  Cahiers Céline, 1976– .
  Revue Célinienne, 1979– .

Deubel, Léon
Bulletin, 1927–?.
Diderot, Denis
Diderot Studies, 1949– .
Cahiers Diderotiens, 1978– .
Dinesen, Isak
Blixeniana, 1976– .
Dostoevsky, Fyodor
Dostoevsky Research Association,
1971– .
International Dostoevsky Society. *Bulletin*, 1972– .
Droste-Hülshoff, Annette von
Jahrbuch der Droste-Gesellschaft,
1947– .
Kleine Beiträge zur Droste-Forschung,
1971– .
Schriften der Droste-Gesellschaft,
1929– .
Du Bellay, Joachim
Amis du Petit Lyré, 1960–?.
du Bos, Charles
Cahiers Charles du Bos, 1956– .
Dudevant, Mme. (George Sand)
Bulletin de Liaison, 1977– .
Newsletter, 1978– .
Dumas, Alexandre
Association des Amis d'Alexandre
Dumas. *Bulletin*, 1971(?)– .
Dumasian, 1956–60.

Eichendorff, Baron Joseph
Aurora: Eichendorff-Almanach, 1953–69.
Aurora: Ein Romantischer Almanach,
1929–43.
*Aurora: Jahrbuch der Eichendorff-
Gesellschaft*, 1970– .
Éluard, Paul. See Grindel, Eugène.
Erasmus, Desiderius
Erasmus in English, 1970– .
Erasmus Studies, 1973– .
Erckmann, Émile
Bulletin, 1914–32.
Ernst, Paul C. F.
Jahresgabe, 1971– .
Mitteilungen der Paul-Ernst-Gesellschaft,
1936–40; 1968(?)– .
Wille zur Form, 1957–65; 1970– .
Erwin von Steinbach
Schriften, 1968– .
Studien, 1965– .

Farigoule, Louis H. J. (Jules Romains)
Cahiers Jules Romains, 1976– .
Société des Amis de Jules Romains.
Bulletin, 1974– .
Flaubert, Gustave
Amis de Flaubert. *Bulletin*, 1951–62.

Flaubert, Gustave (continued)
Amis de Flaubert, 1962– .
Fleg, Edmond
Bulletin, 1967– .
Fontane, Theodor
Fontane-Blätter, 1965– .
Fournier, Henri-Alban (Alain-Fournier).
See Rivière, Jacques.
France, Anatole. See Thibault, Jacques
Anatole.
Freytag, Gustav
Gustav-Freytag-Blätter, 1954– .
Fröding, Gustaf
Skriftserie, 1969– .

García Lorca, Federico
García Lorca Review, 1973– .
Gérard de Nerval. See Labrunie, Gérard.
Gide, André
Bulletin des Amis d'André Gide,
1968– .
Cahiers André Gide, 1969– .
Giono, Jean
Bulletin, 1973– .
Giraudoux, Jean
Cahiers Jean Giraudoux, 1972– .
Gobineau, Joseph-Arthur
Études Gobiniennes, 1966– .
Görres, Joseph von
Historisches Jahrbuch, 1880– .
Literaturwissenschaftliches Jahrbuch,
1926–39; 1960– .
Philosophisches Jahrbuch, 1888– .
Goethe, Johann Wolfgang von
Chronik des Wiener Goethe-vereins,
1886–1959.
English Goethe Society, 1886–1912;
1923–39; 1946–71; 1973– .
*Goethe: Neue Folge des Jahrbuchs der
Goethe-Gesellschaft*, 1947–71.
Goethe: Viermonatsschrift, 1938–44.
Goethe: Vierteljahresschrift, 1936–37.
Goethe-Almanach, 1967–71(?).
Goethe-Gesellschaft, Weimar. *Schriften*,
1885–1941; 1949– .
Goethe-Jahrbuch (Tokyo), 1932–?;
1959– .
Goethe-Jahrbuch (Weimar), 1880–1913;
1972– .
Goethezeit, 1969–77.
Jahrbuch der Goethe-Gesellschaft
(Tokyo), 1955–59.
Jahrbuch der Goethe-Gesellschaft
(Weimar), 1914–35.
*Jahrbuch des Freien Deutschen
Hochstifts*, 1902–40; 1962– .
Jahrbuch des Wiener Goethe-vereins,
1960– .
Jahresbericht, 1886– .

Goldoni, Carlo
  Studi goldoniani, 1968– .
Gourmont, Rémy de
  Imprimerie Gourmontienne, 1920–23.
Grillparzer, Franz
  Grillparzer-Forum Forchtenstein,
    1965– .
  Jahrbuch, 1890– .
Grimm, Jacob and Wilhelm
  Brüder Grimm Gedenken, 1963– .
Grindel, Eugène (Paul Éluard)
  Cahiers Paul Éluard, 1972–?.
Groth, Klaus
  Jahresgabe, 1959– .
Guérin, Eugénie and Maurice de
  L'Amitié Guérinienne, 1964– .
Gutenberg, Johannes
  Gutenberg-Jahrbuch, 1926– .

Hauptmann, Gerhart
  Gerhart-Hauptmann-Jahrbuch, 1936– .
Hebbel, Friedrich
  Hebbel-Forschungen, 1907–33.
  Hebbel-Jahrbuch, 1939–43; 1949– .
Hegel, Georg
  Hegel-Jahrbuch, 1961– .
  Hegel-Studien, 1961– .
  Hegel-Studien/Beiheft, 1964– .
  Owl of Minerva, 1969– .
  Recherches Hegeliennes, 1970– .
Heine, Heinrich
  Heine Jahrbuch, 1962– .
  Heine Studien, 1971(?)– .
  Mitteilungen, 1966– .
  Schriften, 1964– .
Hesse, Hermann
  Hermann Hesse Newsletter, 1975– .
Hölderlin, Friedrich
  Hölderlin-Archiv. *Veröffentlichungen*,
    1953– .
  Hölderlin-Jahrbuch, 1947– .
  Iduna, 1944–46.
  Schriften, 1949– .
Hoffmann, August Heinrich (Hoffmann
  von Fallersleben)
  Jahresgabe, 1957(?)– .
  Mitteilungs-Blätter, 1953– .
Hoffmann, Ernst T. A.
  *Mitteilungen der E. T. A.
    Hoffmann-Gesellschaft*, 1938– .
Hofmannsthal, Hugo von
  Hofmannsthal-Blätter, 1968– .
  Hofmannsthal-Forschungen, 1971– .
Hugo, Victor
  Série Victor Hugo, 1978– .
Huysmans, Joris-Karl
  Bulletin, 1928– .

Ibsen, Henrik
  Ibsen Yearbook, 1952– .

Jacob, Max
  Cahiers Max Jacob, 1951–57.
Jaurès, Jean
  *Bulletin de la Société d'Études
    Jaurésiennes*, 1960– .
Jean Paul. See Richter, Jean Paul Friedrich.
Jouvenal, Sidonie-Gabrielle de (Colette)
  *Bulletin de la Société des Amis de
    Colette*, 1966(?)–?.

Kafka, Franz
  *Newsletter of the Kafka Society of
    America*, 1977– .
Kant, Immanuel
  Kant-Studien, 1899– .
Keller, Gottfried
  Jahresbericht, 1932– .
Kierkegaard, Søren
  Cahiers du Centre Søren Kierkegaard,
    1974–75.
  *Kierkegaard Selskabets Populaere
    Skrifter*, 1951– .
  Kierkegaardiana, 1955– .
  *Meddelelser fra Søren Kierkegaard
    Selskabet*, 1949–55.
  *Publications of the Kierkegaard Society,
    Copenhagen*, 1951– .
Kleist, Heinrich von
  *Jahresgabe der Heinrich-von-Kleist-
    Gesellschaft*, 1962– .
  Schriften, 1921–39.
Kolbenheyer, Edwin Guido
  Bauhütten-Brief, 1955–71.
Kostrowitzky, Wilhelm (Apollinaire)
  Flâneur des Deux Rives, 1954–55.
  Que Vlo-Ve?, 1973– .

La Varende, Jean Mallard
  Amis de La Varende, 1963– .
Labrunie, Gérard
  Cahiers Gérard de Nerval, 1978– .
Lagerlöf, Selma
  Lagerlöfstudier, 1958– .
Lamennais, Hugues-Félicité-Robert de
  Cahiers Lamennais, 1975– .
  Cahiers Mennaisiens, 1963– .
Larbaud, Valéry
  Cahiers des Amis de Valéry Larbaud,
    1967– .
Lazare, Bernard
  Cahiers Bernard Lazare, 1957– .
Léger, Alexis (Saint-John Perse)
  Cahiers Saint-John Perse, 1978– .
Lenau, Nikolaus. See Strehlenau, Nikolaus.

Plisnier, Charles (continued)
Études, 1961–69.
Poquelin, Jean-Baptiste (Molière)
Le Moliériste, 1879–89.
Postl, Karl Anton (Charles Sealsfield)
Jahresgabe, 1964– .
Proust, Marcel
Bulletin de la Société des Amis de Marcel Proust et des Amis de Combray, 1950–
Bulletin d'Informations Proustiennes, 1975– .
Cahiers Marcel Proust, 1970– .
Études Proustiennes, 1973– .
Jaarboek (Netherlands), 1974(?)– .
Proust Research Association Newsletter, 1969– .

Raabe, Wilhelm
Jahrbuch der Raabe-Gesellschaft, 1960– .
Mitteilungen, 1911– .
Schriften, 1948–?.
Wilhelm Raabe-Kalender, 1912–14; 1947–48.
Rabelais, François
Amis de Rabelais, 1952– .
Bulletin. Tours, 1951.
Études Rabelaisiennes, 1956– .
Revue des Études Rabelaisiennes, 1903–12.
Racine, Jean
Bulletin de Liaison Racinienne, 1951–58.
Cahiers Raciniens, 1957– .
Jeunesse de Racine, 1958– .
Raimund, Ferdinand
Raimund-Almanach, 1955– .
Ramuz, Charles-Ferdinand
Bulletin, 1961(?)– .
Reinhardt, Max
Publikation der Max Reinhardt-Forschungsstätte, 1970– .
Renan, Joseph Ernest
Annuaire, 1960– .
Bulletin, 1953– .
Cahiers Renan, 1954– .
Études Renaniennes, 1970– .
Renaud, Madeleine
Cahiers Renaud-Barrault, 1953– .
Retté, Adolphe
Bulletin, 1937–?.
Richter, Jean Paul (Jean Paul)
Hesperus, 1951–66.
Jahrbuch, 1966– .
Jean Paul Blätter, 1926–50(?).
Rilke, Rainer Maria
Blätter, 1972– .

Rimbaud, Arthur
Bateau Ivre, 1949–66(?).
Bulletin, 1931–39.
Cahier, 1969– .
Études Rimbaldiennes, 1969–72.
Rimbaud Vivant, 1973– .
Rivière, Jacques
Amis de Jacques Rivière et d'Alain-Fournier. *Bulletin*, 1975– .
Dossiers de la Société, 1975– .
Rolland, Romain
Association des Amis de Romain Rolland. *Bulletin*, 1946– .
Cahiers Romain Rolland, 1948– .
Cahiers Suisse Romain Rolland, 1977– .
Études sur Romain Rolland, 1954– .
Rollinat, Maurice
Bulletin de la Société, 1956– .
Romains, Jules. See Farigoule, Louis H. J.
Roucher, Jean-Antoine. See Chénier, André.
Rouget, Marie Mélanie (Marie Noël)
Cahiers Marie Noël, 1969– .
Rousseau, Jean-Jacques
Annales de la Société Jean-Jacques Rousseau, 1905– .
Bulletin d'Information, 1964– .
Cahiers Jean-Jacques Rousseau, 1971(?)– .
Rückert, Friedrich and Heinrich
Jahresgabe, 1969– .
Rückert-Studien, 1964– .
Ryner, Han. See Ner, Henri.

Saint-John Perse. See Léger, Alexis.
Saint-Simon, Claude-Henri
Cahiers Saint-Simon, 1973– .
Sand, George. See Dudevant, Mme.
Saussure, Ferdinand de
Cahiers Ferdinand de Saussure, 1941– .
Schiller, Friedrich von
Deutsche Schillergesellschaft. *Jahrbuch*, 1957– .
Deutsche Schillergesellschaft. *Veröffentlichungen*, 1905–37; 1948– .
Rechenschaftsbericht, 1897–1941.
Schneider, Reinhold
Mitteilungen, 1974– .
Schriften, 1973– .
Schnitzler, Arthur
Journal of the International Arthur Schnitzler Association, 1961–67.
Schopenhauer, Arthur
Jahrbuch der Schopenhauer-Gesellschaft, 1912–44.
Schopenhauer-Jahrbuch, 1948– .
Schweitzer, Albert
Cahiers, 1959– .

Sealsfield, Charles. See Postl, Karl Anton.
Sjöberg, Birger
 Skrifter, 1962– .
Spire, André
 Cahiers André Spire, 1972– .
Staël, Madame de
 Cahiers Staëliens, 1929–39; 1962– .
Stendhal. See Beyle, Marie Henri.
Storm, Theodor
 Schriften, 1952– .
Strehlenau, Nikolaus (Nikolaus Lenau)
 Lenau-Almanach, 1959–68.
 Lenau-Forum, 1969– .
Strindberg, August
 Meddelanden från Strindbergssällskapet,
  1945– .
Swedenborg, Emanuel
 New Philosophy, 1898– .
 Studia Swedenborgiana, 1974– .
 Transactions, 1934– .

Tagore, Rabindranath
 Tagore Studies, 1969– .
Tardiveau, René (René Boylesve)
 Heures Boylesviennes, 1969– .
Tasso, Torquato
 Quaderni, 1963– .
 Studi tassiana, 1951– .
Teilhard de Chardin, Pierre
 Acta Teilhardiana, 1963– .
 *Cahiers de la Fondation Teilhard de
  Chardin*, 1968– .
 Cahiers Pierre Teilhard de Chardin,
  1958–65.
 Cahiers Teilhardiens, 1972– .
 *Études Teilhardiennes/Teilhardian
  Studies*, 1958– .
 Revue Teilhard de Chardin, 1961– .
 Teilhard de Chardin, 1960–61.
 Teilhard Review, 1966– .
Thibault, Jacques (Anatole France)
 Cahiers Franciens, 1971– .
 Lys Rouge, 1933– .
Tousseul, Jean. See Degée, Olivier.
Trakl, Georg
 Trakl-Studien, 1954– .
Turgenev, Ivan
 Cahiers Ivan Tourgueniev, 1977– .

Unamuno, Miguel de
 Cuadernos de la Cátedra de Unamuno,
  1948– .

Valéry, Paul
 Bulletin des Études Valéryennes,
  1974– .
 Cahiers Paul Valéry, 1975– .
Velde, Henry van de
 Cahiers Henry van de Velde, 1965– .
Vendel, Henri (Henri Nadel)
 Bulletin, 1954–62.
Vergil (Publius Vergilius Maro)
 Proceedings of the Virgil Society,
  1961– .
 Vergilian Digest, 1956–58.
 Vergilian Society Newsletter, 1961–?.
 Vergilius, 1959– .
 Vergilivs, 1938–40.
Verlaine, Paul
 Cahiers Paul Verlaine, 1953–60.
 Nuances, 1934–39.
Verne, Jules
 Bulletin de la Société Jules Verne,
  1935–38; 1967– .
 Jules Verne Voyages, 1978– .
Viaud, Julien (Pierre Loti)
 Cahiers Pierre Loti, 1952– .
Vigny, Alfred Victor
 Bulletin, 1964(?)– .
Vincent of Beauvais
 Vincent of Beauvais Newsletter, 1976– .
Voltaire. See Arouet, François.

Weil, Simone
 Bulletin, 1974– .
Weinheber, Josef
 Jahresgabe, 1956– .
Wolfram von Eschenbach
 Wolfram-Jahrbuch, 1952–56(?).
 Wolfram-Studien, 1970– .

Zola, Émile
 *Bulletin de la Société littéraire des Amis
  d'Émile Zola*, 1910–13; 1922–37.
 Cahiers Naturalistes, 1955– .
Zuckmayer, Carl
 Carl Zuckmayer, 1978– .
Zweig, Stefan
 Blätter, 1958–63.
Zwingli, Ulrich
 Zwingliana, 1897/1904– .

FICTION

Criticism

*Q895. Kearney, Elizabeth I., and Louise S. Fitzgerald, eds. *The Continental Novel: A Checklist of Criticism in English, 1900-66.* Metuchen, N.J.: Scarecrow, 1968. 460pp. Supplement for 1967-80 (1983), 510pp. Z5916.K4   016.8093'3

A guide to twentieth-century criticism (both articles and books) on the novel in France, Spain, Portugal, Italy, Germany, Scandinavia, Russia, and Eastern Europe. Under each country, arrangement is alphabetical by the major author, then alphabetical by the title of the work being criticized, and then alphabetical by the critic's name. There is no author or title index, so it is necessary to know the country of origin. Nationality can be verified, as the experienced student now knows, in *Webster's Biographical Dictionary* (W1080) or some other appropriate source in the section on Biography (W1080-1152).

No annotations, objectionably small type for the names, but information from approximately 250 periodicals, so it is comprehensive. There are, for instance, fifteen pages on André Gide and good coverage of such authors as Mauriac, Proust, Stendhal, Pasternak, Strindberg, Undset, Goethe, Sartre, Boccaccio, Lazarillo de Tormes, Cervantes, Hesse, Kafka, and Zola. Proof that this is a good source for comparative literature research may be seen by noting the studies on Rabelais as a source for *Gulliver's Travels* and as a point of reference to both Joyce and Cicero.

See also

> Drescher and Kahrmann, *Contemporary English Novel* (J541), numerous European reviews and articles
> Lukács, *Studies in European Realism* (G70)
> Walker, *Twentieth-Century Short Story Explication* (G78)

DRAMA

Criticism

*Q897. Palmer, Helen H. *European Drama Criticism, 1900-1975.* 2nd ed. Hamden, Conn.: Shoe String, 1977. 653pp. Z5781.P2   [PN1721]   016.809'2

A comprehensive list of critical books and articles in over four hundred popular and some scholarly periodicals published between 1900 and 1975 in both English and foreign languages. It covers plays of all centuries and all authors from Aeschylus (*Agamemnon*, 458 B.C.) through Corneille, García Lorca, Chekhov, Strindberg, Shaw, Ionesco, Osborne, Genet, Brecht, Eliot, Kjeld Abell, and Aleksandar Popovic. No mention is made of Shakespeare, which is understandable because he is so well researched elsewhere, but why is no criticism listed for Fernando Arrabal, Joe Orton, David Storey, Pedro Salinas, and many others? The book is convenient in scope and size, but reviewers have pointed out many errors in dates and omissions of important critical material. Students must remember that it lists only criticism concerned with the play *as a whole* or with an important or large part of it.

Arrangement is alphabetical by author and then by title of play, with cross-references for pseudonyms and joint authors. No annotations. The editors state that they have used as sources *MLAIB* (D31), *Ess. Gen. Lit. Ind.* (F46), *Index to Little Magazines* (W1429), *McGraw-Hill Encyclopedia of World Drama* (R967), and many others. See the companion volume, *American Drama Criticism* (P804).

See also

Adelman and Dworkin, *Modern Drama* (J555)
Coleman and Tyler (G111), vol. 2
Crowell's Handbook of Contemporary Drama (J561)
Dramatic Criticism Index (J554)
Encyclopedia of World Theater (R970)
Library of Literary Criticism: Major Modern Dramatists (J558)
McGraw-Hill Encyclopedia of World Drama (R967)
Matlaw, *Modern World Drama* (R968)
Modern World Theatre (G116)
Nicoll, *World Drama* (R965)
Reader's Encyclopedia of World Drama (R966)
Salem, *Foreign Drama* (R969)
————, *Guide to Critical Reviews . . . Continental Drama* (J559)
Stratman, *Bibliography of Medieval Drama* (J281)
Twentieth Century Plays in Synopsis (J560)

POETRY

Surveys

Q899. *Medieval Lyric*. Ed. Peter Dronke. 2nd ed. London: Hutchinson, 1978.
    288pp. Paperback. PN691.D7   809.1'4
    This survey of performers and performances of the medieval lyric has chapters on the development of the lyric in various European countries since the ninth century. Numerous quotations in several languages and a very important bibliography.

Austrian Literature

Surveys

*Q900. *Handbook of Austrian Literature*. Ed. Frederick Ungar. New York:
    Ungar, 1973. 296pp. PT155.U5   830'.9'9436
    The only book-length work in English that isolates and dignifies the national literature of Austria, stressing that the literature, like the language and history, is a blend produced by influences from the surrounding countries. The long critical-biographical essays on such authors as Hofmannsthal, Grillparzer, Rilke, Kafka, and Raimund are accompanied by lists of their works, available translations, critical books and articles. Index of titles and names mentioned in the text.

Periodicals

Q901.   *Modern Austrian Literature (MAL)*. Binghamton: State Univ. of New
York, 1968–   . Quarterly. Former title, 1961–67: *Journal of the International Arthur Schnitzler Research Association*.   PT3810.I52
830.9'9436
Analyses, reports, reviews, bibliographies, and research news.
Indexed in *Arts and Hum. Cit. Ind.* (F47), *MLAIB* (D31).

See also

Leo Baeck Institute Library (Q926)
Oxford Companion to German Literature (Q922)
Twayne's World Authors Series (R957), Austrian authors

French Literature

Surveys

Q902.   *Literary History of France*. Ed. John H. Fox. New York: Barnes and
Noble, 1974–   . Vol. 1, pt. 1 (Middle Ages), and pt. 2 (Renaissance
France, 1470–1589). PQ103.L5   [PQ151]   840'.9
A popular history of French literature that examines the trends, briefly summarizes and interprets the important titles, stresses factual information, has a
full index, and supplies bibliographical notes at the end of each chapter. Furthermore, it is pleasant reading.

Basic guides

*Q903.   *Critical Bibliography of French Literature*. Ed. Richard A. Brooks.
Syracuse: Syracuse Univ. Press, 1947–   . In progress. Z2171.C3   016.84
The standard reference work in its field, prepared by hundreds of contributors. This is a critical, selective, and, therefore, extremely useful bibliography
of books and articles that French scholars need to consult. The annotations are
brief but important because they compare as well as criticize studies in
background, genre, poetry, drama, fiction, the better-known authors (such as
Voltaire, Rousseau, Diderot), and foreign influences, including English,
American, German, Italian, and Spanish. Only the volume on the nineteenth
century is lacking. The earlier volumes will probably be updated.

Vol. 1, Mediaeval Period. 1952.
Vol. 2, Sixteenth Century. 1956.
Vol. 3, Seventeenth Century. 1961.
Vol. 3a, Supplement to Seventeenth Century. 1983.
Vol. 4, Eighteenth Century. 1951.
Vol. 4a, Supplement to Eighteenth Century. 1968.
Vol. 6, Twentieth Century. 3 vols. 1980.

*Q904.   Kempton, Richard. *French Literature: An Annotated Guide to Selected
Bibliographies*. Rev. ed. New York: MLA, 1981. 42pp. Z2171.A1.C34

[PQ103]   016.01684

Designed specifically for the graduate student in French literature who needs help in selecting and using specialized bibliographies concerned with reference guides, periodicals, linguistics, reviews, library catalogs, and specific subject areas. Because the author describes the scope and contents of the bibliographies with exceptional care and accuracy and because the little pamphlet is both inexpensive and small enough to slip inside a book or pocket, this will probably soon by owned by all French scholars. Well done.

Q905.   *French Literature: A Student's Guide to Reference Sources.* Ed. Eleanor Brown. 2nd ed. Montreal: McLennan Library, McGill Univ., 1978. 23pp. ERIC no.: ED 096 942. Z2171.M3   [PQ103]   016.01684'08

One of the best in this excellent series of deliberately brief research guides designed especially for students. It describes all the essential, easily available reference books that could be helpful in the study of French literature. Every professor of French should order these, and every student should buy one ($1.67). See ERIC, in the Glossary, for information on the reproduction, distribution, and purchase of these bibliographies. For additional McGill titles, see the Index.

Q906.   *Annotated Bibliography of French Language and Literature.* Ed. Fernande Bassan, Paul F. Breed, Donald C. Spinelli. New York: Garland, 1977. 307pp. Z2175.A2.B38   [PC207]   016.44

Addressed to the English-speaking reader who needs help in untangling the problem of deciding which French reference book is best for which project. Students will appreciate those annotations that accompany some entries; unfortunately, however, too many entries lack this important research aid. But if the student needs a slang dictionary, a source for Canadian-French titles, or a list of international periodicals containing information on French studies, this may help.

Q907.   *Concise Bibliography of French Literature.* Ed. Denis Mahaffey. London: Bowker, 1976. 286pp. Z2171.M33   016.84

A selective list for undergraduates of major works by and about 450 French authors. Arrangement is century by century, but few contemporary authors are included even though the editor is careful to cite recent criticism and information on English translations. Index of authors and anonymous works.

Q908.   Baker, Robert K. *Introduction to Library Research in French Literature.* Boulder, Colo.: Westview, 1978. 137pp. Z2171.B34   016.84

Descriptions and evaluations of the most important histories, biographical sources, encyclopedias, dictionaries, guides to dissertations, and bibliographies of all reference books needed by French students. Frankly introductory, with explanations of the card catalog, classification of French literature in the L.C. and Dewey systems, and warnings about authoritative editions, recent criticism, and good note-taking. Fine for the undergraduate.

*Q909.   Osburn, Charles B. *Research and Reference Guide to French Studies.*

2nd ed. Metuchen, N.J.: Scarecrow, 1981. 570pp. Z2175.A2.O8
[PC2071]   016.44
Entries for concordances, dictionaries, filmographies, surveys, bibliographies, and other reference books useful in the study of French literature and language—about six thousand in all. Numerous cross-references and an excellent, detailed subject index.

The author has also prepared a collection of essays on about forty topics in French language and literature from the Middle Ages to 1970, with summaries, evaluations, bibliographies, and subject indexes that can be used as a source for research topics: *The Present State of French Studies: A Collection of Research Reviews* (1971; 995pp.), with supplement and cumulative indexes (1973; 377pp.). In English, French, German, and Italian. PQ51.08   840.8

Criticism

Q910.   *Modern French Literature: A Library of Literary Criticism*. Ed. Debra Popkin and Michael Popkin. 2 vols. New York: Ungar, 1977. PQ306.M57   840'.009'14

Like the other Library of Literary Criticism publications (see Index), this specializes in quoting long excerpts from contemporary criticism on selected authors. Some professors scoff at, or at best ignore, this kind of study aid, but how can this be anything but an excellent source for quick consultation when it quotes such critics as Arendt, Auden, Bentley, Brée, Brustein, Chesterton, Donoghue, Edel, T. S. Eliot, Ellis, Ellmann, James (H. and W.), Murry, Stein, and Updike? In addition to important French authors such as Malraux, Sartre, Gide, Anouilh, Beckett (yes, the editors claim him), Artaud, Robbe-Grillet, Roland Barthes, Valéry, and others, it includes French-language writers from Russia, Africa, the Caribbean, Canada, Belgium, and Switzerland—168 in all. France has produced more Nobel Prize–winning authors than any other country. This is one way to get at the ideas that have spawned such talent. Chronological arrangement for criticism, a bibliography of works mentioned in the text, a list of authors by country, and much more.

Identification problems

*Q912.   *Oxford Companion to French Literature*. Ed. Sir Paul Harvey and Janet E. Heseltine. Oxford: Clarendon, 1959; rpt. with corrections, 1969. 771pp. PQ41.H3   840.3

Most of the six thousand entries provide brief identification of authors, titles, and allusions, but included also are historical figures, literary characters, theaters, events, literary terms, and occasional quotations. Students should look here when they need quick information about Rabelais's Pantagruel, Offenbach's connection with France, or Zola's "J'accuse." An updated (1976) but condensed version supplies important information on recent developments.

Indexes

Q913.   *French Periodical Index*. Westwood, Mass.: Faxon, 1973–   . Annual.

AI7.F7   016.054'1
Indexes twenty-five periodicals in twenty-six subject categories, including art, film, literature, language, religion, and theater. Location of a specific title is sometimes difficult, however, if the subject is cross-disciplinary and placed in a subject category other than the one the student anticipates. Book and film reviews.

Periodicals with an interest in French literature

Q914.   *Comparative Literature* (T1016)
Comparative Literature Studies (T1017)
L'Esprit Créateur: A Critical Quarterly of French Literature. Lawrence: Univ. of Kansas, 1961–   .
French Review. Champaign, Ill: American Assn. of Teachers of French, 1927–   . See especially vol. 52, no. 6 (May 1979), 894–910, a survey of research tools in French language and literature.
Kentucky Romance Quarterly. Lexington: Univ. of Kentucky, 1954–   . English and Romance languages
Modern Language Journal (W1336)
Modern Language Notes (Q890)
Modern Language Quarterly (H149)
Modern Philology (H150)
PMLA (H152)
Romance Notes. Chapel Hill: Univ. of North Carolina, 1959–   . Several languages.
Romance Philology. Berkeley: Univ. of California Press, 1947–   . Several languages.
Romanic Review. New York: Columbia Univ., 1910–   . Several languages.
Studies in Philology (J321)
Studies in Twentieth Century Literature (Q891)
Symposium (T1015)
Yale French Studies. New Haven: Yale Univ., 1948–   .

Additional reference sources containing information on French literature

Q915.   *French VI, VII,* and *XX.* New York: French Inst. Comprehensive bibliographies of current scholarship.
Livres du Mois (D36)
Malclès (A7)
Periodicals—Continental (Q890–93)
Streeter, *Eighteenth Century English Novel in French Translation* (J392)
Theatre Research International (G119)
Twayne's World Authors Series (R957), French authors

German Literature

Surveys

*Q916. *Literary History of Germany.* Ed. Kenneth J. Northcott and Robert T. Llewellyn. New York: Barnes and Noble, 1970– . In progress. PT35.L57   830'.9

A literary history that gives proper consideration to the social, political, and economic pressures shaping authors and their work. Reviewers quarrel with the theories and interpretations of this history, but not with the facts. It includes German and Austrian literature and examines the cultural backgrounds, the major writers, their important works, and influential movements and schools. Numerous quotations illustrate the discussions. Four of the projected eight volumes have been published:

   Vol. 4: 1720–1775. 1977. 240pp.
   Vol. 6: 1795–1830. 1981. 276pp.
   Vol. 7: 1830–1890. 1975. 214pp.
   Vol. 8: 1890–1945. 1978. 302pp.

Q917.   *Introductions to German Literature.* Ed. August Closs. 4 vols. New York: Barnes and Noble, 1967–69. PT91.I52   830.9

Pending completion of the title described in Q916, this introduction will be valuable for one main reason: Almost half is devoted to bibliographies of general studies and individual authors. It provides brief facts about authors' lives, a list of their most important works, and selected criticism. Undergraduates, especially, will appreciate this simplified survey from medieval to twentieth-century literature. Some of the volumes are being reprinted by Greenwood (Westport, Conn.).

Basic guides

Q918.   *German Literature: An Annotated Reference Guide.* Ed. Uwe K. Faulhaber and Penrith B. Goff. New York: Garland, 1979. 410pp. Z2231.F38   [PT85]   016.83

The first comprehensive English-language guide to German literature, with two thousand annotated entries of original works, translations, criticism, dissertations, Continental periodicals and reviews, and studies relating to German folklore, cultural history, art, and music. Some annotations and cross-references. Author-subject-title index.

Q919.   *German Literature: A Guide to Reference Sources.* Ed. Kendall Wallis. 2nd ed. Montreal: McLennan Library, McGill Univ., 1981. 14pp. ERIC no.: ED 096 942.

Careful descriptions of the most important German reference books. See ERIC, in the Glossary, for information on purchasing bibliographies in this series. For additional McGill titles, see the Index.

Criticism

Q921.   *Library of Literary Criticism: Modern German Literature*. Ed. Agnes K. Domandi. 2 vols. New York: Ungar, 1972. PT401.D6   830'.9'0091

The most convenient source for a quick overview of twentieth-century opinion on more than two hundred modern German novelists, dramatists, and poets such as Kafka, Rilke, Brecht, Hesse, Dürrenmatt, and Grass. Selections are quoted from reviews and criticism in scholarly periodicals, books, newspapers, and literary magazines. Hermann Hesse is given thirteen pages, for instance, with quotations from criticism written between 1915 and 1971.

Identification problems

*Q922.   *Oxford Companion to German Literature*. Ed. Henry Garland and Mary Garland. New York: Oxford Univ. Press, 1976. 977pp.   PT41.G3   830'.3

All the important facts about German, Austrian, and Swiss literature from the 800s to the 1970s, with an interdisciplinary approach. Like the other Oxford Companions (see Index), this specializes in brief explanations of trends and philosophies (such as the Aufklärung of the eighteenth century), biographical sketches (including Lenau, Hölderlin, B. Traven, Sealsfield), plot summaries (such as Hesse's *Narziss und Goldmund*), terms, and abbreviations. Numerous cross-references.

Periodicals

*Q924.   *Journal of English and Germanic Philology: A Quarterly Devoted to the English, German, and Scandinavian Languages and Literatures (JEGP)*. Urbana: Univ. of Illinois Press, 1897– . Quarterly. PD1.J7   430.5

Articles and numerous book reviews on such varied subjects as Kierkegaard, Milton, Icelandic *exempla*, Thomas Mann, Jonson, Dinesen, Kant, Pinter, Yeats, Ibsen, and David Lindsey. Interest has traditionally been in the relation between Germanic and English-American language and literature, but the journal's scope is now broad and the Anglo-German unannotated literary bibliography ceased in 1970. Index to vols. 1–50 in vol. 51. The text is in English and German.

Indexed in *ABELL* (D32), *Abst. Eng. Stud.* (E38), *Arts and Hum. Cit. Ind.* (F47), *Bk. Rev. Ind.* (W1559), *Current Bk. Rev. Cit.* (W1564), *Hum. Ind.* (F45), *Index to Bk. Rev. Hum.* (W1560), *MLAIB* (D31), *Romantic Movement: A . . . Bibliography* (J443).

Q925.   *German Quarterly (GQ)*. Cherry Hill, N.J.: American Assn. of Teachers of German, 1928– . 4/yr. PF3001.G3

Articles, reviews, and an annual "Bibliography Americana Germanica." Index for vols. 1–10 (1928–37).

Indexed in *Arts and Hum. Cit. Ind.* (F47), *Bk. Rev. Ind.* (W1559), *Current Bk. Rev. Cit.* (W1564), *Ed. Ind.* (W1225), *Index to Bk. Rev. Hum.* (W1560), *Language and Lang. Beh. Abst.* (W1332), *MLAIB* (D31).

Q926.   *Leo Baeck Institute Library and Archives News*. New York: Leo Baeck

Inst., 1975– . Irregular.
An excellent source for information on German, Austrian, Yiddish, and
Exile Literature.

Additional reference sources for information on German literature

Q927. Köttelwesch, Clemens. *Bibliographie der deutschen Sprach- und Literaturwissenschaft.* Frankfurt am Main: Klostermann, 1945– . Annual.
Modern Language Notes (Q890)
Monatshefte, 70, no. 3 (1978), 239–53, a survey of German research
tools
Twayne's World Authors Series (R957), German authors

Italian Literature

Basic guides

Q928. *Italian Literature: A Guide to Reference Resources.* Ed. Kendall Wallis.
2nd ed. Montreal: McLennan Library, McGill Univ., 1979. 8pp. ERIC
no.: ED 096 942. Z2351.M3 [PC1025] 016.85 Former title: *Student's Guide to Reference Sources in Italian Language and Literature.*
Descriptions of guides, encyclopedias, dictionaries, biographical sources,
and other books useful to the student of Italian literature. See ERIC, in the
Glossary, for information on the purchase of bibliographies in this series. For
additional McGill titles, see the Index.

Identification problems

*Q929. *Dictionary of Italian Literature.* Ed. Peter Bondanella and Julia Conaway Bondanella. Westport, Conn.: Greenwood, 1979. 621pp.
PQ4006.D45 850'.3
The only up-to-date guide to Italian literature that is written expressly for
the English-speaking reader: (1) brief biographies and summaries of Italian writers
and their works from the twelfth century to the present, ranging from Machiavelli
and Leopardi to Bassani and Quasimodo; (2) extensive cross-references to literary
groups within a movement or genre; (3) comparisons with other literatures and
disciplines; (4) a subject index; and (5) a chronological chart of a thousand years
of literature, history, religion, science, and the arts. Sorely needed and highly
recommended, it is the "Oxford Companion" of Italian literature.

Q930. Writers of Italy Series. New York: Columbia Univ. Press, 1974– .
Good introductory studies to material that is not well covered elsewhere.
Volumes published so far include:

Ludovico Ariosto	Eugenio Montale
Baldassare Castiglione	Italo Svevo
Giacomo Leopardi	Guiseppe Ungaretti
Alessandro Manzoni	

See also

Modern Language Notes (Q890)
Twayne's World Authors Series (R957), Italian authors

Russian Literature

Surveys

*Q932. Slonim, Marc. *Outline of Russian Literature*. New York: Oxford Univ.
Press, 1958. 235pp. PG2951.S53   891.709
The distilled summary of a vast subject—reliable scholarship and good
reading for students who need to find out a great deal in very little time. Students
who want a more detailed study should go to Slonim's original two volumes
from which he drew this outline: *The Epic of Russian Literature from Its Origins
through Tolstoy* (New York: Oxford Univ. Press, 1950; 367pp.) and *Modern
Russian Literature from Chekhov to the Present* (New York: Oxford Univ. Press,
1953; 467pp.).

Q933. *Literatures of the Soviet Peoples: A Historical and Biographical Survey.*
Ed. Harri Jünger. New York: Ungar, 1970. 482pp. PN849.R9.J813
809.8'947
A survey of Soviet, Russian, and related literatures—such as Estonian,
Georgian, Ukrainian—from their beginnings to the present day. Important
because it supplies generally inaccessible biographical information (though brief)
and because it reveals official (socialist) contemporary opinion of major and minor
authors including Turgenev, Yevtushenko, Sholokhov, Gorki, and Ehrenburg.
Notable omissions include Solzhenitsyn and Bulgakov.

Q934. Brown, Edward J. *Russian Literature since the Revolution*. Rev. ed. Cambridge, Mass.: Harvard Univ. Press, 1982. 424pp. Paperback.
PG3022.B7   891.7'09'004
Suitable for the beginner in twentieth-century Russian literature, especially since it extends its discussion into the 1970s, which Slonim (Q932) does not
do. This mentions briefly the main events in the lives of the authors, including
political pressures, and even more briefly summarizes plots and themes, but it
is easy reading and, therefore, has its value. Brown discusses Akhmatova, Yevtushenko, Babel, Ehrenburg, Sholokhov, Pasternak, the Union of Soviet Writers,
which all Russian writers must join, and other subjects of current importance.

Basic guides

Q935. *Russian Literature: A Student's Guide to Reference Sources.* Montreal:
McLennan Library, McGill Univ., 1973. 13pp. ERIC no.: ED 096 942.
Brief descriptions of books that students of Russian literature might need
to use, including biographies, histories, and dictionaries. See ERIC, in the
Glossary, for information on the purchase of the bibliographies in this series.
For additional McGill titles, see the Index.

Identification problems

*Q937. Harkins, William E. *Dictionary of Russian Literature.* New York: Philosophical Library, 1956; rpt. Westport, Conn.: Greenwood, 1971. 439pp. PG2940.H3   891.7'09

Still the most convenient source for quick answers and long discussions of any subject relating to Russian literature, including literary criticism, journalism, philosophy, and theater. Students who need to do more extensive research will have to go to the excellent third edition, in English translation, of the *Great Soviet Encyclopedia* (New York: Macmillan, 1970–79), which is owned by 600,000 Russian libraries, institutions, and individuals.

Periodicals

Q938. *Russian Literature Triquarterly (RLT).* Ann Arbor, Mich.: Ardis, 1971– . 3/yr. PG2901.R86   891.7'08

Translations, poetry, critical essays, reviews, and special issues on authors, eras, and genres. The text is in English, and there is an index for 1971–76. Indexed in *Arts and Hum. Cit. Ind.* (F47), *MLAIB* (D31).

See also

Modern Slavic Literatures   (Q942)
Twayne's World Authors Series (R957), Russian authors
Who Was Who in the USSR (W1108)
Who's Who in the USSR (W1097)

Scandinavian Literature

FICTION

Q939. *Eight Scandinavian Novelists: Criticism and Reviews in English.* Ed. John Budd. Westport, Conn.: Greenwood, 1981. 192pp. Z2559.B82 829'.5

Devoted to the examination and explanation of eight of Scandinavia's most influential novelists—Lie, Hamsun, Moberg, Lagerkvist, Laxness, Garborg, Lagerlöf, and Undset—five of whom won the Nobel Prize—with biographical sketches, lists of translations, and selective bibliographies of critical books, articles, dissertations, and reviews. Index to authors, editors, and translators.

Periodicals

*Q940. *Scandinavian Studies (SS).* Lawrence, Kans.: Allen, 1911– . Quarterly. Soc. for the Advancement of Scandinavian Studies. PD1505.S6 439.506273

Scholarly articles on philological and linguistic problems of the Scandinavian language and literature, medieval and modern. Papers and research are based on material in the original language. The annual "American-Scandinavian Bibliography" of 1972–74 has since 1975 been expanded to include all English

material, books, articles, and reviews. Author index.
   Indexed in *ABELL* (D32), *Arts and Hum. Cit. Ind.* (F47), *Current Bk. Rev. Cit.* (W1564), *Hum. Ind.* (F45), *Index to Bk. Rev. Hum.* (W1560), *MLAIB* (D31).

See also
   Journal of English and Germanic Philology (Q924)

Slavic Literature

Criticism

*Q942. *Library of Literary Criticism: Modern Slavic Literatures.* Ed. Vasa D.
   Mihailovich et al.   New York: Ungar, 1972–76.   PQ501.M518
   891.7'09'004

   Vol. 1: Russian Literature. 1972. 424pp.
   Vol. 2: Bulgarian, Czechoslovak, Polish, Ukrainian, and Yugoslav
   Literatures. 1976. 720pp.

   Criticism of twentieth-century authors that in many cases is unavailable
elsewhere and in some cases is translated for the first time. Most of the authors
are well known in our country, but others have so far received recognition only
in their own land. All viewpoints are presented, from socialist to anticommunist.
Over two hundred pages are given to criticism of Polish literature, for example,
with several selections on the Nobel prize-winning poet Czeslaw Milosz. This
is a significant contribution to our knowledge of Eastern Europe. Excellent
reviews.

See also
   Russian Literature (Q932–38)

Spanish Literature

Surveys

Q943.   Stamm, James R. *Short History of Spanish Literature.* Rev. ed. New
   York: New York Univ. Press, 1979. 285pp. PQ6033.S7   860'.9
   A survey suitable for undergraduates who need quick information on the
major authors and historical development of Spanish literature. Stamm analyzes
early epic poetry, figures such as Don Quixote and Celestina, theater by Lope
de Vega and Tirso de Molina, and the poetry of Garcilaso, Góngora, and the
Spanish mystics. Easy reading.

Basic guides

Q944.   Bleznick, Donald W. *A Sourcebook for Hispanic Literature and*

> *Language: A Selected, Annotated Guide to Spanish, Spanish-American, and Chicano Bibliography, Literature, Linguistics, Journals, and Other Source Materials.* 2nd ed. Metuchen, N.J.: Scarecrow, 1983. 304pp.
> Z2695.A2.B55   [PC4071]   016.86

A veritable "sourcebook," with information on basic dictionaries, encyclopedias, histories, translations, quotations, journals, and biographical aids. Simple and concise. Supplement it with the excellent McGill University reference guide *Hispanic Literature: A Guide to Reference Sources*, ed. Valerie Mayman (Montreal: McLennan Library, 1982; 18pp.), and Hensley C. Woodbridge, *Spanish and Spanish-American Literature: An Annotated Guide to Selected Bibliographies* (New York: MLA, 1983; 74pp.).

Identification problems

*Q945. *Oxford Companion to Spanish Literature.* Ed. Philip Ward. New York: Oxford Univ. Press, 1978. 627pp. PQ6006.093   860'.3

The first comprehensive guide to Spanish literature in English, from Roman times to the present. This has two outstanding features: special attention to living writers, such as Arrabal, Arreola, Borges, Delibes, and Mihura, and more bibliographical information than the other Oxford Companions (see Index). Entries on critics, philosophers, theologians, literary movements, style, authors, and titles. Scope includes Basque, Catalan, and Galician literatures as well as Castilian in Spain, Central and South America, the Philippines, and all other Spanish-speaking countries. The scholar and layman have never before had so convenient a source for this material.

Periodicals

Q947. *Journal of Spanish Studies: Twentieth Century.* Manhattan: Kansas State Univ., 1973–80. 3/yr. PQ6001.J68   860'.9'006

Critical articles on the literature of Spain and Spanish America. In English or Spanish. After the publication of vol. 8, this incorporated into *Anales de la literatura contemporanea.*

Indexed in *Arts and Hum. Cit. Ind.* (F47), *MLAIB* (D31).

Additional reference sources for information on Spanish literature

Q948. *Bibliography of Hispanic Women Writers* (W1636)
Bibliography of Picaresque Literature (G87)
Modern Language Notes (Q890)
Renaissance Spain and Its Literary Relations (T1012)
Teschner, Richard V. "Hispanic Research Tools: The SRTNHILL Report to the NEH." *Literary Research Newsletter*, 4, no. 3 (1979), 129–52. See *LRN* (W1421).
Twayne's World Authors Series (R957), Spanish authors

R

World Literature

General

Surveys

*R950. *World Literature since 1945: Critical Surveys of the Contemporary Literatures of Europe and the Americas.* Ed. Ivar Ivask and Gero von Wilpert. New York; Ungar, 1973. 724pp. PN771.I9   809'.04

A contemporary, reliable collection of surveys on twenty-eight different world literatures, such as Canadian, Hungarian, Danish, Polish, Latin American, and Yiddish. Each critic considers the social and political background and cites dozens of authors and hundreds of titles. The survey of German literature, for instance, is seventy-five pages long and is followed by a six-page bibliography of titles by and about the authors and their works. Leads from the author index into the surveys supply the reader with useful biographical information. A valuable, unique source.

*R951. Zinberg, Israel. *A History of Jewish Literature.* 12 vols. Trans. and ed. Bernard Martin. Cleveland: Press of Case Western Reserve Univ., 1972–79. PJ5008.Z5313   809'.889'24

This major contribution to scholarship examines the historical development of Jewish literature from tenth-century Spain to nineteenth-century Russia, with numerous quotations, summaries of individual works, brilliant interpretations, and polished style. Originally published between 1929 and 1937 and here translated with the addition of extensive, important notes on the scholarship of the last forty years.

See also

Jewish Writers of North America (A8.1)

277

Identification problems

*R953. *Cassell's Encyclopaedia of World Literature.* Ed. John Buchanan-Brown. Rev. ed. 3 vols. New York: Morrow, 1973. PN41.C3   803

Students regard this as a favorite library source for concise yet detailed information. It has much longer, more scholarly discussions than those in the *Reader's Encyclopedia* (W1402) or the Oxford Companions (see Index). The entries are signed by illustrious contributors (including Tillotson, Opie, Vinaver, Saroyan, Pinto, Jeffares) and often are several pages long. "Printing and Publishing," for instance, is given sixteen pages.

Vol. 1 contains histories of the national literatures, schools, and movements (including Africa, India, the West Indies, Brazil, Yiddish) and definitions of literary terms and genres (including mythology and literature, and sacred books). Vols. 2–3 contain biographies of writers and brief mention of their works. Do not overlook at the end of each entry the editors' recommendations of other surveys, critical works, bibliographies, and anthologies. These are research shortcuts.

Summaries

R955.   *Masterplots: 2010 Plot Stories and Essay Reviews from the World's Fine Literature.* Ed. Frank N. Magill. Rev. ed. 12 vols. Englewood Cliffs, N.J.: Salem, 1976. PN44.M33   809

The rewritten synopses and essay reviews of Magill's four earlier series are admittedly not scholarly, but they are successful in their stated purpose: to provide maximum information in minimum time. Entries are arranged alphabetically by title, with information on genre, type of plot (pastoral, allegorical, realistic), time and location of action, first appearance, principal characters, brief critique on the theme, a two- or three-page summary of the contents, and in some cases a general discussion of the author's other works (Boswell's *London Journal: 1762–1763*, for example). The author-title index is in vol. 12.

Scope is broad: from Homer to Pinter, from poetry to the picaresque novel, from Shakespeare's plays to *Alice in Wonderland*, from Latin America to the Orient. More than a thousand authors are represented, but emphasis is given to recent literature (forty-three Nobel Prize winners).

R956.   Magill, Frank N. *1,300 Critical Evaluations of Selected Novels and Plays.* 4 vols. Englewood Cliffs, N.J.: Salem, 1978. PN44.M344   809'.92'4

These are one- to three-page commentaries on the titles summarized in *Masterplots* (R955). Professors should know about this work because they may see Magill's words coming back to them on students' papers. Everyone should use such sources with caution, but they are admittedly convenient for finding out, quickly, what Lyly's *Endymion* is all about, or for getting an idea, quickly, of how the fifteenth-century mystery play dramatizes the biblical story of Abraham and Isaac. Author and title indexes.

Series

*R957. Twayne's World Authors Series (TWAS). Boston: Twayne, 1966–
Over 630 surveys have been published so far of outstanding authors from thirty-six countries all over the world including Australia, China, France, Nigeria, India, and the West Indies. About a hundred more are in preparation. Twayne's current publications are usually listed in the most recent *PTLA* (W1172), but out-of-print or out-of-stock titles are often omitted. The list below includes all titles Twayne has ever published in this series. For an explanation of the series' intent and scope, see Twayne's United States Authors Series (P720).
Indexed in *MLAIB* (D31).

Argentina
Jorge Luis Borges
Manuel Gálvez
Eduardo Mallea
Ernesto Sábato
Domingo Faustino Sarmiento
Alfonsina Storni

Australia
Marjorie Barnard and M. Barnard
Eldershaw
Louis Becke
Eleanor Dark
Frank Dalby Davison
Robert D. FitzGerald
Miles Franklin
Adam Lindsay Gordon
Xavier Herbert
Henry Kendall
Henry Lawson
Bernard O'Dowd
Vance and Nettie Palmer
Andrew Barton Paterson
Henry Handel Richardson
Kenneth Slessor
Christina Stead
Douglas Stewart
Randolph Stow
Price Warung (William Astley)

Austria
Martin Buber
Heimito von Doderer
Sigmund Freud
Franz Grillparzer
Adalbert Stifter
Georg Trakl

Brazil
Graciliano Ramos
João Guimarães Rosa

Canada
Earle Birney
Morley Callaghan

Canada (continued)
Canadian Fiction
Bliss Carman
John Coulter
Frederick Philip Grove
Ralph Gustafson
Margaret Laurence
Malcolm Lowry
Peter McArthur
Brian Moore
James Reaney
Gwen P. Ringwood
Mazo de la Roche
Sinclair Ross
Charles Sangster
A. J. M. Smith
Ethel Wilson

Chile
Eduardo Barrios
José Donoso
Luis Durand
Juan Godoy
Pedro Prado

China
Book of Songs
Chiang Kuei
Chiang Yen
Chin Sheng-t'an
Chou Tso-jen
Feng Chih
Hsiao Hung
Hsin Ch'i-chi
Kao Shih
Kuan Yün-shih
Kung Tzu-chen
Li Ch'ing-chao
Li Ho
Li Ju-chen
Li Po-yuan
Li Yü
Liang Chien-wen Ti
Liu Tsung-yuan
Lu you

China (continued)
Meng Hao-jan
Pa Chin
P'I Jih-Hsiu
Shen Ts'ung-wen
Su Man-shu
Ts'ao Yü
T'seng P'u
Tu Fu
Tung Yüeh
Wang Wei
Wen I-to
Wu Ching-tzu
Yang Wan-Li
Yuan Chen

Colombia
Tomás Carrasquilla
Jorge Isaacs
José Asunción Silva

Cuba
Lino Novás Calvo

Denmark
Kjeld Abell
Hans Christian Andersen
Georg Brandes
H. C. Branner
Meïr Goldschmidt
Vilhelm Grønbech
Martin A. Hansen
The Heibergs
William Heinesen
Ludvig Holberg
Jens Peter Jacobsen
Johannes Jörgensen
Søren Kierkegaard
Henrik Pontoppidan

Finland
Johan Ludvig Runeberg

France
Arthur Adamov
Jean Anouilh
Guillaume Apollinaire
Louis Aragon
Antonin Artaud
Jacques Audiberti
Barbey d'Aurevilly
Honoré de Balzac
Maurice Barrès
Roland Barthes
Charles Baudelaire
Pierre Beaumarchais
Simone de Beauvoir
Henry Becque

France (continued)
Georges Bernanos
Nicolas Boileau
Paul Bourget
André Breton
Buffon (G. L. le Clerc)
Michel Butor
Albert Camus
Louis-Ferdinand Céline
Blaise Cendrars
René Char
François Chateaubriand
André Chénier
Chrétien de Troyes
Paul Claudel
Jean Cocteau
August Comte
Benjamin Constant
Tristan Corbière
Pierre Corneille
Fernand Crommelynck
Agrippa D'Aubigné
Alphonse Daudet
Denis Diderot
Joachim Du Bellay
Georges Duhamel
Alexandre Dumas, père
Marguerite Duras
Paul Éluard
Fénelon (Salignac de la Mothe)
Gustave Flaubert
Charles Fourier
Anatole France
Théophile Gautier
Jean Genet
André Gide
Jean Giono
Jean Giraudoux
Goncourt Brothers
Julian Green
José-Maria de Heredia
Victor Hugo
Joris-Karl Huysmans
Eugène Ionesco
Jean de la Bruyère
Choderlos de Laclos
Madame de Lafayette
Alphonse Lamartine
Valéry Larbaud
Count Lautréamont
J. M. G. Le Clézio
Charles Leconte de Lisle
Tristan L'Hermite
Pierre Loti
Maurice Maeterlinck
Jean Mairet
Joseph Marie de Maistre
François Xavier de Maistre

France (continued)
Stéphane Mallarmé
André Malraux
Marie de France
Jacques Maritain
Pierre Marivaux
Roger Martin du Gard
Guy de Maupassant
François Mauriac
André Maurois
Prosper Mérimée
Henri Michaux
Molière (J. B. Poquelin)
Michel Montaigne
Charles Montesquieu
Henry de Montherlant
Alfred de Musset
Gérard de Nerval
Charles Nodier
Marcel Pagnol
Étienne Pasquier
Charles Péguy
Benjamin Péret
Charles Perrault
Saint-John Perse
Francis Ponge
Jacques Prévert
Marcel Proust
François Rabelais
Jean Racine
Ernest Renan
Pierre Reverdy
Arthur Rimbaud
Romain Rolland
Jules Romains
Pierre de Ronsard
Edmond Rostand
Jean Rotrou
Jean-Jacques Rousseau
Antoine de Saint Exupéry and David
    Beaty
Charles-Augustin Sainte-Beuve
Nathalie Sarraute
Paul Scarron
Maurice Scève
Eugène Scribe
Madeleine de Scudéry
Madame de Sévigné
Georges Simenon
Claude Simon
Madame de Staël
Stendhal
Hippolyte Taine
Claude Tillier
Paul Valéry
Paul Verlaine
Boris Vian
Alfred de Vigny

France (continued)
Jean Villiers de l'Isle-Adam
François Villon
Voltaire
Émile Zola

Germany
Ernst Barlach
Jacob Biedermann
Heinrich Böll
Sebastian Brant
Bertolt Brecht
Clemens Brentano
Hermann Broch
Martin Buber
Georg Büchner
Gottfried August Bürger
Wilhelm Busch
Paul Celan
Alfred Döblin
Drama of the Storm and Stress
Friedrich Dürrenmatt
Günter Eich
Joseph von Eichendorff
Georg Forster
Max Frisch
Stefan George
German Baroque Novel
German Baroque Poetry
German Dadaist Literature
German Expressionist Drama
German Expressionist Poetry
German Poetic Realism
Johann Wolfgang Goethe
Gottfried von Strassburg
Christian Dietrich Grabbe
Günter Grass
Grimmelshausen
Johann Georg Hamann
Friedrich Hebbel
G. W. F. Hegel
Hermann Hesse
Rolf Hochhuth
Ernst Jünger
Franz Kafka
Georg Kaiser
Karl Kraus
Nikolaus Lenau
Gotthold Ephraim Lessing
Heinrich Mann
Klaus Mann
Thomas Mann
Karl Marx
Eduard Mörike
Christian Morgenstern
Neidhart von Reuental
Novalis
Martin Opitz

Germany (continued)
Oswald von Wolkenstein
Wilhelm Raabe
Ferdinand Raimund
Jean Paul Friedrich Richter
Friedrich Schiller
Friedrich Schlegel
Angelus Silesius
Theodor Storm
Ludwig Thoma
Ernst Toller
Georg Trakl
Walther von der Vogelweide
Richard Wagner
Frank Wedekind
Christoph Martin Wieland
Wolfram von Eschenbach
Carl Zuckmayer
Arnold Zweig

Greece
Alcaeus
Archilochos
Aristophanes
Aristotle
Petros Brailas-Armenis
Callimachus
Chariton
Clement of Alexandria
Anna Comnena
Epicurus
Herondas
Hippocrates
Homer
Paisius Ligarides
Longus
Yannis Manglis
Kostis Palamas
Takis Papatsonis
Plutarch
Procopius
Dionysios Solomos
Theocritus
George Theotokas
Aristotelis Valaoritis
Elias Venezis
Xenophon of Ephesus

Guatemala
Miguel Angel Asturias
Rafael Arévalo Martínez

Hungary
Mihály V. Csokonai
Imré Madách
Kálmán Mikszáth
Ferenc Molnár
Sándor Petöfi

Iceland
Halldór Laxness
Snorri Sturluson

India
Mulk Raj Anand
Subramanya Bharati
Bhartrhari
Bhabani Bhattacharya
Nirad C. Chaudhuri
Kālidāsa
The Mahābhārata
Manohar Malgonkar
Jawaharlal Nehru
Munshi Prem Chand
Raja Rao
Khushwant Singh
Rabindranath Tagore

Italy
Saint Thomas Aquinas
Ludovico Ariosto
Dante Alighieri
Antonio Fogazzaro
Ugo Foscolo
Saint Francis of Assisi
Francesco Guicciardini
Alessandro Manzoni
Lorenzo de Medici
Petrarch
Clemente Rebora
Giovanni Verga
Elio Vittorini

Japan
Takizawa Bakin
Matsuo Bashō
Masamune Hakucho
Kaneko Mitsuharu
Shiga Naoya
Mori Ōgai
Dazai Osamu
Koda Rohan
Natsume Soseki
Ishikawa Takuboku

Latin Literature
Horace
Petronius
Quintilian
Seneca

Mexico
Ignacio Manuel Altamirano
Mariano Azuela
Emilio Carballido
Heriberto Frías
Carlos Fuentes

Mexico (continued)
   Enrique González Martínez
   Sor Juana Inéz de la Cruz
   Carlos Pellicer
   Jaime Torres Bodet
   Xavier Villaurrutia

Netherlands
   Desiderius Erasmus
   Daniel Heinsius
   François Hemsterhuis
   Jean Le Clerc
   Macropedius
   Multatuli
   Jacques Perk
   Janus Secundus
   Benedict de Spinoza
   Hendrik van Veldeke

New Zealand
   James K. Baxter
   D'Arcy Cresswell
   Janet Frame
   Jane Mander
   R. A. K. Mason
   John Mulgan
   New Zealand Drama
   Frank Sargeson
   William Satchell

Nigeria
   Chinua Achebe
   Wole Soyinka
   Amos Tutuola

Norway
   Johan Borgen
   Jonas Lie
   Sigrid Undset
   Tarjei Vesaas

Paraguay
   Augusto Roa Bastos

Peru
   José Santos Chocano
   El Inca Garcilaso de la Vega
   Juan Carlos Onetti

Poland
   Contemporary Polish Poetry, 1925–1975
   Maria Dabrowska
   Witold Gombrowicz
   Jan Kochanowski
   Ignacy Krasicki
   Adam Mickiewicz
   Cyprian Norwid
   Jan Parandowski

Poland (continued)
   Wladyslaw Stanislaw Reymont
   Henryk Sienkiewicz
   Joseph Wittlin

Puerto Rico
   René Marqués

Rhodesia
   Arthur Shearly Cripps

Romania
   Vasile Alecsandri
   Ion Barbu
   Ion Luca Caragiale
   Duiliu Zamfirescu

Russia
   Anna Akhmatova
   E. A. Baratynsky
   Konstantin Batyushkov
   Alexander Bestuzhev-Marlinsky
   Anton Chekhov
   N. G. Chernyshevskii
   Feodor Dostoevsky
   Sergey Esenin
   Afanasy Fet
   Denis Fonvizin
   Vsevolod Garshin
   Nikolay Gogol
   Ivan Goncharov
   Nikolay Gumilev
   Nikolay Karamzin
   Valentin Kataev
   Ivan Krylov
   Alexander Kuprin
   Nikolay Leskov
   Nikolai Nekrasov
   Alexander Ostrovsky
   Boris Pasternak
   Alexander Pushkin
   Alexander Solzhenitsyn
   A. K. Tolstoy
   Gleb Uspensky
   Vasily Zhukovsky

South Africa
   Roy Campbell
   Nadine Gordimer
   Uys Krige
   H. W. D. Manson
   Ezekiel Mphahlele
   Alan Paton
   William Plomer
   Thomas Pringle
   William C. Scully
   Francis Carey Slater
   Pauline Smith

Spain (continued)
  Spanish Sacramental Plays
  Manuel Tamayo y Baus
  Santa Teresa de Avila
  Juan Timoneda
  Tirso de Molina
  Bartolomé de Torres Naharro
  Diego de Torres Villarroel
  Miguel de Unamuno
  Valencian Dramatists of Spain's Golden
    Age
  Juan Valera
  Ramón del Valle-Inclán
  Lope de Vega
  Gil Vicente
  Cristóbal de Villalón
  Cristóbal de Virués

Sweden
  Lars Ahlin
  C. J. L. Almqvist
  Hjalmar Bergman
  Ingmar Bergman
  Lars Gyllensten
  Eyvind Johnson
  Pär Lagerkvist
  Vilhelm Moberg
  Östen Sjöstrand
  August Strindberg
  Emanuel Swedenborg

Switzerland
  Conrad Ferdinand Meyer
  Charles-Ferdinand Ramuz

Uruguay
  Juan Carlos Onetti
  Javier de Viaña

Venezuela
  Mariano Picón Salas

West Indies
  V. S. Naipaul
  Derek Walcott
  West Indian Novel
  West Indian Poetry

Yiddish Literature
  Sholom Aleichem
  Yankev Glatshteyn (Jacob Glatstein)
  Mendele Mocher Sforim
  Isaac Bashevis Singer

Yugoslavia
  Antun Gustav Matoš
  Francè Prešeren

Zimbabwe
  Arthur Shearly Cripps

Periodicals

R959. *Literature East and West (LE&W)*. Austin, Tex:: Literature East and West (University Sta., Box 8107), 1953– . Quarterly. PN2.L67 805.L77651
  Official publication of the Oriental-Western Literary Relations Group of the MLA. Critical articles, poetry, short stories, and reviews, with special issues on selected subjects such as Chinese literary criticism, Korean literature, and African literature.
  Indexed in *ABELL* (D32), *MLAIB* (D31).

*R960. *WLWE (World Literature Written in English)*. Arlington: Univ. of Texas, 1962– . 2/yr. Sponsored by MLA. PR1.W65   820'.9
  Interested in critical works and bibliographies written in English but from non-British and non-American sources. A recent issue contained several articles from Africa on Doris Lessing and others on the literature of Canada, New Zealand, Australia, West Indies, and New Guinea. A special number (Nov. 1975) is devoted to a study of Indian literature written in English.
  Indexed in *ABELL* (D32), *Am. Hum. Ind.* (P738), *Arts and Hum. Cit. Ind.* (F47), *MLAIB* (D31).

*R961. *World Literature Today (WLT)*. Norman: Univ. of Oklahoma Press,

1977 (vol. 51)– . Quarterly. Former title, 1927–76: *Books Abroad: An International Literary Quarterly*. Z1007.B717   028.1

Essential reading for anyone in the field. Articles, commentaries, and outstanding book reviews (about 275 in every issue) concerning all nations of the world and all genres including fiction, poetry, surveys, and bibliographies. Annual index. Its epigram: "There can be no question of the nations thinking alike; the aim is simply that they shall grow aware of one another . . . and . . . may at least tolerate one another" (Goethe).

Indexed in *ABELL* (D32), *Arts and Hum. Cit. Ind.* (F47), *Bk. Rev. Ind.* (W1559), *Current Bk. Rev. Cit.* (W1564), *Hum. Ind.* (F45), *MLAIB* (D31).

FICTION

Periodicals

R963.   *International Fiction Review (IFR)*. Fredericton: International Fiction Assn., Univ. of New Brunswick, 1974– . 2/yr. PN1   805

Articles and reviews of such internationally known authors as Bulgakov, Le Clézio, Dinesen, Hawkes, Lu Hsün, Lampedusa, Powys, Unamuno, and Welty. Annual index.

Indexed in *Am. Hum. Ind.* (P738), *Arts and Hum. Cit. Ind.* (F47), *MLAIB* (D31).

See also

Science-Fiction Studies (G100)
World Historical Fiction Guide (G83)

DRAMA

Surveys

*R965.   Nicoll, Allardyce, ed. *World Drama: From Aeschylus to Anouilh*. 2nd ed. New York: Barnes and Noble, 1976. 965pp. PN1721.N52   809'.2

A fine collection of essays by specialists who survey the state of dramatic scholarship in their own countries, including Africa, the Spanish-speaking nations, Eastern Europe, and Australia. This edition contains a one-hundred-page chapter on drama written between 1945 and 1973. When point of view is important, this is the source to use. No bibliographies, however.

Encyclopedias

*R966.   Gassner, John, and Edward Quinn. *The Reader's Encyclopedia of World Drama*. New York: Crowell, 1969. 1030pp. PN1625.G3   809.2

Concerned with drama as literature, not as theater (see *Oxford Companion to the Theatre*, G117, for that aspect). The long articles, written and signed by experts, are accompanied by bibliographies at the end of each entry and by many illustrations. A lengthy chronological appendix (100pp.), "Basic Documents in Dramatic Theory," includes the *Poetics* of Aristotle and the essays of Jonson, Goethe, Hegel, Coleridge, Strindberg, Susanne Langer, and Northrop Frye.

Long entries discuss literary terms, playwrights, specific works, and national drama—Germany's contribution to the theater from the Middle Ages to the present, for example—giving titles, authors, characteristics, and development. Scope is wide, from an explanation of Plato's concept of tragedy to a five-page entry on O'Neill that includes a biographical sketch, a chronological study of his works and contributions, and a bibliography citing standard editions of his plays, outstanding biographies, and selective criticism. Cross-references lead from the author entry to title entries for major plays and also to entries for such subjects as realism, expressionism, and naturalism. If you're at all interested in literature, you'll want this volume around the house, for leisure browsing as well as for consultation.

R967.   *McGraw-Hill Encyclopedia of World Drama.* 5 vols. 2nd ed. New York: McGraw-Hill, 1984. PN1625.M3   809.2
Synopses of plays, biographies, critiques, bibliographies with dates of performance and publication, and two thousand illustrations. This has a refreshingly contemporary format and approach—readable, attractive, and to the point.

*R968.   Matlaw, Myron. *Modern World Drama: An Encyclopedia.* New York: Dutton, 1972. 960pp. PN1851.M36   809.2'34
This international source book on plays, dramatists, terms, and national drama since the late nineteenth century emphasizes drama as literature rather than as theater. Students may find synopses, brief evaluations, and publishing facts on certain recent drama that is not covered by Gassner and Quinn (R966) or the *McGraw-Hill Encyclopedia* (R967). Character index.

THEATER (STAGE)

Criticism

R969.   Salem, James M. *A Guide to Critical Reviews: Foreign Drama, 1909–1977.* 2nd ed. Metuchen, N.J.: Scarecrow, 1979. 420pp. Z5781.S16   [PN2277.N5]   016.809'2
This bibliography of modern foreign drama produced on the New York stage from 1909 to 1977 lists 1,300 plays by 206 dramatists from Great Britain, the Continent, Canada, South Africa, and Puerto Rico. Like the other Salem publications (see below), it indexes only the most popular periodicals that are certain to be available in all libraries, so it has its limitations as well as its advantages, but if beginning students need readable, convenient criticism on Bolt, Schnitzler, Rattigan, Pinero, Orton, Molnar, Feydeau, Strindberg, Zweig, and a host of others, this will be an appropriate source. Good appendixes provide information on the plays and playwrights. For instance, *Otherwise Engaged*, by Simon Gray, was best play of 1976–77 and was reviewed in about twenty articles.

The editors wisely recommend use of the *MLAIB* (D31), *Modern Drama* (J555), *Theatre Journal* (G118), *Bulletin of Bibl.* (C29), and other specialized sources for more scholarly needs, but this is the handiest one-volume source available for popular reviews. See four other volumes in this series by Salem: *British and Continental Drama from Ibsen to Pinter* (J559), *American Drama* (P805), *The Musical* (P806), and *The Screenplay* (W1242).

Encyclopedias

*R970. *Encyclopedia of World Theater: With 420 Illustrations and an Index of Play Titles.* Ed. Martin Esslin. New York: Scribners, 1977. 320pp. PN2035.E52   792'.03

A notable contribution to scholarship by a well-known theater critic. Esslin gives good coverage to cabaret, music halls, playwrights, designers, and other facets of theater life, especially in Eastern Europe. This revision of the earlier *Friedrichs Theaterlexikon* (1969) provides information on five thousand plays and contains facts not found in the *Oxford Companion to the Theatre* (G117).

Additional reference sources that include information on world literature

R971.   *American Literary Scholarship* (P734)
Besterman, *World Bibliography of Bibliographies* (C25)
Commonwealth Literature (N645–52)
Cyclopedia of World Authors (W1123)
Encyclopedia of World Literature in the 20th Century (J523)
Epic and Romance Criticism (G127)
Reader's Adviser (A4)
Thompson, *Key Sources in Comparative and World Literature* (T1024)
Twentieth Century Writing (J524)
World Authors, 1950–70 (W1124.7)

African Literature

Basic guides

*R972. *Black African Literature in English: A Guide to Information Sources.* Ed. Bernth Lindfors. Vol. 23 of Gale Information Guide Library (A8). Detroit: Gale, 1979. 482pp. Z3508.L5.L56   [PR9340]   012.28

This excellent exhaustive guide to 3,300 books, articles, and theses on four hundred black African authors largely replaces Abrash (R974) but not Jahn and Dressler (R977) because its focus is on books *about* literature, language, authors, teaching, censorship, publishing, research, and other literature-related subjects. Four indexes cover authors, titles, subjects, and geographical areas.

R973.   Zell, Hans M., Carol Bundy, and Virginia Coulon. *A New Reader's Guide to African Literature.* 2nd ed. New York: Africana, 1983. 400pp. Paperback. PN849.A35   809'.8869

This will help the student who needs a brief biography and photograph of Chinua Achebe—the most prominent novelist writing in Africa today—or abstracts of politically oriented books, addresses of book dealers and publishers, an annotated list of periodicals or children's books, a list of articles on African literature or of creative works from Kenya.

Arranged by language, country (south of the Sahara), and author (black Africans), with annotations for works in English and French and citations for reference and critical material. Supplements to the first edition appeared in *Africana Journal* (New York: Africana, 1970–). Zell, Bundy, and Coulon have also produced a second edition of *A Reader's Guide to Contemporary African Literature* (New York: Holmes and Meier, 1983; 576pp.).

R974.   Abrash, Barbara. *Black African Literature in English since 1952, Works and Criticism.* New York: Johnson, 1967. 92pp. Z3508.L5.A25   016.82

This pioneer work is now largely superseded by Lindfors' *Guide* (R972) for critical works, but is still important for its information on book reviews, a good introduction explaining the social and linguistic problems of African literature, the location of stories in anthologies, and lists of works by black Africans writing in English. Its scope covers drama, negritude, the English language, and such authors as Chinua Achebe and Wole Soyinka of Nigeria, and James Ngugi of Kenya.

R975.   *African Literature: A Student's Guide to Reference Resources.* Montreal: McLennan Library, McGill Univ., 1977. 7pp. ERIC no.: ED 096 942.

If brief, best, and inexpensive is what the student needs, this is the source to use. See ERIC in the Glossary for information on purchasing bibliographies in this series. For additional McGill titles, see the Index.

Bibliographies of primary works

*R977.   Jahn, Janheinz, and Claus P. Dressler. *Bibliography of Creative African Writing.* Millwood, N.Y.: KTO, 1975, c1971. 446pp. Z3508.L5.J28   016.8088'996

Still the most inclusive list of African literature, this includes factual information on 2,176 creative sub-Saharan works (books, plays, travel, and poetry in forty African and twelve European languages), with a few citations for reviews. Exceptionally fine indexes by language, translations, country, and author, and a map of languages. *PBSA* (W1075) says this is "a lesson in careful bibliography." The text is in English, French, German, and native languages. See also R972–74.

Series

R978.   African Writers Series (AfrWS). Ed. Chinua Achebe. London: Heinemann Educational, 1962– .

Dedicated to the publication of African literature that would otherwise be inaccessible to the English-speaking world. Over one hundred titles have been published so far.
Indexed in *MLAIB* (D31).

Periodicals

*R980.   *African Literature Today (ALT).* London: Heinemann Educational, 1968– . Annual. PL8010.A4   896

Analyses of works by African authors "not to save readers from making their own judgments, but to provide starting points for personal appreciation and evaluation." Related critical and reference works are also cited. Current international bibliography of African writing in books and periodicals.

Indexed in *ABELL* (D32), *Arts and Hum. Cit. Ind.* (F47), *Current Bk. Rev. Cit.* (W1564), *Hum. Ind.* (F45), *MLAIB* (D31).

*R981.   *Research in African Literatures (RAL)*. Austin: Univ. of Texas, 1970– . Quarterly. PL8010.R46   809'.896

Official organ of the African Literatures Division of MLA, international and interdisciplinary. Interested in oral and written literature, with special emphasis on surveys of research (completed and in progress), bibliographies, reports of library holdings, school curricula, and critical articles. Book reviews and news notes. In English and French.

Indexed in *ABELL* (D32), *Arts and Hum. Cit. Ind.* (F47), *Hum. Ind.* (F45), *MLAIB* (D31).

Additional reference sources containing information on African literature

R982.   *ABELL* (D32), African language
African Authors (W1132)
Afro-American Literature (P835-70)
CLA Journal (H142)
Cassell's Encyclopaedia of World Literature (R953)
Critical Writings on Commonwealth Literatures (N645)
Dictionary of Oriental Literatures (R985)
Humanities Index (F45)
Index to Commonwealth Little Magazines (N647)
Journal of Commonwealth Literature (N650), annual regional bibliographies
Lindfors, Bernth. "Researching African Literatures." *Literary Research Newsletter*, 4, no. 4 (1979), 171–80. See *LRN* (W1421).
MLAIB (D31), vol. 1, English II, and vol. 2, African Literatures
Nicoll, *World Drama* (R965)
Penguin Companion to Classical, Oriental, and African Literature (R986)
Salem, *Foreign Drama* (R969)
Twayne's World Authors Series (R957), Nigeria and Rhodesia
Who's Who in African Literature (W1099)
World Bibliography of African Bibliographies (C25)
World Literature Today (R961)
World Literature Written in English (R960)

Asian Literature

Basic guides

R983.   *Guide to Oriental Classics.* Ed. Theodore De Bary and Ainslie T. Embree. 2nd ed. New York: Columbia Univ. Press, 1975. 259pp. Paperback. Z7046.C65   [PJ307]   016.89

The current interest in Oriental philosophy makes this a timely guide. The quality of the contents, critical and technical, makes it important and eminently readable. Subjects vary from the general (Buddhism, Sanskrit poetry, and Zen) to the specific (the Koran, the Vedas, Mahabharata, haiku, Tagore, Confucius, and Lao Tzu). The explanations are brief, but they include information on critical works and available translations. At the end of every entry several questions are listed for use in class discussions or themes.

R983.1.   *Asian Literature in English: A Guide to Information Sources.* Ed. George L. Anderson. Vol. 31 of Gale Information Guide Library (A8). Detroit: Gale, 1981. 336pp. Z3001.A655   [PR9410]   016.895

A guide to general studies and to works by and about individual authors of Asia. Reviewers have located occasional errors and omissions.

*R984.   *A Guide to Eastern Literatures.* Ed. David M. Lang. London: Weidenfeld and Nicolson, 1971. 501pp. PJ307.L3   809.8'95

Absolutely indispensable. This is an evaluative survey of the historical background and main trends of all major Middle Eastern and Far Eastern literatures: Arabic, Jewish, Persian, Turkish, Armenian, Ethiopic, Indian, Chinese, Tibetan, Korean, Japanese. Fine bibliographies are provided for each area, and all major authors have a biographical-critical entry. Furthermore, its good readable prose is well stocked with surprising information about sophisticated cultures and universal ideas.

Encyclopedias

*R985.   *Dictionary of Oriental Literatures.* Ed. Jaroslav Průšek. 3 vols. New York: Basic, 1974. PJ31.D5   808.8

Choice (W1557) rates this as absolutely top-notch, prophesying that it will not be superseded for many years: "scholarship . . . is very sound." Coverage extends to all of Asia and the Near and Far East, from Turkey to the Soviet provinces, the Arab countries, India, Korea, Mongolia, and West and North Africa. It includes information on works by and about individual authors, major anonymous works, literary forms and genres, schools and movements. It also locates available translations and selected critical studies in English and European languages. Each author is identified with dates, a biographical sketch, and a brief summary of contributions to literary history.

R986.   *Penguin Companion to Classical, Oriental, and African Literature.* New York: McGraw-Hill, 1969. 361pp. PA31.P4   809

Other sources are better for classical subjects, but this is certainly convenient for Oriental, African, Byzantine, and other less accessible identification problems. Chatterji, Jataka, Tchernichowski, Eybers, the Palestinian Talmud, and hundreds of other entries of literary interest.

Series

R988.   Asian Literature Bibliography Series. Boston: Hall, 1973–   .

.1 China

Classical Chinese Fiction: A Guide to Its Study and Appreciation. Ed. Winston L. Y. Yang et al. 1978. 302pp. Z3108.L5.Y29   [PL2625] 016.8951'3

Guide to Chinese Poetry and Drama. Ed. Roger B. Bailey. 1973. 100pp. Z3108.L5.B34   016.8951'1'008

Guide to Chinese Prose. Ed. Jordan D. Paper. 1973. 173pp. Z3108.L5.P34   016.8951'8'08

Modern Chinese Fiction: A Guide to Its Study and Appreciation. Ed. Winston L. Y. Yang et al. 1980. 240pp.

These trim little books will probably do more than decades of artful propaganda to impress on insular Americans the value of other cultures. Each volume has an illuminating introduction to the history, cautiously worded annotations with favorable and unfavorable comments, bibliographies, a glossary, an index, a pronunciation guide, and a chronological table. A most interesting series.

.2 Japan

Guide to Japanese Drama. Ed. Leonard C. Pronko. 1973. 125pp. Z3308.L5.P76   016.8956'2'008

Guide to Japanese Poetry. Ed. J. Thomas Rimer and Robert E. Morrell. 1976. 151pp. Z3308.L5.R54   [PL782.E3]   016.8956'1'008

Guide to Japanese Prose. Ed. Alfred H. Marks and Barry D. Bort. 1975. 150pp. Z3308.L5.M37   [PL782.E8]   016.8956'3'008

No other sources are so informative and so convenient for information on Japanese literature. These surveys open up a whole new field to the receptive, inquiring student. The historical introductions are followed by long discussions of the most important books in the field, with summaries of the novels, and, in the books on poetry and drama, appraisal of both primary and secondary works.

Additional reference sources for Asian literature

R989.   *ABELL* (D32)

Bibliography of Oriental Bibliography (C25)

Cassell's Encyclopaedia of World Literature (R953)

Journal of Commonwealth Literature (N650)

MLAIB (D31), vol. 1, English II: Ceylon, India, Malaysia, Oceania, Pakistan, Philippines, West Indies; vol. 2: Near, Middle, and Far East

Modern Drama (J563)
Twayne's World Authors Series (R957), sections on China, India, Japan

South American and Latin American Literature

Surveys

R990.   *Outline History of Spanish American Literature*. Ed. John E. Englekirk. 4th ed., rev. New York: Irvington, 1981. 327pp. Paperback. PQ7081.I5   860'.9

Surveys of specific periods and genres are followed by biographical sketches and lists of books by and about each important author of that era or genre. Excellent bibliographies for further study and an author index. A good source for the beginning student or the scholar in a hurry.

Criticism

R991.   *Twentieth-Century Spanish-American Novel: A Bibliographic Guide*. Ed. David W. Foster. Metuchen, N.J.: Scarecrow, 1975. 227pp. Z1609.F4.F68   [PQ7082.N7]   016.863

The only available bibliography of criticism on the twentieth-century Spanish-American novel. Good coverage, alphabetically arranged, for Gallegos (Venezuela), García Márquez (Colombia), Sábato (Argentina), Vargas Llosa (Peru), Azuela (Mexico), and about fifty-five other novelists. No annotations, however, and regrettable omissions of bibliographical data.

R992.   *Library of Literary Criticism: Modern Latin American Literature*. Ed. David W. Foster and Virginia R. Foster. 2 vols. New York: Ungar, 1975. PQ7081.F63   860'.9

Latin American literary criticism in English has been all but impossible to locate. This outstanding compilation helps to correct that regrettable void in scholarship. About 140 living authors from South and Central America are assessed here in extracts taken from one hundred international periodicals and books. John Barth criticizes Borges, Updike criticizes Cabrera Infante, but most are Spanish-speaking critics, newly translated.

R993.   Herdeck, Donald E. *Caribbean Writers: A Bio-Bibliographical-Critical Encyclopedia*. Washington, D.C.: Three Continents, 1979. 943pp. PN849.C3.C3   809'.89729

Indispensable because it covers an area that has not been treated thoroughly in any other reference book. The logically important, the obscure, the emerging author will be identified here as well as the internationally and justly famous. Entries are arranged by language, with biographical information and lists of journals, general studies, and primary and secondary works for about two thousand writers, many of whom were published only by small presses in their native lands.

R994.   *West Indian Literature: An Index to Criticism, 1930–1975.* Ed. Jeanette B. Allis. Boston: Hall, 1983. 353pp. Z1502.B5   [PR9210] 016.820'9'9729

Information on native and foreign books, articles, essays, and newspaper clippings criticizing the literature of formerly British Caribbean islands and Guyana.

Periodicals

R994.1.   *Latin American Literary Review (LALR).* Pittsburgh: Carnegie-Mellon Univ., 1972– . 2/yr. L860.5

Devoted to the literatures of Latin America and Latin American minorities in the United States, with articles, reviews, poetry, short stories, plays, and their translations. Occasional special issues, as on Hispanic Caribbean literature (1980). Indexed in *Arts and Hum. Cit. Ind.* (F47), *MLAIB* (D31).

Additional reference sources for South American and Latin American literature

Bibliography of Hispanic Women Writers (W1636)
Bibliography of Picaresque Literature (G87)
Bleznick (Q944)
CLA Journal (H142), Caribbean writers
Diacritics (W1365)
Eighteenth Century: A Current Bibliography (J374)
Journal of Modern Literature (J530)
Journal of Spanish Studies (Q947)
MLAIB (D31), vol. 2
Nicoll, *World Drama* (R965)
Oxford Companion to Spanish Literature (Q945)
Renaissance Spain and Its Literary Relations (T1012)
Romantic Movement Bibliography (J443)
Twayne's World Authors Series (R957), Argentina, Brazil, Chile, Colombia, Guatemala, Mexico, Paraguay, Peru, Uruguay, West Indies
Twentieth Century Literature (J528)
World Literature since 1945 (R950), Latin America
World Literature Today (R961)

S

Classical Literature

Basic guides

S995. *Classical Studies: A Student's Guide to Reference Resources*. Montreal: McLennan Library, McGill Univ., 1977. 17pp. ERIC no.: ED 096 942. Z7019.M3   016.01648

Carefully selected titles for both preliminary studies and in-depth research. Majors in this field should certainly buy this for their knapsacks. See ERIC, in the Glossary, for information on purchasing bibliographies in this series. For additional McGill titles, see the Index to this guide.

Criticism

S996. *Ancient Writers: Greece and Rome*. Ed. T. James Luce. 2 vols. New York: Scribners, 1982. PA3002.A5   880'.09

A survey of forty-seven authors, including Homer, Pindar, Vergil, Ovid, Plato, and Aristotle, with a comprehensive index and lists of recent studies for each author.

S997.   Classical World Bibliographies. New York: Garland, 1978–   .

.1   *Greek Drama and Poetry*. 1978. Z7023.D7.C58 [PA3131] 016.881

.2   *Philosophy, Religion, and Rhetoric*. 1978.   Z7129.G7.C58 [B171]   016.18

.3   *Roman Drama and Poetry and Ancient Fiction*. 1978. 387pp. Z7026.C53   [PA6003]   016.87

These reprints of bibliographical surveys from *Classical World* (Pittsburgh: Duquesne Univ., 1907–   ) summarize the state of scholarship and analyze the most important books and articles. Subjects include recent scholarship on Ovid, Horace, satire, the ancient novel, Aristotle's *Poetics*, Aristophanes and Old

Comedy, and Greek Lyric Poetry. The lack of indexes, however, and the very small print are deterrents to enthusiastic research. More recent information is found in *L'Année Philologique* (S1005).

S998.   *Greek and Roman Authors: A Checklist of Criticism.* Ed. Thomas Gwinup and Fidelia Dickinson. 2nd ed. Metuchen, N.J.: Scarecrow, 1982. 294pp. Z7016.G9   016.88'009

The best and quickest source for criticism of the seventy most famous Greek and Roman classical authors. This could be called a supplement to *MLAIB* (D31) because, while *MLAIB* does include some ancient literature such as Egyptian and Sanskrit, and some medieval and Neo-Latin works, it excludes all of classical Greek and Latin. This draws mainly on scholarship completed between 1930 and 1970, indexing articles from about one hundred periodicals for a total of four thousand items from Aeschylus to Xenophon. See Grant (W1124.5) for more recent information on Greek and Latin authors who wrote between 800 B.C. and A.D. 1000.

Identification problems

*S1000.   *Oxford Classical Dictionary.* Ed. Nicholas G. Hammond and Howard H. Scullard. 2nd ed. Oxford: Clarendon, 1977, c1970. 1176pp. DE5.09 913.38003

Emphasis is on biography and literature, but many entries give explanations for terms, places, and events. The index to names of people mentioned in the text is a valuable feature. "Zealots," for instance, is not listed alphabetically in the main text, but the index refers to the entry for "Jews," where Zealots are identified as members of a nationalist party in Judea that aimed at recovering political independence.

Many scholars prefer this to the *Oxford Companion to Classical Literature* (S1001) because they believe it is more thorough and scholarly. The Daedalus entry in this work, for instance, is at least three times longer than the one in the *Oxford Companion* and cites many Greek and historical sources and five titles for further study. Grant (W1124.5) brings the bibliographies up to date and has much longer biographical sketches, so students may want to consult his work for more complex problems.

S1001.   *Oxford Companion to Classical Literature.* Ed. Sir Paul Harvey. Oxford: Clarendon, 1937; rpt. with corrections, 1980. 468pp. DE5.H3 913.38

Explanations of the classical allusions that recur in modern literature. Thousands of proper names, titles, terms, and items of historical, political, social, geographical, and religious interest. Adonis, Daedalus, the epic, the satires of Juvenal, and the position of women in Greece are illustrations of the type of entry that is so valuable to literature students. Many scholars prefer the *Oxford Classical Dictionary* (S1000) because of its bibliographies and its longer entries written and signed by authorities. See *Greek and Roman Authors* (S998) for criticism of the works.

*S1002. *Crowell's Handbook of Classical Drama.* Ed. Richmond Y. Hathorn. New York: Crowell, 1967. 350pp. PA3024.H35   882.003
A handbook with the expected plot summaries, proper name identifications, and literary term definitions. It gives special care, however, to the details and analyzes as well as summarizes the plays. It provides much more information on all aspects of drama than two other sources with which it overlaps somewhat: *Oxford Classical Dictionary* (S1000) and *Crowell's Handbook of Classical Literature* (New York: Crowell, 1964). Animated prose, witty and perceptive.

S1003. *Who's Who in Greek and Roman Mythology.* Ed. David Kravitz. New York: Potter, 1975. 246pp. BL715.K7   292
Unequalled for its clarification of the tangled family relationships of the gods. Indispensable for the crossword puzzle fan.

Periodicals

S1005. *L'Année Philologique: Bibliographie Critique et Analytique de l'Antiquité Gréco-Latine.* Paris: Belles Lettres, 1924– . Annual. Z7016.M35.A   016.88
The only comprehensive current bibliography that covers classical studies. In French, with some German, English, and Italian material.

Additional reference sources for information on classical literature

S1006. *Classical Rhetoric for the Modern Student* (W1606)
Coleman and Tyler (G111), vol 2, Classical Plays
Epic and Romance Criticism (G127)
Funk and Wagnalls Standard Dictionary of Folklore (W1272)
Greek and Latin Authors, 800 B.C.–A.D. 1000 (W1124.5)
Library of Literary Criticism: Greek and Latin Literatures in Modern Criticism. New York: Ungar. In preparation
Palmer (Q897)
Penguin Companion to Classical, Oriental, and African Literature (R986)
Twayne's World Authors Series (R957), Latin literature
Year's Work in Mod. Lang. Stud. (W1328)

T

Comparative Literature

Students who are interested in comparative literature will find that periodicals and bibliographies that specialize in Continental literature will frequently contain scholarship useful in the field of comparative studies. They should, therefore, also consult the sources listed in Continental Literature (Q884–948).

Surveys

*T1007. *Comparative Literary Studies: An Introduction*. Ed. Siegbert S. Prawer. New York: Harper, 1973. 180pp. PN871.P7   801'.9

Choice (W1557) predicts that this will be the standard text for years. The editor's thesis is that any national literature is enriched by comparison with other literatures. As convincing evidence, he offers hundreds of examples from literature, such as Brecht's dependence on Shelley and Balzac's on Cooper; the pervasive themes from Greek literature in, for example, O'Neill, Anouilh, and Sartre; and the problematical essence of a "good" translation. Brilliant. Readable.

Basic guides

**T1009. Baldensperger, Fernand, and Werner P. Friederich. *Bibliography of Comparative Literature*. New York: Russell, 1960, c1950. 705pp. Z6514.C7.B3   016.809

An international bibliography of books and articles from over two hundred periodicals that examine the interaction of national literatures, individual authors, themes, and disciplines. The detailed table of contents offers the best explanation of the arrangement, which is by subject, country, and then alphabetically by critic. It is possible, for instance, to find titles reflecting different opinions from several countries on *Antigone*, pastoral literature, *Don Quixote*, Byron's influence on both specific writers and national cultures, the influences of Christianity, and modern trends. No annotations and no index.

The scope is unique, but the copyright date limits the book's value, of course. The "Annual Bibliography of Comparative Literature" that appeared from 1952 to 1970 in the *Yearbook of Comparative and General Literature* (T1014) and that has since been cumulated into one volume (see also T1014) kept scholars informed of activity during those years. *YCGL* currently publishes specialized bibliographies or essay reviews to assist in this area.

*T1010. *Comparative and General Literature: A Student's Guide to Reference Resources*. Ed. Margaret Carroll. 2nd ed. Montreal: McLennan Library, McGill Univ., 1977. 26pp. ERIC no.: ED 096 942. Z6525.M3 [PN523] 016.016809

Unquestionably the easiest source to consult for guidance in comparative literature research problems. This is manageable in size and carefully annotated. It has good subject arrangement for genre studies, biographical questions, surveys, period or thematic studies, periodicals, interdisciplinary problems, and all bibliographies. The student who needs more information can go to Baldensperger and Friederich (T1009) and the annual bibliographies (T1014). See ERIC, in the Glossary, for information on purchasing the bibliographies in this series. For additional McGill titles, see the Index to this guide.

T1011. *Post-Symbolist Bibliography*. Comp. Henry Krawitz. Metuchen, N.J.: Scarecrow, 1973. 284pp. Z6520.S9.K7 016.809'04

One section lists criticism on symbolism as a theory and a movement, another concerns national literature, and a third includes comparative studies on individuals such as Eliot, Guillén, Jiménez, Lorca, Rilke, Stevens, Valéry, and Yeats. Students miss so much if they have never been led to useful reference books like this.

T1012. *Renaissance Spain and Its Literary Relations with England and France: A Critical Bibliography*. Comp. Hilda U. Stubbings. Nashville: Vanderbilt Univ. Press, 1969. 138pp. Z6514.C7.S78 016.809

Designed for college students and professors interested in the relations between Spanish, French, and English literatures and cultures from the sixteenth to the eighteenth centuries. The 364 entries in this work are carefully evaluated and annotated, with mention of favorable or unfavorable book reviews and good or bad authorial decisions as to adequate indexes and bibliographies.

Students who want to investigate the rise of the novel in eighteenth-century England should look here to trace English translations and popularity of the sixteenth-century Lazarillo de Tormes and seventeenth-century Don Quixote. The possibilities for important research are bountiful.

The author's scholarship must be complimented. The selections are genuinely "comparative" studies, and the comments are discerning and carefully phrased.

Periodicals

*T1014. *Yearbook of Comparative and General Literature (YCGL)*. Bloomington: Indiana Univ., 1952– . Annual. PN851.Y4

The source to consult for all comparative literature scholarship completed since Baldensperger and Friederich compiled their *Bibliography of Comparative Literature* in 1950 (T1009). This publication has two important features: first, the occasional lists (since 1960) of English translations published in about thirty selected periodicals in the United States. These lists include literary works published originally in Anglo-Saxon, Afrikaans, Oriental, Indic, and Latin as well as all the European languages. Until 1970 they cited only novels, short stories, and plays published in the United States, but since 1971 they have included translations published abroad and book-length literary criticism. The second important feature is the annual bibliography of current comparative literary scholarship that flourished from 1952 to 1970, and its replacement, the highly specialized bibliographies or essay reviews on specific subjects. All nineteen annual supplementary bibliographies have been published in one volume, *Bibliography of Comparative Literature, 1950-1970, Cumulative Indexes*. This, plus the current essay reviews of comparative literature scholarship, vastly increases the usefulness of Baldensperger and Friederich's pioneer work.

Examples of the interdisciplinary, international articles to be found in the periodical are a review of research from 1955-65 on the influence of the Bible on European literature, a study of musico-literary research in the last two decades, the social significance of literature as art, and "Some American Contributions to World Literature" (1977).

Indexed in *ABELL* (D32), *Abst. Eng. Stud.* (E38), *Am. Hum. Ind.* (P738), *MLAIB* (D31), *Romantic Movement: A . . . Bibliography* (J443).

T1015. *Symposium: A Quarterly Journal in Modern Foreign Literatures*. Washington, D.C.: Heldref, 1946– . Quarterly. PB1.S9   405

International coverage, with articles on Valéry, Hesse, Alarcón, Croce, Tomashevsky, Borges, T. S. Eliot, Dürrenmatt, a comparison of Leopardi and Unamuno, and a special issue on film. Reviews of worldwide publications; no news or notes. For years it featured an annual bibliography on the relations between literature and science, including botany, astronomy, medicine, anthropology, and psychology, but this is now appearing in *Clio* (W1303).

Indexed in *ABELL* (D32), *Arts and Hum. Cit. Ind.* (F47), *Current Bk. Rev. Cit.* (W1564), *Hum. Ind.* (F45), *Index to Bk. Rev. Hum.* (W1560), *MLAIB* (D31).

*T1016. *Comparative Literature (CL)*. Eugene: Univ. of Oregon, 1949– . Quarterly. PN851.C595   805.C7373

Official journal of the American Comparative Literature Association. The editors maintain that "transcending the barriers of language and national culture, the peoples of the world have a vast common heritage of literary themes, types, movements, styles." The scholarly, well-documented articles illustrate this point, for they discern relationships between, for example, Spee and Vergil; Dante, Rossetti, Pound, and Eliot; Ovid and seventeenth-century England; Dickens and the French; Yeats and Goethe; Lope de Vega and Titian. Long book reviews and an annual index. Cumulative index for vols. 1-15 (1949-63).

Indexed in *ABELL* (D32), *Abst. Eng. Stud.* (E38), *Arts and Hum. Cit. Ind.* (F47), *Bk. Rev. Ind.* (W1559), *Current Bk. Rev. Cit.* (W1564), *Hum. Ind.* (F45), *Index to Bk. Rev. Hum.* (W1560), *MLAIB* (D31), *Romantic Movement: A . . . Bibliography* (J443).

T1017. *Comparative Literature Studies (CLS)*. Urbana: Univ. of Illinois Press, 1963– . Quarterly. PN851.C63   809
Articles on literary history and the history of ideas—for example, the impact of American literature on French writers, a comparison of Proust and Faulkner, and a survey of Russian formalism and French Structuralism.
Indexed in *ABELL* (D32), *Abst. Eng. Stud.* (E38), *Arts and Hum. Cit. Ind.* (F47), *Bk. Rev. Ind.* (W1559), *Current Bk. Rev. Cit.* (W1564), *Hum. Ind.* (F45), *Index to Bk. Rev. Hum.* (W1560), *MLAIB* (D31), *Romantic Movement: A . . . Bibliography* (J443).

T1018. *Comparative Drama (CompD)*. Kalamazoo: Western Michigan Univ., 1967– . Quarterly. PN1601.C66   809.2
International and interdisciplinary criticism of dramatic literature from the Greeks, medieval drama, and Shakespeare to Auden and Krapp. Reviews and annual index. A cumulative index is in preparation.
Indexed in *ABELL* (D32), *Abst. Eng. Stud.* (E38), *Arts and Hum. Cit. Ind.* (F47), *Current Bk. Rev. Cit.* (W1564), *Hum. Ind.* (F45), *Index to Bk. Rev. Hum.* (W1560), *MLAIB* (D31).

T1019. *ACLA Newsletter*. Binghamton: State Univ. of New York, 1967– . 2/yr. PN855.A512
Official organ of the American Comparative Literature Association. Reports of association activities; news, notes, and book reviews. For other periodicals sponsored by ACLA, see *Encyclopedia of Associations* (W1045).

Background reading for comparative literature

T1020. Clements, Robert J. *Comparative Literature as Academic Discipline: A Statement of Principles, Praxis, Standards*. New York: MLA, 1978. 342pp. Paperback. PN865.C57   809
This is "the first sustained exposition of the principles, practices, and standards of comparative literature." It discusses "the origins and dimensions of the discipline, establishment and maintenance of a department, pedagogical approaches, textbooks, examinations, dissertations, department evaluation, academic diplomacy and politics, and the future of the discipline." Bibliography and index.

T1021. Corstius, Jan Brandt. *Introduction to the Comparative Study of Literature*. New York: Random, 1968. 212pp. Paperback. PN871.B7
This panoramic view of literature and history uses hundreds of authors, titles, countries, and philosophies to illustrate the inevitable interaction of human thought. A good place to begin. Useful bibliographies follow each chapter.

T1022. Weinstein, Arnold L. *Vision and Response in Modern Fiction*. Ithaca, N.Y.: Cornell Univ. Press, 1974. 282pp. PN3503.W39   809.3
Analyses and comparisons of English, American, and Continental novels by such authors as Balzac, Dickens, Kafka, Joyce, and Butor.

T1023. Weisstein, Ulrich W. *Comparative Literature and Literary Theory: Survey and Introduction.* Bloomington: Indiana Univ. Press, 1974. 352pp. PN874.W413   809
". . . undoubtedly the best book of its kind"—René Wellek.

Additional reference sources for information on comparative literature

T1024. *ABELL* (D32)
American Comparative Literature Association (W1045)
Bibliography of Picaresque Literature (G87)
Books Abroad (R961)
Campbell, *Masks of God* (W1284)
Continental Novel (Q895)
Cumulative Author Index for Poole's Index (J417)
Eighteenth-Century: A . . . Bibliography (J374)
Eighteenth-Century Studies (J381)
Essays in Literature (H147)
Fisher, *Medieval Literature of Western Europe* (J255)
Funk and Wagnalls Standard Dictionary of Folklore (W1272)
Genre (G58)
Gerstenberger and Hendrick (W1475), Comparative and European Literature
Guide to Eastern Literatures (R984)
Journal of Medieval and Renaissance Studies (J270)
Journal of Popular Culture (W1500)
MLAIB (D31), vol. 1, General III
Modern Language Notes (Q890)
Modern Language Quarterly (H149)
Modern Slavic Literatures (Q942)
New CBEL (J175), section entitled "Literary Relations with the Continent" in each volume
Philological Quarterly (H154), since 1971, comparative and interdisciplinary studies
Philosophy and Literature (W1490)
Romantic Movement: A . . . Bibliography (J443)
Romantic Movement Bibliography, 1937-1970 (J443)
Sources du travail bibliographique (A7)
Streeter, *Eighteenth Century English Novel in French Translation* (J392)
Studies in Philology (J321)
Studies in Romanticism (J446)
Thompson, George A., Jr. *Key Sources in Comparative and World Literature: An Annotated Guide to Reference Materials.* New York: Ungar, 1982. 383pp.
Wellek and Warren, *Theory of Literature* (W1399)
World Literature Today (R961)
Year's Work in Modern Language Studies (W1328)
York Dictionary of . . . Literary Terms (W1413)

W

Literature-Related Subjects

Abbreviations and Acronyms

Most scholarly reference books include in their preliminary pages an alphabetical list of all abbreviations used in the text (see the front of this guide, for example). These lists are found both in standard bound volumes such as the *New CBEL* (J175, J227, J363, J415, J511) and in continuing publications such as

> *ABELL* (D32)
> *MLAIB* (D31)
> *Philological Quarterly* (H154)
> *Victorian Studies* (J470)
> *Year's Work in English Studies* (D33)
> —and many other familiar literary reference works

When language or literature students find an unfamiliar abbreviation like *SFS*, *JHI*, or *EIC*, they should look first in the front of the book they are using, then in any of the above titles if they are convenient, or in one of the following sources:

W1025. Periodical Title Abbreviations. Ed. Leland G. Alkire, Jr. 4th ed. 3 vols. Detroit: Gale, 1983. Supplements. Z6945.A2.W34   050'.1'48

The most comprehensive and most recent source available. Note the number of volumes and the copyright date. More than five times larger than the first edition, this identifies 55,000 abbreviations for periodicals in all fields and all countries, but it emphasizes language, literature, and linguistics. Letter-by-letter arrangement. In vol. 1, the abbreviations are followed by the titles; in vol. 2, the titles by the abbreviations; vol. 3 lists new periodical title abbreviations. Annual supplements cumulate all previous supplements.

W1026. *Acronyms, Initialisms, and Abbreviations Dictionary.* Ed. Ellen T.

Crowley. 9th ed. 3 vols. Detroit: Gale, 1984. P365.G3   423'.1

This alphabetical list will be useful to belabored Americans who cannot keep up with the flood of shortcuts like LASER, DEW line, or ASCAP—300,000 entries from many different languages. Vol. 2, *New Acronyms*, the annual paperback supplement, contains several thousand additional entries. Vol. 3, *Reverse Acronyms*, lists the complete title and then the condensation. Librarians cannot get through the day without this.

Addresses

If language and literature students need to locate a former professor, or if they want the present address of an important dignitary, they can consult several sources that specialize in current information:

W1028. *National Faculty Directory—1984: An Alphabetical List, with Addresses, of about 600,000 Members of Teaching Faculties at Junior Colleges, Colleges, and Universities in the United States and at Selected Canadian Institutions.* 14th ed. 3 vols. Detroit: Gale, 1983. L901.N34 378.1'2'02573

The recent copyright date, wide coverage, and computer programming make this the best source for addresses of full-time and part-time teaching faculty at over three thousand institutions. Six-month supplement.

*W1029. *PMLA: Directory.* New York: MLA. Annual (Sept.).

This annual directory provides addresses for the 28,000 members of the Modern Language Association, all important publishers, literature-related societies and organizations, the chairmen of four-year and two-year institutions, ethnic studies programs, language programs, and women's studies programs. It is responsible for printing the statistics of the organization, the names of administrators and prize-winners, statements on MLA policies and procedures, and reports of the regional MLA groups. It also lists and describes the various opportunities for fellowships and grants as well as the dates of forthcoming conferences. The section on professional news, notes, and comments is the first part all educators read in every issue of *PMLA* (H152). Professors should have this directory within reach at all times.

W1030. *Writers Directory, 1984-86.* 6th ed. Detroit: Gale, 1983. 1081pp. PS1.W73   808

This directory lists over fifteen thousand living authors who write in English, with their occupations, home and professional addresses, pseudonyms, awards, bibliographies, and publishers. It has two unique features: It locates additional biographical information in fifteen other sources, and it adds a yellow-page section that arranges authors by subject (Novels, Mystery, Science Fiction, Literature, Biography, etc.).

W1031. *Directory of American Poets and Fiction Writers.* New York: Poets and

Writers (201 W. 54th St.), 1980. 208pp. PS129.P6   810'.9'0054

A happy combination of two earlier publications: *Directory of American Fiction Writers* and *Directory of American Poets*. Its objective is to help program planners get in touch with the 4,800 authors listed here with their addresses and a summary of their accomplishments. Poets who want to give readings and novelists who want to supplement their income with lectures will make sure they are listed in this directory. Organizations such as P.E.N. in New York and the Florida Writers' Conference at the University of Florida will then be able to write or phone these authors who, as the editors have found, have an annual residency change rate of twenty-five percent. The same publishers also produce a newsletter for this audience, *Coda* (W1524).

See also

> *Academic Who's Who* (W1147)
> *Contemporary Authors* (W1127)
> *Contemporary Dramatists* (W1128)
> *Contemporary Literary Critics* (W1360)
> *Contemporary Novelists* (W1130)
> *Contemporary Poets* (W1129)
> *Current Biography* (W1115)
> *Directory of American Scholars* (W1146)
> *Living Black American Authors* (W1133)
> *National Playwrights Directory* (W1140)
> *Selected Black American Authors* (W1134)
> *Who's Who* biographical dictionaries in specific regions or professions (W1091–1113, W1126)

Anonymous Literature and Pseudonyms

**W1033. Halkett, Samuel, and John Laing. *Dictionary of Anonymous and Pseudonymous English Literature*. 6 vols. inc. supplement; index and supplement; vol. 8, 1900–1950; vol. 9, addenda to vols. 1–8. Edinburgh: Oliver and Boyd, 1926–62. Z1065.H17   014'.2

Halkett, Samuel, and John Laing. *A Dictionary of Anonymous and Pseudonymous Publications in the English Language*. Ed. John Horden. 3rd ed. Harlow, Eng.: Longman, 1980–   . In progress (vol. 1, 1475–1640; 271pp.). Z1065.D5

The most comprehensive source for identifying authors of books and pamphlets published anonymously or pseudonymously. No attempt is made to cover articles in periodicals. Students should look here, for example, if they come across references to such anonymous works as *McFingal, a Modern Epic Poem* (1775). The entries are arranged alphabetically by title and include bibliographical information, identification of author, and authority for assigning the correct author such as the *British Museum Catalogue* (B13) and the *L.C. Catalog* (B10).

The third edition coordinates all previous information, rewrites every entry, and devotes each volume to a specific historical period. It provides an entry for every work published anonymously or pseudonymously for which the authorship has been established, conjectured, or mistakenly asserted. Whenever possible it makes cross-references to the incomplete new edition of *STC* (J306). Vol. 1 lists (1) four thousand publications by title, (2) an index of authors, translators, and editors, (3) pseudonyms, and (4) tables of equivalent numbers found in Greg (J339), the *STC*, and Allison and Rogers (rpt. London: Dawson, 1964).

W1034. Sharp, Harold S. *Handbook of Pseudonyms and Personal Nicknames.* 2 vols. Metuchen, N.J.: Scarecrow, 1972. Supplement (1975), 2 vols. Supplement (1982), 295pp. Z1041.S43   929.4
Sharp concentrates on authors but also includes popes, kings, actors, musicians, and statesmen of the Western world from the Greek Golden Age to the present for a total of 105,000 entries. Much easier to use than Halkett and Laing (W1033) but not so scholarly.

W1035. *Dictionary of Literary Pseudonyms: A Selection of Popular Modern Writers in English.* Ed. Frank Atkinson. 3rd ed. London: Bingley, 1982. 305pp. Z1065.A83   808'.03'21
A necessary complement to the other titles in this section, which tend toward the historical, this identifies over 9,500 names and pseudonyms of twentieth-century authors writing in English.

Additional sources for pseudonyms

American and British Theatrical Biography (W1138)
American Bibliography (P717.2), Bristol's index, and P717.10, Cooper's index
Author Bibliography of English Language Fiction (G61)
Baker's Biographical Dictionary of Musicians (W1445)
Bergquist, *Three Centuries of English and American Plays* (G113)
Bibliography of Crime Fiction (G85)
Block, *English Novel, 1740–1850* (J390)
Bradley, *Book Collector's Handbook* (W1164)
British Library. *General Catalogue* (B14)
Computer Abstracts (W1190)
Computing Reviews (W1191)
Dictionary of American Biography: Including Men of the Time (W1087)
Eichelberger, *Guide to Critical Reviews of U.S. Fiction, 1870–1910* (P787)
Library of Congress Catalog (B10)
McBurney, *Checklist of English Prose Fiction, 1700–39* (J388)
Myers, *Dictionary of Literature in the English Language* (W1122)
National Union Catalog (B10–11)
Poetry by American Women (W1648)
Science Fiction Story Index (G96.1)
Slocum, *Biographical Dictionaries* (W1084.1)
Wellesley Index to Victorian Periodicals (J466)

Wright, *American Fiction* (P778)
—and many of the carefully edited author bibliographies such as those on Whittier and Hawthorne.

Art

Basic guides

*W1037. *Relationship of Literature and Painting: A Guide to Information Sources.* Ed. Eugene L. Huddleston and Douglas A. Noverr. Vol. 4 of American Studies Information Guide Series (A8.1). Detroit: Gale, 1978. 184pp. Z5069.H84.N66   016.75913

An interesting approach that should appeal to literature students and professors alike. This is essentially a checklist of poems that react to paintings, but the prosaic succumbs to the poetic when the introduction explains why poets respond intensely to art, while artists are seldom inspired by poetry. The book also includes excerpts from previously published pairings and an annotated bibliography of additional sources concerning the relations between literature and painting. Indexes of authors, painters, paintings, books, poems, and first lines of poems.

Identification problems

*W1038. *Encyclopedia of World Art.* 15 vols. and index. New York: McGraw-Hill, 1959–68. Guide to encyclopedia (1968), 38pp. Supplement (1983), 500pp. N31.E4833   703

A production of quality, intellectually and aesthetically. It encompasses every phase of art including architecture, sculpture, and painting, in fact, all objects from the most primitive to the most civilized of all ages and all countries. The entries are long, scholarly, signed monographs with comprehensive bibliographies, and the contributors are specialists from many parts of the world. The English translation is different from the original Italian edition in that it adds about three hundred short biographical sketches.

The first half of each large volume is text; the last half includes pertinent color and black-and-white plates. The entry under "American Cultures," for instance, has numerous subdivisions (geographical, chronological, specific types of art that are once again divided chronologically) and then hundreds of plates to illustrate textual references. All art lovers will wish they could own this.

Volume 15 is an analytical index of proper names, places, works of art, styles, techniques, and periods. References are to both the text and the plates.

W1039. *McGraw-Hill Dictionary of Art.* Ed. Bernard S. Myers. 5 vols. New York: McGraw-Hill, 1969. N33.M23   703

All lower schools as well as colleges and universities should own this popular work. It has an attractive format, a low price, and an abundance of color and black-and-white illustrations for such varied entries as Sacre Coeur, Rubens, Saarinen, Turner, Warwick Castle, and Stonehenge.

Authority is evident in the quality of the articles, many of which are signed and have bibliographies. The range of interest is broad, from artists' biographies to archaeological digs, definitions of art terms, explanation of techniques, specific museums and academies, periods (Prehistoric, Baroque, Colonial American), and schools of painting (Barbizon). Earnest students can, for instance, look here when they realize they need information on Botticelli in order to understand William Carlos Williams' poem "Botticellian Trees."

W1040.   *Oxford Companion to Art.* Ed. Harold Osborne. Oxford: Clarendon, 1970. 1277pp. N33.O9   703
A handbook designed for nonspecialists and limited, therefore, to preliminary information and references to other sources for further study. Subjects range from biographical facts (on John Constable, for example), Gothic art (with illustrations), Romanticism in the Visual Arts, and terra cotta, to Pre-Columbian Arts of the Andes. Art majors and art lovers should own this.

W1041.   Boucher, François. *20,000 Years of Fashion: The History of Costume and Personal Adornment.* New York: Abrams, 1966. 441pp. GT510.B6713   746.9'09
Information about the clothing, jewels, textiles, and accessories of all countries and all centuries, with definitions for unfamiliar terms like "crinoline" and "pattens." The numerous sketches and richly colored reproductions of works by Ingres, Van Eyck, Titian, and Dior, for instance, help to clarify allusions that students may find in literature.

Indexes

*W1042.   *Art Index: A Cumulated Author and Subject Index to a Selected List of Fine Arts Periodicals.* New York: Wilson, 1929– . Quarterly. Z5937.A78   016.7
This author and subject listing (no titles) indexes 200 periodicals and annuals as well as museum and art association publications. It lists articles and other information on art in the broadest sense of the word including archaeology, architecture, graphic arts, decoration, painting, sculpture, landscaping, motion pictures, ceramics, photography, and related subjects. Exhibitions are listed under the artist's name, and reviews are under both the subject and the author or artist reviewed.
Art Index is the source to consult for articles and books on Turner and the Pre-Raphaelites, illuminated manuscripts, the Frick collection in New York, Sartre's connection with art, or the name of a periodical that contains a reproduction of Vermeer's *The Cook.* It is also one of the best sources for information on the motion picture industry, its festivals, music, photography, theaters, and individual films that have been commended or criticized for their aesthetic techniques.

Periodicals

W1043.   *Journal of Aesthetics and Art Criticism (JAAC; JA).* Cleveland:

American Assn. for Aesthetics, Cleveland Museum of Art, 1941– .
Quarterly. N1.J6
Concerned with the interrelations of literature, music, art, psychology, and
the visual arts, including such subjects as symbolism, structuralism, fiction and
the real world, and Hazlitt on painting. Annual current bibliography. The
cumulative index for 1941–76 (vols. 1–35) will permit interesting studies on how
the definition of and stress on "aesthetics" has changed over the years.
Indexed in *ABELL* (D32), *Art Ind.* (W1042), *Arts and Hum. Cit. Ind.* (F47),
Bk. Rev. Dig. (W1558), *Bk. Rev. Ind.* (W1559), *Film Literature Ind.* (W1252),
Hum. Ind. (F45), *Index to Bk. Rev. Hum.* (W1560), *MLAIB* (D31), *Music Ind.*
(W1456), *Psych. Abst.* (E39).

See also
Who's Who in American Art (W1102)

Associations and Societies

W1045. *Encyclopedia of Associations.* 18th ed. 5 vols. Detroit: Gale, 1983.
HS17.G334   061'.3
This convenient source provides information on the addresses, officials, and
purposes of associations that might be of interest to students of literature. They
might want to know, for instance, that the American Comparative Literature
Association sponsors a newsletter (T1019), a yearbook (T1014), and two quarterly
journals (T1016 and T1017). Easy to use: Vol. 1, National Organizations, has
a proper name, subject, and key word index for its subject arrangement; vol.
2 is a geographic and executive index by state and city; and vol. 3, a periodical
supplement published between editions, provides information on the newest
organizations and projects.

W1046. Early English Text Society (EETS). England: Oxford Univ. Press,
1864– .
This international organization publishes two or three volumes a year of
pre-1558 texts not otherwise available in good editions. Some of these editions
are facsimiles; almost all add comments, a glossary, marginal notes, and indexes
that are valuable aids for reading and interpretations. There are 285 volumes
in the original series, 126 in the extra series, and several supplementary texts.
An interesting example of an EETS publication is *The History of Reynard
the Fox*, trans. from the Dutch original by William Caxton, ed. Norman F. Blake
(London: Oxford Univ. Press, 1970). Extensive scholarship is well demonstrated
in the 170 pages, 61 of which are devoted to an introduction and bibliography
and 58 to notes and glossary. See W1435 for microtext information.
Indexed in *MLAIB* (D31).

Additional scholarly associations
—that publish journals, directories, reports of meetings, and research of interest to literature students:

W1047. American Antiquarian Society (P717, P717.1-.2, P717.4, P717.7)
  American Association of Teachers of French (Q914)
  American Association of Teachers of German (Q925)
  American Bibliographical Center (E43, W1632)
  American Committee for Irish Studies (K588)
  American Comparative Literature Association (T1014, T1016-17, T1019)
  American Council of Learned Societies (J247, J262, W1146, W1437)
  American Dialect Society (P748, W1337)
  American Folklore Society (W1278)
  American Indian Historical Society (P877)
  American Humor Studies Association (P746)
  American Library Association (A3, A5, G96.1, G129, G137, H157, P802, W1313, W1324, W1557)
  American Literary Translators Association (W1628)
  American Name Society (H151)
  American Psychological Association (E39)
  American Society for Eighteenth-Century Studies (J373-74, J381)
  American Society for Theatre Research (P812)
  American Studies Association (P745)
  American Theological Library Association (F53)
  Antiquarian Booksellers Association of Japan (W1165)
  Association for Scottish Literary Studies (L623)
  Association for Studies in American Indian Literatures (P880)
  Association of College and Research Libraries (H157, J418, W1557)
  Association of Research Libraries (W1213)
  Bibliographical Society (London) (J306, J339, W1074)
  Bibliographical Society of America (P713, W1075)
  Bibliographical Society of Northern Illinois (W1073)
  Bibliographical Society of the University of Virginia (J324, P717.3)
  British Council (J180)
  British Film Institute (W1267)
  British Library (B13-14, D36, J373, J408)
  Canadian Library Association (N663, N674)
  Center for . . . American Indian (P873)
  Center for Medieval and Early Renaissance Studies (J236)
  Centre for Medieval Studies (Toronto) (J248, J282)
  Checklists in the Humanities (J213, J348)
  Children's Literature Association (W1186)
  College English Association (W1597)
  Committee on Scholarly Editions (W1179)
  Conference on British Studies (J304, J368, J457)
  Eighteen Nineties Society (J471)

English Association (London) (D33, J185)
ERIC (see Glossary)
Folklore Society (London) (W1279)
Helen Dwight Reid Educational Foundation—Heldref (G56, T1015, W1601)
Institute for Scientific Information (F47)
International Arthurian Society (J267)
International Fiction Association (R963)
International Ligue of Antiquarian Booksellers (W1165)
International Linguistic Association (W1338)
International Society for Eighteenth-Century Studies (J381)
Irish American Cultural Institute (K593)
Leo Baeck Institute (Q926)
Library Association (London) (A6, E43, F49)
Library Association (Wales) (M634)
Linguistic Society of America (W1335)
Medieval Academy of America (J254, J265)
MELUS: Society for the Study of the Multi-Ethnic Literature of the U.S. (P753)
Milton Society of America (J314)
Modern Humanities Research Association (D32, W1328)
Modern Language Association (see MLA, Index)
Modern Language Society (Helsinki) (J274)
Modern Poetry Association (P822)
National Council of Teachers of English (W1598–1600)
National Education Association (W1197)
National Federation of Modern Language Teachers Associations (W1336)
Northeast Victorian Studies Association (J474)
Pipe Roll Society (see Glossary)
Pontifical Institute of Medieval Studies (Toronto) (J271)
Popular Culture Association (W1265, W1500)
Renaissance Society of America (J313)
Research Society for Victorian Periodicals (J473)
Royal Historical Society (W1201)
Science Fiction Research Association (G99)
Scottish Text Society (W1435)
Shakespeare Association of America (J316)
Societas Bibliographica (C25)
Society for the Advancement of Scandinavian Studies (Q940)
Society for the Study of Medieval Languages and Literature (J273)
Society for the Study of Midwestern Literature (P754)
Society for the Study of the Multi-Ethnic Literature of the U.S. (P753)
Society for the Study of Southern Literature (P755)
Society for Theatre Research (J210)

Additional sources for information on literary societies

Oxford Companions (see Index)

PMLA (H152), Sept. issue, Directory of Useful Addresses, and Forthcoming Meetings and Conferences

Sources of Serials (W1477)

Atlases and Tour Guides

*W1049. *Oxford Literary Guide to the British Isles.* Comp. Dorothy Eagle and Hilary Carnell. Oxford: Clarendon, 1980, c1977. 413pp. PR109.E18 914.1'04

This and the *Reader's Encyclopedia* (W1402) should be on the desk of every literature student (and in the suitcase of everyone traveling to England). Tunbridge Wells, Penshurst Place, Trinity College, Nether Stowey, the Lake District, Tintagel, Fleet Street, Gad's Hill, and hundreds of other places are identified and linked with every literary figure who ever lived there, visited the area, or mentioned the name. An index of about nine hundred authors leads to over twelve hundred related geographical entries. A bibliography, maps, and color illustrations and portraits encourage peripatetic scholars to further exploration. This book should be twice as big. It is not for anyone in a hurry, as more than one reader has said. The publisher has just announced the completion of another equally welcome traveler's aid, *The Oxford Illustrated Literary Guide to the United States* (ed. Eugene Ehrlich and Gorton Carruth).

W1050. Daiches, David, and John R. Flower. *Literary Landscapes of the British Isles: A Narrative Atlas.* New York: Paddington, 1979. 287pp. PR109.D34   820'.9'941

Daiches' essays on the lives, times, and literature of some 240 authors give this book a kind of stature, but as a traveling companion or conversation piece this is neither so exciting nor so impressive as Eagle and Carnell (W1049). Hardy's hills, Brontë's moors, the Lake District, a variety of schools, and much more. Restricted to deceased authors.

W1051. *Atlas of English Literature.* Ed. Clement T. Goode and Edgar F. Shannon. New York: Century, 1925; rpt. Folcroft, Pa.: n.p. (Box 182), 1973. 136pp. PR109.G6   820'.9

This chronological arrangement of maps of England, Ireland, Scotland, Italy, and London, from the Anglo-Saxon period to 1900, shows the location of birthplaces, burial sites, and any location referred to in literature. The student can see, for instance, where Shelley is buried, where the Canterbury pilgrims journeyed, and where the Romans built their camps and roads.

An index of proper and place names enables students to look up Byron, Wordsworth, and Keats and then turn to the maps to see where they lived and traveled. The early copyright date does not detract from the value of this title at all.

W1052. *Literary Tour Guide to the United States: Northeast.* Ed. Emilie C. Harting. New York: Morrow-Quill, 1978. 218pp. PS144.N65.H3 917.4'04'4

Literary Tour Guide to the United States: South and Southwest. Ed. Rita Stein. New York: Morrow-Quill, 1979. 189pp. PS144.S67.S75 917.5'04'4

Literary Tour Guide to the United States: West and Midwest. Ed. Rita Stein. New York: Morrow-Quill, 1979. 221pp. PS144.W47.S75 917.8'04'3

Travelers of a literary bent consider these an essential part of their luggage. Faulkner, Wolfe, Hemingway, Poe, Twain, Cather, London—a guide to their homes and haunts, their journeys, memorabilia, and museums.

Author Bibliographies

W1053. This is the fastest-growing field in publishing, and of real measurable value. Why leaf through dozens of catalog cards, genre studies, or period bibliographies when some farsighted, hardworking bibliographer has already gathered the information on the person you're investigating and has published it in one convenient volume? Certain publishers are bringing these out as fast as they can be prepared, including the annotated secondary bibliographies from Scarecrow Press (W1054), the G. K. Hall Reference Guides (W1055), the Gale Information Guide Library (A8), a few of uneven quality by Garland, and the fine Northern Illinois University Press publications on Hardy, Conrad, Gissing, George Moore, Maugham, Shaw, Lawrence, Wells, E. M. Forster, Pater, Galsworthy, and Jeremy Taylor.

Author bibliographies contain selective or comprehensive lists of primary and/or secondary materials and as much other information relating to the author as the editors are inspired to collect—pseudonyms, location of manuscripts, problems of scholarship, review of research, chronologies of life and works. They are, of course, the ideal place to begin with any critical, textual, or biographical problem. In the card catalog they will be indicated by a subject heading "Bibliographies" in capital letters or red ink at the top of the author card. If the library uses the Dewey system, these author bibliographies will probably be in the 012 section. The L.C. system places them in the Z8000 division.

Unfortunately, no recent, comprehensive bibliographies exist for many authors. Researchers will, therefore, have to look through several sources to cumulate a workable list of material for their own use. One of the best sources for ongoing information on author bibliographies used to be *ABELL* (D32). In 1975 this listed 223 different articles or books containing primary or secondary titles relating to authors, including those found in *American Literary Realism* (P747), *Bulletin of Bibliography* (C29), and numerous author journals such as the *Evelyn Waugh Newsletter* and the *James Joyce Quarterly*. In 1976 the coverage in this section of *ABELL* shifted to bibliographies of subjects, genres, and periods, so now it is necessary to scan for author bibliographies in the "Authors" section at the end of *ABELL*'s chronological sections.

In addition to the sources already mentioned above, many other reference books contain partial or comprehensive bibliographies of works by or about individual authors:

Section A. General Guides: A4, A8
Section B. National Literatures: B10–14, 17, 20
Section C. Bibliographies of Bibliographies: C25–29
Section D. Annual Bibliographies: D31–33
Section G. Genres: G75–79, 81–83, 85–91, 95–96, 103, 107–09, 111, 113, 125–27, 138
Section J. English Literature:
  Guides: J174–75
  Series: J180–81
  Author Newsletters: J195
  Fiction: J201–04
  Drama: J209, 212–13
  Poetry: J216
  Old English: J227–28, 231, 236, 241
  Medieval: J255, 257, 260–63, 267–68, 281, 283
  Renaissance: J302–03, 306, 311, 316–17, 319, 323–24, 334–39, 343–48, 355
  Restoration: J363–67, 369–70, 373–75, 384, 386–92, 399–401, 403, 408
  Nineteenth Century: J415, 423, 426–27, 429–30, 437–44, 458–62, 464–66, 470–71, 477–80, 485, 488–89
  Twentieth Century: J511–14, 519–20, 528, 530, 535–45, 551–57, 563, 569–70
Section K. Irish Literature: K580–88, 597, 600, 605–06
Section L. Scottish Literature: L620, 624, 627
Section M. Welsh Literature: M634, 636, 640
Section N. Commonwealth Literature: N645, 647, 650, 654–57, 659–60, 663–66, 668–69, 676, 687–88, 691
Section P. American Literature: P702, 709–18, 720–22, 727–31, 734, 737–38, 744, 747, 754–55, 761, 772, 777–78, 780–84, 786–87, 792–93, 795–97, 804, 809, 836–38, 847–48, 856–62, 868–70, 872, 878
Section Q. Continental Literature: Q893, 895, 897, 903–07, 917–18, 939
Section R. World Literature: R950, 957, 972–74, 977, 981, 983.1, 988, 992, 994
Section S. Classical Literature: S996–98, 1005
Section T. Comparative Literature: T1009, 1014
Section W. Literature-Related Subjects:
  Autobiographies: W1056–58
  Biographies: W1085–88, 1115, 1119–22, 1127–32, 1134
  Books in Print: W1170, 1173
  Children's Literature: W1180, 1185
  Dissertations: W1211–15
  Film: W1236
  Goldentree Bibliographies: W1291

Library Collections: W1313–20
Literary Criticism:W1356
Periodicals: W1476
Philosophy: W1485
Psychology: W1509
Religion: W1543–44
Review of Research: W1556
Series: W1575
Translations: W1624–25
Women's Studies: W1630–37, 1644–45, 1647.1, 1648–49
Works in Progress: W1650

W1054. Author Bibliographies Series. Metuchen, N.J.: Scarecrow, 1969–   .
Author bibliographies in the Scarecrow series claim to include all works by and/or about the author. The accuracy and value of each volume, however, depend entirely on the skill and fortitude of the compiler. At the least, they are a logical starting point for researchers, who can later judge the volume's unique contribution compared with that of other reference books on the author.

Horatio Alger, Jr.	John Hawkes
Sherwood Anderson	Nathaniel Hawthorne
Jean Anouilh	Lillian Hellman
John Barth	William Dean Howells
John Berryman	Henry James
Sir John Betjeman	Ben Jonson
Anthony Burgess	Jack Kerouac
Lord Byron	Norman Mailer
George Washington Cable	Christopher Marlowe
Christine de Pisan	Herman Melville
Wilkie Collins	Arthur Miller
Joseph Conrad	Henry Miller
August Derleth	John Milton
James Dickey	Iris Murdoch and Muriel Spark
Benjamin Disraeli	John G. Neihardt
Paul Laurence Dunbar	Sylvia Plath
T. S. Eliot	Katherine Anne Porter
Ralph Ellison	Alain Robbe-Grillet
Ralph Waldo Emerson	Philip Roth
William Everson	John Ruskin
William Faulkner	Marquis de Sade
Henry Fielding	May Sarton
E. M. Forster	Georges Simenon
Four French Dramatists	John Steinbeck
Philip Freneau	Algernon Swinburne
Robert Frost	Henry David Thoreau
Northrop Frye	Leo Tolstoy
Federico García Lorca	E. B. White
Jean Genet	Walt Whitman
Allen Ginsberg	Elie Wiesel
Paul Goodman	Tennessee Williams
Graham Greene	Yvor Winters
Robert Greene	

*W1055. Reference Guides. Boston: Hall, 1974– . Irregular.

In this rapidly expanding series of annotated bibliographies on individual authors or specific subjects, all significant reviews, articles, books, and parts of books are described, cross-referenced, and arranged chronologically, making it possible to trace changes in the critical response. Quality in any series varies, of course, but *Choice* (W1557), *Literary Research Newsletter* (W1421), and other review boards have generally rated these reference guides as useful, at the least, and in some cases, as far superior to other available sources. Those few volumes that have no subject indexes are useless for students who need a subject approach, however. The topics range from women in America, early Anglo-Saxon studies, a Chaucer dictionary, the Bible as literature, Melville's foreign reputation, and Beckett's manuscripts to a concordance of Wilfred Owen. Some are being updated in *Resources for American Literary Study* (P761). Annotated bibliographies have been published on the following authors:

Henry Adams
Louisa May Alcott
Kingsley Amis
Maxwell Anderson and S. N. Behrman
Sherwood Anderson
W. H. Auden

James Baldwin
John Barth, Jerzy Kosinski, and Thomas
    Pynchon
John and William Bartram, William Byrd
    II, and St. John de Crèvecoeur
Saul Bellow
John Berryman
John Braine and John Wain
Charlotte and Emily Brontë
Van Wyck Brooks
Charles Brockden Brown
William Wells Brown and Martin R.
    Delany
Sir Thomas Browne and Robert Burton

James Branch Cabell
Truman Capote
John Cheever
Charles W. Chesnutt
John Clare
Samuel L. Clemens (Mark Twain)
Samuel Taylor Coleridge
William Congreve
E. E. Cummings

Thomas De Quincey
John Dos Passos
Michael Drayton and Samuel Daniel
Theodore Dreiser

Early Puritan Writers
Jonathan Edwards
George Eliot

Sir Thomas Elyot and Roger Ascham
English Renaissance Theater
George Etherege

William Faulkner
Henry Fielding
John Fowles
Robert Frost
Henry Blake Fuller and Hamlin Garland

David Garrick
Elizabeth Gaskell
Oliver Goldsmith
Zane Grey

Joel Chandler Harris
Bret Harte
William Hazlitt
Joseph Heller
Lillian Hellman
Ernest Hemingway
John Hersey and James Agee
Thomas Hobbes
Langston Hughes and Gwendolyn Brooks
J.-K. Huysmans

Washington Irving
Christopher Isherwood

Henry James (3)
William James
Thomas Jefferson
Sarah Orne Jewett
James Weldon Johnson and Arna Bontemps
Ben Jonson (2)

Charles Kingsley

Sidney Lanier, Henry Timrod, and Paul
    Hamilton Hayne

Sinclair Lewis
Jack London
Robert Lowell
Malcolm Lowry

Andrew Marvell
Herman Melville
Edna St. Vincent Millay
Arthur Miller
Kenji Mizoguchi
Marianne Moore
Alfred de Musset

Vladimir Nabokov
Anaïs Nin
Frank Norris

Flannery O'Connor and Caroline Gordon
John Osborne

Harold Pinter
Sylvia Plath and Anne Sexton
Edgar Allan Poe
Katherine Anne Porter and Carson
  McCullers
William Sidney Porter (O. Henry)

Ishmael Reed
Samuel Richardson
Jacob A. Riis
Edwin Arlington Robinson
Theodore Roethke
Christina Rossetti

Dorothy L. Sayers

Sir Walter Scott
Seventeenth-Century American Poetry
Seventy-Five Writers of the Colonial South
Richard Brinsley Sheridan
James Shirley
William Gilmore Simms
Louis Simpson
Tobias Smollett
C. P. Snow
Robert Southey
Harriet Beecher Stowe
Jesse Stuart
William Styron
John Millington Synge

Three Victorian Travel Writers: Butler,
  Stevenson, and Mrs. Trollope
Three Virginia Writers: Johnston, Page,
  Troubetzkoy
Three Writers of the Far West

Robert Penn Warren
Eudora Welty
Edith Wharton and Kate Chopin
Walt Whitman
Roger Williams
William Carlos Williams
Thomas Wolfe
Virginia Woolf
William Wordsworth
Richard Wright
Sir Thomas Wyatt and Henry Howard, Earl
  of Surrey
William Wycherley

Autobiographies and Diaries

W1056. Batts, John Stuart. *British Manuscript Diaries of the Nineteenth Century: An Annotated Listing.* Totowa, N.J.: Rowman, 1976. 345pp.
Z6611.B6.B38   016.941081'092'2
  This chronological and alphabetical list of three thousand diaries will be
of particular interest to nineteenth-century scholars. The editor describes the
contents of each diary and gives the reader information about its author and
its present location.

W1057. Kaplan, Louis. *A Bibliography of American Autobiographies.* Madison:
Univ. of Wisconsin Press, 1961. 372pp. Z1224.K3   016.92
  The first comprehensive bibliography of American autobiographies, each
one briefly evaluated, described, and located in a library for the inquiring scholar.
Coverage ranges from Samuel Clemens' tale of his life as a miner and a journalist to Jack Black's account of his escape from Folsom Prison in 1903. Texts
are now available on microfiche. This has been supplemented and updated by

A Bibliography of American Autobiography, 1945-1980, ed. Mary Louise Briscoe (1982; 384pp.), with expanded coverage of women and ethnic groups.

W1058.   Matthews, William, comp. *British Autobiographies: An Annotated Bibliography of British Autobiographies Published or Written before 1951.* Berkeley: Univ. of California Press, 1955. 376pp. Paperback: Hamden, Conn.: Archon, 1968. Z2027.A9.M3   016.920042
   The best source, especially for studies of minor authors whose complete works may be difficult to locate. Entries range from Kipling to Elizabeth Barrett Browning and Ellen Terry, from "Writers" (with chronological divisions for easy location) to "World Wars" and "Working-Class Life."
   The same author also compiled:

British Diaries: An Annotated Bibliography of British Diaries Written between 1442-1942 (1967). 339pp.
Canadian Diaries and Autobiographies (1950). 130pp.
American Diaries: An Annotated Bibliography of American Diaries (1945). This is currently being expanded into vol. 1, 1492–1844 (Detroit: Gale, 1983), and vol. 2, 1845–1980, in progress.
American Diaries in Manuscript, 1580-1954: A Descriptive Bibliography (Athens: Univ. of Georgia Press, 1974). 176pp. Particularly interesting because it contains unpublished items and brief annotations.

Additional reference sources for information on autobiographies

W1059.   *ABELL* (D32)
   Autobiographies of American Women: An Annotated Bibliography, ed. Dolores Gros-Louis (Bloomington: Indiana Univ. Press). In preparation.
   Biographical Books, 1950-1980 (W1084)
   Biography Index (W1085)
   Black Americans in Autobiography (P870.1)
   Cinema Booklist (W1230)
   Literature of the Film (W1232)
   Prose Studies (G105)
   Survey of Contemporary Literature (J518)
   Twentieth Century British Literature (J512)

Awards

W1060.   *Grants and Awards Available to American Writers.* 12th ed. New York: P.E.N. American Center, 1982–83. 79pp. PN171.P75.G73   001.4'4
   For $$$$$$. If your work has been recognized by a periodical or critic as possessing quality and promise, if you have had some training, if you have lots of courage and determination, write to P.E.N. American Center, 156 Fifth Avenue, New York, NY 10010, enclose two dollars, and consider their suggestions. Also available: *Grants and Awards Available to Foreign Writers* (1973).

W1061. *Awards, Honors, and Prizes: An International Directory*. Ed. Paul
    Wasserman. 5th ed. 2 vols. Detroit: Gale, 1982. AS8.W38 001.4'4
    Vol. 1 describes over five thousand awards in the United States and Canada
for literature, art, film, religion, and all fields in which people attempt to excel,
including MLA's James Russell Lowell prize, the *Explicator* award, and the Martin
Luther King, Jr., award. The second volume gives information on awards granted
by over sixty other countries. Names of donors and information on eligibility
are provided for the optimistic reader. Two supplements keep it up to date.
    Access is easiest through the subject index. Under "Literature," for instance,
is a reference to the Brandeis University award for outstanding contributions
to the fine arts, music, literature, and theater arts ($1,000 for each category).

W1062. *Literary and Library Prizes*. Ed. Olga S. Weber and Stephen J. Calvert.
    10th ed. New York: Bowker, 1980. 651pp. PN171.P75.L5 807.9
    The best source for names of several thousand authors and librarians who
have won prizes during the past few decades. The 450 international awards are
described, the requirements explained, and the value cited. Aspiring young
authors should look here. There might be some money in it.

See also

    Grants Register (W1217)
    PMLA (H152), Sept. issue, Fellowships and Grants
    Scholarships, Fellowships and Loans News Service (W1220)

Bibliography—Books and Printing

Basic sources

*W1064. Gaskell, Philip. *A New Introduction to Bibliography*. New York: Ox-
    ford Univ. Press, 1972; corrected rpt. 1979. Z116.A2.G27 686.2'09
    A worthy successor to the half-century reign of McKerrow's *Introduction
to Bibliography* (W1065). At the earliest opportunity, graduate students in
methods of research courses and specialists in bibliography should read this exhaustive survey of printing practices and problems. It is an accepted text for
graduate courses because it covers almost five centuries of hand- and machine-
press printing information (1500–1800, 1800–1950), cites numerous examples
and problems, features many illustrations, and provides bibliographic essays for
further studies on all subjects relating to book production and the determination of a text in its most accurate form. Its special value is its simple explanation
of the difficult technique of analytical bibliography. This is a sorely needed bit
of scholarship, and it is extremely well done.

*W1065. McKerrow, Ronald B. *An Introduction to Bibliography for Literary
    Students*. Oxford: Clarendon, 1967, c1927. 359pp. Z1001.M16 010
    For many years this was the undisputed definitive study of analytical

bibliography, "the relation of the printed book to the written word of the author." Focusing mainly on the Shakespearean period, McKerrow examines the mechanical side of book production in order to detect the problems and pitfalls experienced during the transition from manuscript to printed text.

All serious students of literature should become familiar with this. They will need to understand McKerrow's bibliographical terms and his definitions for the parts of a book (catchword, colophon, foliation), the printing process, problems of dating, distinction between editions, compositors' errors, and decoration. Of particular value are the appendixes on the most famous publishing houses, development of different kinds of type, abbreviations and contractions used in early books, techniques of using color, and Elizabethan handwriting. There is no adequate substitute for this indispensable reference book, although Gaskell's *New Introduction to Bibliography* (W1064) contains the discoveries and wisdom of more recent scholarship.

*W1066. Bowers, Fredson T. *Principles of Bibliographical Description*. Princeton: Princeton Univ. Press, 1949; rpt. New York: Russell, 1962. 505pp. Z1001.B78   010.1

Scholars may quibble about some minor points, but in general this is still the definitive statement on the procedure and problems of constructing accurate bibliographical descriptions. What begins as science—recording the physical makeup of a book—results in art, for the facts are then used as a basis for authoritative textual analysis, the accumulation of valuable library holdings, and the study of literary and publishing history. Not for the dilettante, however; only the scholar with time, patience, and the desire to be *sure*.

W1067. *Esdaile's Manual of Bibliography*. Ed. Roy Stokes. 5th ed. Metuchen, N.J.: Scarecrow, 1981. 417pp. Z1001.E75   010

The fifth edition of the classic by Arundell Esdaile, still important for its historical survey of "the book"—the materials, machines, and people responsible for its existence.

W1068. Blumenthal, Joseph. *The Printed Book in America*. Boston: Godine, 1977. 250pp. Z208.B56   686.2'0973

A fine survey of the art of printing in America written by a distinguished craftsman with anecdotes, numerous plates, a five-page bibliography, and a thorough index. See also Blumenthal's *Art of the Printed Book, 1455-1955* (Boston: Godine, 1973; 192pp.).

Identification problems

*W1069. Glaister, Geoffrey A. *Glaister's Glossary of the Book: Terms Used in Papermaking, Printing, Bookbinding and Publishing, with Notes on Illuminated Manuscripts and Private Presses*. 2nd ed. Berkeley: Univ. of California Press, 1979. 551pp. Former title: *Encyclopedia of the Book*. Z118.G55   655.03

An indispensable source of well-illustrated, authoritative information on over four thousand terms that are frequently heard in the literature classroom:

Richard Tottel, the Three Mountains Press, Kelmscott Press, *Book of Kells*, illumination process, offprints, the Mazarin Bible, Stationers' Company, quarto, woodcut, proof correction symbols, and hundreds more. *TLS* (W1563) judges the glossary "a prodigious achievement."

W1070. *Bookman's Glossary*. Ed. Jean Peters. 6th ed. New York: Bowker, 1983. 223pp. Z118.B75   010'.3
The elusive item might be found here: antiquarian book trade definitions, foreign phrases, computerized typesetting jargon, bookselling terms, proper names, everything from "AAs" to "zinco" (a type of etching). The list of recommended reading is helpful, and the table of proofreader's marks is excellent. Teachers who grade papers and students who write them should memorize it.

Series

W1071.   Great Bibliographers' Series. Metuchen, N.J.: Scarecrow, 1974– .
Each volume is a collection of essays by a famous bibliographer on the theory, practice, and problems of bibliographic research. Colleagues wrote the accompanying biographical sketches and assessments, and the bibliography of the subject's works is usually the only acceptable one in existence even though in some cases sharp criticism has been leveled against its accuracy and arrangement. Volumes have been completed on Ronald B. McKerrow, Alfred W. Pollard, Thomas F. Dibdin, Douglas C. McMurtrie, and Michael Sadleir; forthcoming volumes will focus on William Blades, Henry Bradshaw, and Fielding Garrison. A welcome testimonial to deserving scholars.

Indexes

*W1072. *Annual Bibliography of the History of the Printed Book and Libraries*. The Hague: Nijhoff, 1973– . Annual. Z117.A55   016.00155'2
An annual international bibliography of books, reviews, and articles from about four thousand periodicals on the history of books and libraries, printing and publishing, illustrating, binding, collecting, and all other aspects of the art. Arranged by subject, with a name index that encourages studies of specific writers. Like all other bibliographies, this has the inevitable human errors and judgmental omissions, so students would be wise to consult other sources if they are trying to solve a troublesome bibliographical problem. They might consult *Studies in Bibliography* (W1076) for pre-1973 scholarship, for instance, and *ABELL* (D32) for current coverage because of its numerous means of access by author, century, subject, and subject subdivisions. They should also try *MLAIB* (D31), *Hum. Ind.* (F45), and *Brit. Hum. Ind.* (F49).

Periodicals

W1073.   *AEB: Analytical and Enumerative Bibliography*. DeKalb: Northern Illinois Univ., 1977– . Quarterly. Bibliographical Soc. of Northern Illinois. Z1007.A115   016.05
Scholarly articles, notes, and reviews on analytical and enumerative bibliography, textual criticism, textual studies, editorial problems, and publishing

history. Its annual index to reviews of bibliographical publications is now published separately (see W1569 for an annotation).
Indexed in *Am. Hum. Ind.* (P738), *MLAIB* (D31).

*W1074. *Library: Transactions of the Bibliographical Society.* London: Oxford Univ. Press, 1899– . Quarterly. Z671.L69   010.5
The patriarch in matters bibliographical. Articles on McKerrow's and Greg's ideas of the substantive edition, on the fallacy of the "ideal" copy, and on lost books of Tudor England; bibliographical notes on corruptions, coauthorships, presses, and variants; mercilessly honest comments on recent books; lists of important articles in recent periodicals. Basic to any book collector.
Indexed in *ABELL* (D32), *Arts and Hum. Cit. Ind.* (F47), *Index to Bk. Rev. Hum.* (W1560), *Lib. Info. Sci. Abst.* (E43), *Lib. Lit.* (F53), *MLAIB* (D31).

*W1075. *Papers of the Bibliographical Society of America (PBSA).* New York: BSA, 1904– . Quarterly. Z1008.B51.P   010.6
Influential scholarship on every phase of bibliography has appeared in this journal, the most respected of the American publications.
Indexed in *ABELL* (D32), *Abst. Eng. Stud.* (E38), *Arts and Hum. Cit. Ind.* (F47), *Current Bk. Rev. Cit.* (W1564), *Hum. Ind.* (F45), *Index to Bk. Rev. Hum.* (W1560), *Lib. Info. Sci. Abst.* (E43), *Lib. Lit.* (F53), *MLAIB* (D31), *Romantic Movement: A . . . Bibliography* (J443).

*W1076. *Studies in Bibliography (SB).* Charlottesville: Univ. Press of Virginia, 1949– . Annual. Z1008.V55   010.6275549
Interested especially in analytical bibliography, with many articles and notes on the history, printing, editing, and description of books, the unpredictable inadequacies of compositors, editorial decisions concerning authorial errors, newly discovered manuscripts, the vagaries of booksellers, and similar problem areas. During the years 1949–71 it featured an annual, international checklist of bibliographical scholarship that was the best available at that time. When it ceased, the *Annual Bibliography of the History of the Printed Book* (W1072) picked up and expanded the coverage. At the present time *ABELL* (D32) is considered the best source for scholarship on bibliographical matters. In 1976, 1977, and 1978 *SB* published additions and corrections for the second edition of Wing (J370). Several articles by G. Thomas Tanselle that originally appeared here are now available in one convenient volume: *Selected Studies in Bibliography* (Charlottesville: Univ. Press of Virginia, 1979; 506pp.).
Indexed in *ABELL* (D32), *Abst. Eng. Stud.* (E38), *MLAIB* (D31).

Background reading

W1078.   Dunkin, Paul S. *Bibliography: Tiger or Fat Cat?* Hamden, Conn.: Archon, 1975. 120pp. Z1001.D83   010
This clever treatise on analytical bibliography will dismay some professors and delight all students.

Additional reference sources
—that may contain further scholarship on books and bibliography or that are customarily used in conjunction with the above titles:

W1079. *ABELL* (D32)
Blanck, *Bibliography of American Literature* (P713)
Book Collecting (W1153-69)
Bowers, Fredson T. "Greg's 'Rationale of Copy-Text' Revisited." *SB* 31 (1978), 90-161. See *SB* (W1076)
Bulletin of Bibliography (C29)
Center for Editions of American Authors (W1177)
Center for Scholarly Editions (W1179)
Editing the Middle English Manuscript (W1615)
Evans, *American Bibliography* (P717)
Goff, *Incunabula in American Libraries* (J261)
Illustrators (W1297-99)
Index to Reviews of Bibliographical Publications (W1569)
Literary Research Newsletter (W1421)
MLAIB (D31), vol. 1, General V, and national subdivisions
Proof (P760)
Publishers and Publishing (W1514-25)
Regents Renaissance Drama Series (J342)
Regents Restoration Drama Series (J402)
Resources for American Literary Study (P761)
Short-Title Catalogue, 1475-1640 (J306)
Short-Title Catalogue, 1641-1700 (J370)
Tanselle, G. Thomas. "The Concept of Ideal Copy." *SB* 33 (1980), 18-53. See *SB* (W1076)
———. "Recent Editorial Discussion and the Central Questions of Editing." *SB* 34 (1981), 23-65. See *SB* (W1076)
Textual Criticism (W1610-23)

Biography
For a detailed outline of the subject headings and titles discussed in this section, see the Short-Title Table of Contents in the front of this guide. In general, the arrangement proceeds from the most commonly used and most easily available to the more specific needs of various disciplines and professions.

Because there are literally dozens of different kinds of biographical dictionaries, you must

1.   FIRST examine the KNOWN FACTS about the person you are investigating (dates, nationality, profession; alive or dead, famous or obscure, man or woman);
2.   THEN consider the TYPE OF INFORMATION that you need (brief facts, historical survey, lengthy discussion, list of critical works, contemporary

opinion); and

3.   FINALLY, you must decide what TYPE of book will give you the information you need (comprehensive encyclopedia, specialized
biographical dictionary, bibliography, directory, index, periodical,
annual).

IF you know nothing about your subject except the name and the probability of
historical importance,
IF you need only a few brief facts,
IF you have very little time,

THEN you will look in a GENERAL source that has BROAD coverage, like one of the
following titles:

*W1080. *Webster's Biographical Dictionary*. Springfield, Mass.: Merriam, 1980.
1697pp. CT103.W4   920'.02
    The most respected one-volume source for brief biographical information
on about forty thousand important people of all periods, races, nationalities,
religions, and occupations. Some entries include information as recent as the
mid-1970s but others need to be brought up to date. It includes, for instance,
Chou En-lai, Joan of Arc, Machiavelli, and Jimmy Carter, but not Golda Meir.
The tables in back of the book are a convenient source for the names of notable
persons in many countries: diplomatic agents to Great Britain, justices of the
Supreme Court, members of the Hall of Fame for Great Americans, rulers of
England and Scotland, prime ministers, popes, and poets laureate. This is also
a good source for pronunciation of unfamiliar names such as John Keble (ē)
and T. E. Hulme (hūm).

W1081. *New Century Cyclopedia of Names*. 3 vols. New York: Appleton,
1954; rpt. Englewood Cliffs, N.J.: Prentice-Hall, 1977.   AG5.N28
909
    Valuable because of its unusually comprehensive scope. Brief entries on
over 100,000 names, places, historical events, literary works and characters, works
of art, mythological references, and legendary persons and places, with the important added feature of pronunciation for all names.

W1082. *McGraw-Hill Encyclopedia of World Biography*. 12 vols. New York:
McGraw-Hill, 1973. CT103.M27   920'.02
    This attractive, comprehensive work is designed for undergraduates and
families. The appearance invites browsing: large white pages with clear type,
numerous photographs and illustrations. The contents invite repeated use: one-
page biographical sketches, signed entries, evaluations of selected best sources
for further study, and an interest in all centuries, countries, and professions.
Coverage includes Bierce, Billy the Kid, Bizet, James Baldwin, Arnold (Matthew and Hap), and Armstrong (Louis and Neil). This is a good example of
the recent trend in publishing to couch scholarship and learning in format and
terms that will encourage further scholarship and learning.

W1083.   *Webster's American Biographies.* Ed. Charles Van Doren. Springfield,
Mass.: Merriam, 1979. 1233pp. CT213.V36   920'.073

A popular source for information on popular Americans, living and dead.
The Kellys explain it all: entries for Ellsworth (the painter), William (Bessemer
steel process), Emmett (clown), Grace (the princess and actress), Walt (the
"Pogo" cartoonist), and "Shipwreck" (the flagpole sitter). Not a complement
to the *DAB* (W1087), to be sure, but it does include women, Westerners, Indians, and Afro-Americans, so it might be useful.

IF you have time to read an entire biography but do not know which one, or even
which person, to select,
THEN this is the book you may need:

W1084.   *Biographical Books, 1950-1980.* Ed. Gertrude Jennings. New York:
Bowker, 1980. 1557pp. Z5301.B68   [CT104]   016.92'002

Biographical Books, 1876-1949. 1983. 1400pp.

These index over 75,000 full-length biographies, autobiographies, letters,
and journals concerning over 30,000 persons, with full bibliographical data so
the reader can purchase or borrow the book. Author, title, and vocation index.

IF your subject is A GROUP OF PERSONS (such as Irish authors) rather than an individual or
IF you need guidance in selecting the biographical dictionary that will be most
appropriate for your needs,

THEN you might want to use the librarian's favorite source:

*W1084.1 Slocum, Robert B. *Biographical Dictionaries and Related Works: An
International Bibliography of Collective Biographies, Bio-Bibliog-
raphies, Collections of Epitaphs, Selected Genealogical Works, Dictionaries of Anonyms and Pseudonyms, Historical and Specialized
Dictionaries, Biographical Materials in Government Manuals,
Bibliographies of Biography, Biographical Indexes, and Selected Portrait Catalogs.* Detroit: Gale, 1967. 1056pp. Supplement 1 (1972),
852pp. Supplement 2 (1978), 922pp. Z5301.S55   016.92

The scope of this briefly annotated guide to twelve thousand biographical
dictionaries is explained by a long subtitle of the sort that Gale fancies for many
of its publications. The book is extraordinarily easy to use because of (1) its arrangement by country (from Afghanistan to Yugoslavia) and vocation (from the
arts to technology) and (2) its enormous author, title, and subject indexes with
entries such as "Irish authors" and "Missionaries." This will not help you if
you need specific books on Sherwood Anderson; it *will* help you if you want
general biographical dictionaries about famous men from Ohio (Cleveland or
Cincinnati but not Camden). And it *will* help you if you want books about
authors from Kentucky, West Virginia, or Iowa, poets from Michigan, or a
Nebraska literary map and guide (all of which were published in the 1960s).
No cumulated index, unfortunately, so the reader must consult all three volumes.

IF you want COMPREHENSIVE biographical information from books or articles about   people, no matter who they were, what their profession was, or when or   where they lived,
IF you are making a SURVEY OF TRENDS over the last thirty years,
IF you need a RECENT biographical study,

THEN this is probably the best source to use:

*W1085. *Biography Index: A Cumulative Index to Biographical Material in Books and Magazines.* New York: Wilson, 1946–   . Quarterly, with annual and three-year cumulations. Z5301.B5   016.92
    A quarterly index that locates biographical material in current books in English and in about 2,600 periodicals, arranges it by subject, and provides profession and occupation indexes in each volume. If students have to find, for instance, a list of the most recent articles, books, and essays about the life of Alexander Solzhenitsyn or William Blake, they should use this source. It is a good place to begin, too, if they know nothing except that the person has gained some fame in sports or politics, the arts or the sciences, modern times or ancient Greece, Tulsa or Timbuktu.
    Coverage includes all pure biographies, critical material of biographical significance, autobiography, letters, obituaries, pictorial works, and juvenile literature. Works of collective biographies are fully analyzed, and biographical chapters in nonbiographical books are included—an eminently valuable feature. *Authors* (W1119) is a specialized source that also analyzes books for biographical information on literary figures.
    Because birth and death dates are always cited and because this is published quarterly, it is a good source for settling questions of exactly when (or if) a notable person died recently. It was one of the first reference books to record, for example, the deaths of Anaïs Nin, Paddy Chayefsky, Katherine Anne Porter, John Cheever, Roman Jakobson, Hannah Arendt, and Vladimir Nabokov. See also the *New York Times Index* (F50), *New York Times Obituaries Index* (W1148), and *Annual Obituary* (W1148) on this problem.

IF you are investigating FAMOUS ENGLISH MEN AND WOMEN—and if they are DEAD, THEN you may find them in this source:

*W1086. *Dictionary of National Biography* (*DNB*). Ed. Leslie Stephen and Sidney Lee. 21 vols. London: Smith, Elder, 1908–09; rpt. London: Oxford Univ. Press, 1937–38. Eight supplements, the latest of which extends coverage through 1970. DA28.D47   920.042
    The standard source for English biography from earliest times through 1970. The articles are scholarly, usually accurate, signed, and accompanied by bibliographies that frequently indicate the location of the subject's papers and memorabilia. All noteworthy inhabitants of the British Isles and colonies, including Americans of the Colonial period, are included. In the twentieth century only those persons who have made some distinct contribution to history and who have died are included. Whether the student needs concise, authoritative information on the life and contributions of Cardinal Wolsey, Lady

Lucy, Countess of Bedford, Beerbohm, Belloc, T. S. Eliot, Bertrand Russell, or Virginia Woolf, this is the source to consult. The latest supplement to the *DNB* contains entries for 745 persons who died between 1961 and 1970. Like all previous supplements, it also contains a cumulative index from 1901.

The Concise Dictionary of National Biography, 2nd ed. (London: Oxford Univ. Press, 1974–82; 2 vols.) provides quick access to the many volumes and supplements, vol. 1 covering from the beginnings to 1900, and vol. 2 from 1901 through 1970.

Latest corrections and additions for the years 1923–66 have been cumulated from the *Bulletin of the Institute of Historical Research* (Boston: Hall, 1969; 212pp.). May this quell, at least temporarily, the triumphant indignation of those few critics who revel in finding a bent straw in the haystack.

Some of the biographies in the *DNB* have been updated and revised in the light of twentieth-century research in a potentially valuable series that is complete with recent bibliographies, indexes, and photographs (see *Lives*, W1144). Its reliability has yet to be tested with extensive use, however.

IF you are investigating FAMOUS AMERICANS—and if they are DEAD, THEN this source may give you the information you need:

W1087.   *Dictionary of American Biography (DAB)*. New York: Scribners, 1928–58. 20 vols. with index and seven supplements, the latest of which (1981) extends coverage through 1965. *Concise DAB*, 3rd ed. complete to 1960 (1980), 1333pp. E176.D563   920'.073

Reliable biographical information on over seventeen thousand deceased persons who have made significant contributions to the history and culture of America. As in the *DNB* (W1086), the entries are written and signed by authorities who have the knowledge and skill to make historical assessments. Each entry has a bibliography to aid further research, and many note the location of manuscripts. The most recent supplement includes a cumulated index for all twentieth-century biographees.

Other ways to approach the persons discussed in the main volumes are suggested by several indexes which are arranged by birthplace, schools attended, profession, topic, and contributor. Beginning with the sixth supplement, coverage is extended to persons from film, sports, jazz, and the sciences. The *DAB* now honors such a variety of names as George Lyman Kittredge, Alexander Woollcott, Hendrik Van Loon, Ida Tarbell, George Patton, John Livingston Lowes, Ellen Glasgow, Lou Gehrig, Theodore Dreiser, George Washington Carver, Stephen Vincent Benét, Robert Benchley, George Ade, W. E. B. Du Bois, Max Weber, E. M. Forster, Ian Fleming, and John Dover Wilson.

An earlier work by the same title is unparalleled for identification of minor nineteenth-century figures, including their pseudonyms (subtitled *Including Men of the Time*: Boston: Osgood, 1872; rpt. Detroit: Gale, 1974; 1019pp.). The third abridged version of the *DAB* and its first six supplements through 1960 are certainly useful in the office and home, but unfortunately they place the 1951–60 biographies in a separate alphabetical listing. An index to the basic set and the first seven supplements is now available in paperback.

IF you are investigating a FAMOUS AMERICAN WOMAN—and if she is DEAD, THEN you may be able to locate some biographical information in this source:

*W1088. *Notable American Women, 1607-1950: A Biographical Dictionary.* Ed. Edward T. James and Janet W. James. 3 vols. Boston: Belknap, 1971. Paperback, 1974. CT3260.N57   920.72'0973

   Vol. 4: *The Modern Period.* Ed. Barbara Sicherman and Carol Hurd Green. 1980. 800pp. Paperback. CT3260.N573   920.72'0973

Modeled after the *DAB* (W1087), which included only seven hundred women when the first three volumes were published in 1971 with fifteen thousand entries. Vol. 4 was sponsored by NEH to extend coverage to women who died between 1951 and 1975. Feminists and authors of history and historical fiction will be especially pleased that this now provides long, scholarly studies ranging from Virginia Dare (born 1587 in Virginia) to Mary Baker Eddy, Margaret Mitchell, Eleanor Roosevelt, Plath, Sandoz, O'Connor, Hurston, Suckow, Hansberry, Wilder, Sexton, Gilbreth, Cadilla de Martínez, and almost eighteen hundred other women of whom the world can be justly proud. The historical survey by Janet W. James traces the determined efforts of these women to enter professions, hold offices, and gain the respect that has so often been denied them. See also Women's Studies (W1630–49.1).

IF you need BRIEF FACTS on some CURRENTLY IMPORTANT person,
IF you are not sure of the nationality or profession,
IF you do not know which biographical dictionary to use,

THEN this may be the shortcut you need:

W1089. *Biographical Dictionaries Master Index.* Ed. Dennis La Beau and Gary C. Tarbert. 3 vols. Detroit: Gale, 1975-77. Supplement 1 (1979), 638pp. Supplement 2 (1980), 450pp. Z5305.U5.B56   920'.073
   Over one million celebrities in one hundred biographical dictionaries are indexed here so that the researcher can tell immediately whether to go to one of the fifty *Who's Who* publications (W1091-1113) or to a source that focuses on a specific profession. Search in a *specific* biographical dictionary is usually preferred if the discipline is known. Use the *American and British Theatrical Biography* (W1138), for instance, if the person in question is in the theater.
   For certain identification problems, this is unquestionably a first source. Keep in mind that it emphasizes living Americans and that it overlaps the coverage of *Index to All Books* (Chicago: Marquis, 1984; 2 vols.), which is a guide to ten *Who's Who* publications.
   The publisher of the *Master Index* has also produced an eight-volume work that it states is the index's second edition with a different title: *Biography and Genealogy Master Index: A Guide to More Than 3,200,000 Listings in Over 350 Current and Retrospective Who's Who and Other Works of Collective Biography* (1980-81), and Supplements (5 vols., 1981-83), ed. Miranda C. Herbert and Barbara McNeil. The supplements add 1,630,000 citations. Reviewers have objected both to the price ($750 plus $385 for the supplements)

and to the size, claiming that most libraries not only will be unable to afford such a purchase but also will not own most of the 350 biographical dictionaries indexed. Over half of the indexed titles are important enough to be listed in Sheehy (A5), however, and eighty-four percent of the entries lead to those books that Sheehy lists. Furthermore, seventy-two percent of the names are identified in only one biographical dictionary, so the second edition does indeed make a notable contribution to identification. Emphasis is on the United States, but there is some coverage of Canada, Africa, and Australasia.

IF the person you are investigating is currently ALIVE and WELL-KNOWN,
IF you know the nationality or profession,
IF you need only BRIEF FACTUAL INFORMATION,

THEN you should look for the *Who's Who* type of biographical dictionary that contains vital statistics but no evaluation. If you do not know which *Who's Who* to use, see if your library owns *Index to All Books* (W1089) or *Biographical Dictionaries Master Index* (W1089). Both are guides to *Who's Who* publications and may contain the name of your subject.

W1091. *Who's Who.* London: Black, 1849– . Annual. DA28.W6   920'.042
  This generally does not include Americans. Most of its subjects are English, but a few persons from the Continent are mentioned.

W1092. *Who's Who in America.* Chicago: Marquis, 1899– . Annual (42nd ed., 2 vols., 1982–83). E663.W56   920.073
  The best source for current information about important Americans and some famous international persons. It now also includes a list of people covered by the regional volumes for the United States, such as *Who's Who in the Southeast.* Professional and geographic area index (1982).

W1093. *Who's Who in American Politics.* New York: Bowker, 1967– . Biennial. E176.W6424   320'.0922

W1094. *Who's Who of American Women.* Chicago: Marquis, 1958– . Biennial. E176.W647   920.72'0973

W1095. *Who's Who among Black Americans.* 2nd ed. Northbrook, Ill.: n.p. (3202 Doolittle Drive), 1978. E185.96.W52   920'.073

W1096. *International Who's Who.* London: Europa, 1935– . Annual (47th ed., 1983–84). CT120.I5   920.01
  The best one-volume biographical dictionary for internationally famous people of all professions. It is of course particularly useful for those countries without a national *Who's Who.*

W1097. *Who's Who in the USSR.* 2nd ed. New York: Scarecrow, 1966. 1189pp. DK275.A1.W53   920.047   See also W1108.

W1098.   *Who's Who in the Theatre: A Biographical Record of the Contemporary Stage.* Ed. Ian Herbert. 17th ed. 2 vols. Detroit: Gale, 1981. Supplements (1982, 1983), with cumulative index. PN2012.W5

W1099.   *Who's Who in African Literature: Biographies, Works, Commentaries.* Tübingen: Erdmann, 1972. 406pp. PL8010.J33   809.896
In addition to the expected *Who's Who* features, this provides photographs, an important appendix arranged by language and by country, and lists of histories and surveys for the student who wants to do further research on these 420 African authors. Good format, carefully edited.

W1100.   *International Authors and Writers Who's Who.* 9th ed. Detroit: Gale, 1982. 1093pp.   Z1010.I57   808
Personal and career information on twelve thousand authors, including the poets who were previously listed in the following entry.

W1101.   *International Who's Who in Poetry.* 5th ed. Totowa, N.J.: Rowman, 1977. 750pp. PS324.I5   928
Important appendixes of poets laureate, awards, recordings, societies. In 1982 this publication was incorporated into the ninth edition of *International Authors and Writers Who's Who* (W1100).

W1102.   *Who's Who in American Art.* 14th ed. New York: Bowker, 1980. 977pp. N6536.W5   709'.22
Currently active American, Canadian, and some foreign artists, collectors, museum officials, and patrons. Index by state and city, and index of exhibitions. Cumulative necrology.

W1103.   *International Who's Who in Music and Musicians' Directory.* 9th ed. Detroit: Gale, 1980. 960pp. ML106.G7.W4   780'.92'2
Especially useful for locating facts about twentieth-century European composers not included in Baker (W1445), Thompson (W1450), Anderson (W1451), or Vinton (W1452).

The *Who's Who* type of biographical dictionary has proven to be so useful that publishers are now including historical figures and literary characters:

W1105.   *Who's Who in the New Testament.* New York: Holt, 1971. 448pp. Paperback (1977). BS2430.B67   225.92'2

W1106.   *Who's Who in the Old Testament.* New York: Holt, 1971. 448pp. Paperback (1977). BS2430.B67   225.92'2

W1107.   Fines, John. *Who's Who in the Middle Ages.* New York: Stein and Day, 1980, c1970. 218pp. Paperback. D115.F5   940.1'0922
Pleasant reading, witty, informal, but not well documented, so there is no way to distinguish fact from fiction.

W1108. *Who Was Who in the USSR*. Metuchen, N.J.: Scarecrow, 1972. 677pp. CT1212.I57   920.047   See also W1097.

W1109. *Who Was Who on Screen*. 3rd ed. New York: Bowker, 1983. 788pp. PN1998.A2.T73   791.43'028'0922

W1110. *Who Was Who in the Theatre, 1912-1976*. 4 vols. Detroit: Gale, 1978. PN2597.W52   792'.028'0922

W1111. *Who Was Who among English and European Authors, 1931-1949*. 3 vols. Detroit: Gale, 1978. PN451.W5   809'.043

W1112. *Who's Who in Dickens*. Ed. John Greaves. London: Elm Tone, 1972. 232pp. PR4589.G75   823.8

W1113. *Who's Who in Shakespeare*. Ed. Peter Quennell and Hamish Johnson. New York: Morrow, 1973. 288pp. PR2989.Q4   822.3'3

————and many other *Who's Who* sources designed for specific regions, eras, or professions.

IF you are investigating persons whose accomplishments since 1940 have been NEWSWORTHY, and
IF they are prominent in a PROFESSION such as politics, sports, education, movies, science, business, or the arts,

THEN they will probably be included in this popular reference book:

*W1115. *Current Biography*. New York: Wilson, 1940– . Monthly except December, with annual cumulations. CT100.C8   920.02
   This work has a specific and limited purpose: to provide biographical information on people currently in the news, whether they are important in the arts, religion, science, business, politics, or sports. Students will enjoy reading the informal, brisk accounts. They will find, too, that this is usually the only source of information on currently newsworthy names. Each entry gives dates, pronunciation of the subject's name if it is difficult, photograph if available, and a summary of publications and contributions. Bibliographical information is provided for further study in books and popular magazines. Obituary references are included for the recently deceased.
   Since 1943 every volume has included a cumulative index that itself cumulates at 1950, 1960, 1970 and 1980. Since there is also a cumulative index for 1940–70, students are easily directed to the volume that includes information on their subject. Each volume is arranged alphabetically by name and has a profession index and necrology. Current information is thus always available on celebrities such as Jessamyn West, Wallace Stegner, Ansel Adams, Michael Landon, Alan Alda, Stephen Spender, Samuel Hayakawa, Andrew Young, John Fowles, Arthur Fiedler, Noam Chomsky, Jesse Jackson, Joyce Carol Oates, Ingmar Bergman, Robert Penn Warren, Donald Sutherland, and Elizabeth Hardwick.

IF you are investigating persons who are or have been PROMINENT in a PROFESSION, THEN you may be wise to look for a PROFESSIONAL BIOGRAPHICAL DICTIONARY such as those devoted to literature (W1117–34), theater (W1138–42), history (W1144), education (W1146–47), or other specific areas (W1152).

LITERATURE, for instance, has numerous specialized companions, handbooks, and directories that will contain brief factual data on literary figures:

W1116.   *Caribbean Writers* (R994)
Cassell's Encyclopaedia of World Literature (R953)
Dictionary of British and American Women Writers, 1660–1800 (W1641)
Dictionary of Italian Literature (Q929)
Dictionary of Oriental Literatures (R985)
Dictionary of Russian Literature (Q937)
Directory of American Poets and Fiction Writers (W1031)
Eight Scandinavian Novelists (Q939)
Guide to Eastern Literatures (R984)
Guide to Oriental Classics (R983)
Handbook of Austrian Literature (Q900)
Oxford Classical Dictionary (S1000)
Oxford Companion to American Literature (P736)
Oxford Companion to Canadian Literature (N670)
Oxford Companion to Children's Literature (W1181.2)
Oxford Companion to Classical Literature (S1001)
Oxford Companion to English Literature (J178)
Oxford Companion to French Literature (Q912)
Oxford Companion to German Literature (Q922)
Oxford Companion to Spanish Literature (Q945)
Oxford Companion to the Theatre (G117)
Oxford History of Australian Literature (N653)
Pelican Guides to European Literature (Q885)
Penguin Companion to European Literature (Q888)
Penguin Companion to . . . Oriental, and African Literature (R986)
Reader's Encyclopedia (W1402)
Southern Writers (P711)
Writers Directory (W1030)

Indexes of biographical material about authors

W1117.   *Author Biographies Master Index: A Consolidated Guide to Biographical Information concerning Authors Living and Dead as It Appears in a Selection of the Principal Biographical Dictionaries Devoted to Authors, Poets, Journalists, and Other Literary Figures.* Ed. Barbara McNeil and Miranda C. Herbert. 2nd ed. 2 vols. Detroit: Gale, 1984. Supplement 1 (1984), 700pp. Z5304.A8.A88   [PN452]   809'.016
This is obviously a central source. Use it to find out quickly which book to consult if the other titles in this section do not seem appropriate. It is the key to 300,000 authors of every era who are identified in 225 English-language biographical dictionaries, including the Oxford Companions, the Library of

Literary Criticism volumes, the Crowell handbooks (see Index), the Wilson volumes (W1124), *Contemporary Authors* (W1127), and dozens of specialized works on women, blacks, Catholics, Southerners, Irish, German, Latin American, Spanish, and Slavic literature, and others. Note that this does for all *writers* what *Biographical Dictionaries Master Index* (W1089) does for living Americans of other disciplines. Neither title pretends to lead to scholarship of any great depth, but both can be helpful in solving stubborn identification problems.

W1118. *Index to Literary Biography*. Ed. Patricia P. Havlice. 2 vols. Metuchen, N.J.: Scarecrow, 1975. First supplement, 1983. Z6511.H38 016.809

Overlaps to some extent with *Author Biographies Master Index* (W1117), but because Havlice used several foreign biographical dictionaries in her search for information on 68,000 authors, she identifies more individuals in that area. She also supplies the authors' nationality and area of specialization as well as the birth and death dates (as does *Biography Index*, W1085). The entry for Vachel Lindsay, for instance, identifies him as an American poet, 1879–1931, and then lists ten biographical dictionaries the student can consult for additional information. The supplement adds facts on 53,000 authors culled from fifty-seven reference books published between 1969 and 1981.

W1119. Combs, Richard E. *Authors: Critical and Biographical References, a Guide to 4700 Critical and Biographical Passages in Books*. Metuchen, N.J.: Scarecrow, 1971. 221pp. PN524.C58 016.809

Combs analyzes five hundred books for literary criticism and biographical material on fourteen hundred authors of all countries and centuries including Claudel, Coleridge, Bunyan, Dreiser, Genet, McCullers, Pasternak, Sophocles, and Turgenev. See also *Biography Index* (W1085) and *Essay and General Literature Index* (F46) for analyses of books.

General information on authors

*W1120. *Great Writers of the English Language*. Ed. James Vinson. 3 vols. New York: St. Martin's, 1979. PR106.G9 820'9

Like the Contemporary Writers Series (W1128–30, W1360), this is an appropriate source for students who need only an overview of an author's worth, a few biographical facts, a list of reliable biographies and critical works, and a brief assessment of the contribution to literature (about two pages in toto). The most famous novelists, poets, and dramatists from Chaucer to Hemingway are included here. This is as easy to use as *Webster's Dictionary*, and students should consult it with equal frequency, purpose, and satisfaction.

*W1121. *Dictionary of Literary Biography*. Ed. Matthew J. Bruccoli. Detroit: Gale, 1978– . In progress (1983, 40 vols. on American and English authors).

American Renaissance in New England is the first of a multivolume series that will cover several periods, movements, and nationalities. It will emphasize especially the research and trends developed since the publication, 1928–1936, of the *DAB* (W1087) and will supplement the basic information found in *Contemporary Authors* (W1127) with a more analytical and historical point of view.

This first volume includes almost one hundred biographical-critical entries, long essays on leading figures like Dickinson and Thoreau, chronologies,

photographs, facsimiles, a list of periodicals, and supplementary readings.
Vol. 2, *American Novelists since World War II* (1978) examines Cheever, Barthelme, Nabokov, O'Connor, Pynchon, Hawkes, and seventy others. The Second Series (vol. 6, 1980) includes Singer, Plath, Steadman, and many more.
Vol. 3, *Antebellum Writers in New York and the South* (1979) covers sixty-seven authors of the period 1820 to 1860, including minor figures such as Cooke, Beecher, Dana, and Timrod as well as Melville, Poe, and Whitman.
Vol. 4, *American Writers in Paris, 1920-1939* (1980) surveys the Lost Generation of ninety-nine great and small from Hemingway to Barney.
Vol. 5, *American Poets since World War II* (2 vols., 1980).
Vol. 7, *Twentieth-Century American Dramatists* (2 vols., 1981).
Vol. 8, *Twentieth-Century American Science Fiction Writers* (2 vols., 1981).
Vol. 9, *American Novelists, 1910-1945* (3 vols., 1981).
Vol. 10, *Modern British Dramatists, 1900-1945* (2 vols., 1982).
Vol. 11, *American Humorists, 1800-1950* (2 vols., 1982).
Vol. 12, *American Realists and Naturalists* (1982).
Vol. 13, *British Dramatists since World War II* (2 vols., 1983).
Vol. 14, *British Novelists since 1960* (2 vols., 1983).
Vol. 15, *Modern British Novelists, 1930-1959* (2 vols., 1983).
Vol. 16, *Beats: Literary Bohemians in Postwar America* (2 vols., 1983).
Vol. 17, *Twentieth-Century American Historians* (1983).
Vol. 18, *Victorian Novelists after 1885* (1983).
Vol. 19, *British Poets, 1880-1914* (1983).
Vol. 20, *British Poets, 1914-1945* (1983).
Vol. 21, *Victorian Novelists before 1885* (1983).
Vol. 22, *American Writers for Children, 1900-1960* (1983).
Vol. 23, *American Newspaper Journalists, 1873-1900* (1983).
Vol. 24, *American Colonial Writers, 1606-1734* (1984).
Vol. 25, *American Newspaper Journalists, 1901-1925* (1984).
Vol. 26, *American Screenwriters* (1984).
Each volume contains a cumulative index to all previous volumes. The final volume in the series will be a comprehensive index for all volumes.
In 1980 the publishers initiated the *Dictionary of Literary Biography Yearbook*. This updates some of the earlier entries with comments on their most recent writings and adds new entries on newly prominent authors such as William F. Buckley, Jr., Robert Fitzgerald, Nancy Hale, Stephen King, and Tillie Olsen. In 1984 the publishers announced a series on Italian literature since 1960.
The value of each individual entry of course depends on the skill and dedication of the contributing critics, most of whom are reputable scholars, but the project's goal is commendable—five thousand American authors, with other nationalities to follow. If editorial standards remain high, this could become the standard source to use until the *DAB* moves in with its final benediction.

*W1122. *Dictionary of Literature in the English Language from Chaucer to 1940.* Ed. Robin Myers. 2 vols. Oxford: Pergamon, 1970. National Book League. 968pp. Z2010.M9   016.82

Dictionary of Literature in the English Language from 1940-1970. Oxford: Pergamon, 1978.   519pp.   Z2010.M92 [PR471]

016.82'08'00914

Ostensibly a short-title checklist of primary works, this is actually a treasure chest of generally inaccessible biographical information. The 1970 volumes contain entries on 3,500 authors, from Chaucer and Benjamin Disraeli to the detective novelist John Dickson Carr, who have written in English, no matter where they lived—England, America, Belgium, Canada, Ceylon, China, Holland, India, New Zealand, South Africa, and other parts of the world. The 1978 volume ranges from Leon Edel, Irving Wallace, and William F. Buckley to Art Buchwald. It reports on more authors than does the St. Martin's Contemporary Writers Series (W1128-30, W1360), locating biographical and bibliographical information on authors of many small countries who are not well covered elsewhere. It also contains a list of literary prize winners (1940-73) and a list of literary journals arranged by country. Since the years 1940-70 are still in the process of being assessed for their literary and intellectual achievements, Myers' assessments are certain to be influential.

Arrangement of all three volumes is by author, with dates, pseudonyms, a brief biographical sketch, a chronological list of the most important bibliographies and first editions, and selected sources for further biographical information. Because the editor has provided a geographical and chronological index, as well as an author-title index, this source can answer questions such as "Who were the first writers in America?" and "Has South Africa produced many active authors during its political upheavals?" Coverage includes poets, dramatists, novelists, scientists, historians, lawyers, and statesmen who have contributed in some way to literary history.

W1123.   *Cyclopedia of World Authors*. Ed. Frank N. Magill et al. 3 vols. Rev. ed. Englewood Cliffs, N.J.: Salem, 1974. Alternate title: *Masterplots Cyclopedia of World Authors*. PN451.M36   803

Brief discussions of the lives and works of the 750 authors who are included in *Masterplots* (R955). This places them in their proper historical background and shows how their works relate to one another. It is certainly convenient for getting an overview of their contributions, even though some professors scorn it as too "popular" (and too easy to plagiarize).

Additional sources for information on authors

W1124.   The Wilson biographical dictionaries, which are found in most schools, are easy to use, but students must beware: The older publications occasionally contain inexact information.

.1   *American Authors, 1600-1900*. Ed. Stanley J. Kunitz and Howard Haycraft. New York: Wilson, 1938. 846pp. PS21.K8   928.1

.2   *British Authors before 1800*. Ed. Stanley J. Kunitz and Howard Haycraft. New York: Wilson, 1952. 584pp. PR105.K9   928.2

.3   *British Authors of the Nineteenth Century*. Ed. Stanley J. Kunitz and Howard Haycraft. New York: Wilson, 1936. 677pp. PR451.K8   928.2

.4   *European Authors, 1000-1900*. Ed. Stanley J. Kunitz and Vineta Colby. New York: Wilson, 1967. 1016pp. PN451.K8

.5 *Greek and Latin Authors, 800 B.C.–A.D. 1000: A Biographical Dictionary.* Ed. Michael Grant. New York: Wilson, 1980. 492pp. PA31.G7 880'.9 920

Biographical sketches, critical comments, chronological list of authors by century—all the information needed by beginning students. For criticism, see *Greek and Roman Authors* (S998) and *Ancient Writers: Greece and Rome* (S996).

.6 *Twentieth Century Authors.* Ed. Stanley J. Kunitz and Howard Haycraft. New York: Wilson, 1942. 1577pp. Supplement, ed. Stanley J. Kunitz and Vineta Colby (1955). Updated necrology, 1973. PN451.K84 809'.04

.7 *World Authors, 1950–70.* Ed. John Wakeman. New York: Wilson, 1975. 1593pp. Supplement, 1970–1975 (1980), 894pp. Supplement, 1975–80, ed. Vineta Colby, in preparation. PN451.W3 809'.04

Some authors wrote parts of their own entries, but all receive brief evaluations, and a few critical studies are suggested. The coverage of minor and foreign authors is a particularly important contribution because sheer economics precludes their appearance in most easily available biographical dictionaries.

See also

American Writers before 1800 (P712.4)
Fifty Western Writers (P712.3)

Biographical sources for nineteenth-century authors

W1125. Allibone, S. Austin. *A Critical Dictionary of English Literature and British and American Authors Living and Deceased from the Earliest Accounts to the Latter Half of the Nineteenth Century.* 2 vols. Philadelphia: Lippincott, 1886, c1854. Supplement, 1891. Z1224.A43 R928

This most enduring of the early biographical dictionaries is still used extensively and confidently for special problems such as the identification of minor authors and pseudonyms. About 46,000 persons are listed in the main volumes and another 37,000 in the supplement. The awesome introduction is actually a brief course in early English literary history, especially important because of its authentic nineteenth-century point of view. The author was, even at that time, complaining about the rapid rate of literary production, which he said rivaled the acceleration in speed of travel and mechanical inventions.

Biographical sources for twentieth-century authors

*W1126. *Who's Who in Twentieth-Century Literature.* Ed. Martin Seymour-Smith. New York: Holt, 1976. 414pp. PN451.S4

Written by a man who dares to say what he thinks: that Barth is "a crushing bore," that O'Connor is "a mind-haunting case," that Singer remains largely untranslated because "he is—like Borges—exquisitely sensitive on the subject of the mutilation of his texts." This, in other words, is not a typical *Who's Who* but a very personal (blunt, impassioned, perceptive, outrageous, sacrilegious, provocative) interpretation of the life and works of twentieth-century British, American, and European authors from Freud and Fromm to McLuhan and Rand, with numerous cross-references. You will enjoy this book.

*W1127. *Contemporary Authors: A Bio-Bibliographical Guide to Current Writers in Fiction, General Nonfiction, Poetry, Journalism, Drama, Motion Pictures, Television, and Other Fields.* Detroit: Gale, 1962– . Semiannual (vol. 110, 1984). Cumulative indexes. Z1224.C615 928.1

This is the best available source for up-to-date, accurate, concise information on contemporary authors and media personalities from many countries. The only criterion for admission is that the author must have had at least one book published by a reputable publisher or have made some contribution to the screen, television, radio, or newspaper. This is a logical source, therefore, for obscure or newly prominent persons. The brief sketches provide every kind of personal fact: education, family, positions, awards, a remarkably complete list of published books and articles, home address, hobbies, work in progress, films, many easily available sources for further study, and, perhaps most important of all, "Sidelights," an analysis of the author's literary contributions with comments by other writers as well as statements by the subject of the entry. It refutes, for instance, the persistent story that Beckett was Joyce's secretary, states that Erle Stanley Gardner's books sell twenty thousand a day including Sunday, and quotes Allen Ginsberg's religion as "Hindu-Buddhist-Jewish-Muslim-Christian."

The major assets are currency and accuracy. The semiannual issues keep current with newly established authors (about 3,500 are added each year), and the earliest volumes are being extensively revised to bring the information up to date. Every sketch in these revised volumes has been submitted to the author for verification of the facts, and the bibliographies and "Sidelights" have been expanded. In 1983 the editors claimed that their work covered 77,000 writers, many of whom are not found in any other biographical reference work.

Extremely easy to use. Look up the author's name in the latest cumulated index and go to the proper volume. Later volumes will, of course, have the more currently popular personalities such as Julia Child (food), Marcia Brown (children's literature), John Jacob Niles (folk songs), Fellini (film), Alex Haley (*Roots*), Earl Wilson (columnist), and Walter Cronkite (newscaster).

*W1128. *Contemporary Dramatists.* Ed. James Vinson and Daniel L. Kirkpatrick. 3rd ed. New York: St. Martin's, 1982. 1104pp. PR737.V5   822'.9'1409

Modern drama enthusiasts might begin their research with this convenient volume because it assembles basic facts on about three hundred world-renowned living playwrights: selected primary and secondary bibliographies, brief biographical information, comments by the authors themselves, and a one- or two-page evaluation of the themes, characters, locale, style, and worth. Necrology and title index. Reliable. Revised every five years. For similar coverage of other genres, see *Contemporary Novelists* (W1130), *Contemporary Poets* (W1129), *Contemporary Literary Critics* (W1360), and *Great Writers of the English Language* (W1120).

*W1129. *Contemporary Poets.* Ed. James Vinson. 3rd ed. New York: St. Martin's, 1980. 1804pp. Z2014.P7.C63 [PR603.C6] 821'.9'109

Extensive improvements over earlier editions include (1) the addition of many new poets for a total of 850, (2) the inclusion of recent biographies, critical works, collections of poems, and statements by the poets themselves, and (3) the deletion of those poets who have failed to fulfill their promise or who have died. Facts about accomplishments and evaluations of important poems (with frequent quotations to illustrate ideas and style) make this an especially helpful source for students who are struggling with a relatively unknown name. Like others in the Contemporary Writers Series (W1128 and W1130), this contains an appendix with evaluations and bibliographies of major post-war authors who have died but whose reputations are essentially contemporary. This overlaps somewhat with *Twentieth Century Writing* (J524). Students can also try *Contemporary Authors* (W1127), *Biography Index* (W1085), or other biographical dictionaries specializing in a specific century or genre.

*W1130. *Contemporary Novelists.* Ed. James Vinson. 3rd ed. New York: St. Martin's, 1982. 750pp. PR883.V55 823'.03

Brief biographical facts, bibliographies, location of manuscripts, authors' comments, and signed critical essays for six hundred novelists and short story writers who have published in English since 1940, including Updike, Bellow, Roth, Malamud, Algren, Salinger, Porter, Knowles, Heller, and Fowles.

That the information is both accurate and well written is not surprising. The contributors themselves are scholars and authors: Walter Allen, A. Norman Jeffares, Louis Rubin, Mark Schorer, and many more. Revised every five years. This might be a good place for students to begin their research even though it will not contain sufficient material for in-depth study.

Two bio-bibliographical dictionaries of specialized novelists have recently been edited by Vinson and Daniel L. Kirkpatrick: *Twentieth-Century Romance and Gothic Writers* and *Twentieth-Century Western Writers* (Detroit: Gale, 1982).

See also

Addresses (W1028–31)
Biographical Dictionary of Modern Yiddish Literature (W1539)
Encyclopedia of World Literature in the 20th Century (J523)
Longman Companion to Twentieth Century Literature (J525)
Twentieth Century Writing (J524)

Biographical sources for black authors

*W1131. *Black American Writers, Past and Present: A Biographical and Bibliographical Dictionary.* Ed. Theressa Gunnels Rush, Carol Fairbanks Myers, and Esther Spring Arata. 2 vols. Metuchen, N.J.: Scarecrow, 1975. Z1229.N39.R87 016.8108'08'96073

Neither comprehensive nor consistent in its treatment of about two thousand black American authors, but a very good beginning for a definitive biographical dictionary of the future. Students will find brief lists of the more important works by and about the authors, biographical information on some but not all of them, direct quotations from interviews and correspondence, and photographs. Authors include W. W. Brown (the first black American to earn his living by writing), Zora Neale Hurston (versatile, prolific, well-published, but still not granted the literary reputation she deserves), Gwendolyn Brooks, Chesnutt, Ossie Davis, Du Bois, Katherine Dunham, and hundreds more. Well edited and in some cases more complete than Turner's Goldentree Bibliography (P838).

W1132. *African Authors: A Companion to Black African Writing*. Ed. Donald E. Herdeck. 2nd ed. Washington, D.C.: Black Orpheus/Inscape, 1974. 605pp. PL8010.H38   809'.89'6
A variety of valuable materials not available in other sources. This contains bio-bibliographical sketches of six hundred authors writing in many languages, with photographs, a collection of critical essays, quotations, indexes by chronology, genre, country, and language. An interesting, readable book.

W1133. *Living Black American Authors: A Biographical Directory*. Ed. Ann A. Shockley and Sue P. Chandler. New York: Bowker, 1973. 220pp. PS153.N5.S5   810'.9'896073
"Directory" here means a compilation of vital statistics: dates, education, experience, publications, and address in *Who's Who* style. About 425 authors are included, from Jupiter Hammon and Phillis Wheatley in the eighteenth century to Don L. Lee, Sonia Sanchez, Arna Bontemps, and Nikki Giovanni in the twentieth. Title and black publisher indexes. Needs to be updated.

W1134. *Selected Black American Authors: An Illustrated Bio-Bibliography*. Ed. James A. Page. Boston: Hall, 1977. 398pp. PS153.N5.P3   810.9'896
About 450 of the most prominent black American writers from colonial times to the present are listed here with extensive factual information on their lives and works. Especially helpful: the suggestions to students for research projects. Title and subject indexes, photographs, addresses, and a list of sources for further research.

See also
Afro-American Fiction (P856)
Afro-American Novel (P859)
Black American Fiction (P857)
Black American Writers (P836)
Black Poets of the United States (P866)
Invisible Poets (P867)
Southern Writers: A Biographical Dictionary (P711)
Who's Who among Black Americans (W1095)
Who's Who in African Literature (W1099)
—and others in African literature (R972–82) and Afro-American Literature (P835–70)

Biographical sources for the theater

*W1138. *American and British Theatrical Biography: A Directory*. Ed. J. Peter
   Wearing. Metuchen, N.J.: Scarecrow, 1979. 1013pp. PN2285.W42
   792'.0295
   About fifty thousand people are identified here with stage names,
pseudonyms, dates, theatrical occupations, and titles of forty-eight additional
books where more biographical information may be obtained. There is no more
comprehensive master index on this subject. Coverage extends to all American
and British and some foreign personalities who have been connected in any way
with the theater. Well edited, with ample cross-references.

W1139. *Notable Names in the American Theatre*. 2nd ed. Detroit: Gale, 1977.
   1250pp. PN2285.N6   790.2'0973
   A revised edition of the respected *Biographical Encyclopedia and Who's
Who of the American Theatre*, this includes detailed biographical sketches of
about 2,600 theatrical figures, seventy percent of whom do not appear in *Who's
Who in the Theatre* (W1098). It includes a list of critical works for students
who need more information; a necrology of eight thousand persons connected
with the theater, from Aeschylus to John Garfield; an index of ten thousand
New York productions; year-by-year lists of awards; and essays explaining the
important theater companies. Almost everyone and everything of significance
can be found here, but certain sharp-eyed critics have noted a few omissions.

W1140. *National Playwrights Directory*. Ed. Phyllis Johnson Kaye. 2nd ed.
   Detroit: Gale, 1981. 507pp. PS129.K3   812'.025'73
   More than a directory, because, in addition to biographical sketches of about
five hundred living American dramatists from Abrash to Zugsmith, it gives brief
synopses of three thousand recent plays as well as production information for
interested drama groups (see also G109–10). This is also one of the few sources
that provide photographs (see *Encyclopedia of World Literature in the 20th Century*, J523; *African Authors*, W1132; *Current Biography*, W1115; and others
listed in the Index of this guide). Some important dramatists are not included,
however, so students may have to consult other sources. Title index.

*W1141. *Biographical Dictionary of Actors, Actresses, Musicians, Dancers,
   Managers, and Other Stage Personnel in London, 1660–1800*. Ed.
   Philip H. Highfill, Jr., et al. 12 vols. Carbondale: Southern Illinois
   Univ. Press, 1973–   . In progress. Vols. 1–2 (1973); 3–4 (1975); 5–6
   (1978); 7 (1982). PN2579.H5   790.2'092'2
   The publishers of *The London Stage, 1660–1800* (J400) have produced
another gold mine for research scholars. When completed, this will provide nearly
complete information on more than 8,500 people who were connected in any
way with theaters, operas, fairs, and concert halls of the Restoration and eighteenth century. The series is particularly notable for its engravings, drawings,
maps, theater plans, portraits, and views of London. Solid scholarship and
eminently readable. Scholars who are fretting for bibliographies will have to wait
for the final volume.

*W1142. *Contemporary American Theater Critics: A Directory and Anthology of Their Works.* Ed. M. E. Comtois and Lynn F. Miller. Metuchen, N.J.: Scarecrow, 1977. 979pp. PN1707.9.C6   792'.9

Everything is here for the theater buff who knows that the critics often make or break a play: facts about the American Theatre Critics Association; a list of books and articles about theater criticism in general; brief information (occasionally inaccurate) about the critics; reprints of their reviews of plays, musicals, films, and dance recitals as they appeared in journals and newspapers or were heard over radio and television; and good indexes of titles, authors, theater groups, and newspapers.

This is the only reference book devoted to biographies of and selected criticism by American theater critics. Browsing is a pleasure. Be on the alert for updating supplements.

See also

> *Crowell's Handbook of Contemporary Drama* (J561)
> *Oxford Companion to the Theatre* (G117)
> Performing Arts (W1468-72)
> *Who Was Who in the Theatre* (W1110)
> *Who's Who in the Theatre* (W1098)
> World Literature (R965-68, R970)

Biographical sources for history

*W1144. *Lives of the Tudor Age, 1485-1603.* Ed. Ann Hoffmann. London: Osprey, 1976- . DA317.H65   942.05'092'2

Using the *DNB* (W1086) as its primary source, this attractive (expensive) series brings up to date (more successfully in some cases than in others) the biographies of hundreds of persons who had an impact on their age. It is, therefore, a convenient first source for recent, generally accurate information from the late twentieth-century viewpoint. Some foreign figures. Each volume contains timely bibliographies, illustrations, and indexes of professions, titles, and all names mentioned in the text. Other volumes in the series:

> *Lives before the Tudors.* In preparation.
> *Lives of the Stuart Age, 1603-1714.* Ed. Edwin Riddell. 1976. 500pp. CT781.L35   920'.041
> *Lives of the Georgian Age, 1714-1837.* Ed. William Gould. 1978. 516pp. CT781.L35   920'.041
> *Lives of the Victorian Age.* In preparation.

For specific historical periods, see works such as the *Who Was Who* biographical dictionaries (W1105-11) and Allibone (W1125).

Biographical sources for education

*W1146. *Directory of American Scholars.* 8th ed. 4 vols. New York: Bowker, 1982. American Council of Learned Societies. LA2311.C23   923.733

About forty thousand biographies of United States and Canadian scholars in history, English, law, speech, drama, languages, linguistics, philosophy, and religion. Cross-references are provided for those with cross-disciplinary interests. Information is brief (area of specialization, birth, education, awards, positions, publications, and current address). Students trying to locate contemporary professors or authors in the humanities should look here as well as in the annual *PMLA* Directory of the MLA (W1029) and the *National Faculty Directory* (W1028). For example, the student could learn here that J. Hillis Miller, the noted Victorian critic, was, at the time this was printed, at Yale University. A geographic index lists the biographees with their areas of specialization.

W1147. *Academic Who's Who: University Teachers in the British Isles in the Arts, Education, and Social Sciences.* 2nd ed. Detroit: Gale, 1975. 784pp. L915.A658   001.3'092'2
Facts about the lives and professional achievements of professors in the British Isles.

IF your subjects are nationally or internationally FAMOUS,
IF they died DURING THE LAST CENTURY, and
IF you need a SHORT SUMMARY of their lives and accomplishments,

THEN you might find enough information in an obituaries index:

W1148. *New York Times Obituaries Index, 1858-1968.* New York: New York Times, 1970. 1136pp. Index II, 1969-1978 (1980), 131pp. CT213.N47 929.3
A computer-prepared list of over 353,000 obituaries of prominent people of the world. Students should consult this if they need to locate anything from a death date to brief biographical information or contemporary public opinion on notables of the past century, including T. S. Eliot, Randall Jarrell, Albert Schweitzer, Oscar Wilde, Charles Darwin, Albert Camus, and Robert Browning.
Recent death dates are often a sticky reference problem (quickly now, did the poet laureate Cecil Day Lewis die in 1977 or 1976?). The most convenient general, current sources for verification of such problems are the *New York Times Index* (F50), *Biography Index* (W1085), and *Annual Obituary* (New York: St. Martin's, 1981–   ). The next best is a specialized professional source such as *Index to Literary Biography* (W1118) or *Notable Names in the American Theatre* (W1139), which will not, however, provide you with the latest information.

W1149. *Obituaries from the* Times (London). Reading, Eng.: Newspaper Archive Developments, 1975–   . In progress. CT120.017   920'.02
Selected obituaries from the *Times* are now being compiled and reproduced in volume form. They are unaltered, unsigned, and very British in their eulogies to their heroic dead. This is an excellent source for contemporary objective evaluations and factual details on British and foreign celebrities, more than half of whom are not included in the *DNB* (W1086) or other easily accessible biographical dictionaries. Volumes published so far (1983) cover the years 1951-60, 1961-70, and 1971-75.

Periodicals concerned with biography as a genre

W1151. *Biography: An Interdisciplinary Quarterly*. Honolulu: Univ. Press of Hawaii, for the Biographical Research Center, 1978– . Quarterly.
CT100.B54 920'.005

Articles and reviews of biographical studies and reference materials, essays on the theory and methods of biography as a genre, and an annual bibliography of works about biography.

Indexed in *America* (E43), *Arts and Hum. Cit. Ind.* (F47), *Hist. Abst.* (E43), *MLAIB* (D31).

Additional biographical information

—may also be found in many titles listed in the sections on American literature (such as P721) and English literature (such as J180) as well as in the following reference books:

W1152. ADDRESSES (W1028–31)
AMERICAN INDIAN LITERATURE
   Indians of Today (P876)
   Reference Encyclopedia of the American Indian (P875)
ART
   Encyclopedia of World Art (W1038)
   McGraw-Hill Dictionary of Art (W1039)
   Oxford Companion to Art (1040)
   Who's Who in American Art (W1102)
AUTOBIOGRAPHIES (W1056–59)
BIBLIOGRAPHY
   Great Bibliographers' Series (W1071)
BIOGRAPHY as genre
   ABELL (D32)
   MLAIB (D31)
CANADIAN LITERATURE
   Dictionary of Canadian Biography (N671)
   Oxford Companion to Canadian History and Literature (N670)
CHILDREN'S LITERATURE
   Children's Authors and Illustrators (W1184)
   Oxford Companion to Children's Literature (W1181.2)
   Twentieth Century Children's Writers (W1181.1)
CLASSICAL LITERATURE
   Ancient Writers: Greece and Rome (S996)
   Crowell's Handbook of Classical Drama (S1002)
   Greek and Latin Authors (W1124.5)
   Oxford Classical Dictionary (S1000)
   Oxford Companion to Classical Literature (S1001)
   Who's Who in Greek and Roman Mythology (S1003)
DATES (W1199–1204)
FILM
   Actor Guide to the Talkies (W1250)
   Dictionary of Film Makers (W1248)
   Film Directors and Genre (W1236)

343

FILM (continued)
Filmgoer's Companion (W1245)
Oxford Companion to Film (W1244)
Who Was Who on Screen (W1109)
HISTORY
DAB (W1087)
DNB (W1086)
Dictionary of the Middle Ages (J247)
Encyclopedia of World History (W1292)
Oxford Companion to American History (W1294)
Webster's Guide to American History (W1295)
ILLUSTRATORS
Ray, *Illustrator and the Book in England* (W1297)
Book Illustrators in Eighteenth-Century England (W1298)
IRISH LITERATURE
Dictionary of Irish Biography (K590)
Dictionary of Irish Literature (K592)
Dictionary of Irish Writers (K591)
Irish Writers' Series (K589)
LITERARY CRITICISM
Contemporary American Theater Critics (W1142)
Contemporary Literary Critics (W1360)
Nineteenth-Century Literary Criticism (J421)
MUSIC
Baker's Biographical Dictionary of Musicians (W1445)
Contemporary American Composers (W1451)
Dictionary of Twentieth-Century Composers (W1450)
International Cyclopedia of Music and Musicians (W1447)
New Grove Dictionary of Music and Musicians (W1446)
New Oxford History of Music (W1443)
Oxford Companion to Music (W1448)
NEW ZEALAND LITERATURE
New Zealand Literature to 1977 (N694)
PHILOSOPHY
Encyclopedia of Philosophy (W1485)
PSYCHOLOGY
Encyclopedia of Psychology (W1510)
RELIGION
Dictionary of the Bible (W1548)
Encyclopaedia of Religion and Ethics (W1542)
Encyclopedia Judaica (W1544)
International Standard Bible Encyclopedia (W1546)
New Catholic Encyclopedia (W1543)
Oxford Dictionary of Saints (W1552)
Oxford Dictionary of the Christian Church (W1551)
SCIENCE FICTION
Encyclopedia of Science Fiction (G93)

SCIENCE FICTION (continued)
   Masters of Science Fiction (G95)
   Science Fiction and Fantasy Literature (G89)
   Science Fiction Writers (G91)
   Who's Who in Science Fiction (G92)
SOCIAL SCIENCES
   International Encyclopedia of the Social Sciences (W1578)
WOMEN'S STUDIES
   American Women Writers (W1630)
   Black Women Novelists (W1647)
   Index to Women of the World (W1640)
   Women in Literature (W1634)
—and other titles described in the subject or national literature sections.

Book Collecting

Basic guides

*W1153. *Book Collecting: A Modern Guide.* Ed. Jean Peters. New York:
   Bowker, 1977. 288pp. Z987.B68 020'.75
   Impressive essays by stellar bibliophiles on rare books, manuscripts, auctions, descriptive bibliography, fakes and forgeries, the role of the scholar/collector, reference books useful in the field, and the organization and care of a collection. The chapter on "The Literature of Book Collecting" is, for its length, definitive at the present time. These essays will be required, revered reading by book collectors for many years.

*W1154. *Collectible Books: Some New Paths.* Ed. Jean Peters. New York:
   Bowker, 1979. 294pp. Z987.C58 020'.75
   All book lovers will find excellent background information in these essays by experienced collectors and book dealers on types of bindings, books in series, film books, paperbacks, photography as illustration, book catalogs, publishers' imprints, and other problem areas.

*W1155. Winterich, John T., and David A. Randall. *A Primer of Book Collecting.* 3rd ed. New York: Crown, 1966, c1928. 228pp. Z992.W78
   020'.75
   A scholarly version of the international whodunit—clever, amusing, and filled with good advice about how to judge prices and how to engineer a prudent purchase. The authors seem to have an endless store of delightful anecdotes for the fledgling "accumulator" of precious books. These stories range from Jeffers, who paid to have his first book printed and then gave away or burned all copies, to Poe, whose first edition of *Tamerlane* is worth thousands of dollars even though almost no one ever reads it. Pleasant company, hard to put down.

W1156. Tannen, Jack. *How to Identify and Collect American First Editions:*

A Guide Book. New York: Arco, 1976. 147pp. Z987.T27   020'.75
This reliable introduction to book collecting was written by a man who for
fifty years was co-proprietor of New York's Biblo and Tannen book shop. It contains definitions of book-collecting terms, various methods of identifying first
editions, problems encountered when acquiring collections such as science fiction
or illustrated books, and discussions of reference books that are useful to book
collectors.

W1157.   *Book Collector's Fact Book*. Ed. Margaret Haller. New York: Arco,
1976. 271pp. Z118.H34   020'.75
Amateurs "of moderate means" (the editor's words) will be grateful for
the concise, clear definitions of terms used in printing, publishing, book illustration, history of the book, bibliography, book cataloging, and bookselling. A
more detailed index would have provided additional ways to get at the contents. Seasoned collectors will still want to consult Carter (W1158) and Winterich
and Randall (W1155).

*W1158.   Carter, John. *ABC for Book-Collectors*. 5th ed. New York: Knopf,
1974, c1952. 208pp. Z1006.C37   020'.75
Simple enough for the beginner, but the unusual clarity, good humor, and
liberally illustrated definitions will reinforce even the most advanced scholar's
knowledge that research must be careful and can be pleasant.

W1159.   *Book Browsers' Guide to Secondhand and Antiquarian Bookshops*.
Ed. Roy H. Lewis. 2nd ed. London: David and Charles, 1982. 184pp.
Z326.L48   658.8'09'07057
Another book for the traveler's suitcase (see *Oxford Literary Guide*, W1049).
This takes a shopping tour from Fleet Street to Llandudno to St. Andrews, from
converted garages and market stalls to haunted houses and third century B.C.
stone structures. Fascinating.

W1160.   *Modern Book Collecting*. Ed. Robert A. Wilson. New York: Knopf,
1980. 270pp. Z987.W49   020.75
Personal friendships with W. H. Auden and Marianne Moore, personal experience as owner of the Phoenix Book Store in New York, authorship of
bibliographies on Stein, Corso, and Levertov, training as publisher of many more
author bibliographies—these are the qualifications offered by the author of this
primer to book collecting that focuses mainly on first editions of recent American
authors. Unexpected features include a list of publishers and their printing
idiosyncrasies, a list of author bibliographies (see W1053-55), a chapter on collecting as an investment, a glossary defining terms used in book collecting, a
list of book shops specializing in modern first editions, caveats on dealers, auctions, and fashions. The author's enthusiasm is contagious—a dangerously
fascinating book.

Directories

*W1161. *American Book Trade Directory: Retailers, Wholesalers, and Publishers in the United States and Canada, Dealers in Foreign Books.* New York: Bowker, 1915– . Annual (29th ed., 1983). Bimonthly updating service. Z475.A5   655.5

All the information necessary to carry on the business of collecting and selling books: names and addresses in the United States, Great Britain, Canada, and Ireland of publishers, book shops, societies, antiquaries, auctioneers, clubs, periodicals, exporters and importers. All serious book collectors will have to use this. The complementary volume *International Book Trade Directory* (New York: Bowker, 1979) gathers similar information from 165 countries.

Book prices

*W1162. *American Book-Prices Current: A Record of Literary Properties Sold at Auction in England, the United States, and in Canada.* New York: American Book-Prices Current, 1895– . Annual. Z1000.A51   018'.3

A record of selected American, Canadian, English, and European sales of books, manuscripts, and autographs. It includes information on the author, title, edition, place and date of publication, size, condition, and place and date of sale, with catalog number and price. Occasional discussions of the most important auctions of the year, chronologies of the sales, and lists of auction houses. Book collectors use this constantly.

*W1163. *Bookman's Price Index: A Guide to the Values of Rare and Other Out-of-Print Books (BPI).* Detroit: Gale, 1964– . Annual. Z1000.B74   018.B724

Book collectors use this basic guide with two caveats in mind: (1) The prices cited are those established by one enterprising book dealer, unlike the prices found in an auction record, which voices the opinion, favorable or unfavorable, of at least two buyers, and (2) printed prices can lag far behind the current value, which is often the victim (or protégé) of fashion, the economy, war, and politics (national, international, and marital). The set contains about 750,000 entries so far, arranged alphabetically by author with description, condition, dealer's name, catalog number, and price of books offered for sale during the year in the United States, Canada, England, Ireland, Switzerland, and other countries.

W1164. Bradley, Van Allen. *The Book Collector's Handbook of Values, 1982-1983.* 4th ed. New York: Putnam, 1981. 624pp. Z1029.B7   016.09

An alphabetical author-title listing with important notes by the author on about twenty thousand nineteenth- and twentieth-century books in English that have sold for twenty-five dollars or more in the secondhand market. Pseudonyms are cross-referenced. This gets out of date rapidly, of course, but book collectors still consult it regularly because it gives the price range and recent auction records if available.

Dictionaries

W1165. Hertzberger, Menno. *Dictionary for the Antiquarian Booktrade in French, English, German, Swedish, Danish, Italian, Spanish, and Dutch.* Paris: International Ligue of Antiquarian Booksellers, 1956. 190pp. Z282.5.D5   070.5'03

Book collecting is an international trade. This indispensable dictionary lists all the words commonly used in printing, publishing, binding, analyzing, and describing books and gives their equivalents in eight languages. In 1977 the Antiquarian Booksellers Association of Japan produced an edition that includes Japanese terms (202pp.; first ed., 1962).

Periodicals

*W1166. *A B Bookman's Weekly: The Specialist Book Trade Weekly (AB).* Clifton, N.J.: n.p. (Box AB), 1969–   . Annual yearbooks. Former title, 1948–69: *Antiquarian Bookman.* Z999.A01.A1   010.5

The single most important periodical for current news in book collecting. Contains announcements of old, new, rare, used, and out-of-print books; personal advertisements for the sale and purchase of specific books; book reviews; illustrations; and an index every six months. It is noticeably prompt in publishing obituaries of renowned book collectors.

Indexed in *Bk. Rev. Ind.* (W1559), *Current Bk. Rev. Cit.* (W1564), *Lib. Lit.* (F53).

W1167. *American Book Collector (ABC).* New York: Moretus, 1950–76; 1980–   . 6/yr. Z987.A2.A48   010.5

The oldest of the periodicals devoted to news and notes on the world of book collecting. The pre-1976 format was more journalistic and less scholarly than its counterpart in England, *Book Collector* (W1168). Its editors favored a lively, informal tone with lots of pictures, big print, and articles on popular subjects such as Sherlock Holmes, Tarzan, World War II sea stories, and early children's books. The 1980 periodical, which supersedes *Book Collector's Market,* is more traditional in subject, scope, and treatment.

Indexed in *ABELL* (D32), *Abst. Eng. Stud.* (E38), *Bk. Rev. Ind.* (W1559), *Current Bk. Rev. Cit.* (W1564), *Ed. Ind.* (W1225), *MLAIB* (D31).

*W1168. *Book Collector (BC).* London: Collector Ltd., 1952–   . Quarterly. Z990.B6   020'.75

The leading English publication in the field, with reports on recent auctions and exhibitions, articles on collections and publishers, news of expensive books and latest catalogs, book reviews, and a valuable exchange of queries and answers.

Indexed in *ABELL* (D32), *Abst. Eng. Stud.* (E38), *Arts and Hum. Cit. Ind.* (F47), *Bk. Rev. Ind.* (W1559), *Brit. Hum. Ind.* (F49), *Current Bk. Rev. Cit.* (W1564), *Index to Bk. Rev. Hum.* (W1560), *Lib. Info. Sci. Abst.* (E43), *MLAIB* (D31), *Romantic Movement: A . . . Bibliography* (J443).

Additional reference sources for information on book collecting

W1169. *ABELL* (D32), Book Production, Collecting, Binding, Design, and Selling
Bibliography—Books and Printing (W1064–79)
Blanck (P713), descriptions of primary works
Bleiler, *Checklist of Science-Fiction* (G89)
Eighteenth-Century Short-Title Catalogue (J373)
English Literary Journal to 1900 (J190)
Evans (P717)
First Printings of American Authors (P714)
Library Collections (P841–43, W1313–24)
Literary Research (T1415–21)
MLAIB (D31), vol. 1, General V, Bibliographical
Mikolajczak, Michael A. "Selective Bibliography on Special Collections in the Academic Library," *Literary Research Newsletter*, 3 (1978), 28–31. See *LRN* (W1421)
NUC (B10–11), for many verification problems
Pollard and Redgrave (J306)
Publishers and Publishing (W1514–25)
Science Fiction and Fantasy Literature (G89)
Sheehy (A5), reference books on watermarks, printers' marks, guides (pp. 23–25)
Wing (J370)

Books in Print

*W1170. *Books in Print* (*BIP*). Vols. 1–3: Authors; vols. 4–6: Titles and Publishers. New York: Bowker, 1948– . Annual (fall). Z1215.P972 015.73

A cumulation from over thirteen thousand United States publishers of 600,000 titles that currently are, or shortly will be, available. Each entry includes date, publisher, price, and L.C. number so that students, teachers, and librarians can find out whether they will be able to get the book they want and how much it will cost. Occasional errors and omissions, but that is to be expected in a production of this size. Paperback editions are sometimes cited, but *Paperbound Books in Print* (W1466) is a better source for that problem. Publishers' names and addresses are listed at the back of the last volume. Bibliographic Retrieval Services (BRS) made this available online in 1981 with a data base that can be searched by author, title, publisher, and eighty thousand Library of Congress subject headings (see the Glossary, computerized literature search).

The cutoff date is July of each year, but an annual supplement appears in the spring, and the student who needs more recent information can consult *Forthcoming Books* (P717.19, bimonthly), *Weekly Record* (P717.18), or *American Book Publishing Record* (P717.18, monthly, annual, five-year, and multiyear cumulations).

W1171. *Subject Guide to Books in Print,* [———]: *An Index to the Publishers'
Trade List Annual.* 2 vols. New York: Bowker, 1957– . Annual.
Z1215.P971   015

About 62,000 subject categories help the researcher locate all currently
available books, new and old—hardback, paperback, trade books, textbooks,
adult books, and juveniles. This contains exactly the same titles found in *Books
in Print* (W1170), but here they are arranged by subject.

W1172. *Publishers' Trade List Annual (PTLA).* 5 vols. New York: Bowker,
1872– . Annual. Z1215.P97   015.73

PTLA is a cumulation of about two thousand publishers' catalogs in
alphabetical order, with smaller publishers listed in a supplementary section of
yellow pages. Students can find out, for instance, how many Norton Critical
Editions have been produced (about one hundred) and whether they include
Hawthorne's *Scarlet Letter* (yes: 2nd ed., 1978, $12.95 hardback and $2.95 paperback). Not all publishers contribute to this publication, however, so students
must be prepared to go to *Books in Print* (W1170), the *Cumulative Book Index*
(D35), or other comprehensive sources. See also Paperback Books (W1466–67).

W1173. *British Books in Print.* 2 vols. London: Whitaker, 1874– . Annual.
Z2001.B74   015.B862

Similar to *Books in Print* (W1170), but restricted to the 325,000 books
presently available from publishers in Great Britain. Other countries of course
provide the same service for their books: *Australian Books in Print, African Books
in Print, Les Livres disponibles,* and many more. There is even an *International
Books in Print,* 2nd ed. (Ridgewood, N.J.: Saur, 1981) that lists all books written in English but published outside the United States and England. It lists
about 100,000 titles and overlaps somewhat with *CBI* (D35).

See also
   CBI (D35)
   Forthcoming Books (P717.19)
   Publishers Weekly (P717.17)
   Weekly Record (P717.18)

Censorship

W1174. *Banned Films.* Ed. Edward de Grazia and Roger K. Newman. New
York: Bowker, 1982. 532pp.

The history of movie censorship, the role of the Supreme Court, and analyses
of 122 films banned for political, religious, moral, or sexual reasons—a convincing investigation well argued by two concerned citizens, one a lawyer and the
other a historian.

W1175. Haight, Anne Lyon. *Banned Books: 387 B.C. to 1978 A.D.* Rev.
Chandler B. Grannis. 4th ed. New York: Bowker, 1978. 196pp.

Z1019.H15   O98'.1

A history of book suppression laws and practices, with an annotated chronology of over three hundred books, excerpts from court decisions, statements ranging from Milton to our current U.S. Supreme Court, and a survey of trends. Lest anyone think that the major problems of censorship are over, note that in 1978 Missouri banned the 1969 edition of the *American Heritage Dictionary*, and that in 1979 a high school teacher was fired because he insisted on teaching Aldous Huxley's *Brave New World*.

W1176.   *Index on Censorship*. London: Oxford Univ. Press, 1972–   . 6/yr.

This literary magazine, according to its information officer, publishes cases, commentary, and examples of the work of writers from all over the world who are banned or censored for political reasons. Especially important is its policy of publishing works for the first time in English, including that by Vaculik and Kundera (Czechoslovakia); Konwicki, Brodsky, and Zinoviev (USSR); Fuchs (East Germany); Ding Ling and Wei Jingsheng (China); Juan Carlos Onetti (Uruguay); Kim Chi Ha (South Korea); Abdellatif Laabi (Morocco); and Mtutuzeli Matshoba (South Africa).

See also

Oxford Companion to English Literature (J178)
Perrin (W1622)

Center for Editions of American Authors (CEAA)

W1177. An MLA program with grants from the National Endowment for the Humanities that was dedicated to the preparation and publication of definitive editions of nineteenth-century American authors whose texts over the years had been corrupted by intentional or unintentional alterations. The CEAA was dissolved in 1976 and replaced with the Center for Scholarly Editions (W1179), a similar organization with the same purpose—to produce accurate editions—but a wider scope that includes English and foreign language as well as American authors of all centuries.

Over 140 volumes have so far been edited with the original CEAA stamp of approval, and others that began production under that organization are entitled to receive its unique seal. In returning the text to the author's original intention, editors involved in the CEAA project first had to locate all available editions, manuscripts, and notes concerning the work and its author. Only then could they establish a copy text, determine the correct version, and prepare a final edition with detailed explanations and justifications (see the entry in the Glossary that defines a critical edition).

The university presses that undertook this project were California (Twain's papers), Virginia (Stephen Crane), Harvard (Emerson and William James), Ohio State (Hawthorne), Indiana (Howells), Wisconsin (Irving), Princeton (Thoreau), Kent State (Charles Brockden Brown), Northern Illinois (James Russell Lowell), New York University (Whitman). There were also several MLA-CEAA associated editions: Northwestern and Newberry Library (Melville), Iowa and California

(Twain's works), Southern Illinois (John Dewey), State University of New York (Cooper), and University of South Carolina (W. G. Simms). The *CEAA Newsletter* (1968–76) reported regularly on new editions and policies.

In 1974 the South Carolina Apparatus for Definitive Editions, an extension of the CEAA that focused on bibliographical and textual material necessary for definitive editions of twentieth-century works, produced its first volume, *The Great Gatsby*.

The CEAA program provoked an explosive interchange of accusations between editors who defended their policies and critics who claimed the editorial apparatus so encumbered the text that it was impossible to read:

Mumford, Lewis. "Emerson behind Barbed Wire." *New York Review of Books*, 18 Jan. 1968, pp. 3–5.

Professional Standards and American Editions: A Response to Edmund Wilson. New York: MLA, 1969. 28pp.

Publishers Weekly, 29 July 1968, pp. 29–30; 11 Jan. 1971, pp. 47–48.

Saturday Review, 10 June 1967, pp. 30, 69–70.

Statement of Editorial Principles and Procedures: A Working Manual for Editing Nineteenth-Century American Texts. Rev. ed. New York: MLA, 1972. Bibliography. 25pp.

Time, 1 Nov. 1968, pp. 73–74.

Wilson, Edmund. *The Fruits of the MLA*. New York: New York Review, 1968. 47pp.

Center for Scholarly Editions (CSE)

W1179.   The MLA created the Center for Scholarly Editions in 1976 to formulate and encourage high editorial standards in all literature, thus replacing the CEAA (W1177), which confined itself solely to editions of nineteenth-century American authors. The CSE committee works with both editors and publishers to produce works that "are based on a thorough study of the variant forms of the texts, are prepared through the consistent application of explicitly announced editorial principles, record all emendations to the copy text introduced by the editors, and are scrupulously and repeatedly proofread to prevent unintentional alterations" (CSE open letter, 29 May 1979). Its emblem of approval has been granted to works by Blake, Brown, Conrad, Cooper, Dewey, Emerson, Frederic, Howells, Irving, Noland, Russell, Shelley, Twain, and Whitman. It is interested in editorial projects not only in English and American literature but also in other languages and in all historical periods in which the theory of copy text is a consideration.

The Committee on Scholarly Editions is appointed by the Executive Council of the MLA. One of its duties is to reach scholars who are willing to act as consultants and inspectors on specific editorial projects. These scholars are paid a modest sum for their time and expenses by the editors and publishers who request their services. Other independent inspectors are also acceptable; their reports on the completed work need only meet satisfactorily the items stated in the CSE's "Guiding Questions" (see below).

The CSE offers advice, free of charge, to any scholar on large or small editorial projects, such as the multivolume editions of Conrad or Peirce and the single volume of the Shelley journals. It also sponsors programs at the annual MLA conference, acts as a clearinghouse for the exchange of information between editors and publishers, and solicits and distributes guidelines for active editions. The project was supported by the National Endowment for the Humanities until May 1979 and is now sponsored by the MLA. Headquarters is at the MLA office, 62 Fifth Ave., New York, NY 10011.

See also

> Bibliography—Books and Printing (W1064–79)
> CSE open letter to MLA members (29 May 1979). New York: MLA.
> *Center for Scholarly Editions: An Introductory Statement.* New York: MLA, 1978. Reprint from *PMLA*, Sept. 1977. 15pp.
> *Guiding Questions for Editors, Publishers, and Inspectors.* Rev. ed. New York: MLA, 1982. 9pp.

Children's Literature
Basic guides

*W1180. Haviland, Virginia, et al. *Children's Literature: A Guide to Reference Sources.* Washington, D.C.: Library of Congress, 1966. 341pp. First supplement (1972), 315pp. Second supplement (1977), 413pp. Third supplement (1982), 279pp. Z1037.A1.H35   016.8098928

Careful selection and personal evaluations make this international, comprehensive guide indispensable to teacher and student alike. The author's confidence in her books is apparent. She knows the contents, and she is excited about the possibilities. Arrangement is by subject and author. The book includes histories, bibliographies, fiction, nonfiction, general studies, an index, illustrations, and lively annotations.

W1181. *Fifteen Centuries of Children's Literature: An Annotated Chronology of British and American Works in Historical Context.* Ed. Jane Bingham and Grayce Scholt. Westport, Conn.: Greenwood, 1981. 536pp. Z1037.A1.B582   [PN1009.A1]   028.52

From sixth-century Latin manuscripts to popular twentieth-century titles, an astonishing collection of 750 entries with evaluations of their contribution to children's literature. Well edited, with a historical survey, a list of periodicals, information on collections, library locations, and author and title indexes.

W1181.1 *Twentieth Century Children's Writers.* Ed. Daniel L. Kirkpatrick. 2nd ed. New York: St. Martin's, 1983. 1500pp.

About seven hundred biographical entries, with a title index to ten thousand books. Revised every five years.

W1181.2 *Oxford Companion to Children's Literature.* Ed. Humphrey Carpenter and Mari Prichard. New York: Oxford Univ. Press, 1984. 500pp.

Two thousand entries covering fairy tales, folklore, characters, genres, historical developments, and biographies for authors, illustrators, printers, and publishers. A valuable contribution.

Criticism

W1182. *Children's Literature Review.* Detroit: Gale, 1976– . Annual.
PN1009.A1.C5139   028.52

Excerpts of criticism on about forty authors, with brief biographical and critical notes and references to other sources. Cumulative indexes to authors, titles, and critics. Like the other Gale publications, it is easy to use, designed for the average student, and remarkably reliable.

Indexes

W1183. *Children's Book Review Index.* Detroit: Gale, 1975– . Annual.
Master cumulation, 1969–1981, 4 vols. (1982).   Z1037.A1.C475
028.52

Cumulates into one volume the reviews that appear in the 325 periodicals indexed by *Bk. Rev. Ind.* (W1559). Convenient and accurate. Title index. The master cumulation expands coverage to four hundred periodicals.

W1184. *Children's Authors and Illustrators: An Index to Biographical Dictionaries.* 3rd ed. Ed. Adele Sarkissian. Detroit: Gale, 1981. 667pp.
Z1037.A1.L2   016.809

"Kiddie Lit" is generally a required course for education majors who intend to become elementary school teachers. As teachers, they should be familiar with all the books that children want and need to read. They will, therefore, be exceedingly grateful for this index, for it locates biographical information on about ten thousand children's authors and illustrators. Once they have learned to use it themselves, their next step, as creative teachers, is to get their students in the habit of using it regularly for their own needs. And that, to put it quite simply, is the ultimate goal of all good librarians—to illustrate the convenience and usefulness of their collection so that their researchers (students or professors) will go out and teach others. James H. Fraser has compiled a companion guide to manuscript collections of children's authors and illustrators (New York: Saur, 1980).

Periodicals

*W1185. *Phaedrus: An International Journal of Children's Literature Research.*
Marblehead, Mass.: Phaedrus, 1973– . 3/yr. Z1037.A1.P5   028.52

This first-class scholarly journal devotes two issues a year to reports from various countries, with bibliographical surveys and reviews that greatly facilitate research in the field. For instance, the Spring 1979 issue was entitled "Latvian Children's Literature in Exile, 1945–1979." Index for vols. 1–5.

Indexed in *MLAIB* (D31).

*W1186. *Children's Literature: An International Journal (ChildL).* New Haven:
Yale Univ. Press, 1972– . PN1009.A1.C514   028.505

This annual of the MLA Division on Children's Literature and the Children's Literature Association includes articles, reviews, bibliographies, notes on dissertations, awards, symposia, and ideas for research. A quality journal with international interests. Index to vols. 1–5 in vol. 6.

Indexed in *MLAIB* (D31).

See also
> *ABELL* (D32), since 1975 (vol. 50), "Literature for Children" in the section on English literature
> *MLAIB* (D31), since 1976, vol. 1, General IV, Themes and Types

Composition and Grammar

Brief rules and clear instructions make these two books invaluable to the student of English:

*W1188. Strunk, William, Jr., and Elwyn B. White. *The Elements of Style.* 3rd ed. New York: Macmillan, 1979. 85pp. Paperback. PE1408.S772 808

> *Practical English Handbook.* Ed. Floyd C. Watkins et al. 6th ed. Boston: Houghton, 1982. 352pp. Paperback. Workbook, 2nd ed. (1982). PE1408.W37   808'.042

Simplicity comes first. Accuracy and clarity follow. No matter which grammar handbook the student may select—and many other time-tested favorites are available—one rule will be dominant: practice, practice, practice.

See also
> Teaching Resources (W1597–1609)
> *Words into Type* (W1587)

Computer Research

Basic guides

W1189. Oakman, Robert L. *Computer Methods for Literary Research.* Rev. ed. Athens: Univ. of Georgia Press, 1984. 256pp. PN73.024 802'.8'5

Required reading for all scholars who expect to remain in the field of literature. After a greatly simplified explanation of how computers accept, process, and return information, individual chapters expand on computer possibilities and problems in compiling concordances and dictionaries, editing texts, analyzing an author's style, and cataloging the collections of archives and libraries. Anyone investigating this field should certainly use the accompanying bibliographies.

W1190. *Computer Abstracts.* Jersey, British Channel Islands: Technical Information, 1957– . Monthly. Z6654.C17   510.78

Under the subject headings "Linguistics" and "Education" are abstracts of articles concerned with new techniques in measurement and evaluation. Under "Information Retrieval" the literature student will find entries for computer approaches to library catalogs, books for the blind, and machine-readable bibliographies.

W1191.   *Computing Reviews.* New York: Assn. for Computing Machinery, 1960– . Monthly. QA76.C5854   001.6'05

Computer-based studies are here briefly evaluated so the student can look under the subject heading "Humanities," for instance, and see the results of work done on language translations, comparative linguistics, growth patterns in E. E. Cummings' sonnets, anonymous works, mixed authorship (such as the Book of Isaiah), and the syntactic structure of Old English poetry.

Periodicals

W1192.   *Computers and the Humanities (CHum).* Osprey, Fla.: Paradigm, 1966– . 6/yr. Z699.5.H8.C65

Articles, abstracts, book reviews, and notices; twice a year a report of work in progress; index with entries for literary subjects such as concordances, Shakespeare's works, and *Pilgrim's Progress*; and an annual international bibliography with a section on language and literature. Author-subject index to vols. 1–5 (1966–71).

Indexed in *ABELL* (D32), *Abst. Eng. Stud.* (E38), *America* (E43), *Am. Hum. Ind.* (P738), *Arts and Hum. Cit. Ind.* (F47), *Computing Reviews* (W1191), *Current Contents* (F47), *Hum. Ind.* (F45), *Language and Lang. Beh. Abst.* (W1332), *MLAIB* (D31), *Music Ind.* (W1456), and many scientific services.

See also

> *ABELL* (D32), Language, Literature, and Computers (56 entries in the 1978 volume)
>
> Glossary in this guide: computerized literature search, ISBD, ISSN, Library of Congress card number, Lockheed Dialog, MARC, OCLC, online information retrieval, RLG, word processing
>
> *Library Literature* (F53), Information Retrieval
>
> *Literary Research Newsletter*, 5, no. 1 (1980), special issue on computers and literary research. See *LRN* (W1421)
>
> *MLAIB* (D31), vol. 1, General IV, Computer-Assisted Research (28 entries in the 1980 volume)

Concordances

W1194.   Dozens of concordances are now available for authors of all centuries, genres, and nations. During the last decade they have become increasingly important as research tools in studies of imagery, prevailing themes, stylistic development, and every aspect of language. What many students do not know is that concordances can be inaccurate and that inaccuracies will lead to erroneous conclusions about the author's work. Before using a concordance, knowledgeable scholars evaluate it on the following points:

> 1. What edition of the author's works did the editor use? Unless it was a definitive or variorum edition designed to establish the author's final intention, students will have to be aware that errors by typesetters, well-meaning editors, and bowdlerizing great-aunts can so corrupt the text that the words, spelling, punctuation, syntax, and, therefore,

meaning are no longer the author's. The concordance then has to be used with caution. See "textual criticism" in the Glossary to this guide for a further explanation of this problem.

2. What does the editor do about variant readings?
3. What is the editorial policy for variant spellings (Saint or St.)? For misspellings?
4. What is the policy for rejected stanzas? (As in Byron's *Don Juan*.)
5. What does the editor do about capital letters? (Extremely important in Hawthorne, who used them for emphasis.)
6. Does the editor include a frequency list? (It seems significant that the word that appears most frequently in Emily Dickinson's poetry is "I"—1,682 times. In Yeats it is "man," then "love," "heart," and "eyes.")
7. Does the editor suggest new areas of study that the concordance has made possible? (Such as Chaucer's "fowl" imagery in *The Canterbury Tales*, Shakespeare's references to Parliament or religion, and Milton's references to women in his prose.)
8. Is it computer-compiled and, therefore, only as good as its programmer? Is the programmer a literary scholar as well as a computer expert?

Students should remember that there are concordances not only to the works of an author (Hopkins, Wallace Stevens, D. H. Lawrence) but also to individual titles (the Bible, *Finnegans Wake*) and groups of titles (certain sonnet sequences of the Renaissance). They should also watch the catalogs of a few publishers, such as the following, who specialize in producing concordances:

Scarecrow: Joyce, Roethke, Hart Crane, Thomas.
Gale: O'Neill, *Paradise Lost*, plays and prefaces of Shaw, E. B. Browning, essays of Francis Bacon, poems of Pope, sayings in Franklin's *Poor Richard*, *The Great Gatsby*, poetry of Stephen Crane and Langston Hughes.
Cornell Univ. Press: poems of Swift, Mandelstam, Dickinson, Ben Jonson, Samuel Johnson, Arnold, and Sidney; plays and poems of Racine, García Lorca, and Yeats; plays of Congreve; writings of Blake, Jean de la Fontaine, and Herbert; Byron's *Don Juan*; Pascal's *Pensées*; *Beowulf*; *Anglo-Saxon Poetic Records* (J235); *On the Origin of Species*.
Garland: Meredith; *Jane Eyre*; Keats; *The Good Soldier* (Ford); Conrad (fifteen novels); Hawthorne (five novels); Emerson (five essays); Pound's *Cantos*; *Wuthering Heights* (Brontë); *Moby-Dick* (Melville); Lewis Carroll (poetry).

Copyright

To locate the copyright date of a book, look first on the verso of the title page. There the year will usually be indicated in one of the following ways:

copyright 1981   ©1981   c1981

The copyright date is not the same as the publication date, which is usually printed at the bottom of the title page along with the name of the publisher and is often a year or two later than the copyright date. The publication date is usually cited in reference works and critical studies. Where both are cited, they appear in this form:

1980[c1978]   or   1980, c1978

See the Glossary for further information on copyright laws. The following three entries provide more detailed explanations:

*W1196. Peters, Marybeth. *General Guide to the Copyright Act of 1976.* Washington, D.C.: U.S. Copyright Office, 1977. 142pp. KF2989.73.P4
Summarizes the historical background of copyright laws, illustrates the advantages of a single federal system, and explains the problems with anonymous works, various kinds of subject matter, copyright protection, transfers of ownership, termination, scope of exclusive rights, royalties, infringement, and other subjects with which teachers need to be familiar. In the back of the book is a brief (6pp.) guideline for quick classroom reference. This depository item will be found in most depository libraries in the United States (see the Glossary).

W1197. *The New Copyright Law: Questions Teachers and Librarians Ask.* Washington, D.C.: National Education Assn., 1977. 76pp. Paperback. KF2995.A43   346'.73'0482
This booklet answers timely questions about duration of copyright, registration, fair use, spontaneity, cumulative effect, videotaping, transparencies, and penalties. Clear explanations in simple terms.

*W1198. Achtert, Walter S. "The New Copyright Law." *PMLA,* 93 (1978), 572–77.
A brief but important explanation of how the revised copyright law of 1976 affects authors and teachers, including the sticky problem of quoting from unpublished works and the significance of the date 1 January 1978 for all copyright holders. This will answer most routine questions. Bibliography.

See also

MLA Handbook (W1584)
Oxford Companion to English Literature (J178), pp. 921–31
Thorpe, *Use of Manuscripts* (W1321)

Dates

W1199. *Famous First Facts: A Record of First Happenings, Discoveries, and Inventions in the U.S.* Ed. Joseph N. Kane. 4th ed. New York: Wilson, 1981. 1350pp. AG5.K315   031
A tempting book for the browser. Did you know that the first automobile fatality was in 1899 and that the first air-conditioned factory was built in 1902? This book of records includes nine thousand "firsts," with the source of information cited for each entry.

There are several indexes, by year, day, person's name, subject, and geographical location. Arrangement is by subject, so search is easy.

W1200. *Everyman's Dictionary of Dates.* 6th ed., rev. London: Dent, 1980. 518pp. D9.D5   903

One of the best sources because of its universality in geography as well as in subject, in events as well as in biography. It clarifies, for instance, the nine periods of Gothic architecture (1066–1600) and lists chronologically the earliest English cathedrals and universities. It is always wise, however, for the sake of accuracy, to check dates in at least two sources.

*W1201. Powicke, Frederick M., and Edmond B. Fryde. *Handbook of British Chronology.* 2nd ed. London: Royal Historical Soc., 1961, c1939. 565pp. DA34.P6   942.002

Powicke and Fryde provide the names, dates, and pertinent facts, in historical order, of all officeholders of England, Ireland, Scotland, and Wales including clergy, nobility, state officials, members of Parliament, and representatives to church councils. Each section is prefaced with an explanation of the problems encountered in deciphering the early records and with descriptions of the duties of the various offices. Sources of information and titles for further study are frequently mentioned in the text. It contains the names, for instance, of the chief secretary of Ireland before and after Edmund Spenser, the treasurer during the reign of Henry VIII, and the children of Henry II and Eleanor of Aquitaine.

W1202. Collison, Robert, ed. *Dictionary of Dates.* 2nd ed. New York: Transatlantic Arts, 1967. 428pp. D11.5.C6   903

Worldwide in scope. The main section is an alphabetical listing of persons, places, and events, and the second section is chronological by day of the year. Most entries have two or three lines of information, so students will use this only for quick reference questions. Keep in mind that this needs updating and enlarging.

W1203. *Historical Tables: 58 B.C.–A.D. 1978.* Ed. Sigfrid H. Steinberg. 10th ed. New York: St. Martin's, 1979. 269pp. D11.S8   902'.02

A tabular presentation of history from the Roman Empire and its contact with England to the election of Pope John Paul II in 1978. Convenient for comparison-and-contrast projects.

W1204. *American Book of Days.* Ed. Jane M. Hatch. 3rd ed. New York: Wilson, 1978. 1214pp. GT4803.D6   394.2'6973

Information about holidays, festivals, anniversaries, civil rights, human rights, women's rights, political events, catastrophes, inventions, wars, Christian and Jewish holy days, and all events important to the development of the United States. About seven hundred long, detailed entries in chronological order explain the origins of the celebrations and trace their development through the ages.

Additional sources that contain dates for specific subjects

Chronologies. See Index

Encyclopedia of World History (W1292), chronological

Holman, *A Handbook to Literature* (W1406), outline of literary history, English and American, pp. 561–627

Oxford Companion to American Literature (P736), chronological index of literary and social development, 1577–1965

Oxford Companion to English Literature (J178), perpetual calendar, pp. 932–56

Oxford History of English Literature (J174), chronological tables in every volume (20–40pp.)

Birth and death dates:

Afro-American Poetry and Drama (P868)

American Bibliography, Bristol's index (P717.2) and *Imprints* (P717.12)

Author Bibliography of English Language Fiction (G61)

Bartlett, *Familiar Quotations* (W1527)

Bibliography of Crime Fiction (G85)

Biography Index (W1085)

Black American Writers (P842)

CARD CATALOG!

Dictionary of Oriental Literatures (R985)

Evans, *Dictionary of Quotations* (W1529)

Index to Black American Literary Anthologies (P848)

Index to Literary Biography (W1118)

Index to Women of the World (W1640)

New York Times Obituaries Index (W1148)

Nineteenth-Century Literary Criticism (J421)

Poetry by American Women (W1648)

Sabin (P718)

—and many, many more

Dictionaries

*W1205. *Oxford English Dictionary (OED)*. Oxford: Clarendon, 1933. 12 vols., supplement and bibliography. Supplement, ed. Robert W. Burchfield: vol. 1 (A–G), 1972; vol. 2 (H–N), 1976; vol. 3 (O–S), 1982; vol. 4 (T–Z), scheduled for 1985, with an extensive bibliography of works cited in the entries of all four volumes. Former title, 1888–1933: *New English Dictionary (NED)*. PE1625.M7   423

Almost fifty years of labor were required to compile every word used in the English language from the earliest records to the present, with all relevant facts about their form and 1,800,000 quotations to illustrate their usage and their meaning changes over the centuries. This examination of the language on historical principles shows, for instance, how "day's eye" in A.D. 1000 became "daisy" by the fifteenth century and how "silly" originally meant deserving of pity, or plain, rustic. The supplements use quotations from American, Canadian, British, Scottish, and West Indian newspapers and periodicals. They include contemporary religious, political, and social terms, even if offensive, and in every way keep up to date with the language. Rubik's cube is here, and Queen Mum, and OK. For any question concerning an author's intention in the use of a word, or for any problem in derivation or spelling, this is the source to use. An authoritative and remarkably entertaining masterpiece. Corrections and additions to the *OED* are published occasionally in *Notes and Queries* (J187).

W1206. *Dictionary of American English on Historical Principles (DAE)*. Ed. William A. Craigie and James R. Hulbert. 4 vols. Chicago: Univ. of Chicago Press, 1938–44. PE2835.C7   427.9
This historical dictionary shows with dated quotations how English words have been used in America since the seventeenth century. It does not pretend to be complete, so little slang and no new words are included, but it is interesting to trace the use of terms such as Brahmin, copperhead, civil rights, consarn, and conniption fit. This should be used as a supplement to the *OED* (W1205).

W1207. *Oxford Dictionary of English Etymology*. Ed. Charles T. Onions. Oxford: Clarendon, 1966; corrected rpt. 1969. 1025pp.   PE1580.05   422.03
The standard etymological dictionary of the English language. It contains word origins, dates, definitions, and explanations in chronological order to show how each word has appeared in different forms in different countries and how its meaning has changed over the centuries. Needs updating.

W1208. *Barnhart Dictionary of New English since 1963*. Ed. Clarence L. Barnhart et al. Bronxville, N.Y.: Harper, 1973. 512pp. PE1630.B3   423
Second Barnhart Dictionary of New English. Ed. Clarence L. Barnhart et al. Bronxville, N.Y.: Harper, 1980. 520pp.

Each volume covers a limited number of years, so students must use both when looking for definitions of new terms. The *Second Barnhart*, for instance, focuses on six thousand words that appeared in the language between 1973 and 1979, with their date of entry, citations, and usage notes. Everyone knows the meaning of such terms as grass, bad trip, aerosol, and acupuncture, but how about ding-a-ling, WASP, Parkinson's Law, agoraphobia, Europort, and Earth Day? The main problem with these dictionaries, which include thousands of terms illustrated with quotations from current literature, is that what started as a five-minute search for a definition turns into an hour of fascinating reading.

If by any chance these should prove to be unproductive, try another guide to all the words an American of the 1980s is likely to see or hear, including slang and informal terms (such as holding pattern, jump ship, sudden death, and Hovercraft): *Oxford American Dictionary*, comp. Eugene Ehrlich et al. (New York: Oxford Univ. Press, 1980; 816pp.; PE2835.09   423). Students will appreciate the pronunciation system (by letter of the alphabet rather than phonetic symbols) and the explanatory notes that distinguish correct from incorrect usage

361

(lend or loan? oral or verbal? continuously or continually?). Another hour of good reading.

W1209. *Webster's Ninth New Collegiate Dictionary.* Rev. ed. Springfield, Mass.: Merriam, 1983. 1563pp. PE1628.W4.M4   423

This prestigious work contains over 22,000 new words and meanings. It is based on *Webster's Third New International Dictionary* and includes biographical and geographical sections, a list of foreign words, even a table of metric measures. Put this right beside your typewriter.

W1210. *Dictionary of Americanisms on Historical Principles (DA).* Ed. Mitford M. Mathews. 2 vols. Chicago: Univ. of Chicago Press, 1951. Abridgment (1966), 304pp. PE2835.D5   427.9

Concerned solely with those words that the United States has added to the English language such as coinages, foreign words, and any term given unique meaning by American usage. Each entry gives dates and examples from contemporary newspapers, journals, or books showing how the word has been used at various times since it first appeared. This is more limited in scope than the *Dictionary of American English* (W1206), but it contains more recent terms and also many revisions of the earlier work.

See also

Anglo-Saxon Dictionary (J233)
Dictionary of Old English (J248)
English-Old English . . . Dictionary (J234)
Johnson, Dictionary of the English Language (J376)
Middle English Dictionary (J264)

Dissertations

Basic sources

W1211. *Comprehensive Dissertation Index, 1861–1972.* 37 vols. Vols. 29–30: *Language and Literature.* Ann Arbor, Mich.: Xerox University Microfilms, 1973. Annual supplements. Z5053.X47   013'.379

The *only* source that provides access to all 417,000 dissertations in all disciplines granted in the United States and some foreign institutions since the first three doctorates were granted at Yale in 1861. In the section on *Language and Literature* the outstanding aspect is the generous key-word arrangement. "The Hopkins Handbook" (Patterson; Univ. of Florida 1970) can be located through both Hopkins and Handbook, and "Biblical Symbolism in the Latin Poetry of the Twelfth Century" (Richard H. Green; Univ. of California, Berkeley 1950) is listed under Biblical, Symbolism, Latin, Poetry, and Twelfth. Each entry cites the source of its information. Students should look for the volume and page number of *DA* and *DAI* (W1214) if they want to read an abstract.

*W1212. McNamee, Lawrence F., ed. *Dissertations in English and American*

Literature: Theses Accepted by American, British and German Universities, 1865-1964. New York: Bowker, 1965. Supplement 1, 1964-1968 (1969), 450pp. Supplement 2, 1969-1973 (1974), 690pp. Z5053.M32   016.82

This definitive accumulation of facts from 260 cooperating universities takes a chronological and genre approach to dissertations. It has an index to major authors, code letters for subjects and universities, a cross-index from literary authors to dissertation authors, and an alphabetical list of authors of dissertations. Entries include author, title, university codes, and date.

Literature students should certainly come here when they are trying to decide on a dissertation subject. Trends are immediately apparent: The Romantic poet John Clare, for instance, inspired only one dissertation between 1865 and 1964 and one between 1964 and 1968, but no fewer than seven from 1969 to 1973. And *A Midsummer Night's Dream* prompted one in German in 1902 on fairies, one in 1955 on the animals, one in 1965, and five between 1969 and 1973.

Supplement 1 supplies the astonishing information that between 1964 and 1968 American universities produced thirty-nine percent of the total number of dissertations written during the previous eighty-eight years. It also introduces two new features. The codes of universities now include the total number of dissertations produced—497 for New York University, for example, and 107 for the University of Florida. And the cross-index of authors now cites the area code as well as the subject and the name of the author.

Supplement 2 adds seven thousand more dissertations to the nineteen thousand in the previous volumes. It also provides the news that Faulkner is now second only to Shakespeare as the most popular subject, that the longest and shortest dissertations are 3,977 and 38 pages, that state universities are producing far more dissertations than private institutions, and that, for the first time, coverage is extended to several Canadian and Australian universities.

See also sources for specific areas such as Woodress for *Dissertations in American Literature* (P737), Altick and Matthews for Victorian literature (J465, which extends to Austrian, French, and Swiss dissertations), and *American Dissertations on the Drama* (P810).

W1213. *American Doctoral Dissertations, [———].* Ann Arbor, Mich.: University Microfilms, 1964- . Annual. Assn. of Research Libraries. Former title, 1955-64: *Index to American Doctoral Dissertations.* Z5055.U49.A62

Claims to be a complete listing of all dissertations from American and Canadian universities, including those abstracted in *DAI* (W1214), but the editors are limited to information from commencement programs sent by cooperating institutions. Arranged by broad subject with no analytical subject index, so efforts to find a listing for O'Connor, for instance, are often fruitless.

Abstracts

*W1214. *Dissertation Abstracts International: Abstracts of Dissertations Available on Microfilm or as Xerographic Reproductions (DAI).* Ann Arbor, Mich.: University Microfilms, 1969- . Monthly, with annual cumulated author index. Former titles, 1938–51: *Microfilm Abstracts*; 1952–69: *Dissertation Abstracts* (*DA*). Z5053.D576

A compilation of over half a million dissertation abstracts submitted to the publisher by over four hundred cooperating universities (students should note this important limitation). The dissertations themselves are available for purchase as microfilm or xerographic prints, but this reference book has an additional purpose: to assist (1) graduate students who want only to read dissertation summaries, (2) Ph.D. candidates who need a manageable survey of dissertation research in their field, and (3) acquisition librarians who must decide whether or not the film is worth purchasing. The September 1979 volume, for instance, shows that Flannery O'Connor was the subject of one dissertation during that month, but the key-word title index lists it under Flannery, not O'Connor.

DAI is arranged by subject and then by dissertation author, with each entry containing all bibliographical information. Key-word title index and author index in each volume. The first twenty-nine volumes have been cumulated in W1215.

*W1215. *Dissertation Abstracts International Retrospective Index, Vols. I–XXIX (1938–69)* (*DAI*). Ann Arbor, Mich.: Xerox University Microfilms, 1970. Z5053.D572

One way to approach the first twenty-nine volumes of *Dissertation Abstracts*, which with vol. 30 became *Dissertation Abstracts International* (W1214). (See also *Comprehensive Dissertation Index*, W1211.) Entry is by discipline and general category (as Literature—Modern) and then by key word of the title, so the student can find, for example, how many dissertations have been written on the humours of Ben Jonson. Because subject headings and cross-references are not always reliable, students should be prepared to look under several key words. Each entry refers to the volume and page number of *DA*, where the students can read and judge the value of the dissertation before purchasing the microfilm.

See also

> *American Dissertations on the Drama* (P810)
> *Critical Writings on Commonwealth Literatures* (N645)
> *Dissertations in American Literature* (P737)
> *Guide to Doctoral Dissertations in Victorian Literature* (J465)
> *Guide to Serial Bibliographies* (C30)
> *Western American Literature* (P772)
> Works in Progress (W1650)

Education

Basic guides

W1217. *Grants Register*. Ed. Craig A. Lerner. New York: St. Martin's, 1970–   .

Every two years (9th ed., 1985–87). LB2338.G7   378.33

Comprehensive information about scholarships, grants, prizes, and awards in many countries and subject areas for American graduates, professionals, and advanced scholars. In addition to the two thousand opportunities that are explained briefly, there is a bibliography for further exploration. Arrangement is alphabetical, but students may also approach the problem through the subject index (under Humanities, Literature, English) or the index of awards and awarding bodies, which, for example, lists the Folger Shakespeare Library as offering a senior fellowship of $15,000. Numerous cross-references.

Better, but fewer, descriptions of grants may be found in the *Annual Register of Grant Support* (Chicago: Marquis, 1966–   ). The literature subject heading leads to details of financial awards given by the Academy of American Poets, *Atlantic Monthly*, the Berkshire Theatre Festival, Bread Loaf Writers' Conference, *Explicator* Literary Foundation, P.E.N., and other organizations that might be interested in determined authors.

W1218. *Barron's Profiles of American Colleges.* 13th ed. Woodbury, N.Y.: Barron's Educational, 1978–   . 946pp. Update service. L901.F5 378.73

Information on financial aid, programs of study, and scholastic requirements in several hundred institutions in the United States. Regional editions.

W1219. Lovejoy, Clarence E. *Lovejoy's College Guide: A Complete Reference Book to Some 3,600 American Colleges and Universities.* New York: Simon, 1940–   . Irregular. Paperback. LA226.L6   378.73

A comprehensive directory with factual information on American colleges and universities.

W1220. *Scholarships, Fellowships and Loans News Service and Counselor Information Services.* Arlington, Mass.: Bellman, 1980–   . 6/yr. LB2338.S36   378.3'0973

Announcements of new student aid programs and explanations of government plans and foundation requirements, with addresses so the student can write directly to the agency for further information. The best possible source for the latest developments. It even includes book reviews on new publications in the field.

*W1221. *World of Learning.* 2 vols. Detroit: Gale, 1947–   . Annual (33rd ed., 1982–83). AS2.W6   060

An indispensable source for the latest information on 24,000 colleges, museums, and libraries, and their collections, galleries, research institutes, and all cultural, educational, and scientific interests, worldwide, arranged by country and name of institution. In Great Britain, for instance, the University of Aberdeen is listed with telephone number, names of all officials and professors, their addresses, titles of publications of the university, and associated colleges. The latest editions include "open" or "free" universities that enable students to work at home through correspondence, radio, and television courses.

Abstracts

*W1223. *Resources in Education (RIE)*. Washington, D.C.: National Inst. of Education, 1975– . Monthly, with cumulations twice a year. Former title, 1967–74: *Research in Education*. Z5813.R4   016.37078

Designed to gather, summarize, index, and disseminate the thousands of unpublished articles, conference papers, individual projects, and reports of seminars and workshops that might be of interest to the educational community even though they have never attained the stature of published form. Since 1981 each issue has contained a special highlights page listing the titles and bibliographic information of fifteen to twenty specially selected publications developed by the sixteen ERIC clearinghouses. (See ERIC in the Glossary of this guide for an explanation of the parent organization and procedure.)

RIE is successful partly because the subject headings are minutely detailed, generously descriptive, and identical to those used by *CIJE* (W1224) so that students can easily look for additional material in education journals. They are much more likely to locate highly specialized material in these sources than in *Ed. Ind.* (W1225). The quality of the material is another matter, however. Some of it is admirable (see the McGill University bibliographies as described in W1326), but too many entries are hastily prepared seminar papers or pseudoacademic efforts to pad out the author's personnel folder. These are unworthy of publication and a waste of the taxpayer's money.

*W1224. *Current Index to Journals in Education (CIJE)*. Phoenix: Oryx, 1969– . Monthly, with cumulations twice a year. Z5813.C8 016.370'5

This monthly index of about 775 education-related journals operates as part of the Educational Resources Information Center (see ERIC in the Glossary). Because it analyzes published material and uses the same subject headings as those for unpublished works indexed by *RIE* (W1223), students can be certain that most of the pertinent material is accessible to them. Workers at sixteen specialized clearinghouses in the United States search for the material, read and abstract it, and then record the bibliographical information. Highly respected and in constant use.

Indexes

*W1225. *Education Index (Ed. Ind.)*. New York: Wilson, 1929– . 10/yr., with quarterly and annual cumulations. Z5813.E23   016.3705

Old Reliable. This comprehensive reference source indexes 350 education-related periodicals by subject and author. It includes a few subject headings that may help the literature student.

Periodicals

W1227. *Journal of College Placement*. Bethlehem, Pa.: College Placement Council, 1940– . Quarterly. LB2343.5.A15

Perhaps the most important title in this guide. The focus is narrow and critical: employment for the college graduate. Subjects range from the value of on-campus interviews to the effect of pertinent course work on the career (it does matter), résumé evaluation, the technique of interviewing an employer, and even "Career counselling for the obscure, the meek, and the ugly." Reviews of books that guide decisions students will face when they look for and try to keep a job. Annotated index for 1948–70. Professors who care about their students will read this.

Indexed in *Current Ind. Jour. Ed.* (W1224), *Ed. Ind.* (W1225).

See also

Awards (W1060–62)
Biography (W1146–47)
Computer Abstracts (W1190)
Computing Reviews (W1191)
Directory of American Scholars (W1146)
PMLA: Directory (W1029), Sept.
Prospects for the 70's (W1310)
Teaching Resources and Methods (W1596–1604)

Encyclopedias

*W1228. *New Encyclopaedia Britannica*. 15th ed. 30 vols. Chicago: Benton, 1974. AE5.E363   031

The new *Britannica* serves two functions: It is a reference book for quick answers or preliminary surveys, and it is an instrument of education for extensive study. The Propaedia volume is a 780-page outline of all knowledge with cross-references to long discussions in the Macropaedia set of nineteen volumes. This approach would be suitable for broad questions like "What can I learn about religion since the Reformation?" For the same question, the Micropaedia (10 vols.) provides a short entry on Luther, for instance, with many cross-references. Researchers may have to handle several volumes before they find the desired subject heading and entry. Critics have belabored this point.

Literature students will be particularly interested in vol. 10 of the Macropaedia. There they will find "Linguistics" (pp. 993–1013), "Literary Criticism" (pp. 1037–41), and "Literature" (pp. 1041–1264), with entries ranging from one column on New Zealand and Katherine Mansfield to three pages on German literature in the eighteenth century and seven pages on American literature of the twentieth century.

Specialized encyclopedias

—with priority for research problems in specific areas:

American Indian (P875)	Music (W1446–47)
Art (W1038–39)	Philosophy (W1485)
Folklore (W1272)	Religion (W1542–44, W1546)
History (W1293)	Russian studies (Q937)
Literature (J523, R953, W1402–05)	Social Sciences (W1578)
Middle Ages (J247)	

Film

Basic guides

*W1229. Armour, Robert A. *Film: A Reference Guide*. Westport, Conn.: Greenwood, 1980. 251pp. PN1993.45.A75   791.43'029

This review of research explains and evaluates the best reference books on film history, film in relation to fiction or drama, film and society, major films and film artists, periodicals, international influences, and relevant areas. Because it emphasizes the popular aspects, it can be used as a classroom text as well as a reference book.

*W1230. *Cinema Booklist*. Ed. George Rehrauer. Metuchen, N.J.: Scarecrow, 1972. 473pp. Supplement 1 (1974), 405pp. Supplement 2 (1977), 470pp. Z5784.M9.R42   016.79143

Important because it has a good editor as well as a good idea. A cumulated index in supplement 2, for instance, leads to entries in all three volumes. This lists, annotates, and recommends the best and most recent biographies, autobiographies, books on the art and history of filmmaking, scripts, indexes, bibliographies, surveys of national efforts, musicals, and science fiction. Students should be given assignments in this easy-to-use source. The success rate will be high.

*W1231. *Film Book Bibliography, 1940-1975*. Ed. Jack C. Ellis et al. Metuchen, N.J.: Scarecrow, 1979. 764pp. Z5784.M9.E44   [PN1994]   016.79143

A noticeably reliable list of 5,400 books and dissertations on the history, technique, interpretation, and personalities of the film published since the one and only volume of the *Film Index* was produced in 1941 (see W1232). This is more comprehensive than Dyment, but students should consult both for thorough coverage of the early years of film. Subject and then chronological arrangement, with some annotations. Title, name, and subject indexes. Extremely well done.

*W1232. *Literature of the Film: A Bibliographical Guide to the Film as Art and Entertainment, 1936-1970*. Ed. Alan R. Dyment. London: White Lion, 1975. 398pp. Z5784.M9.D9   016.79143

The *Film Index* (New York: Wilson, 1941) was, by unanimous agreement, an excellent research tool, but it was never completed. This picks up where that work left off (1936), annotating about thirteen hundred books (not articles) concerned with cinema as art, its history, biographies, autobiographies, critical studies, screenplays, technique, and film categories such as the comedy, the western, and the musical. Books of this type go out of date quickly, of course. More recent information can be found in Ellis (W1231) and the latest issues of *Cinema Booklist* (W1230) and *Film Review Digest Annual* (W1239).

W1233. *Film Study: A Resource Guide*. Ed. Frank Manchel. Rutherford, N.J.:

Fairleigh Dickinson Univ. Press, 1973. 422pp. Z5784.M9.M34
791.43'07
Still valuable for its history of film's relations with fiction, biography,
sociology, and war; for its discussion of film's stereotypes, themes, and techniques; and for its evaluations of hundreds of titles that will help in all these
areas. It was designed specifically for teachers who are faced with the problem
of how to go about teaching film but is now superseded in many ways by Armour's guide (W1229).

*W1234. *American Film Institute Catalog.* New York: Bowker, 1971– . In
progress (vols. 3–4, 1976). PN1998.A57   016.7'9143'0973
When completed, this multivolume set will be the definitive work on factual information concerning American motion pictures made between 1890 and
1970. Vols. 1 and 2 (1653pp.) provide descriptions, credits, and subject indexes
for every feature film produced between 1921 and 1930. The entry for *Abie's
Irish Rose*, for instance, includes the date, number of reels and feet, names of
cast and production staff, a short summary of the plot, and a list of pertinent
subject headings that students might have found in the subject index while looking for ideas: Irish, Rabbis, Priest, Soldiers, Jews, Veterans, Marriage—Mixed,
Prejudice. If students need more material on Prejudice, they will find thirteen
other motion pictures listed under that heading in the subject index. Vols. 3
and 4 cover the years 1961–70 (2244pp.). Reviewers so far have been able to
come up with only one more request: They wish the excellent indexes were even
more detailed to permit additional means of access.

W1235. *Literature and Film: An Annotated Bibliography, 1909–1977.* Ed.
Jeffrey E. Welch. New York: Garland, 1981. 315pp.
Designed especially for students who want to investigate the relation be-
tween films and literature. Arranged chronologically and then alphabetically by
critic. Indexes of critics and films. Keep this up to date with *Literature/Film
Quarterly* (W1266).

Series

W1236.   Film Directors and Genre. Boston: Hall, 1977– . In progress. 200pp.
Brief biographical sketches, critical surveys of film themes and techniques,
chronological listing of films and works, annotated guides to writings about the
director, and author and title indexes appear in each of these research guides
to information:

Robert Aldrich	Stanley Kubrick
Lindsay Anderson	Akira Kurosawa
Ingmar Bergman	David Lean
Stan Brakhage	Richard Lester
Charles Chaplin	Ernst Lubitsch
Walt Disney	Sidney Lumet
Federico Fellini	George Méliès
Robert Flaherty	Sam Peckinpah
Jean-Luc Godard	Arthur Penn
Buster Keaton	Roman Polanski

Jean Renoir
Alain Robbe-Grillet
Ken Russell
John Schlesinger
Dziga Vertov
Peter Watkins

Orson Welles
Billy Wilder
Frederick Wiseman
William Wyler
—and others

W1237. Twayne's Filmmakers Series. Boston: Twayne, 1978–   . Approximately 8/yr. Former title: Twayne's Theatrical Arts Series.

Critical studies of important figures and their achievements in the performing arts. Subjects include

Lindsay Anderson
Luis Buñuel
Frank Capra
René Clair
Francis Ford Coppola
Abel Gance
Jean-Luc Godard
Samuel Goldwyn
Sacha Guitry
Grigori Kozintsev
Fritz Lang
Joseph Losey
Anthony Mann
Lewis Milestone
Mike Nichols
Laurence Olivier
G. W. Pabst

Pier Paolo Pasolini
Sam Peckinpah
Sidney Pollack
Nicholas Ray
Karel Reisz
Alain Resnais
Leni Riefenstahl
Nicolas Roeg
Ken Russell
Max Scheler
John Schlesinger
Douglas Sirk
Surrealism and American Feature Films
François Truffaut
Peter Watkins
Billy Wilder
William Wyler

Reviews

W1238. *Selected Film Criticism.* Ed. Anthony Slide. 7 vols. Metuchen, N.J.: Scarecrow, 1982–83.

1896–1911. 1982. 134pp.
1912–1920. 1982. 325pp.
1921–1930. 1982. 335pp.
1931–1940. 1982. 292pp.
1941–1950. 1983. 280pp.
1951–1960. 1984.
Foreign Films, 1930–1950. 1984.

Reprints of film reviews as they were published between 1896 and 1950.

*W1239. *Film Review Digest Annual.* Ed. David M. Brownstone and Irene M. Franck. Millwood, N.Y.: KTO, 1976–   . Annual. PN1995.F465 791.43'7

Resembles the *Book Review Digest* (W1558) in that each annual volume contains excerpts from about fifteen hundred reviews that appeared originally in a variety of American, British, and Canadian publications. Since it aims to be a convenient source for quick identification, it indexes only a few selected newspapers and popular periodicals such as *Films in Review* and the *Village Voice*. Quotations from fourteen reviews of *The Last Tycoon* are cited, for instance, to give readers a general idea of its critical reception. This source does have its value, therefore, even though it is slow to appear and is not scholarly.

*W1240. *New York Times Film Reviews, 1913-1978.* 11 vols., including indexes. New York: Arno, 1970-   . Supplements every two years. PN1995.N4   809.23

For a panorama of film history since before World War I, consult this chronological arrangement of reproductions of 22,500 reviews as they originally appeared in the *New York Times*. The contents are easily accessible through the detailed index of titles, producing and distributing companies, actors, and other persons cited in the film. Articles concerning outstanding and award-winning films are included as are lists of the ten best movies since 1924 (according to the *Times*), winners of the New York Film Critics' Circle since 1935, and photographs of famous actors and actresses. For reviews of *current* films see "Motion Pictures" in the *New York Times Index* (F50) and other sources listed at the end of this section.

W1241. Bowles, Stephen E. *Index to Critical Film Reviews in British and American Film Periodicals together with an Index to Critical Reviews of Books about Film.* 3 vols. in 2. New York: Burt Franklin, 1975. Z5784.M9.B64   [PN1995]   791.43'01'6

The special focus is on reviews and books about films, especially those of the 1950s and 1960s. Only twenty-nine periodicals are indexed, however, so this source is helpful but not comprehensive.

W1242. Salem, James M., ed. *A Guide to Critical Reviews: The Screenplay from The Jazz Singer to Dr. Strangelove.* 2 vols. New York: Scarecrow, 1971. Supplement 1, 1963-80 (1982), 698pp. Z5782.S34   016.809'2

A bibliography of reviews (not scholarly articles) that appeared in popular American and Canadian periodicals and in the *New York Times* from 1927 to 1963. More recent reviews of movies can be located in the sources listed at the end of this section. The editors have not attempted to index scholarly journals, only those popular titles that are found in most libraries and are therefore accessible to most students.

Coverage is excellent—about twelve thousand American and important foreign films with, for instance, fifteen entries on *Tom Jones*. Several lists of award winners may be found in the back of the book.

Arrangement is alphabetical by title. Dates of production are included. No quotations from the reviews—only information that will help the student locate the original article. See four other volumes in this series by Salem:

American Drama, 1909-1969 (P805)
The Musical, 1909-1974 (P806)
British and Continental Drama from Ibsen to Pinter (J559)
Foreign Drama, 1909-1977 (R969)

Identification problems

*W1243. Katz, Ephraim. *The Film Encyclopedia*. New York: Crowell, 1982, c1979. 1266pp. PN1993.45.K34   791.43'03

Emphasis is on the recent, the American, and the exhaustive details of technology, biography, and history. This is the most comprehensive and scholarly of the numerous film encyclopedias. It contains entries for the histories of national cinema (Soviet Union, Italy, etc.), for filmmakers and filmmaking, for inventions, equipment, organizations, terms, and biographies of hundreds of stars and production staff. The author says he spent ten hours of research for every hour of actual writing. This can be used with confidence.

W1244. *Oxford Companion to Film*. Ed. Liz-Anne Bawden. New York: Oxford Univ. Press, 1976. 767pp. PN1993.4509   791.43'03

A reliable source for facts about the life of a director (such as Jean-Luc Godard) or composer (such as Ernest Gold), for brief summaries of international landmark films, for definitions of film terminology, for films as art and as political weapon, for identification of specific production companies or film periodicals, for surveys of national contributions, or for a few excellent stills from the movies. This is discriminating company. If it is here, it is important. If it is not here, check Katz (W1243), Halliwell (W1245), the American Film Institute catalog (W1234), and other titles in this section.

W1245. Halliwell, Leslie. *The Filmgoer's Companion*. 7th ed. New York: Scribners, 1980. 745pp. Paperback. PN1993.45.H3   791.43'03

A convenient reference book for the layman with brief, very brief, information on actors, directors, musicians, and all important movie personalities as well as on individual films, technical terms, censorship, and other items of interest to the movie fan. Emphasis is on English and American films, with only a little information on foreign films or television. Index of fictional characters, a list of themes mentioned in the main text, and a checklist of recommended books, but no subject index. The *Oxford Companion to Film* (W1244) discusses many of the same subjects, usually in a more discursive and perceptive manner, but this may occasionally supply important facts or clues because of its greater number of entries—ten thousand.

W1246. ———. *Halliwell's Film Guide*. 3rd ed. New York: Scribners, 1982, c1981. 1153pp. Paperback. PN1993.45.H27   791.43'03

Complements Halliwell's *Companion* (W1245) by supplying facts, synopses, and comments on eight thousand films, including those made for television. Other books provide longer summaries, and still others cite more facts, but this is a convenient one-volume source for brief, basic, accurate information. Halliwell's enthusiasm is refreshing.

W1247. Sadoul, Georges. *Dictionary of Films*. Trans. Peter Morris. Berkeley: Univ. of California Press, 1972, c1965. 432pp. PN1993.45.S3213 791.43'03

Important because it summarizes and criticizes twelve hundred of the most influential films from all over the world. No other source is so comprehensive.

W1248. ———. *Dictionary of Film Makers*. Trans. Peter Morris. Berkeley: Univ. of California Press, 1972, c1965. 288pp. PN1993.45.S313 791.43'03

Brief but discerning comments on the significant role played in the development of the film by one thousand producers and directors such as the American DeMille, the Russian Dovzhenko, the Austrian Stroheim, the Swedish Bergman, and the Japanese Mizoguchi. See also the Hall series on film directors (W1236) and Twayne's Filmmakers Series (W1237).

W1249.   Dimmitt, Richard B. *A Title Guide to the Talkies*. 2 vols. Metuchen, N.J.: Scarecrow, 1965. Supplement, 1964 through 1974, ed. Andrew A. Aros (1977), 336pp. PN1998.A6695   791.43'01'6

One specific purpose: to help students locate the novel, play, or short story on which the movie was based. *The Big Wave*, for instance, starred Sessue Hayakawa in 1961 and was based on the book by Pearl Buck published in 1948. The first two volumes list films made from 1927 through 1974. The supplement initiated the listing of distribution companies, entries for directors, year of issue, and foreign films exhibited in the United States. *Literature/Film Quarterly* (W1266) and *Literature and Film: An Annotated Bibliography, 1909–1977* (W1235) are also concerned with adaptations from prose to film.

W1250. ———. *An Actor Guide to the Talkies*. 2 vols. Metuchen, N.J.: Scarecrow, 1967. Supplement, 1965 through 1974, ed. Andrew A. Aros (1977), 781pp. PN1998.A6694   016.79143

An alphabetical title list of 11,500 American and foreign films made from 1949 through 1974 with names of the characters and actors and other production facts. The indexes list actors and actresses alphabetically to permit a study of their roles over the years.

Indexes—Current

*W1252. *Film Literature Index: A Quarterly Author-Subject Index to International Periodical Literature of Film with Expanded Coverage of Television Periodical Literature*. Albany, N.Y.: Film and Television Documentation Center, 1973– . Quarterly. Annual cumulation. Z5784.M9.F45   791.43'01'6

The very best film literature index, with excellent coverage, clear arrangement, and accurate indexing of even minor news notes. The most recent issue (vol. 9 for 1981) locates scholarly articles and book reviews in three hundred film and 125 general international periodicals and arranges them under one thousand subject headings such as Popular Culture, *Casablanca*, Social Values, Frank Capra, and Goldie Hawn. This is a most welcome research aid that will be invaluable when the publishers are finally able to produce it more quickly. It overlaps to some extent with the *International Index* (W1253), but the arrangement is different, so students should consult both for complete coverage. Use this to bring *New Film Index* (W1255) up to date.

W1253. *International Index to Film Periodicals [————]: An Annotated Guide*. Ed. Michael Moulds. London: St. James, 1972- . Annual. Z5784.M9.I49   016.79143

This annual locating file to the contents of about eighty international film periodicals is especially strong in foreign languages. The editors wisely add a few more periodicals to their coverage each year, thus making the index more and more valuable. Critical works are listed under the title of the film. The indexes of directors, authors, and subjects lead to entries on interviews, biographies, general works, histories, and information on festivals and associations. Cross-references could be improved, however. This and *Film Literature Index* (W1252) are the major keys to international criticism and reviews in the cinema.

Indexes—Retrospective

*W1255. *New Film Index: A Bibliography of Magazine Articles in English, 1930-1970*. Ed. Richard D. MacCann and Edward S. Perry. New York: Dutton, 1975. 522pp. Z5784.M9.M29   011

For factual information on films, go to the *American Film Institute Catalog* (W1234). For books about films, go to *Cinema Booklist* (W1230), *Film Book Bibliography* (W1231), or *Literature of the Film* (W1232). For reviews of films, go to *Film Review Digest Annual* (W1239) and others. But for *articles* about film as art and entertainment, use either this or Gerlach (W1257), which overlap only slightly. Arrangement is by subject (Education about Films, Writers, Europe since 1930, Biography, Restraints), with the articles listed chronologically under each heading to illustrate development and trends. This means that browsing is compulsory, but browsing can be productive. A detailed table of contents and a proper name index alleviate the problem. To keep this up to date, go to *International Index to Film Periodicals* (W1253) or *Film Literature Index* (W1252).

W1256. *Retrospective Index to Film Periodicals, 1930-1971*. Ed. Linda Batty. New York: Bowker, 1975. 425pp. Z5784.M9.B39   791.43'05

Complements the *International Index to Film Periodicals* (W1253), which currently indexes the fourteen journals indexed retrospectively here. Lists critical articles, film and book reviews, subjects, names of important individuals, and titles of films. Easy to use, but readers should be aware that, in spite of the title, coverage is limited almost entirely to the 1950s and 1960s.

W1257. *Critical Index: A Bibliography of Articles on Film in English, 1946-1973, Arranged by Names and Topics*. Ed. John Gerlach and Lana Gerlach. New York: Teacher's Coll. Press, 1974. 726pp. Z5784.M9.G47   016.79143

This index to the contents of about one hundred film and general periodicals is unique because it is arranged by 175 subjects (Myth, Literary Figures, American Indians, Blacks, Supernatural) and by name (Antonioni, Bergman, Richardson, Warhol), with brief descriptive phrases, author and film-title indexes, and appendixes. The directions are complicated, however, and the computer production is difficult to read. Browsing is almost impossible because any subject search must begin in the introduction's "Dictionary of Topics." And fifteen of the twenty-two periodicals are also indexed by *New Film Index* (W1255).

W1258. *Film Criticism: An Index to Critics' Anthologies.* Ed. Richard Heinz-kill.   Metuchen, N.J.: Scarecrow, 1975.   151pp.   PN1995.H4 016.79143'7

Similar to the *Essay and General Literature Index* (F46) in that it locates individual essays and reviews buried in anthologies and arranges them according to subject. In this source, the student can look up *Midnight Cowboy* and see that seven different collections contain criticism of that film. The scope is strictly limited, however, to anthologies that contain the work of a single critic.

Indexes

—with special sections on film and other aspects of the motion picture industry:

Art Index (W1042), under "Moving Pictures," with subdivisions on music, festivals, individual films, and specific features that encourage aesthetic studies

Bibliographic Index (C28), entries under "Actors," "Moving Pictures," and others

Biography Index (W1085), under index of professions: "Actors," "Motion Picture Directors," and others

Essay and General Literature Index (F46), under "Moving Pictures," with subdivisions on criticism, acting, production, reviews, their relation to literature, religion, education

New York Times Index (F50), under "Motion Pictures," best for recent reviews because it is published twice a month

Readers' Guide (F48), under "Moving Pictures," particularly good for reviews on individual titles, which it lists alphabetically

Periodicals

W1260. *American Film: Journal of the Film and Television Arts.* Washington, D.C.: American Film Inst., 1975– . 10/yr. PN1993.A617   791.43'05

An important periodical with reviews, notes, articles by professional film critics, and reports on film festivals and activities of the institute.
Indexed in *Arts and Hum. Cit. Ind.* (F47), *Index to Bk. Rev. Hum.* (W1560).

W1261. *Film Comment.* Brookline, Mass.: Film Comment, 1962– . Quarterly. PN1993.F438   791.43'05

Scholarly comments from cultural and historical points of view on every phase of the international motion picture industry: directors, screenwriters, festivals, foreign films, realism, and other -isms. Emphasis is on the best, with frequent reviews and interviews. Annual index.
Indexed in *Arts and Hum. Cit. Ind.* (F47), *Bk. Rev. Ind.* (W1559), *Current Bk. Rev. Cit.* (W1564), *Film Literature Ind.* (W1252), *Hum. Ind.* (F45), *Readers' Guide* (F48).

W1262. *Film Culture.* New York: n.p. (Box 1499), 1955– . Quarterly.
PN1993.F44   791.43'05
An aggressive, well-established journal with the voice of the little magazine
(W1423-30)—independent, imaginative, innovative, and encouraging to the
lover of the experimental film. Criticism, interviews, notes, reviews, illustrations.
Indexed in *Art Ind.* (W1042), *Arts and Hum. Cit. Ind.* (F47), *Current Bk.
Rev. Cit.* (W1564), *Film Literature Ind.* (W1252).

W1263. *Film Quarterly.* Berkeley: Univ. of California Press, 1945– . Quarter-
ly. PN1993.H74
Objective, analytical, scholarly articles, with long, important film and book
reviews, interviews, and an annual survey of international scholarship on the film.
Indexed in *Art Ind.* (W1042), *Arts and Hum. Cit. Ind.* (F47), *Bk. Rev.
Ind.* (W1559), *Current Bk. Rev. Cit.* (W1564), *Film Literature Ind.* (W1252),
Hum. Ind. (F45), *Readers' Guide* (F48).

W1264. *Filmfacts.* Los Angeles: Univ. of Southern California, 1938– .
2/month. PN1995.F48
Long synopses, critiques, and excerpts from favorable and unfavorable
reviews. Before buying overpriced tickets or writing an important paper, read
this to see how the experts judge the film. Annual index and list of film award
winners. Illustrations.

W1265. *Journal of Popular Film and Television.* Washington, D.C.: Heldref,
1978– . Quarterly. Popular Culture Assn. Former title, 1972–78: *Journal of Popular Film.* PN1993.J66   791.43'05
This scholarly journal has been well received by its academic readers and
contributors. Articles, reviews, and bibliography. Index for 1972–77 (see W1500).
Indexed in *Art Ind.* (W1042), *Arts and Hum. Cit. Ind.* (F47), *Film
Literature Ind.* (W1252).

*W1266. *Literature/Film Quarterly (LFQ).* Salisbury, Md.: Salisbury State Coll.,
1973– . Quarterly. PN1995.3.L57   791.43'05
Scholarly and impressive. This is designed especially for the literature stu-
dent, who will find that the scope ranges from Tolstoy, Hawthorne, Faulkner,
Dickens, Greene, Vonnegut, Mann, and Capote to Dante. A 1973 issue, for
instance, was devoted to critical articles on film adaptations of Shakespeare—
Polanski and *Macbeth*, Kozintsev and *Hamlet*, Olivier and *Othello*, and
Hollywood's numerous attempts at *Romeo and Juliet*. The *Title Guide to the
Talkies* (W1249) lists other films that have been made from prose works. See
also *Literature and Film: An Annotated Bibliography, 1909–1977* (W1235).
Indexed in *ABELL* (D32), *Arts and Hum. Cit. Ind.* (F47), *Film Literature
Ind.* (W1252), *Hum. Ind.* (F45), *MLAIB* (D31).

*W1267. *Sight and Sound: The International Film Quarterly.* London: British
Film Inst., 1932– . Quarterly. PN1993.S56   791.43'05
The major publication for British films has a variety of interesting features,

including dynamic editorial policies, a handsome format, letters, articles, reviews, and photographs. Highly respected and frequently quoted. Circulation: 32,000. Indexed in *Art Ind.* (W1042), *Arts and Hum. Cit. Ind.* (F47), *Bk. Rev. Ind.* (W1559), *Brit. Hum. Ind.* (F49), *Current Bk. Rev. Cit.* (W1564), *Film Literature Ind.* (W1252), *Hum. Ind.* (F45).

Additional reference sources for information on film

W1268. *Banned Films* (W1174)
Basic Books in the Mass Media (W1431)
Encyclopedia of Mystery (G86)
Film: A Guide to Reference Sources. Ed. Jewel Lowenstein. Montreal: McLennan Library, McGill Univ., 1982. 17pp.
French XX (Q915)
Guide to Dance in Film (W1470.3)
Journal of Modern Literature (J530), Film as literature
Kane, Leslie. "Current Survey of Reference Sources in Film and Television." *Reference Services Review*, 7, no. 1 (1979), 37–42. See *RSR* (W1569.1)
Library Journal (New York: Bowker, 1875–   ), Cinema
MLAIB (D31), vol. 1, General IV, Cinema
tdr: the drama review (J564)
Who Was Who on Screen (W1109)

Folklore, Mythology, and Legend

Surveys

W1270.   Brunvand, Jan H. *Folklore: A Study and Research Guide*. New York: St. Martin's, 1976. 144pp. Z5981.B78   [GR66]   016.398

A survey of American folklore, its characteristics, research problems and possibilities, and an explanation of general and specific reference works useful in the field. A chapter on the preparation of a research paper helps to make this a suitable text for the beginning student. Author index only. A detailed author-title-subject index should be included in the second edition.

Basic guides

*W1271. *American Folklore: A Bibliography, 1950–1974*. Ed. Cathleen C. Flanagan and John T. Flanagan. Metuchen, N.J.: Scarecrow, 1977. 406pp. Z5984.U6.F55   [GR105]   016.398'0973

Concerned solely with the *verbal* folklore of America (United States, Canada, Mexico, the Caribbean). This lists 3,600 titles relating to ballads, songs, tales, myths, legends, superstitions, beliefs, cures, proverbs, riddles, and folk speech. Because it has too few annotations and no subject, regional, or ethnic indexes, the book is not as convenient as it could and should be. Students might prefer to use *Native American Folklore, 1879–1979: An Annotated Bibliography*, ed. William M. Clements and Frances M. Malpezzi (Athens: Ohio Univ. Press, 1984; 240pp.).

Identification problems

*W1272. *Funk and Wagnalls Standard Dictionary of Folklore, Mythology, and Legend.* New York: Funk and Wagnalls, 1972. 1236pp. GR35.F8 398.03.F98

Probably the best folklore dictionary for quick reference. Recurring motifs, terms, names, dates, and important works are explained; sources and reference materials are cited; national folklore, myths, and twelve major world religions are discussed fully; and many entries are signed. Randomly selected subject headings include betel-nut chewing, cannibalism, Celtic folklore, fallen angels, the Fisher King, infanticide, Johnny Appleseed, Leda, and religious folk music. A readable, fascinating book.

Series

W1273. Folklore of the British Isles. Totowa, N.J.: Rowman, 1974–   .

A geographical series drawing on oral and written sources in the Scottish Highlands, Lake District, Cotswolds, Isle of Man, Warwickshire, Ireland, and other areas. Scope ranges from legends, supernatural beliefs, songs, humor, place-names, and holidays to just plain gossip. Interesting, entertaining, and valuable. A similar series by Garland (New York) focuses on such subjects as folklore and literature in the British Isles and the United States, American immigrant folklore, Jewish and South American Indian folklore.

Abstracts

W1274. *Abstracts of Folklore Studies* (*Abst. Folklore Stud.*). Austin: Univ. of Texas, 1963–75 (vols. 1–13). Quarterly. GR1.A52   398'.05

Scholars regret its passing, because this abstracted almost a thousand articles a year from several hundred international periodicals including *Medium Aevum* (J273), *SEL* (J320), *Critique* (J545), *Modern Philology* (H150), and *Time*. The abstracts are signed, and full citation is provided so the student can consult the complete work if the abstract sounds interesting. Cumulative indexes by title, author, and subjects such as alchemy and Africa.

Indexed in *ABELL* (D32).

Indexes

W1275. *Index to Fairy Tales, 1949–1972, Including Folklore, Legends, and Myths in Collections.* Ed. Norma O. Ireland. Westwood, Mass.: Faxon, 1973. 741pp. Fourth supplement, 1973–77 (1979), 259pp. Z5983.F17.I73 398.2'01'6

The best way to locate an individual tale that has been anthologized even if you know only the title, the subject, or one of the characters. Occasional inaccuracies crop up, but numerous cross-references and two thousand subject headings help determined students find what they need. For complete coverage, use all supplements and the original *Index* published in 1926.

W1276. Thompson, Stith. *Motif-Index of Folk Literature: A Classification of Narrative Elements in Folktales, Ballads, Myths, Fables, and Medieval*

Romances, Exempla, Fabliaux, Jestbooks, and Local Legends. 6 vols. Bloomington: Indiana Univ. Press, 1955–58. GR67.T52   398.012
This is a numerically cross-referenced index to mythological and supernatural motifs found throughout literature. "Dragon" in the index, for instance, leads to vol. 1 (A2468.3) and a list of related subjects found in folklore all over the world. The bibliography has been revised (1976; 38pp.).

Periodicals

*W1278. *Journal of American Folklore (JAF)*. Washington, D.C.: American Folklore Soc., 1888– . Quarterly. GR1.J8   051
"Folklore" in the broadest sense of the word, with articles on the Holy Grail, Chaucer's Wife of Bath, Irish ballads, castes in India, Schiller's *William Tell*, Afro-American legends, and elves. The lengthy book and record reviews are highly respected by researchers and teachers. From 1949 through 1963 it featured an annual bibliography of scholarship that ceased publication when *Abstracts of Folklore Studies* was created (see W1274). Analytical index to vols. 1–70, ed. Tristram P. Coffin (1958).
Indexed in *ABELL* (D32), *America* (E43), *Arts and Hum. Cit. Ind.* (F47), *Bk. Rev. Ind.* (W1559), *Current Bk. Rev. Cit.* (W1564), *Hist. Abst.* (E43), *Hum. Ind.* (F45), *MLAIB* (D31), *Music Ind.* (W1456).

*W1279. *Folk-lore*. London: Folklore Soc., 1878– . 2/yr. GR1.F5
Articles on Stonehenge, Faroese legends, Russian folk theater, Danish ballads, and similar subjects; news, reviews, and letters to the editor.
Indexed in *ABELL* (D32), *Arts and Hum. Cit. Ind.* (F47), *Brit. Hum. Ind.* (F49), *Current Bk. Rev. Cit.* (W1564), *Hum. Ind.* (F45), *Index to Bk. Rev. Hum.* (W1560), *MLAIB* (D31).

W1280. *Southern Folklore Quarterly (SFQ)*. Gainesville: Univ. of Florida, 1937– . Quarterly. GR1.S65   398.0975
Articles, book reviews, and notes. *MLAIB* (D31) has taken over the annual bibliography that *SFQ* featured from 1937 to 1972 of books and articles on all aspects of folklore in the Americas, including that of Spanish- and Portuguese-speaking nations.
Indexed in *ABELL* (D32), *Arts and Hum. Cit. Ind.* (F47), *Hum. Ind.* (F45), *Index to Bk. Rev. Hum.* (W1560), *MLAIB* (D31), *Music Ind.* (W1456).

Background reading

*W1282. Bulfinch, Thomas. *Bulfinch's Mythology: The Age of Fable, The Age of Chivalry, Legends of Charlemagne*. New York: Crowell, 1970. 980pp. BL310.B82   398.2   [291.B933]
Close, careful interpretations (not literal translations) of primary material including Ovid, Vergil, Norse and Greek myths, Beowulf, and all stories related to King Arthur and Charlemagne.

W1283. Campbell, Joseph. *The Hero with a Thousand Faces*. Cleveland: World

(Meridian), 1949. 416pp. Paperback. BL313.C28   291'.13
Fascinating, important, but difficult, for it requires the reader to be familiar with thousands of obscure references and allusions,

W1284.   ——. *The Masks of God: Creative Mythology.* 4 vols. New York: Viking, 1959–68. Paperback. BL311.C272   291.13
This landmark in comparative mythology considers the human preoccupation with ancient anonymous myths, especially as it is evidenced in the works of Joyce, Dante, Mann, and Eliot. Reading this will take fortitude, but it is without doubt a permanent contribution to scholarship. Other titles helpful in this field will be found in Comparative Literature (Section T).

*W1285. Frazer, Sir James. *The Golden Bough: A Study in Magic and Religion.* 1 vol., abridged edition. New York: Macmillan, 1963. 864pp. Paperback. Originally published in 13 vols. in 1896. BL310.F72   291
Important because it focused scholarly attention on the pervading influence of custom and beliefs. As a source of information on folklore, superstitions, and religious beliefs throughout the world, it is without equal, but students should be aware that some of its accounts and arguments originated with travelers and have proved to be unreliable.

See also

ABELL (D32), 286 entries in the 1978 volume
Bibliography of Canadian Folklore (N669.1)
Gerstenberger and Hendrick (W1475)
MLAIB (D31), vol. 1, 3,359 entries in the 1980 volume
Who's Who in Greek and Roman Mythology (S1003)
—and several state or national folklore publications including
  Appalachian South
  Australian Tradition
  Indiana Folklore
  Kentucky Folklore Record
  Mid-South Folklore
  Mississippi Folklore Register
  New York Folklore
  North Carolina Folklore Journal
  Seattle Folklore Society Newsletter
  Tennessee Folklore Society Bulletin
  Western Folklore

Foreign Phrases

*W1287. *Dictionary of Foreign Words and Phrases in Current English.* Ed. Alan J. Bliss. New York: Dutton, 1966; rpt. with corrections, London: Routledge, 1977. 389pp. Paperback. PE1670.B55   423.1
A historical account of the infiltration of foreign words into the English language; an explanation of how foreign words and phrases are used now; statistics

on frequency and nationality; quotations; pronunciation; plurals; and feminine forms. These and other topics in the absolutely first-rate introduction are not to be missed, and neither is the appendix with its list of words by nationality and century. Thousands of well-researched entries. A scholarly achievement.

W1288.   *Dictionary of Foreign Terms.* Rev. Charles Berlitz. 2nd ed. New York: Crowell, 1975. 368pp. PE1670.M3   422'.4
A revision of Christopher Mawson's venerable first edition (1934). About fifty languages including African and American Indian are represented here with fifteen thousand words and phrases. Old-timers with sound Greek and Latin foundations have oft remarked that such books are especially useful to the current younger generation, which has deprived itself of the advantages of a liberal education and so cannot handle foreign languages with ease.

W1289.   *Dictionary of Foreign Phrases and Abbreviations.* Ed. Kevin Guinagh. 3rd ed. New York: Wilson, 1982. 288pp. Paperback. PE1670.G8   418
Guinagh's alphabetically arranged dictionary of foreign terms should be used by the student who finds an unfamiliar reference, for example, to A.M.D.G. in Hopkins' poetry or to Cantab. when studying Milton.

See also
Dictionary of Foreign Quotations (W1537)

Goldentree Bibliographies in Language and Literature

*W1291. Goldentree Bibliographies in Language and Literature. Ed. Osborne B. Hardison, Jr. Arlington Heights, Ill.: AHM, 1966–   . In progress. Paperback. Formerly published by Appleton (Meredith).

Harold B. Allen, *Linguistics and English Linguistics* (W1325)
Charles F. Altieri, *Modern Poetry* (J569)
Arthur E. Barker, *The Seventeenth Century: Bacon through Marvell* (J302)
Albert C. Baugh, *Chaucer* (J257)
David Bevington, *Shakespeare* (1978)
Donald F. Bond, *The Age of Dryden* (J365)
———, *The Eighteenth Century* (J364)
Wayne C. Booth and Gwin J. Kolb, *The British Novel through Jane Austen* (J200)
Jerome H. Buckley, *Victorian Poets and Prose Writers* (J489)
Charles A. Carpenter, *Modern British Drama* (J551)
Harry Hayden Clark, *American Literature: Poe through Garland* (P710)
Richard Beale Davis, *American Literature through Bryant* (P709)
Richard Harter Fogle, *Romantic Poets and Prose Writers* (J439)
Vernon Hall, *Literary Criticism: Plato through Johnson* (W1356)
James Holly Hanford, *Milton* (J366)

C. Hugh Holman, *The American Novel through Henry James* (P783)
John L. Lievsay, *The Sixteenth Century: Skelton through Hooker* (J303)
E. Hudson Long, *American Drama from Its Beginnings to the Present* (P795)
Jack W. Marken, *American Indian: Language and Literature* (P872)
William Matthews, *Old and Middle English Literature* (J228)
Blake Nevius, *The American Novel: Sinclair Lewis to the Present* (P784)
Irving Ribner, *Tudor and Stuart Drama* (J334)
Darwin T. Turner, *Afro-American Writers* (P838)
Ian P. Watt, *The British Novel: Scott through Hardy* (J479)
Paul L. Wiley, *The British Novel: Conrad to the Present* (J537)

History

*W1292. Langer, William L., comp. *Encyclopedia of World History*. 5th ed.
   Boston: Houghton, 1972. 1569pp. D21.L27   902.02
   This scholarly one-volume encyclopedia originally went through twenty editions in Germany and now includes the work of many noted historians. Its approach is chronological, with both long and short discursive entries. An excellent, authoritative source of miscellaneous information on, for instance, the eight Crusades, the spread of Greek culture, and America before Columbus. Maps, genealogical tables, and a 200-page index of persons, places, and events increase the value of this encyclopedia, which should ideally be available on every student's desk.

*W1293. *Dictionary of American History*. Ed. Louise B. Ketz. 7 vols. and index. Rev. ed. New York: Scribners, 1976–78. Abridgment (1983), 1140pp. E174.D52   973'.03
   Information on subjects relating to political, economic, sociological, industrial, and cultural history, but no biographies. Those of course are found in the *DAB* (W1087). Many events and popular terms are included, such as Andrews' Raid of 1862, the Berlin Wall, Indian-American-Native Cultures, and Bills of Credit in the eighteenth century. All articles are signed, and many have brief bibliographies for further study. Students should consult the excellent analytical index first because it lists items under every possible heading.

W1294. *Oxford Companion to American History*. Ed. Thomas H. Johnson. New York: Oxford Univ. Press, 1966. 906pp. E174.J6   973.03
   Brief information on any subject or person significant in the founding and growth of the nation, but emphasis is on the historical rather than the literary importance of the writers.

W1295. *Webster's Guide to American History: A Chronological, Geographical, and Biographical Survey and Compendium*. Springfield, Mass.: Merriam, 1971. 1428pp. E174.5.W4   973
   Maps, illustrations, tables on all subjects from presidents to popular songs,

and an index of all names and titles mentioned in the text help to make this an excellent one-volume source of historical information.

See also

Clio (W1303)
Dates (W1199–1204)
Historical Abstracts (E43)
History of Jewish Literature (R951)
Journal of the History of Ideas (W1305)
Literary History of France (Q902)
Literary History of Germany (Q916)
New Literary History (W1306)
Outline History of Spanish American Literature (R990)
Outline of Russian Literature (Q932)
World Literature since 1945 (R950)

Illustrators

W1297. Ray, Gordon N. *The Illustrator and the Book in England from 1790 to 1914*. New York: Oxford Univ. Press, 1976. 336pp. NC978.R37 741.64'0942

No other book covers this period, the greatest in fine book production in England. The author, publisher, and printer have prepared a laudable tribute to an art that sheer economics has forced almost out of existence. This describes the contents and format of 333 beautifully illustrated books, with essays on people and subjects related to their publication. It is in every way a tribute to its title, a quality book for collectors and book lovers: impressive binding, the finest paper, large pages and print, and exquisite reproductions of the art of Kate Greenaway, the Dalziel brothers, Thackeray, Lear, Blake, William Morris, the illustrations of Walter Crane for Hawthorne, those of Doyle for Ruskin and Thackeray, Rackham for Irving, Beardsley for Malory, Wilde, and Pope, Sullivan for Carlyle and Tennyson, George du Maurier for *Punch*, and Phiz for Dickens. You will spend a lot of time here.

W1298. *Book Illustrators in Eighteenth-Century England*. Ed. Hanns A. Hammelmann and Thomas S. R. Boase. New Haven: Yale Univ. Press, 1975. 120pp. NC978.H28   741.092'2

The era of Tonson, Fuseli, Burney, Gravelot, Hayman, Hogarth, and Stothard. Numerous illustrations. Impressive and entertaining.

*W1299. *Book Illustration and Decoration*. Ed. Vito J. Brenni. Westport, Conn.: Greenwood, 1980. 191pp. Z5956.I44.B7   016'.74164

The first and only guidebook that covers book illustration from ancient times to the present. Everything is listed here for the inquiring student or artist who needs to find helpful books, essays, theses, reference works, histories, biographies, contributions from various countries, and important titles in children's literature. Author and subject indexes.

Interdisciplinary Studies

Basic sources

W1300. *Bibliography on the Relations of Literature and the Other Arts.* Hanover, N.H.: Dartmouth Coll., 1952– . Annual. Z6511.M628 PN53.B5 016.700'8

Specializes in information on books and articles that relate literature, in theory and in application, to the visual arts, film, and music. This MLA project was published in mimeograph form from 1953 to 1973, then was a feature in *Hartford Studies in Literature* (W1307) from 1974 to 1976, and now is produced by Dartmouth and distributed at the MLA conference. A cumulation for 1952–67 was published in 1968 (rpt. New York: AMS, 1977).

W1301. *Literature and Society, 1961–65: A Selective Bibliography.* Ed. Paul J. Carter and George K. Smart. Coral Gables, Fla.: Univ. of Miami Press, 1967. 170pp. MLA. Z6511.M62 016.8099'33

————, *1956–1960.* Univ. of Miami Press, 1962. Annotated, with subject index. 71pp. Reprint, 1973.

————, *1950–1955.* Univ. of Miami Press, 1956. Annotated, with subject index. 57pp.

An alphabetical list of books and articles that "seem to reveal some literary expression of history, sociology, philosophy, religion, political science, folklore, aesthetics, psychology, publishing and communications" (Preface). Analytical index.

Periodicals

*W1303. *Clio: An Interdisciplinary Journal of Literature, History, and the Philosophy of History (Clio).* Fort Wayne, Ind.: Indiana Univ.– Purdue Univ., 1971– . Quarterly. AS30.053 901.9'05

Articles on a variety of authors, such as Joyce, Ben Jonson, Henry James, Verne, Arnold Bennett, Dostoevsky, Auerbach, Steinbeck, and Wordsworth. Even more important, it features hard-to-find items like "Relations of Literature and Science: A Bibliography," which appears annually (for earlier coverage of literature and science, see *Symposium*, T1015, and Dudley, W1573). Reviews of important books, and a cumulative index every two years which experienced researchers use with gratitude as a speedy, accurate, handy shortcut to the contents. Ideally, every periodical should cumulate its contents regularly.

Indexed in *ABELL* (D32), *Arts and Hum. Cit. Ind.* (F47), *Hum. Ind.* (F45), *Index to Bk. Rev. Hum.* (W1560), *MLAIB* (D31), *Phil. Ind.* (W1489), *Romantic Movement: A . . . Bibliography* (J443).

W1304. *Critical Inquiry (CI).* Chicago: Univ. of Chicago Press, 1973– . Quarterly. NX1.C64 700'.9

Predictions are that this will be called a major voice of the 1970s. This thought-provoking periodical specializes in crossing the disciplines: fiction, Bible,

film, poetics, marriage, music, *l'art pour l'art*, Sessions, Abrams, Welty, Burke, *Citizen Kane*, Sontag, Marlowe, Marx, and an entire issue on metaphor (Autumn 1978).
Indexed in *ABELL* (D32), *Abst. Eng. Stud.* (E38), *Am. Hum. Ind.* (P738), *Film Literature Ind.* (W1252), *MLAIB* (D31).

*W1305. *Journal of the History of Ideas: An International Quarterly Devoted to Intellectual History (JHI)*. Philadelphia: Temple Univ., 1940–   . Quarterly. B1.J75   105
Ideas as expressions of interrelationships between literature, the arts, religion, social sciences, and political and social movements. This intellectual journal maintains an enviable reputation for considering the provocative issue: the religion of Hume, Bartram and nature, Amicus Plato, the concept of Arcadia, and whether or not *verum* is *factum*. Annual index and cumulative indexes for vols. 1–25, 26–30, 31–35, 36–40.
Indexed in *ABELL* (D32), *Abst. Eng. Stud.* (E38), *Arts and Hum. Cit. Ind.* (F47), *Bk. Rev. Ind.* (W1559), *Current Bk. Rev. Cit.* (W1564), *Hum. Ind.* (F45), *Index to Bk. Rev. Hum.* (W1560), *MLAIB* (D31), *Phil. Ind.* (W1489).

W1306. *New Literary History: A Journal of Theory and Interpretation*. Baltimore: Johns Hopkins Univ. Press, 1969–   . 3/yr. PR1.N44   820.1
The nature of literature and how it relates to other disciplines and to society. Coverage extends to articles on the hero, the evolution of style, myth, hermeneutics, European and world literatures, historical interpretations, theory in film and the novel, medieval literature and contemporary theory (1979), and other subjects concerned with the relations of literature and history. International contributors. Cumulative index for vols. 1–10 (1969–79). Cumulative indexes every five years thereafter.
Indexed in *ABELL* (D32), *Abst. Eng. Stud.* (E38), *Arts and Hum. Cit. Ind.* (F47), *Film Literature Ind.* (W1252), *Hum. Ind.* (F45), *MLAIB* (D31).

W1307. *University of Hartford Studies in Literature: A Journal of Interdisciplinary Criticism*. West Hartford, Conn.: Univ. of Hartford, 1977–   . 3/yr. Former title, 1969–79: *Hartford Studies in Literature*. PN.H3   805
This journal's interest in interdisciplinary literary criticism extends to philosophy, theology, cinema, and psychology. Subjects range from *David Copperfield* (the novel and the film) to a psychoanalytic study of Calderón, a metaphysical approach to Sartre's *The Wall*, Hamlet, Defoe, James, Joyce, and Hesse. The annual bibliography on the relations between literature and the other arts, which it featured through 1977, has since that time appeared as a separate publication (W1300).
Indexed in *ABELL* (D32), *Am. Hum. Ind.* (P738), *Arts and Hum. Cit. Ind.* (F47), *MLAIB* (D31).

Background reading

W1310. Finestone, Harry, and Michael F. Shugrue. *Prospects for the 70's:*

English Departments and Multidisciplinary Study. New York: MLA, 1973. 246pp. PE66.F5   420'.7'11

This collection of essays proposes new directions for the study and teaching of English.

See also: Interdisciplinary material in the following reference sources:

W1311. Altholz, *Victorian England: 1837-1901* (J457)
    American Quarterly (P745)
    Annual Bibliography of Victorian Studies (J464)
    Bulletin of Research in the Humanities (H141)
    Cumulative Author Index for Poole's Index (J417)
    Danziger and Johnson, *Critical Reader* (W1409)
    Eighteenth Century: A Current Bibliography (J374)
    Eighteenth-Century Life (J380)
    Eighteenth-Century Studies: An Interdisciplinary Journal (J381)
    Encyclopaedia of Religion and Ethics (W1542)
    Encyclopedia of Philosophy (W1485)
    Georgia Review (H148)
    Humanities Index (F45)
    Improving College and University Teaching (W1601)
    International Encyclopedia of the Social Sciences (W1578)
    Journal of Aesthetic Education (W1602)
    Journal of Aesthetics and Art Criticism (W1043)
    Journal of Medieval and Renaissance Studies (J270)
    Kirschke, James J. "Methodology in the Study of Literature and the Other Arts." *Literary Research Newsletter*, 2, no. 2 (1977), 64-76. See *LRN* (W1421)
    Literature and Psychology (W1511)
    Modern Fiction Studies (J544)
    Oxford Companion to German Literature (Q922)
    Philosophy and Literature (W1490)
    Psychoanalysis, Psychology, and Literature: A Bibliography (W1509)
    Reader's Encyclopedia (W1402)
    Relations of Literature and Science: A Selected Bibliography (W1573)
    Relationship of Literature and Painting (W1037)
    STTH: Science/Technology and the Humanities (W1574)
    Symposium (T1015)
    Wellek and Warren, *Theory of Literature* (W1399)
    Yearbook of Comparative and General Literature (T1014)

Interlibrary Loan

W1312. When students need to borrow material from another library, they will be asked to write all pertinent information about their requests on a special interlibrary loan card. This is given to an interlibrary loan librarian who then has the task of verifying all the details. Correct title, spelling, initials of the author's name, publication date, edition, publisher, volume, issue, series, page numbers if it is an article, and, equally important, the *source* of this information must be included on the request form that is sent to the lending library. Accuracy is essential for obvious reasons. If the student fails to specify the first edition, for instance, the lending library may send the third edition, wasting time, effort, and money.

The sources used for verifying bibliographical information depend on the form, genre, nationality, and publication date of the item. Librarians might have to go to several different reference books to verify the facts on, for instance, the microfilm of a dissertation written in 1972, an American newspaper dated 1804, a volume of letters privately printed in Dublin in 1921, or the handwritten manuscripts of Gerard Manley Hopkins' poems. Most of the sources that librarians use for verification searches are included in this guide with evaluative annotations to explain their scope and purpose:

NUC (B10–11), *Brit. Mus. Cat.* (B13), Wright (P778), Ash (W1315), Downs (W1313–14), de Ricci (J262), Goff (J261), the Stratman bibliographies (J209, 211, 281, 401, 799, 803), *ULS* (W1479), *NST* (W1478), *Brit. U.-C. of Per.* (W1480), *New CBEL* (J175), *STC* (J306, 370), and many others including those listed in Library Collections (W1313–24).

After the facts have been verified, the next task is to locate first a library that owns a copy, and then a library that will lend one. Many libraries, students will find, do not release any of their holdings (such as Folger, Oxford, Cambridge, John Crerar), while others lend only certain items. As students use these bibliographies for their own reference problems, they will learn to interpret the bibliographical details and to note the library locations provided in the entries.

Library Collections

Economy and scholarly efficiency encourage most large libraries to develop extensive holdings in areas that represent the primary interests of their faculty, alumni, and donors. They then publish catalogs describing their holdings so that scholars all over the world will know what is available at their institution. G. K. Hall of Boston and the American Library Association are two of several publishers who specialize in preparing library catalogs. Students should certainly consult these catalogs if they need detailed descriptions of important collections in such areas as African and Afro-American studies, theater, folklore, Latin American studies, religion, or rare books. The section on Interlibrary Loan (W1312) provides information on how to borrow from or gain access to these collections.

A few of the most famous library holdings are

Folger (Washington, D.C.): seventy-nine First Folios (British Library has five)
Houghton (Harvard): Keats
Huntington (San Marino, Calif.): incunabula (first in the Western Hemisphere) and *STC* books (second only to the British Library)

Pierpont Morgan Library (New York): manuscripts and incunabula (seventy Caxtons)
New York Public Library: nineteenth-century English and American literature
University of Illinois: Victorian
University of Texas: eighteenth century and Romantics
Yale University: eighteenth century

Guides to library catalogs

**W1313. Downs, Robert B. *American Library Resources: A Bibliographical Guide*. Chicago: American Library Assn., 1951. Supplement, 1950–61 (1962), 428pp. Supplement, 1961–70 (1972), 256pp. Supplement, 1971–80 (1981), 224pp. Cumulative index, 1870–1970, ed. Clara Keller (1981), 96pp. Z1002.D6   016.016

The first source to consult when trying to locate author or subject collections of any discipline in United States libraries because it lists 3,400 catalogs and other finding aids that actually describe the individual library holdings. "Victorian Literature" in the index, for example, leads to entries for library catalogs of the extensive holdings at the University of Illinois, the University of Texas at Austin, and the Huntington Library. And the Maxwell Anderson entry cites a 175-page catalog describing his papers at the University of Texas at Austin. The obvious caveat: If the collection has not been honored with a published catalog, it will not be listed here but may be cited in Ash's *Subject Collections* (W1315).

W1314.   Downs, Robert B. *British and Irish Library Resources: A Bibliographical Guide*. 2nd ed. New York: Mansell, 1981. 420pp. Title of first edition: *British Library Resources*. Z1002.D63   016.016

This guide to British and Irish library catalogs, special collections, archives, directories, and other records might help scholars locate information on specific authors or subjects such as Ruskin, Robin Hood, Arnold Bennett, Dante, and Luther. Researchers wish that the indexes of these two books by Downs indicated minor as well as major collections.

Location of collections

**W1315. Ash, Lee. *Subject Collections: A Guide to Special Book Collections and Subject Emphases as Reported by University, College, Public, and Special Libraries and Museums in the United States and Canada*. 5th ed. New York: Bowker, 1978. 1184pp. Z731.A78   026'.00025'7

Even small library collections are cited in this alphabetically arranged subject guide to the holdings of eleven thousand libraries and museums, and the address and librarian's name are given to facilitate correspondence. Students of Gerard Manley Hopkins, for instance, can either write to or go to the College of Notre Dame in Maryland to use its Hopkins collection of 115 volumes, manuscripts, pictures, 250 periodicals, and family letters. And Carl Sandburg students will discover that his works have been collected by four libraries: Dickinson College and the Universities of Illinois, Virginia, and Delaware. The fourth edition of this book, however, shows that Sandburg collections exist at two additional libraries, the Universities of North Carolina and Texas at Austin, and that Gonzaga University has a Hopkins collection, also, so students would be wise to heed the editor's advice and consult both editions for complete coverage.

Ash also edits a quarterly journal entitled *Special Collections* that describes specific holdings in various subject fields and explains how to go about locating additional information.

W1316.   *Subject Collections in European Libraries*. Ed. Richard C. Lewanski. 2nd ed. London: Bowker, 1978. 495pp. Z789.L4   026'.00094

Similar in concept to Ash's guide for American libraries (W1315), but this identifies six thousand *European* libraries that specialize in collecting works, criticism, and memorabilia on specific individuals or subjects. Probably only the advanced scholar will need this.

**W1317. *American Literary Manuscripts: A Checklist of Holdings in Academic, Historical, and Public Libraries, Museums, and Authors' Homes in the United States*. Ed. J. Albert Robbins. 2nd ed. Athens: Univ. of Georgia Press, 1977. 387pp. Z6620.U5.M6   [PS88]   016.81

The current interest in textual studies, definitive editions, critical editions, facsimiles, descriptive and analytical bibliography is making this book increasingly important because it locates in six hundred American libraries the manuscripts and papers of about 2,800 authors. We expect Harvard to own the collected papers of 1,585 authors, but it is more than surprising to discover that Oklahoma University has collections on 258 authors, Western Kentucky on 109, Brigham Young on 267, and Indiana on 997. The search for manuscripts has led to interesting caches in town historical societies, private homes (Steinbeck's and Lindsay's), parks, abbeys, and even the U.S. Military Academy (Faulkner).

Authors' names are listed alphabetically with symbols indicating library locations and a numerical count of the books and other memorabilia available. No annotations and no evaluations, so, unless the library has prepared a special catalog for its collection, researchers have no way of judging its potential value to their projects except by writing. The accompanying bibliography of additional source material provides some help in this area.

This checklist does not claim to be all-inclusive, because some major libraries failed to reply to the queries and many others have never prepared an inventory of their special collections. Almost one hundred people worked on this second edition, and four hundred names were added, including some Canadians and Australians, but the obvious omission of many important author collections is regretted by seasoned scholars who have to find out the hard way about their existence. Even worse, it is misleading to novices who may accept this work as definitive. It is not, as more than one critic has noted.

The *National Union Catalog of Manuscript Collections* (W1320) and the *Directory of Archives* (W1319) perform similar functions but have a different scope.

**W1318. *Index of English Literary Manuscripts*. Ed. John Horden et al. 5 vols. London: Mansell, 1980–   . In progress (vol. 1, 1980; vol. 4, 1982). Z6611.L7.I5   [PR83]   016.82'08

This scholarly project lists, describes, and locates about fifty thousand literary manuscripts, including a large number of unpublished works, owned by private and public collections in the United Kingdom, Europe, and America. More than 270 British and Irish writers who flourished from 1450 to 1900 will be included in this index. Vol. 1, parts 1 and 2 ($300), examines the manuscripts of seventy-two major English authors who lived between 1450 and 1625. Vol. 4, parts 1 and 2, is concerned with authors of the nineteenth century. The last volume will be an index to titles and first lines of the works.

W1319.   *Directory of Archives and Manuscript Repositories in the United States*. Washington, D.C.: National Historical Publications and Records Commission, 1978. 905pp. Former title: *Guide to Archives and Manuscripts in the United States*, ed. Philip M. Hamer. CD3020.U54   016.091'025'73

An attempt to organize information on collections of documents, photographs, oral history interviews, and other source material on a wide range of subjects in 3,250 libraries and archival agencies of the United States. It cites but regrettably does not describe, for instance, the Tennyson collections at Yale, Harvard, and Duke so that students who need Tennyson manuscripts or microfilm will know where to write for possible assistance but not what they can hope to find. Arrangement by state and city permits a geographical as well as a subject approach, and information on addresses, phone numbers, and hours encourages correspondence. Excellent comprehensive index to subjects and proper names.

Brief descriptions of these library collections may be found in Ash (W1315). The most detailed descriptions are in special catalogs published by the libraries themselves such as that for the Schomburg Collection at the New York Public Library (P843). These special library catalogs are listed and described in Downs (W1313–14).

**W1320. *The National Union Catalog of Manuscript Collections*. Washington, D.C.: Library of Congress, 1959–   . Annual; projected publication form: COM microfiche (see Glossary). Z6620.U5.N3

Locates letters, manuscripts, and assorted memorabilia in 35,500 selected specific collections found in 950 public and private American libraries, giving the name of the collector, the description, location, and approximate numerical size of the collection. Because the coverage is so vast, only the most diligent literary scholar will need to consult this source, but keep in mind, for instance, that the subject index shows some Flannery O'Connor letters reposing in the Washington and Lee University Library and others in the Joint University Library in Nashville. The thirteen volumes are unwieldy but they do contain keys to uncirculated and unpublished treasures.

W1321.   Thorpe, James E. *The Use of Manuscripts in Literary Research: Problems of Access and Literary Property Rights*. 2nd ed. New York: MLA,

1979. 40pp. Z692.M28.T47   026'.091
The perplexing problems of how to locate and use manuscripts and how to enlist the cooperation of private and specialized library collectors is here clearly explained with updated information on the right to photocopy, publish, and quote. Of particular value is the chapter on the revised 1976 copyright law, which cites the basic principles of ownership, transfer, infringement, and foreign literary rights. Additional information for more complex situations may be found in the section on Copyright (W1196–98).

Periodicals

W1322. *Manuscripta.* St. Louis: St. Louis Univ. Library, 1957– . 3/yr. Z6602.M3
Articles on illuminated manuscripts, computer aids, the annual conference on manuscript studies; occasional reviews of English Renaissance textual studies; notes and comments; and reviews.
Indexed in *ABELL* (D32), *Abst. Eng. Stud.* (E38), *Am. Hum. Ind.* (P738), *Arts and Hum. Cit. Ind.* (F47), *Index to Bk. Rev. Hum.* (W1560), *MLAIB* (D31).

W1323. *Manuscripts (MSS).* Newton, Mass.: Manuscript Soc., 1953– . Quarterly. Former title, 1948–53: *Autograph Collectors' Journal.* Z41.A2.A925 091.505
Focus is on the collection, preservation, research possibilities, illustrations, and provenance of manuscripts. Autograph hunters read this eagerly. Cumulative index to vols. 1–11.
Indexed in *MLAIB* (D31).

Additional sources for information on manuscripts and collections

W1324. Fiction
   Contemporary Novelists (W1130)
   English
   de Ricci, *Census of Medieval and Renaissance Manuscripts* (J262)
   Dictionary of National Biography (W1086)
   Greg, *Bibliography of the English Printed Drama* (J339)
   Howard-Hill, *Shakespearian Bibliography* (J337)
   Index of Middle English Verse (J283)
   Ker, *Catalogue of Manuscripts Containing Anglo-Saxon* (J229)
   Manual of the Writings in Middle English (J260)
   New CBEL (J175)
   Stratman, *Bibliography of English Printed Tragedy, 1565–1900* (J209)
   ———, *Bibliography of Medieval Drama* (J281)
   Irish
   Guide to Irish Resources (K588)

American
Black American Writers (P842)
Carter, John. "The Private Library in America." *American Libraries*,
Dec. 1973, pp. 665–67.
Dictionary Catalog of the Schomburg Collection (P843)
Dictionary of American Biography (W1087)
Goff, *Incunabula in American Libraries* (J261)
Kaplan, *Bibliography of American Autobiographies* (W1057)
Library and Information Science Abstracts (E43)
Library Literature (F53), Acquisitions, Special Collections,
Manuscripts, Archives
Literary History of the United States (P701)
Resources for American Literary Study (P761)
Sabin, *Bibliotheca Americana* (P718)
Schatz, *Directory of Afro-American Resources* (P841)
Wright, *American Fiction* (P778)
General
Annual Bibliography of the History of the Printed Book (W1072)
College and Research Libraries (Chicago: American Library Assn.,
1939–   ), News from the Field, "Acquisitions" in the annual
index
Journal of Modern Literature (J530), annual review issue
World of Learning (W1221)

Linguistics

Basic guides

*W1325. *Linguistics and English Linguistics*. Ed. Harold B. Allen. 2nd ed.
Goldentree Bibliographies (W1291). Arlington Heights, Ill.: AHM,
1977. 175pp. Paperback. Z7001.A4   [P121]   016.41
The most convenient bibliography of scholarship on linguistics, with information on three thousand books and articles and some reviews. Students
should use this as a basic source and keep it up to date with the annual Linguistics
volume of *MLAIB* (W1329) and *Year's Work in Modern Language Studies*
(W1328). Cant, bilingualism, reading, grammar, history, biographies of linguists,
phonetics, dialects, growth and peculiarities of vocabulary, teaching, translation, idioms, and dozens of other subject areas are cited. Like all other Goldentree Bibliographies, this is intended as an aid to students. Only the best critical
works are included, therefore, and the most dependable carry asterisks. A critical
author index, but no annotations.

W1326. *Linguistics: A Student's Guide to Reference Resources*. Ed. Maryna
Nowosielski. Montreal: McLennan Library, McGill Univ., 1977. 20pp.
ERIC no.: ED 096 942.   Z7005.M3   [P121]   016.01641
The best feature of this source, which was prepared especially for students

and is only one of an excellent series of bibliographies, is that it includes information on languages other than English—American Indian, for example. Because of the careful descriptions and evaluations of guides, surveys, word counts, glossaries, teaching aids, special studies, and bibliographies, many students may prefer this to W1325. For more information on the series, see ERIC in the Glossary. For additional McGill titles, see the Index.

W1327. McMillan, James B. *Annotated Bibliography of Southern American English*. Coral Gables, Fla.: Univ. of Miami Press, 1971. 173pp. Z1234.D5.M32   016.427'9'75

Students should look for reference books like this when they begin work in specific areas. It is an exhaustive bibliography with a subject approach to critical works and their journal reviews. Besides historical studies there are sections on Phonology, Morphology, Place Names, Personal Names, Figurative Language, Word-Play, and, of most interest to literature students, Literary Dialect, which has entries on Welty, Poe, Lanier, Rawlings, Cable, Negro Dialect, and other subjects of regional concern.

Annual bibliographies
—that will keep the preceding sources up to date

*W1328. *Year's Work in Modern Language Studies* (*YWMLS*; *Year's Wk. Mod. Lang. Stud.*). Leeds: Maney, for the Modern Humanities Research Assn., 1930–   . Annual (vol. 44, 1982). PB1.Y45   405.8

A work of art in itself. Every year internationally known scholars summarize and criticize the world's studies in medieval Latin and Neo-Latin, Romance languages (including South and Central American), Celtic languages (including Irish, Welsh, and Scottish Gaelic), Germanic, and Slavonic languages. Its outstanding feature is the author and subject index, which locates—and suggests to the alert, inquiring student—subject areas for further research, not only in linguistic studies but also in such topics as "The Absurd in Twentieth-Century Russian Literature," "The Circe Theme in Beckett," "Aesthetics in Lessing," "Violence in Genet," "Feminism and the English Novel," "Folklore and Ibsen," Kafka and the Law, and realism in world literature. Each national literature is divided into chronological periods, then genres, individual authors, and linguistics. Indispensable for the scholar of modern languages and literatures. Indexed in *Brit. Hum. Ind.* (F49), *MLAIB* (D31).

*W1329. *MLA International Bibliography of Books and Articles on the Modern Languages and Literatures, Vol. 3, Linguistics*. New York: MLA, 1970–   . Paperback. Z7006.M64   016.4

Since 1969 the *MLAIB* (D31) has published a separate volume for the year's scholarship on linguistics. This does not claim to be comprehensive even though it indexes hundreds of books and periodicals and in 1980 contained 14,173 entries. Further search is recommended in *Year's Work in Modern Language Studies* (W1328) and *Bibliographie Linguistique* (Utrecht: Spectrum, 1949–   ). Coverage extends to festschriften and scholarship on theoretical and descriptive linguistics, comparative and historical linguistics, and all languages of the world.

Dictionaries

W1330. *Dictionary of Language and Linguistics.* Ed. R. R. K. Hartmann and
F. C. Stork. New York: Wiley, 1972. 302pp. Paperback. P29.H34
410'.3

Serious students should buy this highly recommended dictionary of hundreds of terms used in linguistics, whether philological, structural, transformational, or rhetorical. Many cross-references, both to other entries and to the subject bibliography in the back of the book.

Series

W1331. Studies in Language. Ed. Noam Chomsky and Morris Halle. New
York: Harper, 1966– . Irregular (vol. 7, 1977).

Technical studies such as *Inquiries into the Origin of Language* (1976), designed expressly for the linguistics scholar.

Abstracts

W1332. *Language and Language Behavior Abstracts (LLBA; Language and
Lang. Beh. Abst.).* La Jolla, Calif.: Sociological Abstracts, 1967– .
Quarterly. Z7001.L15   016.4

Summarizes the contents of about a thousand periodicals, papers, monographs, and transactions in over thirty languages. It thus makes manageable the scholarship of all disciplines related to the nature and use of language, such as anthropology, speech, applied linguistics, rhetoric, psycholinguistics, education, and communication services. Indexed by author, subject, book reviews, and source. Annual cumulated index; cumulation for 1967–71. Broad or narrow computer searches are provided by the staff for a modest fee.

W1333. *Language Teaching and Linguistics: Abstracts.* London: Cambridge
Univ. Press, 1975– . Quarterly. Former title, 1968–74: *Language-
Teaching Abstracts.* Z5814.E59.L3   [PB35.L32]   407

Abstracts of articles and book reviews in three hundred international journals that focus on the theory and method of teaching foreign languages, the psychology of language learning, and general and applied linguistics. Annual cumulated index.

Periodicals

W1334. *Current Trends in Linguistics.* The Hague: Mouton, 1963– . Irregular
(vol. 14, 1977). P25

Each volume assesses the current state of scholarship in a specific area. Vol. 10, for instance, is entitled *Linguistics in North America.*

*W1335. *Language (Lg).* Washington, D.C.: Linguistic Soc. of America,
1925– . Quarterly. P1.L3   405

This highly specialized, very technical periodical is concerned with grammar in all languages. Cumulative index every five years; index for vols. 1–50

(1925–74) in vol. 50, no. 4, pt. 2.
   Indexed in *ABELL* (D32), *Arts and Hum. Cit. Ind.* (F47), *Current Ind. Jour. Ed.* (W1224), *Hum. Ind.* (F45), *MLAIB* (D31), *Psych. Abst.* (E39), *Year's Wk. Eng. Stud.* (D33).

*W1336. *Modern Language Journal* (*MLJ*). Madison: Univ. of Wisconsin Press,
   1916–   . 6/yr. PB1.M47   407
   Devoted to the problems of language: teaching, use, correction, contrast, change, translation, and—the perennial thorn—the requirement of foreign languages in the curriculum. Articles, reviews, bibliographies, and notes focus on methods of teaching. Annual index. The best in the field.
   Indexed in *ABELL* (D32), *Bk. Rev. Dig.* (W1558), *Bk. Rev. Ind.* (W1559), *Current Bk. Rev. Cit.* (W1564), *Current Ind. Jour. Ed.* (W1224), *Ed. Ind.* (W1225), *Index to Bk. Rev. Hum.* (W1560), *MLAIB* (D31).

W1337.   *Publication of the American Dialect Society* (*PADS*). University: Univ.
   of Alabama Press, 1944–   . 2/yr. PE1702.A5
   Articles on dialects, place names, new terms, influences, and the use of dialect in literature.
   Indexed in *ABELL* (D32), *Language and Lang. Beh. Abst.* (W1332), *MLAIB* (D31).

W1338.   *Word: Journal of the International Linguistic Association.* Worcester,
   Mass.: Clark Univ., 1945–   . 3/yr. P1.W65
   Articles on history, theory, and research in all phases of linguistic studies and analysis. Reviews.
   Indexed in *MLAIB* (D31).

Additional periodicals that often contain information on linguistics

   American Speech (P748)
   English Language Notes (J186)
   English Studies (H145)
   Journal of English and Germanic Philology (Q924)
   Modern Language Notes (Q890)
   Modern Language Quarterly (H149)
   Scandinavian Studies (Q940)
   Studies in Philology (J321)

Background reading

*W1339. Baugh, Albert C., and Thomas Cable. *A History of the English
   Language*. 3rd ed. Englewood Cliffs, N.J.: Prentice-Hall, 1978, c1957.
   438pp. PE1075.B3   420'.9
   The most highly respected study of the internal and external history of the English language, with its foreign infiltrations, social and legal pressures, industrial and economic contributions. The latest edition includes new developments in sociolinguistics, an examination of twentieth-century trends, a current bibliography, and a workbook.

*W1340. Bloomfield, Leonard. *Language*. Rev. ed. New York: Holt, 1961, c1914. 564pp. P121.B5   400

An unparalleled and unchallenged introduction to the development of language, with painstaking discussions of the complexities of dialects, borrowings, syntax, vowels, and a thousand other distinctions.

W1341. Bolinger, Dwight L., and Donald A. Sears. *Aspects of Language*. 3rd ed. New York: Harcourt, 1981, c1968. 352pp. Paperback. P106.B59   410

An inquiry into how individuals learn and use their language, with new material on psycholinguistics, sociolinguistics, anthropological linguistics, and developmental linguistics. It covers traditional, structural, transformational, stratificational, and tagmemic approaches to language. The author also discusses acquisition of language, usage, style, writing and reading, and much more. Bibliography, pp. 321–34.

W1342. Burkett, Eva M. *American English Dialects in Literature*. Metuchen, N.J.: Scarecrow, 1978. 223pp. Z1234.D5.B87   016.428'00973

This survey of American regional dialects and their appearance in literature includes references to dialect studies, discussions of writers who have used these dialects, and lists of their works.

W1343. Chomsky, Noam. *Syntactic Structures*. The Hague: Mouton, 1978, c1957. 117pp. P291.C5   415

The acknowledged basis for the transformational-generative grammarians. Even though some students find Chomsky obscure, they soon learn that it is politically wise to be familiar with his theories. A reviewer's simplification that other reviewers will relish: Just as science proposes abstract theories that are tested against observable reality, so Chomsky proposes that in language, also, there is a universal grammar and universal rules by which all people know their language.

W1344. Dillard, Joey L. *Black English: Its History and Usage in the United States*. New York: Random, 1972. 361pp. Paperback. PE3102.N4.D5   427'.9'73

A survey of the history, influences, vocabulary, structure, grammar, and future of black English. Bibliography, pp. 315–47. Well received by reviewers. Dillard has written two more books that deserve consideration: *All-American English* (1976) and *American English* (1980).

W1345. Fries, Charles C. *Structure of English: An Introduction to the Construction of English Sentences*. London: Longman, 1977, c1952. 304pp. PE1375.F75   425.2

The major text on structural grammar. Plans for an earlier book delegated one chapter to "the sentence." Here it is explored fully. A note to the apprehensive beginner: This is interesting reading.

W1346.   Hill, Archibald A. *Introduction to Linguistic Structures: From Sound to Sentence in English.* New York: Harcourt, 1958. 496pp. PE1105.H5 425

This classic in language analysis contains step-by-step exploration and explanation.

W1347.   Hymes, Dell, ed. *Language in Culture and Society: A Reader in Linguistics and Anthropology.* New York: Harper, 1964. 764pp. P25.H9   401

A convenient collection of almost sixty essays by experts in the field.

W1348.   Katzner, Kenneth. *The Languages of the World.* New York: Funk and Wagnalls, 1975. 374pp. P201.K35   400

A pleasure to read, and of special interest to the layman who is curious about the other peoples of our world. It contains general information on about five hundred of the three or four thousand languages spoken today, with charts showing relationships, essays on characteristics, examples of the actual script, and translations. A country-by-country survey in the back of the book is equally interesting. Index.

W1349.   Lehmann, Winfred P. *Historical Linguistics: An Introduction.* 2nd ed. New York: Holt, 1973, c1962. 273pp. P121.L45   409

A good place to begin, with a minimum of technical information, an annotated bibliography, and definitions of symbols. Equally valuable is Lehmann's *Descriptive Linguistics* (New York: Random, 1976; 339pp.).

W1350.   Lockwood, David G. *Introduction to Stratificational Linguistics.* New York: Harcourt, 1972. 365pp. Paperback. P123.L56   415

Begins with the premise that language is a communication tool concerned with the articulation and decoding of concepts and goes on to explore the theory that "relationships form the most appropriate characterization of a language" (p. 3).

*W1351.   Mencken, H[enry] L. *The American Language: An Inquiry into the Development of English in the United States.* 4th ed. New York: Knopf, 1938, c1919. 799pp. Supplement 1 (1945), 775pp. Supplement 2 (1948), 933pp. PE2808.M4   427.9

Written by a controversial figure with a brilliant mind, flawless memory, discerning vision, unflagging curiosity, fluent pen, and caustic tongue. Mencken traces American speech from its earliest days, when the English lamented its barbarisms, to contemporary times, when the American dialect has finally become a dominant influence. This readable classic conveys, with numerous examples and an inimitably keen wit, the wonder of variety and change. Mencken's theories and style are themselves studied in an excellent periodical, *Menckeniana* (Baltimore: Enoch Pratt Free Library, 1962–   ).

*W1352. Pyles, Thomas. *The Origins and Development of the English Language*. 3rd ed. New York: Harcourt, 1982. 383pp. PE1075.P9 420'.9

The best available history, with numerous interesting anecdotes, explanations, and examples. Use this in conjunction with *Problems in the Origins and Development of the English Language*, ed. John Algeo (New York: Harcourt, 1982; 3rd ed.; 288pp.).

W1353. Sapir, Edward. *Language: An Introduction to the Study of Speech*. New York: Harcourt, 1921. 242pp. P105.S2   400

Language is defined, analyzed, and classified, with historical trends and conflicting influences in this classic that everyone, including elementary school teachers and all mothers, should read.

Additional reference sources for information on linguistics

ABELL (D32)
American Literature and Language (A8.1)
Anglo-Saxon Dictionary (J233)
Bibliographic Index (C28)
Computer Abstracts (W1190)
Computing Reviews (W1191)
Dictionaries (W1205–10)
Dictionary of Old English (J248)
Directory of American Scholars (W1146), vol. 3
Fry, *Beowulf* (J242)
Fundamental Reference Sources (A3)
Hawkes, *Structuralism and Semiotics* (W1381)
Jones and Ludwig, *Guide to American Literature* (P707)
Language and Language Behavior Abstracts (W1332)
Metaphor (W1412)
Middle English Dictionary (J264)
Psychological Abstracts (E39)
Rubin, *Bibliographical Guide to the Study of Southern Literature* (P711)
Year's Work in English Studies (D33), English language

Literary Criticism

STEP 1 in literary criticism is to read the primary material.

STEP 2 is to remind yourself that there are fashions in literary criticism just as there are in hemlines. The wise critic retains an appropriate humility in judgment.

STEP 3 is to read the following books:

W1354. Crews, Frederick C. *The Pooh Perplex: A Freshman Casebook*. New York: Dutton, 1963. 150pp. Paperback. PR6025.I65.W65   823.912

This will alert you to the pitfalls of pedantry, emphasize the necessity for retaining your perspective, and prove that a few scholars still have a sense of humor and the wisdom to turn it on themselves.

W1355.   Lindenberger, Herbert S. *Saul's Fall: A Critical Fiction*. Baltimore: Johns Hopkins Univ. Press, 1979. 258pp. PN165.L5   818'.5'407

Perhaps the next generation of literary scholars will heed the wisdom of this modest proposal for dispensing with the excesses of certain contemporary editors and critics. The current generation seems beyond salvation. What strange intellectual pomposity compels intelligent people to vie for the most difficult way to explain the most refined thought. Hail Strunk and White! Hail Shakespeare! Hail Fair Reason! This is a spoof, an elaborate critical edition of a non-existent play complete with barbed acknowledgments, anatomized chronology and introduction, pseudocritical essays, inane letters, ludicrous snapshots, poems, music, and dear little puffy clouds drifting about the title page. What aspect of "Saul" is this—the dreamer, the transition figure, the neurotic, the overreacher? This will be rejected by those who need to consider its message.

Basic guides

W1356.   Hall, Vernon. *Literary Criticism: Plato through Johnson*. Goldentree Bibliographies (W1291). New York: Appleton (Meredith), 1970. 119pp. Paperback. Z6514.C97.H3   016.809

International, but frankly biased toward English publications; comprehensive, indexing about 120 periodicals; chronological, going from Aristotle to Aquinas, Saint Bede, Chaucer, Bacon, Du Bellay, Michelangelo, Tasso, Hobbes, Hume, Leibniz, Rousseau, and dozens of other English and European writers. The vast coverage alone—in both centuries and the number of people—makes this a valuable source. Important items carry asterisks, but there are no annotations.

Criticism

W1357.   *Magill's Bibliography of Literary Criticism: Selected Sources for the Study of More Than 2,500 Outstanding Works of Western Literature*. Ed. Frank N. Magill. 4 vols. Englewood Cliffs, N.J.: Salem, 1979. Z6511.M25   [PN523]   016.8

Hailed by busy students because it locates criticism of 2,500 works from *Gilgamesh*, Aeschylus, and Boccaccio to Auchincloss, Borges, Cary, and Updike. Citations only—no excerpts, abstracts, or annotations. Arrangement is alphabetical by author, then title, then critic. Even a title index for those students who cannot remember the author's name. But scholars will note some important omissions and will point to the worthy primary and secondary bibliographies that already exist for many of the authors and titles. Still, this is convenient.

W1358.   *The Critical Temper: A Survey of Modern Criticism on English and American Literature from the Beginnings to the Twentieth Century. A Library of Literary Criticism*. Ed. Martin Tucker. 3 vols. New York: Ungar, 1969. Supplement (1980), 550pp. PR83.C764   820.9

Vol. 1: *From Old English to Shakespeare*; vol. 2: *From Milton to Romantic Literature*; vol. 3: *Victorian Literature and American Literature*.

This excellent source for a quick overview of literary accomplishments, critical opinion, and trends in literary taste contains passages from twentieth-century criticism on authors of all eras. It is a welcome supplement to Moulton's *Library of Literary Criticism* (W1359), which in general gathers criticism only to the beginning of the twentieth century. All major authors and titles are included, from Alfred the Great and *Beowulf* to Mark Twain and Sidney Lanier. Vol. 4 cumulates extracts from criticism of the past ten years and adds a few more authors such as Mary Wollstonecraft and Charles W. Chestnutt. Critical passages are taken from scholarly journals, monographs, biographies, and books. As an aid to the student, there is a brief introductory paragraph for each author and a list of standard editions and biographies.

W1359. Moulton, Charles Wells. *The Library of Literary Criticism of English and American Authors*. 8 vols. Buffalo: Moulton, 1901–05. Rev. Martin Tucker (New York: Ungar, 1975; 4 vols.). PR83.M73   820.9

A compilation of quotations from notable persons living between 680 and 1904 who made memorable comments on their contemporaries or predecessors. Extremely useful in studying trends in literary criticism, for it indicates the status of authors in their own time and down through the centuries. Gerard Manley Hopkins, for example, is not mentioned at all in the volumes that cover the Victorian period, but Roger Ascham was highly respected by Elizabeth I, who said in 1568 that she would rather throw ten thousand pounds into the sea than lose him.

The revision, *Moulton's Library of Literary Criticism*, includes some criticism published to 1914, adds a few authors whose reputations have become established (such as Meredith and Lear), and deletes some dated material. Students may have to go back to Moulton for minor authors who are currently unpopular. It also provides lists of each author's works and selected critical studies to 1964. For more recent criticism, see W1358.

This has proved such a useful approach to criticism that several similar pubications have appeared recently:

English and American (W1358)	*Modern Dramatists* (J558)
Greek and Latin (S1006)	*Modern French* (Q910)
Modern American (P732)	*Modern German* (Q921)
Modern Black Writers (P845)	*Modern Latin American* (R993)
Modern British (J517)	*Modern Romance* (Q887)
Modern Commonwealth (N646)	*Modern Slavic* (Q942)

Identification problems

*W1360. *Contemporary Literary Critics*. Ed. Elmer Borklund. 2nd ed. Detroit: Gale, 1982. 600pp. PS78.B56   801'.95'0922

Wit, candor, clarity, and warmth are evident in this companion volume to *Contemporary Poets* (W1129), *Contemporary Novelists* (W1130), and *Contemporary Dramatists* (W1128). The difference here is that this is the work of one experienced critic rather than of many contributors. Its chief purpose is to supply straight interpretations of literary theories, but it also gives brief biographical facts, addresses, and bibliographies for major critics whose names appear repeatedly in literary research: Abrams, Bloom, Booth, F. Crews, Daiches, Ellmann, Empson, Frye, Kazin, Leavis, Ransom, Richards, Tate, Trilling, Wellek, Winters, and one hundred others. This is a good place, for instance, to obtain a capsule explanation of *The Mirror and the Lamp* and to chuckle over the professional sparring of highly competitive scholars. Numerous quotations from the critics illustrate their style and stance and provide an excellent opportunity to compare and weigh the most interesting literary theories of the twentieth century. No Continental critics are included, unfortunately.

Series

W1361.   Critical Heritage Series. Boston: Routledge, 1968– .

Generally good reviews for this series because it assembles hard-to-locate selections from early criticism on an expanding list of famous authors:

Joseph Addison and Richard Steele	Henrik Ibsen
Matthew Arnold	Samuel Johnson
W. H. Auden	James Joyce
Samuel Beckett	John Keats
Arnold Bennett	Rudyard Kipling
William Blake	D. H. Lawrence
The Brontës	Christopher Marlowe
Robert Burns	Andrew Marvell
Lord Byron	Herman Melville
Thomas Carlyle	George Meredith
Geoffrey Chaucer (2)	John Milton
Anton Chekhov	William Morris
John Clare	Vladimir Nabokov
Arthur Hugh Clough	George Orwell
Samuel Taylor Coleridge	Walter Pater
Wilkie Collins	Alexander Pope
Joseph Conrad	Ezra Pound
James Fenimore Cooper	John Wilmot, 2nd Earl of Rochester
George Crabbe	John Ruskin
Stephen Crane	Sir Walter Scott
Daniel Defoe	William Shakespeare (6)
Charles Dickens	George Bernard Shaw
John Donne	Percy Bysshe Shelley
John Dryden	John Skelton
George Eliot	Robert Southey
T. S. Eliot	Edmund Spenser
William Faulkner	Laurence Sterne
Henry Fielding	Robert Louis Stevenson
Ford Madox Ford	Jonathan Swift
E. M. Forster	Algernon Charles Swinburne
Georgian Poetry, 1911–22	William Makepeace Thackeray
George Gissing	Leo Tolstoy
Oliver Goldsmith	Anthony Trollope
Thomas Hardy	Mark Twain
Nathaniel Hawthorne	Evelyn Waugh
Ernest Hemingway	John Webster
George Herbert	H. G. Wells
Aldous Huxley	

Walt Whitman	Virginia Woolf
Oscar Wilde	Thomas Wyatt
William Carlos Williams	William Butler Yeats

W1362. Readings in Literary Criticism. Coral Gables, Fla.: Univ. of Miami Press, 1972– .

This series specializes in collecting excerpts written *by* famous authors *about* famous authors. Vol. 17, for instance, contains criticism written by Randall Jarrell, Allen Tate, William Carlos Williams, Richard Poirier, and others on Robert Lowell. An interesting by-product: We find out as much about Jarrell, Tate, and company as we do about Lowell.

Jane Austen	Christopher Marlowe
William Blake	Herman Melville
Charlotte and Emily Brontë	Edgar Allan Poe
Geoffrey Chaucer	Alexander Pope
Emily Dickinson	Ezra Pound
Ralph Waldo Emerson	Upton Sinclair
Nathaniel Hawthorne	Wallace Stevens
Henry James	Mark Twain
John Keats	Walt Whitman
D. H. Lawrence	Virginia Woolf
Robert Lowell	William Butler Yeats

W1363. Regents Critics Series. Lincoln: Univ. of Nebraska Press, 1963– .

A total of seventeen volumes in this series have been published so far (1984), including studies on the literary criticism produced by:

Arnold Bennett	Edgar Allan Poe
Joseph Conrad	Alexander Pope
Dante Alighieri	Russian Formalists
John Dryden	Charles Sainte-Beuve
Ralph Waldo Emerson	George Bernard Shaw
Ford Madox Ford	Percy Bysshe Shelley
Samuel Johnson	Sir Philip Sidney
George Henry Lewes	Oscar Wilde
James Russell Lowell	William Wordsworth

W1364. Twentieth Century Views (TCV). Englewood Cliffs, N.J.: Prentice-Hall, 1962– .

Students should not confuse this series, which specializes in the collection of critical essays on important authors, with another series by the same publisher, which collects essays on important titles such as *Crime and Punishment*, *The Trial*, and *The Pardoner's Tale* (Twentieth Century Interpretations, 1967–   ). When students and librarians are trying to decide whether to purchase Twentieth Century Views, they can look in a volume which reprints their indexes: *Reader's Index to the Twentieth Century Views: Literary Criticism Series, Vols. 1–100* (1973), 682pp.

Aeschylus	James Baldwin
Edward Albee	Charles Baudelaire
Sherwood Anderson	Samuel Beckett
Matthew Arnold	Saul Bellow
Jane Austen	William Blake

The Brontës
Robert Browning
Miguel Cervantes
Anton Chekhov
Samuel Taylor Coleridge
Joseph Conrad
Contemporary Women Novelists
James Fenimore Cooper
Stephen Crane
E. E. Cummings
Daniel Defoe
Detective Fiction
Charles Dickens
Emily Dickinson
John Dos Passos
Fyodor Dostoevsky
John Dryden
George Eliot
T. S. Eliot
Ralph Ellison
Euripides
William Faulkner
Henry Fielding
F. Scott Fitzgerald
John Forster
Benjamin Franklin
Robert Frost
Jean Genet
Graham Greene
Thomas Hardy
Nathaniel Hawthorne
Ernest Hemingway
Hermann Hesse
A. E. Housman
Aldous Huxley
Henrik Ibsen
Eugene Ionesco
LeRoi Jones
James Joyce
Franz Kafka
John Keats
Arthur Koestler
D. H. Lawrence
Literature of Horror and the Supernatural
Norman Mailer
Bernard Malamud
Christopher Marlowe

Herman Melville
Arthur Miller
John Milton
Modern American Theater
Modern Black Novelists
Modern Black Poets
Modern British Dramatists
Modern Chicano Writers
Molière
Marianne Moore
Sean O'Casey
Eugene O'Neill
George Orwell
Boris Pasternak
Harold Pinter
Edgar Allan Poe
Alexander Pope
Katherine Anne Porter
Thomas Pynchon
Samuel Richardson
Science Fiction
William Shakespeare (3)
Alexander Solzhenitsyn
Sophocles
John Steinbeck
Stendhal
August Strindberg
Jonathan Swift
Lord Tennyson
William Makepeace Thackeray
Theatre of Black Americans
Dylan Thomas
Henry David Thoreau
Mark Twain
John Updike
Vergil
Robert Penn Warren
H. G. Wells
The Western
Walt Whitman
Tennessee Williams
Thomas Wolfe
Women Writers of the Short Story
Virginia Woolf
William Wordsworth
W. B. Yeats

Indexed in *Arts and Hum. Cit. Ind.* (F47), *MLAIB* (D31).

Periodicals

W1365.   *Diacritics: A Review of Contemporary Criticism.* Baltimore: Johns
Hopkins Univ. Press, 1971– . Quarterly. PN80.D5   805
Concerned with criticism, its achievements in the past and its current problems. Discussions by critics about other Anglo-American, Latin American, and European critics and their theories; numerous review articles; interviews;

letters. International contributors.
  Indexed in *ABELL* (D32), *Abst. Eng. Stud.* (E38), *Am. Hum. Ind.* (P738),
Arts and Hum. Cit. Ind. (F47), *Film Literature Ind.* (W1252), *MLAIB* (D31).

W1366. *Style*. DeKalb: Northern Illinois Univ., 1967– . Quarterly. PE1.S89
  This highly specialized publication focuses on such subjects as Kierkegaard's
word clusters, the oral tradition in Stapleton, metaphor in various works, prosody, the language of science and politics, problems in translation, the effect
of structure and settings, and interpretation of concrete poetry. Articles and
reviews only. Annual international bibliography of the year's research on style
in English and European literature. Occasional special bibliographies such as
"Psychology and Style" (1975), with over eight hundred entries.
  Indexed in *ABELL* (D32), *Arts and Hum. Cit. Ind.* (F47), *Index to Bk.
Rev. Hum.* (W1560), *Language and Lang. Beh. Abst.* (W1332), *MLAIB* (D31).

Background reading

*W1367. Auerbach, Erich. *Mimesis: The Representation of Reality in Western
  Literature*. Garden City, N.Y.: Doubleday, 1953, c1946. 498pp.
  Paperback. PN56.R3.A83   809
  A masterpiece of criticism that all students should ponder over and absorb
even though many years may pass before they appreciate the wisdom and
brilliance of the writer. Auerbach dissects and expounds on the epic technique
in a scene from the *Odyssey*, Boccaccio and the nascence of Italian prose, chan-
sons de geste, medieval drama, Dante's didacticism, Rabelais and the interpretation of Pantagruel, Montaigne, heroes and tragedy in Shakespeare, Dulcinea,
Virginia Woolf.

W1368. Bateson, Frederick W. *The Scholar-Critic: An Introduction to Literary
  Research*. Boston: Routledge, 1972. 202pp. PN73.B3   801'.95
  Bateson encourages literature students to be independent, objective, even
skeptical—to use the critics but to distrust them.

*W1369. Blackmur, Richard P., ed. *The Art of the Novel*. New York: Scribners,
  1934. 348pp. PS2112.A3   813.46
  A collection of the critical prefaces written by Henry James for the famous
New York edition of his works.

W1370. Bloom, Harold. *The Anxiety of Influence: A Theory of Poetry*. New
  York: Oxford Univ. Press, 1973. 157pp. Paperback. PN1031.B53
  809.1
  This has been called outrageous and perplexing; it is certainly stimulating.
It examines influences such as that of Milton on Wordsworth and argues that
this itself is poetic history.

W1371. Culler, Jonathan D. *Structuralist Poetics: Structuralism, Linguistics, and
  the Study of Literature*. Ithaca, N.Y.: Cornell Univ. Press, 1976. 301pp.

PN98.S7.C8   801'.95
A lucid, reasonable introduction to structuralism in both linguistics and literary criticism. Its thesis: that interpretation of literature is not enough, that we must investigate why we arrive at these interpretations. An important feature is its selective bibliography of books and articles.

*W1372. Eliot, T[homas] S[tearns]. *The Sacred Wood: Essays on Poetry and Criticism*. New York: Barnes and Noble, 1928. 171pp. Paperback. PN511.E44   801
Contains the famous essay "Tradition and the Individual Talent," which every student should read.

W1373. Empson, William. *Seven Types of Ambiguity*. 3rd ed. London: Chatto, 1953. 258pp. Paperback. PN1031.E5   808.1
Scrutinizes the connotations and associations of metaphor in poetry, an approach that is always interesting and usually valid, at least for the writer.

*W1374. Frye, Northrop. *Anatomy of Criticism: Four Essays*. Princeton: Princeton Univ. Press, 1957. 383pp. Paperback. PN81.F75   801
This thoughtful argument in favor of total criticism considers all influences and succeeds in becoming an influence itself.

*W1375. ———. *The Educated Imagination*. Bloomington: Indiana Univ. Press, 1964. 159pp. Paperback. PN45.F7
Excellent—a memorable, quotable little masterpiece. Frye reminds us that the end of literary teaching is not to admire the literature but to transfer the imaginative energy from literature to the student.

*W1376. Gardner, Helen. *The Business of Criticism*. Oxford: Clarendon, 1959. 157pp. PN85.G33
Six lectures survey the past and present role of literary critics and urge them to retain a sense both of history and of their own importance.

W1377. Grebstein, Sheldon, ed. *Perspectives in Literary Criticism: A Collection of Recent Essays by American, English, and European Literary Critics*. New York: Harper, 1968. 395pp. PN511.G69   809
Fiedler, Frye, Winters, Valéry, and other international critics explain approaches to the criticism of literature: the historical (Auerbach and Tillyard), formalist (Leavis and Richards), sociocultural (Arnold), psychological (Aristotle and Coleridge), and mythopoeic (Frye).

*W1378. Guerin, Wilfred L., et al. *A Handbook of Critical Approaches to Literature*. 2nd ed. New York: Harper, 1979. 350pp. Paperback. PN81.G8   801.95
An up-to-date, college-level examination of various methods of approaching literature: psychological, formalistic, mythological, feminist, history of ideas, biographical, historical, and others. Intelligent and reasonable. Glossary.

W1379.   Hall, Vernon. *A Short History of Literary Criticism*. New York: New
York Univ. Press, 1963. 184pp. Paperback. PN86.H3   801.9
Elementary, but a good starting place for the undergraduate.

W1380.   Hartman, Geoffrey H. *Beyond Formalism: Literary Essays, 1958–1970*.
New Haven: Yale Univ. Press, 1970. 396pp. Paperback. PN710.H32
809
This collection of thoughtful and thought-provoking essays examines the
interplay of literary history and literary criticism, with discussions of formalism,
structuralism, politics, language, and the works of numerous authors, such as
Milton, Hopkins, Frye, and Malraux. You may not agree with the details, but
you should read this.

W1381.   Hawkes, Terence. *Structuralism and Semiotics*. Berkeley: Univ. of
California Press, 1977. 192pp. P146.H3   808
Choice (W1557) says this is "the best companion-volume" among the recent studies of structuralism. Hawkes takes the historical approach from Vico
to Barthes and semiology, discussing the theories of the intervening American
and Russian figures as they apply to linguistics, anthropology, and literature.
Fine bibliography.

*W1382. Hough, Graham. *An Essay on Criticism*. New York: Norton, 1966.
179pp. Paperback. PN81.H53   801'.95
This has been judged as "rarely wise." In assessing the role of the critic,
Hough advocates a consciously controlled balance between the literal and the
allegorical. This is a reasonable, provocative book, a book to think about and
to come back to at quiet moments. The author has even numbered his paragraphs
to facilitate classroom or lakeside discussion. Special.

W1383.   Langer, Susanne K. *Philosophy in a New Key: A Study in the Sym-
bolism of Reason, Rite, and Art*. 3rd ed. Cambridge, Mass.: Harvard
Univ. Press, 1957. 313pp. Paperback. BF458.L3   153
An inquiry into the ways in which people try to give meaning to their lives.

W1384.   ———. *Feeling and Form: A Theory of Art*. New York: Scribners,
1953. 431pp. Paperback. BF458.L29
Ruminations on the aesthetic—theory, application, and effect.

W1385. Leavis, Frank R. *The Common Pursuit*. London: Chatto, 1952. 307pp.
PR99.L35   820.4
Leavis' collection of essays has provoked a variety of responses, mostly fiery.
Consideration of and disagreement with his propositions is splendid mental
exercise.

*W1386. Lewis, C[live] S[taples]. *An Experiment in Criticism*. Cambridge, Eng.:
Cambridge Univ. Press, 1961. 142pp. Paperback. PN85.L48
An exhortation not to use art but to receive it, to surrender to it so that
we may gain a vision and understanding of how others see.

*W1387. Longinus. *On Great Writing (On the Sublime)*. Trans. and introd.
   Georges M. A. Grube. Indianapolis: Bobbs-Merrill, 1957. 66pp.
   PN203.L6   808
   "After Aristotle, Longinus" is an aphorism that all students of literature
should remember. This is a fine translation by a noted authority in the field.
The fifteen-page introduction is of great value in explaining translation problems,
the elusive nature of the subject, and the question of dating and authorship.
Helpful biographical index.

*W1388. Lovejoy, Arthur O. *The Great Chain of Being: A Study of the History
   of an Idea*. New York: Harper, 1936. 376pp. Paperback. B105.C5.L6
   An erudite, philosophical examination of the logical, universal continuity
of ideas—which means that its arguments are long, complex, and extremely important. Some parts of this book are fascinating (the genesis in Plato, acceptance in the eighteenth century), and others are difficult to follow (the conflict
in medieval thought), but students should struggle with it until they raise
themselves to its level. It is a classic.

*W1389. Ransom, John Crowe. *The New Criticism*. Norfolk, Conn.: New Directions, 1941. 339pp. PN1031.R3   801'.951
   A treatise against impressionistic literary criticism and in favor of a close
reading of the imagery and diction of the text itself. See also Ransom's *The
World's Body* (G135).

W1390. Richards, Ivor A. *Practical Criticism: A Study of Literary Judgment*.
   London: Paul, Trench, 1929. 375pp. Paperback. PN1031.R48
   The author submitted thirteen unidentified poems to his classes, categorized
their stock responses, irrelevancies, "flabby" thoughts, and other floundering
attempts at analysis, and then tried to draw conclusions about poetry and people. His annotated list of the ten major difficulties in arriving at valid criticism
applies to students and critics alike. Do we want valid interpretations of the
author's intention or unfettered, imaginative musings?

W1391. ———. *Principles of Literary Criticism*. 5th ed. New York: Paul, Trench,
   1934. 298pp. Paperback. PN81.R5   801
   This has been deemed more a psychological study of our responses to
literature and the arts than a consideration of the purely literary aspects of
criticism. Slow but important reading.

*W1392. Schiff, Hilda, ed. *Contemporary Approaches to English Studies*. New
   York: Barnes and Noble, 1977. 105pp. PE25.C6   820'.9
   This slim little volume is important because its authors focus on literature's
role in the 1970s. It is a collection of essays by such critics as Jonathan Culler,
George Steiner, and Leon Edel. Ever the realist, Edel selects as spokesmen for
his ideas three Greek philosophers who solemnly debate the poetics of biography
as they stand on the steps of the British Library and surreptitiously ogle girls
flitting by in their summer dresses.

*W1393. Thorpe, James E., ed. *Relations of Literary Study: Essays on Interdisciplinary Contributions*. New York: MLA, 1967. 151pp. Paperback. PN45.R39   809

Essays by Frye, Edel, Crews, J. Hillis Miller, and others on the warp and woof of literature, history, myth, biography, psychology, sociology, religion, and music. These assessments of the 1960s will be the target for zesty comparative studies when MLA's second collection of interdisciplinary essays arrives in the classroom: *Interrelations of Literature*, ed. Jean-Pierre Barricelli and Joseph Gibaldi (New York: MLA, 1982; 320pp.). Culler, Weisstein, Mast, Calinescu, and eleven other contemporary authors respond to the current pressure for "humanist" scholarship in their discussions of linguistics, the visual arts, film, politics, and other paths of human righteousness.

W1394.   Trilling, Lionel. *The Liberal Imagination: Essays on Literature and Society*. Garden City, N.Y.: Doubleday, 1950. 293pp. Paperback. PS3539.R56.L5   814'.5'2

A collection of fine essays about liberalism in literature before 1950, in Anderson, Fitzgerald, Huck Finn, the Immortality Ode, the Kinsey Report. In his introduction the author refers to conservative and reactionary impulses as being only "irritable mental gestures which seek to resemble ideas." Those "gestures" have become movements of the masses, but the book is still historically important.

W1395.   Watson, George. *The Study of Literature: A New Rationale of Literary History*. New York: Scribners, 1969. 237pp. Paperback. PN81.W3   801'.95

A word to the wise is sufficient. Students need to consider Watson's premise that literature must be studied in the context of its time, that every author *does* have a purpose, and that the "relevant" only confirms existing values whereas we, as educators, are obliged to cultivate judgment by comparison.

*W1396. ———. *The Discipline of English: A Guide to Critical Theory and Practice*. New York: Macmillan, 1978. 125pp. PR21.W3   808'.042

An examination of the trends in literary criticism and a proposal of what its true function should be. Reviewers have termed this "sensible," a compliment that Watson will surely prize. At the core of this book is his belief that reading, writing, and speaking our native language require systematic, intensive training.

W1397.   Wellek, René. *Concepts of Criticism*. New Haven: Yale Univ. Press, 1963. 403pp. Paperback. PN85.W38   801.9

In this important survey an experienced scholar of literary history, criticism, and theory dicusses the baroque, romantic, and realistic elements in research and points out the weaknesses of mid-twentieth-century efforts to encompass the total field of criticism.

*W1398. ———. *A History of Modern Criticism, 1750-1950.* 4 vols. New Haven: Yale Univ. Press, 1955-65. PN86.W4   801
Unquestionably the best.

*W1399. Wellek, René, and Austin Warren. *Theory of Literature.* Rev. ed. New York: Harcourt, 1956. 375pp. Paperback. PN45.W36   801
This study of literary theory and form was eminently successful when it first appeared, but it covers so much territory that even graduates sometimes find its arguments elusive. Numerous allusions and examples, however, make it useful for comparative studies as well as for advanced literature courses. It is one of the important works of literary criticism in the twentieth century.

W1400. Wimsatt, William K., Jr., and Cleanth Brooks. *Literary Criticism: A Short History.* New York: Knopf, 1957. 755pp. Paperback. PN86.W5
Erudite. Exhaustive. A very long "short history."

Additional reference sources
—for information on literary criticism:

ABELL (D32), English Literature, Literary History and Criticism
American Literary Scholarship (P734), Themes and Topics
Contemporary Literary Criticism (J516)
Interdisciplinary Studies (W1300-11)
Library of Literary Criticism:
   Greek and Latin Literatures (S1006)
   Modern American Literature (P732)
   Modern Black Writers (P845)
   Modern British Literature (J517)
   Modern Commonwealth Literature (N646)
   Modern Dramatists (J558)
   Modern French Literature (Q910)
   Modern German Literature (Q921)
   Modern Latin American Literature (R993)
   Modern Romance Literatures (Q887)
   Modern Slavic Literatures (Q942)
"Literary Criticism," by Frye, in Thorpe (W1419)
Literature Criticism from 1400 to 1800. Detroit: Gale, 1983-   . In progress.
MLAIB (D31), vol. 1, General II
Nineteenth-Century Literary Criticism (J421)
Regents Renaissance Drama Series (J342)
Regents Restoration Drama Series (J402)
Twentieth-Century Literary Criticism (J515)
Year's Work in English Studies (D33), chap. 1

Literary Encyclopedias

Basic sources

—for identification of proper names, titles, allusions, and other items encountered in literature.

*W1402. Benét, William Rose. *The Reader's Encyclopedia.* 2nd ed. New York: Crowell, 1965. 1118pp. PN41.B4   803   Third edition in preparation.

A source of international, interdisciplinary information, with dates, digests of plots, identification of characters and places, illustrations, literary allusions, biographical information about authors and notable persons, historical and sociological trends, and countless other basic facts on art, music, psychology, mythology, and philosophy. It contains, for instance, brief identification of the Psalms, *Typee*, Miss Havisham, Hogarth, the Fenian cycle, and Robin Hood. This should be on the student's desk at all times, a one-volume substitute for the twelve Oxford Companions (see Index).

W1403. *Webster's New World Companion to English and American Literature.* Ed. Arthur Pollard. New York: World, 1973. 850pp. Paperback. PR19.W4   820'.3

A good place to begin. The brief comments on themes and style are even more helpful than the biographical sketches, and the bibliographies of best critical works will guide the student into profitable research. Coverage extends to many living authors as well as to occasional artists, musicians, philosophers, critics, literary schools, and movements. Entries are signed, suggesting an authoritative opinion.

W1404. *Cyclopedia of Literary Characters.* Ed. Frank N. Magill. New York: Harper, 1963. 1280pp., plus indexes. Alternate title: *Masterplots Cyclopedia of Literary Characters.* PN44.M3   803

Brief identification of sixteen thousand characters from about thirteen hundred literary works of all cultures and periods. Arrangement is alphabetical by title of the work and then by character in order of diminishing importance, with pronunciation of difficult names and both author and character indexes to facilitate search. If students want, for instance, the names of the principal characters in *Dr. Zhivago*, they can look under the title. And if they are unable to recall which of Cooper's novels starred Natty Bumppo, they can look in the character index.

Students should note that these are not only explanations but also evaluations of the characters' motivation, development, and flaws. They should read them critically, therefore, and be prepared to welcome valid interpretations and to disagree with tenuous proposals.

Additional reference sources

—for identification of names and terms in special subject areas:

W1405. Anonymous Literature and Pseudonyms (W1033–35)
Black Plots and Black Characters (P846)
Bondanella, *Dictionary of Italian Literature* (Q929)
Cassell's Encyclopaedia of World Literature (R953)
Companion to Scottish Literature (L630)
Crowell's Handbook of Classical Drama (S1002)
Dictionary of British and American Women Writers (W1641)
Dictionary of Oriental Literatures (R985)
Encyclopedia of World Literature in the 20th Century (J523)
Esslin, *Encyclopedia of World Theater* (R970)
Film (W1243–50)
Gassner, *Reader's Encyclopedia of World Drama* (R966)
Guide to Oriental Classics (R983)
Harkins, *Dictionary of Russian Literature* (Q937)
Index to Women of the World (W1640)
Longman Companion to Twentieth Century Literature (J525)
McGraw-Hill Encyclopedia of World Drama (R967)
Matlaw, *Modern World Drama* (R968)
More Women in Literature (W1634)
Oxford Classical Dictionary (S1000)
Oxford Companion to American History (W1294)
Oxford Companion to American Literature (P736)
Oxford Companion to Art (W1040)
Oxford Companion to Canadian Literature (N670)
Oxford Companion to Children's Literature (W1181.2)
Oxford Companion to Classical Literature (S1001)
Oxford Companion to English Literature (J178)
Oxford Companion to Film (W1244)
Oxford Companion to French Literature (Q912)
Oxford Companion to German Literature (Q922)
Oxford Companion to Music (W1448)
Oxford Companion to Spanish Literature (Q945)
Oxford Companion to the Theatre (G117)
Oxford History of Australian Literature (N653)
Penguin Companion to Classical, Oriental, and African Literature (R986)
Penguin Companion to European Literature (Q888)
Reference Encyclopedia of the American Indian (P875)
Twentieth Century Children's Writers (W1181.1)
Ungar, *Handbook of Austrian Literature* (Q900)
Who's Who in Greek and Roman Mythology (S1003)
Women in Literature (W1634)
—and most of the entries in Biography (W1080–1152) and Addresses (W1028–31).

Literary Handbooks

Basic sources

—for definitions of terms and concepts used in the evaluation of literature.

*W1406. Holman, Clarence Hugh. *A Handbook to Literature*. 4th ed. Indianapolis: Bobbs-Merrill, 1980. 537pp. Paperback. PN41.H6   803
   The best investment a literature student can make. It is based on the original edition by William Thrall and Addison Hibbard, but every entry has been rewritten, two hundred entries have been added to the third edition (total 1,560), and the analysis now tends to be critical rather than historical.

   No other source provides more authoritative brief explanations of literary terms such as "semiotics" and "symbolism," genres such as confessional poetry and the comedy of manners, philosophical classifications like Platonism and Augustinianism, prosodic terms such as "heroic couplet" and "rhyme royal," names such as Abbey Theatre, little magazines, theater of the absurd, Mabinogian tales, and Electra complex.

   The appendixes are equally valuable: an outline of English and American literary history interspersed with historical events from Celtic Britain to the present (55pp.) and lists of the winners of the Nobel Prize from 1901 to 1978 and of the Pulitzer Prize from 1918 to 1979. This handbook belongs on every student's desk.

W1407. Beckson, Karl E., and Arthur F. Ganz. *Literary Terms: A Dictionary*. 2nd ed. New York: Farrar, 1975. 280pp. PN44.5.B334   803
   All the literary terms that students will ever encounter are illustrated with hundreds of appropriate quotations and references to literary works, authors, and critics. Entries range from "kitsch" (Kahlil Gibran and Jonathan Livingston Seagull) to "structuralism" (Barthes, Jakobson, Lévi-Strauss) and "poetic justice" (Thomas Rhymer and Oscar Wilde). Additional sources are sometimes cited for students who need more information. Careful scholarship and readable prose; therefore, one of the best literary handbooks.

W1408. Cuddon, John A. *A Dictionary of Literary Terms*. Rev. ed. London: Deutsch, 1979. 761pp. PN41.C83   803
   Definitions and illustrations for about two thousand terms from the obscure ("kasa") to the familiar ("sprung rhythm"). The author gives special attention to the origins of the terms and provides numerous cross-references but no bibliographies. Readable and amusing as well as learned.

W1409. Danziger, Marlies K., and W. Stacy Johnson. *The Critical Reader: Analyzing and Judging Literature*. New York: Ungar, 1978. 199pp. PN83.D28   801'.95
   A slightly revised edition of the editors' out-of-print *Introduction to the Study of Literature* (Boston: Heath, 1965). This updates some entries and adds a few more—brief discussions of structuralism, semiology, and other currently

popular subjects. To say that it is entertaining, pleasant reading is only to underline the effectiveness of its discussion of comedy and tragedy, allegory and satire, prosody, character, and plot, problems of textual accuracy, and interdisciplinary studies with psychology, history, and sociology.

The authors have organized a compendium of basic literary terms into a well-developed argument for accuracy in usage, with all the subtleties explained and ramifications illustrated. This would be excellent for students who admit they are foggy on the connotations of, for instance, "symbolism" (quick, now, give a crystal-clear definition of the term). It is essential for teachers who want to know all the answers to all the questions their students are going to ask.

W1410. Fowler, Roger, ed. *Dictionary of Modern Critical Terms*. London: Routledge, 1973. 208pp. PN41.F6   801'.95

This specializes in defining and illustrating rhetorical terms: -isms, genres, critical concepts, and currently popular labels for style and structure. It does not, therefore, duplicate the brief entries found in most other literary handbooks. Its short essays (written by twenty-seven different contributors) concern structuralism, semiotics, pornography, modernism, the hero, foregrounding, criticism (meta- , extrinsic, intrinsic, etc.), and other puzzling issues that require some thought and exploration.

W1411. Scott, Arthur F. *Current Literary Terms: A Concise Dictionary of Their Origin and Use*. London: Macmillan, 1965; rpt. New York: St. Martin's, 1979 with revisions. 324pp. PN44.5.S3   803

Emphasis is on whittling down the definition to the briefest possible statement. Reviewers agree that neither clarity nor accuracy is forsaken. Entries range from caricature, doggerel, and Mrs. Grundy to, literally, the kitchen sink. Numerous quotations from recent publications illustrate the usage of each term. A fine bibliography, and an index of the quoted authors (a handy item when you need to fatten up a speech, promote a paper, or engage in some other form of felicitous name-dropping).

W1412. Shibles, Warren A. *Metaphor: An Annotated Bibliography and History*. Whitewater, Wis.: Language, 1971. 414pp. Z7004.M4.S5

Shibles' introduction explains that metaphors are common, almost unconscious, vehicles of communication in literature, sculpture, music, film, philosophy, even geometry. He defines 104 characteristics of metaphor. It has a "temporal" aspect and has much to do with expectation; it is a summary of an experience; it gives old words new functions; it does not stand for something else — it *is* itself, and any sterile interpretation of it robs it of its subtlety and its life; commas and question marks are metaphorical; one might say that Dylan Thomas died of metaphors; and so on into an avant-garde philosophy of imagination and truth that has interesting parallels with that of Keats.

The 300-page annotated bibliography is arranged alphabetically by critical authors such as Abrams, Burke, Ellmann, Feidelson, Jung, Nietzsche, Richards, Wallace Stevens, Wellek, Wimsatt, and many more.

An index of works on metaphor; a fifty-page index of terms and names mentioned in the annotations (allegory, Anglo-Saxon, Aristotle); a forty-page index of the various uses of metaphor (as adjective, art, intuited). This book will improve the scholarship of every student and teacher.

W1413.   *York Dictionary of English-French-German-Spanish Literary Terms and Their Origin.* Ed. Saad Elkhadem. Fredericton, N.B.: York, 1976. 154pp. PN41.E4   803
Designed especially for the comparative literature student, with definitions, translations, and indexes. Nothing else like it. An indispensable book.

Additional reference sources for literary terms and handbooks

W1414.   Bibliography—Books and Printing (W1064–79)
Clayton, Thomas. "Literary Handbooks: A Critical Survey." *Literary Research Newsletter*, 5, no. 2 (Spring 1980), 67–87. See *LRN* (W1421)
Literary Encyclopedias (W1402–05)
Oxford Companions (see Index)
Princeton Encyclopedia of Poetry and Poetics (G128)
Prosody (W1504–08.1)

Literary Research

Basic sources

*W1415. Altick, Richard D. *The Art of Literary Research.* 3rd ed. Rev. John J. Fenstermaker. New York: Norton, 1981. 318pp. PR56.A68 808'.023
The combination of wit and wisdom makes for delightful reading. This is about "the joy of finding" and "a sense of history."

*W1416. ———. *The Scholar Adventurers.* New York: Free Press, 1966, c1950. 338pp. Paperback. PR56.A7   820.72
Guaranteed to instruct and amuse à la Horace, *utile et dulce*, this book is an excellent example of our claim that research is a fascinating pursuit. The author obviously has enjoyed his profession, and he knows how to pass on this enthusiasm to his readers. He unravels the maze of Boswell's missing papers, Wordsworth's girl friend in France, the criminal record of the collector of the King Arthur legends, and sundry other literary mysteries.

W1417. Barzun, Jacques, and Henry F. Graff. *The Modern Researcher.* 3rd ed. New York: Harcourt, 1977. 378pp. Paperback. D13.B334   808'.023
The editors' first principle is that every researcher is a historian; the second is that all research is a series of decision-making crises; and the third, that all searchers must have certain virtues: a respect for accuracy, love of order, logic,

honesty, self-awareness, and imagination. The book is written accordingly, with chapters on fact-finding, verification, patterns, idea-handling, influence of other disciplines, data banks, and the art of writing plain, simple, clear, lucid, rhythmic prose (more difficult than you think). Up-to-date bibliography.

W1418.   Beaurline, Lester A. *A Mirror for Modern Scholars: Essays in Methods of Research in Literature*. New York: Odyssey, 1966. 395pp. Paperback. PN85.B34   801.95
Graduate students will want to consult this collection of important essays by Greg, Harkness, Edel, Allen, Matthiessen, Kermode, Booth, McKerrow, and others.

*W1419.   Gibaldi, Joseph, ed. *Introduction to Scholarship in Modern Languages and Literatures*. New York: MLA, 1981. 143pp. Paperback. PB35.I57   402
Six timely essays focus on the purpose, problems, methods, and procedures involved in contemporary literary and linguistic scholarship. Graduate students, especially, will benefit from the experience and sound conclusions of the noted contributors: Winfred P. Lehmann, G. Thomas Tanselle, Barbara K. Lewalski, Lawrence Lipking, Paul Hernadi, Wayne C. Booth, and Joel Conarroe. The earlier edition with essays by William G. Moulton, Fredson Bowers, Robert E. Spiller, and Northrop Frye is still of interest for historical and comparative purposes: *Aims and Methods of Scholarship in Modern Languages and Literatures*, ed. James E. Thorpe (New York: MLA, 1970; 84pp.).

Periodicals

*W1421.   *Literary Research Newsletter (LRN)*. Brockport: State Univ. of New York Coll., 1976– . Quarterly. PN73.L57   809
The only periodical created especially for professors and librarians who want to exchange ideas on how to teach bibliography and methods of research to literature students. The articles, reviews, and bibliographies are written by professionals who have had teaching and research experience. A special issue in 1981 on teaching research methods includes an annotated bibliography on research paper instruction (ed. James E. Ford; *LRN* 6, nos. 1–2, Winter-Spring 1981, 3–65). Annual index. For additional information on *LRN* see the Index of this guide.
Indexed in *ABELL* (D32), *Am. Hum. Ind.* (P738), *Am. Lit. Schol.* (P734), *Arts and Hum. Cit. Ind.* (F47), *Index to Bk. Rev. Hum.* (W1560), *MLAIB* (D31), *Year's Wk. Eng. Stud.* (D33).

See also

Bibliography—Books and Printing (W1064–79)
Book Collecting (W1153–69)
Literary Criticism (W1354–1400)
Textual Criticism (W1610–23)

Little Magazines

Surveys

*W1423. *Little Magazine in America: A Modern Documentary History.* Ed. Elliott Anderson and Mary Kinzie. Yonkers, N.Y.: Pushcart, 1979. 770pp. PN4878.3.L5   051

An important collection of essays on small presses and selected periodicals such as the *Kenyon Review* and *Paris Review.* Photographs and an annotated bibliography of little magazines that is the best available at the present time (pp. 666–750).

W1424. *Little Magazine: A History and a Bibliography.* Ed. Frederick J. Hoffman et al. 2nd ed. Princeton, N.J.: Princeton Univ. Press, 1947; rpt. Millwood, N.Y.: Kraus, 1967. 450pp. PN4836.H6

About eighty percent of the most important authors of the twentieth century were first published in little magazines, those "fiercely independent, financially shaky, non-commercial, non-traditional ventures with an extremely limited list of paying subscribers" (publ.). Witty and full of facts that are not found elsewhere. This is still a priority source in spite of its copyright date.

Directories

*W1425. *International Directory of Little Magazines and Small Presses.* 18th ed. (1982–83). Paradise, Calif.: Dustbooks, 1973–   . Approximately 450pp. Paperback. Former title, 1965–73: *Directory of Little Magazines and Small Presses.* Z6944.L5.D5   051'.025

A reference book for literature students, a buying guide for librarians and collectors, and a security blanket for aspiring poets and novelists. It contains information about three thousand periodicals that specialize in publishing material by newcomers, with addresses, names of editors, price, frequency of publication, circulation, number of pages, special interests, payment, and reply information. The introduction to one of the earlier editions contains good advice: "If you don't know what a SASE is, then you've really no business using this Directory" (self-addressed stamped envelope for return of the manuscript). A subject index (folklore, Haiku, prison, quotations), a United States regional index (thirty-two little magazines in Wisconsin, including the *Holy Cow!*), and a distributors index. More information may be found in *Index to Little Magazines* (W1429) and Mass Media (W1431).

Indexes

W1427. *Comprehensive Index to English-Language Little Magazines, 1890–1970.* Ed. Marion Sader. Series 1, 8 vols. Millwood, N.Y.: Kraus, 1975. Z6944.L5.S23   016.051

The eight volumes indicate that this will probably be the first place to come when searching for material in one hundred little magazines of American and world literatures. Arrangement is by author's name only, with works by and about each writer listed thereafter. Book reviews are listed under both the book's author and the reviewer. Not comprehensive, however, so students who want complete coverage must also consult the next two entries and Goode's *Index to Commonwealth Little Magazines* (N647). Work has started on a second series that will index an additional number of titles.

W1428. *Index to American Little Magazines, 1900-1919: To Which Is Added a Selected List of British and Continental Titles for the Years 1900-1950, Together with Addenda and Corrigenda to Previous Indexes.* Ed. Stephen H. Goode. 3 vols. Troy, N.Y.: Whitston, 1974. AI3.I54

   Index to American Little Magazines, 1920-1939. Troy, N.Y.: Whitston, 1969.

   Index to American Little Magazines, 1940-1942. New York: Johnson, 1967.

   Index to American Little Magazines, 1943-1947. Denver: Swallow, 1965.

   The editor states that these titles will ultimately be incorporated into one final cumulation with other existing indexes and with indexes to titles not yet treated, thus giving fine documentary coverage to five hundred little magazines of the first half of the twentieth century.

*W1429. Index to Little Magazines (Index to Lit. Mag.). Denver: Swallow, 1948-78(?). Every two years. AI3.I54

   An important source because it indexed thirty to fifty periodicals that were not covered by *Readers' Guide* (F48), *Humanities Index* (F45), and other indexing services. It continued the work by Goode that is described in W1428. The normal publication lag was six years, and the 1968-69 volume was not published until 1978. Authors and subjects are arranged alphabetically. Reviewers state there is only about a twenty percent chronological overlap with Goode, so the careful researcher will use both sources.

   In 1975 coverage of these periodicals, plus another forty titles, was picked up by *Access: The Supplementary Index to Little Magazines* (Evanston, Ill.: Burke; 3/yr.). Even though it has increased its coverage to 150 periodicals, only about four percent of the sturdiest little magazines in the United States are currently being indexed. Much more remains to be done.

Additional reference sources
—for information on little magazines:

W1430. *American Poetry Review* (P821)
   Basic Books in the Mass Media (W1431)
   Index to Commonwealth Little Magazines (N647)
   Little Magazines in America (A8)
   Silet, Charles L. P. "Annotated Checklist of Articles and Books on American Little Magazines." *BB*, Oct.-Dec. 1977, pp. 157-66, 208.
   See *BB* (C29)

Mass Media

W1431. *Basic Books in the Mass Media: An Annotated, Selected Booklist Covering General Communications, Book Publishing, Broadcasting, Editorial Journalism, Film, Magazines, and Advertising.* Ed. Eleanor Blum. 2nd ed. Urbana: Univ. of Illinois Press, 1980. 426pp. Z5630.B55   016.3022'3

A well-annotated bibliography of 1,179 titles (almost all post-1971) that might be useful to literature students who are interested in the communication gap between author and audience, whether in advertising, editorials, journalism, publishing, or broadcasting. This is interested not in the history of the subject but in the function and effect.

See also

Film (W1229–68)
Index to Little Magazines (W1429)
International Directory of Little Magazines (W1425)
Publishers (W1514–25)

Microtext

Basic sources

**W1434. *Subject Guide to Microforms in Print, Incorporating International Microforms in Print.* Westport, Conn.: Microform Review, 1961–   . Annual, with supplements. Z1033.M5.S8   011

Only imagination and timidity will limit the ways in which students can use to their advantage this subject index to the author-arranged *Guide to Microforms in Print*. Because this functions like *Books in Print* (W1170), students can look under "English Literature," for instance, and see that currently available are microforms for the Caedmon manuscript ($10), the Dickens papers (including original letters and annotated proofs), complete runs of numerous expensive periodicals, and many out-of-print materials. No dissertations (see W1214–15). The only remaining task is to convince the library to purchase the microform. Not cheap, but when no other copy is available, essential.

W1435. *National Register of Microform Masters.* Washington, D.C.: Library of Congress, 1965–   . Irregular. Z1033.M5.N3   011

A location list of library materials (foreign and domestic books, pamphlets, serials, foreign dissertations) that have been filmed and for which master negatives exist. Libraries use it as a location and purchasing list. Since 1970, arrangement has been alphabetical rather than by L.C. number, so scholars can now look up, for instance, specific titles published by the Early English or Scottish Text Societies and see if microtext is available for examination. Cumulation for 1965–75, 6 vols. The current publication form of the *Register* is paperback, but it will soon be converted to COM microfiche (see Glossary).

W1436.   *Newspapers in Microform*. Washington, D.C.: Library of Congress, 1948–   . Annual. Former title, 1948–67: *Newspapers on Microfilm*. Z6945.U515b   [PN4731]   016.07

A location list of both negative and positive microfilms of thousands of newspapers. Since 1978, an annual publication for the United States and foreign countries has supplemented the original volumes (1948–72) and their cumulations (1973–77). Arrangement is by state and city or by country and city, so the student who wants to do research on, for example, Marjorie Kinnan Rawlings, can look up Florida, then Palatka, Gainesville, or other cities where Rawlings might have been an item of interest and find out which newspapers are available on microtext for examination. Coverage is surprisingly far-reaching. A Finnish student found that all five newspapers in her small hometown were included.

The current publication form of the catalog is paperback, but it will soon be converted to COM microfiche (see Glossary).

W1437.   *British Manuscripts Project: A Checklist of the Microfilms Prepared in England and Wales for the American Council of Learned Societies, 1941–45*. Washington, D.C.: Library of Congress, 1955; rpt. 1968. Z6620.G7.U5   016.025179

This location list to microfilm in the major libraries of England and Wales of valuable and rare material includes the Cotton collection, numerous Rolls, parts of the collections of Oxford and Cambridge Universities, and some private collections. Index by name (Aquinas, Bede, Becket) and geographical location (Hastings, Spain). Both librarians and scholars use this to check the availability of microfilm for purchase and loan.

**W1438.   *English Books, 1475–1640: A Partial List by STC Numbers*. Ann Arbor, Mich.: University Microfilms, 1937–   . Irregular. Alternate title: *Early English Books*. Z2002.E2

A guide to film reproductions of the works listed in Pollard and Redgrave's *STC* (J306). As the reel is purchased, many librarians enter the reel number next to the appropriate title in the *STC* so that scholars will know the film is available. Most large libraries pay a fixed fee each year and receive the film automatically as it is produced.

This monumental project will be many years in the making because (1) some titles are not available in the cooperating libraries, and (2) even if the titles are available, frequently the parent library is concerned about possible loss or damage to the rare book and is unwilling to release it for the photographic process.

**W1439.   *English Books, 1641–1700: A Partial List by Wing Numbers*. Ann Arbor, Mich.: University Microfilms, 1961–   . Irregular. Alternate title: *Early English Books*. Z2002.U583

See W1438 for further information on this guide to film reproductions of the works listed in the Wing *STC* (J370).

Periodicals

W1441. *Microform Review.* Westport, Conn.: Microform Review, 1972– .
        Quarterly. Z265.M565   025.17'9

Book lovers don't like it, and scholars are reluctant to use it, but microform is here to stay. Its advantages—compact size, durability, availability, and low cost—outweigh other considerations. *Microform Review* reports on all the latest developments, with articles, reviews, and notes on new publications in microform, analyses of usage and lack of usage, and bibliographies. One survey suggests that if scholars face the choice of reading the desired material in microform or not reading it at all, they will, however reluctantly, choose microform. Statistics indicate that the number of users increases every year and that, in many state institutions especially, the number of microforms now equals or exceeds the number of bound volumes. Annual index; five-year cumulations of reviews arranged by subject.

Indexed in *Current Bk. Rev. Cit.* (W1564), *Current Ind. Jour. Ed.* (W1224).

See also

Bergquist, *Three Centuries . . . .: A Checklist* (G113)
Early American Imprints Project (P717.4)
Freedley and Nicoll, *English and American Plays of the Nineteenth Century* (J429, P801)
Wells, *Three Centuries of English and American Plays, 1500–1830* (G112)

Music

Surveys

*W1443. *New Oxford History of Music.* 11 vols. London: Oxford Univ. Press,
         1954– . In progress. ML160.N44   780.9

This is a worldwide survey of music from earliest times to the present. Eight volumes of the projected eleven have been published so far (1–5, 7–8, 10). Unique feature: Records are being prepared to accompany each volume.

Identification problems

*W1444. Apel, Willi. *Harvard Dictionary of Music.* 2nd ed. Cambridge, Mass.:
         Belknap, 1979, c1969. 935pp. Paperback. ML100.A64   780'.3

Music students still prefer this one for quick, accurate references. No biographies are included because they can be found in *Baker's Biographical Dictionary of Musicians* (W1445) and other biographical sources. The definitions of all terms and theories are unquestionably scholarly and comprehensive. Excellent bibliographies include even periodical literature.

*W1445. *Baker's Biographical Dictionary of Musicians.* Ed. Nicolas Slonimsky.
         7th ed. New York: Schirmer, 1984. 2200pp. ML105.B16   780'.92'2

Music students say this is one of the best sources for concise, accurate, and often amusing information on composers, performers, publishers, patrons, critics, scholars, and teachers of all centuries and all nations. Do not fail to read the editor's entertaining account of his efforts to extract elusive and often embarrassing information about his subjects. Mozart was not buried in a wild snowstorm that kept all his "friends" away (records show it was a mild day with a gentle west wind); Marinuzzi was not assassinated (he died in bed); Wagner did go to jail (for nonpayment of a debt). Each entry includes vital statistics and an evaluation of the subject's life and contributions; pseudonyms; an explanation of the themes of the most important works; background notes on environmental, historical, political, and family influences; and a bibliography for further study.

This is an especially important source for all deceased musicians because the facts are accurate and the evaluations are perceptive. The updated seventh edition now includes twelve thousand biographies from Michael Haydn to Michael Jackson, from Bach to the Beatles. One thousand new entries have been added, and many of the bibliographies have been revised. "Baker's" is still the best in its field.

*W1446. *New Grove Dictionary of Music and Musicians*. Ed. Stanley Sadie. 6th ed. 20 vols. Washington, D.C.: Grove's Dictionary of Music, 1980. Paperback. Former title: *Grove's Dictionary of Music and Musicians*, ed. Eric Blom. ML100.N48   780.3

For over a century this has been the unchallenged single authority for information on the whole field of music from 1450 to the present. Emphasis has traditionally been on England, but the sixth edition has greatly enlarged its coverage of the United States and the international scene. Because *Grove's* has always taken pride in its scholarship, it located 2,500 different experts to write the 22,500 signed articles, most of which have extensive bibliographies including research up to the late 1970s. Musical terms are defined, musical forms and methods explained, instruments and important works discussed at length. Historical background, portraits, characteristics, excerpts from scores, bibliographies, editions of works, and a valuable, exhaustive catalog of works with title, date, and classification for each composition are included in each of the 16,500 biographical articles. Literature students will find here a longer account (24pp.) of the life and works of Henry Purcell, who was greatly admired by Gerard Manley Hopkins, than in either the *Oxford Companion to Music* (W1448) or the *International Cyclopedia of Music and Musicians* (W1447). See W1450-52 for more recent information. And for a complimentary, highly analytical review of *Grove's*, see *Choice* (W1557), Feb. 1981, pp. 762-66.

W1447. *International Cyclopedia of Music and Musicians*. Ed. Bruce Bohle. 10th ed. New York: Dodd, 1975. 2511pp. ML100.T47   780'.3

This eminently readable tome is designed for the layman as well as for the musician. Experts from many nations have contributed lengthy signed articles on the life and works of famous composers from all countries and all times, from Beethoven and Aaron Copland to the contemporary Dutch composer-critic Flothius. The editor also provides detailed studies of influences of, for example, radio on music and entries on such varied subjects as music societies, specific concert halls, schools, performers, orchestras, and publications. Not much attention is given to contemporary developments, however. As a reference source, this is more detailed than the *Oxford Companion to Music* (W1448) but not so scholarly as *Grove's* (W1446).

W1448. *Oxford Companion to Music*. Ed. Percy A. Scholes. 10th ed. London: Oxford Univ. Press, 1970. 1189pp. ML100.S37   780'3
   In addition to the expected brief entries on composers, performers, scholars, instruments, terms, and important compositions, this companion contains summaries of operas, many illustrations, a pronunciation glossary, and an outline that organizes the entries into a logical lesson plan for individual study. If students need a brief clarification of a critic's reference to Milton's "Mozartean smoothness," this is the source to use. If they want to clarify their understanding of Hopkins' sonnet to Purcell, the seventeenth-century composer of church and instrumental music, they will find a two-column summary of Purcell's life, education, and official duties as well as a survey of the type of music he wrote, while the *International Cyclopedia of Music and Musicians* (W1447) gives him eight double-column pages. This will probably be superseded by the *New Oxford Companion to Music*, ed. Denis Arnold (1983; 2 vols.).

Contemporary music

W1450. *A Dictionary of Twentieth-Century Composers (1911–1971)*. Ed. Kenneth Thompson. New York: St. Martin's, 1973. 666pp. ML118.T5   016.78'0904
   This volume provides information about Bartók, Debussy, Hindemith, Mahler, Prokofiev, Rachmaninov, Schoenberg, Sibelius, Stravinsky, and other established twentieth-century composers. It contains brief biographical sketches, lists of their works, pertinent dates, publishing information, and criticism. For earlier composers, see W1445–48.

*W1451. *Contemporary American Composers: A Biographical Dictionary*. Ed. E. Ruth Anderson. 2nd ed. Boston: Hall, 1982. 570pp. ML390.A54   780'.92'2
   Important because it emphasizes contemporary composers who have worked in America, including many minor figures not found elsewhere. Over four thousand born after 1870 are here identified with brief biographical facts and a list of major works.

W1452. Vinton, John. *Dictionary of Contemporary Music*. New York: Dutton, 1974, c1971. 834pp. ML100.V55   780'.904
   Most books in this section emphasize the traditional and the established; only this and the previous entry focus on the contemporary. Excellent for national music (Israel), composers (Copland), and all phases of popular music.

Opera

*W1453. *Kobbé's Complete Opera Book*. Ed. Earl of Harewood. 9th ed. London: Putnam, 1976. 1694pp. MT95.K52   782.1'3
   This edition begins with summaries of Purcell and Handel operas and

continues through to the 1970s with Britten (108pp.) and Tippett. Its scope has been widened substantially from 237 operas in the previous edition to more than three hundred, including entries on early opera, the Czech school, and the opera of Dvorák, but many contemporary works have regrettably been omitted. Arrangement is first chronological, then by author, and then by title, with information on the cast, plot, performance, dates, and comments by both composer and critics. The literature student might be interested in reading about Gay's *Beggar's Opera*, Verdi's *Otello*, *Macbeth*, or *Falstaff*, Wagner's *Tristan und Isolde*, or musical versions of Molière or *Billy Budd*.

W1454. Mordden, Ethan. *Opera in the Twentieth Century: Sacred, Profane, Godot.* New York: Oxford Univ. Press, 1977. 368pp. ML1705.M67 782.1'09
Traces rise of modern music drama from Wagner to *Jonny Spielt Auf* and *The Bassarids*. Entries on Puccini, Poulenc, Britten, Henze, the twelve-tone experiments of Schoenberg and Berg, *War and Peace*, and *Death in Venice*.

W1455. *Twentieth Century Opera in England and the United States.* Ed. Cameron Northouse. Boston: Hall, 1976. 392pp. ML128.04.N7 016.7821
One of the few reference books that cover contemporary English-language opera, this has a chronological list of about 2,500 works and a valuable appendix. Students will be interested in the index of operas based on literary works.

Indexes

*W1456. *Music Index: A Subject-Author Guide to Current Music Periodical Literature.* Detroit: Information Coordinators, 1949– . Monthly. ML118.M84
Cross-references under "Literature" and "Music" lead to entries on such subjects as the Bible, Don Juan and Faust legends, Folklore, Mythology, Poetry, and Prose. Critical works are also listed for Fiction and Jazz, Romance, Beckett, Joyce, songs in *Wuthering Heights*, and *Don Quixote*. International coverage of about three hundred journals.

See also

International Who's Who in Music and Musicians' Directory (W1103)

Paleography

W1457. Dawson, Giles E., and Laetitia Kennedy-Skipton. *Elizabethan Handwriting, 1500–1650: A Guide to the Reading of Documents and Manuscripts.* Chichester, Eng.: Phillimore, 1981, c1968. 131pp. Z5115.E5.D38   421.7
Numerous facsimiles and illustrations for students who need to learn to read the original material.

W1458. Denholm-Young, Noël. *Handwriting in England and Wales.* 2nd ed.

Cardiff: Univ. of Wales Press, 1964. 102pp. Z115.E5.D4
An expert who was associated with the Bodleian Library for many years traces the development of handwriting, the vagaries of punctuation and abbreviations, the dating and identification of manuscripts. Numerous plates and a bibliography.

*W1459. Gelb, Ignace J. *A Study of Writing*. 2nd ed. Chicago: Univ. of Chicago Press, 1963. 319pp. Paperback. P211.G37   411
Gelb discusses the origins and uses of writing and provides numerous illustrations and tables. Reviews of this work were mixed: Some called it "definitive"; others complained about the excess of "personal opinion." Bibliography, pp. 254–68.

*W1460. Hector, Leonard C. *The Handwriting of English Documents*. 2nd ed. Dorking, Eng.: Kohler, 1980, c1966. 136pp. Z115.E5.H4   421.7
A history of handwriting with explanations of materials and techniques, scribal problems and textual solutions. Subjects range from descriptions of vellum, paper, quills, inks, languages, letterform, numerals, abbreviations, scribal conventions, punctuation, and errors to all the styles of handwriting (archive, business, bastard, free, secretary, humanistic, and others). Numerous plates of the manuscripts are accompanied by transcripts so students can test their ability to read the early styles.

W1461. Judge, Cyril B. *Specimens of Sixteenth-Century English Handwriting Taken from Contemporary Public and Private Records*. Cambridge, Mass.: Harvard Univ. Press, 1935. 18pp., with facsimiles. Z113.U4
Helpful illustrations of the many styles of sixteenth-century handwriting.

W1462. Parkes, Malcolm B. *English Cursive Book Hands, 1250–1500*. Rev. ed. Berkeley: Univ. of California Press, 1980. 84pp., with 24pp. of plates. Z115.E5.P37   417'.7
A standard work on late medieval English manuscripts, with fifty examples accompanied by transcriptions, notes explaining the terminology, an index, and an updated bibliography. This can be an uninspiring subject, but when professors coordinate an assignment in any one of the books in this section with a Renaissance musical instrument program, a costume film, and live readings in early English, their students have no trouble remembering the feeling, if not the facts, of the era itself.

W1463. Ullman, Berthold L. *The Origin and Development of Humanistic Script*. Rome: Edizioni di Storia e Letteratura, 1960. 197pp. Z114.U4
Specialists in medieval and Renaissance literature will be interested in Ullman's explanation of the evolving fashions in scribal handwriting (the book hand). He traces changes from the Roman Empire to Carolingian script in France during the eighth century, then to Gothic in the thirteenth and the highly refined, legible, humanistic script that was developed in fourteenth-century Renaissance Italy. This script was a response to the needs of the times. More students were reading more books, and even Petrarch himself complained that

the excessive abbreviations and tiny handwriting in medieval manuscripts were hard on his aging eyes. The careful analysis and numerous reproductions will help everyone working in this field.

W1464.   ———. *Ancient Writing and Its Influence*. Toronto: Univ. of Toronto Press, 1980, c1932. 238pp. Paperback. Z105.U4   411'.09
Excellent for a broad survey of the entire field up to modern times, but fewer illustrations than Ullman's other text (W1463).

See also

Catalogue of Manuscripts Containing Anglo-Saxon (J229)
Gaskell (W1064)
McKerrow (W1065)

Paperback Books

*W1466. *Paperbound Books in Print*. New York: Bowker, 1955–   . 3 vols. (2 vols., Spring; updating cumulation, Fall). Z1033.P3.P32
Lists about 200,000 currently available and forthcoming paperback books with price and publisher. Author, title, and subject arrangement makes access easy, as does a publishers and distributors index. If teachers want their classes to study Dorothy Sayers' translation of Dante's *Divine Comedy*, for instance, they should first consult this to be sure there is an inexpensive edition available. (There is.) The *CBI* (D35) often includes information on paperback editions, but it does not attempt to be comprehensive.

W1467.   *Paperbacks in Print*.   London: Whitaker, 1960–   .   Annual. Z1033.P3.P359
Similar to *Paperbound Books in Print* (W1466), but restricted to publications in Great Britain.

Performing Arts

Basic guides

*W1468. *Performing Arts Books in Print: An Annotated Bibliography*. Ed. Ralph N. Schoolcraft. New York: Drama Book Specialists, 1973. 761pp. Z6935.S34   016.7902.
Supersedes the earlier and now outdated *Theatre Books in Print* (1966). Brief annotations describe international publications (mainly in English) on the theater, film, television, radio, dance, musicals, puppets, technical arts relating to dramatic productions, and mass media in all countries and all centuries. The author and title indexes lead to such subjects as Isadora Duncan, Andy Warhol, Covent Garden, Fellini, Goethe, Greek tragedy, Russian ballet, *The Reader's Encyclopedia of World Drama* (R966), and the Stanislavski system. Like many other computer-produced publications, this was evidently bedeviled by deadlines. A large "supplement" in the back of the book brings the main section up to

date. More recent information can be found in the *Annotated Bibliography of New Publications in the Performing Arts*, its quarterly supplement.

This does not overlap to any great extent with Whalon's *Performing Arts Research* (W1470.1), which is arranged by *type* of reference book rather than by subject, a form more conducive to browsing. Both are annotated. Whalon's contains more recent publications, but students should consult both for comprehensive research. See also G115-16.

W1469. *Guide to the Performing Arts*. Comp. Sara Y. Belknap. Metuchen, N.J.: Scarecrow, 1957-67. Comp. Louis Rachow: 1968-69. ML118.G8

Indexes about fifty periodicals concerning the theater, opera, dance, television, symphony orchestras, instruments, musical and dramatic events, folk music, international news, and illustrious persons. The literature student can find articles about the opera versions of Pushkin's *Boris Godunov* and Steinbeck's *Of Mice and Men*, music in Shakespeare, Laurence Olivier's acting in Shakespeare, criticism of Bertolt Brecht, Dürrenmatt, Lady Mary Montagu, Eugene O'Neill, Shaw, Strindberg, and an opera and a play based on Tolstoy's *War and Peace*.

Series

*W1470. Performing Arts Information Guide Series (PAIGS). Detroit: Gale, 1976- . In progress.

.1 *Performing Arts Research*. Ed. Marion K. Whalon. 1976. 280pp. Z6935.W5   016.7902

.2 *Stage Scenery, Machinery, and Lighting*. Ed. Richard Stoddard. 1977. 274pp. Z5784.S8.S79   [PN2091.S8]   016.792'025

.3 *Guide to Dance in Film*. Ed. David L. Parker and Esther Siegel. 1978. 220pp. GV1779.P37   793.3

.4 *American Stage to World War I*. Ed. Don B. Wilmeth. 1978. 275pp. Z1231.D7.W55   [PN2221]   016.792'0973

.5 *Theatre and Cinema Architecture*. Ed. Richard Stoddard. 1978. 368pp.

.6 *Theatrical Costume*. Ed. Jackson Kesler. 1979. 308pp.

.7 *American and English Popular Entertainment*. Ed. Don B. Wilmeth. 1980. 465pp.

.8 *American Actors and Actresses*. Ed. Stephen M. Archer. 1983. 710pp.

Most of these titles are annotated and international with either geographical or chronological arrangement and a variety of indexes. Some begin with particularly helpful essays that explain the unique research problems in the area and point out the research possibilities. As is true of all series, some volumes are more reliable and more comprehensive than others.

Indexed in *MLAIB* (D31).

Periodicals

W1472. *Performing Arts Resources (PAR)*. New York: Drama Book Specialists,

1975–   . Annual. Z6935.P46   016.7902'08
Articles describing guides to archives, analyses of individual collections, and surveys of reference books and training programs. The result is a general assessment of the state of research in drama, film, radio, and television. Cumulative index in each new volume.
Indexed in *MLAIB* (D31).

Periodicals

This section includes only those reference books that are concerned with listing, describing, or locating periodicals. For individual periodicals that deal with a specific national literature, subject, century, or genre, see the Index or the appropriate literature or subject section.

Basic sources

*W1474. *MLA Directory of Periodicals: A Guide to Journals and Series in Languages and Literatures*. New York: MLA, 1979–   . Every other year. Pl.Al.M62   [Z7006.M58]   016'.405
A directory of the three thousand journals and series currently indexed in the *MLAIB* (D31). The up-to-date publishing information on each title is convenient for librarians and readers, and the editorial and manuscript submission information is appreciated by literary scholars who want to locate appropriate vehicles for their publications. They will probably find everything they need in this specialized source and will not have to go to the *Directory of Publishing Opportunities in Journals and Periodicals*, 5th ed. (Chicago: Marquis, 1981; 844pp.), which, because it strives to cover all disciplines, includes only the more important literary periodicals. There are indexes by subject, specific language, editors, sponsoring organizations, and MLA abbreviations. Paperback edition, listing periodicals published in the United States and Canada (1984; 294pp.).

W1475. Gerstenberger, Donna L., and George Hendrick. *Fourth Directory of Periodicals Publishing Articles on English and American Literature and Language*. Denver: Swallow, 1975. 234pp. Paperback. Z2015.P4.G4
The *MLA Directory of Periodicals* (W1474), with its vast coverage of highly specialized literary publications, is generally preferred, but Gerstenberger and Hendrick's aging directory does have two advantages—it is paperback and it is inexpensive. Professors and students who are interested in publishing their research may even want to purchase it, for it gives the address, price, frequency, sponsor, and editors of almost five hundred alphabetically arranged literary periodicals. After describing the major fields of interest so that contributors will know what kind of material to send each periodical, it lists their form of payment, copyright rules, manuscript requirements of numbers of copies, footnoting, length, and, inevitably, the self-addressed stamped envelope (SASE) for return of the manuscript.
Would-be authors will find periodicals that represent states (*Alabama Review*), countries (*New South African Review*), genres (*Modern Drama*), eras (*Medieval Studies*), and people (*James Joyce Quarterly*).

427

*W1476. *Author Newsletters and Journals: An International Annotated Bibliography of Serial Publications Concerned with the Life and Works of Individual Authors.* Ed. Margaret C. Patterson. Vol. 19 of Gale Information Guide Library (A8). Detroit: Gale, 1979. 497pp. Z6513.P37   [PN4836]   016.809

A guide to over one thousand publications that contain criticism, bibliographies, reviews, and news relating to 435 authors from twenty-eight countries including Chaucer, Claudel, Jeffers, Hesse, and Dostoevsky. Unique and important, because often these newsletters and journals are the only source of information on unpublished or unrecorded manuscripts, special library collections, memoirs, interviews, and other personal material. Authors are listed first alphabetically with their periodicals, then by country and century. Title index. Since 1982, the contents have been updated annually in *Serials Review* (W1482).

*W1477. *Ulrich's International Periodicals Directory: A Classified Guide to Current Periodicals, Foreign and Domestic.* 22nd ed. 2 vols. New York: Bowker, 1983. Every other year. Z6941.U5   011

Entries for almost four thousand language and literature titles in this multidisciplinary directory of about 65,000 American and European periodicals. It provides information on their addresses, frequency, circulation figures, special features such as book reviews and bibliographies, and, most important, facts about where the periodical is indexed and abstracted (E38–43, F45–53). If, for instance, students have to locate an article they think may have appeared several years ago in the *Sewanee Review*, they can save time by consulting *Ulrich's*, which shows that the *Sewanee Review* is indexed by *Abst. Eng. Stud.* (E38), *ABELL* (D32), *Current Contents* (F47), and *Hum. Ind.* (F45). Students will also find, unfortunately, that *Ulrich's* is plagued with errors and omissions, for, in fact, the *Sewanee Review* is also indexed by *Bk. Rev. Ind.* (W1559), *Index to Bk. Rev. Hum.* (W1560), and *MLAIB* (D31).

Since 1977, a quarterly supplement has tried to keep *Ulrich's* up to date. A more professional source for title changes or any other publication irregularity is the monthly *Serials Updating Service* (W1483).

Sources of Serials, 2nd ed. (New York: Bowker, 1981; 1547pp.), a companion volume to *Ulrich's*, lists about 63,000 publishers and organizations issuing serials in 181 countries. This will solve many frustrating problems faced by acquisitions departments and researchers. Another Bowker publication, *Irregular Serials and Annuals*, supplies information on titles that are published less frequently. The ninth edition for 1984 contains 34,000 titles. It, too, is kept up to date by *Ulrich's Quarterly*.

In 1981 the Bibliographic Retrieval Services (BRS) made *Ulrich's* and *Irregular Serials* (including over 10,000 ceased titles) available online with 385 subject headings and monthly updating. The computer can now do in seconds a complex search that formerly might have taken many hours. See the Glossary in this guide, computerized literature search.

**W1478. *New Serial Titles, 1950–70: A Union List of Serials Commencing Publication after December 31, 1949 (NST).* 4 vols. Washington, D.C.: Library of Congress, 1973. Monthly, with quarterly, annual, and five-year cumulations (1971–75 and 1976–80); since 1984, available on COM microfiche (see Glossary). Z6945.U5.S42

Even the most obscure periodical is now relatively easy to locate in about nine hundred United States and Canadian libraries for verification or interlibrary loan purposes. The monthly subject index was useful for students who wanted to locate new literature or linguistics periodicals, but it ceased in 1980 (cumulation for 1950–70). The best source for serial changes (in title, address, frequency, price, etc.) is *Serials Updating Service* (W1483). For information on periodicals that began publication before 1950, see *Union List of Serials* (W1479).

**W1479. *Union List of Serials in Libraries of the United States and Canada (ULS).* 3rd ed. 5 vols. New York: Wilson, 1965. Z6945.U45

Use this for information on 226,000 periodicals with a pre-1950 *initial* publication date that students may not have in their own library. It is a location guide, in other words, to "serials" (continuing publications) owned by about nine hundred libraries that might be willing to lend or copy material for scholars. See *New Serial Titles* (W1478) for periodicals that began publication in 1950 or later. See Interlibrary Loan (W1312) for loan procedures.

**W1480. *British Union-Catalogue of Periodicals: A Record of the Periodicals of the World, from the Seventeenth Century to the Present Day, in British Libraries (Brit. U.-C. of Per.).* 4 vols. London: Butterworths, 1955–58. Supplement to 1960 (1970). Z6945.B87

Periodicals are elusive, the preface says. They are also fragile, notoriously short-lived, generally inexpensive, and, therefore, expendable. This work is important because it records titles, known publication dates, and libraries where British periodicals of all eras can be seen and used: 140,000 titles in 440 libraries. Since June 1981 the quarterly *Serials in the British Library* has listed all new serial acquisitions and issued annual cumulations on microfiche. Beginning students will not use this often, but the experienced researcher recognizes the value of its unique scope. For comparable publications covering American periodicals and libraries, see *Union List of Serials* (W1479) and *New Serial Titles* (W1478).

Periodicals concerned with periodicals

*W1482. *Serials Review.* Ann Arbor, Mich.: Pierian, 1975– . Quarterly. PN4832.S47   016.05

Features articles analyzing the history and influence of important periodicals such as *American Literature* (see vol. 4, no.2, 1978); reports on new and defunct periodicals; numerous reviews of new and old literary periodicals, abstracting services, almanacs, and indexes. Cumulative index of titles reviewed in vols. 1–5 (1975–79). No other source pays such scrupulous attention to the content and quality of serial publications. Really fine editorial work.

Indexed in *Bk. Rev. Ind.* (W1559).

W1483. *Serials Updating Service.* Westwood, Mass.: Faxon, 1973– . Monthly,

with quarterly and annual cumulations.   Z6941.S47   [PN4801]
016.05

Registers all changes in the publishing information of all periodicals: title
or price changes, cessations and births, new format, new editors, different frequency. Ask your acquisitions or reference librarian to consult this if your favorite
periodical suddenly disappears.

Additional reference sources

—for information about periodicals:

W1484.   *ABELL* (D32), Bibliography, subsections on newspapers and periodicals
Choice (W1557), feature articles on periodicals, new and old
Chielens, *Literary Journal in America* (P740–41)
Greene, Donald J. "Periodical Publication in Post-Restoration and
Eighteenth-Century Studies." *Scriblerian*, 11, no. 2 (Spring 1979),
87–91. See J384
Kribbs, *Annotated Bibliography of American Literary Periodicals,
1741–1850* (P742)
MLAIB (D31), English, American, and Commonwealth literatures,
subsections on periodicals
Nineteenth-Century Periodical Press in Britain (J420)
Periodical Title Abbreviations (W1025)
Victorian Periodicals Review (J473)
White, *English Literary Journal to 1900* (J190)

Philosophy

Basic sources

*W1485.   *Encyclopedia of Philosophy*. Ed. Paul Edwards. 8 vols. New York: Macmillan, 1967; rpt. 1972 in 4 vols. B41.E5   103

A favorite source, because it is surprisingly readable, for interdisciplinary,
international information on the philosophy of the East and the West, all centuries, all countries, and all theories. It is by and about mathematicians,
physicists, biologists, sociologists, moral reformers, and religious thinkers. It is
also about Medieval Philosophy, Miracles, Metaphor and Tension, Myth,
Mysticism, and Nihilism.

The entries are written and signed by scholars who have tried to be authoritative and yet not polemical. The biographical entries emphasize contributions
to philosophy. Extensive bibliographies, both primary and secondary, accompany most of the articles so that the student can go on to further research.

Students of the Reformation, for instance, would benefit from reading what
this book has to say about Martin Luther. Or, after reading *Passage to India*,
they might note the similarities between the philosophies of Forster and Hegel.
Or, they might be interested in the thesis that Machiavelli was concerned not
with good and evil but with political and military efficiency, stating that although
all political organizations die, the well-organized live longer.

W1486. Lacey, Alan R. *A Dictionary of Philosophy*. Boston: Routledge, 1978, c1976. 239pp. B41.L32 103
Choice (W1557) proclaims this outstanding. Lacey's emphasis is on terminology, his extensive bibliographies for further study are commendable, and the treatment is scholarly. For longer explanations and for biographical entries, go to *Encyclopedia of Philosophy* (W1485).

W1487. *Dictionary of Philosophy and Religion, Eastern and Western Thought*. Ed. William L. Reese. Atlantic Highlands, N.J.: Humanities, 1980. 644pp. B41.R43 103
This extremely well-organized encyclopedic dictionary focuses on the analysis of ideas and beliefs ranging from Abelard and epistemology to logic, pragmatism, Bertrand Russell, and B. F. Skinner. Paragraphs are numbered so that cross-references lead directly to further discussion of the same subject. A brief definition of *tabula rasa*, for instance, refers to the entry for John Locke, paragraph 1, where there is a full elaboration of Locke's well-known interpretation of the concept. Selected as an outstanding reference book of 1980.

Summaries

W1488. *Masterpieces of World Philosophy in Summary Form*. Ed. Frank N. Magill. New York: Harper, 1961. 1166pp. B21.M3 108.2
A chronological summary of philosophical works from Confucius and Aristotle to Bergson, Whitehead, and Tillich. The glossary, title index, and subject index make this extremely easy to use, as are Magill's other publications (see Index). Students may not have time to read all of Locke, Kant, and Aquinas, but they will at least have an opportunity, with this book, to become familiar with the theories of these influential thinkers so they can better understand the literature that reflects their influences.

Indexes

W1489. *Philosopher's Index: An International Index to Philosophical Periodicals and Books (Phil. Ind.)*. Bowling Green, Ohio: Bowling Green State Univ., 1967– . Quarterly, with annual cumulations. Z7127.P47 016.105
The contents of over three hundred scholarly publications in English, French, German, Spanish, and Italian are here analyzed by author and subject, some of which (Heidegger, Literature, Metaphor, for instance) will help the more imaginative literature student. Unusual features: an author index that contains abstracts of the articles, and a book review index. A retrospective three-volume set published in 1978 indexes United States publications for 1940–76, and a similar set of 1980 indexes non-United States publications for 1940–66.

Periodicals

*W1490. *Philosophy and Literature*. Baltimore: Johns Hopkins Univ. Press, 1976– . 2/yr. PN2.P5 809
An unexpectedly diverse range of interests centered on the relation between philosophy, the literary arts, theater, and film: Augustine's *Confessions*, *Crime*

and Punishment, Camus's *L'Étranger*, Woolf's *To the Lighthouse*, and Buñuel's films. Articles and reviews; annual index and annual bibliography.
Indexed in *ABELL* (D32), *Am. Hum. Ind.* (P738), *Arts and Hum. Cit. Ind.* (F47), *MLAIB* (D31), *Phil. Ind.* (W1489).

See also
> *Philosophy, Religion, and Rhetoric* (S997.2)
> *Studies: An Irish Quarterly* (K598)

Popular Culture

Basic sources

W1497. *Handbook of American Popular Culture*. Ed. M. Thomas Inge. 3 vols.
Westport, Conn.: Greenwood, 1978–81. E169.1.H2643   301.2'1
Critical essays on such currently important subjects as comic art, children's literature, film, science fiction, radio, stage, editorial cartoons, popular poetry, best-sellers, and propaganda. The approach is generally historical and always scholarly, with surveys of completed research and available reference books. Favorable reviews, but occasional typographical errors. A revised edition is in preparation.

Abstracts

W1498. *Abstracts of Popular Culture: A Quarterly Publication of International Popular Phenomena* (*Abst. Pop. Cult.*). Bowling Green, Ohio: Bowling Green State Univ., Popular Press, 1976–77; 1983(?)–   . Quarterly.
Z7164.S66.A27   [HN17.5]   016.909
Very broad coverage of about six hundred periodicals concerned with film, television, folklore, family, sports, and so forth. Subject index. The editorial policies have not been well planned, so more than a little determination and luck are needed to locate the desired information. In 1977 the editors announced that the publication was temporarily suspended.

Periodicals

*W1500. *Journal of Popular Culture* (*JPC*). Bowling Green, Ohio: Bowling Green State Univ., Popular Press, 1967–   . Quarterly. P87.J67 [AP2.J8325]
The official publication of the Popular Culture Association and the Popular Culture sections of MLA and Midwest MLA. Articles on a startling variety of showstoppers: the history of the Mickey Finn, the Barbie doll as the ultimate swinging single, subversive elements in Alice's Wonderland, and a study of advice-to-the-lovelorn columns. What is the academic world coming to?
Popular Abstracts (1978; 257pp.), which is an annotated index for *JPC*, 1967–77, also indexes two other periodicals published by the Popular Press: *Journal of Popular Film* (1972–77) and *Popular Music and Society* (1971–75).
Indexed in *ABELL* (D32), *Arts. and Hum. Cit. Ind.* (F47), *Bk. Rev. Ind.* (W1559), *Current Bk. Rev. Cit.* (W1564), *Film Literature Ind.* (W1252), *Hum. Ind.* (F45), *MLAIB* (D31).

See also
American Humor (P746)
Folklore (W1270–71, W1274, W1278–80)
Science Fiction (G88–101), selected titles

Pronunciation

W1501.   Jones, Daniel. *Everyman's English Pronouncing Dictionary.* 14th ed.,
rpt. with corrections. London: Dent, 1981. 560pp. PE1137.G53
421'.52
A respected guide to the current pronunciation of 45,000 words and 15,000
proper names, but the use of the International Phonetic Alphabet will probably
send many students to the *NBC Handbook of Pronunciation* (W1502).

*W1502. *NBC Handbook of Pronunciation.* Ed. James F. Bender. 3rd ed. New
York: Crowell, 1964. 418pp. PE1137.B573   421.5
Not an arbitrary or prescriptive standard for pronunciation, but a record
of how words actually are pronounced by educated persons in the United States
(a fourth edition is badly needed). It includes proper names in the news, frequently mispronounced words, and words from all centuries and disciplines—
twenty thousand alphabetized entries. Send one to your local radio announcer.

W1503. Kenyon, John S., and Thomas A. Knott. *A Pronouncing Dictionary
of American English.* 2nd ed. Springfield, Mass.: Merriam, 1953. 484pp.
PE1137.K37   421.5
A general purpose guide to pronunciation, based on the International
Phonetic Alphabet.

Additional sources that may help in pronunciation problems

Asian Literature Bibliography Series (R988)
Contemporary Authors (W1127)
Current Biography (W1115)
Cyclopedia of Literary Characters (W1404)
New Century Cyclopedia of Names (W1081)
Oxford Companion to Classical Literature (S1001)
Webster's Biographical Dictionary (W1080)

These books will correct the mispronunciation of names frequently used
by literature students: Wieland (Veeland), Magdalen College, Oxford, and
Magdalene College, Cambridge (both pronounced maudlin), Northánger Abbey (hard g), David Dáiches (Day shes), Cholmondeley (chumley), Lytton
Strachey (Litton Strachey, not ck), Mónaco, Marjorie Kinnán Rawlings, Geoffrey
Keynes (Canes), William Cowper (Cooper), Thomas Carlýle, and Bácchae (back
ee).

Prosody

Basic guides

*W1504. *English Versification, 1570–1980: A Reference Guide with a Global Appendix.* Ed. Terry V. F. Brogan. Baltimore: Johns Hopkins Univ. Press, 1981. 832pp. Z2015.V37.B76   016.821'009

At last. An annotated list of six thousand international studies about the theory and practice of versification in English poetry from the Renaissance to 1980. Each work is summarized, described, evaluated, cross-referenced, classified by subject, and indexed by poet and critic. Separate sections discuss the rhythm of prose, sources in the classics, the relation between music and verse, and concrete poetry. It is now possible to view the historical development of and complex influences on the poet's use of sound, meter, rhythm, stanza, line, syntax, and word selection. Bibliography, pp. 743–49.

Handbooks

*W1505. Deutsch, Babette. *Poetry Handbook: A Dictionary of Terms.* 4th ed. New York: Funk and Wagnalls, 1974; rpt. Harper, 1982. 203pp. PN44.5.D4   808.1'01'4

Unique in that numerous examples from 180 different poets illustrate every definition. Imagism has Williams, haiku has Moritake, objective correlative has Eliot, Welsh forms have Rolfe Humphries, and each quotation is essential to the definition, for, as the author says in her preface, the words in a poem exceed their definition. This is one of the few reference books that have sparkle, warmth, and a really good idea in every line. Do not miss her "By Way of Preface" and "A Word to the Beginner."

W1506. Fussell, Paul. *Poetic Meter and Poetic Form.* Rev. ed. New York: Random, 1979. 208pp. PE1505.F78   808.1

This convincing exhortation for close reading is designed for the reader who wants to feel poetry. The brief history of meter and form uses illustrations from English poetry with clarity and wit. It shows, for example, how poets establish a rhythm and then deliberately break it to disturb the reader into a recognition of some change in the form or intent of the words themselves. Poetry lovers will always be grateful they purchased this.

W1507. Malof, Joseph. *A Manual of English Meters.* Bloomington: Indiana Univ. Press, 1970; rpt. Westport, Conn.: Greenwood, 1978. 236pp. PE1505.M3   426

All literature students should own this, for it is a detailed but methodical collection of facts about metrical analysis with which they should be familiar. Definitions, explanations, and illustrations clarify every aspect of prosody from simple iambic pentameter to brachycatalectic lines, from feminine endings to hemistichs.

W1508. Shapiro, Karl, and Robert Baum. *A Prosody Handbook.* New York:

Harper, 1965. 214pp. PN1042.S57   416

Prosody made easy in the simplest terms possible. The explanations progress from syllables to feet to lines to stanzas, and excerpts from poems accompany every explanation. The authors show that the movement of a line—and hence its meaning—varies with the arrangement of its sounds and that, therefore, the prosody must be considered simultaneously with the theme, imagery, and structure. Would that all professors of literature could read this. Why do so many of them teach a poem as if it were an essay?

A detailed glossary, a selected bibliography arranged chronologically from Aristotle's *Poetics* (G120) in 350 B.C. to works in the 1960s, and an index of poetic terms help to make this a scholarly as well as an enlightening text.

W1508.1   Wimsatt, William K., ed. *Versification: Major Language Types*. New York: New York Univ. Press, for MLA, 1972. 252pp. PN1042.W52 416

Sixteen essays on versification from classical Chinese and Biblical Hebrew to the modern languages including Celtic, Spanish, French, and English. The critics take into consideration the literary-cultural background of the various countries, and they approach the subject from different interests such as descriptive, historical, and philological. Bibliographies for each chapter. An especially fine list of scholarship for English prosody.

See also

Literary Handbooks (W1406–14)
Oxford Companions (see Index)
Princeton Encyclopedia of Poetry and Poetics (G128)
Reader's Encyclopedia (W1402)

Psychology

Basic sources

W1509.   *Psychoanalysis, Psychology, and Literature: A Bibliography*. Ed. Norman Kiell. 2nd ed. 2 vols. Metuchen, N.J.: Scarecrow, 1982. 1296pp. Z6514.P78.K53   [PN56.P93]   016.801'92

A welcome revision that contains five times the entries provided by the first edition. Its range is enormous, beginning with an article written in 1790 on Hamlet and ending with scholarship completed in 1980. The chapters focus on autobiography, biography, diaries, drama, fairy tales, film, folklore, myths, poetry, wit, and similar themes. Readers can start either in the subject index, with entries on, for instance, Hesse, the Hero, Homosexuality, Sadism, and Symbolism, or in the table of contents (Myths and Legends: see Don Juan, Oedipus, Sphinx). An exciting, stimulating book that will appeal to imaginative, creative writers. Additional information can be found in *American Imago* (W1512) and *Literature and Psychology* (W1511).

W1510.   *Encyclopedia of Psychology*. Ed. Hans J. Eysenck. 3 vols. New York:

Herder, 1972; rpt. Continuum, 1982. BF31.E522   150'.3
International in subject and authority—so much so, in fact, that it is being
published in five languages. Contents range from brief definitions to long, signed
essays with bibliographies for further study.

Periodicals

*W1511. *Literature and Psychology (L&P)*. Teaneck, N.J.: Fairleigh Dickinson
Univ., 1951–81; Sept. 1983– . Quarterly. MLA. PN49.L5
Concerned with literary criticism on any modern or classical work that has
a psychological approach. The articles have a broad range covering Yeats, Dracula,
Thomas Chatterton, Henry James, Virginia Woolf, Hemingway, B. Traven,
Faulkner, Webster, Spenser, Hardy, Dickens, Zola, Swift, and of course (since
we are of the worldly-wise twentieth century) the "old-fashioned" Victorians.
The long book reviews, such as the one on the study of Emily Dickinson by
Cody, have the same psychological focus.
The annual annotated bibliography that supplemented the first edition of
Kiell (W1509) was a valuable contribution until it ceased in 1970. It is still useful
for retrospective searches because it indexes over 150 periodicals and leads to
articles on Langland, Albee, Austen, Ruskin, Stephen and Bloom. The editor's
flair for the dramatic is refreshing: endpapers by Blake, Dürer, Doré, and modern
artists. Cumulated index to vols. 1–10 (1951–60) and 11–15 (1961–65).
Indexed in *Arts and Hum. Cit. Ind.* (F47), *Current Bk. Rev. Cit.* (W1564),
Hum. Ind. (F45), *MLAIB* (D31), *Romantic Movement: A . . . Bibliography*
(J443).

W1512. *American Imago: A Psychoanalytic Journal for Culture, Science and
the Arts (AI)*. Detroit: Wayne State Univ. Press, 1939– . Quarterly.
BF1001.A49
A cross-disciplinary journal that frequently contains articles of interest to
the imaginative literature student. Recent issues, for instance, featured studies
on Proust, Freud, Agamemnon's dream, Sartre, symbolism of the bird, Conrad
Aiken, *Star Wars*, and Billy Budd.
Indexed in *ABELL* (D32), *Abst. Eng. Stud.* (E38), *Arts and Hum. Cit. Ind.*
(F47), *Film Literature Ind.* (W1252), *MLAIB* (D31), *Psych. Abst.* (E39).

See also
Psychological Abstracts (E39)
Style (W1366)

Publishers and Publishing

Surveys

W1514. Madison, Charles A. *Irving to Irving: Author-Publisher Relations,
1800–1974*. New York: Bowker, 1974. 279pp. PN155.M27   808'.02
Not a definitive study, because it could include more examples and be better documented, but important because it examines the relations between authors

and publishers, the inevitable economic pressures, the growth of the literary agent, and the current corporate control of publishing. Case histories of Washington Irving, Twain, Alcott, Henry James, Frost, Santayana, Conrad, Millay, and twenty others.

*W1515. Tebbel, John W. *History of Book Publishing in the United States.* 4 vols. New York: Bowker, 1973–81. Z473.T42   070.5'0973

Twenty years in the making, extraordinarily detailed, and strongly recommended by all reviewers, who hail its author as the Gibbon of the book publishing trade. Tebbel explores, without mercy, the economics of mergers, competitive editors, paperback booms, and academic presses. In his fourth volume, *The Great Change, 1940–80* (830pp.), he shows himself to be a master of intrigue as well as of good prose style.

Basic guides

W1517. *Book Reviewing: A Guide to Writing Book Reviews for Newspapers, Magazines, Radio, and TV by Leading Book Editors, Critics, and Reviewers.* Ed. Sylvia E. Kamerman. Boston: Writer, 1978. 215pp. PN98.B7.B6   808'.066'0281

How to write a review—organization, style, and approach—with lists of reference books, awards, and other encouraging material. It is important largely because it was assembled by the editor of *The Writer* (Boston: Writer, 1877–   ; circulation: 50,000).

W1518. *Scholars and Their Publishers.* Ed. Weldon A. Kefauver. New York: MLA, 1977. 59pp. Paperback. Z286.S37.S34   070.5

For the publish-or-perish generation. A collection of essays by university press administrators discussing standards, economic limitations, contracts, new methods of printing, academic pressures, and readers. Depressing.

Directories

*W1520. *Literary Market Place: The Directory of American Book Publishing (LMP).* New York: Bowker, 1940–   . Annual (Dec.). Paperback. PN161.L5   655.473

An alphabetical, geographical, and topical listing of the most active book publishers in the United States and Canada. It supplies names of officers and selected personnel so that writers will know how to address their manuscripts and gives the number of titles produced by each publisher during the preceding year so writers will be able to assess their chances of being accepted. It also cites reviewers and columnists, and lists book clubs, awards, Braille publishers, and every other type of information needed by authors, librarians, and book traders. Students will look here, for instance, if they want to find the address of a literary agent who could locate a publisher for their manuscript. Name index. The *International Literary Market Place* covers similar material in about 160 foreign countries.

W1521. *Writer's Market.* Cincinnati: Writer's Digest, 1930–   . Annual.

Paperback. PN161.W83   029.6

Where to sell what you write. This topical listing of over four thousand book and magazine publishers includes information on their manuscript specifications, the number of copies and words, scope of subjects, mailing instructions, payment. It is a good source of information for all those threatened with the publish-or-perish ultimatum because it lists agents, organizations, awards, notes on freelancing, consumer publications, trade, technical, and professional journals, freelance markets and services.

*W1522. *Scholar's Market: An International Directory of Periodicals Publishing Literary Scholarship.* Ed. Gary L. Harmon. Columbus: Ohio State Univ. Libraries, 1974. 736pp. Z6513.H37 [PN1]   805

This comprehensive, classified reference book provides the name, address, contents, manuscript submission details, and rate of payment of 848 markets actively publishing materials from literary scholars. Professors who are serious about their profession should know about this one.

W1523. *Publishers' International Directory.* 11th ed. 2 vols. Ridgewood, N.J.: Saur, 1984. Z282.P78   070.5'025

This source is arranged geographically to locate 180,000 publishers in 190 countries, with addresses and publishing specialties. This is the best source for identification of foreign publishers, especially the small and remote.

Periodicals

*W1524. *Coda: Poets and Writers Newsletter.* New York: Poets and Writers, 1973– . 5/yr. PS128.C63   810'.9

News on where to publish what, editors' preference for specific kinds of material, opportunities for awards and contests, and other information vital to the author's existence. This has been called the *Wall Street Journal* of writers. See also its *Directory* (W1031).

Indexed in *Am. Hum. Ind.* (P738).

W1525. *Publishing History.* Teaneck, N.J.: Somerset, 1977– . 2/yr. Z280.P8 658.8'09'0705

Interested in all aspects of publishing in the English-speaking world: the relation between publisher and author, the influence of the publisher on literary trends, publishing as a reflection of social and cultural influences, publishing and politics, and publishing economic history.

See also

ABELL (D32)
Addresses (W1028–31)
Author Newsletters
   American (P777)
   Canadian (N685)
   Continental (Q893)
   English (J195)

Irish (K600)
Scottish (L627)
Welsh (M640)
Bibliography—Books and Printing (W1064–79)
Book Collecting (W1153–69)
Books in Print (W1170), vol. 6, publishers' addresses
Composition and Grammar (W1188)
Little Magazines (W1423–30)
MLA Directory of Periodicals (W1474)
MLAIB (D31), vol. 1, General VI, Miscellaneous
Periodicals (W1474–84)
PTLA (W1172)
Style Manuals (W1584–87)

Quotations

To locate the author and source of a quotation, follow this procedure:

1. First look up the key words (nouns, verbs, or their synonyms) in all editions of Bartlett (W1527).
2. Then try Stevenson (W1528), Evans (W1529), *Magill's Quotations* (W1535), *The Oxford Dictionary* (W1530), or other general collections of quotations.
3. Look in *Granger's Index to Poetry* (W1536) if you suspect the quotation is the title or first line of a poem. This will also locate the entire poem for you in an anthology.
4. If you have no success in the previous titles, try the *Oxford English Dictionary* (W1205) under the key words.
5. If the quotation can be traced to a specific period, try to locate a book specializing in that period, such as Whiting (W1532–33) for early English proverbs.
6. If you know or suspect the author's identity, try a concordance of the collected works, if there is one.
7. If you suspect the quotation is from the Bible, try a Bible concordance.
8. Should all of these attempts prove fruitless, either ascribe the quotation casually to any play by Shakespeare or write to the *New York Times*. Either move will produce an immediate response.

Basic sources

*W1527. Bartlett, John. *Familiar Quotations: A Collection of Passages, Phrases, and Proverbs Traced to Their Sources in Ancient and Modern Literature*. 15th ed. Boston: Little, 1981. 1540pp. Paperback. PN6081.B27   808.88'2

The undisputed sovereign of all reference works, with 22,500 quotations from 2,500 authors in this, its fifteenth edition. As usual, it is arranged chronologically by author, from those of ancient Egypt to Milton Friedman and Stevie Wonder (Steveland Judkins Hardaway), and then by selections from their works in chronological order (except for the Bible and anonymous entries). Readers can thus easily compare contemporaries and trace development of thought. The author's birth and death dates are included as well as the title and date of the selection. Students should also observe the footnotes, which often trace the history of analogous thoughts and events relating to the remarks.

The key-word index includes over a hundred thousand entries to assist in locating half-remembered quotations. Students should remember that they may have to look up several key words (nouns, verbs, and synonyms) before finding the quotation, so they should begin with the most important or most unusual noun and then, if that is not productive, go on to the lesser words.

W1528. Stevenson, Burton E. *The Home Book of Quotations, Classical and Modern*. 10th ed. New York: Dodd, Mead, 1967; rpt. 1984. 2816pp. PN6081.S73 808.88'2

This edition includes statements from people of all ages and all countries up to Khrushchev and John F. Kennedy. The minutely detailed subject index is aided by author and key-word and -phrase indexes, so teachers can easily locate poems to support a theme.

W1529. Evans, Bergen. *Dictionary of Quotations*. New York: Delacorte, 1968. 2029pp. PN6081.E9 808.88'2

The editor has added a refreshing personal touch to this reference book with his witty introduction and informal running comments.

Students can locate quotations by looking up the key words or general subjects in the subject index. If they need a quotation to reinforce an idea, they can start with the topical index. Its chronological arrangement will illustrate the development of the idea. Current interpretation of "ambition," for instance, can be traced from the fourteenth century through Shakespeare, Bacon, Dryden, Burke, Bierce, and Wharton. The author index includes birth and death dates.

W1530. *Oxford Dictionary of English Proverbs*. Rev. Frank P. Wilson. Oxford: Clarendon, 1970. 930pp. Abridgment (1982), 256pp. PN6421.09 398.9'2'03

A prestigious authority with ten thousand proverbs alphabetically arranged by the first important word, with full quotations, source, and date.

W1531. Tilley, Morris Palmer. *Dictionary of the Proverbs in England in the Sixteenth and Seventeenth Centuries*. Ann Arbor: Univ. of Michigan Press, 1950; rpt. New York: AMS, 1983. 854pp. PN6420.T5

A definitive collection of proverbs as they appeared in English literature during the sixteenth and seventeenth centuries. Quotations from Shakespeare are identified in a separate index. Still essential for work in this field.

W1532. Whiting, Bartlett J. *Proverbs, Sentences, and Proverbial Phrases from English Writings Mainly before 1500*. Cambridge, Mass.: Belknap, 1968. 733pp. PN6083.W45 808.88'2

Key words (first important noun or verb in the quotation) are arranged alphabetically with the complete quotation, source, and date listed in chronological order. The indexes of important words and of proper names will facilitate thematic studies.

W1533. ———. *Early American Proverbs and Proverbial Phrases*. Cambridge, Mass.: Belknap, 1977. 555pp. PN6426.W5   398.9'21

Washington, it seems, invited someone to take "Pott Luck" with him in 1776, and even in 1634 people dreamed of their "castles in the air." This work cumulates the favorite sayings of early Americans, generally biblical, generally utilitarian rather than fanciful, some literary, and some popular. See also Whiting and Archer Taylor's *Dictionary of American Proverbs and Proverbial Phrases, 1820–1880* (Cambridge, Mass.: Belknap, 1958; 418pp.).

W1534. *Peter's Quotations: Ideas for Our Time*. Ed. Laurence J. Peter. New York: Morrow, 1977. 540pp. PN6083.P4   808.88'2

For the contemporary speaker, writer, humorist, and philosopher (home, office, classroom, or laboratory), this is a treasury of wit. No documentation, unprofessionally broad subject headings that make it difficult to locate a specific quotation, a bewildering cross-referenced Table of Contents, but worth every penny. The author's most notorious book is *The Peter Principle* (c1969).

W1535. *Magill's Quotations in Context*. Ed. Frank N. Magill. New York: Harper, 1965. 1230pp. Second series: New York: Harper, 1969. 1350pp. PN6081.M292

The first series contains about two thousand quotations, and the second, about fifteen hundred more, arranged alphabetically with lengthy interpretations of their meaning. These summaries frequently provide convenient clues to the prevailing themes of an author's works.

Indexes

*W1536. *Granger's Index to Poetry*. 7th ed. New York: Columbia Univ. Press, 1982. 1329pp. PN1022.G7   808.81'0016

The latest edition of this indispensable poem-locator indexes titles, first lines, authors, and subjects of 40,000 poems in 248 anthologies published between 1970 and 1981. Earlier editions cover earlier anthologies. Each entry in the title and first-line indexes includes a symbol for the anthology in which the entire poem may be found. Some libraries put the call number beside the anthology titles that are listed in the front of the book. Included are listings for classical poets as well as for the Bible, Shakespeare, and moderns like Ferlinghetti, Dickey, Duncan, and Wilbur. The 4,500 subject headings include ecology, social protest, and black, Native American, Chicano, and Hispanic poets. Comprehensive as this is, students must remember to use numerous other sources when attempting to locate obscure quotations (see preceding entries in this section).

Foreign quotations

W1537. *Dictionary of Foreign Quotations*. Ed. Robert Collison and Mary

441

Collison. New York: Facts on File, 1980. 448pp. PN6080.C54   080
The only source of its kind, with quotations in their original language followed by the English translation. Entries are arranged by subject. The name index will help students who want quotations from specific persons.

See also

Foreign Phrases (W1287-89)
Treasury of Jewish Quotations (see W1539)

Religion

Basic guides

*W1538. *Reader's Guide to the Great Religions.* Ed. Charles J. Adams. 2nd
ed. New York: Macmillan, 1978. 521pp. Z7833.A35 [BL80.2]
016.2
The modest term "reader's guide" does not do justice to this admirable survey. Thirteen essays, in English, European, and Oriental languages, discuss and appraise the most notable books, articles, reference sources, and periodicals that are concerned with the world's great religions, including primitive and ancient beliefs; the religions of China, Japan, and South America; and Hinduism, Buddhism, Sikhism, Judaism, Christianity, and Islam. The two indexes are to names and subjects.

W1539. *Student's Guide to Reference Resources for Jewish Studies.* Montreal:
McLennan Library, McGill Univ., 1972. 10pp. ERIC no.: ED 096 942
Z6375.M26 [DS102]   016.910'039'24
A convenient, reliable source for students who need help with questions relating to Jewish literature. This describes and evaluates such titles as the *Cyclopedia of Modern Hebrew Literature*, *Biographical Dictionary of Modern Yiddish Literature*, *Treasury of Jewish Quotations*, and the *Index to Jewish Periodicals*. See ERIC, in the Glossary, for information on the purchase of bibliographies in this series. For additional McGill titles, see the Index.

W1540. Batson, Beatrice. *Reader's Guide to Religious Literature.* Chicago:
Moody, 1968. 188pp. BR85.B425   809.9'35'2
The approach by century makes this a unique aid for students who need a brief, convenient, readable survey of religious literature.

Encyclopedias

W1542. *Encyclopaedia of Religion and Ethics.* Ed. James Hastings. 13 vols. New
York: Scribners, 1961, c1908-26. BL31.E44   203
"Religion" and "ethics" in the broadest sense of the words: beliefs, customs, superstitions, philosophies, standards, and values. It encompasses theology, anthropology, mythology, folklore, sociology, and economics with such a broad topic approach that it is absolutely necessary to use the index to locate all facets of the subject. There are, for instance, ten pages on Arminianism,

forty on ancestor worship, and long studies on the concept of the hero through-out history, including the antihero in Algonquin Indian legend and the trickster Loki in Scandinavian myth. Entries discuss the similarities and differences be-tween the Hindu and the Christian concepts of heaven, burial of the dead, chang-ing ideas of good and evil, Huguenots, Harpies, Luther, Locke, Toynbee, Baillie, Lang, and thousands of other subjects. The articles are written and signed by scholars, and comprehensive bibliographies are generally included. This reference book is for the serious student only. Dilettantes will not be interested.

*W1543. *New Catholic Encyclopedia.* 15 vols. Washington, D.C.: Catholic Univ. of America, 1967. Supplements (1974, 1979). BX841.N44 282'.03

The best ready reference source for extensive scholarly studies on all sub-jects relating to the Catholic religion: the life and works of famous persons, im-portant events, theories, terms, buildings, and conferences. Thomas Aquinas is given fifteen double-column pages, with a detailed analysis of his scholarship and a long bibliography. The history of the Thirty-Nine Articles explains the political and social pressures that caused their alteration. Bring this up to date with a service that specializes in locating religious literary material, the *Catholic Periodical and Literature Index* (Haverford, Pa.: Catholic Library Assn., 1930–), which, for instance, usually contains items on Flannery O'Connor.

*W1544. *Encyclopedia Judaica.* 16 vols. New York: Macmillan, 1972. DS102.8.W496   296'.03

In this truly inspired piece of scholarship all aspects of Jewish life, knowledge, history, culture, and beliefs are presented by the most respected authorities. Read the articles on the Holocaust and Jewish history. They are difficult to put down and impossible to forget.

Bible

*W1546. *International Standard Bible Encyclopedia (ISBE).* Ed. Geoffrey W. Bromiley. 4 vols. Rev. ed. Grand Rapids: Eerdmans, 1979– . Vol. 1 (1979); vol. 2 (1981). BS440.16   220.3

A respected companion for over six decades, now revised to take into ac-count recent textual alterations and exciting archaeological discoveries. The editors and contributors are international and interdenominational. The work defines and explains every term and every topic relating to biblical study, every person and place, every doctrine and practice. Pronunciation, original languages, transla-tions, variants, definitions, cross-references, bibliographies, maps, and illustra-tions. Unquestionably an impressive work that will retain its respected position for many years to come.

*W1547. *Interpreter's Bible.* 12 vols. New York: Abingdon, 1951–57. BS491.2.I55   220.7

Twelve years in the making, a composite effort by 125 international scholars of the twentieth century, this book has a bias that is frankly liberal Protestant. It features signed entries, long bibliographies, maps, and a valuable introduction explaining editorial problems and policy.

The arrangement is unique. Each book of the Bible is treated separately. After a lengthy discussion of the book's position in the canon, its background, dating, structure, theological implications, outline, and a selected bibliography, the text is presented in brief passages for close examination. Each page is divided into four sections, the top half presenting the King James and Revised Standard Versions, the middle giving an exegesis or literal summary, and the bottom pointing out the relevancies and citing illustrations and examples to clarify the meaning. When studying MacLeish's *J.B.*, for example, the student might want to consult this for an overview of the background and thesis of the Book of Job. A shorter version is available: *Interpreter's Dictionary of the Bible: An Illustrated Encyclopedia* (4 vols., 1962, and supplement, 1976). The important supplement adds new subject headings, updates information, and rewrites outmoded entries.

W1548. Hastings, James, ed. *Dictionary of the Bible*. Rev. Frederick C. Grant and Harold H. Rowley. New York: Scribners, 1963. 1059pp. BS440.H5 220.3

Not a condensation of the *Interpreter's Bible* (W1547) and not an abridgment of Hastings' monumental *Encyclopaedia of Religion and Ethics* (W1542) but a dictionary with relatively short, signed entries explaining allusions, terms, themes, structure, laws, characters, places, events, quotations, even studies of style. Convenient for quick reference, and unquestionably authoritative.

This edition is based on the Revised Standard Version of the Bible, with references to the Authorized Version and the Revised Version. There are no bibliographies but many cross-references. A few titles are mentioned in the text for further study. The sixteen colored maps are accompanied by an index of place names.

W1549. *A Dictionary of Biblical Allusions in English Literature*. Ed. Walter B. Fulghum, Jr. New York: Holt, 1965. 291pp. Paperback, 1983. PR145.F8   820.93

Fulghum's dictionary has one purpose: to explain allusions in the Bible that everyone recognizes and most misunderstand, such as "the voice of the turtle," "through a glass darkly," and "coat of many colors." This and Hastings' *Dictionary of the Bible* (W1548) are essential sources that underline the extent to which our thoughts have been permeated with biblical lore, usually without our knowledge.

Dictionaries

W1551. *Oxford Dictionary of the Christian Church*. Ed. Frank L. Cross and Elizabeth A. Livingstone. 2nd ed. New York: Oxford Univ. Press, 1983, c1974. 1550pp. BR95.08   208

An awesome list of well-qualified contributors wrote entries for such subjects as the Second Vatican Council, John Knox, Augustine of Hippo, grace and free will, and the historical attitude of the church toward celibacy. There are important bibliographies at the end of each entry. Consistently fine reviews for this well-edited handbook.

W1552. *Oxford Dictionary of Saints*. Ed. David H. Farmer. New York: Oxford Univ. Press, 1978. 448pp. Paperback. BX4659.G7 [F37] 270
Students have been waiting for this one for years. No other convenient, readable source of this kind exists. The author, a former Benedictine monk, examines the lives and artistic or literary memorials of about one thousand saints of England, Ireland, Scotland, and Wales, including Oliver Plunket, Patrick, Thomas More, Margaret of Antioch, and Philip Howard. He also includes bibliographies for further study and appendixes concerned with peripheral subjects. An interesting, enlightening contribution to literature and life.

Summaries

W1553. *Masterpieces of Catholic Literature in Summary Form*. Ed. Frank N. Magill. New York: Harper, 1964. 1134pp. BX885.M2 208.2
For students who finally realize that they will never have time to read everything. These are summaries of famous Catholic statements from earliest times to Pope John XXIII's "Pacem in Terris" (1963). The chronological arrangement shows the trends and changes in philosophy and theology, and each entry is preceded by a précis of the author's work, dates, and principal ideas. Here the student can read summaries of titles that are constantly mentioned in literature classes such as Augustine's *City of God*, Thomas Aquinas' *Summa Theologica*, and Boethius' *Consolation of Philosophy*.

W1554. *Masterpieces of Christian Literature in Summary Form*. Ed. Frank N. Magill. New York: Harper, 1963. 1193pp. BR50.M22 208.22
Summaries of Hooker's *Treatise on the Laws of Ecclesiastical Polity*, Erasmus' *Praise of Folly*, Blake's *Songs of Innocence and Experience*, and the works of Bunyan, Jonathan Edwards, Jeremy Taylor, and all historical, philosophical, and devotional literature that has been a product of Christianity. Coverage extends to about three hundred books that are considered the most influential in the development of Protestantism. Arrangement is chronological, with author, title, and category indexes. Helpful subheadings summarize the principal ideas.

See also
> *Who's Who in the New Testament* (W1105)
> *Who's Who in the Old Testament* (W1106)

Review of Research

W1556. The quickest way to survey trends of scholarship on any given author
or era is to locate a review of research written by a reliable scholar who is qualified to compare past and present criticism, evaluate editions and ideas, select the best, pan the rest, and pass on to the reader a brief summary of all worthy research that pertains to the field.

Reviews of research sometimes appear as an annual feature in periodicals or other serial publications:

American Literary Scholarship (P734)

Shakespeare Survey (J319)
Studies in English Literature (J320)
  Winter—Renaissance
  Spring—Elizabethan and Jacobean drama
  Summer—Restoration and Eighteenth century
  Autumn—Nineteenth century
Victorian Poetry (J490)
  Year's Work in Victorian Poetry
  Year's Work in English Studies (D33)

Reviews of research are also published as separate volumes:

English literature
Medieval
  Present State of Scholarship in Fourteenth-Century Literature (J294)
  Fisher, *Medieval Literature of Western Europe* (J255)
  Powell, *Medieval Studies* (J253)
  Severs and Hartung, *Manual of the Writings in Middle English* (J260)
Renaissance
  Present State of Scholarship in Sixteenth-Century Literature (J305)
  Logan and Smith, *Predecessors of Shakespeare* (J343)
  ———, *Popular School* (J344)
  ———, *New Intellectuals* (J345)
  ———, *Later Jacobean and Caroline Dramatists* (J346)
  Fordyce, *Caroline Drama* (J347)
Romantic
  Jordan, *English Romantic Poets* (J437)
  Houtchens, *English Romantic Poets and Essayists* (J438)
Victorian
  Ford, *Victorian Fiction* (J477)
  Stevenson, *Victorian Fiction* (J478)
  DeLaura, *Victorian Prose* (J485)
  Faverty, *Victorian Poets* (J488)
Poetry
  Dyson, *English Poetry* (J216)
Fiction
  Dyson, *English Novel* (J204)
Drama
  Wells, *English Drama* (J212)
Anglo-Irish literature
  Finneran, *Anglo-Irish Literature* (K581)
American literature
  American Women Writers (W1635)
  Bryer, *Sixteen Modern American Authors* (P728)
  Gross and Wertheim, *Hawthorne, Melville, Stephen Crane* (P731)
  Inge, *Black American Writers* (P836)
  Sherman, *Invisible Poets: Afro-Americans* (P867)
  Woodress, *American Fiction, 1900–1950* (P782)
  ———, *Eight American Authors* (P730)

Classical literature
   Classical World Bibliographies (S997)
Film
   Armour, *Film: A Reference Guide* (W1229)
Religion
   Reader's Guide to the Great Religions (W1538)

By consulting these and similar sources regularly, students and professors can become familiar with the best critics, keep up with the latest scholarship, and use the capsulized information as a catalyst for their own teaching and research.

Reviews

Books

1. Reviews of a *popular* book can usually be located either in comprehensive sources such as

   Cumulative Book Review Index, 1905-1974 (W1565)
   New York Times Book Review Index, 1896-1970 (W1561)

or, if the book was published within the past few months or years, in the latest issues of

   Book Review Digest (W1558)
   Book Review Index (W1559).

2. The *scholarly* book presents more of a problem. The first volumes have just been published of the

   Combined Retrospective Index to Book Reviews in Humanities Journals, 1802-1974. Ed. Evan I. Farber. 10 vols. Woodbridge, Conn.: Research Publications, 1982–   .

This will index all reviews published during the past century in about two hundred humanities periodicals, listing them by author, critic, and title. A similar fifteen-volume index that began publication in 1979 with citations from 460 periodicals for one million reviews in history. political science, and sociology has received highest praise for everything but its price ($1,200). If the humanities version does manage to prevail over all economic adversities, we predict it will rank only after the *New CBEL* (J175) and *MLAIB* (D31) in value and usefulness. Meanwhile, students who want reviews of scholarly books must follow a simple three-step procedure:

   consider the date and subject of the book itself (new? old? scholarly? popular?),
   become familiar with the available book review indexes, annuals, and periodicals that are described in this section, and
   decide which indexes, annuals, and periodicals would logically be interested in the book they are researching.

3. Without exception, the first thing to note, when trying to find a book

review, is the publication date of the book itself. This date is essential because reviews will naturally have been written soon after the first appearance of the book, and most book review sources are published in annual or more frequent volumes except for the *Cumulative Book Review Index* (W1565) and the *New York Times Book Review Index, 1896-1970* (W1561), mentioned above. The publication date can be found in

> the card catalog
> *Books in Print* (W1170)
> *Cumulative Book Index* (D35)
> *National Union Catalog* (B10-11)
> *New CBEL* (J175)
> —or other appropriate bibliographies.

It can also be found in the book itself at the bottom of the title page along with the publisher's name and location (the imprint). In a paperback edition, the original publication date of the hardback is usually found on the verso of the paperback's title page. Students must remember that they need the date of the hardback to locate a review because that tells them when the review would have been written.

4. Because book review sources must necessarily limit their scope, the next step is to consider the contents of the book itself. Is it of general interest or strictly scholarly? Is it twentieth-century fiction or a new edition of Chaucer's poetry? Would the review appear in a professional literary journal or in a popular periodical? Is it a play, a reference book, a periodical, a best-seller? Recently published or an old-timer?

5. The final step is to examine the book review sources and decide which would be the logical source for reviews on this particular book. Here are some of the possibilities:

*W1557. *Choice.* Chicago: American Library Assn., 1964– . Monthly (one in July-Aug.). Assn. of College and Research Libraries. Cumulated photographic reprints of the reviews in vols. 1–10 (1964–74) in 8 vols. and index (Totowa, N.J.: Rowman, 1976–77). Z1035.C5   028

All professors and students who are on library committees should scan this regularly, for it specializes in evaluating and advertising new books and some nonprint material (computer software, video, etc.) of interest to college and research libraries. Because this is published eleven times a year, with unexpectedly frank evaluations written by 2,600 experts (eighty percent with Ph.D.'s), it is an extremely important and reliable source for keeping up with new academic publications, which in 1980 totaled over eight thousand in all fields. It has two outstanding features: All books are compared with existing scholarly works, and recommendations for or against purchase are made. Every May the best of these books are selected and listed in a special article, "Outstanding Academic Books," which is accepted as a reliable means of keeping Sheehy (A5) up to date.

Most issues contain a feature article describing new periodicals as well as a bibliographic essay on a specific subject such as "Writing Down Under: Recent Literature from Australia, New Zealand, and the Pacific Islands" (vol. 14,

1977, 19–31). Experienced research students learn to look for these ready-made reference aids.

A serious handicap in the individual issues is the absence of an index to subjects or genres. *Choice*'s index is to titles and authors only, so the reader must search page by page through the reference section and English and American literature entries. A cumulative index is published annually in February. The ten-year cumulative index is arranged by subject: vol. 1—reference and humanities; vol. 2—language and literature (comparative, classical, English, American, Germanic); vol. 3—literature (Romance, Slavic, and others), performing arts, philosophy, religion; vols. 4–8—the sciences, history, education, and others; vol. 9—index for authors, titles, and broad subject—so broad, in fact, that it is almost useless. Scholars would like to see a finely detailed subject index in the next cumulation.

Indexed in *Bibl. Ind.* (C28), *Bk. Rev. Dig.* (W1558), *Bk. Rev. Ind.* (W1559), *Current Bk. Rev. Cit.* (W1564), *Lib. Lit.* (F53).

*W1558. *Book Review Digest* (*Bk. Rev. Dig.*). New York: Wilson, 1905– . 10/yr., with quarterly and annual cumulations. *Author/Title Index, 1905–74* (1976). Z1219.C96   028.1

For reviews of books that have received some measure of popular acclaim. To be included, fiction must have been reviewed at least three times and nonfiction four times in eighteen months by the eighty-three participating scholarly and popular periodicals. Arrangement is alphabetical by author (including pseudonyms), and each entry includes a description of the book, an abstract of the contents, and favorable and unfavorable excerpts from the reviews.

The subject and title index in each volume cumulates every five years. The four-volume author-title index for 1905–74 cumulates the names and titles from all those years into one alphabetical list by author, compiler, editor, translator, and some pseudonyms. This good editorial planning helps the scholar who wants to work with a specific author or title. Literature students should look in *Book Review Digest* if they want to examine the critical response to Stephen Crane's short stories entitled *Tales of War* edited by Fredson Bowers for CEAA (W1177) in 1972, or to scan excerpts from several reviews of Harry Crews's recent novel, *A Childhood*. This source not only indicates reception at the time of publication but also provides a convenient way to determine whether the book or the reviews are worth reading in their entirety.

*W1559. *Book Review Index* (*Bk. Rev. Ind.*). Detroit: Gale, 1965– . 6/yr., with annual cumulations. Z1035.A1.B6

Much more comprehensive than the *Bk. Rev. Dig.* (W1558) in number of periodicals indexed (about four hundred) and number of titles listed (80,000 reviews of 40,000 new books in 1982). Students should remember this source when they need reviews for books other than best-sellers because it includes titles that have been reviewed only once. No excerpts or abstracts are provided, however—only bibliographical information so the student can go read the entire review. Coverage is extensive: fiction, nonfiction, humanities, social sciences, librarianship, bibliographies, juvenile books, and new periodicals. Scope ranges from scholarly journals like *PQ* (H154) to popular magazines like *Esquire*, *Ms.*, and *Rolling Stone*. Title index in each annual volume since 1976. The ten-year cumulation, *Book Review Index, 1969–1979* (1980–81, 7 vols.), has a cumulated title index for the half-million books reviewed.

*W1560. *Index to Book Reviews in the Humanities* (*Index to Bk. Rev. Hum.*). Detroit: Thomson, 1960– . Annual. Z1035.A1 [163] 028.1
No excerpts from reviews, but comprehensive in both number and type of journals covered. Over 685 scholarly and some popular publications are examined in the fields of art and architecture (but not archaeology), biography, drama and dance, folklore, language, literature, music, philosophy (but not religion), travel (but not, since 1970, history), and literary research.
Arrangement is alphabetical by author, with citations to reviews listed under each name. Inclusion is not confined to books published during the current year but extends to previous years as well, so the student must check several volumes to get all the reviews on a single title. Of interest to literature majors is the fact that coverage now extends to several author newsletters, linguistics journals, and specialized titles such as *Studies in the Novel* (G66).

W1561. *New York Times Book Review Index, 1896–1970*. 5 vols. New York: Arno, 1973. AN.N561
A gold mine for students who are interested in the trends in literary criticism, social taste, and artistic temper during the twentieth century. The five volumes of 800,000 entries are arranged as indexes by author, title, reviewer, subject, and category. This means that we now have a superior source for well-written reviews of important books and that we can survey, trace, and compare American attitudes from the Edwardian era to Kilroy and the freaks. Think what pop culture enthusiasts will do with the four columns of entries on sex, which progress from the prim "Alleged preoccupation with sex in French Fiction" of 1907, to 1970's *Everything You Always Wanted to Know about Sex, but Were Afraid to Ask*. Someone will inevitably trace critical opinion of Eliot, Hesse, Sinclair Lewis, or Cummings over half a century. Someone else will voice an opinion on the sporadic reviews of Joyce's *Ulysses*. And others will find axes to grind in weighing the Humor of 1900 and 1970, Children's Fiction of 1896 (five titles) and 1969 (five columns), or the uncertain influence of a critic by the name of Ellen Lewis Buell, who wrote reviews for thirty-four years (25 pages of entries). Who was she? The reviews themselves are now available in one monumental accumulation covering 1896–1979: $7,320.

*W1562. *New York Review of Books* (*NYRB*). New York: New York Review, 1963– . 22/yr. AP2.N6552 028.1'05
Robert Lowell, Irvin Ehrenpreis, Robert Heilbroner, Richard Ellmann, Flannery O'Connor, Stephen Spender, Ivan Turgenev, Joseph Heller, and all the important names in literature and literary criticism will be found here. Good prose, worthy ideas, prestige, and, therefore, a decided influence on the general reception and sale of the reviewed books. Index for 1963–75.
Indexed in *ABELL* (D32), *Arts and Hum. Cit. Ind.* (F47), *Current Bk. Rev.*

Cit. (W1564), *Film Literature Ind.* (W1252), *MLAIB* (D31), *Readers' Guide* (F48).

*W1563. *Times Literary Supplement (TLS)*. London: Times, 1902–   . Weekly. *TLS Index, 1902-1939* (1978). 2 vols.

Timely, responsible, witty, and impeccable in style and reputation. It reviews all manner of literature from a new edition of Flaubert's letters to a new biography of Katherine Mansfield—about twenty literary titles in each issue. Of special interest to academics are letters to the editor from irate authors who have suffered at the hands of *TLS* reviewers. Literary historians may also find valuable criticism in the early twentieth-century issues where in 1902 readers complained indignantly about errors in the *DNB* (W1086), and a delightfully comic, tongue-in-cheek review takes W. D. Howells to task for his stinging criticism of heroines in fiction.

The cumulated index of 350,000 entries arranged by title, subject, and name is especially important because the *Book Review Digest* (W1558) did not begin indexing *TLS* until 1917 and even then included information on only a few reviews.

Indexed in *ABELL* (D32), *Arts and Hum. Cit. Ind.* (F47), *Brit. Hum. Ind.* (F49), *Current Bk. Rev. Cit.* (W1564), *Film Literature Ind.* (W1252), *Hum. Ind.* (F45).

W1564. *Current Book Review Citations (Current Bk. Rev. Cit.)*. New York: Wilson, 1976–   . Monthly except August, with annual cumulations.
Z1035.A1.C86   016.0281

Not so helpful to the literature student as the title suggests, because, aside from adding a few library reviewing sources, this does nothing more than cumulate book reviews from about twelve hundred periodicals already indexed by the other Wilson indexes: *Readers' Guide* (F48), *Hum. Ind.* (F45), *Ed. Ind.* (W1225), *Art Ind.* (W1042), *Soc. Sci. Ind.* (W1579), and four others unrelated to literature. Experience seems to indicate that the *Bk. Rev. Ind.* (W1559) may be superior in accuracy, currency, and coverage of literary periodicals, but this still should be consulted if the subject is interdisciplinary.

W1565. *Cumulative Book Review Index, 1905-1974 (Cum. Bk. Rev. Ind.)*. 6 vols. Princeton, N.J.: National Library Service, 1975. Z1035.A1.N3
Alternate title: *National Library Service Cumulative Book Review Index*.
This author-title index to all reviews cited in *Bk. Rev. Dig.* (W1558), *Choice* (W1557), *Library Journal* (W1268), and *Saturday Review* should be a great time-saver, but reviewers have found many errors and omissions. Their advice: Use the title index because the author index is not reliable, or, even better, go directly to the *Bk. Rev. Ind.* (W1559) or *Bk. Rev. Dig.* (W1558).

W1566. *Review.* Charlottesville: Univ. Press of Virginia, 1979–   . Annual.
PR14.R38   820.9
This annual publication specializes in reviewing scholarly works in English and American literature. Some articles focus on new editions such as the Wesleyan edition of Fielding and the revised *STC, 1475-1640* (J306); others examine

current critical work on specific authors such as Milton, Melville, and Faulkner. Most are careful judgments, discerning and accurate, but occasionally, in their zeal to achieve "rigorous" reviewing, "frankly and boldly" (preface), the articles succumb to the delicious temptations of hyperbole and humor and ensnare themselves in their own inaccurate accusations. Sheehy's *Guide to Reference Books* (A5), as one example, is seldom consulted by scholars for *evaluations.* It is unequaled for its *descriptions* of the contents and publishing history of reference works, but one has to read a good many entries before finding such a word as "important." The latest supplements do quote occasionally from introductions and prefaces, but that is not true "evaluation." *Review's* stated policy is commendable, however. When criticism's aim is scholarship, it succeeds; when its aim is derision, it judges itself to be something less worthy.

Indexed in *Arts and Hum. Cit. Ind.* (F47).

Reviews of plays and films

W1567. Samples, Gordon. *How to Locate Reviews of Plays and Films: A Bibliography of Criticism from the Beginnings to the Present.* Metuchen, N.J.: Scarecrow, 1976. 114pp. Z5781.S19 [PN1707] 016.791

Locating reviews of plays and films should never again be a problem. Use of this reference source should unquestionably be included in all drama, film, bibliography, and methods of research courses. It lists leading theater and film periodicals, reference guides, study guides, and indexes and devotes chapters to special subjects such as synopses. All titles are annotated. For additional reviews of films, see W1570.9.

Reviews of reference books

W1568. *American Reference Books Annual.* Littleton, Colo.: Libraries Unlimited, 1970– . Annual. Z1035.1.A55   011'.02

The most prestigious of the agencies devoted exclusively to reviewing reference books. The convenient subject arrangement leads to women's studies, ethnic studies, film, theater, literature, and all areas of the arts, humanities, and sciences. In the 1979 volume, for instance, students can find reviews of McKenna's *Irish Literature, 1800–1875* (K582, "a treasure-house"), *Contemporary Literary Critics* (W1360, "admirable"), and *Biographical Dictionary of Actors . . . 1660–1800, vols. 5 and 6* (W1141, "indispensable"). The 1981 volume contains reviews for over seventeen hundred reference books, not only more in number than any other review source but also more timely, for most of the titles are reviewed within a year or two of their publication. Furthermore, each entry includes citations for additional reviews in other sources.

Cumulative indexes to vols. 1–4 (1970–74), vols. 5–10 (1975–79), and vols. 11–15 (1980–84) serve as an independent, nearly complete list of the authors, subjects, and titles of all worthy reference books published during those years in the United States. Very important. Every literary scholar should scan this as soon as it is received by the library.

Indexed in *Bk. Rev. Ind.* (W1559), *Index to Bk. Rev. Hum.* (W1560).

W1569. *Index to Reviews of Bibliographical Publications.* Troy, N.Y.: Whitston, 1976– . Annual. Z1002.I57   028.1

A reference source that specializes in locating reviews solely of bibliographical publications. This is a splendid idea, but the time delay of several years between the first appearance of the volume being reviewed and the publication of this annual limits its value severely. Because most scholars and librarians need prompt analysis and evaluation, this will be useful for retrospective searches only, especially since much of the same material is indexed regularly by *Bk. Rev. Ind.* (W1559) and *Index to Bk. Rev. Hum.* (W1560). Five indexes to the contents, but the subject headings are so broad (followed only by numbers, no identifying phrases) that they may discourage even the most stalwart researcher. Most students will probably continue to seek the prompt assistance of *American Reference Books Annual* (W1568) because it makes a point of reviewing scores of indexes, bibliographies, and other reference books within a year or two of their publication, and, in addition, it locates reviews in other sources.

The index first appeared in the scholarly periodical *AEB* (W1073), then was published separately, 1976–78, by G. K. Hall, Boston, and since 1979 has been published by Whitston.

See also these additional sources for reviews of reference books

W1569.1 *American Literary Scholarship* (P734)

> *Choice* (W1557), monthly reviews and annual list of outstanding reference books
>
> *College and Research Libraries* (A5), Jan. and July issues, a column devoted to reviews of newly published reference books, written by the master of research materials, Eugene P. Sheehy
>
> *Literary Research Newsletter* (W1421), several reviews of recent research publications in every quarterly issue
>
> *Reference Services Review* (Ann Arbor, Mich.: Pierian, 1973–), reviews in every quarterly issue

Additional sources for reviews in special subject areas

W1570. Reviews can sometimes be found only in periodicals or books that focus on a specific area or subject. Because the preceding book review sources necessarily have limited scope, students must be prepared to use their imagination if they are searching for the less well-known title. And to find timely reviews soon after they are published, the researcher must go directly to the current issues of the relevant periodical because indexing services require six months to five years to gather, list, and print review information. The following sources might help those students who are looking for reviews in special areas:

.1   American Literature

American Humanities Index (P738)
American Literary Realism (P747)
American Literary Scholarship (P734)
American Literature (P744)

Black American Fiction (P857)
Black American Literature Forum (P850)
Black American Playwrights (P860)
Black Dialogue (P851)
California Quarterly (P750)
Early American Literature (P751)
Eichelberger, *Guide to Critical Reviews* (P787)
Great Lakes Review (P752)
New England Quarterly (P756)
Northwest Review (P757)
Phylon (P853)
Salem, *Guide to Critical Reviews: American Drama* (P805)
Sewanee Review (P762)
Southwest Review (P767)
Studies in American Fiction (P788)
Studies in American Humor (P769)

.2   Art

Art Index (W1042)

.3   Author Newsletters

American (P777)
Canadian (N685)
Continental (Q893)
English (J195)
Irish (K600)
Scottish (L627)
Welsh (M640)

.4   Commonwealth Literature

Anglo-Welsh Review (M638)
Annual Bibliography of Scottish Literature (L620)
Australian Literary Studies (N660)
Bibliotheck (L622)
Canadian Book Review Annual (N672)
Canadian Literature (N676)
Canadian Periodical Index (N674)
Dalhousie Review (N678)
Gnarowski (N666)
Hermathena (K594)
Index to Australian Book Reviews (N658)
Index to Commonwealth Little Magazines (N647)
Irish University Review (K596)
Journal of Commonwealth Literature (N650)

Lecker and David (N669)
Scottish Literary Journal (L623)
Studies: An Irish Quarterly (K598)
Studies in Scottish Literature (L625)
Tamarack Review (N681)
University of Toronto Quarterly (N683)
West Coast Review (N682)

.5   Comparative Literature

Comparative Drama (T1018)
Comparative Literature (T1016)
Journal of English and Germanic Philology (Q924)
Literature East and West (R959)
Renaissance Spain and Its Literary Relations (T1012)
Symposium (T1015)
Yearbook of Comparative and General Literature (T1014)

.6   Education

Education Index (W1225)
Scholarships, Fellowships and Loans News Service (W1220)

.7   English Literature

General
  British Book News (J180)
  Howard-Hill (C26)
  Studies in English Literature (J320)
Medieval Literature
  Bibliographical Bulletin (J267)
  Bibliography of Medieval Drama (J281)
  Bibliography of Publications on Old English Literature (J231)
  Fry, *Beowulf* (J242)
  Medievalia et Humanistica (J272)
  Medium Aevum (J273)
  Neuphilologische Mitteilungen (J274)
  Speculum (J265)
Renaissance Literature
  English Literary Renaissance (J311)
  Renaissance Quarterly (J313)
  Seventeenth-Century News (J314)
  Shakespeare Newsletter (J315)
  Shakespeare Quarterly (J316)
  Shakespeare Studies (J318)
  Shakespeare Survey (J319)
  Shakespearean Research and Opportunities (J317)

Restoration and Eighteenth-Century Literature
  Eighteenth Century: A Current Bibliography (J374)
  Eighteenth Century: A Journal of Theory (J379)
  Eighteenth-Century Studies (J381)
  English Literature, 1660–1800 (J375)
  Restoration (J383)
  Restoration and 18th Century Theatre Research (J403)
Nineteenth-Century Literature
  Bibliographies of Twelve Victorian Authors (J462)
  English Literature in Transition (J471)
  Keats-Shelley Journal (J444)
  Nineteenth-Century Fiction (J422)
  Nineteenth Century Readers' Guide (J468)
  Nineteenth-Century Theatre Research (J430)
  Palmer's Index to the Times (J419), which contains, for instance,
    numerous entries for reviews on Hardy's *Tess of the D'Urbervilles* when
    it was published in 1891
  Poole's Index (J416)
  Romantic Movement (J443)
  Slack (J459)
  Studies in Romanticism (J446)
  Victorian Newsletter (J472)
  Victorian Periodicals Review (J473)
  Victorian Poetry (J490)
  Victorian Studies (J470)
  Wellesley Index (J466)
Twentieth-Century Literature
  Contemporary Literature (J529)
  Journal of Modern Literature (J530)
  Parnassus (J571)

.8   Fiction

Modern Fiction Studies (J544)
Novel (G64)
Studies in Short Fiction (G80)
Studies in the Novel (G66)

.9   Film

American Film (W1260)
Art Index (W1042)
Bowles, *Index to Critical Film Reviews* (W1241)
Essay and General Literature Index (F46)
Film Comment (W1261)
Film Criticism (W1258)
Film Culture (W1262)

Film Literature Index (W1252)
Film Quarterly (W1263)
Film Review Digest Annual (W1239)
Filmfacts (W1264)
International Index to Film Periodicals (W1253)
Journal of Popular Film (W1265)
Literature/Film Quarterly (W1266)
New York Times Film Reviews (W1240)
New York Times Index (F50)
Readers' Guide (F48)
Retrospective Index to Film Periodicals (W1256)
Salem, *Guide to Critical Reviews: The Screenplay* (W1242)
Selected Film Criticism (W1238)
Sight and Sound (W1267)

.10   Linguistics

Language and Language Behavior Abstracts (W1332)
Language Teaching (W1333)
Modern Language Journal (W1336)
Word (W1338)

.11   Literary Research

Literary Research Newsletter (W1421)

.12   Music

Music Index (W1456)

.13   Philosophy

Philosopher's Index (W1489)

.14   Science Fiction

Science Fiction Book Review Index (G97–98)
Science-Fiction Studies (G100)

.15   Theater

Black American Playwrights (P860)
Black Theatre (P864)
Gohdes, *Literature and Theater* (P800)
Hatch, *Black Image* (P862)
Modern Drama (J555)
Modern Drama (Toronto) (J563)

New York Theatre Critics' Reviews (P807)
New York Times Theater Reviews (P808)
Salem, *Guide to Critical Reviews: American Drama* (P805)
————, *Guide to Critical Reviews: British and Continental Drama* (J559)
————, *Guide to Critical Reviews: Foreign Drama* (R969)
————, *Guide to Critical Reviews: The Musical* (P806)
tdr: the drama review (J564)
Theatre Journal (G118)
Theatre Research International (G119)

.16   World Literature

Black African Literature (R974)
International Fiction Review (R963)
Journal of English and Germanic Philology (Q924)
Literature East and West (R959)
Research in African Literatures (R981)
Russian Literature Triquarterly (Q938)
Scandinavian Studies (Q940)
World Literature Today (R961)
—and many, many more.

See also

ABELL (D32), an exceptionally comprehensive source for reviews of scholarly
works in English and American literature with, for example, fifteen
reviews listed for Wimsatt and Brooks, *Literary Criticism: A Short History*
(W1400)

Arts and Hum. Cit. Ind. (F47), reviews of books, films, records, art ex-
hibits, television and radio programs, and dance, music, and theatrical
performances

Hum. Ind. (F45), especially for interdisciplinary studies

Microform Review (W1441)

New York Times Index (F50), issued twice a month with listings for reviews
found in the Sunday issue. Students must remember that there are no
entries under *R* for "Reviews"—only under specific subjects such as
"Books," "Motion Pictures," "Plays and Operas."

Readers' Guide (F48), under the author of the book reviewed

Year's Wk. Eng. Stud. (D33), especially for its reviews of selected scholarly works in specific fields of English and American literature

Science and Literature

W1573. *Relations of Literature and Science: A Selected Bibliography,*
1930–1967. Ed. Fred A. Dudley. Ann Arbor, Mich.: University Microfilms, 1968. 137pp. Z6511.D8   016.809
   Concerned with "the literary impact of scientific thought," not with the
psychological aspects (see *Literature and Psychology*, W1511, for that approach),

and not with the history and philosophy of science. Arrangement is chronological, with subdivisions for general studies, centuries, and individual authors. Compiled from the annual bibliographies that appeared originally in *Symposium* (T1015) and from an earlier MLA publication with the same title. To update this, see *Relations of Literature and Science: A Bibliography of Scholarship, 1970-1980*, ed. Walter Schatzberg (Worcester, Mass.: Clark Univ. Press, 1981; 27pp.; MLA). See *Clio* (W1303) for current bibliographies.

W1574. *STTH: Science/Technology and the Humanities*. Melbourne: Florida Inst. of Technology, 1977– . 3/yr. AS30.S16
    Interested in creating a dialogue between the sciences and the humanities, especially the psychological, sociological, and aesthetic aspects.

See also
    Clio (W1303), annual bibliography on literature and science
    Symposium (T1015)

Series

W1575. Students who have advanced to the research stage in literature do not
    need to be told that any series will inevitably include a few excellent
publications, a larger number of adequate but uninspired titles, and an occasional three or four that everyone (especially the publisher) wishes had never been granted the honor of publication. A sweeping denigration of the series concept, however, is not only unjust but unwise, because most series are designed to fulfill specific needs of a specific audience, and if those needs are answered excellently or adequately by most of the volumes, then the project has been successful. And at the least, the most conspicuous failures may inspire some energetic, indignant scholar to capitalize on the efforts of the pioneer who made the first bold strokes on the blank canvas, however bumbling they may have been. Discrimination is the key. The quality of each volume in a series depends entirely on the qualifications of the author and the sincerity of his or her efforts.

American Authors Logs Series (P723)
American Critical Tradition (P724)
Approaches to Teaching Masterpieces (W1596)
Asian Literature Bibliography Series (R988)
British Author Series (J182)
British Book News (J180)
British Writers and Their Work (J180)
Checklists in the Humanities and Education (J213, J348)
Contemporary Writers Series (W1128-30, W1360)
Critical Essays on American Literature (P725)
Critical Heritage Series (W1361)
Critical Idiom Series (G55)
Essential Articles Series (J183, J243)
Film Directors and Genre (W1236)
Folklore of the British Isles (W1273)

Gale Information Guide Library (A8)
Great Bibliographers' Series (W1071)
Hall, G. K., Reference Guides (W1055)
Introductions to Twentieth-Century American Poetry (P817)
Irish Writers' Series (K589)
McGill University Reference Guides (see Index)
Makers of the Nineties (J471)
Masters of Science Fiction and Fantasy (G95)
Northern Illinois University Press Bibliography Series (see Author
   Bibliographies, W1053)
Oxford History of English Literature (J174)
Oxford University Press Select Bibliographical Guides (J204, J212, J216)
Performing Arts Information Guide Series (W1470)
Pittsburgh Series in Bibliography (W1616)
Plays by Renaissance and Restoration Dramatists (J341)
Plots and Characters Series (W1590)
Poet and His Critics (G129)
Poets on Poetry. University of Michigan, 1978–   .
Readings in Literary Criticism (W1362)
Regents Critics Series (W1363)
Regents Renaissance Drama Series (J342)
Regents Restoration Drama Series (J402)
Routledge Critics Series. Boston: Routledge, 1972–   .
Scarecrow Author Bibliographies (W1054)
Serif Series (G90, G99, P722)
Twayne's English Authors Series (J181)
Twayne's Filmmakers Series (W1237.1)
Twayne's Theatrical Arts Series (W1237.1)
Twayne's United States Authors Series (P720)
Twayne's World Authors Series (R957)
Twentieth Century Interpretations (W1364)
Twentieth Century Views (W1364)
Ungar Series in Modern Literature. New York: Ungar, 1969–   .
Ungar Series in World Dramatists. New York: Ungar, 1970–   .
University of Minnesota Pamphlets on American Writers (P721)

Slang

*W1576. Partridge, Eric. *A Dictionary of Slang and Unconventional English.*
   7th ed. 2 vols. in 1. New York: Macmillan, 1970. 1520pp.
   PE3721.P322   427.09

Slang terms, colloquialisms, solecisms, catchphrases, a few nicknames, and
vulgarisms are arranged in alphabetical order, with an explanation of their origin
and changes in meaning, dates, quotations, and reference sources. Such words
as bobby, dandy, humbug, smithereens, rave, and thousands of others are
defined and placed in their historical context. Because Partridge used many
editions of early dictionaries as well as the *OED* (W1205) and numerous

specialized glossaries (as for military terms), the scope is extremely comprehensive in both the chronological and the linguistic sense.

*W1577. Wentworth, Harold, and Stuart B. Flexner. *Dictionary of American Slang*. 2nd ed. New York: Crowell, 1975. 766pp. PE2846.W4 427'.09

The second edition adds numerous regionalisms and colloquialisms, terms from the prohibition era, jazz, the armed forces, business, politics, entertainment, teenagers, the beat generation, even taboo words of four letters (or more). The resulting compendium is both amusing and astonishing, especially since the sociocultural influences that produced the slang are brilliantly analyzed in an accompanying essay. The updated bibliography might be of interest to literature as well as linguistics majors because it lists items on Nelson Algren, Maxwell Anderson, Richard Bissell, Morris Bishop, and other authors.

Social Sciences

W1578. *International Encyclopedia of the Social Sciences*. 17 vols. New York: Macmillan, 1968. Biographical supplement, vol. 18 (1979). H40.A2.I5 300'.3

This highly respected work is especially useful for interdisciplinary studies because it covers anthropology, economics, geography, history, law, political science, psychology, sociology, statistics, and related areas. Literature students would use this text, for instance, if they were studying nineteenth-century backgrounds and needed an explanation of the term "mercantilism." The articles are signed (evidence of authority) and most are accompanied by bibliographies. This is a good source for biographical material on interdisciplinary notables, especially since the publication of the 820-page supplement which adds 215 biographies for such figures as Arendt, Allport, Leakey, Kennan, Lovejoy, Niebuhr, Russell, Skinner, and Toynbee.

W1579. *Social Sciences Index* (*Soc. Sci. Ind.*). New York: Wilson, 1974– . Quarterly, with annual cumulations. AI3.S62 016.3

Author and subject entries to 307 periodicals that focus on anthropology, psychology, sociology, history, and related subjects. Crossdisciplinary studies of such authors as Henry James and T. S. Eliot will be indexed here. Book reviews are in a separate section in the back of each issue, arranged by author of the book. Similar studies for the years previous to 1974 are found in *Soc. Sci. Hum. Ind.* (F51).

Speeches

W1580. *Speech Index*. 4th ed. Metuchen, N.J.: Scarecrow, 1966. Supplement, 1966–80 (1982), 484pp. AI3.S85

The main volume indexes about 350 collections of speeches and arranges the contents by name and subject, ranging from Mark Antony's orations to Zola's appeal for Dreyfus, exhortations on education and labor unions, presidential addresses, Bella Abzug, Dakota Indians, and science and the humanities. The supplements add information on recent speeches and on newly located speeches of the past.

Style Manuals

*W1584. Gibaldi, Joseph, and Walter S. Achtert. *MLA Handbook for Writers of Research Papers*. 2nd ed. New York: MLA, 1984. 221pp. Paperback. PE1478.M57   808'.02

The second edition of the *MLA Handbook* introduces a new system of documentation for research papers in the humanities (by parenthetical references in the text keyed to a list of works cited), provides instructions for other systems, and gives explicit directions on the technique of preparing a research paper, from the initial idea to correction symbols on the final version. Numerous examples illustrate the instructions. Students should memorize them. When the basic facts of spacing, punctuation, and form of bibliographies and quotations are mastered, the typing becomes easier, the research quicker, the awareness of other scholars' errors keener, and the confidence surer. Students will benefit in accuracy, efficiency, and scholarship.

MLA Handbook style is required by almost all literary and many other scholarly journals. To be certain of editors' specifications, scholars should consult the *MLA Directory of Periodicals* (W1474) before preparing their manuscripts for a specific journal.

*W1585. *Chicago Manual of Style: For Authors, Editors, and Copywriters*. 13th ed. Chicago: Univ. of Chicago Press, 1982. 738pp. Former title: *A Manual of Style*. Z253.U69   686.2'24

Everyone who is now or plans to become a student, teacher, and/or author in any discipline whatsoever should be thoroughly familiar with this, for it has all the necessary information on proofreaders' marks, capitalization and punctuation, abbreviations, use of foreign languages, alphabetizing, symbols, manuscript preparation, a glossary of technical terms, and an analytical index. Generally referred to as the Chicago Style Manual, this has thirty-six pages on the art and strategy of drawing up footnotes and bibliographies, and another forty-six pages on the form of the entries. Use this to supplement the *MLA Handbook* (W1584), which gives a commendable 110 pages to documentation. Professional writers generally own both books.

W1586. Turabian, Kate L. *Student's Guide for Writing College Papers*. 3rd ed. Chicago: Univ. of Chicago Press, 1977. 272pp. Paperback. LB2369.T82   808'.042

Remarkably clear explanations and illustrations for awkward footnotes and complex bibliographies, a detailed index leading to numbered paragraphs, and a list of reference works that is badly out of date. Some professors prefer to use this as the authority on the technique of preparing research papers rather than the *MLA Handbook* (W1584). Students will have to act accordingly.

*W1587. *Words into Type.* Ed. Marjorie E. Skillin and Robert M. Gay. 3rd ed. Englewood Cliffs, N.J.: Prentice-Hall, 1974. 585pp. PN160.S52 808'.02
   All the problems of copy editing: proofreaders' marks, typing form, capitalization (in all languages), spelling, division of words, abbreviations, and grammar. Scholars who publish or wish to publish should have this on their desk.

Summaries

Basic sources
*W1589. Kolar, Carol Koehmstedt. *Plot Summary Index.* 2nd ed. Metuchen, N.J.: Scarecrow, 1981. 544pp. Z6514.P66.K63   809
   The dedication in the first edition indicates the value of this book. It will indeed be useful to students in a hurry, especially at examination time, because it locates summaries of plots of all important works from Homer's *Iliad* to musical comedies of the 1970s. The title index shows that *The Sound and the Fury* is summarized in four different reference books; the author index indicates that seventeen of Faulkner's novels have been summarized in various sources. Plays, poems, short stories, and essays are also included. Perhaps students should look here before deciding which authors and books they want to investigate! If used with discretion, this can be an acceptable, helpful source.

W1590. Plots and Characters Series. Ed. Robert L. Gale. Hamden, Conn.: Archon, 1965-   . In progress.
   Extremely long (too long) summaries of selected fiction—for example, twelve pages on Charlotte Brontë's *Villette*. Admittedly a timesaver, but this questionable asset will unquestionably be abused by the lazy and the dull. The entries include lists of characters and brief descriptions of their roles plus all their nicknames, patronymics, surnames, and first names, an understandably valuable feature for the Russian novels. They also include biographical information on historical figures and brief chronologies of the authors' life and works. Perhaps of some use to some professors as a memory refresher, but keep these away from students.

   Fiction of Henry James. 1965. 207pp.
   Fiction and Sketches of Nathaniel Hawthorne. 1968. 259pp.
   Fiction and Poetry of Edgar Allan Poe. 1970. 191pp.
   Works of Mark Twain. 2 vols. 1973.
   Fiction of Jane Austen, the Brontës, and George Eliot. 1976. 282pp.
   Fiction of William Dean Howells. 1976. 306pp.
   Fiction of Theodore Dreiser. 1977. 152pp.
   Major Russian Fiction. 2 vols. 1977-78.
   Fiction of James Fenimore Cooper. 1978. 346pp.

> *Fiction of Eighteenth-Century English Authors.* 2 vols. 1977–78.
> *Classic French Fiction.* 1981. 253pp.
> *Works of Joseph Conrad.* Projected for 1985.

W1591.   Magill, Frank N., ed. *Masterplots.* New York: Salem, 1954– . Title
    varies: *Masterplots Annual Review.* PN44.M36

Essay reviews of outstanding books published in America, one hundred titles each year through 1976 and two hundred since 1977, when it also initiated a subject, rather than an alphabetical, arrangement. Unquestionably convenient, but not a substitute for the author's own words and work. For updated, selected reprints of these titles, see J518. For additional similar projects by Magill, see the Index.

Additional sources

W1592. Brief summaries of many well-known novels, short stories, plays, essays,
          and poems may be found in the section on Literary Encyclopedias (W1402–05). For brief summaries of critical works, see Abstracting Services (E38–43). Encyclopedias in specific subject areas such as Gassner and Quinn, *Reader's Encyclopedia of World Drama* (R966), should also be consulted for brief summaries and evaluations of important individual works. Other summaries may be found in the following specialized sources:

> *Afro-American Poetry and Drama* (P868)
> *American Indian in Short Fiction* (P878)
> *Canadian Fiction* (N687)
> *Encyclopedia of Mystery and Detection* (G86)
> *Illinois! Illinois!* (P780)
> *Ireland in Fiction* (K603)
> *Magill's Quotations in Context* (W1535)
> *Masterpieces of Catholic Literature in Summary Form* (W1553)
> *Masterpieces of Christian Literature in Summary Form* (W1554)
> *Masterpieces of World Philosophy in Summary Form* (W1488)
> *Masterplots . . . from the World's Fine Literature* (R955)
> *Modern World Theatre* (G116)
> *National Playwrights Directory* (W1140)
> *Survey of Contemporary Literature* (J518)
> *Survey of Science Fiction Literature* (G94)
> *1,300 Critical Evaluations of Selected Novels and Plays* (R956)
> *Twentieth Century Plays in Synopsis* (J560)
> *Women and Literature* (W1642)
> —and others that are indexed in the *Plot Summary Index* (W1589)

Synonyms

*W1593. *Webster's New Dictionary of Synonyms.* Rev. ed. Springfield, Mass.:
       Merriam, 1978, c1973. 909pp. PE1591.W4   423'.1

This dictionary discriminates between synonyms and near synonyms by defining their different implications and citing their use in works by famous authors.

It explains, for instance, the subtle difference between surmise and assume, intermittent and recurrent, accumulate and amass and hoard. Antonyms as well as analogous words are included to assist in the distinction of meanings. In entries where no discriminating explanation is supplied, the starred synonym indicates that the reader should turn to that word for further information.

A lengthy introduction explains the historical and linguistic problems, and the list of quoted authors includes their dates and profession. Many quotations are taken from works by the best contemporary writers and from periodicals in American and British literature. The purist, the linguist, the conscientious professor, the careful writer should own this one. They will find the joy of enlightenment in every entry.

*W1594. *Webster's Collegiate Thesaurus*. Springfield, Mass.: Merriam, 1976. 944pp. PE1591.W38   423'.1

Many students will find this completely new thesaurus easier to use than the venerable Roget (W1595). This is for writers who want more than just an appropriate word. It is for discriminating purists who will use the comparisons and contrasts as a means of clarifying their own thoughts and improving the intellectual quality of their prose as well as their literary style. The entry for "excellent," for instance, begins with a definition, then gives an illustration in a sentence, several synonyms (ranging from "bang-up" to "dandy"), related words (from "rum" to "nobby"), idioms, contrasting words and antonyms, only one of which will be exactly what the purist needs. Buy a copy.

W1595.   *Roget's International Thesaurus*. Ed. Robert L. Chapman. 4th ed. New York: Crowell, 1977. 1317pp. Paperback. PE1591.R73

The unabridged edition is the wisest purchase for students of literature because this is a lifetime investment, a quick way to increase one's vocabulary, to sharpen style and meaning, to avoid dull language, to encourage accuracy. Up to date, with modern terms.

Teaching Resources and Methods

Series

W1596. Approaches to Teaching Masterpieces of World Literature. Ed. Joseph Gibaldi. New York: MLA, 1981- . In progress.

1. *Approaches to Teaching Chaucer's* Canterbury Tales. Ed. Joseph Gibaldi. 1981. 175pp. Paperback. PR1874.G5   821'.1

2. *Approaches to Teaching Dante's* Divine Comedy. Ed. Carole Slade. 1982. 177pp. Paperback. PQ4371.A6   851'.1

Each volume in this new series will be devoted to teaching a major work (or group of related works) and will include (1) a discussion by the editor about the texts and major issues surrounding the teaching of the work and (2) a series of essays by teachers on their methods of teaching the work. Forthcoming: *Don Quixote, Beowulf,* and *David Copperfield*.

Periodicals

W1597. *CEA Critic (CEA)*. Shreveport: Centenary Coll. of Louisiana, 1939– .
2/month (Nov.–May). PE1011.022

Articles on teaching English at the college level, book reviews, news, and notes. The same subscription covers the *CEA Forum*, the quarterly official publication of CEA.

Indexed in *ABELL* (D32), *Abst. Eng. Stud.* (E38), *Am. Hum. Ind.* (P738), *Arts and Hum. Cit. Ind.* (F47), *MLAIB* (D31).

*W1598. *College Composition and Communication (CCC)*. Urbana: NCTE, 1950– . 4/yr. PE1001.C6   808'.042'0711

This official journal of the Conference on College Composition and Communication publishes articles on the theory, practice, and teaching of composition, including its relation to literature, language, and logic. Particularly important because since 1973 it has provided an annual bibliography that abstracts the year's significant books and articles on composition and the teaching of composition.

Indexed in *ABELL* (D32), *Current Bk. Rev. Cit.* (W1564), *Current Contents* (F47), *Current Ind. Jour. Ed.* (W1224), *Ed. Ind.* (W1225), *Language and Lang. Beh. Abst.* (W1332), *MLAIB* (D31).

*W1599. *College English (CE)*. Urbana: NCTE, 1939– . 8/yr. (Sept.–April). PE1.C6   420.5

Official journal of the NCTE. Articles on the teaching and interpretation of language and literature. "Comment and Response" is one of its more important features.

Indexed in *ABELL* (D32), *Abst. Eng. Stud.* (E38), *Arts and Hum. Cit. Ind.* (F47), *Current Bk. Rev. Cit.* (W1564), *Current Contents* (F47), *Current Ind. Jour. Ed.* (W1224), *Ed. Ind.* (W1225), *Index to Bk. Rev. Hum.* (W1560), *Language and Lang. Beh. Abst.* (W1332), *MLAIB* (D31), *Romantic Movement: A . . . Bibliography* (J443).

W1600. *English Journal (EJ)*. Urbana: NCTE, 1912– . 9/yr. PE1.E5   420.5

Designed to assist those interested in the art of teaching, especially at the secondary and undergraduate levels. Numerous bibliographies, usually annotated, for timely topics such as science fiction and computers.

Indexed in *ABELL* (D32), *Abst. Eng. Stud.* (E38), *Bk. Rev. Ind.* (W1559), *Current Contents* (F47), *Current Bk. Rev. Cit.* (W1564), *Current Ind. Jour. Ed.* (W1224), *Ed. Ind.* (W1225), *Film Literature Ind.* (W1252), *MLAIB* (D31).

W1601. *Improving College and University Teaching*. Washington, D.C.: Heldref, 1953– . Quarterly. L11.I4

This interdisciplinary publication focuses on teaching techniques: preparation, incentives, innovations, programs, research, evaluation, and development. Cumulative index to vols. 1–10 (1953–62).

Indexed in *Current Bk. Rev. Cit.* (W1564), *Ed. Ind.* (W1225).

W1602. *Journal of Aesthetic Education*. Champaign: Univ. of Illinois Press, 1966– . Quarterly. N1.J58   701.1707
Focusing on literature and related arts, this debates the problems of teaching and the needs of society.
Indexed in *ABELL* (D32), *Arts and Hum. Cit. Ind.* (F47), *Current Ind. Jour. Ed.* (W1224), *Ed. Ind.* (W1225), *Film Literature Ind.* (W1252), *Hum. Ind.* (F45), *Phil. Ind.* (W1489), *Psych. Abst.* (E39).

W1603. *Teaching English in the Two-Year College*. Greenville, N.C.: East Carolina Univ., 1974– . 3/yr. PE1065.T4   807'.1173
Articles on teaching composition, creative writing, technical writing, and literature, reviews of new texts, and news items.
Indexed in *Current Ind. Jour. Ed.* (W1224).

W1604. *Use of English*. St. Albans, Eng.: Hart-Davis Educational, 1949– . 3/yr. PE1001.U84
A literature-oriented education journal concerned with methods of teaching and learning good English. Circulation: 3,000.
Indexed in *British Education Index, Current Ind. Jour. Ed.* (W1224).

Background reading—Teaching composition and rhetoric

W1605. *Options for the Teaching of English: Freshman Composition*. Ed. Jasper P. Neel. New York: MLA, 1978. 120pp.
Writing programs at universities in Virginia, Texas, Washington, Iowa, Arizona, California, Michigan, Rhode Island, Wyoming, New York, and Missouri—the course structure, teaching and grading policies, subjects, faculty assignments, and details of special problems and solutions. Similar situations exist in every school in the country. This is guaranteed to give ideas and encouragement to everyone who teaches composition.

W1606. Corbett, Edward P. J. *Classical Rhetoric for the Modern Student*. 2nd ed. New York: Oxford Univ. Press, 1979, c1971. 672pp. PN175.C57 808
A practical recommendation for teaching writing: Imitate the classics and practice constantly. Bibliography of primary and secondary sources pertaining to classical rhetoric (pp. 632–41).

W1607. Hirsch, Eric D. *Philosophy of Composition*. Chicago: Univ. of Chicago Press, 1977. 200pp. PE1403.H57   808'.001
A scholarly approach to the teaching of composition. A query into the features of written and spoken speech. An exhortation for readability ("efficiency of communication"). A search for a way to assess the effectiveness of teaching. The author makes a statement that the younger generation refuses to accept: Writing is a craft in itself, not a mere by-product of the subject matter under discussion.

W1608. Tate, Gary, ed. *Teaching Composition: 10 Bibliographical Essays*. Fort Worth: Texas Christian Univ. Press, 1976.   304pp.   Paperback.

PE1403.T4   808.042

Essays discuss works, from Plato to the present, that might help majors who, trained exhaustively in the appreciation of literature, are going to end up teaching composition. See also the annual bibliographies on the teaching of composition in *College Composition and Communication* (W1598).

W1609.   *The Writing Teacher's Sourcebook.* Ed. Gary Tate and Edward P. J. Corbett. New York: Oxford Univ. Press, 1981. 348pp. PE1404.W74 808'.042'071173

A collection of thirty-two outstanding essays by Booth, Kinneavy, Shaughnessy, and other experts on the teaching and writing of composition. Subjects include the training of teachers, the selection of teaching aids, and the uses of grammar and rhetoric. This will be useful (and encouraging) to anyone who teaches composition. The annotated bibliography offers suggestions for further study.

See also

Composition and Grammar (W1188)
Education Index (W1225)
Fries, *Structure of English* (W1345)
Prospects for the 70's (W1310)
Literary Research Newsletter (W1421)
Modern Language Journal (W1336)
Sociological Abstracts (E40)

Textual Criticism

Basic sources

**W1610.   Gaskell, Philip. *From Writer to Reader: Studies in Editorial Method.* New York: Oxford Univ. Press, 1978. 264pp. PN162.G3   808'.02

Using works by Milton, Swift, Dickens, Joyce, Hawthorne, Stoppard, and others, Gaskell illustrates how a scholarly editor can establish an authoritative "critical" text from earlier editions that have been corrupted through a variety of intentional or unintentional alterations. These alterations, as we all know, may have been inflicted on the manuscript by weary or hung over typesetters, well-intentioned widows, unethical friends, and mercenary or puritanical publishers. The duty of editor and professor is to ascertain the actual words of the author, not the intermediaries, so that history can judge the author's ability, not theirs. Gaskell is excellent, even though many critics disagree with him on certain details. Put this on the required reading list for all advanced literature students.

**W1611.   *British Bibliography and Textual Criticism: A Bibliography.* Vols. 4 and 5 of *Index to British Literary Bibliography* (C26). Oxford: Oxford Univ. Press, 1979. Z2011.A1.H68   [PR83]   016.6588'09'07

British Literary Bibliography and Textual Criticism, 1890–1969: An

Index. Vol. 6 of *Index to British Literary Bibliography* (C26). Oxford: Oxford Univ. Press, 1980. 864pp. Z2011.A1.H68   [PR83] 016.82

Three of a projected seven-volume project that will provide, when completed, "a guide to the literature which enumerates works on topics likely to be of concern to students of British literary history, or which describe the conditions under which British books were produced and disseminated, with consequent effects on their texts." Over eight thousand titles in vol. 4, six thousand in vol. 5. Vol. 6, the index, makes accessible all the information in the four volumes published so far—names, titles, and subjects. It will of course have to be revised when the last remaining volume in the set is finally published (vol. 3). A valuable, important work.

W1612.   Thorpe, James E. *Principles of Textual Criticism*. San Marino, Calif.: Huntington Library, 1972. 209pp. Paperback. PR65.T5   801'.959

All future teachers of literature should read this. It does make a difference whether Paul Morel (in Lawrence's *Sons and Lovers*) "whispered" or "whimpered" at the moment of his decision, just as it does made a difference, although this is not a point made by the author, whether Paul's last name is accented on the first or last syllable. The book, in short, is focused on accuracy of the text—the spelling, wording, forms of words, punctuation, paragraphing, capitalization. Thorpe stresses how these "minor" questions of the author's final intention can radically alter the meaning of the work.

Teachers should know, for instance, that Dickens wrote two endings to *Great Expectations* (tearfully Victorian and traditionally Cinderella) and students should consider the effect of both of them because it has to do with literary and social criticism, psychology, ethics, and dollars. Awareness of these authorial and editorial pressures leads to awareness of the power of the single word, and hence, without any straining of the imagination, to the power of press, television, and advertising. Scholarship is not removed from life.

PMLA (H152) originally printed one chapter of this book under the title "Aesthetics of Textual Criticism" (Dec. 1965). It was later offprinted and sold separately by MLA.

W1613. *Evidence for Authorship: Essays on Problems of Attribution*. Ed. David V. Erdman and Ephim G. Fogel. Ithaca, N.Y.: Cornell Univ. Press, 1966. 559pp. PR61.E7   809

Put this on the required browsing shelf for courses in bibliography and methods of research. English majors must of course learn to be aware of textual problems such as the possibility of contradictions between internal and external evidence, the import of stylistic evidence, statistical analysis, and cumulative effect. A gratifying number of examples from literature, including Johnson, Sidney, More, and *Christabel*.

W1614. Dearing, Vinton A. *Principles and Practice of Textual Analysis*. Berkeley: Univ. of California Press, 1974. 256pp. P47.D43   001.55'2

Dearing's step-by-step explanation of the problems involved in textual editing is important because it was written by a person who learned the hard way, as textual editor of *The Works of John Dryden*. This will be valuable to anyone who is particularly interested in the use of the computer in editing.

W1615. Moorman, Charles. *Editing the Middle English Manuscript*. Jackson: Univ. Press of Mississippi, 1975. 107pp. PR275.T45.M6   820'.9'001
Moorman's practical manual explains the problems and solutions involved in editing early manuscripts, from deciphering the handwriting and the language to the final published version.

Series

W1616. Pittsburgh Series in Bibliography. Pittsburgh: Univ. of Pittsburgh Press, 1972–   . In progress.
A series of descriptive bibliographies (see Glossary) designed by and for the textual critic. The goal is to provide detailed descriptions of all printings of all English editions, with numerous illustrations and bibliographies for the works of such authors as Hawthorne, Hart Crane, Stevens, Berryman, Fitzgerald, O'Neill, Lardner, Marianne Moore, O'Hara, Fuller, Hammett, Ross Macdonald and Kenneth Millar, Chandler, Dreiser, Wolfe, Cozzens, Thoreau, and Emerson. The lists include separate publications, chapters within books, articles in periodicals or newspapers, quotations, translations, movies, and occasional important criticism.

W1617. The annual conference on editorial problems at the University of Toronto has produced the following collections of essays (New York: Garland):

Editing Sixteenth-Century Texts. Ed. Richard J. Schoeck. 1965. 137pp. PN162.E3   808'.02
Editing Nineteenth-Century Texts. Ed. John M. Robson. 1966. 145pp. PN62.E3   808'.02
Editing Eighteenth-Century Texts. Ed. Donal I. B. Smith. 1967. 132pp. PN162.E3   808'.02
Editor, Author and Publisher. Ed. William J. Howard. 1968. 121pp. PN155.E3   808'.2
Editing Twentieth-Century Texts. Ed. Francess G. Halpenny. 1969. 103pp. PN162.E3   808'.02
Editing Seventeenth-Century Prose. Ed. Donal I. B. Smith. 1970. 142pp. PN162.C62   801'.95
Editing Texts of the Romantic Period. Ed. John D. Baird. 1971. 125pp. PN162.C62   808'.02
Editing Canadian Texts. Ed. Francess G. Halpenny. 1972. 124pp. PN162.C62   801'.95
Editing Eighteenth-Century Novels. Ed. Gerald Eades Bentley, Jr. 1973. 109pp. PN162.C62   801'.95
Editing British and American Literature, 1880–1920. Ed. Eric W. Domville. 1974. 108pp. PN162.C62   801'.95
Editing Renaissance Dramatic Texts: English, Italian, and Spanish. Ed. Anne Lancashire. 1975. 140pp. PN162.C62   801'.95
Editing Medieval Texts: English, French, and Latin Written in England. Ed. A. G. Rigg. 1976. 136pp. PN162.C62   091'.0942

Editing Nineteenth-Century Fiction. Ed. Jane Millgate. 1977. 128pp. PN162.C62   802'.95

Editing Correspondence. Ed. J. A. Dainard. 1978. 124pp. PN162.C62 801'.956

Editing Illustrated Books. Ed. William F. Blissett. 1979. 125pp. PN162.C62   808'.02

Editing Sixteenth- and Seventeenth-Century Poetry. 1980.

Background reading

W1619. Bowers, Fredson T. "Textual Criticism." In Thorpe (W1419), pp. 28–54.

W1620. Brack, O. M., and Warner Barnes, eds. *Bibliography and Textual Criticism: English and American Literature, 1700 to the Present.* Chicago: Univ. of Chicago Press, 1969. 345pp. Paperback. PR77.B7   820.9
A collection of important articles on a difficult subject.

W1621. Gottesman, Ronald, and Scott Bennett, eds. *Art and Error: Modern Textual Editing.* Bloomington: Indiana Univ. Press, 1970. 306pp. PN162.G63   808.02
Essays on controversial problems of all kinds: the "good" and "bad" quartos of Shakespeare, the varying degrees of reliability in the manuscripts of Hawthorne and Twain and John Stuart Mill, the life history of one sentence in Joyce's *Finnegans Wake.* Graduate students and professors should browse through this so they will learn to be more critical of the editions they purchase for their classes.

W1622. Perrin, Noel. *Dr. Bowdler's Legacy: A History of Expurgated Books in England and America.* Garden City, N.Y.: Atheneum, 1969. 226pp. Paperback. Z1019.P4   098
An amusing, fact-laden account of efforts to clean up the classics, from "Out, crimson spot!" to Huck Finn's sweat and hogwash. This is good leisure-time reading.

W1623. Tanselle, G. Thomas. "Textual Scholarship." In Gibaldi (W1419), pp. 29–52.

Additional reference sources for information on textual criticism

ABELL (D32)
Bibliography—Books and Printing (W1064–79)
Censorship (W1174–76)
Computer Abstracts (W1190)
Computing Reviews (W1191)
Editing the Romantics Newsletter (J447)
Glossary (Section Y), definitions for terms used in textual criticism
Howard-Hill (C26, J337)
MLAIB (D31), vol. 1, General V

Princeton Encyclopedia of Poetry and Poetics (G128), Textual Criticism
Proof (P760)

Translations

Basic sources

*W1624. *Translations: A Student's Guide to Reference Sources in the Humanities.* Montreal: McLennan Library, McGill Univ., 1977. 15pp. ERIC no.: ED 096 942

The best student-oriented selective source for information on important literary translations including Oriental, European, Yiddish, and medieval sources. See ERIC, in the Glossary, for information on the purchase of bibliographies in this series. For additional McGill titles, see the Index.

W1625. *Index Translationum (International Bibliography of Translations).* Paris: UNESCO, 1932–40, 1948–   . Annual (vol. 31: 1978, published in 1982). Z6515.T7.I42   016

The 1976 volume (1006pp.) cites over 50,000 translated books in sixty-one countries. Arrangement is by nation, with major subject headings such as Philosophy, Education, Biography, and Literature. Access to the first twenty-one volumes has been improved since the publication of the *Cumulative Index to English Translations, 1948-1968,* 2 vols. (Boston: Hall, 1973), but there are still no cross-references between volumes, and inconsistencies abound. The five-year lag in publication is unavoidable.

W1626. *Translation and Translators: An International Directory and Guide.* Ed. Stefan Congrat-Butlar. New York: Bowker, 1979. 241pp. PN241.C749   418'.02

The only handy guidebook in this field, with a survey of the history and problems, sections on awards, training, legislation, and journals, and a directory of names and languages.

Periodicals

W1627. *Translation.* New York: Translation Index, 1977–   . Quarterly. Articles, recommendations, UNESCO reports, and bibliographies. Indexed in *ABELL* (D32), *MLAIB* (D31).

W1628. *Translation Review.* Richardson: Univ. of Texas (Box 688), 1978–   . 6/yr. American Literary Translators Assn. PN886.T7

Interviews with eminent literary translators; articles on the theory and practice of translation; reviews of all major books translated into English; and lists of translations in progress.

Indexed in *Arts and Hum. Cit. Ind.* (F47).

Additional reference sources for information on translations

Bergquist, *Three Centuries* (G113)
Bibliographic Index (C28)
Bibliographical Bulletin (J267), International Arthurian Society
Bibliography of Crime Fiction (G85)
Bibliography of Picaresque Literature (G87)
Block, *English Novel, 1740–1850* (J390)
Checklist of English Prose Fiction, 1700–39 (J388)
Computer Abstracts (W1190)
Computing Reviews (W1191)
Concise Bibliography of French Literature (Q907)
Dictionary of Oriental Literatures (R985)
German Literature (Q918)
Guide to Eastern Literatures (R984)
Guide to Oriental Classics (R983)
Handbook of Austrian Literature (Q900)
MLAIB (D31), vol. 1, General IV, Translation
Medieval Studies (J253)
Modern Slavic Literatures (Q942)
New CBEL (J175)
Reader's Adviser (A4)
Reader's Guide to African Literature (R973)
Renaissance Spain and Its Literary Relations (T1012)
Russian Literature Triquarterly (Q938)
Sourcebook for Hispanic Literature (Q944)
Speculum (J265)
Yearbook of Comparative and General Literature (T1014), occasional lists of translations

Women's Studies

Basic sources

*W1630. *American Women Writers: A Critical Reference Guide from Colonial Times to the Present*. Ed. Lina Mainiero. 4 vols. New York: Ungar, 1979–82. Paperback, 2 vols. (1983). PS147.A4   810'.9'9287

The first comprehensive reference work devoted to one thousand American women writers from Colonial times to the present, with critical assessments, a complete list of their works, a selected list of criticism, and hard-to-find biographical data. This is a convenient and, we are proud to say, distinguished source for quick information on all authors, but especially so for the obscure or neglected. Hallie Quinn Brown, a lecturer and educator whose childhood home was in the Underground Railroad, is included as well as Kay Boyle, Rachel Carson, Nikki Giovanni, and Margaret Wise Brown, whose children's books have sold millions of copies. Vol. 4 includes an index to all names and subjects mentioned in the text. (A note for future publishers: Spare us the author's initial; use the full name. It has to do with respect, honor, gratitude, scholarship, and good manners.) Some reviewers have noticed factual errors and misspellings.

W1631.   *American Women Writers: An Annotated Bibliography of Criticism*. Ed. Barbara A. White. New York: Garland, 1977. 126pp. Z1229.W8.W45 [PS147] 016.81'09'9287
Concentrates on the criticism published on American women writers of fiction, poetry, and drama — *not individuals, but women writers in general*. Good points: careful annotations and a feisty introduction. Serious weakness: no efficient way to find out what is in the book because there is no subject index and the chapter titles are not descriptive.

W1632.   *Articles on Women Writers, 1960–1975: A Bibliography*. Ed. Narda L. Schwartz. Santa Barbara, Calif.: American Bibliographical Center, 1977. 236pp. Z2013.5.W6.S37 [PR111] 016.82'09'9287
A locator list to criticism in periodicals and dissertations concerning six hundred women writers of all literary forms from the Middle Ages to the present. Particularly important for less-known authors such as Eliza Haywood, Mary Davys, or Margaret Cavendish, who are not carefully researched elsewhere. This is a good beginning and easy to use, but it has no annotations, no cross-references, indistinct arrangement, and a mixture of popular and scholarly sources.

W1633.   Backscheider, Paula, et al. *An Annotated Bibliography of Twentieth-Century Critical Studies of Women and Literature, 1660–1800*. New York: Garland, 1977. 287pp. Z2012.B13 [PR449.W65] 016.809'89287
Part of this book concerns the treatment of women in literature of the eighteenth century, particularly in the works of Cleland, Defoe, Fielding, Richardson, Smollett, and Sterne. The remainder is a bibliography of works by and about sixty-five women writers of the period from Wollstonecraft to Williams. A good beginning, but students must remember that it is selective and that much more remains to be done. It can be updated by the annual bibliographies in *Women and Literature* (W1645) and *Eighteenth-Century Studies* (J381). See also W1634 for women characters.

W1634.   *Women in Literature: Criticism of the Seventies*. Ed. Carol Fairbanks Myers. Metuchen, N.J.: Scarecrow, 1976. 256pp. Z6514.C5.W645 [PN56.W6] 809'.933'52
More Women in Literature. 1979. 465pp.

The first volume is a list of 2,800 books, articles, dissertations, and reviews published between 1970 and 1975 concerned with women characters in literature. It lists critical works about their roles, and then it cites biographies for and interviews with about three hundred of their authors, mostly American, but a few Canadian, British, and European. Its coverage is rather sketchy—only six articles on Tillie Olsen, nineteen on the Canadian Margaret Laurence, and fourteen on Zora Neale Hurston—but at least it was a beginning. It was soon supplemented in the indispensable *Bulletin of Bibliography* (C29) with "Women in Literature: A Selected Bibliography" (July-Sept. 1978, pp. 116–22, 131). And in 1979 a second volume appeared entitled *More Women in Literature*, which includes writers from the sixth century B.C. to 1977, one thousand in all. Few other books cover this subject (see W1644–45 and part of W1633). Much more needs to be done, however, because these volumes have no annotations, no subject index, no accessible arrangement, and no criteria for selection.

*W1635. *American Women Writers: Bibliographical Essays*. Ed. Maurice Duke, Jackson R. Bryer, and M. Thomas Inge. Westport, Conn.: Greenwood, 1983. 434pp. Z1229.W8.A44 [PS147] 016.81'09'9287
Critical surveys of the research completed on twenty-four writers from Bradstreet to Hurston.

W1636. *Bibliography of Hispanic Women Writers*. Ed. Norma Alarcón and Sylvia Kossnar. Bloomington, Ind.: Chicano-Riqueño Studies, 1980. 86pp. Z1609.L7.A45 [PQ6055] 016.86'09'9287
This compilation of selected entries from the volumes for 1922 through 1978 of the *MLAIB* (D31) contains six pages of entries for Santa Teresa and Sor Juana, seven pages for Pardo Bazán, and nine pages for Mistral. Recognition is at last given to a host of other major and minor poets who, as the introduction points out, seem to exist generation after generation, almost as a subculture that is intent on harboring its own treasured values and in voicing its own concept of how the world is and should be.

Identification problems

*W1640. *Index to Women of the World from Ancient to Modern Times: Biographies and Portraits*. Ed. Norma O. Ireland. Westwood, Mass.: Faxon, 1970. 573pp. Z7963.B6.I73 016.92072
A comprehensive index to information on every important woman who ever lived with their dates, nationality, profession, and a list of biographies. Sappho, Hannah More, Dorothy Thompson, Harriet Beecher Stowe, Willa Cather, Anne Bradstreet, and many more. A good first source, especially since the *DAB* (W1087), *DNB* (W1086), and most standard biographical dictionaries have been consistently weak on entries for either the famous or the infamous woman. See also W1088, W1630, W1632, W1635–37, W1641, and W1644–49 for identification problems.

W1641. *Dictionary of British and American Women Writers, 1660–1800.*

Ed. Janet Todd. Totowa, N.J.: Rowman, 1984. 375pp.
A biographical dictionary of eighteenth-century British and American
women writers.

Summaries

W1642. *Women and Literature: An Annotated Bibliography of Women Writers*.
   3rd ed. Cambridge, Mass.: Women and Literature Collective, 1976.
   212pp. Z5917.W6.S46   [PN3401]   016.80883'9'352
Brief summaries of the most important books written by women, from the
tragic *Coquette* in America (1797) to *Notes from a Spanish Prison* (1975). The
editors (female) undoubtedly enjoyed writing it, and female reviewers praise
it, but some parts are decidedly feminist. Good reference books are without bias.
Geographical and chronological divisions. Author and broad subject indexes.

Abstracts

W1644. *Women Studies Abstracts*. Rush, N.Y.: Rush, 1972–   . Quarterly.
   Z7962.W65   016.30141'2'05
Literature, art, biography, sex roles, and religion are some of the subject
headings found in this index of seven hundred periodicals. Scope ranges from
Mary, Queen of Scots, to Anaïs Nin, Emily Dickinson, May Sarton, and the
women in Dostoevsky, James, *Hamlet*, Austen, Hemingway, and Jong. Subject
and author indexes cumulate annually.

Periodicals

W1645. *Women and Literature (W&L)*. New York: Holmes and Meier, 1975–   .
   2/yr, 1975–78; quarterly, 1979; annual, 1980–   . Former title,
   1972–74: *Mary Wollstonecraft Newsletter*. PN481.W65   809'.933'52
This scholarly periodical is concerned with women writers and the literary
treatment of women of all eras, with bibliographies and articles on George Sand,
Mary Shelley, E. M. Forster, Flannery O'Connor, women and television, and
related subjects. It is international in scope, with a special interest in European
women. When it was a quarterly, two issues were devoted to women and
literature; one to a special topic, such as contemporary novelists and film; and
one to an annual international bibliography, 600 to the present, which indexed
over five hundred periodicals and included about 2,500 entries. Corrected,
augmented bibliographies from all the early issues have been published in book
form (New York: Holmes and Meier, 1981; 550pp.). The new annual focuses
on a single theme and extends to film as well as literary history and criticism.
The 1981 volume, for example, is concerned with the images of man in literature
and film produced by women.
   Indexed in *Am. Hum. Ind.* (P738), *Arts and Hum. Cit. Ind.* (F47), *Hum.
Ind.* (F45), *MLAIB* (D31).

W1646. *Journal of Women's Studies in Literature (JWSL)*. Montreal: Eden,
   1979–   . Quarterly. PR115   809'.933'52
Scholarly articles on the contributions made by women poets, novelists,

and dramatists.

Indexed in *Am. Hum. Ind.* (P738), *MLAIB* (D31).

FICTION

W1647.   *Black Women Novelists: The Development of a Tradition, 1892-1976.*
Ed. Barbara Christian. Westport, Conn.: Greenwood, 1980. 275pp.
PS374.N4.C5   813'.09'9287

Favorable reviews greeted this long-awaited survey of the contributions of
the black woman novelist. It examines the work of Harper, Hurston, Petry,
Marshall, Morrison, Walker, and many other imaginative, talented women who
had the determination to surmount their difficulties and then felt an obligation
to relate them. Well done.

DRAMA

W1647.1 *American Women Dramatists of the Twentieth Century: A Bibliography.* Ed. Brenda Coven. Metuchen, N.J.: Scarecrow, 1982. 244pp.

A major contribution to research on 133 American women dramatists.

POETRY

W1648.   *Poetry by American Women, 1900-1975: A Bibliography.* Ed. Joan
Reardon and Kristine A. Thorsen. Metuchen, N.J.: Scarecrow, 1979.
681pp. Z1229.W8.R4   [PS151]   016.811'008

A list of 5,500 women poets who have published one or more volumes of
poetry, for a total of 9,500 volumes. This is the only source providing such information, and it has proved so popular that the editors are planning a supplement. They have located titles, dates, pseudonyms, and maiden names of such
poets as Bates, Boyle, Miles, Millay, Plath, Rich, Riding, Teasdale, Wakoski,
Widdemer, and Wyse. The result is an impressive tome that may inspire a dissertation or two. And, we hope, many more volumes of poetry.

FILM

W1649.   *Women and Film: A Bibliography.* Ed. Rosemary R. Kowalski.
Metuchen, N.J.: Scarecrow, 1976.   278pp.   Z5784.M9.K68
[PN1995.9.W6]   016.79143

The best approach to the contents is through the subject index, which leads
to annotated citations for books and articles on women as performers, filmmakers,
characters on the screen, columnists, and critics. The director Dorothy Arzner,
for example, has been the subject of thirty-one critical works; Shirley Clarke,
twenty-nine; Maya Deren, twenty-eight; and Penelope Gilliatt, eighteen.

Additional reference sources for information on women

W1649.1 *Notable American Women* (W1088)

Novels in English by Women, 1891-1920: A Preliminary Checklist.
Ed. Janet Grimes and Diva Daims. New York: Garland, 1981–   .
Vol.   1   (1981),   805pp.   Z2013.5.W6.G75   [PR830.W6]
016.823'912

PMLA (H152), Sept. issue, Women's Studies Programs

Who's Who of American Women (W1094)

Works in Progress

W1650.   The professor who needs to publish and the student who is getting
ready to write a dissertation want most of all to avoid duplicating work
that has already been done by some other scholar. Of inestimable assistance in
this situation are these periodicals that feature regular announcements of research
in progress:

African Literature
  Research in African Literatures (R981)
American Literature
  American Literature (P744), dissertation coverage ceased in 1979
  American Quarterly (P745), including dissertations
  Early American Literature (P751), including dissertations
  Journal of American Folklore (W1278), including dissertations
  Western American Literature (P772)
Computers
  Computers and the Humanities (W1192)
English Literature
  Annual Bibliography of Victorian Studies (J464)
  Australian Literary Studies (N660)
  Chaucer Review (J268)
  English Literature in Transition (J471)
  14th Century English Mystics Newsletter (J269)
  Johnsonian News Letter (J382)
  Keats-Shelley Journal (J444)
  Medieval Studies (J271)
  Neuphilologische Mitteilungen (J274)
    Chaucer Research in Progress
    Middle English Research in Progress
    Old English Research in Progress
  Old English Newsletter (J236)
  Scriblerian and the Kit-Cats (J384)
  Speculum (J265)
  Victorian Newsletter (J472), including dissertations
  Victorian Periodicals Review (J473)
  Victorian Studies Bulletin (J474)
  Wordsworth Circle (J445)
Theater
  Nineteenth-Century Theatre Research (J430)
  Research Opportunities in Renaissance Drama (J349)
  Restoration and 18th Century Theatre Research (J403)
  Shakespearean Research and Opportunities (J317)
  Theatre Journal (G118)
Translations
  Translation Review (W1628)

478

X

Decimals, Dewey, Logic,
and the Library of Congress

The arrangement of books on library shelves must of necessity be logical. Whether the classification system is that of the Library of Congress, Dewey, or some special identification code designed to serve a specific, local purpose, students may be certain that it is based on a logical arrangement of subjects. The sooner they become familiar with the system used in their special field, the more comfortable they will be with the card catalog, serials catalog, reference area, and general library collection. They will know that each symbol in the call number has a specific meaning, and they will locate area, shelf, and title much more easily. Even more important, they will be able to reap the profits of educated browsing.

Large libraries favor the Library of Congress system because it accommodates both comprehensive and minute classification of material. It provides unlimited expansion of subject divisions, for example, compared with the one hundred in Dewey. No two of its divisions are identical in their construction, however, and it contains few mnemonic devices — both of which are important advantages in the Dewey system.

Dewey Decimal Classification System

— A LOGICAL OUTLINE of all knowledge by subject, nationality, genre, and chronological era,

— WITH BUILT-IN MEMORY AIDS to help the student locate an individual book or a general subject area on the library shelf.

Ten minutes spent analyzing the logic of this system will illustrate how the student can learn to find many books without even having to consult the card catalog. Note, for instance, that throughout many subject and geographical divisions the numbers often indicate national groups:

1 American
2 English
3 German and Scandinavian
4 French
5 Italian
6 Spanish and Portuguese
7 Latin
8 Greek
9 Celtic, Slavic, Semitic, Asian, African, and American Indian

1. Major subject divisions of the Dewey System by 100s

000–099 General Works, including
    Library Science   020
    Encyclopedias   031 (1 for American)
                    032 (2 for English), etc.
    Journalism   070

100–199 Philosophy, including
    Psychology   150

200–299 Religion, including
    Bible   220 (an example where the 2 does
                    not refer to English)
    Mythology   291

300–399 Social Science, including
    Social Problems   304
    Economics   330
        Natural Resources   333
    Law   340
    Education   370
    Folklore   398

400–499 Language, including
    English   420 (2 for English)
    German   430 (3 for German)
    French   440 (4 for French)
    Italian   450 (5 for Italian)
    Spanish   460 (6 for Spanish), etc.

500–599 Science, including
    Biology   570
    Zoology   590
        Reptiles   598.11

600–699 Useful Arts, including
Medicine   610
Physical Education   613
Agriculture   630
Forests   634.9

700–799 Fine Arts, including
Architecture   720
Painting   750
Photography   770
Moving Pictures   778
Music   780

800–899 Literature (note similarities with 400s, Language)
General Histories   809
American   810 (1 for American)
English   820 (2 for English)
German   830 (3 for German)
French   840 (4 for French)
Italian   850 (5 for Italian)
Spanish   860 (6 for Spanish), etc.

900–999 History (note similarities with 400s and 800s)
Geography and Travel 910
in Europe   914
in England and Wales 914.2 (2 for England)
in Germany   914.3 (3 for Germany)
in France   914.4 (4 for France)
in Italy   914.5 (5 for Italy)
in Spain   914.6 (6 for Spain), etc.
in North America   917
in the United States   917.3
Ancient History   930
Europe—History   940
England—History   942 (2 for England)
Germany—History   943 (3 for Germany)
France—History   944 (4 for France)
Italy—History   945 (5 for Italy)
Spain—History   946 (6 for Spain)

2. Subdivisions by 10s

Each of the above major subject divisions of 100 units is subdivided into units of ten. In literature, as described above, this subdivision indicates nationality:

810 American Literature
820 English Literature
830 German Literature

840 French Literature
850 Italian Literature
860 Spanish Literature, etc.

3. Divisions by genre

Each nationality subdivision of ten units has smaller units to indicate genres:

810 American Literature
811 American Poetry
812 American Drama
813 American Fiction
814 American Essays
815 American Speeches
816 American Letters
817 American Satire
818 American Collections
819 American, General Information

The same system is applied to each country:

821 English Poetry
832 German Drama
843 French Fiction, etc.

4. Chronological subdivisions

In literature classification, the number *after* the decimal point indicates a chronological subdivision, with the lowest numbers indicating the earliest literature:

821	English poetry for *all* centuries
821.3	John Donne and other seventeenth-century poets
821.8	Tennyson and other nineteenth-century poets
821.91	Dylan Thomas and other twentieth-century poets

5. Book numbers

The second line of the book's identification is called the book number. This
is composed of the first letter of the author's last name and a specific number
that will identify all the author's works so they will be found in one place on
the library shelf after they have been assigned the proper subject and
chronological numbers.

The works of the following poets, all of whom wrote in the early seventeenth century, are, therefore, easily distinguishable:

821.3   John Donne's works
D685

821.3
H536   George Herbert's works

821.3
J81   Ben Jonson's works

6. Title subdivisions

Because each work must be distinguished from others by the same author, the first letter of the first important word in the title is placed immediately after the author number. For example, let us analyze the call number of Charles Dickens (1812–70), English novelist:

800 Literature
  820 English Literature
    823 English Literature, Fiction
    823.8 English Literature, Fiction—Nineteenth Century, Victorian Period

Dickens has been assigned the author number D548. All his novels, therefore, have the basic call number 823.8
               D548

His individual novels are identified by adding the first letter of the title to his author number:

823.8
D548b   *Bleak House*

832.8
D548d   *David Copperfield*

823.8
D548g   *Great Expectations*

823.8
D548o   *Oliver Twist*

823.8
D548ol   *Old Curiosity Shop*

823.8
D548ou   *Our Mutual Friend*

7. Critical works

A critical work is indicated in many libraries by a capital Y (or X or other designation) following the author number:

823.8
D548Yhar   A critical work *about* Dickens written by a critic whose name begins with "har" (such as Hardwick)

8. Edition numbers

The edition number is indicated at the end of the line containing the author number:

All poems by William Butler Yeats, an English, twentieth-century poet, have this call number	821.91 Y41
A critical work about Yeats's poems adds a capital "Y"	821.91 Y41Y
A critical work about Yeats by Ellmann adds an "e"	821.91 Y41Ye
A second edition of this same critical work adds a "2"	821.91 Y41Ye2

Library of Congress Classification System

Because the Library of Congress classification system is based on letters, numbers, and the infinite variety of ways in which numbers and letters can be combined, it is superior to Dewey's system in its ability to identify and locate millions of books in thousands of areas. Furthermore, libraries on the L.C. system are automatically provided with detailed schedules and continuous expansions. It is, therefore, being adopted by an increasing number of libraries whose expanding collections require a more flexible structure than Dewey can provide without the creation of unwieldy call numbers. Although it does not have the memory aids of the Dewey system, it is based on the same logical progression from the general to the specific, so researchers will be able, after a little experience, to predict the location of subjects and even specific books in their special areas.

1. Organization of the major divisions

Each major division of knowledge is designated by a capital letter. Class A is reserved for general works; classes B–P are the humanities and the social sciences; classes Q–V are science and technology; and class Z is bibliography.

These major classes of knowledge have subclasses which are identified by the addition of a second capital letter. For example, class P (Language and Literature) has subclasses that group books according to specific literary forms and nationalities:

PA	Classical languages and literatures
PN	Literary history and collections
PR	English literature
PS	American literature

It is important to remember, however, that all aspects of a subject are not necessarily grouped together in one class. Any part of a subject that has a specific focus is generally placed in that specific discipline class. For example, *general* biography that has no specific subject orientation is placed in class CT; general *local* biography is placed in history classes D, E, or F; and biography that is concerned with a specific subject is placed in that subject class.

The major *subject* classes such as class P (Language and Literature) are generally subdivided, where necessary, by country or place (a decided advantage for scholars who want to take a comparative approach). This system is reversed (that is, classified first by *country* and then subdivided by subject) when that approach is more useful (in class J, government and politics, for example).

The principle of arrangement within each subject class follows a general but not identical pattern. The divisions that appear first are the "external" forms such as

Periodicals
Societies
Collections
Encyclopedias
Dictionaries.

These are followed by "internal" subdivisions such as

Theory
History
Biography
Research

and then by

General works.

Each subdivision is further subdivided into subject areas that progress from the general to the specific, logically where possible, but alphabetically where that order is more useful.

The greatest merit of the L.C. system is its ability to expand and, therefore, to accommodate an unlimited number of new subjects and titles. The following outline illustrates some of the possibilities in the major divisions:

A   GENERAL REFERENCE BOOKS
    AC   Collections of individual writers arranged by language
    AE   Encyclopedias
    AG   Dictionaries
    AI   Indexes
    AP   Periodicals

B   PHILOSOPHY, PSYCHOLOGY, RELIGION
    BL   Religion
            300–325 Mythology
    BM   Judaism
    BQ   Buddhism
    BR   Christianity
            1690–1725 Biography
    BS   Bible

C AUXILIARY SCIENCES OF HISTORY
   CC   Archaeology
   CD   Archives
   CS   Genealogy
   CT   Biography (except for biography associated with a particular subject)
             93–206 Collections (General, Universal)
             210–3150 National biography
             3200–3910 Biography of women

D HISTORY: GENERAL AND OLD WORLD
             204–849 Modern history
             901–1075 Europe (General)
   DA   Great Britain
             20–690 England
             700–745 Wales
             750–890 Scotland
             900–995 Ireland
   DB   Austria
   DC   France
   DD   Germany
   DE   Mediterranean area
   DK   Russia
   DP   Spain

E–F HISTORY: AMERICA
   E   31–46 North America
             51–99 Indians
             186–199 Colonial history
             456–655 Civil War
             740–   Twentieth century
   F   1–975 U.S. local history

G GEOGRAPHY, ANTHROPOLOGY, RECREATION
             149–570 Voyages and travels
             1000.3–3122 Atlases
   GR   Folklore
             72–79 Folk literature (General)
             430–940 Folklore relating to specific subjects
   GT   Manners and customs (General)
             2400–5090 Private and public life (Marriage, Death, Holidays)

H SOCIAL SCIENCES
J POLITICAL SCIENCE
K LAW
L EDUCATION

M MUSIC
    ML   Literature of music
           159–3795 History and criticism, including biographies of individual composers

N FINE ARTS
           400–4040 Art museums, arranged by country, with subarrangement by city
           7475–7483 Art criticism
           7575–7624 Portraits
    NA   Architecture
    NB   Sculpture
    ND   Painting
           2890–3416 Illuminating of manuscripts and books

P LANGUAGE AND LITERATURE (treated as one discipline except for PQ, PR, PS, and PT, where the languages are given separate classifications)
           101–409 Language (General)
           201–297 Comparative grammar
           311 Prosody
    PA   Classical languages and literatures—Greek and Latin, including the modern versions
    PB–PH Modern European languages
           PC Romance languages
           PD Germanic languages
           PE English language
    PJ–PL Oriental and Eastern Asian languages and literatures
    PN   LITERARY HISTORY (General) and Collections
           80–99 Criticism
           101–245 Authorship
           441–1009 Folk literature, fables, romances
           1010–1551 Poetry
           1560–1590 Performing arts—show business, theater, radio, television
           1600–3299 Drama
           3311–3503 Prose and prose fiction
           4400 Letters
           4520 Essays
           6011–6790 Collections
                6080–6095 Quotations
                6099–6110 Poetry
                6110.5–6120 Drama
                6147–6231 Wit, Satire
    PQ   ROMANCE LITERATURES
    PR   ENGLISH LITERATURE
    PS   AMERICAN LITERATURE
    PT   GERMANIC LITERATURES

PZ FICTION AND JUVENILE LITERATURE (Note, however, that some libraries classify fiction as literature.)
1-4 Fiction in English, including foreign fiction translated into English

Q SCIENCE
R MEDICINE
S AGRICULTURE
T TECHNOLOGY
TR Photography
U MILITARY SCIENCE
V NAVAL SCIENCE

Z BIBLIOGRAPHY, LIBRARY SCIENCE (contains all bibliography concerned with a specific subject except that for music and law, which is placed in class M, Music, and class K, Law)
4-8 History of books
105-115 Paleography
116-265 Printing
266-276 Bookbinding
278-549 Bookselling and publishing
881-980 Library catalogs
987-997 Private libraries, Book collecting
1001-8999 Bibliography
1041-1107 Anonyms and pseudonyms
1201-4980 National bibliography
5051-7999 Subject bibliography
8001-8999 Personal bibliography

2. Basic points for literature students

The foregoing outline illustrates the main features of subject identification in the L.C. system:

a. One letter of the alphabet indicates the broad subject area (such as P for Literature).
b. Two letters indicate the subclasses (such as PR for English literature).
c. Numbers following these letters range from 1 to 9999 and designate still smaller areas within these classes.

The average class number in the L.C. system, therefore, generally has not more than two letters and four numbers: PR1509 includes all Anglo-Saxon authors and their works. These class numbers may be expanded indefinitely to accommodate new topics, however, by adding decimal points and/or alphabetical-topical numbers (often referred to as Cutter numbers after the inventor).

In class P (literature) the numbers 1 through 9999 indicate genre and author studies. Logic and convenience would naturally require that these subdivisions be in part arranged chronologically. And so it is that English literature, for example, allocates to individual authors from the beginning of English literary history to the twentieth century the numbers PR1509 (Anglo-Saxon authors and works) through PR6076 (PR6045.072 is Virginia Woolf). Letters and numbers that follow the decimal point indicate additional subdivisions alphabetically by subject or form, or by state or country:

PN6110   Special collections of poetry
PN6110.S6   Sonnets

A basic pattern prevails in these literature classes. Each subject is subdivided first into general books, then into chronological periods, and then into literary forms. Individual authors are arranged by chronological period with one exception: Since the English Renaissance section is already a chronological division, the authors are divided according to literary form—poetry, prose, and drama. Earliest authors, therefore, are presented first, with their dates and a designated L.C. number. Listed under each author, with additional specific numbers, are

the collected works and their translations,
separate works, their translations and criticism,
periodicals,
indexes,
biographies, and
general criticism (which is further subdivided into general and special topics such as drama, humor, love).

Several items are important for literature students who want to browse intelligently among the library shelves:

Translations generally follow the original work in alphabetical order by language, adding distinctive numbers for each language:
.L3   original
.L313   English translation
.L314   French translation
.L315   German translation, etc.
Criticism of separate works follows translations and is arranged alphabetically by author.
Biography receives special treatment, as we noted earlier. English literature (Colonial), for example, has a subdivision for *collected* biography, but biography and criticism of *individual* authors are scattered throughout PR1800–6076. That is, individual authors who write in English, no matter whether they are Colonials or whether they live in Europe, are classed according to their chronological period, not in the local arrangement.
Shakespeare, Dante, Cervantes, and a few other important authors have special, detailed arrangements because of the enormous amount of scholarship available. Shakespeare, for instance, is given all the numbers

from PR2750 to PR3112.

Even though authors have been assigned numbers in class P (Literature), the student will occasionally find some of their works elsewhere, when essays, for instance, focus on a specific subject and therefore must be placed in that specific subject class or when authors began their writing career with a collection of essays that required an AC classification and later turned to novels and poetry, which placed them in class P (Literature).

The "author" number in literature classification is composed of (1) a letter (generally the first letter of the last name, but sometimes the second letter, as in the literature classes of the twentieth century, where a great many authors have the same first letter: see Jack London, below) and (2) a number or numbers that indicate the alphabetical sequence of the rest of the name:

Saint	.S2
Scott	.S37
Smith	.S6
Sullivan	.S9

These numbers are not identical in each national or chronological literature section, but the numerical principle is the same. In most cases, authors are assigned a single number to distinguish them from all other authors:

PS	American literature
PS3523	twentieth century
PS3523.O46	Jack London

In other cases, however, an author is either so prolific or so favored with critical works of one kind or another that more than one number is given. Browning, for instance, has forty-eight different numbers, much to the dismay of many scholars who would prefer to find all related works on one shelf in the library.

The author number is followed by the "title designation," which is simply the first one or two letters of the title of the book (if it is in the PZ section), or the first letter of the title (in the original language) followed by numerals chosen to keep the titles alphabetically arranged on the shelf. Jack London's *Call of the Wild*, for instance, would in some libraries receive this classification number: PS3523.O46C3. In other libraries, it would be identified in this manner: PZ3.L846C35.

3. Fiction in the PZ division

Libraries that use PZ for fiction rather than the literature classification conform to the following guidelines:

a. PZ includes all English and American fiction and also all foreign fiction translated into English. It is a good system for browsing, but it annoys scholars who want to study all the works of one particular author (not just the fiction) because they must also check the literature classifications (PR and PS).

b. PZ1 includes collections by more than one author of novels and short stories in English. The original language takes precedence over the English translation. Italian short stories accompanied by an English translation, for instance, are found in PQ (Romance literatures).

c. PZ3 includes fiction in English by individual authors, whether English is the original language or a translation.

d. PZ4 includes authors who began to publish in English in 1951 or later. Authors who were originally classified in PZ3 will continue to be classified there even though they are still publishing. Authors who wrote nonfiction before 1951 but did not begin writing fiction until 1951 or later, and authors of fiction who were first translated into English in 1951 or later are placed in PZ4.

e. Authors will be found in PZ3 or PZ4, not both.

f. Authors who write in more than one language will have each title classed in its original language.

g. All fiction in English or translations into English are not necessarily placed in PZ3 or PZ4. Editions accompanied by criticism, rare editions, or other distinctive works are placed in the regular literature classes from PA to PT. For example, the German original of Erich Maria Remarque's *Arc de Triomphe* has the call number PT2635.E68A67, but the call number for the English translation is PZ3.R2818Ar.

h. Since PZ is wholly fiction and juvenile literature (without translations, criticisms, and biography), its classification system is simple. The PZ number (PZ1, PZ2, PZ3, or PZ4) is followed by a decimal point and then the author number and the title designation (see the examples in the previous paragraph).

The main thing to remember is that the Library of Congress classification system is based on a logical pattern that progresses from the most general to the most specific. Students can, therefore, soon learn to locate an American author's biography, an English author's letters, or a collection of satire. Logic and convenience are guidelines in the Library of Congress system just as they are in the Dewey, and familiarity with both systems is the mark of an experienced scholar.

Subject Headings

These sample subject headings illustrate the subdivisions for period, form, and geographical location used in most card catalogs, indexes, abstracting services, and bibliographies. Note that in the card catalog the subject headings at the top of the card are capitalized or printed in red—and sometimes both.

AFRO-AMERICAN FOLK-LORE—GEORGIA
AMERICAN FICTION—18TH CENTURY
AMERICAN LITERATURE—BIBLIOGRAPHY
AMERICAN LITERATURE—CATHOLIC AUTHORS
BLACKS—BIOGRAPHY
ENGLISH BALLADS AND SONGS—HISTORY AND CRITICISM
ENGLISH LANGUAGE—VERSIFICATION
IRISH NEWSPAPERS
IRISH-AMERICAN NEWSPAPERS
MINORITIES—U.S.
MYTHOLOGY, WELSH
PERIODICALS—ABBREVIATIONS OF TITLES
PHILOSOPHY, ORIENTAL
PHONETIC ALPHABET
RUSSIAN LITERATURE IN FOREIGN COUNTRIES
SOUTHERN STATES—HISTORY—CIVIL WAR
SWEDEN—HISTORY—1905-
THEOLOGY—DICTIONARIES
WAR AND LITERATURE
WIT AND HUMOR (MEDIEVAL)

The Alphabet: New York Precedes Newark

Most library card catalogs and reference books use word-by-word alphabetiza-
tion (note the title of this section). Certain notable exceptions like the *Encyclopaedia Britannica* (and, for practice, Abbreviations and the Glossary of
Bibliographical Terms in this guide) prefer the letter-by-letter arrangement,
however, so students should become familiar with both methods. Note that in
the following example of word-by-word alphabetizing all numbers and abbreviations are filed as if they were spelled out, that "Mc" is filed as if it were "Mac,"
that the initial article (the, a, an) is ignored, that books by an author are filed
before books about an author, that historical subjects are arranged chronologically, that the real name is preferred over the pseudonym, that an author's dates
are provided:

Bookbinding
Books—Bibliography
Books—Dictionaries
Books and Book-Collectors
Clemens, Samuel Langhorne (1838–1910)
EUROPE—HISTORY—18th CENTURY
EUROPE—HISTORY—1945-
Kennedy, John Fitzgerald (as author)
KENNEDY, JOHN FITZGERALD (as subject)
McCarthy, Joseph

MacKenzie, Norman
Mr. Smith Goes to Washington
Moby-Dick
New Amsterdam
New York
Newark
Newton, Isaac
The Oxford English Dictionary
St. Paul, Minnesota
San Francisco
Twain, Mark. See Clemens, Samuel Langhorne
200 Contemporary Authors

Since the American Library Association's new filing rules were adopted in January 1981, all libraries have had to decide whether to retain the traditional method just described or to adopt the ALA rules for filing "as-is" rather than "as-if"— that is, *not* to file abbreviations as if they were spelled out, *not* to spell out numbers but to place them in numerical order before the letter *A* (or after the letter Z), *not* to use real names if the pseudonym is more familiar. In some libraries, including the Library of Congress, the old system will be retained for the old catalog, and the new system will apply only to new acquisitions and a new catalog. In other libraries, old and new filing rules will be combined in one catalog with numerous cross-references leading to the established main entry. Furthermore, students will find that some libraries divide the card catalog into as many as three alphabetical sections because they prefer to have separate files for authors, titles, and subjects. And that in others the card catalogs have been totally or partially replaced by microprint (film or fiche) which is usually also divided by author, title, and subject. All of this has been the result of our need to automate and simplify so that enormous amounts of material can be handled quickly and without error. Within a few years students will think of these catalogs and alphabetizing problems as items of historical interest. Computerized literature searching, COM, OCLC, and Lockheed Dialog information retrieval will be the norm (see Glossary). Then we will look back on the card catalog as we do on the covered wagon—as old-fashioned, inefficient, but absolutely indispensable in its day.

The Catalog Card

1. Dewey Decimal System

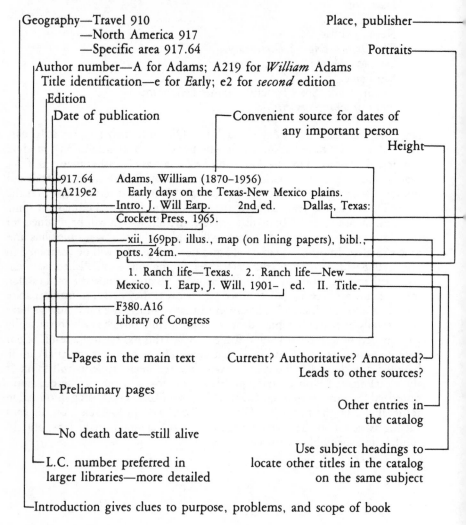

COMPOSITE CARD WITH FICTIONAL INFORMATION TO ILLUSTRATE ALL POSSIBILITIES.

2. Library of Congress card

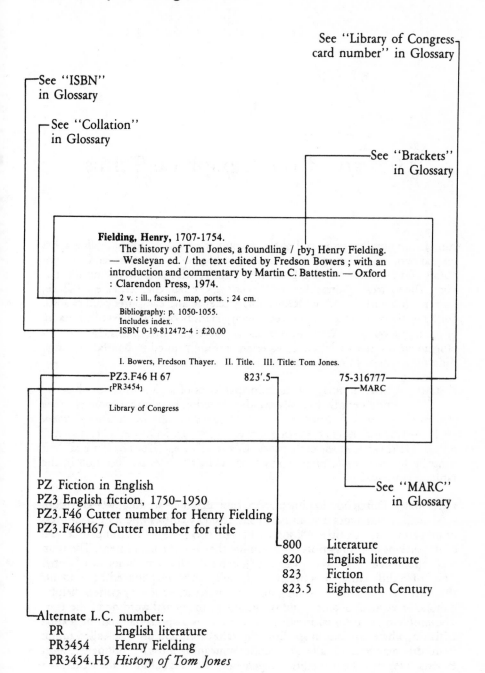

See "Library of Congress card number" in Glossary

See "ISBN" in Glossary

See "Collation" in Glossary

See "Brackets" in Glossary

Fielding, Henry, 1707-1754.
 The history of Tom Jones, a foundling / ₍by₎ Henry Fielding.
— Wesleyan ed. / the text edited by Fredson Bowers ; with an
introduction and commentary by Martin C. Battestin. — Oxford
: Clarendon Press, 1974.
 2 v. : ill., facsim., map, ports. ; 24 cm.
 Bibliography: p. 1050-1055.
 Includes index.
 ISBN 0-19-812472-4 : £20.00

 I. Bowers, Fredson Thayer. II. Title. III. Title: Tom Jones.

PZ3.F46 H 67   823'.5   75-316777
₍PR3454₎   MARC

Library of Congress

PZ Fiction in English
PZ3 English fiction, 1750–1950
PZ3.F46 Cutter number for Henry Fielding
PZ3.F46H67 Cutter number for title

See "MARC" in Glossary

800   Literature
820   English literature
823   Fiction
823.5 Eighteenth Century

Alternate L.C. number:
PR   English literature
PR3454   Henry Fielding
PR3454.H5 *History of Tom Jones*

495

Y

Glossary of Bibliographical Terms

Almost two hundred terms and names encountered in the study of bibliography, textual criticism, old manuscripts, books, early printing practices, and contemporary computer research are listed here with concise definitions and illustrations. The sources are Greg, Bowers, McKerrow, Gaskell, Glaister, Peters, Esdaile, Carter, Blumenthal, and numerous library science and computer publications. For definitions of literary terms, see Literary Handbooks (W1406–14). Because of the numerous abbreviations, phrases, and foreign terms in this Glossary, arrangement is letter by letter. Cross-references are printed in **boldface** the first time they appear in each entry.

abstract A brief summary of the principal ideas of a given text; an objective abridgment that ideally avoids evaluation or editorial comment. See *Abstracts of English Studies* (E38), *Dissertation Abstracts International* (W1214–15), and other abstracting services (E38–43). Some periodicals such as *PMLA* (H152) and, in the early issues, *Chaucer Review* (J268) have asked their contributing authors to prepare abstracts of their articles for inclusion in the table of contents.

accidentals Differences in punctuation, capitalization, spelling, word division, and italics that must be considered by editors when, in the process of preparing the **definitive edition** of a given work, they must compare several of its **editions** or **manuscripts** to determine the author's final intent. The term was popularized by W. W. Greg in 1949 in his article "The Rationale of Copy-Text." He differentiated between accidentals, which may indeed be accidents that have crept into the text during many exposures to careless typesetters, helpful editors, or virtuous spouses, and **substantives**, the actual wording of the text. The problem of authorial intent in accidentals is a special concern of **textual criticism**, where fashions in spelling, capitalization, and other so-called minor items that may certainly affect the author's meaning must be considered. Most experts agree that the first edition is generally the best authority for accidentals (if it is set from an authoritative manuscript) because it has not had a chance to be adulterated by either intentional changes or accidents and, therefore, is probably closest to the author's intent. Editors of the definitive edition are obligated, however, to examine every variant of these accidentals and determine whether it might have been the author's. They should explain their decisions and policy on these textual problems in both the introduction and the notes.

addendum, addenda   A supplement to a book; something added.

A.L.S.   Autograph letter, signed; a letter wholly in the handwriting of the author.

analytical bibliography   A detailed description of the **watermarks**, paper, **cancels**, **signatures**, binding, ink, initials, **factota**, **press figures**, ornaments, **catchwords**, size and spacing of type. Such a description requires a careful physical examination by an expert to determine how the book was manufactured. This type of analysis is used in problems of dating and authorship and in studies of early printing-house practices. Cf. **descriptive bibliography**.

annotated bibliography   A list of works that includes a brief summary and/or description of each title. These annotations are sometimes evaluative, their chief aim being to inform readers of the contents so they can decide whether the work might be helpful in research. See **abstract**.

apocrypha   Writings of questionable authorship or authenticity that are not generally accepted in the **canon** of an author. The Shakespeare apocrypha and the Chaucer apocrypha, for instance, contain works that have been doubtfully, or mistakenly, attributed to them over the centuries. Of the fifty Elizabethan plays **ascribed** to Shakespeare since the seventeenth century, only three have any serious claim to his name: *Two Noble Kinsmen*, *Sir Thomas More*, and *Edward III*.

ascription   An educated guess that a certain work was written by a certain author, usually made when there is insufficient factual proof of authorship but substantial **internal evidence** that the author might have written the work. See the comment on Shakespeare in the previous entry.

association copy   A copy of a book that was once owned either by its author or by some famous person. These copies are usually quite expensive, partly because they are coveted by enthusiastic critics who want to study the marginal notes and doodling.

attribution   See **ascription**.

author bibliography   A list of works by and/or about an individual author. Because recent interest in research has promoted the publication of literally hundreds of author bibliographies, the researcher's first step should be to determine whether there is a new or forthcoming bibliography devoted to the author. Some libraries using the Dewey Decimal system place author bibliographies in alphabetical order in the 012 section so they will be easy to find. The Library of Congress system usually places author bibliographies in the Z8000 category, unless they are related to a specific subject area. The best and most scholarly author bibliographies include pseudonyms, a chronology of life and works, annotations, and information on reviews, films, recordings, and location of manuscripts. See W1053-55.

bastard title   A shortened title that is sometimes placed on the **half-title page**.

bibliographical ghost   (1) A publication that is believed to have existed or to have been planned for publication (that is, it has been cited in publishers' catalogs, auction records, library catalogs, or casual literature) but no copy has ever been found to substantiate the records; or (2) a title or name that never existed and that appears in some publications as a deterrent to wholesale copying by other bibliographers. There is one in this book.

bibliography   (1) A list of books and/or articles. This may be a compilation according to **author** (such as the Faulkner bibliography), subject (see *Metaphor*, W1412), **nation** (*Cumulative Book Index*, D35), or chronological period (Sadleir's *XIX Century Fiction*, J480). In form it may be **enumerative**, **analytical**, or **descriptive**. (2) In another sense, "bibliography" may refer to the art of describing a book's physical characteristics, its authorship, and the history of various editions.

black letter type   Dark, heavy, ornate type used in early printed books because it was similar to the handwriting popular in Germany when the printing press was invented there about 1450. This Gothic or Old English form was gradually replaced in the sixteenth century by the style that is still in use today, the Italian or roman.

blurb   A publisher's description of a book—generally unduly flattering.

Bodley, Sir Thomas (1545-1613)   A sixteenth-century book collector whose library formed the core of the Bodleian Library at Oxford University, where Edward VI had dismantled earlier holdings of the 1300s.

book hand   The remarkably legible, uniform handwriting used by professional medieval and Renaissance **scribes** on **manuscripts**.

bowdlerize   To omit words, scenes, or passages that seem offensive. The term comes from an English family named Bowdler who, for prudish reasons, expurgated and published dozens of books, some of which bore little resemblance to their original form. The most famous of the Bowdlers was Thomas (1754-1825), a physician who in 1818 published an expurgated version of Shakespeare. Recommended reading: a witty, readable account by Perrin, *Dr. Bowdler's Legacy* (W1622).

Bowers, Fredson   The author of *Principles of Bibliographical Description*, an authoritative study with valuable modifications of **McKerrow**'s earlier work and perhaps better for nineteenth- and twentieth-century books. See Bowers (W1066) for a full annotation and Gaskell (W1064) for a more recent examination of bibliographical problems and scholarship.

brackets   Brackets around any word or sign indicate that the item was not a part of the original text but was supplied by someone editing the text. In the description of a **title page**, for instance, brackets around an item mean that item was not printed on the original title page and had to be supplied by the cataloger or bibliographer. On the sample L.C. card in this guide's explanation of the Library of Congress system, the word [by] has been inserted to avoid confusion with the title. Similarly, if the publication date of the book is omitted from its usual place at the bottom of the title page, the cataloger may find it mentioned in another part of the book and will enclose it in brackets: [1982].

broadside   A large undivided sheet of paper printed on one side only, such as the advertisements on theater billboards.

©, c   Abbreviation for **copyright**, usually found on the **verso** of the **title page** followed by the date: ©1974 or c1974. See Copyright (W1196–98).

ca., c., circa (Latin for 'about')   Used before approximate dates or figures.

calendar   The Julian (Old Style) calendar was introduced by Julius Caesar in 46 B.C. It was replaced by the Gregorian (New Style) calendar in Europe in 1582 and in England and America in 1752, when September 2 was followed directly by September 14 to correct a discrepancy in time.

calligraphy   The art of fine handwriting.

call number   The unique identifying numbers and letters assigned to a library book to distinguish it from all others and to assist in locating it on the shelf. See also **pressmark**.

cancel   Any substitution for the original part of a book, the original being called a "cancelland." If this substitution occurs before publication, there will be two or more **states** of the **edition**; if it occurs after publication, there will be two or more **issues** of the edition.

canon   The total accepted list of books by a given author. See **apocrypha**.

catchword   A word used by printers of early books to ensure accuracy in typesetting and assembling. At the lower inner margin of the last line of type on a printed page, the first word of the next page (the catchword) is printed to guide the arrangement of pages in the **forme** for the press and then, by extension, the assembling of the **gatherings** by the binder.

Caxton, William (c.1422–91)   Accomplished translator and English printer who, when he was living in Bruges in 1474–75, printed the first book in English, *Recuyell of the Historyes of Troye*. In 1476 he moved to London, where he printed nearly eighty more books including the works of Malory, Chaucer, Boethius, and Gower. His assistant and successor, Wynken de Worde, produced work of lower quality.

CEAA   See Center for Editions of American Authors (W1177).

cf.   Confer (Latin for "compare"). Suggests dissimilarity, as "Fair papers, cf. foul papers." This is not to be confused with "See also," which refers readers to other entries concerned with their subject.

chain-lines   The widely spaced markings left on paper by the wires on which the pulp is laid. Chain-lines may be up to one inch apart, as opposed to **wire-lines**, which are close together. They are always parallel with the shorter dimension before the original sheet is folded, so they will be found running vertically in the **leaf** of a **folio** and horizontally in the leaf of a **quarto**.

chapbook   Small, cheap ("chap") pamphlets containing popular tales, jests, ballads, and poems that were sold originally by chapmen, or hawkers, not booksellers. Their low price and familiar content was responsible for their popularity from the Renaissance to the early nineteenth century. Our closest modern counterpart is the pulp magazine. The word is now often used to refer to small books containing poems, ballads, tales, or religious tracts.

checklist   A bibliography with only brief information for each title, as opposed to the detailed information found in a **descriptive** or **annotated bibliography**. See also **short title**.

codex, codices   A term reserved usually for early **manuscript** books dating from the first century A.D. in which the text was written on leaves hinged in book form rather than on long **rolls** of **papyrus**. See **leaf**.

collate   To compare two or more **editions**, **impressions**, **states**, or any versions of a work, word by word and line by line, in order to record the differences. See **Hinman collator**. Also, to assemble in proper numerical or logical order; to analyze and describe the physical makeup of a book. In verifying the completeness of a rare book, "collate" means to examine the gathered **signatures** to see that all are included and in proper order.

collation   As used by librarians this term refers to the section of the catalog card that describes the book—the size, number of volumes, number of pages, illustrations, maps, and other added material.

colophon   A note found at the end of early printed books (sometimes with an identifying picture or mark—see **device**) that gives the name of the book, the author, printer, place of printing, and date. In the early sixteenth century this information was transferred to a new invention, the **title page**. The colophon is now used only rarely as a gesture of respect to the printer. Its origin probably lies in the early **scribe**'s custom of signing off his handwritten labors with a Latin cheerio: "The work is finished, and my weary hand has found rest," "The scribe deserves the very best wine," or "Now I've written it all; for Christ's sake give me a drink." See **imprint**.

COM   Computer-output-microform may become the future sole form of publication because of the increasing expense and proliferation of printed matter. COM material is generated directly from the computer without the intervening steps of hardcopy printout and filming that used to be necessary. Increasingly, publishers are storing their texts on the computer and generating COM as their product. Some libraries now have COM catalogs instead of card catalogs as the indexes to their collections.

comp.   Compiler; compiled by.

computerized literature search   Lockheed ("Dialog"), System Development Corporation ("Orbit"), Bibliographic Retrieval Services ("BRS"), and several other vendors now offer access online to computerized bibliographic data bases prepared by commercial or nonprofit organizations. The organizations often use these data bases to produce a printed product such as a cumulating index to periodical literature in a specific field. BRS, for example, now offers online access to three of the most frequently consulted Bowker reference books: *Books in Print* (W1170), *Ulrich's International Periodicals Directory* (W1477), and *American Men and Women of Science*. The *MLAIB* (D31) has since 1978 had online access through the Lockheed Dialog system, which is the largest online information retrieval service in the world, with data bases for *Philosopher's Index* (W1489), *America* (E43), *Historical Abstracts* (E43), *RILM Abstracts*, and many other basic reference sources. *MLAIB* will soon also have access to the BRS system. Full abstracts accepted since July 1980 by *Dissertation Abstracts International* (W1214) became available on Dialog and BRS in the spring of 1984. Many large libraries offer computerized literature search services to students and faculty. The average connect time required for an average search is about ten minutes, and while connect time charges differ with each data base, they usually fall between $15 and $35. See also **online information retrieval**, **OCLC**, **RLG**, and **Lockheed Dialog information retrieval**.

concealed printing   Undifferentiated **editions** or different **impressions** within a given edition that are not so designated on the **title page** and that may have significant **emendations** or corruptions within them that can be unearthed only by analysis of progressive type deterioration, measurement of **gutter margins**, or discovery of resetting by machine **collation**.

concordance   An alphabetical index of all words appearing in a text. Its purpose is to show how each word is used in the context of its own phrase or sentence and thus to permit studies of the author's imagery and themes. See W1194.

conflation   The merging of variant texts into one version in an effort to eliminate all errors and to return the text to the author's final intention. See **critical edition; variorum edition**.

copyright   Public Law 94–553 (U.S. Code, Title 17), a general revision of the Copyright Law of 1909, was passed by the Congress in 1976 and became effective on 1 January 1978. The new law establishes uniform protection for all copyrightable works, whether published or unpublished. Works created after 1 January 1978 are now protected from their moment of creation until fifty years after the author's death, or seventy-five if the work is anonymous. Works that were copyrighted before 1 January 1978 are still protected through the original term of twenty-eight years and then will have the right to renew for an additional forty-seven years. Works that were created but not copyrighted before 1 January 1978 are guaranteed from twenty-five to one hundred years, depending on the conditions of authorship. The main difference between the old and the new law is that (1) a work is now copyrighted as soon as pen is lifted from paper, and (2) copies are now sent to the Library of Congress only when the author wishes to *register* the work and thus have added clout if it is necessary to sue those who abuse the copyright privileges. This law intends to protect both the author and the public. The public should of course have the right to use and read material, but, because one incentive for authorship is royalties, no one should have the right to make unlimited copies of copyrighted works. For a definition of "fair use" and other problems, see Copyright in this guide (W1196–98). The copyright date of a book is usually found on the **verso** of the **title page** and may not be the same as the date found on the **recto**, which is the publication date. If the copyright date is not cited on the verso, it may be mentioned or alluded to in the introduction or text.

copy text   The version of a work that editors use as the basic copy against which all other **editions, impressions, states,** and **issues** are compared in an effort to arrive at the author's final intent. This version is usually considered closest to the author's final intent and may be found in the **manuscript** (if it exists), the first edition (if it was set from the manuscript), or the last edition published during the author's lifetime (if the author is known to have made extensive changes). See **substantives; accidentals; textual criticism; analytical bibliography; variant**.

corrigenda   A list of errors with their corrections. See **errata**.

Cotton collection   The collection of books, **manuscripts,** coins, and medals owned by Sir Robert Bruce Cotton (1571–1631) that is now in the British Library and that contains many unique items from destroyed monasteries. The only **extant** manuscript of *Beowulf*, for example, is still referred to as "Cotton Vitellius A xv" because in Cotton's library it was the fifteenth book on the first shelf of a bookcase adorned with the bust of the Roman emperor Vitellius.

courtesy books   Manuals that prescribed rules for the education and behavior of Renaissance gentlemen—Castiglione's *Il Cortegiano* (1528), for example.

critical edition   An edition for which the editor examines all authoritative **editions** and **manuscripts** of the work, attempts to eliminate all errors, and makes editorial corrections and **emendations** for the express purpose of producing a text as close as possible to the author's final intent. Good critical editions will explain the choice of **copy text**, the editorial decisions on **accidentals** and **substantives**, and the problems encountered in **collating** the several versions. Within the past decade, a few enterprising publishers have responded to the current interest in and preference for accurate texts by preparing popular, classroom-oriented versions of critical editions of the classics. About one hundred have been published by Norton (New York) including Henry James's *The American*. Its text is based on an examination of the five printed versions that appeared during James's lifetime and is preceded by his Preface to the New York edition (1907). The editors trace the textual history of the novel. They provide a list of substantive **variants** and emendations, a **facsimile** manuscript page showing James's method of revision, and a list of the installments of the novel as they appeared in the *Atlantic*. Twenty-one American and English reviews reflect contemporary critical reception. And extracts from correspondence and articles by James and others serve as background and source material. Viking (New York) is embarking on a similar series of popular critical editions. For more scholarly efforts, see the Regents Renaissance and Restoration Drama Series (J342 and J402), the Center for Scholarly Editions (W1179), and the Center for Editions of American Authors (W1177). Twayne (Boston) has already published seventeen volumes of Irving's works and four of Howells' that have received the approval of the Center for Editions of American Authors.

CSE   See Center for Scholarly Editions (W1179).

cumulative index   An index that combines all previous indexes into one single alphabet to facilitate research. See, for example, the cumulative index for 1940–70 of *Current Biography* (W1115).

definitive edition   An **edition** that, as a result of careful scholarly research, is considered as close to the author's final intent as possible. This research may involve **analytical bibliography**, **descriptive bibliography**, and **textual criticism**. See, for example, the University of California Press's definitive edition of Mark Twain's published works.

depository library   About 1300 libraries in the United States are designated as U.S. Government depositories. There can be two depository libraries per Congressional district, plus additional depositories in law school, court, and government agency libraries. Materials included in the depository program are those published by the U.S. Government Printing Office, plus some materials printed at agency printing plants around the country. In most states, there is a "regional" depository that receives the entire output of the program and serves as a collection of last resort for the other libraries in the state; the "partial" depositories select which types of materials to add to their collections. By law, deposited materials must be made available to the general public during the normal operating hours of the library in which they are housed.

descriptive bibliography   Close, detailed analysis of a book's format, **pagination**, binding, and **title page** to distinguish it from other **editions**, **impressions**, and **issues**. See Pittsburgh Series in Bibliography (W1616). Cf. **analytical bibliography**.

device   The printer's or publisher's mark or sign, such as the Viking ship or the Harper torch, which helps to identify the work. The device may appear either on the **title page** or on the last page of the book. In old books its condition or shape may assist in dating the work. See **colophon**.

duodecimo (twelvemo; 12mo)   A small book about 7¾ inches tall in which the original large sheet of paper has been folded to make twelve leaves. See **leaf**; **folio**; **quarto**; **gathering**.

edition   The entire number of copies of a book set from a single typesetting regardless of whether they are run off at one time or different times. See **impression**, **printing**, **issue**, **state** for special conditions of an edition. When type is reset or when numerous changes are made in the text or content of the book, the edition is given a new number to distinguish it from all previous editions.

EETS   Early English Text Society (see W1046).

emendation   An editorial guess; a correction (either documented or **silent**) of some part of the text that the editor believes is not what the author actually meant to write. These errors could have crept in as a result of faulty handwriting, faulty copying, or well-intended tampering. With emendations, editors attempt to return the text to what they believe was the author's final intent. In the eighteenth century, Theobald made a generally approved emendation when he suggested that Madame Quickly's reference to the dying Falstaff in the First Folio, "and a Table of greene fields," was probably a corruption of the original words "and 'a babbled of green fields." See **variant**.

endpapers   The first and last leaves of a book on which there is usually no printed text and which are added by the binder, the outer **leaf** being pasted to the cover and the inner leaf hanging free. They are sometimes patterned or covered with maps.

enl. Enlarged, as in a new **edition**; revised and enlarged (rev., enl.).

enumerative bibliography A list of works that merely cites the basic bibliographical information without annotations or descriptions of the works themselves. Cf. **annotated bibliography**.

ERIC Educational Resources Information Center, an organization which accumulates uncirculated papers, reports, essays, bibliographies, and other research material for the purpose of reproducing and distributing copies through the ERIC Document Reproduction Service. ERIC thus provides a national market for information that might otherwise have no channel to the public. A regularly published index, *Resources in Education* (W1223), lists materials added to the ERIC system, provides an order number, and gives instructions for ordering individual items. Citations to ERIC materials should include the order number (often called the ED number) as, for example, *Shakespeare: A Student's Guide to Basic Reference Sources*, 1977 (ED 151 863). See the Index in this guide for information on the McGill Reference Guides that are available through ERIC. Copies and prices of all ERIC material can be obtained from P.O. Box 190, Arlington, Va. 22210. Many libraries subscribe to the entire ERIC collection on microfiche. ERIC also generates, via a subcontract to a commercial printer, the *Current Index to Journals in Education* (W1224).

errata Mistakes or misprints discovered after the book has been printed. Corrections are noted either on a spare page or on a piece of paper **tipped in** during or after binding. Also called **corrigenda**.

explicit A Latin verb meaning "here ends"; a formal phrase originally used to introduce the closing words or explanation of a **manuscript** or book. Cf. **incipit**.

extant manuscript A **manuscript** that is still in existence, not having been lost or destroyed.

external evidence Evidence depending on factual history, biography, or **analytical bibliography** that is used to help determine authorship, dating, or composition of a work. Cf. **internal evidence**.

facsimile Photographic reproduction of the original **manuscript** or book that enables scholars to note the peculiarities of the author's spelling, capitalization, and style at the time the original was made. A really fine facsimile **edition** also attempts to simulate the exact physical appearance of the original work.

factotum An ornamental block with an opening in the center for a capital letter, which was used in early printed books for decorative purposes, probably in imitation of the beautifully illustrated medieval **manuscripts**. These ornate capital letters are usually found on the opening page or at the beginning of chapters and paragraphs.

fair papers   The corrected copy of a play **manuscript** (usually Elizabethan) as submitted to an acting company with appropriate notes for scenery, action, and production. Cf. **foul papers**.

fascicle   A part of a work published in installments, such as the fascicles of the *Middle English Dictionary* (J264). Cf. **supplement**.

festschrift   A collection of essays written by several authors in honor of a distinguished scholar. The word comes from the German meaning "celebration writing."

fl.   Abbreviation for flourished, used to indicate the productive years of an individual when birth and death dates are unknown, such as Aelius Donatus, a Roman grammarian who wrote literary commentaries on Terence and Vergil, fl. A.D. 333.

foliation   The numbering of a book by leaves rather than pages. Foliation is rare before 1475, when there was no numbering system, and after 1600, when **pagination** became the custom. See **leaf**.

folio (f., ff., fol., fols., 1º, F)   A large book approximately fifteen inches tall in which the original sheet of paper is folded only once to make two leaves (four pages). Additional foldings produce a **quarto, octavo, duodecimo, sixteenmo**, twenty-fourmo, thirty-twomo, forty-eightmo. See **leaf**.

font   Type for printing, which is kept according to style and size in cases, with capitals in the "upper case," and small letters in the "lower case."

fore-edge   The outside edge of a page, opposite the **hinge** or spine.

fore-edge painting   The art of delicate painting on the **fore-edge** of the pages of a closed book; popular in the nineteenth century.

format   The physical make up of a book: **foliation** or **pagination**, style of type, binding, margins, arrangement on the page, size (**folio, quarto, octavo**, etc.).

forme   Assembled type that is arranged in proper page form, enclosed in a chase or frame, and ready for printing. The impression taken from this forme is called a **signature**.

foul papers   The dramatist's original, uncorrected **manuscript** (usually Elizabethan) that was copied and adapted for use by the acting company. Cf. **fair papers**.

foxing   Discolorations or stains on paper, caused by dampness and lack of ventilation.

galley   A long tray used for holding composed type before the pages are numbered and cut. Galley proofs are taken from this tray and examined for errors before the **edition** is run off.

gathering   That section of a book derived from folding and sewing the original large sheet of paper once for a **folio**, twice for a **quarto**, etc. Gatherings may be composed of two or more sheets of paper whereby two sheets folded together would produce a folio in fours and a quarto in eights, three sheets folded together would produce a folio in sixes, etc.

gothic   Heavy black letter type used by early printers like **Caxton**. Its shape quite naturally imitated the standard **book hand** in popular use in the fifteenth and sixteenth century on the Continent.

grangerized   Extra-illustrated books; books to which editors or owners have added extraneous portraits, letters, documents, and drawings, so that sometimes it is necessary to rebind the volume. The term is derived from James Granger, who in 1769 published a *Biographical History of England* with blank leaves so that the purchaser could insert personal mementos.

Gutenberg, Johann (c. 1400–c. 1468)   German inventor of movable type; printer of the first book produced by a printing press, the Gutenberg Bible, about 1450. His invention spread rapidly all over Europe and went with **Caxton** to England in 1476. See **incunabula**.

gutter margin   The inner margin of a book, measurement of which will sometimes reveal **concealed printings** or rebinding.

half-title page   The **leaf** in front of the **title page** which was originally included solely to protect the title page. Since the late seventeenth century, the title, **short title**, or **bastard** title has been placed on the **recto** of this page.

hapax legomenon   A word or form that is found only once in a given language or author, as may occur in the book of Job or works by early prophets and Christians.

head   Top margin of the page of a book.

headpiece   A decoration at the beginning of a chapter or section of a book.

hinge   The spine of a book.

Hinman collator   An optical device adapted by Charleton Hinman from World War II aerial photography. It permits accurate, fast comparison of copies of a work that differ only slightly in the setting of their type. As the viewer looks through a magnifying glass at lighted, alternating images of the two copies, the flickering light and shadow call attention to differences in punctuation or spelling. The machine has been especially valuable in distinguishing between **states** and **issues** and has made notable contributions to the art of producing **definitive editions.**

holograph   A **manuscript** that is entirely in the handwriting of the author.

horn book   The first teaching aid designed especially for children; a small piece of thin wood covered with a piece of paper on which were printed the alphabet, numbers, and prayers. Since paper was expensive, it in turn was covered with a thin piece of horn and framed with metal. The horn book was often provided with a handle so the child could hold it comfortably.

ibid.   An abbreviation of the Latin word *ibidem* ("in the same place") used in notes to indicate repetition of the preceding item. The modern tendency is to avoid Latin terms and to say only "P. 32" instead of "Ibid., p. 32."

ill. or illus.   Illustrated.

illuminated manuscript   A medieval **manuscript** with margins, initial letters, and sometimes the text itself decorated with scrolls, leaves, or other designs in red, blue, green, gold, and/or silver.

impression   See its synonym, **printing.**

imprimatur   A Latin verb meaning "Let it be printed," which indicates that official approval has been granted to the author for the publication of a work; most commonly used in reference to sixteenth- and seventeenth-century publications and to titles approved by the Roman Catholic church.

imprint   The publisher's name, place, and date of publication found at the bottom of the **title page.** The same term is also used to describe the same information when it appears in a bibliographical description of the book. If the date is found anywhere other than on the title page, it is enclosed in **brackets,** as [1859], and if it is not found at all, the **copyright** date is used and indicated in this manner [c1859].

incipit (Latin for "it begins")   A word that is occasionally found at the beginning of **manuscripts** written during the medieval period, when titles were not used and the author or **scribe** wanted to supply a brief introductory explanation of the work. By extension, the term is now used to designate the first line of all texts that have no titles, whether old or modern. Cf. **explicit.**

incunabula, incunabulum   A Latin word meaning "things in the cradle"; books that were printed from movable type before 1500 or 1501. Also called incunable(s). Cf. **manuscript.**

in preparation   A phrase referring to a work that is currently being written. Cf. **in progress.**

in progress   A phrase referring to a work that is currently in the hands of the printer, binder, or editor, being actively prepared for publication. Cf. **in preparation**.

internal evidence   Evidence found within the work itself that helps to assign a date and author, for example, allusions to historical events or notable persons, and distinctive use of imagery or phrasing. Cf. **external evidence**.

interpolation   Insertion of nonauthorial material into a text, sometimes innocently by well-meaning editors who are not concerned with the requirements of a **definitive edition**.

ISBD   International Standard Bibliographic Description. These are international guidelines for catalog cards that make the placement and punctuation of book descriptions standard throughout the world so that even if readers do not understand the language they can locate the facts. The arrangement of bibliographic information in a standard pattern permits its transference in machine-readable form regardless of the language of origin.

ISBN   International Standard Book Number. A distinguishing book number that facilitates purchase from the publisher or book supplier.

ISSN   International Standard Serial Number. A distinguishing number that identifies a **serial** by title and is now usually printed on each issue. The number is helpful in purchasing and identifying as well as in distinguishing between two serials of the same title. In computer search, the ISSN number is often preferred over the title because an incorrect preposition or article, or even a one-word title, will inevitably produce negative results.

issue   Those copies of a book that differ from others of the same **printing** and **edition** because minor changes have been made in the **format** or text *after* the earlier issues of that same printing were published and sold. These differences almost invariably influence the sale (and resale) of the ensuing copies. Major changes would of course require a new edition, and minor changes made *before* publication and sale would result in a different **state** of that printing. See **Hinman collator**.

j   Used in early printing instead of *i* for the final letter, as in *iij* for *iii*.

jestbooks   Collections of witty or satirical jokes or stories that were popular in the sixteenth through eighteenth centuries.

leaf   The leaf of a book equals two pages. From about 1475 to 1600 numbering was according to leaves rather than pages. See **foliation**; **pagination**; **quarto**.

Library of Congress card number An identification number that appears in the lower right-hand corner of catalog cards prepared by the Library of Congress and available for purchase from that agency. The card number was originally a device to aid in the efficient ordering and sale of cards, but since it is unique to a given bibliographic entity, it is now also used in some computerized systems as one of the alternate methods for searching, especially if wording of the title or spelling of the author's name is uncertain. When the number is punched into the terminal, all cataloging information on the book appears on the screen, with the names of all cooperating libraries that own the book. **ISSN** and **ISBN** codes are also used for searching in some systems. See Section X in this guide for a sample of a Library of Congress catalog card and the L.C. card number.

ligature Type combining two or more letters, such as æ.

little magazines Literary journals that are interested in publishing experimental poetry and prose and that are usually limited in both funds and circulation. Harriet Monroe's *Poetry*, founded in 1912, is the most famous, but hundreds of others have come and gone after a few months or years of existence.

Lockheed Dialog Information Retrieval A timesaving service that enables scholars to type on computer terminals their requests for a title or subject search and receive on a video display screen or a printout information that would otherwise have taken several hours to locate in books. This computer system extracts facts from a growing number of sources, including *Comprehensive Dissertation Index* (W1211), *America* (E43), *Encyclopedia of Associations* (W1045), **ERIC**, *Foundation Directory*, *Historical Abstracts* (E43), *Language and Language Behavior Abstracts* (W1332), *Library and Information Science Abstracts* (E43), *MLAIB* (D31), *National Newspaper Index*, *Philosopher's Index* (W1489, including retrospective indexes), *Psychological Abstracts* (E39), and *Sociological Abstracts* (E40). Most large libraries now have a computer terminal that will receive this service (a Dialog-compatible receiver). Requests can also be made by TWX, WATS, and other telephone devices. The average search takes about ten minutes and costs only a few dollars. Lockheed has announced that its customers worldwide will soon have online access to every work cataloged by the Library of Congress. See also **OCLC**, **RLG**, **computerized literature search**, and **online information retrieval**.

majuscule Upper case or capital letters. Cf. **minuscule**.

manuscript In medieval literature any handwritten work; now used especially for the author's own handwritten or typed copy as it was prepared and submitted for publication.

MARC *Ma*chine *R*eadable *C*ataloging. A machine-readable process developed by the Library of Congress for standardizing cataloging information in one main office and producing it on magnetic tape so that it can be distributed to subscribing libraries in the United States and, in adapted forms, overseas, thereby saving repetitious labor. The library sells its MARC magnetic tapes to any bibliographic utility or organization for their own computers and also uses the tapes to generate catalog cards for sale to libraries. See Section X in this guide for a sample catalog card with the identifying Library of Congress card number for that particular book: 75–316777 MARC.

McKerrow, Ronald B. His *Introduction to Bibliography for Literary Students* (1927) is an indispensable, basic work that for many years was the undisputed authority for most questions of bibliography. See W1065 for a full annotation and W1064 for a more recent examination by Gaskell, *New Introduction to Bibliography*.

microtext An increasingly popular means of preserving and using printed material because it is much less expensive and takes up much less room than the original volumes. Microfilm is on reels or cartridges (either 16mm. or 35mm.); 3-by-5 microcards contain small reproductions of dozens of pages; 4-by-6 microfiche sheets and 6-by-9 microcards contain prints of up to a hundred pages of type. See **COM**.

minuscule Lower case, or small letters. Cf. **majuscule**.

monograph A scholarly treatise that makes a close study of a single subject; a work or collection that is not a serial.

MSS (singular, **MS**) Abbreviation for **manuscripts**.

national bibliography A list of all books published in a certain country or language. *CBI* (D35) and the *British National Bibliography* (D36) are examples.

n.d. No date. When the editor makes an educated guess about a date, it is placed within **brackets**: [1742?].

nihil obstat A Latin phrase meaning "nothing hinders," which is printed on the opening pages of a book to indicate official approval of its publication by a Roman Catholic censor.

normalization Justified editorial changes, especially in spelling, for the sake of consistency throughout the text. See **definitive edition**; **emendation**. Cf. **interpolation**.

n.p. No publisher or no place. See also **s.l.** and **s.n.**

OCLC Online Computer Library Center (formerly, Ohio College Library Center), a not-for-profit organization that operates an **online information retrieval service** for libraries. In 1981, it involved two thousand libraries in forty-six states (including the Library of Congress), a staff of five hundred, the bibliographic records of almost seven million books and **serials**, and a multi-million-dollar budget. Video-display terminals in each of the participating libraries connect with a central computer at Columbus, Ohio, which stores and disseminates on demand (for eighty-seven hours a week) machine-readable bibliographic information on all material owned by these libraries. OCLC offers a variety of subsystems, all dependent to some degree on the main data base: interlibrary loan, serials control records, serials union listing, and acquisitions. As each library orders catalog cards via the terminal, that library's special symbol is affixed to the bibliographic record in the data base. Thus, the OCLC data base has become, in effect, a gigantic **union catalog** of the holdings (especially since the late sixties) of a multitude of libraries, large and small, in all parts of the United States. OCLC data is also available in machine-readable form and, as such, is used by some libraries in the production of computerized catalogs that are replacing card catalogs. The very size of the data base makes it invaluable for verifying bibliographic information. Libraries will more and more frequently make this reference tool available for public use as students, scholars, and faculty members become aware of its many uses.

If, for example, your library (1) does not own a book you want to investigate, (2) does not contain reference books that will give you the information you need about this same book, (3) is considering buying this book for you and needs to verify facts, or (4) prefers to borrow it for you, your librarian can punch in a request on a typewriter keyboard (by author, title, **ISSN**, **ISBN**, or **Library of Congress card number**) and within a few seconds see displayed on a small video screen above the keys all the cataloging information that is available on that book—if it is owned by the Library of Congress or any one of the libraries in the system. This online information retrieval system is used to save time in cataloging, to verify dates and spelling, to facilitate interlibrary loan transactions, to obtain lists of all books written by one author, to locate one particular **edition** or one particular journal title, to aid in book selection, to order appropriate catalog cards, and many other services beyond the layman's imagination. Since the fall of 1979, for instance, libraries have been able to obtain instant information not only from a national data base but also from one another via the automated subsystem that handles interlibrary loan questions and answers. Only one more step remains: to put the individual library user online to this revolutionary system. Idle speculations: (1) Will this lead to the demise of the card catalog in even the smallest libraries, and (2) should additional centers be set up to forestall chaos in the event of a catastrophe? See *Library Literature* (F53) for recent information on this subject, *MLAIB* (D31) for an explanation of its online information retrieval services, and *NUC* (B11). See also **RLG**, **computerized literature search**, and, for another example of online information retrieval, **Lockheed Dialog Information Retrieval**.

octavo (8vo, 8⁰, eightvo)   The most common size book (about 9¾ inches tall), in which the original sheet of paper is folded three times to make eight leaves (sixteen pages). See **leaf**; **folio**.

offprint   A separate printing of a small section of a book, but made from the same setting of the type. Publishers sometimes send several offprints to the author of the section as a courtesy.

online information retrieval   Any process whereby a person may obtain information directly from a computer. The entries for **computerized literature search**, **RLG**, **OCLC**, and **Lockheed Dialog Information Retrieval** in this Glossary explain how the system works. See *Library Literature* (F53) for recent information on how it is used in libraries, and entry D31 for an explanation of the online information retrieval services of *MLAIB*.

o.p.   Out of print. All the copies that the publisher originally ran off have been sold, and no more are available. If this situation is temporary, the proper phrase is "out of stock."

pagination   Numbering by page, a practice that did not become common until about 1550. Cf. **foliation**.

paleography   The study and scholarly interpretation of the writing on ancient documents.

palimpsest   A written document that has been used, erased, and reused, perhaps several times over, and that with careful analysis can sometimes lead to the recovery of lost literary works.

papyrus   Paper used from about 3000 B.C. to A.D. 1000, which was made out of thin strips of papyrus grass laid in layers crossways, pressed, pounded, treated with a gum solution, and smoothed. This was formed into a roll that might measure twelve inches by twenty feet and was marked with a reed pen in hieroglyphics. These rolls were kept in clay jars or metal cylinders because papyrus is susceptible to both dampness and dryness. Key words were written on the outside of the containers, which were then stacked on shelves much like those in our modern libraries.

parchment   The carefully prepared skin of sheep that largely replaced **papyrus** as writing material about the fourth century A.D. See **vellum**.

pipe rolls   Town and city records of the Old and Middle English period, which were handwritten on rolled **manuscripts**. The Pipe Roll Society is dedicated to the preservation and reproduction of these records, which are invaluable for research in the life and literature of the times. See **roll**.

pirated edition   An unauthorized **edition** of a work that is published, usually in another country, without the permission of the author. International **copyright** laws now help to protect the author, but pirating still flourishes.

pp. (p., singular) Abbreviation for pages.

preliminary pages The pages at the front of the book that contain the preface, introduction, table of contents, and acknowledgments. They are now usually numbered with small roman numerals.

presentation copy A copy of a book given and signed by the author.

press figures Small numbers in the lower margin of some pages of some seventeenth- to nineteenth-century books which assist in distinguishing different **impressions**, **states**, and **editions**. They should be included in bibliographical descriptions of the books because they inevitably indicate a **variant** of some kind, whether it be concerned with the text itself (as **cancels** or possible extra printings of **offprints**) or with early printing-house practices, such as the employment of more than one person at the type with the resulting need to account for the work accomplished by each one, the irregular arrangement of pages in the **forme** or of paper in the printing process, the involvement of more than one printer, or whole or sectional reimpressions that may not have been completed in one run.

pressmark The identifying number given to a book by libraries. It is placed sometimes on the spine and sometimes inside the front cover. Also called the **shelfmark** or **call number**.

primary source The original document, as opposed to **secondary sources**, which use or criticize the primary source.

printing All those copies of a work that are run off *at one time* on the same setting of the type. If all these copies are sold and the publisher decides to have more copies made on the same typesetting, it is called a second printing. One **edition**, therefore, may have several printings. If extensive changes are made that require a resetting of the type, however, the next run is called a second edition. Synonym: **impression**. See **issue**; **state**.

private press A press that at its own expense prints books for a certain author or authors and circulates the works through unofficial channels. William Butler Yeats's sister, for instance, founded the Cuala Press in order to get his works printed and publicized.

prolegomenon, prolegomena An introductory statement about how a given subject or project is going to be handled.

prompt book The copy of a play adapted from the author's **manuscript** for use on the stage, with stage directions, act and scene divisions, and, occasionally, the name of the actor rather than the character.

provenance The history of ownership of a book, determined by bookplates, **pressmarks**, auction records, booksellers' catalogs, signatures, and coats of arms. An interesting provenance inevitably results in a more valuable book because of the possibility of historically important marginal notes.

Public Records Office (PRO, London)   Location of three-quarters of England's surviving official archives, the product of eight hundred years of government, over fifty million manuscripts. It contains legal papers, tax records, deeds, coroners' reports, letters, records of the Admiralty and most government departments, including the Tower, the Treasury, and the Registry of Wills, foreign and domestic state papers, trial records, and numerous other **primary sources**, which scholars may consult when they need factual information on authors who have had some connection with the government, whether voluntary (such as Arnold, the civil servant) or involuntary (such as Marlowe, the unwilling prisoner).

quarto (Q, 4⁰, 4to)   A book for which the original sheet of paper has been folded twice to make four leaves. See **leaf**; **folio**.

rebus   A picture that suggests either the sound or the meaning of a word or name; used occasionally during the Renaissance in place of a signature.

recto   The right-hand page of an open book. Cf. **verso**.

remainder books   The last remaining volumes of a title that the original publisher decides not to sell directly to primary customers. When the publisher overestimates the sales potential of a book and is left with a supply that does not justify further promotion and warehousing, it then "remainders" these titles to make way for new ones. This generally means that it sells the entire inventory to the highest bidder, who in turn sells the books at a price far lower than the original one. Clever librarians and individuals search for bargains at one of the many remainder houses such as Quality Books, Inc., 400 Anthony Trail, Northbrook, Ill. 60062.

reprint   A copy of a book that is sometimes a **facsimile** (especially if done by photo-offset process), sometimes a new **printing** from an old typesetting, and sometimes a new **edition**, so the purchaser must beware.

rev.   Abbreviation for revised.

RLG   **Research Libraries Group**. A consortium of large libraries interested in resource sharing and non-duplicative collection building. As a basis for their cooperation, the consortium has developed a shared cataloging computerized data base (RLIN, Research Libraries Information Network) and is working with other groups interested in this same type of project such as **OCLC**, WLN (Washington Library Network), California, New York University, the Northwestern automated cataloging system, and about fifteen other groups. The RLG expects to be self-sufficient by 1985. Looking beyond this commendable cooperative effort, we can predict that by the late 1980s all large libraries will be using cable television and mini- and microcomputers to provide information to library patrons in immediate response to their needs. See *American Libraries*, 3, no. 7 (July-Aug. 1982), 450–55.

roll An early document, sometimes on **parchment** and as much as forty feet long, which was rolled rather than cut into pages and sewn in a volume. See **pipe rolls**.

rpt. Abbreviation for **reprint**.

rubric Headings given to chapters or books; notes about the author, date, or **scribe**; initial letters printed in red to make them distinctive from the rest of the book.

running title A line of type that runs across the top of both pages of an open book.

scribe Professional copyist. Used in this Glossary to refer to the skilled pen artists of the Middle Ages who generally lived in monasteries or courts and whose duty it was to copy legal or literary documents in legible, highly stylized handwriting. See **colophon**.

secondary sources Works of criticism or other documents that rely on **primary sources** for their facts and inspiration.

secretary hand The most common style of writing in sixteenth-century England. It was used earlier only in law courts and business. By the end of the seventeenth century it had been supplanted by the much more legible Italian hand.

serial A publication whose parts are issued periodically with no anticipation of cessation, such as *PMLA* (H152). On a catalog card, the title of the serial is always followed by information about the volume numbering and the dates of those volumes, as, for example, vols. 1–20, 1910–30. If the serial is still being published, the date of the first issue is followed by a dash and a space, as *PMLA*, 1884– . If this continuing publication is currently being received by the library, the last volume and year will either not be specified or will read "date" (i.e., up to the current date).

shelfmark See **pressmark**; **call number**.

short title An abbreviated title. A short-title catalog or **checklist** contains only minimum information about each book.

signature A letter or figure (or combination of the two) that is placed by the printer in the **tail margin** of the first **leaf** of each **gathering** to assist the binder in correct assemblage of the numerous sections of the book. Signatures may run from A to Z (usually omitting J, U, and W) and then double the letters: AA, BB, CC, or Aa, Bb, Cc. See also **forme**.

silent emendations Editorial changes that should be made and that do not need to be explained individually either in the introduction or in footnotes. Examples are turned letters, letters of the wrong **font**, words that have been accidentally run together, omitted hyphens, and obvious punctuation errors, such as a comma at the end of a sentence. See **emendation**.

sixteenmo (16mo, 16⁰) A small book about 6¾ inches tall for which the original sheet of paper has been folded four times to make sixteen leaves. See **leaf**; **folio**; **octavo**; **quarto**.

s.l. (sine loco) Place of publication unknown.
s.n. (sine nomine) Name of publisher unknown.
  Abbreviations used in cataloging data since the International Standard Bibliographic Description was established. See **ISBD**.

state Those copies of a book that are run off on a single **printing** of one **edition** but that may have minor differences from another state or states of the same printing because the printer, before offering the book for sale, stopped the presses, made a correction here or an addition there, and then started the presses again. A printing, therefore, may have two or more states if minor textual changes were made *before* publication, and two or more **issues** if minor textual changes were made *after* publication.

stemma The genealogical tree that traces the relation of several versions (generations) of a manuscript back to the original (head of the family). The process of copying a text, whether by hand or machine, seems inevitably to produce **variant** readings, sometimes inadvertently, sometimes by authorial or editorial determination. Examination of the stemma enables the **textual critic** to isolate the different families, thus making it easier to group the variants and, finally, to determine the author's original intent.

subject bibliography A list of books and/or articles devoted to a specific subject, such as *Metaphor* (W1412).

substantives The actual words of the text, as distinguished from **accidentals** (the spelling, punctuation, and capitalization). The difference between the two and the different policies established for their authority are of extreme importance in **textual criticism**, when editors are concerned with producing a **definitive edition**, because after they select a **copy text** they must be willing to accept **variant** readings of substantives from other editions that may have received authorial supervision. They must also be aware that the first **edition** is not always the most authoritative source for the form of the accidentals.

supplement A separate section with additional or corrected material that is added to or published after the original work. Cf. **fascicle**.

tail The bottom margin of a page.

tailpiece   A design placed at the end of a chapter or book.

textual criticism   The examination of all different versions of a work for the purpose of returning the text to the author's final intention. The textual editor will first have to become familiar with all possible facets of the project, collect every **manuscript, edition, state, issue,** and other relevant texts, choose a base text for comparison, compare them all, determine which should be the **copy text,** make **emendations, normalize,** and then write textual notes to explain all problems and decisions. See also Textual Criticism (W1610–23).

thorn   A letter used in Old English writing. It had the sound of *th* and resembled a *y* with a small loop on the right side. Careless handwriting resulted in a change of shape over the centuries and finally produced the linguistically untenable y' and y' that ignorant shopkeepers use for their signs—''Y' Old Chop Suey Shoppe.''

tipped in   Insertion of any **leaf** into a book (**corrigenda,** for example) by applying glue to the inner edge and thrusting it in against the stitching.

title page (t.p.)   The page of a book that contains basic information concerning the title, author, and **imprint** (publisher, place and date of printing), with **copyright** generally found on the **verso.** Information for library catalog cards and for bibliographers is always taken from the title page and its verso, not from the cover or spine. If information is taken from any other part of the book, it is enclosed in **brackets.**

t.p.   Abbreviation for **title page.**

trade book   Usually a hardcover book produced by a commercial publisher and distributed at retail bookstores. Because many copies are printed at one time, the cost is minimal, and librarians can expect to get high discounts. Trade paperbacks are usually priced higher than mass-market paperbacks.

typescript   A typewritten version of a work. If it is the author's original copy, it is equivalent to an original **manuscript.** A copy that the author prepares, and probably corrects or changes, for a publisher or other interested party is called a fair copy typescript, and might easily be the most authoritative copy available, so editors might select this as the **copy text** for a **definitive edition.** A copyist's typescript, however, is a copy prepared by other hands and may have nonauthorial errors or changes, so it would not be so desirable.

union catalog   A central catalog containing information on books (and possibly serials) located in several different rooms or buildings within a given institution or library system. Harvard University, for instance, has over one hundred libraries scattered over its campus, but the main union catalog in

Z
INDEX

Z

Index

Index to titles of reference books and periodicals, editors, criticism, national literatures, chronological periods, genres, subjects, series, and a few authors, such as Wordsworth, Steinbeck, and Goethe, who have had serial publications dedicated to their life and works.

Numbers are entry numbers, not page numbers. Capitalized subject headings lead either to entries in the Literature-Related Subjects section (Section W) or to major divisions in the text such as American Literature or Afro-American Literature (Section P). For alphabetizing rules, see Guidelines for the Reader in the front of this guide.

Index